THE COMPLETE BOOK OF
SOCCER

EDITED BY CHRIS HUNT

FIREFLY BOOKS

Dedicated to Cliff Hunt, a 'Gooner' until the end!

A FIREFLY BOOK

Published by Firefly Books Limited 2006

First printed 2006, reprinted 2008

Publisher Cataloging-in-Publication Data (U.S.)

Hunt, Chris, 1962-
    The complete book of soccer / edited by Chris Hunt.
[384] p. : col. photos. ;   cm.
Includes index.
Summary: A comprehensive look at soccer including player biographies and profiles, stories of legendary coaches and teams, detailed histories of the World Cup and European championships, origins of the game and its rules.
ISBN-13: 978-1-55407-161-6
ISBN-10: 1-55407-161-5
1. Soccer. I. Title.
796.334   dc22   GV943.H86   2006

Library and Archives Canada Cataloguing in Publication

    The complete book of soccer / edited by Chris Hunt. Includes index.
ISBN-13: 978-1-55407-161-6
ISBN-10: 1-55407-161-5
    1. Soccer. I. Hunt, Chris, 1962-
GV943.H95 2006   796.334   C2006-902154-6

Published in the United States by
Firefly Books (U.S.) Inc.
P.O. Box 1338, Ellicott Station
Buffalo, New York 14205

Published in Canada by
Firefly Books Ltd.
66 Leek Crescent
Richmond Hill, Ontario L4B 1H1

A 'MILE AWAY CLUB' PRODUCTION
Edited by Chris Hunt (www.ChrisHunt.biz)
Designed by David Houghton

All photography © Action Images Ltd
Printed and bound in Slovakia

CONTENTS

FOREWORD

Legend has it that Pelé' once described football as the 'beautiful game'. Although the true origins of the saying are shrouded in mystery, no other description of the sport has come close to summing up the true splendour of this simple 11-a-side game.

With its heady mix of bewitching ball wizardry and rabble-rousing high drama, football can thrill and entertain like no other sport. Its history, too, is like a mirror of the history of the turbulent 19th and 20th Centuries. The evolution of the game and the tales of its most talented protagonists are set against a backdrop of the great wars and the political divides that shaped the story of our world. In learning about the idols of yesterday, like West Germany's Fritz Walter, Hungary's Ferenc Puskás and Argentina's Mario Kempes, we also learn so much more.

While each generation of football fans is brought up with its own heroes – today we have Rooney and Ronaldinho, Henry and Schevchenko – it is often in books like this that we discover our heritage, the roots of the game, and the legends that originally inspired our parents, and grandparents before them, to fall in love with the world's best and most popular sport.

This is a book for all of us who have dreamt of glorious victory. It is for those of us who have felt our heart quicken by the counter attack or the anguish of defeat. This book is a celebration of football, the beautiful game that conquered the world!

Chris Hunt
Editor

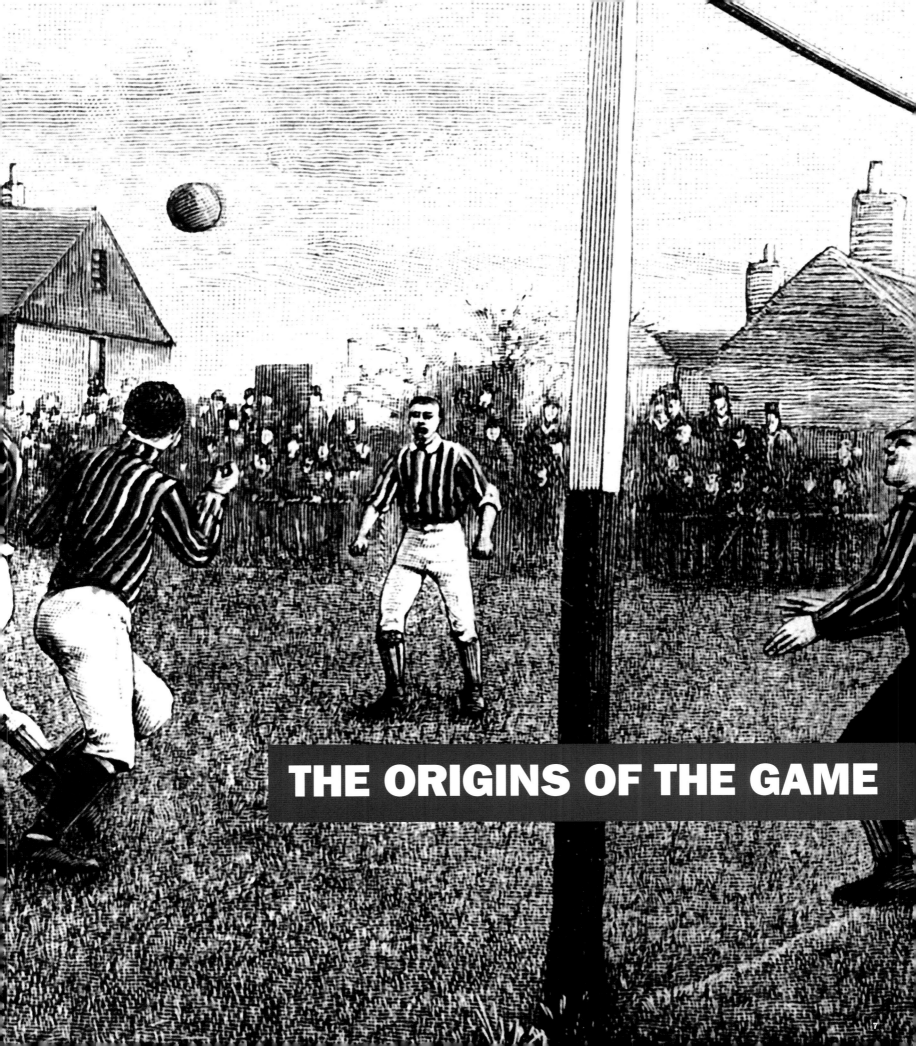

THE ORIGINS OF THE GAME

Above: Part of a 14th Century misericord at Gloucester Cathedral depicts an early example of ball game players. Opposite: A game of 'mob football' on the streets of London in 1721.

THE ORIGINS OF THE GAME

TO WATCH FOOTBALL at the beginning of the 21st Century is to watch a multi-million pound industry that creates global stars out of the most ordinary of people and stirs the emotions of billions of men, women and children around the world. In bars and cafés, homes and schools, from the Amazon to Zanzibar, the conversation is never far from 'the beautiful game'. Hours of TV coverage are devoted not just to showing matches, but to talking about them, endlessly arguing over rules and their interpretation, over tactics used by different coaches, and the relative merits of players. The world is obsessed with football.

But how did it get to this? How did a game so apparently simple become the *raison d'être* for millions, a worldwide religion?

The only thing that can be said with any real certainty about the early origins of football is that a variety of games were played in countries around the world, which involved elements of today's football. Some featured little or no kicking, others lacked a competitive edge, but each embraced something recognisably part of the modern day game.

Recorded in a military manual dating back to the Han Dynasty (200-300 BC), it is usually said that the Chinese Tsu Chu is the earliest form of football known to man, though in truth it more closely resembles a fairground game

than the football we know today. Two nine-metre high bamboo canes were used to suspend a large piece of silk cloth with a hole 30cm-40cm in diameter cut into it. Competitors would then attempt to kick a leather ball filled with hair and feathers through the hole, sometimes with the added difficulty of being pressured by opponents. Tsu Chu, it seems, was played to celebrate the Emperor's birthday. The penalty for losing was death.

Less sinister, and certainly less fatal, was Kemari, a non-competitive Japanese game dating from around the 5th Century AD. Best described as 'keepie-uppies', Kemari was contested among a group of eight players standing in a circle and passing the ball to each other without allowing it to touch the ground. Further south, in the Malay states, they played Sepak Raga, a similar game in which you were permitted to use any part of your body apart from your hands to keep the ball in the air. In South America, in 400 AD, the Mayans played Poktapok, a game between two teams using rubber balls. Much later, the Aztecs had a similar game called Ullamatzli, while in North Africa there was Koura, a Berber ball game probably linked to fertility rights.

It is unlikely that there was any common link among these different games, rather that each civilisation invented its own game with its own rules uninfluenced by people living thousands of miles away. It is difficult, therefore, to sustain the Chinese claim to have

invented football, since the evidence that they took Tsu Chu to the world is at best threadbare. They may not even have invented the world's first ball game – there is actually evidence of ball games being played even earlier, in Greece, where the little-known Pheninda (or Episkyros) is mentioned in the writings of the Greek playwright Antiphanes, who lived in the 4th Century BC. Adding weight to his words is a bas relief at the foot of a marble column in Athens, believed to date from 600 BC, which shows a figure playing a game that looks very much like football. And Episkyros probably did influence later games, not least as the forerunner of Harpastum.

Used as a way of keeping the Roman army fit, Harpastum was played on a rectangular field with the aim of getting the ball over the opponents' boundary line. Kicking was limited and the game was probably more similar to rugby, but the growth of the Roman Empire took the game to new territories and it survived for 700 years. It may even have had some influence on the very early development of football in Britain: it is claimed that victory celebrations after a battle with the Romans in Derby in the 3rd Century involved something resembling a game of 'football'.

Yet despite the claims and counter-claims, none of these games was football as we know it. The game known around the world by that name did not really exist until the mid-19th Century and its home was certainly England.

FOOTBALL MILESTONES

1848: First code of football rules compiled at Cambridge University. The 'Cambridge Rules' helped differentiate football from rugby.

1857 Sheffield FC, the world's oldest club, is formed after two keen cricket lovers, William Prest and Nathaniel Creswick, decided football would be the sport to keep their fitness levels up during the winter.

1862 Notts County, the Football League's oldest side, founded as Nottingham Football Club.

1863 The Football Association formed in London.

1865 Tape introduced between two posts of a goal.

1866 The offside rule altered to allow a player to be onside when three of opposing team are nearer their own goalline.

1867 Queen's Park, the oldest Scottish club, founded.

1869 Goal kicks introduced.

1871 The FA Cup competition is introduced and goalkeepers are first mentioned in the laws.

1872 England and Scotland draw the first ever international 0-0 in Glasgow. Scottish FA is formed. Wanderers win the first FA Cup final, beating Royal Engineers 1-0. Corner kicks are introduced. Le Havre are the first French team to be formed.

1874 Umpires are first mentioned in the laws of the game. Shinguards are also introduced.

1875 The FA make the crossbar obligatory after it had been used in the Sheffield Rules since 1870.

1876 Football Association of Wales is formed. Scotland play Wales for the first time.

1877 The London Association and Sheffield Association agree to use the same rules.

1878 The whistle is introduced by referees.

1879 First international between England and Wales takes place at Kennington Oval, England winning 2-1.

1880 The Irish FA is formed.

1882 The two-handed throw-in is introduced.

1883 First British Home Championship is staged and won by Scotland.

1885 Professionalism is legalised in England. Arbroath beat Bon Accord 36-0, a record for a first-class match.

1886 The awarding of caps for international appearances is approved by the FA.

1887 Preston North End beat Hyde United 26-0 to record the biggest FA Cup score. Football introduced in Russia.

1888 The Football League is formed.

1889 Preston North End win first league and cup 'double'.

1890 The Scottish League is formed.

1891 Devised by Liverpool engineer John Alexander Brodie, goal nets are introduced. The taking of penalties from a penalty line is also introduced.

1893 Genoa, Italy's oldest football club, is formed by British diplomat Sir Charles Alfred Payton and nine of his contemporaries. The club is originally named Genoa Football and Cricket Club.

1894 Scotland adopts professionalism. Referees are given complete control of the game. The first match is played in Brazil between employees of São Paolo railway and a local gas company, while the sport also makes its debut in Austria.

1895 The original FA Cup is stolen in Birmingham and never recovered. It is decided that players taking thrown-ins must be on the touchline.

1896 An unofficial football competition is played at the Athens Olympics, with teams from Denmark, Athens and Izmir taking part.

1897 The Players Union is formed for English and Scottish players. English club side Corinthians tour South America. Juventus are formed and play in pink shirts.

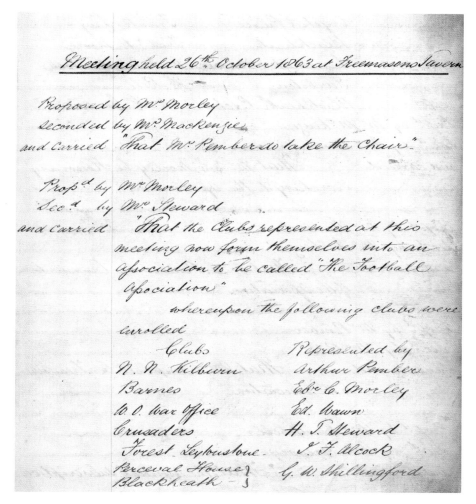

Meeting held 26th October 1863 at Freemasons Tavern

Proposed by Mr Morley
Seconded by Mr Mackenzie
and carried "That Mr Pember do take the Chair".

Propd by Mr Morley
Secd by Mr Steward
and carried "That the Clubs represented at this
meeting now form themselves into an
Association to be called "The Football
Association"
whereupon the following clubs were
enrolled

Clubs	Represented by
N. N. Kilburn	Arthur Pember
Barnes	Ebr C. Morley
W. O. War Office	Ed. Cawn
Crusaders	H. T. Steward
Forest Leytonstone	I. F. Alcock
Perceval House	G. W. Shillingford
Blackheath	

THE FOOTBALL ASSOCIATION RULES 1863

1. The maximum length of the ground shall be 200 yards, the maximum breadth shall be 100 yards, the length and breadth shall be marked off with flags; and the goal shall be defined by two upright posts, eight yards apart, without any tape or bar across them.

2. A toss for goals shall take place, and the game shall be commenced by a place kick from the centre of the ground by the side losing the toss for goals; the other side shall not approach within ten yards of the ball until it is kicked off.

3. After a goal is won, the losing side shall be entitled to kick off, and the two sides shall change goals after each goal is won.

4. A goal shall be won when the ball passes between the goal-posts or over the space between the goal-posts (at whatever height), not being thrown, knocked on, or carried.

5. When the ball is in touch, the first player who touches it shall throw it from the point on the boundary line where it left the ground in a direction at right angles with the boundary line, and the ball shall not be in play until it has touched the ground.

6. When a player has kicked the ball, any one of the same side who is nearer to the opponent's goal line is out of play and may not touch the ball himself, nor in any way whatever prevent any other player from doing so, until he is in play; but no player is out of play when the ball is kicked off from behind the goal line.

7. In case the ball goes behind the goal line, if a player on the side to whom the goal belongs first touches the ball, one of his side shall be entitled to a free-kick from the goal line at the point opposite the place where the ball shall be touched. If a player of the opposite side first touches the ball, one of his side shall be entitled to a free-kick at the goal only from a point 15 yards outside the goal line, opposite the place where the ball is touched, the opposing side standing within their goal line until he has had his kick.

8. If a player makes a fair catch, he shall be entitled to a free-kick, providing he claims it by making a mark with his heel at once; and in order to take such a kick he may go back as far as he pleases, and no player on the opposite side shall advance beyond his mark until he has kicked.

9. No player shall run with the ball.

10. Neither tripping nor hacking shall be allowed, and no player shall use his hands to hold or push his adversary.

11. A player shall not be allowed to throw the ball or pass it to another with his hands.

12. No player shall be allowed to take the ball from the ground with his hands under any pretext whatever while it is in play.

13. No player shall be allowed to wear projecting nails, iron plates, or gutta percha on the soles or heels of his boots.

THE ORIGINS OF the game in England are just as hazy as those elsewhere. Along with the story of the Romans in Derby, comes a tale from Chester of a game played with the severed head of a defeated Dane. Whether either is true is impossible to say, but what is clear is that from around the 12th Century, ball games were a common sight in the towns and villages of the British Isles.

Often these games were for local pride, two teams in a village fighting it out for bragging rights, or neighbouring villages competing in an annual contest, usually staged on Shrove Tuesday (in northern France a similar game called La Soule was played on Shrove Tuesday, Sundays and Saints days, and it has been suggested that the Norman conquest of 1066 brought the tradition to England). But local pride came at a cost, often counted in broken limbs, sometimes in fatalities.

The rules – if there were any – were vague. This was 'mob football', with no limit to the number of men on each side and virtually no method of play illegal. Nor was there necessarily much use of feet in contact with the ball. The general idea was to transport a ball (or pig's bladder) to one or other point within a village, but with so many players, games could last for days. (Annual games are still played today, albeit with less risk to life and limb, in places like Ashbourne in Derbyshire and Haxey in Lincolnshire, where they fight over a hood rather than a ball.)

By the 14th Century, these raucous street games were causing consternation among the authorities. So much so, in fact, that in 1314, King Edward II tried to ban them with the threat of jail. A proclamation was issued: 'For as much as there is great noise in the city caused by hustling over large balls, from which many evils arise, which God forbid; we command and forbid on behalf of the King, on pain of imprisonment, such game be used in the city in future.'

Yet Edward II was just the first of several monarchs to try – and fail – to clamp down on what was fast becoming 'the people's game'. When his son, Edward III, made his own attempt to ban football, he was not just concerned with public order issues but with the distraction football was causing at a time when England was at war with France. His subjects, he argued, should be focusing on more important business, like archery practice. But despite his attempts – and those of monarchs to come – mob football continued to flourish in England (and Scotland) mainly due to the people's desire to play.

Meanwhile in Italy in the 14th Century, the game of Il Calcio had begun to be played in the main square in Florence on the feast day of St John the Baptist, the city's patron saint.

With its roots in the Roman game of Harpastum, Il Calcio was nevertheless closer to modern day football than its ancient predecessor – to begin with, its name came from *calciare*, Italian for 'to kick'.

The game, with its teams dressed in bright colours, was certainly more civilised than its English counterpart. In 1580, a set of rules was published for the first time by Giovanni Bardi, and the game may even have had an influence on the development of football in Britain after a match was played in front of the British Consul. But football in England remained firmly in the hands of the mobs (a character in Shakespeare's 1605 play *King Lear* refers to a 'base football player'). Rough, violent and a nuisance to the authorities, for several centuries no real progress was made in the development of the game.

The turning point came in the mid-19th

Top left: The minutes recording the formation of the Football Association.

Opposite top: A depiction of a football game at the turn of the 18th Century.

Opposite bottom: A team from Harrow public school in the 19th Century.

Above: The 1897 FA Cup final at Crystal Palace.

Below: An advert for equipment from the late 19th Century.

Century. By then, football had long been played in the major public schools of England; the virtues of team play, discipline and exercise were noted by teachers, and the rough and tumble excesses were a joy to the pupils. By their nature more organised, these games allowed for a gradual refinement of the 'rules' to the point where a more sophisticated game was starting to be played.

Still, however, there was no uniformity. Different schools played by their own evolved regulations, dependent on, for example, the area of ground they had at their disposal for games or the whims of the master in charge. Other rules were added piecemeal over the years by each school, so that when two schools faced each other they would adopt the rules of one of the two teams, the other adapting as best they could. But there were too many problems to make this satisfactory.

There were irreconcilable differences, for example, in the degree to which handling was permitted. In some schools running with the ball in your hands was fine, in others only minimal use of the hands was allowed. More controversial was the use of hacking, a technique which essentially involved kicking away at an opponent's shins if he had the ball.

It was not until a group of footballers from various public schools found themselves together at Cambridge University that the first attempt to draw up a uniform set of rules was made. Published in 1848, the 'Cambridge Rules' were by no means universally adopted, but the group of students behind them were to play an important part in both raising awareness of the need for a standardised set

of rules and in persuading various schools and clubs to modify their own rules in order to develop unity.

Other rules were drawn up over the next 15 years (the best known being the 'Sheffield Rules' of 1857 and the 1862 'Rules for the Simplest Game' by Mr Thring, a teacher at Uppingham School), but the breakthrough came in October 1863 when representatives from 11 clubs – Barnes, Blackheath, Blackheath School, Crusaders, Crystal Palace, Forest (later Wanderers), Kensington School, No Names Kilburn, Perceval House, Surbiton and War Office – met to form the Football Association.

Two months later, the Football Association rules were published [see sidebar on previous page], and it was here that rugby and football went their separate ways and the football we know today really began to appear. Some clubs, Blackheath among them, opted to continue with their own game, based more on catching and passing the ball than kicking it, but those that stayed within the FA were determined that their 'football' should be played largely with the feet. For a while there was hope that the two groups – the rugby unionists and the association footballers as they became known – could be brought back under the same umbrella, but when, six years later, the FA banned all handling of the ball, the split became permanent and in 1871 the Rugby Football Union was formed.

The first FA laws were far from perfect – they did not, for example, stipulate the number of players on each side or the duration of the game – and to begin with, many schools and clubs continued to follow their own rules. But

gradually they began to be used all over the country and when, in 1878, the 'Sheffield Rules' were absorbed into a new set of FA rules, uniformity was fast approaching.

In 1886 overall responsibility for the laws of the game passed to the International Football Association Board comprising of one representative from each of the English, Scottish, Welsh and Irish football associations. (Since 1913 FIFA has also had a presence on the board, which now consists of four delegates making up 50 per cent of any vote.)

As the FA grew bigger and stronger, there became apparent a desire among the top teams to test themselves in organised competition. So, at the start of the 1871-2 season, the world's oldest cup competition, the FA Challenge Cup was launched. Based on a knockout competition – Cock House – and played at Harrow School, the inaugural FA Cup saw 15 entries; 13 from the London area, plus Donington School from Lincolnshire and Queen's Park from Glasgow, who were given a bye to the semi-finals because of the distance they had to travel. Sadly, having drawn their semi-final in London, the Scots decided they could not afford to return for the replay, so the first ever final, in 1872, pitted Royal Engineers against Wanderers, who won 1-0.

In October of the same year, England played Scotland in the first ever international match, a 0-0 draw in Glasgow. Just five months later, the Scottish FA was established at a meeting attended by Clydesdale, Dumbreck, Glasgow Eastern, Granville, Queen's Park, Rovers, Third Lanark and Vale Of Leven.

With football's popularity growing in England and attendances at matches rising, it

was not long before the potential financial rewards of football were noted. Spectators, it became apparent, could be charged for admission. And since, unsurprisingly, the more successful teams attracted larger crowds, it was inevitable that ambitious clubs would look for ways to attract better players. There was little the FA could do to hold back the advent of professionalism. Having at first attempted to limit payments to players to 'wages lost' and 'expenses', in 1885 the FA gave in and permitted professional players.

Three years later, it was decided that the growing number of clubs warranted better organisation and the world's first Football League was established with 12 teams taking part: Accrington, Aston Villa, Blackburn Rovers, Bolton Wanderers, Burnley, Derby County, Everton, Notts County, Preston North End, Stoke, West Bromwich Albion and Wolverhampton Wanderers.

The FA was barely 25 years old yet English football had taken huge strides in the development of the game. In the FA Cup it had a glamorous cup competition that drew large crowds, and it had a professional football league with a basic structure in place that would carry the game well into the 20th Century. International football was under way too, with regular fixtures among the four home nations, England, Scotland, Wales and Ireland. But already football was far more than just a British sport. It was still a long way from becoming the most popular pastime in the world, but by the turn of the century, travelling British workers and businessmen had taken football to all four corners of the globe.

Top: Preston, the first double-winners in 1889. Above: Lord Kinnaird, who presided over the first ever international match.

1898 The first Italian football championship played in one day, with Genoa the victors.

1899 Promotion and relegation between English divisions is used for the first time. Barcelona play their first game, against FC Catala.

1900 The German Football Association is founded in Leipzig with 86 member clubs.

1901 The first six figure attendance for an FA Cup final sees Southern League Tottenham draw 2-2 with Sheffield United in front of 110,820 fans at Crystal Palace. Spurs win the replay to become the only non-league side to win the cup. Argentina beat Uruguay in first international between South American countries.

1902 The maximum wage of £4 per week is brought in. Real Madrid are founded. Austria beat Hungary 5-0 in Vienna in the first European international between countries outside of Britain.

1904 World governing body FIFA is formed in Paris.

1905 Goalkeepers ordered to stay on goal line for penalties. The first £1,000 transfer sees Alf Common move from Sunderland to Middlesbrough.

1908 England play Austria in Vienna – their first international against a non-British side. The transfer fee limit is fixed at £350. England win the first official Olympic football gold, beating Denmark in the final.

1910 Argentina win the first unofficial South American championship, in a three-team tournament that also includes Uruguay and Chile.

1912 Goalkeepers banned from handling outside the box.

1916 The founding of the South American Football Confederation.

1919 The four British football associations withdraw from FIFA after refusing to play against any of their recent wartime enemies. They extend their boycott to any nation prepared to play against these countries.

1920 Players cannot be offside from throw-ins.

THE FA CUP

ALL FOOTBALL-PLAYING nations have domestic knockout competitions – Spain's Copa Del Rey, for instance, or Italy's Coppa Italia – but none is older or more prestigious than England's FA Cup. The idea of a cup competition originated in London on July 20, 1871, with a proposal in the offices of The Sportsman by then FA honorary secretary Charles Alcock to establish 'a Challenge Cup... for which all clubs belonging to the Association should be invited to compete'. Fifteen clubs entered the inaugural FA Cup in the 1871-2 season, with Wanderers, a team of ex-public school and university players, making history as 1-0 winners of the first final against Royal Engineers at Kennington Oval, in front of a crowd of 2,000 who each paid one shilling for the privilege.

Since it was conceived as a 'challenge' cup, Wanderers simply defended the trophy the following year against Oxford University. A change of rules ushered in a more competitive tournament but Wanderers still dominated the early years, along with amateur side Old Etonians. Blackburn Rovers then became the dominant force until the turn of the century, when southern non-leaguers Tottenham won in 1901.

For the first 50 years the trophy was played out in a number of venues, including the Oval and Crystal Palace, which hosted the final on 20 occasions, the last time in 1914. The final moved to Old Trafford a year later before the Great War forced its suspension.

Northern clubs held sway – notably Sheffield United, Bradford, Aston Villa and Newcastle United – until the great Arsenal side of the Thirties briefly made their mark. Manchester United registered their first win in 1909 (having first entered in 1886

as Newton Heath) but the club would have to wait until 1948 for a second win. They now hold the FA Cup record with ten wins, followed by Tottenham's eight. In all, 42 different clubs have won the competition.

In January 1922 building started on a permanent venue, Wembley Stadium. It cost £750,000 but it was completed too late to host that year's final. Instead, a year later Wembley began by hosting the famous 'White Horse Final' between Bolton Wanderers and West Ham United, when an over-capacity crowd spilt on to the pitch and were brought under control by a single mounted policeman and his white horse, Billy. Bolton emerged as 3-2 winners when order was restored.

All subsequent FA Cup finals were played at Wembley, excluding the war years (when there were unofficial competitions) until 2000 when the ground was knocked down. The Millennium Stadium in

Cardiff staged the final for the next five years while the new Wembley was being built, with Liverpool winning the first game with a late flurry against Arsenal.

The highest scoring final ever occurred in 1953 when Blackpool beat Bolton Wanderers 4-3 in a stunning comeback. It became known as 'The Matthews Final' after Blackpool's inspirational winger Stanley Matthews, though this is now regarded as rather unfair on Stan Mortensen who scored a hat-trick.

There have been four actual trophies during the competition's existence. The original trophy, smaller than the present one, was stolen from a Birmingham shop window in 1895 and never recovered after Aston Villa had won the competition. The second trophy, an exact replica of the first, lasted until 1910 before being presented to FA president Lord Kinnaird. In 1911 it was replaced by a larger cup and fittingly the Bradford-made trophy was won by Bradford FC. The current cup, played for since 1992, is an exact replica of the third trophy.

FA Cup rules have differed little since World War II, though clubs higher up the league are given byes through the early rounds. Substitutes were finally allowed in 1966-7 and a replay was not necessary until 1970, when the final at Wembley was drawn and to clinch the trophy Chelsea travelled to Old Trafford to beat Leeds.

In 1991-2 penalty shoot-outs were introduced in order to settle replayed games that were still level after extra-time. Fortunately a shoot-out in the final itself did not occur until 2005, when Arsenal beat Manchester United 5-4. It was not a memorable final, as has become the case in recent years. However, some faith was restored in the FA Cup's ability to produce a thriller when West Ham and Liverpool met in 2006. Both teams played attacking football, producing a 3-3 draw with the game eventually settled by penalties in favour of Liverpool. It was easily the best final since 1987, when underdogs Coventry beat Tottenham 3-2.

At the start of the 1994-5 season controversial steps were taken to capitalise on the cup's appeal by introducing sponsorship. The competition remains titled the FA Cup, but AXA, Littlewoods and most recently E.On have paid for the rights to be associated with the world's oldest football cup. Such moves have made traditionalists uncomfortable, especially as the FA Cup has suffered from the dominance of league football in recent years, a symptom of the increased expectations of entering the Champions League and the power of the major Premiership sides.

The competition received a further blow in 1999 when, in an attempt to curry favour for a World Cup bid, the Football Association encouraged the withdrawal of holders Manchester United in order to compete in the World Club Championship.

Since a subsequent relaunch, there has been increased TV exposure, steps to stop clubs switching ties for financial gain to preserve the romance of David vs Goliath encounters, bigger prize money and a guaranteed UEFA Cup place for the winners. In truth, it may never again possess quite the same glory, but with 600 teams entering annually, playing over 500 games on the way to a showcase final that compares to no other, the FA Cup still breeds romance and excitement like no other national cup competition anywhere in the world.

Above: An artist's impression of the 1891 FA Cup final.

Left: Steven Gerrard and Rafael Benítez celebrate victory in the 2006 FA Cup final, scheduled to be the last played at Cardiff's Millennium Stadium.

Opposite top: Queen Elizabeth and King George VI present the FA Cup to Sunderland captain Raich Carter in 1937.

Opposite centre: The original FA Challenge Cup.

Opposite bottom: Newcastle captain Joe Harvey celebrates with the trophy in 1951.

Overleaf: West Ham and Bolton in action at the 1923 FA Cup final at Wembley Stadium.

THE FOOTBALL LEAGUE

THE FOOTBALL ASSOCIATION had been in existence for 23 years before it was considered necessary to create an official league. Before then the nascent English game was strictly amateur, though unofficial payments were made to some players, with matches organised on an ad hoc, 'friendly' basis. The league's instigator was Scotsman William McGregor, an Aston Villa committee member who organised two meetings in London and Manchester in 1888 which brought together the 12 clubs that became the Football League's founder members: Accrington, Aston Villa, Blackburn Rovers, Bolton Wanderers, Burnley, Derby County, Everton, Notts County, Preston North End, West Bromwich Albion, Stoke and Wolverhampton Wanderers.

The idea was to create order and lend structure to the game by guaranteeing fixtures, and revenue, for a dozen professional teams, split equally between the north and the midlands, the south remaining predominantly amateur. Arsenal would become the first southern club to join the Football League in the 1893-4 season.

The first games played under Football League rules took place on September 8, 1888, with points awarded only for wins. This system was rapidly amended to include one point for a draw, remaining in place for the best part of a century until 1981-2, when to improve competition three points were awarded for a win.

Preston North End were the league's inaugural winners, also recording a league and cup 'double', a feat repeated by Aston Villa eight years later and then not achieved again until Tottenham in 1961. In all only six different teams have won the double, the last being Arsenal for the third time in 2002.

The Football League acquired a 12-strong Second Division in the 1892-3 season, by taking over the rival Football Alliance, which featured Nottingham Forest and Crewe Alexandra among others. Promotion and relegation was settled with the top three teams from Division Two playing the bottom three from Division One. This rule was later simplified to stop anomalies.

A third division was established in 1920-1, then divided into regions the following year (Division Three North and Division Three South), creating four divisions. In 1958 it was decided to replace these with national third and fourth divisions, with the top half of each regional division forming the new Division Three, and the bottom half becoming Division Four. This structure was to remain unchanged for 34 years.

The Football League proved to be a huge success, with attendances booming in the years up to World War I. Northern clubs held sway with Newcastle United, Blackburn and Sheffield Wednesday proving the dominant forces. Post-war Londoners Chelsea and Arsenal joined the top flight but neither could break the northern stranglehold until the latter prised manager Herbert Chapman from powerful Huddersfield. He promptly took advantage of a change to the offside law to create a vibrant, attacking team in the 1930s that went on to win five league championships and four FA Cups.

Following another suspension for World War II the Football League restarted and entered into another era of success, the sport attracting massive attendances. Manchester United steadily asserted their influence but just as they appeared to be embarking on a period of domination after two consecutive league titles in 1954-5 and 1955-6, tragedy struck when an air crash robbed them of seven leading players, including captain Roger Byrne and rising star Duncan Edwards. The Munich air disaster occurred because United were returning from a European fixture with Red Star Belgrade. The previous season, despite great resistance from the Football League, United had been the first English club to enter a side in a European competition, reaching the quarter-finals.

The early part of the modern era saw the championship rotate regularly between clubs. A rare victory for London's Tottenham aside though, the north continued to dominate. League football became increasingly attractive to business with regular televised coverage beginning on the BBC in 1964 (in the past it was confined to European and FA Cup finals).

In the mid-Sixties, Liverpool began to establish themselves as a force under Bill Shankly and his successors, Bob Paisley and Joe

Fagan, who brought about an unequalled period of dominance. Liverpool's 1972-3 victory opened the way to 11 titles in 16 years and an overall total of 18, a feat so far unequalled in the game. With Liverpool also taking the commercial lead by announcing a shirt sponsor in 1978, the Football League opened its doors to outside money. While there had been a few short-lived competitions like the Texaco Cup and the Watney Cup, the Football League took the next logical step with the announcement of a three-year deal with Canon in 1983. Further lucrative tie-ins followed. Another idea to generate money came with the revival of the concept of play-offs in 1986-7. Originally a means of helping to reduce Division One from 22 clubs to 20, play-offs proved so successful they still remain.

The 104-year history of the Football League received its greatest blow on February 20, 1992, when 22 clubs announced they were breaking away to form the FA Premier League from the beginning of the 1992-3 season. This was partly a way of revitalising the top flight which had been damaged by a number of catastrophes in the Eighties, including 1985's Bradford fire, the carnage at the Heysel Stadium in Brussels, and 1989's Hillsborough disaster. Football

hooliganism was considered to be out of control, attendances were down, and the game's image was recognised as archaic.

After the birth of the Premier League, the remaining divisions of the Football League were renumbered, with automatic promotion and relegation continuing and the remaining 72 clubs governing themselves. In 2004-5 the Football League followed the Premiership example by rebranding itself, with the bigger clubs in Division One demanding more of the spoils. Coca-Cola announced a three-year sponsorship and the top tier became the Coca-Cola Championship with the other divisions becoming League One and League Two.

Since the establishment of the Premier League, there has been a distinct fissuring between the clubs with the most money and those with lesser resources. Put simply, the richest dominate, with the title rotating between Manchester United, Arsenal and monied newcomers Chelsea. The only surprise in the Premiership era has been the triumph of Blackburn Rovers in 1994-5. Whether the title race in the top tier can ever be as open as it was is doubtful but England's four divisions are as strong as any in Europe.

Above: Liverpool players run around the pitch after beating Arsenal 5-0 to win the league championship in 1964.

Left: Chelsea captain John Terry celebrates winning the English Premier League in 2006.

Opposite top: Winners of the 1897 league and FA Cup double, Aston Villa.

Opposite bottom: Ipswich Town captain Andy Nelson and his manager Alf Ramsey celebrate winning the title in 1962.

THE WORLD GAME

IN 1930, URUGUAY hosted the first football World Cup, featuring 13 nations – France, Mexico, Chile, Argentina, Yugoslavia, Brazil, Bolivia, Romania, Peru, USA, Belgium, Paraguay and the hosts. Fifty years earlier, the competition could not have been played; would not, in fact, have even been dreamed of. But in the late 19th century, football had spread like wildfire, carried around the world by English sailors (to France), engineers (to Spain), schoolteachers (to Switzerland and Germany), textile workers (to Holland), businessmen (to Argentina), students (to Portugal and Uruguay) and Scottish shipyard workers (to Sweden).

As early as 1866, British students were playing football in Portugal. By 1869 it had been introduced to Swiss schools and in 1872, a group of British sailors formed the Le Havre club in France. At around the same time their colleagues were playing the first football games half a world away in Brazil.

British influence can still be seen in the names of clubs around the world – AC Milan (rather than Milano), Athletic (not Atlético) Bilbao, Newell's Old Boys in Argentina, Young Boys of Berne, Corinthians of Brazil and Chile's Everton to name just a few.

But though they undoubtedly played the leading role, it wasn't just the British who helped the game to flourish worldwide. FC Barcelona, for example, who despite borrowing their club colours from the old school of one of several English players who turned out in their first game, were founded by a Swiss, Joan Gamper, who had learned and loved the game at school. Internazionale of Milan (Inter Milan) chose their name because of the cosmopolitan make-up of their team. Yes, the British took football to the world, but it wasn't long before the world adopted football as its own.

In Brazil, Charles Miller, the son of an English father and a Brazilian mother, returned from studying in England with two footballs. Within the space of a year, the five teams Miller had organised for a São Paulo state championship had swelled to 70.

In neighbouring Argentina, River Plate were founded by an Englishman and Boca Juniors by an Irishman, but it was the Italians who oversaw and pushed through the real growth of football there, as they did in Uruguay. Meanwhile, in Africa, colonialists – French, German and Portuguese, as well as English – played their part in introducing the game to the continent.

As football's popularity boomed around the world, so too did its organisation. In 1889, the Dutch and Danish football associations were established. By 1900, the associations of New Zealand, Argentina, Chile, Belgium, Italy, Germany, Switzerland and Uruguay were also up and running, and it was becoming increasingly apparent that, just as individual countries had football associations, so the sport would benefit from an organisation that could oversee the growth of the global game in the 20th Century.

In May 1904, the Fédération Internationale de Football Association – FIFA – came into being, founded by representatives from France, Belgium, Holland, Spain, Sweden and Switzerland. The English FA wrote to say that they could see no need for the new federation.

Above: France set-sail for the inaugural 1930 World Cup, they were one of only four European teams to compete.

Opposite top: Henri Delaunay, the founder of the European Championship.

Opposite bottom: Leônidas and his Brazilian team-mates enjoy a kickabout while waiting for a train during the 1938 World Cup in France.

Right: FIFA president Jules Rimet, the man who established the World Cup and lent his name to its original trophy.

Overleaf: Uruguay and Argentina contest the 1930 World Cup final in Montevideo.

(It would not be the last time that arrogance resulted in the English being missing at the start; in later years, the World Cup, European Cup and European Championship would all begin without the presence of English teams.)

Initially FIFA struggled to make a mark. Within a year the idea of a world championship had been raised, but when the first competition was arranged for 1906 in Switzerland, no-one entered. Yet despite this setback, there was a growing clamour for nations to test themselves against each other. The first opportunity had come at the Olympic Games of 1896, but since the teams taking part came from Denmark, Athens and Izmir, it could hardly be seen as a real international tournament.

The following two Olympics saw football played merely as a demonstration sport, but in 1908 in London the game was finally accepted, with England beating Denmark 2-0 in the final. They repeated the trick four years later with a 4-2 win in Stockholm.

In those early years of the 20th Century, it was the European nations who led the way. By the mid-1920s, however, Europe was being forced to take note of the increasing strength of South American football. Uruguay won the 1924 Olympic title, thrashing Switzerland in the final, and in 1928 they won gold again, beating neighbours Argentina in a replay.

The South Americans had also organised their own international tournament, the Copa América. Initially beginning as an unofficial championship in 1910, featuring Argentina, Uruguay and Chile, the Copa América had developed in to an annual opportunity for the major South American football-playing nations to test themselves against each other. The result was an improvment of standards throughout the continent and the development of tough, competitive teams.

The FIFA president, a Frenchman by the name of Jules Rimet, watched with growing interest. A long-time advocate of a world championship, Rimet now sensed an opportunity to finally get the project off the ground, and when Uruguay offered to host and fund the inaugural World Cup, his dream became reality. Little did Rimet know as he set out for South America with just four European countries agreeing to send teams, that his brainchild would become the biggest sporting event in the world.

FIFA HAD EXPERIENCED massive growth by the 1950s. Founded by the federations in Europe, in its first half-century football's world governing body had become truly global, its role much broader than initially envisaged, with the World Cup now established as the shining symbol of that development. With FIFA's attentions divided across Africa, Asia and the Americas, as well as Europe, the Europeans decided to create their own governing body to more carefully protect their interests and administer to their needs. In June 1954, at a meeting in Basle, Switzerland, UEFA was born.

Almost immediately, a plan was put in place for a national European Championship. The competition had actually been suggested nearly 30 years earlier by Henri Delaunay, a colleague of Jules Rimet at the French Federation, who considered the World Cup a bridge too far, arguing that the logical first step was to create a European Championship. The World Cup had captured FIFA's imagination, however, and the European Championship was duly forgotten, though never by Delaunay.

In fact, Europe was a late starter in having its own international competition. By the time of the first European Championship final in 1960, the Copa América was well established; the first African Nations Cup had kicked-off in 1957, with Egypt beating Ethiopia 4-0 in the final; the inaugural Asian Games had seen India victorious in 1951, with South Korea lifting the Asian Cup five years later; and the first CONCACAF Championship (for North

1957 The Confederation of African Football is founded and Egypt beat Ethiopia 4-0 to become the first African Nations Cup winners.

1958 Just Fontaine of France scores a record 13 goals in six games at the World Cup. Pelé is the youngest ever World Cup winner at 17 and scores twice in the final. Barcelona win the first Inter-Cities Fairs Cup, beating London Select 8-2 on aggregate.

1960 The Soviet Union win the first European Championship, beating Yugoslavia 2-1 in the final. Uruguayan side Peñarol become the first winners of the Copa Libertadores. Real Madrid win the European Cup for the fifth consecutive time, beating Eintracht Frankfurt 7-3. They also win the first World Club Cup, beating Peñarol 5-1 on aggregate.

1961 CONCACAF is founded in North and Central America. Juventus become the first Italian side to be awarded a gold star following their tenth title victory. Tottenham win England's first domestic 'double' of the 20th Century. Fulham's Johnny Haynes becomes the first British player to earn £100 per week. The first British £100,000 transfer sees Denis Law move from Manchester City to Torino. Fiorentina win the first European Cup Winners' Cup, beating Rangers 4-1 on aggregate. Aston Villa are the first League Cup winners.

1963 The West German Bundesliga begins. Prior to this German football had been regional. Tottenham win the Cup Winners' Cup against Atlético Madrid.

1964 Oryx Douala of Cameroon win the first African Champions Club Cup. George Best makes his debut for Manchester United. Alfredo Di Stéfano scores his 49th European Cup goal.

1965 Stanley Matthews is the first footballer to be knighted. The Football League agree to one substitute per team in the event of injury. Arthur Rowley retires with a record 434 goals in the English Football League.

and Central America) had been won by Costa Rica back in 1941.

If the Europeans were slow to organise their first international championship, however, they were the pioneers of international club competitions. The godfather of international club football was an Austrian, Hugo Meisl, who hit upon the idea of a competition between the very best teams from Hungary, Czechoslovakia, Yugoslavia and Austria. He called his creation the Mitropa Cup, from the German for central Europe – Mittel Europa. The format was simple, but ingenious: a two-legged (home and away) knockout with the winners progressing. The first competition, in 1927, was won by Sparta Prague, and in 1929 the Italians took part adding to the prestige. Sadly, World War II halted the competition in mid-flight, and though it

returned in the post-war years, in 1955 the bigger European competitions were already on their way, signalling the beginning of the end. (Amazingly the competition continued until 1991, when Torino lifted the trophy.)

The Mitropa Cup was crucial to the development of international club football (as was the Latin Cup, a competition involving teams from Spain, Italy, Portugal and France, which debuted in 1949). It was the forerunner – in both concept and format – to the competition that would go on to become the richest and most glittering club competition in the world; the European Champions Cup.

The European Cup was actually born out of arrogance – the arrogance, once again, of the English. Their over-the-top response to Wolverhampton Wanderers' victory over Hungary's Honvéd at a waterlogged Molineux

prompted the editor of France's *L'Equipe* to propose what he called a 'proper European club cup', pitching the champions of each country against each other in a knockout format based on the Mitropa Cup.

The English immediately banned champions Chelsea from taking part. But those more familiar with international club competitions, like Real Madrid, Milan and Sporting Lisbon, were enthusiastic, seeing the commercial and sporting benefits of playing against the top clubs from all over Europe. So, in 1955, the European Cup began, with immediate success.

In other circumstances Real Madrid's dominance – they won the first five finals – could have caused the competition to stagnate, but the manner of their victories and the wonderful football they played merely raised the stakes and European football was soon climbing to new heights.

Before long, two other notable European competitions had kicked-off: the Cup Winners' Cup (a knockout between domestic cup winners) and the Inter-Cities Fairs Cup (later to become the UEFA Cup), a competition that owes its origins to an age when industrial trade fairs were held in Europe's major cities. UEFA's idea was to arrange a competition that could be played between select XIs of the cities that hosted these fairs. To begin with the matches were only played when the fairs were taking place, with the result that the first competition kicked off in June 1955 but didn't finish until May 1958, when Barcelona defeated London in the first final.

By the early 1960s, however, all three competitions were annual events and had cemented their places in the European football calendar, broadening the football experience and horizons of all who took part. Their success saw replicas spring up around the world. CONCACAF launched their own Champions Cup in 1962, Mexico's Guadalajara taking the first honours, and the African Champions Cup arrived two years later, with Cameroon's Oryx Douala drawing first blood. The African Cup Winners' Cup followed in 1975 and the CAF Cup (essentially the African federation's version of the UEFA Cup) in 1992. In Asia, a club championship launched in 1967 but lasted just four years before falling apart (partly due to the huge geographical area covered). It returned in 1985 with South Korea's Daewoo Royals triumphant, and it also was joined by a Cup Winners' Cup in 1990.

The Europeans were also responsible for South America's Copa Libertadores. In the mid-Fifties, just as the European Cup was taking off, Henri Delaunay suggested a match between the club champions of Europe and those of South America. The South Americans liked the idea – despite the absence of Africa, Asia and the rest of the Americas, football's powerhouses of Europe and South America considered this a world championship – but before it could take place they needed to establish who the South American champions were. For that, they needed a competition. They came up with the Copa Libertadores, won in its inaugural year, 1960, by Uruguay's Peñarol, who gleefully headed off for a money-spinning tie with the European champions, Real Madrid, in what was known as the Intercontinental Cup, or World Club Cup.

BY THE MID-1960s, the fundamental structure of world and domestic football was established. FIFA was at the head of the global game, with UEFA (Europe), CONCACAF (Central and North America), CAF (Africa), CONMEBOL (South America), AFC (Asia) and OFC (Oceania) each taking control of their own geographical areas and running events such as the international club competitions and continental championships. The national football associations were then in charge of domestic football and their national teams.

In that sense, little has changed. But though the structure remains familiar, football at the beginning of the new millennium is hardly recognisable from the game of 40 years ago. In the Sixties, local heroes mixed with fans on the way to matches, sharing buses, playing for the love of the game and earning a decent, but far from spectacular living. When their careers ended, they would seek other work and many struggled to make ends meet. The history books are full of tragic stories of great footballers, like Brazil's World Cup-winning Garrincha, whose lives ended in the gutter.

In contrast, today's football stars live a life of luxury, hidden away in palatial homes, treated like movie stars with flashy cars and bulging pay packets. When they retire in their 30s, many will never have to work again (some, like Raúl, Ronaldo and Michael Owen, were in that position by their early 20s).

The move towards big wages actually began in South America as long ago as the 1940s, when the best players in the world, like Alfredo Di Stéfano, were lured to earn their fortunes in Colombia's super league. In 1951, however, Colombia (who had been expelled) rejoined FIFA on condition that the foreign players left. Rubbing their hands with glee, Europe's top clubs were quick to capitalise, not least Real Madrid who, led by a Spanish lawyer called Santiago Bernabéu, were determined to become the world's best club. Bernabéu offered the likes of Di Stéfano and Hector Rial up to £10,000 a year. Not surprisingly they

took him up on that offer, laying the foundations for Madrid's early dominance of the European Champions Cup.

Italian clubs followed suit, paying their top players huge salaries in search of glory, but elsewhere in Europe players earned far less. It was not until Jimmy Hill led a revolution in 1961 that the English Football League abandoned its maximum wage for players, while in Germany and Belgium, players were not professional until the mid-Sixties.

But even in the 1970s and 1980s, with wages theoretically limitless and hundreds of

Above: Celtic's Jimmy Johnstone takes on Racing Club in the 1967 World Club Cup.

Opposite: Alfredo Di Stéfano, whose move to the unofficial Colombian super league was an early example of 'player power'.

WERELDBEKER   PRIJS F 1,—

AJAX–INDEPENDIENTE

DONDERDAG
28 SEPTEMBER 1972

OLYMPISCH STADION
AMSTERDAM

Far left: Davie Provan of Rangers defends against Bayern Munich in the 1967 European Cup Winners' Cup final.

Left: The programme from the second leg of the 1972 World Club Cup, which pitted Ajax against Independiente.

professional clubs watched by millions of fans, the idea of millionaire footballers was laughable. It was not until the 1990s that football, the world's most popular sport, finally became a big business.

Throughout the Seventies and Eighties, companies had increasingly used footballers to advertise their products, or made use of sponsorship opportunities to publicise their brand on club shirts or pitchside hoardings. The sport enjoyed a commercial awakening and transfer fees jumped to seven figures and top players reaped the rewards. But it was television that changed football forever.

In the late Eighties and early Nineties, new TV stations across Europe sought to challenge the state channels' monopolies and some of them – Rupert Murdoch's Sky in Britain, Silvio Berlusconi's Mediaset in Italy, and the Kirch group in Germany – saw football, 'the people's game', as the best way to do that. Off the back of a hugely successful 1990 World Cup in Italy, and with hopes that hooliganism was finally coming under control, football was enjoying a boom in popularity and these new TV companies wanted a part of it.

The result was more and more TV coverage of the game with a resultant boost in exposure for any brands associated with clubs and players. What followed was an unseemly scramble as everyone from brewers to fast-food chains and mobile phone companies flocked to associate themselves with 'the beautiful game'.

The sudden commercial interest in the game did not go unnoticed in football's corridors of power. In England, the chairmen of the top clubs saw their opportunity to seize power from the FA and control the rapidly increasing TV revenues. In the 1992-3 season they launched the Premier League.

A year later UEFA followed with the Champions League, a reformatted European Cup guaranteeing more games (and therefore more TV coverage and money) for the top clubs. All of this led to ever-increasing sums of cash flooding into the game. Merchandising sales rocketed, TV contracts were signed for billions of pounds and clubs paid huge transfer fees and unprecedented salaries. In 2001 the commercial boom hit its peak when Real Madrid paid a world record £47 million for one player, France's Zinédine Zidane.

That appears to have been the high water-mark, however. A year later Madrid signed World Cup-winner Ronaldo for £22 million, and in 2003, the world's most marketable footballer, David Beckham, arrived at the Bernabéu for a fee that at most will be £24.5 million. However, many of Europe's top players still earn in excess of £5 million a year, and while Michael Ballack's transfer to Chelsea in the summer of 2006 might have been a free transfer as he was out of contract with Bayern Munich, his reported £120,000 a week salary made him the highest paid player in football history.

It's all a far cry from medieval rabbles or public schoolboys making up the rules as they went along. Who then could have predicted what football would become? Who now can guess what it will be like next century?

THE INCREASING POWER OF FOOTBALL CLUBS

Modern football is often disparagingly referred to as a business but clubs arguably turned into businesses the day Small Heath (now Birmingham City) became the game's first limited company in 1888. The advent of professionalism effectively sanctioned elites in football. Back then the Football Association, concerned about clubs and individuals making a profit out of football, ensured that, 'the right class of men who love football for its own sake' became directors by prohibiting their payment. Limits were also placed on the amount of dividend it was possible for shareholders to earn from clubs, a figure steadily levered up over the years.

This initial attempt by a governing body to control the finances and hence the power of clubs is a microcosm of the tension which has existed in the wider game ever since. In England the great financial sea change of the modern era began with the financial glut created by satellite TV coverage. The 1992 Premier League restructuring was not only a way of revitalising the game but of maximising earning potential, since the newly formed top division gained commercial independence from the Football Association and the Football League, giving it license to negotiate its own broadcast and sponsorship agreements.

The first Sky television agreement was worth £191 million over five seasons. The next contract, negotiated to start from the 1997-8 season, rose to £670 million over four seasons, then £1.024 billion until 2007. After 2007 the TV rights will be split between Sky and Sentanta, achieving a £1.706 billion windfall for the Premiership. With the bulk of funds ending up with the biggest clubs, their ability to challenge the status quo has been hugely enhanced.

This has been mirrored in Europe where major broadcasters have become so influential that there has been a vertical integration, with media companies taking stakes in top clubs. Fininvest, the Italian-listed media group, holds a majority shareholding in AC Milan. In France, Canal+, the broadcaster and media company, holds a controlling interest in Paris Saint-Germain. Meanwhile, in Deloitte's 2006 list of the world's elite clubs, the top 20 were all European, underlining how real power in the world game now resides within the European Union's strongest and richest leagues: the English Premiership, Italy's Serie A, Spain's La Liga and Germany's Bundesliga.

For the biggest, European competition is seen as the holy grail: giant club vs giant club generating major gates while maximising television revenue and business opportunities. Threats of a breakaway league by Europe's top clubs led to the creation of the Champions

League in the early Nineties, but this step was not enough for the elite. In September 2000, 14 leading clubs – Ajax, Barcelona, Bayern Munich, Borussia Dortmund, Inter Milan, Juventus, Liverpool, Manchester United, Marseille, AC Milan, Paris Saint-Germain, Porto, PSV Eindhoven and Real Madrid – established an organisation, G-14, to pursue their interests with voting power weighted in favour of those with the most European Cup wins (ie. Real Madrid get 20 votes: two for each European Cup, one for each UEFA Cup). Four further clubs were subsequently admitted to the caucus (Arsenal, Bayer Leverkusen, Lyon and Valencia), swelling the ranks to 18.

This pressure group is composed of the most powerful clubs in football across seven countries, though even within such a small group there are anomalies. While Manchester United and Juventus can lay claim to domestic dominance in recent years, Inter Milan last won a championship in 1989, Paris Saint-Germain 1994, Bayer Leverkusen, never. So what unites the group is not success but power and the willingness to flex it, in this case against UEFA.

G-14's mission statement, to 'promote cooperation... between G-14 and FIFA, UEFA..., paying special attention to negotiating the format, administration and operation of the club competitions in which the member clubs are involved' betrays its aim: to run the game for its own interests.

Ultimately, G-14 wants professional clubs to have executive representation within UEFA and FIFA. Equally a leaked draft report in 2006 suggested that G-14 wished to ensure its 18 members could participate in Europe's elite club competition every year, creating a closed shop. G-14 is essentially involved in a battle for control of the game. It opposed

UEFA when the Champions League second stage was cancelled in 2003 and is now lobbying for its restoration, but this is a minor skirmish compared to the major battle unfolding in a Brussels court in 2006.

G-14 are bankrolling a compensation case brought by minor Belgian club Charleroi, whose Moroccan midfielder Abdelmajid Oulmers returned from international duty injured. Charleroi claim that with him they would have qualified for the Champions League, but by extension a ruling could mean all players' wages are paid by the national associations when they are called up for international duty. Not a great burden for the major European powers, but one that might instantly cripple World Cup hopefuls like Ivory Coast or Angola, setting African football back to the dark ages.

Karl-Heinz Rummenigge, Bayern Munich chairman and G-14 member, also spoke out in March 2006, threatening to open a further case with FIFA for club compensation after his nation's World Cup competition. The accusation is that FIFA act as a monopoly, taking money from the clubs via hugely successful global competitions.

Given European courts' refusal to make football a special case over claims like the Bosman ruling, it seems that the traditional pyramid structure, whereby the governing bodies ruled the game, might well be overturned in the near future. Few would argue that UEFA and FIFA are selfless or far-sighted, or even that they don't need reform, but their statutes do ensure they make provision for the future health of the game. The likelihood in the short term is that the G-14 clubs will profit enormously, but if they succeed in ring-fencing the game, fans may well vote with their feet. It would not be the first time a golden goose was slaughtered.

Above: As Bayern Munich chairman Karl-Heinz Rummenigge has voiced his opinions in the battle between the major football clubs and the governing bodies of the game.

Opposite top: Zinédine Zidane poses between Real Madrid chairman Florentino Perez and club legend Alfrédo Di Stefano after his transfer to the Bernabéu in 2001.

Opposite bottom: Barcelona celebrate winning the 2006 Champions League final at the Stade de France in Paris.

Right: Manchester United saw their first team squad decimated on a runaway in Munich in 1958.

FOOTBALL DISASTERS

1902: As Scotland play out a 1-1 draw with England, wooden planking gives way under the weight of 20,000 people in Ibrox's new West Stand – 25 fans die and hundreds are injured as the 40-foot high structure crashes to the ground.

1946: More than 65,000 fans are packed into Bolton's Burnden Park for an eagerly anticipated FA Cup sixth round tie with Stoke City. With another 20,000 milling around outside, many force their way into the ground, causing a crush barrier to collapse. Thirty-three people die from asphyxiation and more than 500 are injured, but the game restarts after just 26 minutes, with lifeless bodies still evident round the edge of the pitch.

1949: A plane carrying the entire Torino squad crashes into the Superga hills near Turin following a friendly match in Lisbon, Portugal. The crash is the biggest tragedy Italian sport has ever experienced. Torino had won the Serie A title for the previous four years and their team made up the bulk of Italy's national side. In total, 31 people die, including 18 players. Torino's youth team complete the season and receive the Serie A trophy.

1958: On February 6, Flight BE609, a British European Airways plane, crashes on its third attempt to take off in a blizzard from Munich-Riem airport. On board are the players and officials of Manchester United, plus a number of journalists and supporters. United are returning from a 3-3 draw with Red Star Belgrade which had earnt them a place in the semi-finals, when the plane stops in Munich for a scheduled refuel. The pilot, Captain James Thain, tries to take off for the final leg of the journey but twice has to abort due to engine trouble. When the plane finally takes off at 3.04pm, it fails to reach the required height and crashes into a fence and a house: 23 of the 43 passengers die, including seven United

Below left: The terraces of the Heysel Stadium, where 39 fans died before the 1985 European Cup final.

Below right: A policeman helps an injured fan at Hillsborough Stadium in 1989, on a day when 96 died.

players. Young star Duncan Edwards passes away some 15 days later. A build-up of slush, causing deceleration of the aircraft, is later blamed for the crash.

1964: The fierce South American rivalry between Peru and Argentina spills into the stands as a last minute Peruvian goal is ruled out in an Olympic qualifying match in Lima. The decision sparks mass rioting inside the National Stadium and 318 people are killed, with a further 500 injured. Martial law is put in place for 30 days.

1968: When fans of Boca Juniors drop lit torches on the rival fans of River Plate inside the Monumental Stadium, Buenos Aires, 74 people are killed and 113 are injured. Those at the front of the ensuing melee are crushed to death due to a closed passageway.

1969: El Salvador and Honduras go to war as a result of a World Cup tie in Mexico, which

the Salvadorians won 3-2. Many Salvadorians living in Honduras are attacked and killed before the Salvador government launches a military attack.

1971: A disaster occurs at Ibrox on January 2 when, as a Rangers v Celtic match looks set to end in a goalless draw, Celtic take the lead, prompting a mass exodus of Rangers fans. Although Colin Stein then equalises, Stairway 13 at the ground gives way, resulting in the death of 66 fans. Initially it is speculated that fans trying to get back into the stadium are to blame and this myth is believed for many years.

1982: Some 340 people are killed as Spartak Moscow fans rush back into the Lenin Stadium following a late UEFA Cup equaliser against Dutch side Haarlem. While the incident is played down by police, who insist that just 61 people are dead, a report into the disaster seven years later reveals the real death toll.

1985: With Bradford City fans celebrating their Third Division title win, a loose cigarette end falls in to rubbish underneath Valley Parade's main stand. The wood and asbestos construction is quickly engulfed in flames and, with the exits at the back of the stand locked, 56 people lose their lives. The disaster leads to new legislation to increase safety in British football stadia.

1985: England is hit with a second tragedy in the same year when riots – started by English fans prior to Liverpool's European Cup final against Juventus – result in the death of 39 spectators inside the archaic Heysel Stadium in Brussels, Belgium. As the clashes intensify between the Liverpool section and the Juventus

contingent in the 'neutral' block Z, Juve fans trying to escape the violence cower towards the corner flag at the front of the terracing. Under the intense pressure, a wall collapses and dozens of fans are either crushed or trampled underfoot. As a result, UEFA ban English clubs from European competition indefinitely.

1988: At least 93 fans are killed and more than 100 are injured in Kathmandu in Nepal, when a severe hailstorm leads to a stampede among fans at a game between Jankapur and Mukti Jodha. The fatalities occur because the stadium doors are locked.

1989: Britain's worst sporting disaster occurs when Liverpool fans, eager to get into the ground to see their club's FA Cup semi-final with Nottingham Forest at Hillsborough, converge in a bottleneck outside the Leppings Lane end of the ground. With an estimated 5,000 trying to get in and an increasingly dangerous situation developing, the police decide to open a set of gates that do not have turnstiles. The result is hundreds of fans entering the ground through a narrow tunnel at the rear of the terrace and into two already overcrowded central pens. With

security fences present, many at the front are crushed by the volume of people: 96 die and 766 are injured. As a result, the Taylor Report recommends that all fences are removed from grounds and stadia should become all-seater.

1991: Kaizer Chiefs score a goal against Orlando Pirates, which causes fighting and a stampede at the game in Orkney, near Johannesburg: 40 are killed and over 50 are injured.

1992: Just 15 minutes before Bastia play Marseille in a French Cup semi-final, a temporary metal stand in the Corsican town collapses, leading to the deaths of 15 people. The competition is cancelled for the season.

1993: A plane carrying the Zambian national squad crashes into the sea off Gabon on their way to a World Cup qualifier against Senegal. There are no survivors. The team's best player and captain, Kalusha Bwalya, is not onboard as he was making his own way to the game from Holland, where he was playing for PSV.

1996: A stampede during the all-Central American clash between Guatemala and Costa

Rica results in 84 deaths and 150 injuries in Guatemala City. The Stadio Meteo Flores held 45,000 but 60,000 were present on the day.

2001: Tragedy again strikes a Kaizer Chiefs v Orlando Pirates clash. A stampede outside the Ellis Park stadium in Johannesburg causes the death of 43 people inside, while 126 fans also die in the Accra Stadium in Ghana following a riot during the derby match between Hearts Of Oak and Asante Kotoko.

Above: Celtic manager Jock Stein and Willie Waddell of Rangers lift a body on to a stretcher after the disaster at Ibrox in 1971.

Below: The Kaizer Chiefs team carry a wreath in memory of the fans who died at Johannesburg's Ellis Park stadium in 2001.

FOOTBALL SCANDALS

1900: Burnley goalkeeper Jack Hillman is the first British player suspended from football. He tries to bribe Nottingham Forest to lose. They win 4-0 and Hillman is banned for a year.

1904: Manchester City are fined £250 and their Hyde Road ground is shut for two games after they break transfer rules signing Glossop's Irvine Thornley and Frank Norgrove. Thornley is banned for a season.

1905: Middlesbrough, who have just bought Alf Common in the first £1,000 transfer, are fined £250 and 11 directors are suspended for three years after the club are found guilty of making illegal payments.

1905: Manchester City's Billy Meredith is banned for a season for attempting to bribe Aston Villa's Alec Leake while City are chasing the title.

1906: Some 17 current and former Manchester City players are fined a total of £900, suspended for six months and banned from playing for the club again after accepting illegal payments.

1909: Fulham's George Parsonage is banned for life after asking for a £50 signing on fee from Chesterfield.

1911: Middlesbrough chairman Thomas Poole and manager Andy Walker are banned for trying to fix a game against Sunderland.

1919: Leeds City are wound up by the FA after making illegal payments to players. Leeds United are formed.

Below: An early legend of the game, Manchester City's Billy Meredith was banned for a year in 1905 after being implicated in a match-fixing scandal.

1924: John Browning and Archibald Kyle are handed 60 days' hard labour for trying to fix games between Scottish Division Two clubs Bo'Ness and Lochgelly.

1927: Torino win the Scudetto, only to have their title annulled weeks later when it is alleged that Juventus defender Luigi Allemandi was bribed in a crucial game, even though he actually played quite well in the match. He is banned for life, but the ban is rescinded and he plays on to win the title with Inter Milan and the World Cup with Italy in 1934.

1930: At the 1930 World Cup, hosts Uruguay have a little help with the build-up to their third semi-final goal against Yugoslavia. The ball appears to go out of play, only to be kicked discretely back onto the pitch by a uniformed policeman.

1932: Former Montrose skipper Gavin Hamilton spends 60 days in jail after offering Montrose player David Mooney £50 to fix a home match with Edinburgh City.

1957: Sunderland are hit with a record £5,000 fine from the Football League for illegal payments to players.

1965: Sheffield Wednesday players Peter Swan, Tony Kay and David Layne are exposed for fixing a pools win and placing a £50 bet that correctly predicted their team would beat Ipswich Town 2-0. The scam, masterminded by Mansfield Town's Jimmy Gauld, results in ten players being found guilty of conspiracy to defraud. Gauld is jailed for four years, the others between four and 15 months. The Wednesday trio are also banned from football for life, which is overturned in 1972

1967: Millwall are fined £1,000 after fans attack referee Norman Burtenshaw at The Den.

1968: Port Vale are expelled from the Football League for illegal payments but are immediately re-elected.

1970: The England captain Bobby Moore is arrested in Bogota, Colombia, after being falsely accused of stealing a bracelet prior to the World Cup in Mexico. The England squad have to fly on to Mexico without him and he rejoins the team in time for the tournament.

1970: Derby County qualify for the Fairs Cup but are banned for administrative irregularities.

1971: Fifty-three players from seven West German clubs receive various punishments for match-fixing. Arminia Bielefeld are demoted to a regional league for their involvement, while Kickers Offenbach are stripped of their playing license for two years.

1973: Juventus are accused of using a go-between to try and bribe Francisco Marques Lobo, the referee for their European Cup semi-final game with Derby County.

1974: Polish players accuse their Italian opponents of offering cash incentives to lose a vital World Cup clash between the teams. Italy lose 2-1 and are eliminated.

1974: On the eve of the 1974 World Cup final, German newspaper Bild Zeitung runs the headline 'Cruyff, Champagne and Naked Girls', suggesting there had been a 'naked party' in the swimming pool of the Dutch team's hotel the night before the Brazil game, involving four Dutch players and two German girls. Johan Cruyff's wife keeps him on the phone late into the night before the final.

1977: Manchester United sack their manager Tommy Docherty following his affair with the wife of physio Laurie Brown.

1978: Scottish referee John Gordon and his two linesmen are suspended by the Scottish FA for accepting £1,000 presents from AC Milan prior to their UEFA Cup match with Levski Spartak. The Italian club are fined £8,000 by UEFA.

1978: It is alleged that Peru's game with Argentina at the 1978 World Cup was fixed by the Argentine military government, who shipped 35,000 tons of free grain to Peru, and possibly arms too, while the Argentine central bank unfroze $50 million in credits. Argentina won the game 6-0 and progressed to the World Cup final.

1980: Italy striker Paolo Rossi is banned for two years when it emerges that Perugia's 2-2 draw with Avellino the previous year, in which Rossi scored twice for the former, was fixed by a betting syndicate – 20 players are banned in the same investigation and AC Milan and Lazio are both relegated to Serie B for involvement in the bribery scam.

1982: Standard Liege manager Raymond Goethals and 13 players are banned for life for offering sweeteners to SV Thor Waterschei to ensure they won the Belgium League.

1985: Millwall fans riot at Kenilworth Road, prompting Luton to ban all away fans.

1986: Roma are banned from European competition for a season and president Dino Viola for four years after he tried to bribe the referee in a European Cup semi-final against Dundee United in 1982.

1988: Arsenal midfielder Paul Davis is banned for nine game for breaking the jaw of Southampton's Glenn Cockerill.

1989: Nottingham Forest boss Brian Clough receives a one-year touchline ban for striking a QPR spectator who had run on the pitch.

1990: Division One team Swindon are demoted to Division Three (Division Two on appeal) for irregular payments to players.

1990: Arsenal are deducted two points, Manchester United one, following a mass brawl at Old Trafford.

1990: Bologna's Giuseppe Lorenzo is sent-off after just ten seconds for striking an opponent in a league game against Parma.

1991: Diego Maradona is banned from playing in Italy for 15 months after taking cocaine before a Napoli match. He is also handed a 14-month suspended jail sentence.

1993: Marseille chairman Bernard Tapie bribes opposition players from Valenciennes to guarantee that his club can rest first-team players for the upcoming European Cup final and still clinch the French title. Marseille are stripped of both wins. Tapie is sentenced to two years in prison.

1993: Former Manchester United player Mickey Thomas is jailed for 18 months for printing his own £10 notes.

1994: Diego Maradona is sent home from USA 94 for testing positive for weight loss drug ephedrine.

1995: Eric Cantona is banned from football for nine months following a two-footed, kung-fu attack on Crystal Palace fan Matthew Simmons.

1995: Arsenal sack George Graham after he is found guilty of accepting a £285,000 'bung' from agent Rune Hauge following the transfer of John Jensen to Highbury.

1997: Bruce Grobbelaar, John Fashanu and Hans Segers go on trial for match-fixing. Grobbelaar is accused of taking £40,000 to make sure Liverpool lost to Newcastle in 1993, while Segers and Fashanu's involvement concerns a

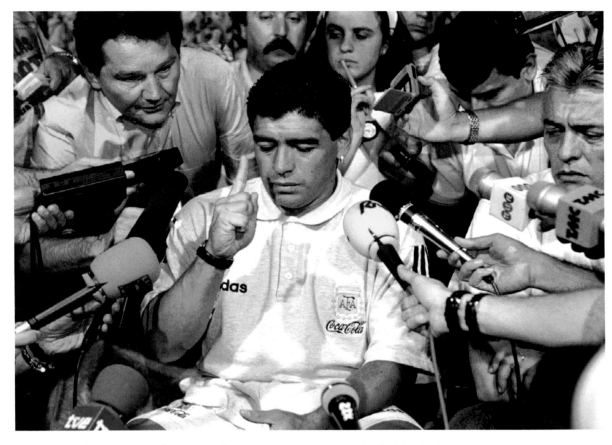

Wimbledon defeat against Manchester United. All three are acquitted.

1997: Anderlecht admit that they gave the referee a £20,000 'loan' prior to the club's UEFA Cup semi-final victory over Nottingham Forest in 1984. Forest start court proceedings.

1999: Chelsea coach Graham Rix is sentenced to prison for having sex with a 15-year-old girl while on first-team duty with the club.

1999: A Malaysian-based betting syndicate is caught trying to install a remote-control device to sabotage the floodlights at Charlton Athletic. Investigations prove floodlight failures at West Ham and Crystal Palace in 1997 were caused by the syndicate.

2001: Dutch stars Jaap Stam, Edgar Davids and Frank de Boer receive bans for testing positive for the banned steroid nandralone.

2003: Faria Alam is dismissed from her job at the FA after it emerges she had affairs with chief executive Mark Palios and England coach Sven-Göran Eriksson.

2003: Manchester United defender Rio Ferdinand is banned for nine months from both club and international football after he fails to attend a drug test.

2004: Referee Ncedisile Zakhe is charged with the murder of Michael Sizani after the Marcelle

coach criticises his penalty decision during a game with Ekuphumuleni in South Africa.

2005: German referee Robert Hoyzer is sentenced to two years and five months in prison, and banned from refereeing for life, following his bid to rig nine matches in a £1.3 million betting fraud in 2004.

2005: Brazilian referee Edilson Pereira de Carvalho is banned for life after being found guilty of taking money from a gambling ring to manipulate results – 11 championship games are declared null and void.

2005: Serie B champions Genoa demoted to Serie C1 after being found guilty of bribing Venezia in the final game of the season.

2006: Paolo di Canio is fined £7,000 for making a facist salute after Lazio's defeat of Roma.

2006: Turkey are ordered by FIFA to play six home matches at a neutral ground and behind closed doors following a fracas after their World Cup play-off elimination against Switzerland.

2006: The Juventus board resigns, as does the President of the Italian football federation, after serious allegations surface of match-fixing in the 2004-5 season. Juventus are punished with relegation to Serie B and a 17-point deduction (they are also stripped of their last two titles). Fiorentina and Lazio are given points deductions after appealing against relegation to Serie B.

Above: Argentina captain Diego Maradona faces the press in Dallas after failing a drug test at the 1994 World Cup.

Left: Manchester United's Eric Cantona attacks a Crystal Palace fan after being abused from the terraces in 1995.

HISTORY OF TACTICS & FORMATIONS

FOOTBALL IS THE world's number one sport. The basic principle of the game has stayed the same – to score more goals than your opponent – but law changes and tactical innovations have led to significant changes in the way that the game is approached by the 22 players on the pitch.

English teams of the amateur era of the 1870s generally lined up with a goalkeeper, a full-back, two half-backs and seven forwards. The half-backs would invariably join the surge forward and some teams even played with eight forwards dispensing with a half-back. The English game was based on the skill of dribbling. Once a player got possession of the ball he would just plough his way forward until either he scored or lost possession. Running in his wake would be his team-mates, 'backing up'. In effect, those 'backing-up' were waiting for the ball to come loose so they could take over possession and continue the surge goalward.

The Scots, meanwhile, played football as a team game, as did the northern English clubs. They played with one less forward and an additional full-back, lining up with a 2-2-6 formation. They even passed the ball to each other. It was no coincidence that they won nine of the first 14 internationals against England, who persevered with their dribbling style. The innovation of passing had the profound effect of diminishing the value of 'dribbling'. Passing the ball was less exhausting than running from one end of the pitch to the other and weaving through a dense mass of players. Heading was

also introduced to the game by Scottish and northern players, while in the amateur university-educated South it was frowned upon.

The next innovation came in England in the 1890s with the evolution of the 2-3-5 'pyramid formation' that had two full-backs with two wider half-backs ahead of them, with a newly-created centre-half in the middle. The five-man attack now had two wide players as wingers in the outside-left and outside-right positions. In the middle was a centre-forward flanked by forwards at inside-right and inside-left, in positions between the wide men and the centre-forward. In this formation the centre-half became the key player. His role was to instigate attacks and his ability to pass and drive forward was priceless.

The quality of passing had got better and better and in 1883 Blackburn Olympic became the first northern working class team to win the FA Cup. Tactically what was so significant about Blackburn's success was that they utilised the width of the pitch and played what was described as a 'wide-passing' game.

The next big tactical change came in the 1920s as a result of a full-back playing for Newcastle United called Bill McCracken. McCracken, along with fellow full-back Frank Hudspeth, adopted the tactic of running up the field with the deliberate and successful intention of catching his opponents' attackers offside. At the time the offside rule was that three players had to be in front of the player receiving the ball. McCracken exploited this

with his regular dashes up field. McCracken was so good at this that Newcastle's fixtures were plagued by as many as 40 stops per game, as free-kicks were constantly awarded for the effective deployment of this offside trap.

The FA changed the offside rule so that only two players needed to be in front of the player receiving the ball, beginning from the 1925-6 season. The effect was immediate, with a staggering 6,373 goals scored in the four divisions of the English Football League. The previous season the figure had only been 4,700. It was great for fans but not so great for managers. The club that was to confront the issue was Arsenal and their new manager Herbert Chapman, who developed what was to become known as the 'WM formation'. The centre-half became a 'stopper' between the two full-backs and ahead of them were the right-and left-halves. If you were to join their positions up the five players would form a 'W'. The 'M' part had the inside-right and inside-left behind the wingers and centre-forward.

The WM formation brought Arsenal unbelievable success. They were to dominate the 1930s, winning the league championship five times and the FA Cup twice. Chapman was blessed with having the right players in the right positions to pull it off. Other English sides who copied the formation – and everyone did – never got to the same heights. Arsenal's WM method was defence-orientated. The Gunners could and did withstand pressure and would counter-attack with pace and

Above left to right: Sandor Kocsis of the Hungarian team that humiliated England 6-3 at Wembley in 1953; Johan Cruyff demonstrates Holland's Total Football of the early Seventies; It took the 4-2-4 formation to enable Brazil and Garrincha to lift the World Cup for the first time.

CRYSTAL PALACE.

Saturday, April 10th, 1897.

FINAL TIE

FOR THE

CHALLENGE CUP of the FOOTBALL ASSOCIATION.

ASTON VILLA.

Colours—
Claret and Light Blue Shirts,
White Knickers.

Goal.
X
WHITEHOUSE.

RIGHT.   **LEFT.**

Backs.

X   X
SPENCER.   EVANS.

Half-Backs.

X   X   X
REYNOLDS.   JAMES COWAN.   CRABTREE.

Forwards.

X   X   X   X   X
ATHERSMITH.   DEVEY.   CAMPBELL.   WHELDON.   JOHN COWAN.

( )

Forwards.

X   X   X   X   X
MILWARD.   CHADWICK.   HARTLEY.   BELL.   TAYLOR.

Half-Backs.

X   X   X
STEWART.   HOLT.   BOYLE.

LEFT.   **RIGHT.**

Backs.

X   X
STORRIER.   MEECHAN.

Goal.
X
MENHAM.

Colours—
Blue Shirts, White Knickers.

EVERTON.

Referee— J. LEWIS (Lancashire).   Linesmen— J. HOWCROFT (Redcar).   A. SCRAGG (Crewe).

Above: Herbert Chapman, seated front right, introduced the WM formation to the world with his Arsenal team.

precision. Once the ball was lost Arsenal went into solid defence mode and awaited the next opportunity to counter-attack. The wing-halves and inside-forwards could switch positions from attack to defence and vice-versa. Creating attacks now became the responsibility of the wingers and the importance of a good crosser of the ball became more apparent, particularly with the change to the corner kick rule which now prevented players from dribbling the ball directly from a corner.

Professionally Arsenal's methods were attracting attention at home and abroad, but supporters hated the Gunners and their success. It was during this period that the club earned the tag 'Lucky Arsenal'. The failing of the WM system, however, was that it was too rigid. Each position was clearly defined, even down to what number you wore on the back of your shirt.

Shirt numbering had been introduced during this period and was based on the 2-3-5 formation, with numbers unofficially allocated to positions as follows: 1 goalkeeper; 2 right full-back; 3 left full-back; 4 right half-back; 5 centre half-back; 6 left half-back; 7 outside-right; 8 inside-right; 9 centre-forward; 10 inside-left; 11 outside-left. Even with the advent of the WM system, the number five centre half-back became a 'stopper'. The rigidity showed itself by the way the wingers hugged the touchline, by the way defenders marked their set opponent, and by the way it was vulnerable to deep crosses.

The death knell for the WM system was sounded in November 1953 by the Hungarian national coach Guzstáv Sebes. The 'Magical Magyars' of Hungary were Olympic champions, unbeaten in over 20 games. Through individual flair and mesmerising team play Hungary inflicted a 6-3 thrashing upon the English, previously undefeated by continental opposition at home. From the start of the match, Hungary's players confused their opponents because they did not play where they were expected to. Nandor Hidgekuti wore the number 9 shirt, a position that would traditionally have been marked by an England centre-half, but when Harry Johnston set off to mark him, he found that Hidgekuti was playing in a deeper role. This allowed the inside-

forwards, Kocsis and Puskás, to push forward goal side of England's wing-halves, who were supposed to be marking them. Space was created and England's defence was in tatters. Hungary had a four-man backline and although not perfect on the night, it did allow the Hungarians to attack or defend with six players.

This system has proved hard to describe and has often been referred to as WW (inverting the attacking 'M' of 'WM'), or 3-3-4 (the centre-forward in midfield and the inside and outside forwards in attack), or sometimes as 3-5-2 (the wingers and centre-forward deemed to be part of a flexible midfield allowing them to attack or defend in numbers). It is also seen as a prototype of the 4-2-4 system that was also played in South America in the 1950s, notably by Flamengo, as well as other Brazilian and South American clubs. Where Hungary's version had failed to lift the World Cup in 1954, the Brazilian version went all the way in 1958. In Brazil, the concept of defence-first football had never taken hold. In the 4-2-4 formation the left-half was paired with the centre-half and these two players did the work of passing and ball-winning in midfield in order to release their wingers and two forwards to devastating effect in attack. It was a game that utilised width, passing and pace and a heavy lacing of individual Brazilian skill.

Brazil's success at the 1958 World Cup launched a wave of copycats across Europe to lesser degrees of success. One place where the flamboyant attack-minded Brazilian style did not take root was in Italy. Italy pursued a different route to winning that unleashed catenaccio (Italian for padlock) on football, utilising a sweeper in a system that lined-up 1-4-3-2. The sweeper was a fifth defender whose presence had two benefits: firstly, it would pack a defence that could smother opposition attacks, and secondly, if anything did get past the back four, then the sweeper would deal with any threat. It also allowed the four defenders to be more effective at man-for-man marking.

Catenaccio had its origins in Switzerland thanks to Austrian coach Karl Rappan who

developed a system known as the 'Bolt', or the 'Swiss Bolt'. The strength of the system was that a team would outnumber the opponents' attack with defenders. When going forward, the players took a 3-3-4 formation with an attacking centre-half and a three-man full-back line that moved well upfield. When possession was lost, all ten outfield players retreated behind the ball, the forwards harrying opponents to slow down the attack and the attacking centre-half turned into a centre-back, from where he could cover the full-backs and provide a 'sliding bolt' to lock out opposing forwards. The system was not widely used but it did reinforce the idea of a retreating defence and a deep-lying defender.

Italy had not resorted to the stopper until 1930s but with catenaccio they were to develop some of the world's best and most ruthless defenders. This defence-minded football has dominated the Italian game ever since, with quality defenders being as prized as star strikers.

In the 1960s England manager Alf Ramsey pioneered a formation that was to change the way that football was played. Until then wingers had been revered and relied upon to create goalscoring opportunities, but England won the 1966 World Cup by throwing convention out of the window. In the run up to the competition Ramsey had become less reliant on wingers, playing a 4-3-3 formation with just one recognised winger playing up front with twin forwards. He used this formation in the early stages of the World Cup, but in the knock-out phase, Ramsey dispensed with the idea of wide men and switched to a 4-4-2 formation, England's Wingless Wonders.

In the final England's four-man midfield saw young Alan Ball on the right and Martin Peters on the left, with the tenacious Nobby Stiles and the supremely talented Bobby Charlton paired in the middle behind a striking partnership of Roger Hunt and Geoff Hurst. Defensively it gave the two full-backs George Cohen and Ray Wilson space to move and each defender now was responsible for defending an area of the pitch, or a zone. The team without wingers and

Right: A pioneer of the 4-4-2 formation, England manager Sir Alf Ramsey talks tactics with Bobby Moore, captain of his Wingless Wonders.

ENGLAND 1870s (1-2-7)

Individual dribbling skills dominated the early English game. A player in possession would plough goalward until scoring or losing the ball. Chasing players – 'backing up' – seized the ball if possession was lost and continued dribbling forward.

SCOTLAND 1870s (2-2-6)

The Scottish game was more team-orientated and geared around passing the ball. A second full-back was also utilised at the expense of a forward player. On the surface it appeared more defensive but it was a superior style to the English dribbling game.

THE PYRAMID SYSTEM (2-3-5)

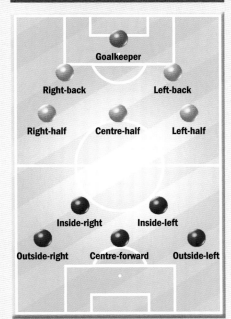

The creation of a centre-half as a free-roaming playmaker was the Pyramid System's dominant feature in the 1880s. It gave width and variation, as epitomised by Blackburn Olympic's 'wide-passing' game at the 1883 FA Cup final. It was also used by 1930 World Cup winners Uruguay.

WM

The centre-half became a centre-back to negate the centre-forward. Full-backs played wider to cancel the threat from the wings. The half-backs dealt with the threat of the inside-right/inside left (thus creating the 'battle for midfield'). Wingers became instigators of attack.

WW (HUNGARY 1950s)

This attacking formation was the undoing of WM. A deep-lying centre-forward was pulled back as a playmaker in midfield, allowing the inside-forwards to push ahead and exploit the space. Often described as a 3-5-2, or a 3-3-4, it is seen as a prototype 4-2-4.

4-2-4

Brazil's 4-2-4 was the attack-minded formation they used at the 1958 World Cup. It utilised width and numbers in attack, through either the midfield or the use of attacking full-backs. The system was geared towards scoring and it relied upon passing and speed.

The Bolt/Catenaccio (1-4-3-2)

A fifth defender, 'a sweeper', was introduced to pack the defence and also clear up if any attacker broke through the back four, who were each responsible for a particular attacker introducing close man-for-man marking.

Wingless Wonders (4-4-2)

Wingers were dropped and a forward was pulled back into midfield to create a 4-4-2 formation. A functional system, it was to lead to more use of overlapping full-backs and the development of striking partnerships.

4-3-3

In this varient of the wingless wonders team, two forwards could support the central striker, but it also gave the full-backs more mobility to attack and overlap. In moments of pressure, the midfield could be bolstered by a forward dropping back.

Total Football (Holland 1974)

The Total Football of Holland was dependent on physical mobility, tactical intelligence and crop of gifted players. Passing, movement and switching positions were the creative driving force behind this development. The attacking sweeper evolved here.

3-4-3

The realisation that you don't need four defenders to mark two attackers led teams such as France having a four-man midfield with twin attackers supported by another forward playing just behind them in the hole.

3-5-2

A formation of flexibility utilised by Argentina in 1986. The wide midfielders provide width in attack and while also packing the midfield to outnumber in central areas and also provide numbers for attack. A variation of 5-3-2, which is more defence orientated with a sweeper.

minus its star striker Jimmy Greaves defeated West Germany 4-2 after extra-time, with Hurst scoring the first-ever World Cup final hat-trick.

After 1966 wingers found themselves having to become midfielders, or they were increasingly overlooked. An alternate 4-3-3 formation became a spin-off but still led to a more defensive game. Rising sides like Leeds United patented the 1-0 win and more than ever the game was focussed on not losing rather than setting out to win. It was all about power, pace and stamina and about stopping the opposition.

Fortunately Holland, a minor football nation that had only just turned professional, had already began moving away from the functional football of Ramsey. In the early 1970s their club sides Ajax and Feyenoord began dominating continental football and in 1974 the national team of Holland exploded onto the world stage with a breathtaking style of play that was termed 'Total Football'. West Germany were also exponents of the style, having won the 1972 European Championship playing that way and going on to win the 1974 World Cup.

The simple premise of Total Football was that any player could play in any position. The consequence of Ramsey's functional football was that other countries were looking for stalwarts to do a job without any flamboyance, but Total Football was educating players to utilise the best of their abilities for the team. During play both Holland and West Germany saw their players interchange positions in full knowledge of what each other was doing. Players simply had to have physical mobility and the tactical intelligence to understand the significance and consequences of what they were doing.

Another innovation was the attacking sweeper that was conceived by West Germany's Franz Beckenbauer. It turned Italy's negative catenaccio into a positive and influential tactic. Ironically, it was reverting to the influential centre-half of the turn of the century.

Despite these innovations, the defence-

orientated 4-4-2 still dominated the game, along with its 4-3-3 variation. By the 1980s, however, teams such as France, West Germany, Denmark and Spain realised there was no need to have four (or even five) defenders marking just two strikers. At the 1984 European Championship France turned to a 3-4-3 formation, with three defenders, four midfielders and three front men, with one of those just playing off the front two. Lacombe and Bellini were the French strikers, with Platini playing just behind them to such devastating effect. France won the title that year beating Spain in the final.

In the 21st century, 4-4-2 still carries credence with many coaches: with a goalkeeper, two attacking full-backs, two centre-backs, and a four-man midfield, including a defensive midfielder often playing in front of the two centre-backs in a holding position, and an

attacking midfielder who will play behind the front two attackers. The other two midfielders are there to link with the full-backs, to provide width and create opportunities.

Alternatives are 3-5-2, 5-3-2 and 4-5-1. Argentina played with three central defenders to win the 1986 World Cup, allowing Diego Maradona free reign behind the front two strikers. In that tournament teams like West Germany played 5-3-2 to protect themselves from the Mexican heat but in normal conditions the two full-backs would act like over lapping wingers to give support to midfield or attack. The 4-5-1 formation, meanwhile, is overtly defensive, with a packed midfield to stifle play, defending en masse with a sole striker ready to pounce on a rare breakaway. It is a formation that was often used by teams lacking resources or the self-belief that they can win by attack.

Above: Franz Beckenbauer reinvented the attacking sweeper in West Germany's answer to Total Football.

Left: Diego Maradona was part of Carlos Bilardo's innovative 3-5-2 formation at the 1986 World Cup.

Far left: France played 3-4-3 in the Eighties, with Michel Platini operating just behind the two strikers.

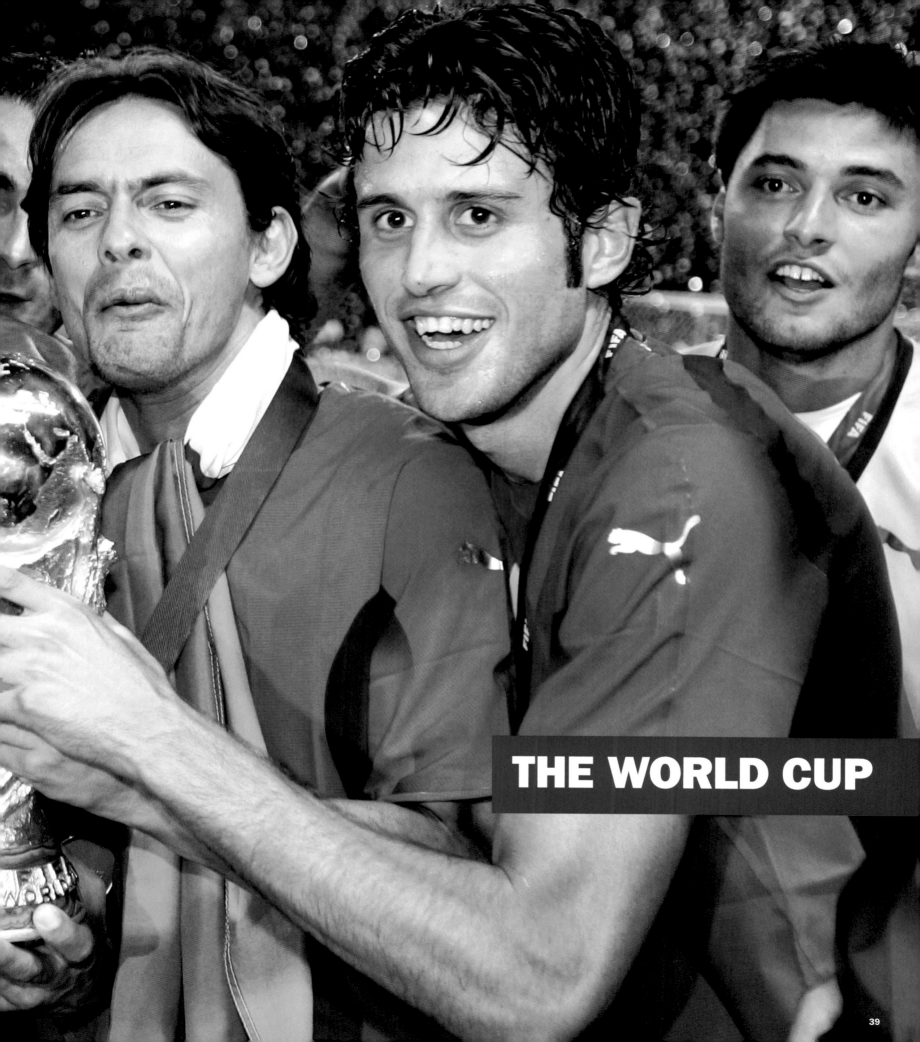

THE WORLD CUP

THE WORLD CUP

There is no other sporting event that captures the imagination across the globe quite like the World Cup. Ever since the first competition in Uruguay in 1930, the tournament has grown in popularity and prestige. But that's not to say it hasn't been without its share of problems. Indeed, the origins of the tournament were so wrapped up in politics that it took 26 years for the idea of a World Cup to become a reality.

During its inaugural meeting in 1904, FIFA agreed that it had the sole right to organise a tournament that brought together the world's strongest national football teams. However, it wasn't until the 1920s that an idea nurtured by FIFA president Jules Rimet and French football administrator Henri Delaunay gained impetus. In the interim the Olympic football tournament had begun to establish itself as a credible competition, and such was its success that a FIFA commission was established in 1927 to examine the creation of a football World Cup. The recommendations struck a chord with FIFA's Executive Committee, and at the 1928 congress, held at the Amsterdam Olympics,

FIFA voted in favour of a football World Cup.

Uruguay beat Argentina in 1928 to retain their Olympic title and proved they were the country most determined to host the inaugural World Cup. Not only did the Uruguayan government offer to build a magnificent new stadium in Montevideo capable of staging a showcase event, but they offered to cover all the travel and accommodation costs of the visiting teams. Rivals Italy, Holland, Spain and Sweden were unprepared to match this offer and withdrew their bids, leaving Uruguay to stage the first World Cup.

On July 13, 1930 the first game of the first World Cup kicked-off in the Pocitos Stadium, Montevideo, France beating Mexico 4-1 amid the snow of a southern hemisphere winter. The tournament was not without its problems. At one stage it seemed that no European sides would be prepared to make the three-week journey by sea. Ultimately just four signed on for the competition, although they were hardly the major football nations of the continent: France, Romania, Belgium and Yugoslavia. It

was the only World Cup not to involve the modern system of qualifying rounds, 13 invited teams competing for the 12-and-a-half-inch solid silver and goldplated prize. The original World Cup trophy was designed by French sculptor Abel Lafleur and based upon one of the great surviving masterpieces of Greek sculpture, Winged Victory of Samothrace.

Since 1934 the 18 tournaments have seen only seven different winners. However, the World Cup has still been punctuated by some dramatic upsets that have helped create football history: the USA's defeat of England in 1950; North Korea beating Italy in 1966; Cameroon's opening match defeat of reigning champions Argentina in 1990; and Senegal's shock victory against holders France in 2002.

The early years of the competition were dogged by controversy. In 1934 holders Uruguay, still upset by the stay-away attitude of the European sides four years earlier, boycotted the tournament in Italy. Rumours also circulated about the many biased refereeing decisions in favour of the hosts. Sadly, not for the last time,

Above from left to right: Brazil captain Cafu lifts the trophy in Yokohama in 2002; England manager Alf Ramsey and captain Bobby Moore admire the Jules Rimet Trophy in 1966; the Italian team parade with the World Cup in Madrid in 1982.

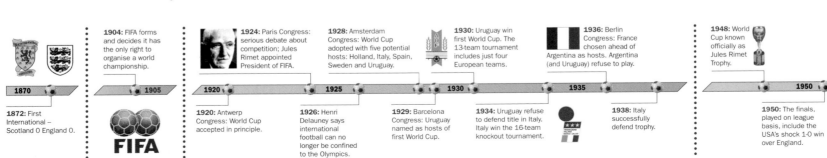

1870
1872: First International – Scotland 0 England 0.

1904: FIFA forms and decides it has the only right to organise a world championship.
1905

1920
1920: Antwerp Congress: World Cup accepted in principle.

FIFA

1924: Paris Congress: serious debate about competition; Jules Rimet appointed President of FIFA.

1926: Henri Delauney says international football can no longer be confined to the Olympics.

1928: Amsterdam Congress: World Cup adopted with five potential hosts: Holland, Italy, Spain, Sweden and Uruguay.
1925

1929: Barcelona Congress: Uruguay named as hosts of first World Cup.

1930: Uruguay win first World Cup. The 13-team tournament includes just four European teams.
1930

1934: Uruguay refuse to defend title in Italy. Italy win the 16-team knockout tournament.

1936: Berlin Congress: France chosen ahead of Argentina as hosts. Argentina (and Uruguay) refuse to play.
1935

1938: Italy successfully defend trophy.

1948: World Cup known officially as Jules Rimet Trophy.
1950

1950: The finals, played on league basis, include the USA's shock 1-0 win over England.

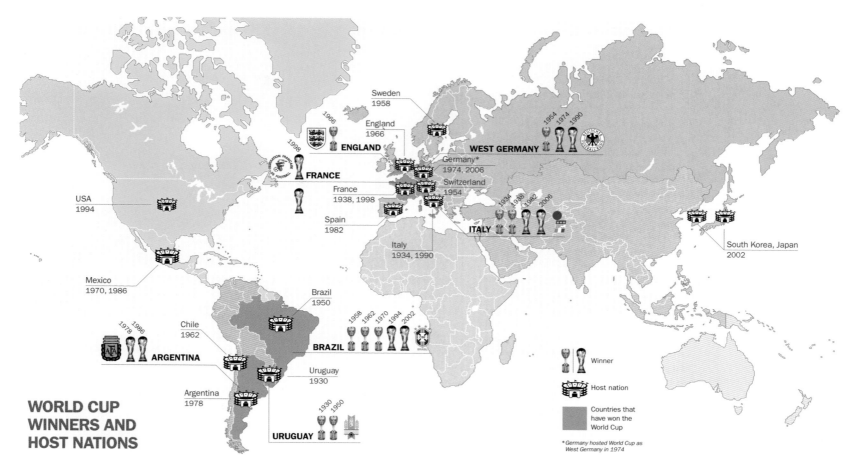

WORLD CUP WINNERS AND HOST NATIONS

the shadow of world politics threatened to eclipse the event, as Italian dictator Benito Mussolini used the World Cup as a showcase for his fascist regime. A straightforward 16-team knockout format was used in 1934, while it was also the first World Cup to host games in more than one city.

The 1938 tournament was played under the clouds of impending conflict. Spain was in the middle of a bloody civil war, while Austria had been annexed by Germany, many of their best players persuaded to change national allegiance.

The World Cup was contested three times in the 1930s before the Second World War put a 12-year stop to the competition. The trophy was renamed the Jules Rimet Cup in 1946, having survived World War II hidden in a shoebox under the bed of Dr Ottorino Barassi, the Italian vice-president of FIFA. In 1950, the World Cup made its comeback in Brazil. To host the event the country built the Maracanã, the largest stadium in the world. It was the first time

England entered the World Cup, although several other countries withdrew on the eve of the competition. This could have resulted in scheduling headaches, but the original draw was retained, leaving a decidedly uneven competition: two groups consisting of four teams, one of three teams, and one of just two.

The World Cup format was rejigged again in 1954. Each group of four in the first round possessed two seeded teams who played only the two unseeded teams in their group. This increased the likelihood of sides ending up with the same number of points, and the need for play-offs meant that 26 games had to be played in just 19 days. It was a system that was never used again. But the constant evolution of the format has not deterred interest.

Throughout its history the number of teams entering has continued to rise: just 38 nations started the 1954 campaign, while 197 nations entered the 2006 competition. In 1974 the World Cup had a new solid gold trophy, three-

time winners Brazil having retained the Jules Rimet Cup in 1970. In 1982, FIFA president João Havelange expanded the field from 16 teams to 24, opening the World Cup to the less established football nations. His expansionist philosophy saw the USA given the tournament in 1994, while in 1998 it was expanded further to include 32 finalists.

The tournament continues to evolve. The 2002 competition in Japan and South Korea marked the first time the World Cup was held in Asia, and the first occasion it had co-hosts, while in 2010 South Africa are due to play hosts.

Today, the World Cup holds the global public under its spell. It was estimated that an audience of over 37 billion people watched the France 98 tournament, including 1.3 billion for the final alone, while over 2.7 million people flocked to the stadiums to watch the 64 matches. After all these years, and despite so many changes in format, the focus of the World Cup still remains the same: to raise aloft the golden trophy.

PLAYER RATINGS

In our coverage of World Cup finals over the following pages, all available footage and match reports have been studied by an independent expert, with players awarded marks out of ten for their performance.

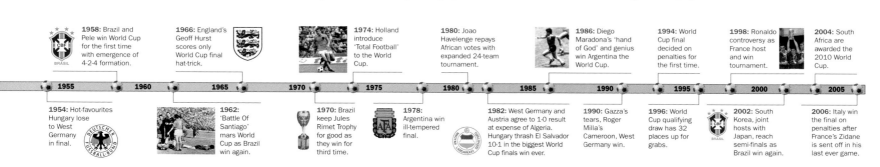

URUGUAY 1930

Above: The opening ceremony of the 1930 World Cup at the Centenary Stadium in Montevideo. Opposite top: Uruguay goalkeeper Enrique Ballestrero watches the ball hit the back of the net in the final. Opposite bottom: despite having only one arm, Hector Castro scored Uruguay's match-winning goal in the final.

FIFA mandarins had been trying to get a world championship off the ground since shortly after the turn of the century, but it wasn't until visionary Frenchman Jules Rimet ascended to the presidency of FIFA after World War I that plans for such a tournament started to take shape, finally receiving a stamp of approval from FIFA's governing congress in 1928. The following year five countries bid to host the tournament – Holland, Italy, Spain, Sweden and Uruguay – with the South Americans eventually winning the vote.

Thirteen countries (out of 41 that boasted FIFA membership) contested the inaugural tournament, with eight hailing from South America: Brazil, Bolivia, Mexico, Argentina, Chile, Peru, Paraguay and Uruguay. The other participants were made up of the United States and a disappointing turn-out from Europe: Yugoslavia, Belgium, France and Romania, who were coached by the country's reigning monarch, King Carol. Several European federations were undoubtedly deterred from competing by the great distance to Uruguay (then only negotiable by boat), while others fulminated that Italy had been overlooked as hosts. None of the British sides entered as they had withdrawn from FIFA in 1928 following a row over the definition of 'amatuerism'.

The rather unwieldy number of teams was split into four pools – four teams in one, three teams in the rest – and the draw itself didn't take place until all the sides had actually arrived in Uruguay. The very first match in a World Cup finals took place on July 13, 1930, and it saw France run out comfortable 4-1 winners over Mexico, their first goal scored by Lucien Laurent in the 19th minute. Disappointingly, the game took place not at the grand Centenary Stadium in Montevideo as planned, because it wasn't yet finished, but in the much smaller Pocitos Stadium in the same city.

France were probably the European side most likely to win the tournament. They had even put four goals past the Mexicans despite being reduced to ten men when their keeper went off injured in the first 20 minutes (no substitutes were allowed at the World Cup until 1970). But any such ambitions came grinding to a halt in their next match, a controversial encounter with Argentina.

The South Americans were leading 1-0, but with the French slowly but surely getting on top it was an advantage that looked increasingly fragile. However, the Brazilian referee, Almeido Rego, blew the whistle for full-time with six minutes still left on the clock and France on the attack, provoking angry scenes and many accusations of foul play. Such was the furore that the referee called the players back out to complete the final six minutes, but by that stage the French had lost their rhythm and the game ended 1-0. Argentina went on to qualify for the semi-finals at a canter. They defeated Chile 3-1, but had been at their most impressive in their previous game, a 6-3 win over Mexico that had boasted three penalties and a hat-trick from young Argentine striker Guillermo Stábile.

Yugoslavia headed Pool 2 after wins over Brazil (2-1) and Bolivia (4-0). They were the only one of the European entrants to make the semi-finals, as Uruguay and the United States took the honours in Pools 3 and 4 respectively. Uruguay didn't concede a single goal as they despatched Peru and Romania, a feat matched by the Americans, who had little difficulty putting Belgium and Paraguay to the sword in two impressive 3-0 victories, the latter featuring at least two goals from Bertram Patenaude (some sources list him as having scored a hat-trick, the first in World Cup history, while others attribute the disputed goal to either Thomas Florie or an own-goal).

Argentina and Uruguay ran up high scores against lesser opposition in the semi-finals, Argentina 6-1 winners against the USA. Uruguay, meanwhile, started their showdown with Yugoslavia slowly, falling behind after four minutes. The lead was short-lived, Pedro Cea equalising after 18 minutes and Pelegrin Anselmo claiming a brace of goals before the interval to make it 3-1, although in the build-up to his second goal the ball had appeared to go out of play, only to be kicked discretely back on to the pitch by a uniformed policeman. Iriarte made it 4-1 with half an hour to play, and Cea completed an extraordinary hat-trick with goals in the 67th and 72nd minutes to cap a crushing victory.

Uruguay and Argentina had met in the Olympic final two years earlier in Amsterdam. Uruguay, also Olympic champions in 1924, ran out 2-1 winners in that encounter, and were too strong again in the first World Cup final. Argentina may have been the reigning South American champions, but they were unable to exact revenge on their great rivals, as Uruguay became the first world champions.

SEMI-FINALS
Argentina 6-1 USA
Uruguay 6-1 Yugoslavia

THIRD PLACE PLAY-OFF
Not held

TOP SCORERS
8 goals: Guillermo Stábile (Argentina)
5 goals: Pedro Cea (Uruguay)
4 goals: Guillermo Subiabre (Chile)

FASTEST GOAL
1 minute: Adalbert Desu (Romania v Peru)

TOTAL GOALS
70

AVERAGE GOALS
3.88 per game

THE FINAL

URUGUAY (1) 4-2 (2) ARGENTINA

Date Wednesday July 30, 1930 **Attendance** 93,000
Venue Centenary Stadium, Montevideo

It was perhaps fitting that the tournament's first hosts should also end up as its first winners, in the country's centenary year. On top after 12 minutes through Pablo Dorado, Uruguay were nonetheless stunned when Carlos Peucelle brought the Argentinians level eight minutes later. Another setback for the hosts arrived in the 37th minute when Argentina took the lead through Stábile – the man who'd go on to be the tournament's highest scorer with eight goals.

Uruguay rallied after the break, Pedro Cea equalising in the 57th minute, and Santos Iriarte snatching a third 11 minutes later. Argentina were unlucky when Pancho Varallo had a shot cleared off the line, and their ill fortune was compounded a minute before the end when Hector Castro snatched the winner.

URUGUAY	
BALLESTRERO	6
NASAZZI	7
MASCHERONI	6
ANDRADE	7
GESTIDO	5
FERNÁNDEZ	5
SCARONE	
CEA	*8
Goal: 57 mins	
DORADO	7
Goal: 12 mins	
CASTRO	7
Goal: 89 mins	
IRIARTE	7
Goal: 68 mins	

ARGENTINA	
BOTASSO	6
DELLA TORRE	5
PATERNÓSTER	5
EVARISTO, J	6
MONTI	7
SUÁREZ	6
VARALLO	6
FERREIRA	5
PEUCELLE	7
Goal: 20 mins	
STÁBILE	*8
Goal: 37 mins	
EVARISTO, M	6

Referee: Langenus (Belgium)

HOW THE TEAMS LINED UP

URUGUAY
COACH: ALBERTO SUPPICCI

Ballesteros
Nasazzi — Mascheroni
Andrade — Fernández — Gestido
Dorado — Scarone — Castro — Cea — Iriarte

ARGENTINA
COACH: AUGUSTO ROUQUETTE

Evaristo, M — Stäbile — Peucelle
Ferreira — Varallo
Suárez — Monti — Evaristo, J
Paternóster — Della Torre
Botasso

Above: The Brazilian entourage and their luggage arrive in Italy for the tournament. Opposite: Eventual winners Italy (top) edged past Spain 1-0 in Florence in the opening round thanks to a goal from Giuseppe Meazza (bottom).

ITALY 1934

Italian dictator Benito Mussolini hoped to use the first World Cup on European soil to further the cause of his fascist regime, but while the tournament can claim to have been a success it was not without controversy. Following the widespread European boycott of the 1930 tournament, the South American nations retaliated with holders Uruguay not even sending a team, and both Brazil and Argentina fielding under-strength sides.

With 32 teams competing, qualification was required before 16 nations reached the preliminary round in Italy. Unlike the 1930 tournament in Uruguay which had been staged solely in Montevideo, eight venues across Italy played host to matches. On May 27, Genoa, Turin, Florence, Milan, Trieste, Rome, Naples and Bologna all witnessed preliminary round action, though naturally it was to be Rome that would eventually stage the showpiece final.

Brazil, Argentina, USA and Egypt were the only non-European countries in the final 16 and all were making the long journey home after just one game. Many of the Argentinian stars had moved to play in the European leagues and not one member of their 1930 team appeared against Sweden in Bologna. However, twice the Argentinians led before a late goal from Kroon sent the Swedes through 3-2. Brazil were barely in the game in Genoa before Spain took total control, leading 2-0 by the break. The South Americans pulled one back but their fate was sealed by Langara's second goal of the match.

France took a shock lead against the second-favourites Austria in Turin, and though Matthias Sindelar levelled, it wasn't until extra-time that Austria's superiority showed – it took a blatantly offside strike from Schall to unsettle the French before Josef Bican decided the match for the Austrians. A late penalty for the French was nothing more than a consolation.

Germany turned around a 2-1 half-time deficit to beat Belgium 5-2 in Florence, the victory owing much to a hat-trick in less than 20 minutes from Edmund Conen. The Dutch, meanwhile, crashed out of the competition 3-2 to Switzerland in Milan.

There were no such problems for favourites Italy against the USA. Angelo Schiavio netted a hat-trick in Rome as the hosts won 7-1. In Naples the first African challenge on the world stage succumbed in the second half as Egypt, who had put 11 goals past Palestine to qualify for the finals, went out of the competition with a 4-2 defeat to Hungary.

In Trieste, highly-fancied Czechoslovakia struggled past Romania. Dobai had given the Romanians the lead shortly before the break, but the Czechs possessed a formidable forward pairing of Antonin Puc and Oldrich Nejedly, who both scored to line-up a quarter-final meeting with the Swiss.

Once again the Czechs did not have it all their own way, falling behind to an early Kielholz goal before Svoboda levelled the tie. Sobotka put the Czechs ahead early in the second-half, but Switzerland hit back and once again it needed Nejedly to find the target seven minutes from time to decide the see-saw match and put Czechoslovakia through to the semi-finals.

Germany and Austria disposed of Sweden and Hungary respectively, but the most remarkable of the quarter-finals saw Italy triumph over Spain in Florence a full 24 hours after the game had kicked-off! The first encounter finished 1-1 and not even extra-time could separate the sides, so the first replay in World Cup history was arranged for the following day. The Spanish made seven changes and the Italians four, but it was another close encounter, ultimately settled in favour of the hosts by prolific Inter Milan marksman Giuseppe Meazza.

There was little respite for Vittorio Pozzo's side and just 48 hours later, having now moved on to Milan's San Siro stadium, they took on Austria's 'Wunderteam' in the semi-finals. A first-half goal from Argentine-born winger Guarita was enough to take Italy through their fourth game in eight days.

The Czechs progressed through the other semi-final in Rome with a 3-1 victory over the Germans and Nejedly took centre stage once again, netting a hat-trick. But this encounter was witnessed by just 13,000 people, some 30,000 less than at the Italy-Austria match.

Four days later Germany did at least salvage some pride by winning the inaugural third place play-off with a 3-2 victory over Hugo Meisl's Austria. But Mussolini and all of Italy had the dream they had longed for with the Azzuri in the final. For the second tournament running the hosts had gone all the way and now only Czechoslovakia stood before Pozzo's men and glory in Rome.

THE FINAL

ITALY (0) **2-1** (0) **CZECHOSLOVAKIA**
(aet; 1-1 at 90 mins)

Date Sunday June 10, 1934 **Attendance** 55,000
Venue Stadio del PNF, Rome

Czechoslovakia were less than ten minutes away from stunning the hosts and winning the World Cup in front of Mussolini. Antonin Puc, suffering with cramp, fired the Czechs ahead with little over 15 minutes remaining and an upset looked on the cards. Italy drew level though, through Raimondo Orsi in the 81st minute, and five minutes into extra-time Pozzo's men grabbed a deserved winner through Angelo Schiavio's fourth goal of the competition.

The final saw Italy's Luis Monti set a unique record, appearing in his second straight final, but for different nations. Four years after finishing a runner-up with the country of his birth, Argentina, Monti was this time celebrating World Cup success with his adopted Italy.

HOW THE TEAMS LINED UP

ITALY
COACH:
VITTORIO POZZO

Combi
Monzeglio · Allemandi
Ferraris · Monti · Bertolini
Meazza · Ferrari
Guaita · Schiavio · Orsi

CZECHOSLOVAKIA
COACH:
CORNEL PETRU

Puc · Sobotka · Junek
Nejedly · Svoboda
Krcil · Cambal · Kostálek
Ctyroky · Zenisek
Plánicka

ITALY	
COMBI	7
MONZEGLIO	5
ALLEMANDI	6
FERRARIS	6
MONTI	7
BERTOLINI	7
MEAZZA	6
FERRARI	7
GUAITA	7
SCHIAVIO ⚽	7
Goal: 95 mins	
ORSI ⚽	*9
Goal: 81 mins	

CZECHOSLOVAKIA	
PLÁNICKA	6
ZENISEK	5
CTYROKY	6
KOSTÁLEK	6
CAMBAL	*9
KRCIL	5
SVOBODA	7
NEJEDLY	6
JUNEK	6
SOBOTKA	6
PUC ⚽	8
Goal: 71 mins	

Referee: Eklind (Sweden)

SEMI-FINALS
Czechoslovakia 3-1 Germany
Italy 1-0 Austria

THIRD PLACE PLAY-OFF
Germany 3-2 Austria

TOP GOALSCORERS
5 goals: Oldrich Nejedly
(Czechoslovakia)
4 goals: Angelo Schiavio (Italy),
Edmund Conen (Germany)

FASTEST GOAL
30 seconds: Ernst Lehner
(Germany v Austria)

TOTAL GOALS
70

AVERAGE GOALS
4.12 per game

FRANCE 1938

The 1938 World Cup brought us Italy, one of the greatest teams of all time, and Leônidas, the Brazilian striker who emerged as the outstanding individual of the tournament. While nobody could argue with Italy's eventual triumph, thanks largely to their outstanding mix of tactical astuteness and pragmatic defending, it was hard luck on Leônidas, known as 'the Black Diamond', that he ended without even a place in the final. As top scorer with seven goals, and with some magnificent performances, he was one of the earliest luminaries of the world game.

Yet Italy's all-round mix of resilience and flair was enough for a second consecutive triumph and confirmed Vittorio Pozzo as the foremost coach of his era. He had led the Italians to World Cup victory four years earlier and sandwiched the Olympic title in between. Who knows how great the Azzurri dynasty could have been but for World War II?

Impending conflict in Europe cast a shadow over the tournament from the outset. Adolf Hitler's Germany had annexed Austria and

Above: The Germans, complete with controversial Nazi salute, line up against Switzerland. Opposite clockwise from top: The captains of Brazil and Poland exchange pennants; Belgian goalkeeper Badjou punches away the ball against France; the teams run out in the same game; the German keeper Raftl makes a save against Swiss striker Abbeglen.

insisted the country's best players join the German side. Several did, but others refused, notably star striker Matthias Sindelar, who committed suicide a year later. Austria were forced to withdraw from the tournament, while Spain too pulled out, racked by civil war.

Champions eight years earlier, Uruguay also stayed at home, while Argentina pulled out over the decision to give the tournament to France. They had wanted to hold it themselves and felt FIFA should have alternated the venue between Europe and South America.

When the tournament finally kicked off, the three outstanding sides, Italy, Brazil and Hungary, were joined in the 16-team format by lesser nations such as Cuba and the Dutch East Indies. The competition was no less exciting for that. Italy needed a Silvio Piola goal in extra-time to win their opening match against Norway to reach the quarter-finals, while Cuba drew 3-3 with Romania and then stunned them by winning 2-1 in the replay. France beat Belgium 3-1, while Czechoslovakia knocked out Holland with a 3-0 win.

Switzerland, in a memorable clash, drew 1-1 with Germany and fell two goals behind in the replay but, despite playing much of the game with only ten fit men after an injury to Aebi, shocked the Germans with four second-half goals to send them home early.

The game of the first round saw Brazil beat Poland 6-5, thanks mainly to Leônidas who even scored one of his goals barefoot, hitting the shot after his boot had come off in the mud. After 90 minutes the game was level at 4-4, but three minutes into extra-time Leônidas scored his second goal to put Brazil ahead. He completed his hat-trick in the 104th minute, although many records indicate that he scored four times. Such was the exceptional nature of his performance that it is often overlooked that just minutes later Polish striker Ernest Wilimowski did, in fact, score four goals, the first player to do so in a World Cup game.

Italy continued their fine form in the quarter-finals by putting out hosts France with a 3-1 win at Colombes; Piola adding two more goals to his tally and captain Giuseppe Meazza dominating in midfield. It meant that for the first time the hosts would not win the World Cup, leaving 58,455 disappointed fans.

Following their attacking exploits in the previous round Brazil showed an ugly side to their game in the clash with Czechoslovakia. A brawl and the sending-off of three players blighted the first match, which ended 1-1, before Brazil won the replay through goals from Leônidas and Roberto. Hungary looked good, beating Switzerland 2-0, while Sweden crushed Cuba 8-0 to complete the final quartet.

In the semi-finals Brazil faced Italy, but Brazil coach Adhemar Pimenta left out Leônidas, a decision that proved their undoing. Some say Leônidas was arrogantly rested for the final, others that he was simply unable to play because of injuries collected in the fierce clash with Czechoslovakia. Whatever the reason, Italy gained the advantage. Gino Colaussi scored shortly after half-time and Giuseppe Meazza added a penalty on the hour. Brazil managed only a consolation goal three minutes from time through Romeu.

In the other semi-final Hungary ended Sweden's run with a 5-1 triumph despite conceding in the first minute. The Swedes' lead lasted 19 minutes before Hungary won through, thanks to Jakobsen's own goal, and strikes by Titkos, Sárosi and a brace from Zsengellér. The forward partnership between Gyula Zsengellér and Gyorgy Sárosi was perhaps the most thrilling in the tournament and revealed its power to devastating effect.

Leônidas returned for the third place play-off and Brazil fell two goals behind to Sweden before fighting back to win 4-2. He scored twice to finish top-scorer with seven. In the final, however, the Italians confirmed their place as one of the greatest sides of all time.

SEMI-FINALS

Italy 2-1 Brazil
Hungary 5-1 Sweden

THIRD PLACE PLAY-OFF

Brazil 4-2 Sweden

TOP GOALSCORERS

7 goals: Leônidas (Brazil)
5 goals: Gyorgy Sárosi (Hungary), Gyula Zsengellér (Hungary), Silvio Piola (Italy)

FASTEST GOAL

35 seconds: Arne Nyberg (Sweden v Hungary)

TOTAL GOALS

84

AVERAGE GOALS

4.67 per match

THE FINAL

ITALY (3) 4-2 (1) HUNGARY

Date Sunday June 19, 1938 **Attendance** 45,124
Venue Stade Olympique de Colombes, Paris

Italy won by a two-goal margin but it was no contest. Pozzo's side were much stronger than Hungary and far more decisive in attack. Colaussi opened the scoring when he collected a Piola cross in the sixth minute and prodded home past Szabó from close range. Titkos immediately equalised, but Hungarian hopes were dashed when Piola scored on 16 minutes, picking up a pass from Meazza to lash the ball high into the net. Colaussi added a third before half-time to put Italy in total control.

The reigning champions defended their lead in the second-half. Sárosi's goal put Hungary back in contention, but when Piola scored with eight minutes remaining, Italy were certain of victory. They were in a class of their own.

ITALY	
OLIVIERI	6
FONI	6
RAVA	7
SERANTONI	7
ANDREOLO	8
LOCATELLI	8
MEAZZA	*9
FERRARI	7
BIAVATI	6
PIOLA ⚽⚽	7
Goal: 16 mins, 82 mins	
COLAUSSI ⚽⚽	7
Goal: 6 mins, 35 mins	

HUNGARY	
SZABÓ	7
POLGAR	6
BIRÓ	7
SZALAY	6
SZÜCS	7
LÁZÁR	6
VINCZE	5
ZSENGELLÉR	6
SAS	6
SÁROSI ⚽	6
Goal: 70 mins	
TITKOS ⚽	6
Goal: 8 mins	

Referee: Capdeville (France)

HOW THE TEAMS LINED UP

ITALY
COACH: VITTORIO POZZO

Olivieri
Foni — Rava
Serantoni — Andreolo — Locatelli
Meazza — Ferrari
Biavati — Piola — Colaussi

HUNGARY
COACH: KAROLY DIETZ

Titkos — Sárosi — Sas
Zsengellér — Vincze
Lázár — Szücs — Szalay
Biró — Polgar
Szabó

BRAZIL 1950

The 1950 World Cup was, in many ways, the oddest of tournaments: withdrawals dominated the build-up, only 13 teams turned up in Brazil, and no final was scheduled by the organisers, the winners to be decided in a second league phase. Even the new Maracanã stadium, built specifically for the tournament, wasn't ready when the first game kicked-off. But in the end the competition produced moments of pure drama and a game that will never be forgotten. The chaotic preparations eventually gave way to some excellent football and one of the greatest clashes the World Cup has ever seen.

The draw itself looked lop-sided, the opening round consisting of two groups of four, one of three and one of two. Argentina were among the many teams to pull-out before the qualifiers, while Scotland and Turkey withdrew after booking a place in the finals. India refused to turn up, according to some reports, because FIFA insisted they wore boots.

All eyes were on Pool 1, where the host nation and highly-fancied outsiders Yugoslavia impressed immediately. With a wonderfully entertaining line-up, boasting a trio of attackers who ranked among the finest in the world – Ademir, Jair and Zizinho – Brazil played skilful and inventive football and were favourites to lift the trophy for the first time in their history. They made a superb start beating Mexico 4-0 in their opener, with Ademir scoring twice. Yugoslavia kept pace with an impressive 3-0 win over Switzerland, maintaining their stunning form with a 4-1 win over Mexico in their second match.

Switzerland surprisingly held Brazil 2-2, but when the two group leaders met in the Maracanã in front of 142,429 spectators, the hosts came out on top with a 2-0 win thanks to goals from Ademir and Zizinho, ensuring Brazil safe passage to the final pool. With only one team to go through, it was harsh on the talented Yugoslavs who went home early.

In Pool 2, England were the biggest attraction, taking part in their first World Cup. The team had lost star players Frank Swift and Tommy Lawton since the war but still boasted Billy Wright, Tom Finney and Stan Mortensen in their ranks. It was an impressive line-up and goals from Mortensen and Wilf Mannion secured a 2-0 win over Chile. It looked as though they would cruise through to the next round but in their second game the United States inflicted one of the most embarrassing defeats in English football history. The USA, who had lost their opening game 3-1 to Spain, recorded a 1-0 win in Belo Horizonte on June 29, with Joe Gaetjens scoring the 38th minute winner. It was a major shock for England, who had assumed their side would reach the final pool at the very least.

England's misery was doubled when Spain beat them 1-0 to reach the final pool with a 100 per cent record. Walter Winterbottom's team returned home thoroughly humiliated.

In Pool 3, holders Italy, Sweden and Paraguay played each other, with Sweden earning an early advantage thanks to a 3-2 win over Italy. The Scandinavians' 2-2 draw with Paraguay in the next match was enough for them to clinch the top spot and Italy's 2-0 win over Paraguay was a mere consolation.

In the absurd two-team Pool 4, Uruguay thrashed Bolivia 8-0 to make the final pool, with Juan Schiaffino catching the eye and Omar Miguez grabbing a hat-trick.

And so to the Final Pool – the World Cup trophy would go to whoever topped the mini-league table. It could have been an anti-climax if one team had wrapped it up early, but in the event it provided perhaps the most thrilling climax to any World Cup, with scorelines and scheduling throwing up an 'unofficial final' in front of the largest football crowd ever.

Certainly the hosts looked the best bet to win when the pool kicked-off, racking up a 7-1 win over Sweden, which included some of the finest attacking football ever seen. Ademir scored four goals in a truly blistering display as his understanding with Jair and Zizinho reached its peak. Next they thrashed Spain 6-1, all three strikers getting on the scoresheet, and Chico hit the target twice. The hosts began to look unstoppable.

Uruguay kept in touch by starting with a 2-2 draw against Spain in a tough physical encounter, and then a 3-2 win over Sweden was enough to retain a slim chance of causing an upset. It meant the final group match, between Brazil and Uruguay, would decide who would win the World Cup. Uruguay needed to win, while Brazil needed only a draw.

As Brazil had played the better football and had home advantage, the result seemed a foregone conclusion, but the unimaginable happened. Uruguay came from behind and hit

a winner with just 11 minutes remaining to leave the crowd shellshocked. The 'Fateful Final' left a bitter feeling in Brazil that remains to this day. Their white kit, deemed not patriotic enough, was replaced four years later by the yellow shirts that they would make famous.

Above: A packed Maracanã hosts its only World Cup. Opposite clockwise from top: Schiaffino equalises for Uruguay in the 'final' against Brazil; Uruguay celebrate; England in action against Chile; Brazil open the scoring against Uruguay.

FINAL POOL

	P	W	D	L	Pts
Uruguay	3	2	1	0	5
Brazil	3	2	0	1	4
Sweden	3	1	0	2	2
Spain	3	0	1	2	1

TOP GOALSCORERS

9 goals: Ademir Menezes (Brazil)
5 goals: Juan Schiaffino (Uruguay), Estanislao Basora (Spain)

FASTEST GOAL

2 minutes: Alfredo (Brazil v Switzerland)

TOTAL GOALS:

88

AVERAGE GOAL

4.00 per game

THE FINAL POOL MATCH

URUGUAY (0) 2-1 (0) BRAZIL

Date Sunday July 16, 1950 **Attendance** 199,854
Venue Maracanã, Rio de Janeiro

Thirty shots at goal, the will of a nation, and 200,000 fans in the stadium – but Uruguay refused to read the script and achieved a remarkable triumph. During a goalless first-half they weathered the storm, their defence doing everything to match the efforts of Brazil's famed attack, before they shocked in the second-half. Friaça scored two minutes after the break, making victory look inevitable, but on 66 minutes Juan Schiaffino swept in an equaliser. Uruguay stood firm and, on the break, Alcides Ghiggia attacked Barbosa's goal and scored from close range to seal a famous victory.

Uruguay had achieved the impossible and the supporters could hardly believe what they had seen. In the most dramatic circumstances, Brazil had yet again failed to lift the World Cup.

HOW THE TEAMS LINED UP

URUGUAY
COACH:
JUAN LOPEZ

BRAZIL
COACH:
FLAVIO COSTA

Máspoli

Gonzáles, M   Tejera

Gambetta   Varela   Andrade

Ghiggia   Peréz   Miguez   Schiaffino   Morán

Chico   Ademir   Friaça

Jair   Zizinho

Bigode   Danilo   Bauer

Juvenal   Augusto

Barbosa

URUGUAY	
MÁSPOLI	*9
GONZÁLES, M	7
ANDRADE	8
TEJERA	7
VARELA	8
GAMBETTA	7
PERÉZ	6
SCHIAFFINO ⚽	7
Goal: 66 mins	
GHIGGIA ⚽	8
Goal: 79 mins	
MIGUEZ	6
MORÁN	6

BRAZIL	
BARBOSA	6
AUGUSTO	6
JUVENAL	7
BAUER	5
DANILO	7
BIGODE	6
ZIZINHO	6
JAIR	6
FRIAÇA ⚽	7
Goal: 47 mins	
ADEMIR	7
CHICO	5

Referee: Reader (England)

SWITZERLAND 1954

Although it came nearly ten years after the end of the Second World War, and was even seen by a privileged few in flickering black and white television pictures for the first time, the 1954 World Cup remained a marginal event, far removed from the global marketing phenomenon it is now. But for all that, the tournament produced some of the most colourful attacking football in its history, with 140 goals shared between 16 teams at an average of over five goals a game. The quarter-final between Austria and their Swiss hosts finished 7-5, the highest aggregate ever for a game at the finals, and several other matches finished with scorelines that appear improbable today.

Switzerland was a logical choice to host the first post-war tournament to be held in Europe, and not simply because it had escaped the devastation sustained across the rest of the continent. FIFA's headquarters were situated in Zurich and 1954 represented the 50th anniversary of its formation.

The Swiss had been granted the tournament at FIFA's first post-war congress in 1946, and they spent eight years building new stadia. However, the finished grounds had small capacities and were not really up to the requirements of such a tournament. Despite this, it was a financial success, the organisers displaying early signs of grasping the World Cup's marketing potential by having special commemorative coins minted.

The qualifying rounds featured the highest number of nations yet, with 38 entries. Sweden and Spain failed to qualify, the latter being beaten by Turkey who automatically became seeds, a ruling that was to have particular significance as the competition unfolded. England and Scotland came through the Home Nations group, though the latter were to lose both their games and make a rapid return. Once again the Soviet Union and Argentina were notable absentees.

Almost inevitably FIFA tampered with the set-up, reverting to a complicated pool phase featuring 16 teams divided into four groups, with two seeded sides in each who would not play each other. At the end the four winners played each other in a knock-out phase, as did the four runners-up. But the system was open to exploitation and the Germans did just that.

It was no surprise to find that Hungary, coached by Gusztáv Sebes, were favourites. This was the era of the 'Magical Magyars'. Two years previously they had been crowned Olympic champions and now their players were at their peak. The line-up was crammed with legends, including the 'Galloping Major' Ferenc Puskás, striker Sándor Kocsis (dubbed 'The Man With The Golden Head'), midfield dynamo Josef Bózsik and deep-lying centre-forward Nandor Hidegkuti.

This was the core of the side that destroyed English pretensions to superiority with a 6-3 win at Wembley in November 1953 (England's first home defeat to a continental side) and a 7-1 pasting in Budapest six months later. The Magyars hammered South Korea 9-0 in their opening game in Zurich and put eight past a deliberately weakened German side, eventually scoring a record 27 goals in the tournament. Sándor Kocsis raced to the Golden Boot with 11 goals, including two hat-tricks.

Hungary's game against Brazil went down in football history for all the wrong reasons. Instead of the classic that it promised to be, the match degenerated into hand-to-hand combat, since dubbed the 'Battle Of Berne'. The bout was refereed by future British television personality Arthur Ellis, who sent-off three players, Hungary's József Bózsik and Brazil's Humberto Tozzi and Nilton Santos, after trouble broke out over a disputed penalty. The game degenerated from this point into violence that continued in the changing rooms after the match, embroiling both managers and even the official delegations.

Above: Santos and Bózsik troop off during the 'Battle of Berne'. Opposite top: Tom Finney gets a header in for England against Uruguay. Opposite bottom: Sandor Kocsis, whose goal put Hungary 2-0 up in their ill-fated final.

England, under Walter Winterbottom, topped a group featuring hosts Switzerland, Belgium and Italy. The side, featuring Billy Wright, Nat Lofthouse, Stanley Matthews and Tom Finney, should have gone further but came unstuck against Uruguay, losing 4-2 with goalkeeper Gil Merrick at fault for three goals. In the end the feeling was that their shattering 7-1 defeat at the hands of Hungary just weeks earlier had destroyed the team's confidence.

West Germany were admitted after their banishment following World War II and rapidly made a mockery of their non-seeding, beating Turkey 4-1, while France, another seeded side, lost to Yugoslavia. German manager Sepp Herberger then exploited the play-off system by electing to send out a weak side against Hungary in the knowledge that the group winners would play Brazil in the knock-out phase, while the runners-up would face Korea or Turkey. His plan worked and Germany duly thrashed Turkey and squeezed past the Yugoslavs 2-0, scoring early on and holding out until a late goal sealed the victory. A 6-1 semi-final victory over Austria sent out an ominous warning.

Hungary's semi-final against holders Uruguay was another memorable encounter that put paid to the South Americans' unbeaten record in the competition, Hungary winning 4-2 in extra-time.

The final looked on paper to be a forgone conclusion. West Germany, unseeded, faced the might of Hungary, who had not lost in 31 games and four years, but the form book was discarded in a fascinating see-saw encounter that saw the Germans come back from 2-0 down to win the trophy for the first time. Hungary were stunned and when the Soviet Union crushed the country's uprising two years later the squad broke up, effectively ending its dominance forever.

SEMI-FINALS
West Germany 6-1 Austria
Hungary 4-2 Uruguay
(aet: 2-2 at 90 mins)

THIRD PLACE PLAY-OFF
Austria 3-1 Uruguay

TOP GOALSCORERS
11 goals: Sándor Kocsis (Hungary)
6 goals: Maximilian Morlock
(West Germany), Josef Hügi
(Switzerland), Erich Probst
(Austria)

FASTEST GOAL
2 minutes: Mamat Suat
(Turkey v West Germany)

TOTAL GOALS
140

AVERAGE GOALS
5.38 per game

THE FINAL

WEST GERMANY (2) 3-2 (2) HUNGARY

Date Sunday July 4, 1954 **Attendance** 62,472
Venue Wankdorf Stadium, Berne

Though carrying an injury, Puskás put his side ahead after only six minutes when he followed up a Kocsis shot. Two minutes later Czibor latched on to a weak back-pass to put them two up, but Morlock reduced the arrears after 11 minutes and a mistake by the Hungarian goalkeeper Grosics in the 18th minute allowed Rahn to equalise.

In the second-half Hidegkuti hit the post, Kocsis the bar, Kohlmeyer cleared off the line and Turek made a succession of great saves. Six minutes from time, winger Rahn picked up a half-hearted clearance, raced to the edge of the box and struck a low shot past Grosics, who appeared to slip. There was more drama when Puskás had a goal disallowed for offside; the Hungarians still arguing after the final whistle.

HOW THE TEAMS LINED UP

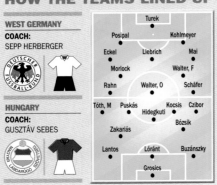

WEST GERMANY
COACH:
SEPP HERBERGER

HUNGARY
COACH:
GUSZTÁV SEBES

WEST GERMANY	
TUREK	*9
POSIPAL	6
KOHLMEYER	7
ECKEL	6
LIEBRICH	6
MAI	7
MORLOCK	7
Goal: 11 mins	
WALTER, F	8
RAHN	8
Goal: 18 mins, 84 mins	
WALTER, O	6
SCHÄFER	7

HUNGARY	
GROSICS	5
BUZÁNSZKY	6
LANTOS	6
BÓZSIK	6
LÓRÁNT	7
ZAKARIÁS	6
KOCSIS	*8
PUSKÁS	6
Goal: 6 mins	
CZIBOR	7
Goal: 9 mins	
HIDEGKUTI	6
TÓTH, M	5

Referee: Ling (England)

Above: One of Just Fontaine's record-breaking tally of 13 goals at the 1958 World Cup, this one part of his hat-trick against Paraguay. Opposite clockwise from top: Pelé beats the Swedish goalkeeper – he was to score twice in the final; John Charles of Wales helps his side edge out Hungary; a 17-year-old Pelé is overcome at the final whistle.

SWEDEN 1958

For fans of the beautiful game, the 1958 World Cup will always be remembered for the birth of a football nation, and in particular of its favourite son, Pelé. Before Sweden '58, Brazil had never won the World Cup. Uruguay had forged a reputation as South America's finest side by twice lifting the trophy, but in 1958 the balance of power shifted. It has yet to shift again. Brazil, for the first of five times, became world champions.

They did so by pioneering a style of play that, in an era when defenders could – and did – get away with kicking the opposition's best players into the crowd, had football writers everywhere purring at its grace and beauty. The first strains of what was to become known as 'Samba football' were born in Sweden. "Where skill alone counted Brazil stood alone," reported The Times of England. "The way each daffodil shirt of theirs pulled the ball down out of the sky, tamed it with a touch of the foot, caressed it and stroked it away into an open space was a joy."

Looking back, it is easy to over-romanticise about Brazil and to think that any team with so much skill, and with arguably the greatest ever player, was bound to succeed. But there was nothing inevitable about it. In the early decades of the World Cup, sides unfamiliar with foreign conditions did not travel well: until this tournament the winners had always been a team from the host continent. Brazil, third in 1938, spurned another great chance in 1950. This time, they meant business and even brought along a psychiatrist.

As for Pelé, while everyone knew he was a bit special, at 17 no-one knew how special. His mere selection remained in doubt, partly because of a niggling injury and partly because some believed he wasn't up to it.

The tournament, though, was something of a watershed. Although there were plenty of

tasty tackles, Sweden marked the end of the more carefree, attack-minded post-war era of international football. In the 1960s, World Cup matches became increasingly cynical affairs characterised by defensive attitudes.

The party began without some familiar names as Uruguay and fellow two-time winners Italy both failed to qualify. For British football though, 1958 remains a high point with all four home nations qualifying for the only time. England, despite the Munich air disaster denying them such talents as Duncan Edwards, Tommy Taylor and Roger Byrne, were the favourites, particularly as they had never lost to any of the teams in their group. But it was to prove a frustrating tournament for Walter Winterbottom's side. Creditable draws against the USSR and Brazil – the first goalless match in World Cup finals history – meant England only had to beat eliminated Austria to advance. But the draws continued and it came down to a play-off with the Soviets in the Ullevi Stadium, where England wilted.

Scotland set the tone for future World Cups by also going out in the first round, but Northern Ireland and Wales both advanced. The Irish, who had drawn 2-2 with West Germany in their group, beat Czechoslovakia in a play-off, a situation Wales were also catapulted into after drawing all three group matches. Inspired by John Charles, they came from behind to beat Hungary 2-1.

Charles was injured for the quarter-finals, where Wales met Brazil. For 70 minutes the Welsh dream lived on as the likes of Garrincha, Didi, Mazzola and Zagalo were continually thwarted. But when Pelé scored the first of his 12 World Cup goals, it was all over.

The big guns were beginning to fire. In the quarter-finals, France ended Irish resistance with a 4-0 thumping. West Germany sneaked home 1-0 against Yugoslavia and Sweden put paid to the Soviet Union 2-0.

Although West Germany, the defending champions, were still in the competition,

THE FINAL

BRAZIL (2) 5-2 (1) SWEDEN

Date Sunday June 29, 1958 **Attendance** 49,737
Venue Rasunda Stadium, Solna, Stockholm

The final was a summit meeting between football's new and old world orders. Heavy rain and a passionate home crowd suggested now wasn't the time or place for South American flair, especially when Liedholm fired the hosts ahead after four minutes. Five minutes later Vavá equalised from Garrincha's cross, then Pelé struck the post and Vavá added a second. Suddenly Sweden were chasing shadows.

The second half was Pelé's. His first goal in the 55th minute combined individual trickery with a rasping volley. Zagalo made it 4-1 before Simonsson restored hope for Sweden. But Pelé had the final word, heading home for a 5-2 win.

The Brazilians were overcome, weeping openly. They sportingly paraded the Swedish flag, bringing the stadium to its feet in acclaim.

HOW THE TEAMS LINED UP

BRAZIL
COACH: VICENTE FEOLA

SWEDEN
COACH: GEORGE RAYNOR

Gilmar

Santos D   Bellini   Orlando   Santos N

Didi   Zito

Garrincha   Vavá   Pelé   Zagalo

Skoglund   Simonsson   Hamrin

Liedholm   Gren

Parling   Gustavsson   Borjesson

Axbom   Bergmark

Svensson

BRAZIL	
GILMAR	6
SANTOS, D	7
BELLINI	6
ORLANDO	7
SANTOS, N	7
DIDI	8
ZITO	7
GARRINCHA	7
VAVÁ	8
Goal: 9 mins, 32 mins	
PELÉ	*9
Goal: 55 mins, 90 mins	
ZAGALO	7
Goal: 68 mins	

SWEDEN	
SVENSSON	5
BERGMARK	6
AXBOM	6
BORJESSON	5
GUSTAVSSON	6
PARLING	7
GREN	*8
LIEDHOLM	7
Goal: 4 mins	
HAMRIN	5
SIMONSSON	7
Goal: 80 mins	
SKOGLUND	5

Referee: Guigue (France)

Sweden and Brazil had emerged as favourites. Sweden underlined their credentials in front of 53,000 fans in Gothenburg when they eliminated West Germany 3-1 in the semi-finals. The Germans hung on until the last ten minutes when the home team scored twice to trigger wild celebrations. It was one of West Germany's darkest World Cup moments. Erich Juskowiak was sent-off for kicking and they were reduced to nine men for a time when another player went off for treatment.

In the other semi-final in Stockholm, Brazil electrified the tournament with a 5-2 defeat of France, who had cruised through their quarter-final and were expected to pose a severe test. For half the match they did but they were blown away when Pelé netted a hat-trick in 23 unforgettable second-half minutes. French striker Just Fontaine had the consolation of scoring 13 goals in the tournament, a record that may never be broken.

The dream final had arrived and the era of Brazilian dominance was about to begin. That they have stayed ahead of their competition ever since, without forsaking their unique poetic style, is a sporting wonder.

SEMI-FINALS

Brazil 5-2 France
Sweden 3-1 West Germany

THIRD PLACE PLAY-OFF

France 6-3 West Germany

TOP GOALSCORERS

13 goals: Just Fontaine (France)
6 goals: Pelé (Brazil), Helmut Rahn (West Germany)
5 goals: Vavá (Brazil), Peter McParland (Northern Ireland)

FASTEST GOAL

90 seconds: Vavá (Brazil v France)

TOTAL GOALS

126

AVERAGE GOALS

3.60 per game

CHILE 1962

🏆 "We have nothing, that is why we must have the World Cup," pleaded Carlos Dittborn, president of the Federación de Fútbol de Chile. FIFA had been looking for an alternative host following the devastating earthquake that caused serious damage and loss of life in Chile in May 1960, but Dittborn's pleas were heeded and Chile kept the World Cup in the end and served up a tournament of extremes, ranging from the appalling 'Battle of Santiago' to the beautiful, crafted performances of the sublime Brazilians.

Local interest in the games wavered wildly, from disappointingly small attendances of under 6,000 at one extreme, to the crowds of over 60,000 who squeezed into the cauldron of Santiago. It was also a World Cup that witnessed the dawn of defensive football. This largely dismal football showpiece reached its nadir with the infamous 'Battle of Santiago' between Italy and hosts Chile. Anti-Italian feeling had been whipped-up in Santiago as a result of the publication of derogatory articles about Chilean life by two Italian journalists. This was in addition to ill-feeling created by Italy's reputation for poaching South American players at both domestic and international level. Indeed, their line-up for the game included Argentinian Humberto Maschio and a veteran of Brazil's previous World Cup campaign, José 'Mazzola' Altafini.

The match, staged in front of a hostile over-capacity crowd in the Estadio Nacional, quickly descended into violence, which English referee Ken Aston failed to control. He did dismiss the Italian Ferrini for retaliation after just eight minutes, although the player refused to leave the field for a further ten minutes and was eventually removed by FIFA officials and the police. Aston also sent-off Ferrini's team-mate David in the second-half, however the referee did nothing when Sánchez, the son of a boxer, retaliated to Maschio's severe foul by breaking the Italian player's nose right in front of a linesman. The disgraceful violence on the field continued and Chile won the game 2-0.

The group stages were dominated by defensive play and excessive violence. After three match days the Chilean press reported there had been 34 serious injuries. Among the casualties was 21-year-old Pelé, the result of a torn muscle from a groin injury sustained in a pre-tournament friendly – Pelé had refused to declare it because of trainer Paolo Amaral's "don't train, don't play" policy.

The opening stages did feature the odd decent match, the most amazing being the Group One clash between the Soviet Union and first time qualifiers Colombia in Arica. Three goals in three minutes gave the Soviets a 3-0 lead by the 11th minute, with two goals from Ivanov sandwiching a single strike from Chislenko. The game looked over, and an Aceros goal ten minutes later did nothing to change that opinion, with Ponedyelnik adding to Colombian woe with a fourth for the Soviets early in the second-half. Colombia, however, staged a magnificent comeback to secure an amazing 4-4 draw, with Coll, Rada and Klinger all scoring. Indeed, Group One provided the most entertaining football of the early stages.

Outside of Santiago the games were poorly attended. The six Group Four matches in Rancagua, for example, attracted an average crowd of just 7,000, the worst attended being England's dull 0-0 draw against Bulgaria.

The quickest goal of the tournament was scored after just 15 seconds, Czechoslovakia's Vaclav Masek putting the ball past Mexican goalkeeper Carbajal, a veteran of three previous World Cups. Mexico won the game 3-1 but Czechoslovakia went on to the final along with group winners and holders Brazil.

Czechoslovakia had built a team around the successful Dukla Prague club with a strategy strongly built on defence. A cautious, counter-attacking team, they had held Brazil to a goalless draw and beaten a disharmonious

Above: Brazil's Garrincha goes past future World Cup winner Ray Wilson in their quarter-final with England. Opposite clockwise from top: Amarildo shows off his skills in the final; Chile's Rojas celebrates his country's last minute third place play-off win against Yugoslavia; Mauro lifts the Jules Rimet trophy after beating Chechoslovakia

Spain 1-0, reaching the quarter-finals on goal average (being used for the first time at this World Cup) by virtue of conceding fewer goals than Mexico, thanks in no small part to Wilhelm Schrojf, the goalkeeper of the tournament. He was in magnificent form, particularly in the quarter-final and semi-final clashes with Hungary and Yugoslavia, a series of magnificent saves keeping his opponents at bay in both games.

Brazil may have suffered the loss of Pelé after two games but they remained unfazed by the loss of their star, having unearthed Tavares Amarildo, who was quickly dubbed 'the white Pelé'. It was Garrincha, though, who was Brazil's inspiration. The father of seven children, he was just as productive on the pitch when creating and scoring goals.

Brazil breezed through their quarter-final in Vinã del Mar, outclassing England who had finished runners-up in Group D. Garrincha, the smallest player on the field, opened the scoring with a header before later setting up Vavá and finding the net again in a 3-1 win.

The semi-final pitched Brazil against hosts Chile in an open game that was streaked with spite. Garrincha gave Brazil a 2-0 lead through a volley and a header, although a Toro free-kick halved the deficit for the hosts before the break.

A Garrincha free-kick was headed home by Vavá just after the interval, but Sánchez converted a penalty to keep Chile in touch. With 13 minutes remaining Zagalo dribbled through the Chilean defence and set up Vavá with another header. Shortly afterwards Chile's Landa was sent-off and only minutes later Garrincha followed, finally retaliating to one of the many kicks he had suffered during the game. Nevertheless, now firm favourites Brazil progressed to the final, where they beat Czechoslovakia 3-1 to retain the trophy.

THE FINAL

BRAZIL (1) 3-1 (1) CZECHOSLOVAKIA

Date Thursday June 17, 1962 **Attendance** 68,679
Venue National Stadium, Santiago

Favourites Brazil named an unchanged side that included Garrincha, despite his semi-final sending-off. FIFA had imposed one-match bans on all of the other five players dismissed during the tournament. The experienced Brazil side included eight members of the team that had won in Sweden in 1958, but still they went 1-0 down to Masopust's opener for the Czechs.

Amarildo scored from an acute angle to equalise within two minutes and the match was closely-fought until the 69th minute when Amarildo's high pass was headed home by Zito.

The match was decided when Czech keeper Schrojf allowed a Djalma Santos high ball to fall through his hands, enabling Vavá to stab home the loose ball for an unassailable 3-1 lead. It was the best match of the tournament.

BRAZIL	
GILMAR	7
SANTOS, D	7
MAURO	7
ZÓZIMO	6
SANTOS, N	6
ZITO ⚽	7
Goal: 69 mins	
DIDI	7
GARRINCHA	6
VAVÁ ⚽	*8
Goal: 77 mins	
AMARILDO ⚽	7
Goal: 17 mins	
ZAGALO	6

CZECHOSLOVAKIA	
SCHROJF	5
TICHY	6
PLUSKAL	7
POPLUHAR	7
NOVAK	6
KVASNAK	6
MASOPUST ⚽	*8
Goal: 16 mins	
SCHERER	5
POSPICHAL	7
KADRABA	6
JELINEK	7

Referee: Latychev (Soviet Union)

HOW THE TEAMS LINED UP

BRAZIL
COACH:
AYMORE MOREIRA

Gilmar
Santos, D   Mauro   Zózimo   Santos, N
Zito   Didi   Zagalo
Garrincha   Vavá   Amarildo

CZECHOSLOVAKIA
COACH:
RUDOLF VYTLACIL

Jelinek   Kadraba   Scherer   Pospichal
Masopust   Kvasnak
Novak   Popluhar   Pluskal   Tichy
Schrojf

ENGLAND 1966

Most England fans remember the 1966 World Cup as their country's greatest sporting triumph, but the tournament itself was characterised by dour, often ugly defending, punctuated by occasional glimpses of brilliance and drama. The hosts England boasted players of the calibre of Bobby Moore, Bobby Charlton and Jimmy Greaves and expectations were high, particularly after coach Alf Ramsey had, on taking the job, promised the nation that his team would lift the trophy.

The draw pitted England against Uruguay, Mexico and France, but the opening game was an anticlimax with the negative Uruguayans blotting out England's sterile attack for a 0-0 draw. England followed this up with a still less than convincing 2-0 win against Mexico, but progress to the second stage was sealed with a 2-0 win against France. The FA had asked Ramsey to drop Nobby Stiles after the game, because of his fierce tackle on Jacky Simon, but the coach stood by his man.

In Group Two West Germany got off to a flying start with a crushing 5-0 win over a Swiss side depleted by internal suspensions. The first surprise came when a physical Argentina beat a Spanish team built around the players of the mighty Real Madrid side. While Spain recovered to beat the Swiss, West Germany faced Argentina and were subjected to the kind of brutal tactics which saw the South Americans pick up a FIFA warning. It did not prevent them progressing though, Argentina clinching qualification against Switzerland in front of a hostile Hillsborough crowd. West Germany, meanwhile, qualified top after an Uwe Seeler goal put Spain out.

Group Three favourites Brazil started well by beating Bulgaria 2-0 with two great strikes from Pelé and Garrincha, though the game was marred by a series of ugly challenges. Hungary, meanwhile, faced Portugal without their first choice goalkeeper, which proved crucial as they lost 3-1. Hungary against Brazil, minus the injured Pelé, was to prove a classic match with the Hungarians showing a flair and skill rarely seen in the finals. Bene gave them the lead after three minutes, then Brazil equalised against the run of play. The second-half saw Hungary step up a gear, with Albert at the heart of their 3-1 win. Portugal finished top after beating Bulgaria and Brazil, and Hungary joined them in the quarter-finals.

Group Four opened at Ayresome Park with the Soviet Union overpowering outsiders North Korea 3-0 and Italy beating Chile 2-0. The English fans warmed to the energetic North Koreans and inspired them to a draw with Chile in their next game. The meeting of the group heavyweights saw a curiously unbalanced Italy run ragged by the Soviets, who were not flattered by their 1-0 win.

Italy faced Korea expecting to overcome their defeat to Russia and qualify in second place, but Italian coach Fabbri picked his slowest defenders and the quick Koreans revelled in the occasion, scoring the winning goal after 42 minutes. Italy were out.

England faced Argentina in the first quarter-final, with Geoff Hurst coming in for the country's best striker Jimmy Greaves, injured in the game with France. Argentina continued their ugly approach and just before half-time the referee lost patience and sent-off Rattin, sparking ten minutes of mayhem as he initially refused to leave the field and then started abusing the crowd. Ten-man

Above: Rattín is sent-off during Argentina's game with England. Opposite clockwise from top: England's Bobby Moore raises the trophy; Portugal's Eusébio leaves three Hungarians behind on his way to the Golden Boot; Soviet keeper Lev Yashin saves from Italy's Sandro Mazzola.

Argentina held out until 13 minutes from time when a header from Hurst put England into the semi-finals. On the final whistle England manager Alf Ramsey was so furious with the performance of the Argentinians – who he later described as 'animals' – that he took to the field, physically preventing his players from exchanging shirts with the opposition.

The second quarter-final was equally unpleasant. Uruguay had looked the better side in an open first-half, but the second-half descended into violence. The Germans reacted to the Uruguayan provocation – Emmerich kicked Troche, only for the Uruguayan to respond with a kick to the stomach. Troche was sent-off and he slapped Uwe Seeler in the face as he left the field. Minutes later Uruguay were down to nine men and Germany cruised home with four goals in the last 20 minutes.

The third quarter-final saw the Soviet Union press the Hungarians into making mistakes, as twice goalkeeper Gelei blundered and the Hungarians went down 2-1.

The most exciting game of the round brought the Koreans and Portugal together,

and unbelievably the Koreans were 3-0 up in just 25 minutes. Then, inspired by Eusébio (he would finish as the tournament's top scorer with nine goals), Portugal began their comeback, with their star scoring twice before half-time. After the break Eusébio scored two more, before Augusto added a fifth.

The first semi-final saw West Germany face the Soviet Union in another bruising encounter. Poor sportsmanship and violent conduct marred the game and the Soviet Union left the pitch with nine men, having lost 2-1.

England's match with Portugal was altogether different. Portugal struggled to breach England's resolute defence and Bobby Charlton was outstanding going forward, scoring in each half to put England two ahead. A penalty pulled one back for Portugal but it was too little too late and England, who had controversially retained Hurst in the line-up over Greaves, were in the final to face West Germany. Ramsey's team were about to fulfil the manager's prediction – and Geoff Hurst, not even a first choice selection at the start of the tournament, was about to write himself into the football history books.

THE FINAL

ENGLAND (1) 4-2 (1) WEST GERMANY
(aet: 2-2 at 90 mins)

Date Saturday July 30, 1966   **Attendance** 93,802

Venue Wembley Stadium, London

The match got off to the worst possible start for the hosts as Haller scored to give the Germans a 12th minute lead. It was short-lived though, as six minutes later a fine header from Geoff Hurst made it 1-1. Both sides continued to press forward in the second-half until, with only 12 minutes left, Peters latched on to a poor clearance to give England the lead. In the final minute West Germany won a controversial free-kick and Weber equalised.

England went into extra-time on the attack and had already gone close twice when Hurst thumped a cross against the underside of the bar, the referee and his linesman giving the goal. In the final minute Hurst broke away to complete the only World Cup final hat-trick.

HOW THE TEAMS LINED UP

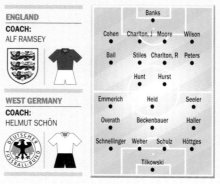

ENGLAND
COACH:
ALF RAMSEY

WEST GERMANY
COACH:
HELMUT SCHÖN

Banks
Cohen Charlton, J. Moore Wilson
Ball Stiles Charlton, R Peters
Hunt Hurst
Emmerich Held Seeler
Overath Beckenbauer Haller
Schnellinger Weber Schulz Höttges
Tilkowski

SEMI-FINALS
West Germany 2-1 Soviet Union
England 2-1 Portugal

THIRD PLACE PLAY-OFF
Portugal 2-1 Soviet Union

TOP GOALSCORERS
9 goals: Eusébio (Portugal)
5 goals: Helmut Haller (West Germany)
4 goals: Geoff Hurst (England), Franz Beckenbauer (West Germany), Ferenc Bene (Hungary), Valeri Porkujan (Soviet Union)

FASTEST GOAL
1 minute: Pak Seung-zin (North Korea v Portugal)

TOTAL GOALS
89

AVERAGE GOALS
2.78 per game

ENGLAND

BANKS	7
COHEN	7
CHARLTON, J	7
MOORE	8
WILSON	6
STILES	6
CHARLTON, R	8
PETERS	7
Goal: 78 mins. Booked.	
BALL	8
HUNT	7
HURST	*9
Goal: 18 mins, 101 mins, 120 mins	

WEST GERMANY

TILKOWSKI	5
HÖTTGES	6
SCHULZ	7
WEBER	7
Goal: 90 mins	
SCHNELLINGER	5
HALLER	*8
Goal: 12 mins	
BECKENBAUER	7
OVERATH	6
SEELER	7
HELD	6
EMMERICH	6

Referee: Dienst (Switzerland)

MEXICO 1970

Against all the odds Mexico 70 turned into a feast of football, and remains the most fondly remembered of all the World Cup competitions. Portents, however, didn't bode well. The problems of the extreme heat of the Mexican summer and the energy-sapping altitude threatened to stifle free-flowing, attacking football, especially in light of FIFA's decision to kick-off many games at midday to appease European broadcasters. Pre-tournament fears of ultra-defensive and violent play, a worrying trend in the game, also threatened to put a negative stranglehold on the competition. But thanks to the colourful flamboyance and daring excellence of the multi-skilled, Pelé-inspired Brazilians, the beautiful game somehow managed to prosper like never before.

The first two qualifying groups saw the Soviet Union, Mexico, Italy and Uruguay come through without any surprises against lesser opposition. The ultra-cautious Italians qualified without conceding a goal, and scoring just two,

Above: Gerd Müller, who scored the winner, in action against England. Opposite clockwise from top left: Germany and Italy in semi-final action; Pelé celebrates; Carlos Alberto lifts the Jules Rimet Cup; Pelé and Bobby Moore swap shirts.

while the Soviet Union finished on top of their group above Mexico on goals scored.

The outstanding match of the group stage was between twice-champions Brazil and the holders England. In a wonderful end-to-end game, famed for Gordon Banks' incredible save from a downward goal-bound Pelé header, Brazil stole the honours with the only goal from the powerful Jairzinho, who was to score in all of Brazil's six matches. Both teams were to progress to the next stage.

In Group 4, despite an early struggle against a spirited Morocco, the West Germans gained maximum points with 'Der Bomber', Gerd Müller, in typically prolific form, knocking in hat-tricks against Peru and Bulgaria.

In León, England were matched against West Germany in the first quarter-final. With goals from Alan Mullery and Martin Peters, England were 2-0 up and in control early in the second-half. However, after a couple of rhythm-disturbing substitutions by Sir Alf Ramsey (Hunter and Bell for Bobby Charlton and Peters) the Germans clawed themselves back into the game, and goals from Franz Beckenbauer and Uwe Seeler took the tie to extra-time. A close-range volley from Müller past second-choice goalkeeper Peter Bonetti (Banks was ill with an upset stomach) finally eliminated the holders.

In the other quarter-finals, hosts Mexico lost out 4-1 to an untypically free-scoring Italy at Toluca, with the talented striker Gigi Riva scoring twice. In Guadalajara, Brazil continued their irrepressible form, getting the better of Peru in a six-goal thriller. In the lowest profile game of this stage, Uruguay narrowly defeated the Soviet Union with an extra-time goal by substitute Esparrago in the Azteca Stadium.

The match of the tournament came in Mexico City where the two European giants, Italy and West Germany, were pitted against each other in a thrilling semi-final. Italy took the lead through Roberto Boninsegna, and in

typical fashion withdrew to protect their lead. It was a tactic that very nearly worked, but an equaliser in the third minute of injury-time from Karl Heinz Schnellinger meant the game was not to be decided within the 90 minutes. Franz Beckenbauer famously remained on the field even with a dislocated shoulder, his arm in a sling strapped to his body. In extra-time the goals kept coming. Müller edged Germany into the lead, while Tarcisio Burgnich and Riva put Italy back in control at 3-2. Müller, the eventual Golden Boot winner, clawed it back to 3-3, before Rivera finally clinched one of the World Cup's most epic struggles for Italy.

The other semi-final pitted the old South American foes, Uruguay against Brazil, in Guadalajara. The Uruguayans took an early lead through Cubilla, and immediately tried to shut up shop. Not an easy task against Mario Zagalo's side, and Brazil were on equal terms late in the first-half when right-half Clodoaldo powered in the equaliser. Despite aggressive tackling from Uruguay, the Brazilians took hold of the game in the second 45 minutes, and goals from Jairzinho and the fabulous Rivelino sealed a 3-1 victory. Late on Pelé almost hit the goal of the tournament, outrageously dummying Mazurkiewicz in the Uruguayan goal, before pulling his shot just wide.

Brazil were to play some of their most open and attacking football in the final, especially significant as Italy were the self-confessed masters of catenaccio, the most defence-minded style of play. The competition was also a personal victory for Pelé. Having threatened to quit football after his treatment at the 1966 tournament, his performances in 1970 stood as a permanent testament to his genius.

The 1970 World Cup was a triumph, and thanks, ironically, to television, a triumph on a global scale. How fitting that Mexico 1970 was to be first tournament to be shown in colour, and thanks to the fantasy football of the Brazilians it was glorious technicolour.

SEMI-FINALS
Italy 4-3 West Germany (aet)
Brazil 3-1 Uruguay

THIRD PLACE PLAY-OFF
West Germany 1-0 Uruguay

TOP GOALSCORERS
10 goals: Gerd Müller (West Germany)
7 goals: Jairzinho (Brazil)
5 goals: Teófilo Cubillas (Peru)

FASTEST GOAL
3 minutes: Ladislav Petras (Czechoslovakia v Romania)

TOTAL GOALS
95

AVERAGE GOAL
2.97 per game

THE FINAL

BRAZIL (1) 4-1 (1) ITALY

Date Sunday June 21, 1970 **Attendance** 107,412
Venue Azteca Stadium, Mexico City

Pelé opened the scoring after 18 minutes, athletically getting his head on the end of Rivelino's cross. Against the run of play, Boninsegna pounced on a careless mistake by Clodoaldo to level the score, but Italy were unable to match the Brazilians in terms of possession. Their skilful play left the Azzurri chasing shadows. In the 66th minute Gerson's left-footed cross-shot found the back of Albertosi's net, followed by Jairzinho's customary goal. The match winner was one of the most loved goals in football history. In a move where eight of Brazil's ten outfield players touched the ball, Jairzinho found Pelé and laid the ball off into the stride of captain Carlos Alberto, who thundered it low into the corner. The Jules Rimet Cup was Brazil's to keep.

BRAZIL	
FÉLIX	6
CARLOS ALBERTO ⚽	7
Goal: 87 mins	
BRITO	6
PIAZZA	6
EVERALDO	7
JAIRZINHO ⚽	8
Goal: 71 mins	
CLODOALDO	7
GERSON ⚽	7
Goal: 66 mins	
TOSTÃO	8
PELE ⚽	*9
Goal: 18 mins	
RIVELINO	7
Booked	

ITALY	
ALBERTOSI	6
BURGNICH	5
Booked	
CERA	6
BERTINI	6
Subbed: 75 mins (Juliano)	
FACCHETTI	6
ROSATO	5
DOMENGHINI	7
DE SISTI	6
MAZZOLA	*8
BONINSEGNA ⚽	7
Goal: 38 mins. Subbed: 84 mins (Rivera)	
RIVA	6
sub: JULIANO	6
sub: RIVERA	5

Referee: Glöckner (East Germany)

HOW THE TEAMS LINED UP

BRAZIL
COACH: MARIO ZAGALO

Félix
Carlos Alberto Brito Piazza Everaldo
Clodoaldo Gerson
Jairzinho Tostão Pelé Rivelino

ITALY
COACH: FERRUCCIO VALCAREGGI

Riva Boninsegna Domenghini
De Sisti Mazzola Bertini
Facchetti Rosato Cera Burgnich
Albertosi

WEST GERMANY 1974

The 1970 finals in Mexico had ended somewhat ignobly for the Europeans, with Italy on the receiving end of a 4-1 demolition from a seemingly unstoppable Brazil. This time, however, European countries found themselves most definitely in the ascendancy and, at the tournament's end, Poland, Holland and West Germany were installed as the world's three best teams. The latter pair contested the final itself, which, under a new system featuring 16 teams and two group stages, was the only proper 'knock-out' game of the tournament.

Although they had struggled slightly during the qualifying stages, Holland, under manager Rinus Michels and boasting a plethora of stars from the all-conquering Ajax club side, cut a swathe through the group stages. Their unique brand of Total Football, in which players switched positions and roles with astonishing versatility, saw them score 14 goals in six games, conceding just one.

They began their first group stage campaign with a comfortable 2-0 win over the very first world champions, Uruguay, both goals coming from Ajax star Johnny Rep. Michels' men followed it up with a goalless draw against Sweden, but bounced back to record an impressive 4-1 rout of Bulgaria (including two penalties from another Ajax man, Johan Neeskens). This was enough for them to top the group and qualify for the last eight along with the Swedes.

A pre-tournament defeat of the West Germans had made Argentina seem a good 'dark horse' bet for glory at the finals, but after only just edging out Italy for a place in the last eight they were effectively dismantled by the inspired Dutch in their opening second group stage game. Goals from Rep, Cruyff (2) and Ruud Krol contributed to the 4-0 landslide. Holland's 2-0 win over East Germany, who had beaten their West German neighbours earlier in the tournament, set up an all or nothing showdown with reigning world champions Brazil: the prize a place in the final.

Without Pelé, who had by now retired, the Brazilians were clearly not the force they had once been. They had scraped through the first stage thanks to goalless draws with Yugoslavia and Scotland, and a 3-0 win over a hapless Zaïre side who had shipped nine against Yugoslavia. However, Brazil had started the second stage with something approaching their old swagger, beating East Germany 1-0, thanks to a second-half strike from Rivelino, and Argentina 2-1, with goals from Jairzinho and Rivelino again. Despite improving form, however, the Brazilians found it impossible to live with a Dutch side approaching the peak

Above: Joe Jordan in action for Scotland during their win over Zaïre. Opposite clockwise from top: Holland captain Johan Cruyff; German Gerd Müller fends off the Yugoslav Maric; Müller again, this time firing home against Poland; Beckenbauer lifts the World Cup in Munich.

of its powers. Two second-half goals, Cruyff's strike in the 65th minute following Neeskens' gorgeous lob in the 50th, saw Holland run out 2-0 winners. The self-destructing Brazilians finish with ten men after the dismissal of Luís Pereira. Holland, many assumed, were well on their way to a first and hugely deserved world championship.

In contrast West Germany started the tournament slowly. After a narrow win over Chile and an unimpressive 3-0 victory against Australia, Helmut Schön's men progressed to the last eight in second place after losing 1-0 to neighbours East Germany. A benefit of the shock result, however, was that they avoided Brazil, Argentina and Holland in the next group stage. Slowly but surely the West German team started to gel.

Spurred on by inspirational skipper Franz Beckenbauer, they started the second group stage impressively – beating Yugoslavia 2-0 thanks to goals from Paul Breitner and the prolific Müller. Even better followed in the shape of a 4-2 victory over Sweden. Finely balanced at 2-2 with 14 minutes left, Jürgen Grabowski and Uli Hoeness put the tie beyond doubt, setting up a crucial final group game with Poland in the process – a match the Germans only needed to draw to advance to their third World Cup final appearance.

The Poles, who had surprisingly eliminated England during the qualifiers, were unbeaten thus far in the tournament and in Grzegorz Lato had a striker who would go on to become its highest scorer, with seven goals, including two in a 3-2 first stage victory over Argentina. He also scored a crucial second-half winner in the 2-1 victory over Yugoslavia that effectively brought Poland face-to-face with the West

Germans for a place in the World Cup final.

It was an exciting but incredibly nervy game for both sides, especially after the kick-off was delayed due to a waterlogged pitch. Poland's best chances came in the first half, Robert Gadocha and the effervescent Lato forcing West Germany's goalkeeper Sepp Maier into a couple of excellent saves. In the second-half it was the turn of Maier's opposite number in the Polish goal, Jan Tomaszewski, to shine. He saved a penalty from Uli Hoeness, but it was to prove in vain. West Germany snatched the winner 14 minutes from time when Hoeness's shot deflected into the path of Müller, who clinically buried it into the back of the net in typical fashion.

A 1-0 third place play-off victory over Brazil (the goal coming courtesy of Lato) was scant consolation for the Poles, who had surely been the tournament's biggest surprise package. The final, however, was now to be contested between hosts West Germany, who hadn't won the tournament since 1954, and Holland, who hadn't even managed to qualify since 1938. Efficiency, organisation and hard work against versatility, vision and precocious talent.

THE FINAL

WEST GERMANY (2) 2-1 (1) HOLLAND

Date Sunday July 7, 1974 **Attendance** 77,822

Venue Olympic Stadium, Munich

Holland got off to the best possible start in this all-European final. After less than a minute had elapsed on the clock, Johan Cruyff was up-ended in the West German penalty area by Bayern Munich's Uli Hoeness. There had never been a penalty awarded in a World Cup final before, but Johan Neeskens calmly slotted the ball past goalkeeper Sepp Maier to put Rinus Michels' side a goal up.

The Dutch continued to dominate but surrendered their lead cheaply in the 25th minute when a surging Bernd Hölzenbein run was bought to an abrupt end by a trip in the Holland penalty area. Paul Breitner duly converted the spot-kick, and the Germans went on to snatch a decisive lead two minutes before half-time through Gerd Müller.

HOW THE TEAMS LINED UP

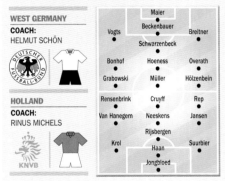

WEST GERMANY
COACH: HELMUT SCHÖN

HOLLAND
COACH: RINUS MICHELS

Maier
Vogts — Beckenbauer — Breitner
Schwarzenbeck
Bonhof — Hoeness — Overath
Grabowski — Müller — Hölzenbein

Rensenbrink — Cruyff — Rep
Van Hanegem — Neeskens — Jansen
Rijsbergen
Krol — Haan — Suurbier
Jongbloed

WEST GERMANY	
MAIER	6
VOGTS	7
Booked: 3 mins	
SCHWARZENBECK	7
BECKENBAUER	9
BREITNER	7
Goal: 25 mins (pen)	
BONHOF	6
HOENESS	6
OVERATH	7
GRABOWSKI	7
MÜLLER	8
Goal: 43 mins	
HÖLZENBEIN	6

HOLLAND	
JONGBLOED	6
SUURBIER	6
RIJSBERGEN	6
Subbed: 69 mins (De Jong)	
HAAN	7
KROL	7
JANSEN	6
NEESKENS	8
Goal: 2 mins (pen). Booked: 39 mins	
VAN HANEGEM	6
Booked: 22 mins	
REP	7
CRUYFF	*9
Booked: 45 mins	
RENSENBRINK	6
Subbed: 46 mins (Van De Kerkhof, R)	
sub: VAN DE KERKHOF, R	6
sub: DE JONG	6

Referee: Taylor (England)

SEMI-FINALS

Replaced by a second round group phase

THIRD PLACE PLAY-OFF

Poland 1-0 Brazil

TOP GOALSCORERS

7 goals: Gregorz Lato (Poland);
5 goals: Johan Neeskens (Holland), Andrzej Szarmach (Poland);
4 goals: Gerd Müller (Germany), Ralf Edström (Sweden), Johnny Rep (Holland)

FASTEST GOAL

80 seconds: Johan Neeskens (Holland v West Germany)

TOTAL GOALS

97

AVERAGE GOAL

2.55 per game

ARGENTINA 1978

When Daniel Passarella hoisted the World Cup aloft in Buenos Aires, it was one of the most romantic and tragic moments in football history. For Argentina, named as hosts back in 1966, just to have staged the event was an achievement given the political turmoil that had prompted several participants to talk of a boycott. To then win the trophy sent the nation ecstatic.

Yet for Holland, whose players endured the victory night celebrations cooped up in their hotel, defeat in the final for the second consecutive time was cruel beyond measure. The country that had illuminated Seventies football and had probably done more to create the modern game than any other, was destined to end the decade without a major honour.

The tournament itself, in the wake of the great Brazil team's performance of 1970 and the Beckenbauer/Cruyff head-to-head of 1974, was not a vintage. Mario Kempes emerged as

Argentina's hero, but not to the extent that Diego Maradona would eight years later. While Argentina 78 lacked a true superstar or a great team, the extreme emotions it generated – not to mention the whiff of scandal – ensured its place in football folklore.

The threatened boycott in protest at General Videla's military regime never materialised and all 16 teams arrived, although Holland's enigmatic Cruyff stayed at home. Like 1974, there was no knockout stage. The top two teams in four groups would progress into a second group stage with the winners going into the final.

Most of the football superpowers had qualified, with the exception of Euro 76 winners Czechoslovakia, the Soviet Union and, for the second consecutive finals, England. British interest centred on Scotland, who assembled perhaps their greatest ever team, but their campaign degenerated into shambles and acrimony. Poor results, coupled with their winger Willie Johnston failing a drugs test, ensured a shameful early exit for Scotland. Only then, when it was too late, did they show what they could do by beating Holland 3-2.

Peru had proven they weren't the expected pushover, while doubts persisted whether Holland without Cruyff could mount a serious challenge. West Germany qualified in equally unimpressive style as runners-up to Poland in perhaps the weakest group.

Brazil, under coach Claudio Coutinho, had gone from poetic to pragmatic. They too were far from convincing, managing only two goals in their first round group, but along with Austria they still squeezed through ahead of Spain and Sweden.

With so many big guns misfiring, the tournament appeared to be opening up. Italy, masters of the defensive approach that characterised football in this era, looked likely to prosper when they topped a group that also included Argentina, France and Hungary. Argentina's 2-1 defeat of France proved the decisive result for second place.

Despite their indifferent showings, all of the favourites had spluttered their way into a second round that fizzed with exciting match-ups. Group A featured European superpowers West Germany, Holland and Italy, plus a useful Austria side gorging itself on the goals of Hans Krankl. Group B included the less fancied Poles and Peru, plus arguably the fiercest rivals in world football – Argentina and Brazil.

When the two met in Rosario, the weight of history and the fear of defeat were too much for either side to bear and the match fizzled out into an ill-tempered 0-0 draw. With both sides having already recorded victories (Brazil had beaten Peru 3-0 and Argentina defeated Poland 2-0), providing both could win their last matches the finalist would be decided on goal difference. When Brazil overcame Poland 3-1, the balance of power appeared to have

Above: Scotland's Archie Gemmill scores his wonder goal against eventual finalists Holland. Opposite clockwise from top left: Daniel Passarella lifts the trophy; the ticker tape welcome as Argentina took to the pitch; top scorer Mario Kempes; Rob Rensenbrink of Holland in action.

swung their way. But owing to some unfair scheduling, Argentina didn't kick-off their final game against Peru in Rosario until 45 minutes after Brazil's game had finished. César Luis Menotti's side had the massive advantage of knowing they had to win by four clear goals to reach the final.

Peru, who had looked so accomplished early in the tournament, at first looked prepared for the challenge, even hitting the post. Then, in one of the most talked about matches in World Cup history, they rolled over and lost 6-0. Rumours had already circulated about some controversial decisions in Argentina's favour against France in the first round, and it was soon alleged that the match with Peru had been fixed by the country's ruling military junta. But when the dust settled, Argentina – 48 years after they had lost the first World Cup to Uruguay – had booked their ticket to the final of their own fiesta.

In the other group, Holland exploded into life with a 5-1 destruction of Austria to take an early stranglehold on the group, while Italy and West Germany drew 0-0. Holland strengthened their hand when, in a repeat of the 1974 final, goals from Haan and Rene van der Kerkhof earned them a useful 2-2 draw with West Germany.

With Italy beating Austria 1-0, the Dutch knew that unless the West Germans could manage a landslide against Austria, a draw with Italy would be sufficient. West Germany, a shadow of their 1974 side, were put out of their misery when they lost 3-2 to the already-eliminated Austrians. Holland did all that was required and more by beating Italy 2-1.

In the third-place play-off, Brazil overcame Enzo Bearzot's Italy 2-1 to maintain the only unbeaten record of the tournament. But in some ways the victory only upset Brazilians even more. For the first time in the competition they had shed their inhibitions and played in the great Brazilian tradition, leaving many to wonder why they left it so late.

SEMI-FINALS

Replaced by a second round group phase

THIRD PLACE PLAY-OFF

Brazil 2-1 Italy

TOP GOALSCORERS

6 goals: Mario Kempes (Argentina)
5 goals: Teófilo Cubillas (Peru), Rob Rensenbrink (Holland)
4 goals: Hans Krankl (Austria), Leopoldo Luque (Argentina)

FASTEST GOAL

31 seconds: Bernard Lacombe (France v Italy)

TOTAL GOALS

102

AVERAGE GOAL

2.68 per game:

THE FINAL

ARGENTINA (1) 3-1 (1) HOLLAND

(aet; 1-1 at 90 mins)

Date Sunday June 25, 1978 **Attendance** 77,260
Venue River Plate Stadium, Buenos Aires

Argentina attempted to unnerve the Dutch by keeping them on the pitch for five minutes before their arrival to a sea of sky blue and white ticker tape. They then objected to a bandage on Rene van der Kerkhof's arm. When play began, high skill mingled with barely restrained violence. Rep wasted a great chance for Holland before Kempes put Argentina ahead on 37 minutes. The Dutch were growing feverish with frustration when, in the 81st minute, substitute Nanninga headed the ball into the net. Then with a minute to go, Rensenbrink struck the foot of the post.

Kempes, the tournament's top scorer, scrambled the hosts back into the lead a minute before the first period of extra-time ended and, with four minutes to go, Bertoni made the game safe.

ARGENTINA	
FILLOL	7
OLGUIN	6
GALVAN	7
PASSARELLA	8
TARANTINI	6
ARDILES	7
Booked: 40 mins. Subbed: 66 mins (Larossa)	
GALLEGO	6
ORTIZ	6
Subbed: 75 mins (Houseman)	
BERTONI	7
Goal: 115 mins	
LUQUE	8
KEMPES	*9
Goal: 38, 105 mins	
sub: LAROSSA	6
Booked: 94 mins	
sub: HOUSEMAN	6
HOLLAND	
JONGBLOED	6
POORTVLIET	5
Booked: 96 mins	
KROL	*8
Booked: 15 mins	
BRANDTS	7
JANSEN	6
Subbed: 73 mins (Suurbier)	
NEESKENS	7
HAAN	6
VAN DE KERKHOF, W	6
VAN DE KERKHOF, R	6
REP	5
Subbed: 59 mins (Nanninga)	
RENSENBRINK	6
sub: NANNINGA	7
Goal: 82 mins	
sub: SUURBIER	
Booked: 94 mins	6
Referee: Gonella (Italy)	

HOW THE TEAMS LINED UP

ARGENTINA
COACH: CÉSAR LUIS MENOTTI

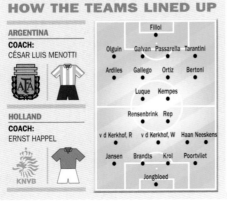

Fillol

Olguin Galvan Passarella Tarantini

Ardiles Gallego Ortiz Bertoni

Luque Kempes

HOLLAND
COACH: ERNST HAPPEL

Rensenbrink Rep

v d Kerkhof, R v d Kerkhof, W Haan Neeskens

Jansen Brandts Krol Poortvliet

Jongbloed

SPAIN 1982

There was a real sense of trepidation as the World Cup jamboree descended on Spain for the 1982 finals. Many doubted Spain's ability to host such a global spectacular and those fears were heightened as the draw descended into chaos. To begin with the balls representing Peru and Chile were accidentally left in the draw when it was FIFA policy to keep them out initially in order to ensure the teams were kept apart from their more illustrious neighbours, Argentina and Brazil.

Scotland, meanwhile, found themselves mistakenly in Argentina's group instead of Belgium, before being moved into the correct grouping with Brazil. The confusion led to a halt in proceedings, then to compound the situation, the cage containing the balls jammed and one split in half.

The critics were given further ammunition with the tournament's expansion to 24 teams. There was a fear that games would descend into a procession as the likes of Kuwait, Honduras and El Salvador took to the stage, while conversely there was every indication that such teams would stifle the opposition and defend for their lives. Thankfully, the inspirational opening ceremony and Belgium's subsequent 1-0 victory against champions Argentina allayed the fears and set the tone for a tournament that would promote the World Cup as a truly global affair.

Brazil were clear favourites. The flair and breathtaking skill – so absent four years earlier – had returned, while in Zico, Socrates, Falcão and Junior, they had a prowess that few could compete with. Their 4-1 victory against Scotland – in which David Narey had the audacity to score first – and a 4-0 win over New Zealand indicated their intention.

Their rivals did not have it so easy. Italy made a less than auspicious start, drawing against Poland and Peru, and their progression was only confirmed in a winner-takes-all game against Cameroon. A Graziani header ensured another draw but, although he had secured a safe passage on goal difference, Italy were being ridiculed back home.

West Germany, another thoroughbred, lost their opener to Algeria, then contributed to one of the most distasteful moments in World Cup history. Having scored against neighbours Austria, and knowing a 1-0 score would ensure the progress of both sides, the second-half descended into farce at the expense of Algeria, whose complaint to FIFA fell on deaf ears.

Spain were also left sweating on their progression as a Gerry Armstrong goal for Northern Ireland stunned the home support, but the 1-0 defeat ensured both teams progressed, with Billy Bingham's side heading the group. The Irish also created history when their winger, Norman Whiteside, became the

Above: England captain Bryan Robson celebrates scoring the tournament's quickest goal. Opposite clockwise from top left: Argentina captain Daniel Passarella; Norman Whiteside on the ball for Northern Ireland; the victorious Argentina squad with the World Cup; Poland's Lato shoots against France in the third place play-off.

youngest player to appear in the finals, aged 17 years and 41 days.

Europe's other leading lights, France and England, were left to battle it out in Group Four. Aggrieved at England's seeding, the French were left to lick their wounds as Ron Greenwood's side put them to the sword with an emphatic 3-1 victory, kicked-off by a Bryan Robson goal in 27 seconds. Further wins against Czechoslovakia and Kuwait served to enhance England's reputation, while the French limped through, helped by a 4-1 defeat of Kuwait, a game remembered for coach Hidalgo's clash with police when a goal was disallowed after the Kuwaitis' claimed they had stopped on hearing a whistle from the crowd.

With the second phase split into four groups of three, and with only the top side guaranteed a semi-final place, victory was imperative in the opening game, certainly in Group C which contained Brazil, Argentina and Italy. The latter's flaccid displays had them installed as elimination fodder, yet goals from Tardelli and Cabrini ensured a 2-1 win against Argentina. With Brazil defeating their South American counterparts – a game that saw Maradona red-carded – the game between Brazil and Italy was billed as the clash of the tournament. The pendulum swung back and forth, yet it was the superlative finishing of Paolo Rossi that ensured Italy's 3-2 victory. His hat-trick, completed 15 minutes from time, created a hero and revitalised a nation.

England's progress, meanwhile, was halted by a lack of firepower. A sterile 0-0 draw against West Germany meant they had to beat Spain by two goals, but with the creativity of Kevin Keegan and Trevor Brooking still absent through injury, another 0-0 prevailed. Both players were desperately plunged into action with 27 minutes remaining, but a clearly unfit Keegan fluffed a simple header that could have provided the impetus so desperately needed.

France and Poland made up the quartet, but it was Italy who had the easiest route to the

final against the Poles, who would sorely miss goalscorer Boniek. Rossi further enhanced his credentials with a goal in either half, and although the 2-0 win raised few eyebrows, the other semi was a classic.

With Platini in sparkling form for France, the game against West Germany finished 1-1 after 90 minutes. Further goals from Giresse and Tresor had the French dreaming of the final, yet Germany refused to quit. Coach Derwall gambled by introducing half-fit captain Rummenigge and, having pulled a goal back in the 106th minute, Fischer then equalised with an overhead kick. The resulting penalty shoot-out went to sudden death and Hrubesch saw the Germans home. The hero was keeper Schumacher, yet he should not have been on the pitch following an appalling challenge on Battiston, which had left the Frenchman unconscious for three minutes.

The incident won the Germans few admirers, and with Italy on an upward spiral, there would be one winner and one hero...

SEMI-FINALS

West Germany 3-3 France (aet)
(West Germany won 5-4 on penalties)
Italy 2-0 Poland

THIRD PLACE PLAY-OFF

Poland 3-2 France

TOP GOALSCORERS

6 goals: Paolo Rossi (Italy)
5 goals: Karl-Heinz Rummenigge (West Germany)
4 goals: Zbigniew Boniek (Poland), Zico (Brazil)

FASTEST GOAL

27 seconds: Bryan Robson (England v France)

TOTAL GOALS

146

AVERAGE GOAL

2.81 per game

THE FINAL

ITALY (0) **3-1** (0) **WEST GERMANY**

Date Sunday July 11, 1982 **Attendance** 77,260
Venue Santiago Bernabéu, Madrid

Italy were favourites to win their third World Cup but, with midfielder Antognoni injured, their anxieties were heightened further when Graziani left the field with an injured shoulder inside the first ten minutes. Things then got even worse when Cabrini became the first player to miss a penalty in a World Cup final. Yet despite the setbacks, Italy shaded a first-half dominated by fouls and the game finally came to life after 57 minutes when Rossi rose highest to connect with Gentile's pin-point cross.

Victory was secured 11 minutes later when Tardelli hit a superb left-foot shot from the edge of the area, and by the time Altobelli hammered home a Conti cross, the game had become a procession. Paul Breitner scored a late consolation but the Germans were left to pay a heavy price for their epic semi-final. Italy claimed their third crown and toasted Rossi, who had become an overnight sensation.

HOW THE TEAMS LINED UP

ITALY
COACH: ENZO BEARZOT

WEST GERMANY
COACH: JUPP DERWALL

ITALY: Zoff; Cabrini, Scirea, Gentile, Collovati; Oriali, Bergomi, Tardelli; Conti, Rossi, Graziani

WEST GERMANY: Fischer, Rummenigge; Littbarski; Dremmler, Briegel, Breitner; Förster, B, Förster, K-H, Stielike, Kaltz; Schumacher

ITALY	
ZOFF	6
GENTILE	7
SCIREA	6
COLLOVATI	7
BERGOMI	7
CABRINI	6
Missed pen: 25 mins	
ORIALI	7
Booked: 73 mins	
TARDELLI	*8
Goal: 69 mins	
CONTI	7
Booked: 31 mins	
GRAZIANI	
Subbed: 8 mins (Altobelli)	
ROSSI	7
Goal: 57 mins	
sub: ALTOBELLI	7
Goal: 81 mins. Subbed: 88 mins (Causio)	
sub: CAUSIO	5
WEST GERMANY	
SCHUMACHER	6
KALTZ	5
STIELIKE	6
Booked: 73 mins	
FÖRSTER, K-H	6
FÖRSTER, B	6
LITTBARSKI	6
Booked: 88 mins	
DREMMLER	6
Booked: 61 mins. Subbed 63 mins (Hrubesch)	
BREITNER	7
Goal: 83 mins	
BRIEGEL	*7
FISCHER	6
RUMMENIGGE	5
Subbed: 70 mins (Muller H)	
sub: HRUBESCH	6
sub: MULLER, H	6
Referee: Coelho (Mexico)	

MEXICO 1986

SEMI-FINALS
Argentina 2-0 Belgium
West Germany 2-0 France

THIRD PLACE PLAY-OFF
France 4-2 Belgium
(aet: 2-2 at 90 mins)

TOP GOALSCORERS
6 goals: Gary Lineker (England)
5 goals: Emilio Butragueño
(Spain), Careca (Brazil), Diego
Maradona (Argentina)

FASTEST GOAL
63 seconds: Emilio Butragueño
(Spain v Northern Ireland)

TOTAL GOALS
132

AVERAGE GOAL
2.54 per game

When Colombia decided they no longer had the financial muscle to host the 1986 World Cup, Mexico stepped into the breach to become FIFA's saviour in what proved to be another troubled episode for the game's governing body. The Mexicans may have hosted an exemplary tournament in 1970, but with their own financial crisis and Mexican unemployment at record levels, the decision looked dubious given the stability provided by the rival USA bid.

When it was revealed that the tournament would be staged by Mexican television network Televisa, whose president was a friend of FIFA president João Havelange, it drew outrage from the Americans. A strained relationship ensued – bombs were even found outside the US Embassy – and to compound the problems, some 25,000 people were killed in a huge earthquake prior to the tournament.

THE FINAL

ARGENTINA (1) 3-2 (0) WEST GERMANY

Date Sunday June 29,1986 **Attendance** 116,026
Venue Azteca Stadium, Mexico City

Argentina proved they were no one-man team as their superior skill and creativity came to the fore against the Germans. With Burruchaga matching Maradona's performance, a 2-0 lead was established through Brown and Valdano. The Germans, who had so successfully stifled their opposition en route to the final, had no answer this time and the South American's were already dreaming of another ticker tape celebration back home.

Yet, as so often in the past, a wounded German animal is a dangerous beast and as the game limped to its conclusion, they finally showed the inventiveness that had been so absent. Two headers inside six minutes, from Rummenigge and Völler, brought the tie level on 80 minutes. But cometh the hour, cometh the man. Maradona's inch-perfect pass found Burruchaga who beat the offside trap to power the ball past Schumacher.

ARGENTINA		
PUMPIDO		6
Booked: 85 mins		
BROWN		8
Goal: 23 mins		
CUCIUFFO		7
RUGGERI		6
OLARTICOECHEA		6
Booked: 77 mins		
GIUSTI		6
BATISTA		7
BURRUCHAGA		*9
Goal: 83 mins. Subbed: 89 mins (Trobbiani)		
ENRIQUE		7
Booked: 81 mins		
MARADONA		8
Booked: 17 mins		
VALDANO		7
Goal: 56 mins		
sub: **TROBBIANI**		5

WEST GERMANY		
SCHUMACHER		5
JAKOBS		5
BERTHOLD		6
FÖRSTER, K-H		6
BRIEGEL		*8
Booked: 62 mins		
MATTHÄUS		7
Booked: 21 mins		
BREHME		7
MAGATH		6
Subbed: 63 mins (Hoeness, D)		
EDER		6
RUMMENIGGE		7
Goal: 74 mins		
ALLOFS		6
Subbed: 46 mins (Völler)		
sub: **HOENESS, D**		6
sub: **VÖLLER**		7
Goal: 80 mins		

Referee: Arppi Filho (Brazil)

HOW THE TEAMS LINED UP

ARGENTINA
COACH: CARLOS BILARDO

Pumpido
Ruggeri   Brown   Cuciuffo
Giusti Batista Burruchaga Enrique Olarticoechea
Valdano Maradona

WEST GERMANY
COACH: FRANZ BECKENBAUER

Allofs   Rummenigge
Briegel Eder Magath Matthäus Berthold
Forster, K-H   Jakobs   Brehme
Schumacher

Mexico simply had to deliver, yet little did they realise that a pint-sized genius from Argentina would play the trump card. Diego Maradona enlightened us all while exorcising the ghosts of Spain 82, when a lunge on Brazilian defender Batista had ended his participation in the second round.

With a record transfer fee of £6.9 million hanging above him, the Napoli midfielder was a marked man, and the succession of fouls inflicted by South Korea gave an indication of the fear he instilled. Yet he destroyed his opponents, setting up goals for Valdano and Ruggeri in a 3-1 Group A victory. A truer test came against champions Italy. No team knew the diminutive star better, yet he shone in a game of intrigue. In the 34th minute he eluded Napoli team-mate Bagni, his low centre of gravity enabling him to score from an acute angle. The goal cancelled out Altobelli's penalty but both teams progressed.

Yet if Maradona created headlines for his on-field exploits, the enthusiasm of the Mexico crowd proved unprecedented: 110,000 filled the Azteca for their opening win against Belgium and the 'Mexican Wave' phenomenon was born. Hero of the hour was Mexican Hugo Sanchez, whose feats were rivalling those of Maradona. Having scored in the 2-1 win, he was equally impressive against Paraguay and the consensus grew that the hosts could go far.

With the high altitude, European nations were given little chance. France were deemed a threat with Platini, Battiston and Bossis providing experience and guile, but a 1-0 win against Canada was less than convincing, while a 1-1 draw with an impressive Soviet Union side left the European champions sweating on their progress. Their eventual qualification had more to do with the ineptitude of Canada and Hungary than their own creativity.

England also made heavy work of ensuring qualification as a 1-0 defeat against Portugal was followed by a sorry draw with Morocco. The 0-0 scoreline created a furore, and with captain Bryan Robson dislocating his shoulder and fellow midfielder Ray Wilkins being sent-off, victory against Poland was imperative. A Gary Lineker hat-trick saved the team as a 3-0 win kept manager Bobby Robson in a job and England in the competition.

Denmark appeared the European side best equipped to succeed in the tournament. An opening 1-0 win against Scotland was just an aperitif for the Michael Laudrup-inspired 6-1 demolition of Uruguay and a shock 2-0 victory over West Germany.

The second phase reverted to a knock-out format once again, with Brazil again looking dangerous. Having cruised through their group against Spain, Algeria and Northern Ireland, their 4-0 demolition of Poland saw a return to the flamboyance of four years earlier. Edinho's third goal, in particular, had the 45,000 Guadalajara crowd mesmerised.

Above: Gary Lineker after his hat-trick against Poland.
Opposite clockwise from top left: Argentina's Jorge Valdano fends off West Germany's Ditmar Jakobs; Diego Maradona celebrates victory against England; Bryan Robson about to dislocate his shoulder against Morocco; Uruguay's Jose Batista is sent-off against Scotland.

The expected nations progressed, with the exception of Denmark and Italy. The Danes had peaked and their emphatic 5-1 defeat at the hands of Spain is best remembered for Emilio Butragueño's four goals. The Italians, meanwhile, succumbed to a much-improved French team. Platini confirmed his class with a casual chip over Galli to set up a 2-0 win.

The French, playing as potential champions, would have to overcome Brazil in the quarter-finals if they had realistic ambitions, and with so much riding on the outcome, a game of cat and mouse ensued. Substitute Zico missed a crucial late penalty and the match was decided by a penalty shoot-out, France winning 4-3 thanks to Fernandez's decider.

Shoot-outs decided three of the quarter-final ties, with West Germany edging past Mexico and Belgium overcoming Spain. The process of elimination led to calls for sudden death football. Yet if this was knee-jerk anger on the part of the losers, their pain was nothing compared to that felt by England following their exit against Argentina.

With the scores level at 0-0, a harmless backpass from Hodge was lobbed towards keeper Shilton only for Maradona to seemingly head home. It appeared that the altitude had helped his elevation, but replays proved he had punched the ball. "A little of the hand of god and a little of the head of Maradona," was how he would refer to it, but his first goal only served to inspire his second, a fantastic solo effort six minutes later which put the game beyond doubt. Lineker's sixth goal of the tournament gave England hope, but the 'hand of God' goal would be the source of dispute between the two countries for many years.

A virtuoso semi-final performance against Belgium, which included two breathtaking second-half goals, restored faith in Maradona and, although West Germany eased past France 2-0, there was little stopping the Argentine. His hands were already on the cup.

ITALY 1990

Italia 90 was the tournament where FIFA appeared to step up its campaign to have the World Cup recognised as a global marketing phenomenon, and no country was more suited to put on a mass footballing circus than Italy. As hosts for the second time, the Italians embarked on a major overhaul of ten stadiums and built two more in Turin and Bari in anticipation of the biggest tournament ever.

Sadly, the quality of play failed to live up to the vast hype and the carefully negotiated corporate endorsements, the competition being characterised by negativity, foul play and penalties. The statistics only underline its sorry reputation: a mere 115 goals were scored at a ratio of 2.21 per game, yet there were a record 16 dismissals and 164 bookings.

The format remained the same as four years previous, with 24 teams competing in six groups of four, the top two teams and the four best third placed teams progressing through to a knock-out second round, then quarter-finals, semi-finals and the final. Some strong teams were notably absent, including the 1986 semi-finalists France, coached by Michel Platini, and rising stars Denmark, but the Republic Of Ireland qualified for the first time.

Mexico and Chile were suspended for breaches of FIFA rules, the former breaking regulations in a youth tournament, the latter after keeper Rojas attempted to fake an injury from a firecracker in a World Cup qualifier against Brazil. The suspension would also rule them out of the 1994 qualifying tournament.

Inevitably the hosts, under Azeglio Vicini, were hot favourites and their smooth progress only emphasised the feeling that their name was on the cup. They won all of their group games, against Austria, United States and Czechoslovakia, playing solid, attacking football without conceding a goal.

The nation also discovered a new Paolo Rossi in the shape of Palermo-born Salvatore 'Toto' Schillaci, a diminutive Juventus striker who rose from the substitute's bench to win the Golden Boot with six goals. Walter Zenga kept a clean sheet for a record 517 minutes, aided by a watertight defence superbly marshalled by Franco Baresi.

The Azzurri dream died against Argentina at the semi-final stage – not for the last time in a penalty shoot-out. Maradona had already attempted to divide the north and south of the country by appealing to Napoli fans to support his side. The hosts finished the tournament unbeaten, but still had to settle for third place while the nation mourned.

Of the other possible contenders, both Brazil and Holland went out tamely in the second round. European champions the Dutch, featuring Gullit, Rijkaard and Van Basten, were the biggest disappointments. Their encounter

Above: Roger Milla was one of the surprise stars of Italia 90. Opposite clockwise from top left: Jurgen Klinsmann and Guido Buchwald enjoy success against Holland; top-scorer Toto Schillaci; Maradona prays for Argentina; Paul Gascoigne in tears after England's semi-final exit.

with old enemy West Germany is best remembered for Frank Rijkaard's rather too literal spat with Rudi Völler. Brazil topped a weak group featuring Sweden, Scotland and Costa Rica, but lacked the firepower to finish off Argentina when they had a chance.

For a while it seemed Cameroon might make history by winning the tournament. Despite being reduced to nine men, the 'Indomitable Lions' beat holders Argentina in a memorable opening encounter and became the first African nation to reach the quarter-finals when they beat Colombia after extra-time. Mixing some vibrant skills with a fairly strong physical presence, their unquenchable spirit was embodied by Roger Milla. A goal-scoring talisman who danced around the corner flag after each of his four strikes as a substitute, Milla was then 38 years old and playing for JS Saint-Pierroise, a local team from Reunion Island. Cameroon's recklessness in the tackle eventually proved their undoing, however, when they allowed England to pull level and win 3-2 in extra-time through two penalties in their quarter-final.

The English had travelled to the World Cup more in hope than expectation, having just scraped through qualification as second best of the second-placed teams in the European groups. Bobby Robson's tenure as national coach had already involved the disastrous European Championship two years earlier and he was vilified by the British tabloid press for his team selections and tactics. However, in Gary Lineker England had a proven goalscorer, there was real creativity in a midfield that featured Chris Waddle and Paul Gascoigne, Mark Wright was a defender who could switch to sweeper, and in Peter Shilton they had a keeper who had not conceded a goal in 540

minutes during qualification. But they made hard work of their group, progressing via two draws and a win, before stumbling past Belgium thanks to David Platt's memorable last minute volley. Their quarter-final defeat of Cameroon was a tense affair, two penalties from Lineker seeing them in to the semi-final.

England's finest performance was in a pulsating encounter with West Germany that remains one of the great World Cup semi-finals, but their failure in the subsequent penalty shoot-out was to leave some deep psychological scars – and inspire at least one successful stage play.

Coached by Franz Beckenbauer, the West Germans were strong in all departments and had Matthäus and Klinsmann both at their peak. However, for all their strengths, they did nothing to help Italia 90 finish on a high. Instead, the tournament got what it deserved in the final: stale, cynical football punctuated by fouls, histrionic diving and petulance. When a penalty against Argentina settled the final in West Germany's favour five minutes before time, the only sensation was relief that another 30 minutes would not have to be endured.

THE FINAL

WEST GERMANY (0) **1-0** (0) ARGENTINA

Date Sunday July 8, 1990 **Attendance** 73,603
Venue Olympic Stadium, Rome

Ranking as the worst final in World Cup history, the game was characterised by negativity and bad sportsmanship. Argentina arrived with a record of a foul every four minutes and were shorn of four players through suspension, but both teams were guilty of deeply cynical play.

West Germany held the upper hand for much of the game but the contest degenerated, Monzon becoming the first player to be sent-off in a World Cup final for a wild lunge at Jurgen Klinsmann. It was no surprise when the match was settled by a spot-kick following a foul by Sensini on Völler. Argentina lost control and two minutes later Dezotti was also sent-off.

Maradona conducted his side's protests and the enduring image is not Matthäus holding aloft the cup but the Argentinian's tear-stained face.

HOW THE TEAMS LINED UP

WEST GERMANY
COACH: FRANZ BECKENBAUER

ARGENTINA
COACH: CARLOS BILARDO

Illgner
Berthold — Kohler — Buchwald — Brehme
Augenthaler
Hässler — Matthäus — Littbarski
Völler — Klinsmann

Dezotti — Maradona
Lorenzo — Troglio — Burruchaga — Basualdo — Sensini
Serrizuela — Simón — Ruggeri
Goycoechea

WEST GERMANY	
ILLGNER	6
AUGENTHALER	6
BERTHOLD	6
Subbed: 75 mins (Reuter)	
KOHLER	7
BUCHWALD	*8
BREHME	7
Goal: 85 mins (pen)	
HÄSSLER	7
MATTHÄUS	7
LITTBARSKI	6
KLINSMANN	6
VÖLLER	6
Booked: 52 mins	
sub: REUTER	6

ARGENTINA	
GOYCOECHEA	5
SIMÓN	6
SERRIZUELA	*7
RUGGERI	6
Subbed: 46 mins (Monzon)	
TROGLIO	5
Booked: 84 mins	
SENSINI	6
BURRUCHAGA	6
Subbed: 54 mins (Calderon)	
BASUALDO	5
LORENZO	5
DEZOTTI	6
Sent-off: 65 mins	
MARADONA	6
Booked: 87 mins	
sub: MONZON	5
Sent-off: 87 mins	
sub: CALDERON	6

Referee: Codesal (Mexico)

SEMI-FINALS

Argentina 1-1 Italy
(aet: Argentina won 4-3 on penalties)

West Germany 1-1 England
(aet: West Germany won 4-3 on penalties)

THIRD PLACE PLAY-OFF

Italy 2-1 England

TOP GOALSCORERS

6 goals: Salvatore Schillaci (Italy)
5 goals: Tomás Skuhravy (Czechoslovakia)
4 goals: Michel (Spain), Roger Milla (Cameroon), Gary Lineker (England), Lothar Matthäus (Germany)

FASTEST GOAL

4 minutes: Safet Susic (Yugoslavia v United Arab Emirates)

TOTAL GOALS

115

AVERAGE GOALS

2.21 per game

USA 1994

In light of their earlier snub in 1986, there was an air of inevitability when the United States were awarded the 1994 tournament. With rivals Morocco and Brazil unable to match the superior infrastructure, a lack of tradition was no barrier as FIFA used the competition to breach their final frontier.

There were concerns that the World Cup would fail to capture the imagination, and the excruciating opening ceremony penalty miss by Diana Ross cemented the apprehension. Yet the tournament would prove successful. Three points for victory ended those lifeless group games, while the introduction of motorised carts for 'injured' players saw feigning decrease. Stadiums were full and only the actions of one player blighted the festival.

Diego Maradona came to America looking to play his third final and, on form, there was every chance the dream could become reality. However, after testing positive for five variants of the stimulant ephedrine, his aspirations and his career were at an end.

THE FINAL

BRAZIL (0) **0-0** (0) **ITALY**

(aet: Brazil won 3-2 on penalties)

Date Sunday July 17, 1994 **Attendance** 94,194

Venue Pasadena Rose Bowl, Los Angeles

Although much was expected, the game was a disappointment in which defences prevailed. Baresi, just three weeks after cartilage surgery, returned to shore up the Azzurri. Normal time saw just one clear opportunity, when Pagliuca pushed Silva's effort on to a post, while Bebeto and Baggio spurned chances in extra-time.

The game went to penalties and Baresi's opening miss set the trend for the drama to follow. Santos missed for Brazil, but after successful spot-kicks from Albertini and Evani for Italy and Romario and Branco for Brazil, the scores were level. Massaro saw his effort stopped by Taffarel, before Dunga converted for Brazil. This left Baggio needing to score but he shot over before bowing his head in despair.

HOW THE TEAMS LINED UP

BRAZIL

COACH:
CARLOS PARREIRA

Taffarel

Jorginho Aldair Marcio Santos Branco

Mazinho Mauro Silva Dunga Zinho

Bebeto Romario

ITALY

COACH:
ARRIGO SACCHI

Massaro Baggio, R

Donadoni Albertini Baggio, D Berti

Benarrivo Maldini Baresi Mussi

Pagliuca

BRAZIL	
TAFFAREL	7
JORGINHO	6
Subbed: 22 mins (Cafu)	
ALDAIR	8
MARCIO SANTOS	*9
BRANCO	7
MAZINHO	6
Booked: 4 mins	
MAURO SILVA	7
DUNGA	7
ZINHO	6
Subbed: 106 mins (Viola)	
BEBETO	7
ROMARIO	8
sub: CAFU	6
Booked: 87 mins	
sub: VIOLA	6

ITALY	
PAGLIUCA	7
MUSSI	6
Subbed: 34 mins (Apolloni)	
BARESI	8
MALDINI	*9
BENARRIVO	7
BERTI	7
BAGGIO, D	6
Subbed: 95 mins (Evani)	
ALBERTINI	7
Booked: 42 mins	
DONADONI	7
BAGGIO, R	6
MASSARO	6
sub: APOLLONI	6
Booked: 41 mins	
sub: EVANI	6

Referee: Puhl (Hungary)

Above: Ray Houghton celebrates his strike against Italy.
Opposite clockwise from top left: Brazil show off their spoils; Baggio and Taffarel experience differing emotions after the decisive penalty; Sweden salute their fans after semi-final defeat; Stoichkov's Bulgaria beat Germany.

The tournament began with Germany taking on Bolivia, and a solitary goal from Klinsmann spared the blushes although it was overshadowed by Bolivian star Etcheverry, red-carded four minutes after coming on as sub.

The dismissal of Spanish defender Nadal also proved costly in the group. Having taken a 2-0 lead against South Korea, the Spaniards conceded late goals and, with their match against Germany ending in stalemate, both superpowers teetered on the brink. Normality resumed as Caminero hit a brace against Bolivia, while Klinsmann took his tally to four in a 3-2 win against the Koreans.

Group A proved equally fascinating. Having defeated Argentina 5-0 away in qualifying, Colombia were tipped to go far. Yet internal bickering and poor preparation caused their downfall, as a 3-1 defeat against Romania and a subsequent loss to the hosts sealed their fate. The USA result had tragic consequences for Colombia as Andrés Escobar, blamed for the defeat after scoring an own-goal, was murdered shortly after his return home.

Despite their tepid qualification form, Brazil opened with a 2-0 victory against Russia, while Romario and Bebeto proved the catalysts of a 3-0 defeat of Cameroon. The Africans came with high expectations following their exploits in 1990, yet returned early after a 6-1 mauling by Russia, Salenko scoring five. Sweden also booked their place with Brolin and Dahlin's Euro 92 momentum carrying them forward.

Prior to Maradona's positive drugs test, Argentina had the look of champions. An emphatic 4-0 defeat of Greece was followed with victory over Nigeria, signalling Batistuta's arrival with three goals. The Africans hailed their own hero, Yekini, whose opener against Bulgaria was his country's first World Cup goal. With Stoichkov scoring twice for Bulgaria against Greece, and Nigeria also defeating the whipping boys, Argentina limped in third.

Italy, led by Roberto Baggio's guile, were regarded as certainties in Group E. Yet when they conceded Ray Houghton's solitary strike for Ireland it meant that victory against Norway was imperative. The sending-off of goalkeeper Pagliuca and injury to Baresi further troubled the Azzurri, yet Dino Baggio's goal ensured progress.

Bickering threatened Holland's Group F chances. A spat between Gullit and coach Advocaat led to the 32-year-old's omission, and a less than convincing 2-1 win against Saudi Arabia confirmed their troubles. The Saudis became the surprise package, beating Morocco 2-1 before Saeed Owairan, 'The Desert Pelé', ran 60 yards through the Belgian rearguard to secure victory and qualification.

The Germans continued their ominous march as Rudi Völler inspired a 3-2 second round win over Belgium, while Spain's emphatic defeat of Switzerland was closer than the 3-0 scoreline suggests.

Two goals from Andersson enhanced his reputation as Sweden edged Saudi Arabia 3-1, while the tie of the round saw Argentina paired with Romania. Ortega did his best to fill Maradona's void, but it was the opposition playmaker, Hagi, who ran the midfield in a 3-2 victory. Argentina had ultimately been let down by their favourite son.

The heat of Orlando cost Ireland – errors by Phelan and Bonner sealed their fate against Holland, while USA's progress ended against Brazil, who had Leonardo sent-off for elbowing midfielder Ramos, who was later diagnosed with a fractured skull.

But what of Baggio? A last-minute equaliser against Nigeria and a subsequent extra-time penalty signalled his arrival, made more significant by Zola's red card.

The final second round clash between Bulgaria and Mexico was delayed when a goalpost collapsed, as did the Latin Americans when Aspe, Benal and Rodriguez missed kicks in the deciding penalty shoot-out.

Seven European sides from eight made the quarter-finals, with Italy in the ascendancy. Dino and Roberto Baggio's goals edged a thriller against Spain, while Brazil and Holland dished up a similarly scintillating show. Romario's drive and Bebeto's cool finish appeared to have won the game, but Bergkamp and Winter replied to set up a grandstand finish, which Brazil won thanks to free-kick from Branco. Bulgaria provided the biggest shock, beating Germany 2-1 with Stoichkov's free-kick and a text-book header by Letchkov, the tournament's star midfielder.

Sweden's tussle with Romania went to extra-time. Stefan Schwarz's sending-off at 1-2 made progression for Scandinavians unlikely, but Andersson's goal took the game to penalties, where Ravelli saved from Belodedici to win. Ravelli was once again inspired against Brazil, but it would be the Brazilians who would meet Italy in the final, who had two goals from Baggio to thank for their 2-1 defeat of Bulgaria.

FRANCE 1998

After the sterile final of 1994, and a tournament which failed to grip the imagination, France 98 came like a breath of fresh air, providing excitement, passion, drama and controversy. While it was the world's best footballer, Ronaldo, who would inflame the passions of the conspiracy theorists in the final, there was plenty of classic football action throughout the tournament.

The competition featured 32 teams, more than ever before, and that meant not only more games, but more sides from Africa, Asia and other emerging regions. Among those making a debut at the finals were Japan, Jamaica, South Africa and Croatia. There was also the introduction of the 'golden goal': if a game went into extra-time, the first goal scored would decide the match.

The hosts came into the tournament under pressure – they had failed to qualify for USA 94 and many claimed they had no strikers. But driven by Zinédine Zidane and his fabulous midfield, as well as the fanatical home support, goals didn't seem a problem in their group as they dispatched South Africa 3-0, Saudi Arabia 4-0, and Denmark 2-1.

Scotland kept up another tradition – giving the good teams a run for their money and flopping against the lesser lights. A narrow defeat to Brazil in the opening match (2-1, with the winner coming from an own-goal by Tommy Boyd) was followed up by a 1-1 draw with Norway, and a 3-0 defeat against Morocco.

England went through the group stage with a 2-0 victory over Tunisia, defeat against Romania thanks to Dan Petrescu's last-minute winner, and a 2-0 win against Colombia. In the other groups the major football nations emerged relatively unscathed, with one major exception. Always a favourite 'outsider' for any title given the exceptional talent within their domestic league, Spain again promised much but delivered very little. They lost a thriller against Nigeria 3-2, drew 0-0 with Paraguay, and made a desperate effort in their last match, Bulgaria ending up on the wrong end of a 6-1 scoreline, but to no avail.

In the second phase, Brazil and Denmark were impressive, Italy and Croatia both crept through 1-0, Germany edged Mexico, the Dutch beat Yugoslavia in a thriller, and France's Laurent Blanc scored the tournament's first 'golden goal' to pip Paraguay.

The match of the round brought together two old foes: England and Argentina. The first-half was simply brilliant, Gabriel Batistuta giving the South Americans an early lead through a penalty before Alan Shearer converted a spot-kick for England. Then came one of those moments that build a reputation, as 18-year-old striker Michael Owen controlled a long pass, raced towards the Argentine goal

Caption: **Above: The Romanian team celebrate progressing to the second round by dyeing their hair blond. Opposite clockwise from top left: Denmark's Brian Laudrup after scoring against Nigeria; France celebrate winning the World Cup on home soil; Michael Owen takes on Argentina's Jose Chamot; Holland's Edgar Davids in quarter-final action against Argentina.**

leaving defenders floundering, and beat Carlos Roa with an unstoppable shot. England stayed ahead until just before the interval, when a clever free-kick routine saw Zanetti equalise.

The second-half saw drama of a different kind, and another of those defining moments. Within minutes of the restart, Diego Simeone brought down David Beckham. While on the ground, the Englishman kicked Simeone on the leg – hardly vicious, but certainly foolish – and the Argentinian went down, perhaps a little too easily. Beckham was sent-off and England had to play the rest of the second-half, and 30 minutes of extra-time, with ten men.

England held their own, even having an effort from Sol Campbell disallowed and a penalty appeal refused. In the deciding penalty shoot-out David Batty saw Roa save his spot-kick and England's dream was over, the fans blaming Beckham rather than Batty.

The World Cup carried on. Perhaps the best quarter-final was played out by Brazil and Denmark – the Europeans being pipped 3-2 thanks to Rivaldo's second-half winner. Holland and Argentina were both reduced to ten men in their game and an early goal apiece was all the scoring until near the end. Then Ariel Ortega was red-carded for head-butting goalkeeper Edwin Van Der Sar, and from the free-kick the ball was played to Dennis Bergkamp who finished with aplomb.

Croatia caused the upset of the round, a late goal from Davor Suker sealing a 3-0 win over Germany. Then the aristocracy of Europe played one of the dullest matches, Italy and France failing to register a goal. The game went to penalties, and when Luigi di Biagio's effort hit the bar, the hosts were through.

The first semi-final saw the debutants from Croatia come up against the hosts. Suker opened the scoring, then the team with no strikers once again relied on a defender to score, this time Lilian Thuram netting his first for his country and then going on to score the winner. The other semi-final was also pure drama. Ronaldo's second-half goal looked enough, until a late Kluivert equaliser for the

Dutch. Neither side could grab the winner and it went to penalties, Brazil winning 4-2.

The dream final was on: champions versus hosts, Ronaldo versus Zidane, style versus substance. What could go wrong?

THE FINAL

FRANCE (2) **3-0** (0) **BRAZIL**

Date Sunday July 12, 1998 **Attendance** 75,000
Venue Stade de France, Paris

The record will show the scoreline, the scorers and the fact that France's Marcel Desailly received his marching orders following a tackle on Cafu. What it won't show is the controversy which threatened to overshadow the final.

Brazil's World Player Of The Year, Ronaldo, wasn't named on coach Mario Zagalo's teamsheet when it was first handed in. An hour later his name was back on it again. It emerged that earlier in the day Ronaldo had suffered from convulsions and was taken to hospital. Zagalo named the team without him but the striker declared himself fit to play. The stadium was in uproar, Brazil – especially Ronaldo – looked lethargic, and Zinédine Zidane conducted the French orchestra to perfection, heading two goals, while Emmanuel Petit scored the breakaway third in the dying moments of the game. The country that had invented the World Cup had finally won it – on home soil!

HOW THE TEAMS LINED UP

FRANCE
COACH: AIME JACQUET

Barthez
Thuram Desailly Leboeuf Lizarazu
Karembeu Deschamps Petit
Zidane
Djorkaeff Guivarc'h

BRAZIL
COACH: MARIO ZAGALO

Bebeto Ronaldo
Rivaldo Dunga Cesar Sampaio Leonardo
Roberto Carlos Aldair Junior Baiano Cafu
Taffarel

SEMI-FINALS
Brazil 1-1 Holland
(aet: Brazil won 4-2 on penalties)
France 2-1 Croatia

THIRD PLACE PLAY-OFF
Croatia 2-1 Holland

TOP SCORERS
6 goals: Davor Suker (Croatia)
5 goals: Gabriel Batistuta (Argentina)

FASTEST GOAL
53 seconds: Celso Ayala (Paraguay v Nigeria)

TOTAL GOALS
171

AVERAGE GOALS
2.67 per game

FRANCE

BARTHEZ	7
THURAM	7
DESAILLY	6
Booked: 48 mins. Sent-off (second booking) 68 mins	
LEBOEUF	7
LIZARAZU	7
DESCHAMPS	7
Booked: 39 mins	
ZIDANE	*9
Goal: 27 mins, 45 mins	
PETIT	8
Goal: 90 mins	
KAREMBEU	7
Booked: 56 mins. Subbed: 56 mins (Boghossian)	
DJORKAEFF	8
Subbed: 74 mins (Vieira)	
GUIVARC'H	6
Subbed: 66 mins (Dugarry)	
sub: **BOGHOSSIAN**	6
sub: **DUGARRY**	7
sub: **VIEIRA**	6

BRAZIL

TAFFAREL	6
CAFU	6
JUNIOR BAIANO	5
Booked: 33 mins	
ALDAIR	6
ROBERTO CARLOS	*7
CESAR SAMPAIO	5
Subbed: 57 mins (Edmundo)	
LEONARDO	5
Subbed: 46 mins (Denilson)	
DUNGA	6
RIVALDO	6
RONALDO	5
BEBETO	5
sub: **DENILSON**	6
sub: **EDMUNDO**	5

Referee: Belqola (Morocco)

KOREA/JAPAN 2002

The 17th World Cup finals in Japan and Korea were the first to be played in Asia, and as if to metaphorically signify a shift in the balance of global football dominance, from the very first game it was a competition full of shocks and surprise results. It was a tournament that saw plenty of countries with established reputations and big name players catch an early return flight home. However, Korea/Japan 2002 was also notable for the emergence of many unfancied countries, such as Senegal, Turkey and South Korea. Despite this, ironically enough, the final was to be played out between the World Cup's two most established and successful sides.

It was World Cup debutantes Senegal who provided the biggest shock, in the opening game, with a 1-0 defeat of the holders and pre-tournament favourites France, with the goal scored by Pape Bouba Diop. In a physical game, the Africans over-powered a jaded looking French team, clearly missing the talismanic presence of an injured Zinédine

SEMI-FINALS

Germany 1-0 South Korea
Brazil 1-0 Turkey

THIRD PLACE PLAY-OFF

Turkey 3-2 South Korea

TOP SCORERS

8 goals: Ronaldo (Brazil)
5 goals: Miroslav Klose (Germany); Rivaldo (Brazil)

FASTEST GOAL

10.8 seconds: Hakan Sükür (Turkey v South Korea)

TOTAL GOALS

161

AVERAGE GOALS

2.51 per game

Above: South Korea watch the penalty shoot-out that will take them through to the semi-finals. Opposite clockwise from top left: Japan's Junichi Inamoto is mobbed by his team-mates after scoring against Russia; Roque Junior and Ronaldinho lift the World Cup; Senegal's goal celebrations after scoring against France; David Beckham gains revenge over Argentina.

THE FINAL

BRAZIL (0) 2-0 (0) GERMANY

Date Sunday June 30, 2002 **Attendance** 69,029
Venue International Stadium, Yokohama

Despite sharing seven World Cup titles between them, Brazil and Germany had never met in the final stages of the tournament. Brazil started favouites but they would have to beat Oliver Kahn, who had conceded just one goal in the tournament. A largely uneventful first half saw two bookings, while Kleberson hit the bar for Brazil and a couple of half-chances fell to Ronaldo. In the 67th minute, however, Kahn spilt Rivaldo's shot into the path of the grateful Ronaldo, who pounced on the ball to score.

He was on the scoresheet again 12 minutes later, curling the ball past Kahn to make it 2-0. Shortly after the final whistle, skipper Cafu, in his third World Cup final, was to lift the trophy to mark Brazil's record-breaking and wholly deserved fifth victory.

BRAZIL

MARCOS	7
LUCIO	8
EDMILSON	8
ROQUE JUNIOR	7
Booked: 6 mins	
CAFU	7
KLEBERSON	7
GILBERTO SILVA	6
ROBERTO CARLOS	6
RONALDINHO	7
Subbed: 85 mins (Juninho)	
RIVALDO	6
RONALDO	*9
Goal: 67 mins, 79 mins. Subbed: 90 mins (Denilson)	
sub: JUNINHO	5
sub: DENILSON	5

GERMANY

KAHN	7
LINKE	6
RAMELOW	7
METZELDER	6
FRINGS	7
JEREMIES	6
Subbed: 77 mins (Asamoah)	
HAMANN	7
SCHNEIDER	*8
BODE	6
Subbed: 84 mins (Ziege)	
NEUVILLE	7
KLOSE	6
Booked: 9 mins. Subbed: 74 mins (Bierhoff)	
sub: BIERHOFF	6
sub: ASAMOAH	6
sub: ZIEGE	5

Referee: Collina (Italy)

HOW THE TEAMS LINED UP

BRAZIL
COACH:
LUIZ FELIPE SCOLARI

Marcos
Lucio   Edmilson   Roque Junior
Cafu   Kleberson   Gilberto   Roberto Carlos
Ronaldinho
Rivaldo   Ronaldo

GERMANY
COACH:
RUDI VÖLLER

Klose   Neuville
Bode   Hamann   Jeremies   Schneider
Metzelder   Ramelow   Linke   Frings
Kahn

Zidane. Indeed, France failed to score a single goal in three qualifying games and were on a plane home much earlier than expected.

Joint favourites Argentina also suffered the ignominy of elimination at the group stage. After a narrow win in their opening game against Nigeria, courtesy of a Gabriel Batistuta header, defeat to England and a draw against Sweden meant the hugely talented Argentine squad were to play no further part in the tournament. The game against England was one of the most eagerly anticipated games of the competition, and saw David Beckham convert the match-winning penalty to gain revenge for his dismissal in the same fixture four years previous.

The much-fancied Portuguese side were the other high-profile casualties at this stage, losing out to both the USA and joint hosts South Korea, who topped their group after having never before won a match at the finals.

An impressive Brazil, looking more assured and confident with every game, and perennial under-achievers Spain were the only two countries to qualify from their respective groups with 100 per cent records, while Slovenia, China and Saudi Arabia went home without a point. Germany's 8-0 demolition of Saudi Arabia was, by quite a margin, the most one-sided of all the games of the tournament. The other group winners were Denmark, Germany, Sweden, Mexico and Japan, much to the delight of an enthusiastic co-host nation.

With Germany and England securing routine wins against Paraguay and Denmark in the opening games of the second round, it was left to South Korea to provide the major upset of this stage. Some controversial refereeing marred their 2-1 golden goal victory over the Italians, which saw golden boy Francesco Totti sent-off for diving, and an apparently good goal ruled out.

Despite the loss of influential captain Roy Keane, who walked out on the squad before they had even arrived at the World Cup, Ireland qualified for the knockout rounds, only to go out on penalties to Spain. The other games at this stage saw wins for USA over Mexico, Senegal over Sweden and Brazil over Belgium, while a headed goal from Turkey's Umit Davala ended the dreams of Japan.

The quarter-final stage consisted of four established football nations (Brazil, Germany, England, Spain), and four inexperienced at this level of competition (USA, South Korea, Turkey and Senegal). Brazil beat England 2-1, countering an opportunistic Michael Owen strike thanks to a freak long-range goal from Ronaldinho. Germany were fortunate to get past USA 1-0, especially after a blatant handball in their own penalty area had gone unnoticed. Turkey secured a golden goal victory over an unlucky Senegal, and South Korea were once again up to their giant-killing antics. This time Guus Hiddink's superbly conditioned and well-drilled team got the better of Spain, but again the victory was not without controversy, the Spanish side furious that two perfectly good goals had been disallowed.

The semi-finals finally saw the established powers assert some domination. Brazil eased past a spirited Turkey 1-0 with a memorable goal from a rejuvenated Ronaldo. Germany narrowly got the better of the co-hosts with a solitary goal from Michael Ballack, who got himself booked and missed the final.

Despite complaints over poor organisation in respect of ticket allocation, the first World Cup outside of Europe and the Americas was superbly staged by the hosts. The wide-eyed enthusiasm of the supporters of both nations is sure to be considered one of the lasting memories of a successful tournament. No respecter of reputations, the 2002 World Cup in Korea/Japan will also be remembered as one when the smaller football nations fought back and nearly succeeded in overthrowing the existing global power base.

GERMANY 2006

After the shocks of the 2002 World Cup that saw outsiders South Korea and Turkey reach the semi-finals, Germany 2006 went some way to restoring the balance of power in favour of the established football nations. Only two of eight quarter-finalists had not previously won the competition, and even the hosts found they were a nation newly invigorated by this tournament after some years in relative decline.

Finding themselves paired in Group A with Ecuador, bitter rivals Poland, and opening game opponents Costa Rica, Germany surprised the doubters, proving an unstoppable force in attack. Lahm scored their opening goal just five minutes after the tournament had kicked-off and by the time the group stages were over, the Germans had racked up eight goals, progressing to the second round with a 100 per cent record.

Brazil cruised through the group stage, but World Footballer Of The Year Ronaldinho seemed a shadow of his best, not benefiting from the defensive play of coach Carlos Alberto Parreira. Ronaldo also appeared out of shape and was even criticised by his country's president.

Under the guidance of the 2002 World Cup-winning coach Luiz Filipe Scolari, Portugal qualified for the second round without dropping a point. In doing so Scolari broke Vittorio Pozzo's 68-year-old record, becoming the first coach to win eight World Cup games in succession (the first seven he achieved with Brazil in 2002). Scolari would ultimately stretch this record to 11 games before the tournament was over.

Spain won all their games and qualified ahead of Ukraine, while Argentina appeared to be in unstoppable form. A 6-0 demolition of Serbia and Montenegro demonstrated their pace and class, with players as talented as Lionel Messi and Carlos Tevez having to settle for substitute appearances. But not all of the seeded nations had it their own way. England topped their group despite some lacklustre performances that even drew criticism from FIFA president Sepp Blatter. Italy's progress looked uncertain after a draw with the USA that saw the Italians lose one man to a red card and the Americans two. An early exit was prevented by victory over the Czechs, Italy salvaging top spot ahead of Ghana.

French fans had called for coach Raymond Domenech to drop his ageing stars in favour of youngsters like Franck Ribéry, the 23-year-old Marseille midfielder with just three substitute appearances to his name. The coach stayed loyal to his stars but included Ribéry, France stumbling through as runners-up to the Swiss after coming alive in their final game against Togo.

While the group stage had thrown up plenty of exciting games, the sudden death football of the second round brought a cautious approach. Argentina's clash with Mexico was an exception. The Mexicans took a sixth minute lead through Marquez, only to see Crespo equalise four

minutes later, but a thunderous left-foot volley from Maxi Rodriguez eight minutes into extra-time secured the win for Argentina.

In a limp encounter in Cologne the Swiss lost on penalties to Ukraine, becoming the first team to exit a World Cup without conceding a goal. A Beckham free-kick made all the difference in a pallid encounter between England and Ecuador, while Italy needed a controversial penalty to beat Australia with the last kick of the game. The hosts put in a workmanlike performance to see off Sweden, while Brazil brushed aside Ghana with little effort, Ronaldo becoming the World Cup's all-time leading goalscorer, with his 15th goal.

In the 700th World Cup finals game, France needed a bit of self-made luck against Spain to be certain of a place in the last eight. Portugal edged through with a Maniche goal against Holland, but it was a fraught encounter that equalled the World Cup record for bookings (16) and broke the record for red cards: Portugal had Deco and Costinha dismissed, while Holland's Boulahrouz and Van Bronkhorst were sent-off.

The Germans were the first team to qualify for the semi-finals. They stunned Argentina with an 80th minute equaliser from Klose, before winning 4-2 in a penalty shoot-out. Portugal also needed penalties to beat ten-man England, who had Rooney sent-off early in the second-half. Italy stepped up a gear to defeat Ukraine 3-0, and in the biggest surprise of the round, Zinédine Zidane – who had retired from international football two years earlier – proved the inspiration his team needed to achieve victory over Brazil.

While the early exit of the holders created headlines, the first semi-final provided a greater shock. Under the shrewd tactical stewardship of Marcello Lippi, the Italians ended German hopes of winning the trophy in the best game of the tournament. Late in extra-time, with penalties just a minute away, defender Fabio Grosso hammered a magnificent first time shot into the back of the net. Just two minutes later, Gilardino played a sublime reverse pass into the path of Del Piero, who had run the length of the field to fire past Lehman with the last kick of the game.

A single Zidane penalty was enough to send France into the final at the expense of Portugal,

giving their World Cup-winning veterans – Thuram, Barthez, Vieira and Zidane – one more chance to shine on the biggest stage.

France and Italy had started slowly, but with both teams approaching top form at just the right time, the final would prove a dramatic encounter.

THE FINAL

ITALY (1) **1-1** (1) **FRANCE**
(aet: Italy won 5-3 on penalties)

Date Sunday July 9 **Attendance** 69,000
Venue Olympic Stadium, Berlin

The 2006 World Cup final was destined to belong to Zinédine Zidane, playing his last game. But by the time the Italians lifted the trophy it was their defender Marco Materazzi who had made the most decisive impact. France took the lead with a seventh minute penalty after Materazzi fouled Malouda in the box, Zidane's chipped spot-kick ricocheting down from the underside of the bar. Just 12 minutes later Materazzi made amends when he rose to head home Pirlo's corner.

Italy remained the more threatening, but in extra-time the best chance came to Zidane, his header pushed over the bar by Buffon. When the end came for Zidane it wasn't as expected: he received a red card for an off-the-ball assault on Materazzi, having knocked the Italian to the floor with a butt to the chest. David Trezeguet struck the only failed penalty of the shoot-out and the trophy was lifted by Italian captain Cannavaro.

Above: Ghana celebrate victory over the Czechs. Opposite clockwise from top left: Marco Materazzi is butted by Zidane in the final; golden boot winner Miroslav Klose; England's Wayne Rooney sees red; Italy's Fabio Grosso with the World Cup.

HOW THE TEAMS LINED UP

ITALY
COACH: MARCELLO LIPPI

FRANCE
COACH: RAYMOND DOMENECH

Buffon
Zambrotta Cannavaro Materazzi Grosso
Pirlo Gattuso
Camoranesi Totti Perrotta
Toni

Henry
Malouda Zidane Ribéry
Vieira Makelele
Abidal Gallas Thuram Sagnol
Barthez

SEMI-FINALS
Germany 0-2 Italy
Portugal 0-1 France

THIRD PLACE PLAY-OFF
Germany 3-1 Portugal

TOP SCORERS
5 goals: Klose (Germany)
3 goals: Crespo (Argentina), Henry (France), Podolski (Germany), Rodriguez (Argentina), Ronaldo (Brazil), Torres (Spain), Villa (Spain), Zidane (France)

FASTEST GOAL
1 min 10 seconds: Asamoah Gyan (Ghana v Czech Republic)

TOTAL GOALS
147

AVERAGE GOALS
2.29 per game

ITALY
BUFFON	7
GROSSO	7
MATERAZZI	7
Goal: 23 mins	
CANNAVARO	8
ZAMBROTTA	8
Booked: 5 mins	
PERROTTA	6
Subbed: 60 mins (De Rossi)	
GATTUSO	6
PIRLO	*9
CAMORANESI	8
Subbed: 86 mins (Del Piero)	
TOTTI	6
TONI	6
Subbed: 60 mins (Iaquinta)	
sub: **IAQUINTA**	6
sub: **DE ROSSI**	6
sub: **DEL PIERRO**	6

FRANCE
BARTHEZ	6
ABIDAL	6
GALLAS	8
THURAM	6
SAGNOL	6
Booked: 12 mins	
MAKELELE	7
Booked: 76 mins	
MALOUDA	5
Booked: 111 mins	
VIEIRA	6
Subbed: 56 mins (Diarra)	
RIBÉRY	8
Subbed: 99 mins (Trezeguet)	
ZIDANE	*8
Goal: 7 mins (pen). Sent-off: 110 mins	
HENRY	7
Subbed: 106 mins (Wiltord)	
sub: **DIARRA**	6
Booked: 75 mins	
sub: **TREZEGUET**	6
sub: **WILTORD**	6

Referee: Eilzondo (Argentina)

WORLD CUP RESULTS

The Centenary Stadium in Montevideo was built especially for the 1930 World Cup finals.

1930 URUGUAY

GROUP 1

France **4-1** Mexico
Argentina **1-0** France
Chile **3-0** Mexico
Chile **1-0** France
Argentina **6-3** Mexico
Argentina **3-1** Chile

	P	W	D	L	F	A	Pts
Argentina	3	3	0	0	10	4	6
Chile	3	2	0	1	5	3	4
France	3	1	0	2	4	3	2
Mexico	3	0	0	3	4	13	0

GROUP 2

Yugoslavia **2-1** Brazil
Yugoslavia **4-0** Bolivia
Brazil **4-0** Bolivia

	P	W	D	L	F	A	Pts
Yugoslavia	2	2	0	0	6	1	4
Brazil	2	1	0	1	5	2	2
Bolivia	2	0	0	2	0	8	0

GROUP 3

Romania **3-1** Peru
Uruguay **1-0** Peru
Uruguay **4-0** Romania

	P	W	D	L	F	A	Pts
Uruguay	2	2	0	0	5	0	4
Romania	2	1	0	1	3	5	2
Peru	2	0	0	2	1	4	0

GROUP 4

USA **3-0** Belgium
USA **3-0** Paraguay
Paraguay **1-0** Belgium

	P	W	D	L	F	A	Pts
USA	2	2	0	0	6	0	4
Paraguay	2	1	0	1	1	3	2
Belgium	2	0	0	2	0	4	0

SEMI-FINALS

Argentina **6-1** USA
Uruguay **6-1** Yugoslavia

THIRD PLACE PLAY-OFF

Not held

FINAL

Uruguay **4-2** Argentina

1934 ITALY

FIRST ROUND

Italy **7-1** USA
Czechoslovakia **2-1** Romania
Germany **5-2** Belgium
Austria **3-2** France
(aet)
Spain **3-1** Brazil
Switzerland **3-2** Holland
Sweden **3-2** Argentina
Hungary **4-2** Egypt

SECOND ROUND

Germany **2-1** Sweden
Austria **2-1** Hungary
Italy **1-1** Spain
(aet)
Italy **1-0** Spain
(replay)
Czechoslovakia **3-2** Switzerland

SEMI-FINALS

Czechoslovakia **3-1** Germany
Italy **1-0** Austria

THIRD-PLACE PLAY-OFF

Germany **3-2** Austria

FINAL

Italy **2-1** Czechoslovakia
(aet)

1938 FRANCE

FIRST ROUND

Switzerland **1-1** Germany
(aet)
Switzerland **4-2** Germany
(replay)
Cuba **3-3** Romania
(aet)
Cuba **2-1** Romania
(replay)
Hungary **6-0** Dutch E. Indies
France **3-1** Belgium
Czechoslovakia **3-0** Holland
(aet)
Brazil **6-5** Poland
(aet)
Italy **2-1** Norway
(aet)
Sweden **w/o** Austria

QUARTER-FINALS

Sweden **8-0** Cuba
Hungary **2-0** Switzerland
Italy **3-1** France
Brazil **1-1** Czechoslovakia
(aet)
Brazil **2-1** Czechoslovakia
(replay)

SEMI-FINALS

Italy **2-1** Brazil
Hungary **5-1** Sweden

THIRD-PLACE PLAY-OFF

Brazil **4-2** Sweden

FINAL

Italy **4-2** Hungary

1950 BRAZIL

POOL 1

Brazil **4-0** Mexico
Yugoslavia **3-0** Switzerland
Yugoslavia **4-1** Mexico
Brazil **2-2** Switzerland
Brazil **2-0** Yugoslavia
Switzerland **2-1** Mexico

	P	W	D	L	F	A	Pts
Brazil	3	2	1	0	8	2	5
Yugoslavia	3	2	0	1	7	3	4
Switzerland	3	1	1	1	4	6	3
Mexico	3	0	0	3	2	10	0

POOL 2

Spain **3-1** USA
England **2-0** Chile
USA **1-0** England
Spain **2-0** Chile
Spain **1-0** England
Chile **5-2** USA

	P	W	D	L	F	A	Pts
Spain	3	3	0	0	6	1	6
England	3	1	0	2	2	2	2
Chile	3	1	0	2	5	6	2
USA	3	1	0	2	4	8	2

POOL 3

Sweden **3-2** Italy
Sweden **2-2** Paraguay
Italy **2-0** Paraguay

	P	W	D	L	F	A	Pts
Sweden	2	1	1	0	5	4	3
Italy	2	1	0	1	4	3	2
Paraguay	2	0	1	1	2	4	1

POOL 4

Uruguay **8-0** Bolivia

	P	W	D	L	F	A	Pts
Uruguay	1	1	0	0	8	0	2
Bolivia	1	0	0	1	0	8	0

FINAL POOL

Uruguay **2-2** Spain
Brazil **7-1** Sweden
Uruguay **3-2** Sweden
Brazil **6-1** Spain
Sweden **3-1** Spain
Uruguay **2-1** Brazil*

	P	W	D	L	F	A	Pts
Uruguay	3	2	1	0	7	5	5
Brazil	3	2	0	1	14	4	4
Sweden	3	1	0	2	6	11	2
Spain	3	0	1	2	4	11	1

THIRD PLACE

Sweden

FINAL (DECIDING MATCH)

Uruguay **2-1** Brazil*

the last game of the Final Pool decided the World Cup.

1954 SWITZERLAND

POOL 1

Yugoslavia **1-0** France
Brazil **5-0** Mexico
France **3-2** Mexico
Brazil **1-1** Yugoslavia
(aet)

	P	W	D	L	F	A	Pts
Brazil	2	1	1	0	6	1	3
Yugoslavia	2	1	1	0	2	1	3
France	2	1	0	1	3	3	2
Mexico	2	0	0	2	2	8	0

POOL 2

Hungary **9-0** South Korea
West Germany **4-1** Turkey
Hungary **8-3** West Germany
Turkey **7-0** South Korea

	P	W	D	L	F	A	Pts
Hungary	2	2	0	0	17	3	4
West Germany	2	1	0	1	7	9	2
Turkey	2	1	0	1	8	4	2
South Korea	2	0	0	2	0	16	0

PLAY OFF FOR 2ND GROUP PLACE

West Germany **7-2** Turkey

POOL 3

Austria **1-0** Scotland
Uruguay **2-0** Czechoslovakia
Austria **5-0** Czechoslovakia
Uruguay **7-0** Scotland

	P	W	D	L	F	A	Pts
Uruguay	2	2	0	0	9	0	4
Austria	2	2	0	0	6	0	4
Czechoslovakia	2	0	0	2	0	7	0
Scotland	2	0	0	2	0	8	0

POOL 4

England **4-4** Belgium
(aet)
England **2-0** Switzerland
Switzerland **2-1** Italy
Italy **4-1** Belgium

	P	W	D	L	F	A	Pts
England	2	1	1	0	6	4	3
Switzerland	2	1	0	1	2	3	2
Italy	2	1	0	1	5	3	2
Belgium	2	0	1	1	5	8	1

PLAY-OFF FOR 2ND GROUP PLACE

Switzerland **4-1** Italy

QUARTER- FINALS

West Germany **2-0** Yugoslavia
Hungary **4-2** Brazil
Austria **7-5** Switzerland
Uruguay **4-2** England

SEMI-FINALS

West Germany **6-1** Austria
Hungary **4-2** Uruguay
(aet)

THIRD-PLACE PLAY-OFF

Austria **3-1** Uruguay

FINAL

West Germany **3-2** Hungary

1958 SWEDEN

POOL 1

West Germany **3-1** Argentina
Northern Ireland **1-0** Czechoslovakia
West Germany **2-2** Czechoslovakia
Argentina **3-1** Northern Ireland
West Germany **2-2** Northern Ireland
Czechoslovakia **6-1** Argentina

Fritz Walter scores West Germany's fifth goal in the 1954 semi-final against Austria.

Pelé, unable to play in the 1962 final because of injury, hugs replacement Amarildo.

	P	W	D	L	F	A	Pts
West Germany	3	1	2	0	7	5	4
Northern Ireland	3	1	1	1	4	5	3
Czechoslovakia	3	1	1	1	8	4	3
Argentina	3	1	0	2	5	10	2

PLAY-OFF FOR 2ND GROUP PLACE
Northern Ireland **2-1** Czechoslovakia (aet)

POOL 2
France **7-3** Paraguay
Yugoslavia **1-1** Scotland
Yugoslavia **3-2** France
Paraguay **3-2** Scotland
France **2-1** Scotland
Yugoslavia **3-3** Paraguay

	P	W	D	L	F	A	Pts
France	3	2	0	1	11	7	4
Yugoslavia	3	1	2	0	7	6	4
Paraguay	3	1	1	1	9	12	3
Scotland	3	0	1	2	4	6	1

POOL 3
Sweden **3-0** Mexico
Hungary **1-1** Wales
Wales **1-1** Mexico
Sweden **2-1** Hungary
Sweden **0-0** Wales
Hungary **4-0** Mexico

	P	W	D	L	F	A	Pts
Sweden	3	2	1	0	5	1	5
Wales	3	0	3	0	2	2	3
Hungary	3	1	1	1	6	3	3
Mexico	3	0	1	2	1	8	1

PLAY-OFF FOR 2ND GROUP PLACE
Wales **2-1** Hungary

POOL 4
England **2-2** Soviet Union
Brazil **3-0** Austria
England **0-0** Brazil
Soviet Union **2-0** Austria
Brazil **2-0** Soviet Union
England **2-2** Austria

	P	W	D	L	F	A	Pts
Brazil	3	2	1	0	5	0	5
Soviet Union	3	1	1	1	4	4	3
England	3	0	3	0	4	4	3
Austria	3	0	1	2	2	7	1

PLAY-OFF FOR 2ND GROUP PLACE
Soviet Union **1-0** England

QUARTER-FINALS
France **4-0** Northern Ireland
West Germany **1-0** Yugoslavia
Sweden **2-0** Soviet Union
Brazil **1-0** Wales

SEMI-FINALS
Brazil **5-2** France
Sweden **3-1** West Germany

THIRD-PLACE PLAY-OFF
France **6-3** West Germany

FINAL
Brazil **5-2** Sweden

1962 CHILE

GROUP 1
Uruguay **2-1** Colombia
Soviet Union **2-0** Yugoslavia
Yugoslavia **3-1** Uruguay
Soviet Union **4-4** Colombia
Soviet Union **2-1** Uruguay
Yugoslavia **5-0** Colombia

	P	W	D	L	F	A	Pts
Soviet Union	3	2	1	0	8	5	5
Yugoslavia	3	2	0	1	8	3	4
Uruguay	3	1	0	2	4	6	2
Colombia	3	0	1	2	5	11	1

GROUP 2
Chile **3-1** Switzerland
West Germany **0-0** Italy
Chile **2-0** Italy
West Germany **2-1** Switzerland
West Germany **2-0** Chile
Italy **3-0** Switzerland

	P	W	D	L	F	A	Pts
West Germany	3	2	1	0	4	1	5
Chile	3	2	0	1	5	3	4
Italy	3	1	1	1	3	2	3
Switzerland	3	0	0	3	2	8	0

GROUP 3
Brazil **2-0** Mexico
Czechoslovakia **1-0** Spain
Brazil **0-0** Czechoslovakia
Spain **1-0** Mexico
Brazil **2-1** Spain
Mexico **3-1** Czechoslovakia

	P	W	D	L	F	A	Pts
Brazil	3	2	1	0	4	1	5
Czechoslovakia	3	1	1	1	2	3	3
Mexico	3	1	0	2	3	4	2
Spain	3	1	0	2	2	3	2

GROUP 4
Argentina **1-0** Bulgaria
Hungary **2-1** England
England **3-1** Argentina
Hungary **6-1** Bulgaria
Argentina **0-0** Hungary
England **0-0** Bulgaria

	P	W	D	L	F	A	Pts
Hungary	3	2	1	0	8	2	5
England	3	1	1	1	4	3	3
Argentina	3	1	1	1	2	3	3
Bulgaria	3	0	1	2	1	7	1

QUARTER-FINALS
Yugoslavia **1-0** West Germany
Brazil **3-1** England
Chile **2-1** Soviet Union
Czechoslovakia **1-0** Hungary

SEMI-FINALS
Brazil **4-2** Chile
Czechoslovakia **3-1** Yugoslavia

THIRD-PLACE PLAY-OFF
Chile **1-0** Yugoslavia

FINAL
Brazil **3-1** Czechoslovakia

1966 ENGLAND

GROUP 1
England **0-0** Uruguay
France **1-1** Mexico
Uruguay **2-1** France
England **2-0** Mexico
Uruguay **0-0** Mexico
England **2-0** France

	P	W	D	L	F	A	Pts
England	3	2	1	0	4	0	5
Uruguay	3	1	2	0	2	1	4
Mexico	3	0	2	1	1	3	2
France	3	0	1	2	2	5	1

GROUP 2
West Germany **5-0** Switzerland
Argentina **2-1** Spain
Spain **2-1** Switzerland
Argentina **0-0** West Germany
Argentina **2-0** Switzerland
West Germany **2-1** Spain

	P	W	D	L	F	A	Pts
West Germany	3	2	1	0	7	1	5
Argentina	3	2	1	0	4	1	5
Spain	3	1	0	2	4	5	2
Switzerland	3	0	0	3	1	9	0

GROUP 3
Brazil **2-0** Bulgaria
Portugal **3-1** Hungary
Hungary **3-1** Brazil
Portugal **3-0** Bulgaria
Portugal **3-1** Brazil
Hungary **3-1** Bulgaria

	P	W	D	L	F	A	Pts
Portugal	3	3	0	0	9	2	6
Hungary	3	2	0	1	7	5	4
Brazil	3	1	0	2	4	6	2
Bulgaria	3	0	0	3	1	8	0

GROUP 4
Soviet Union **3-0** North Korea
Italy **2-0** Chile
Chile **1-1** North Korea
Soviet Union **1-0** Italy
North Korea **1-0** Italy
Soviet Union **2-1** Chile

	P	W	D	L	F	A	Pts
Soviet Union	3	3	0	0	6	1	6
North Korea	3	1	1	1	2	4	3
Italy	3	1	0	2	2	2	2
Chile	3	0	1	2	2	5	1

QUARTER-FINALS
England **1-0** Argentina
West Germany **4-0** Uruguay
Portugal **5-3** North Korea
Soviet Union **2-1** Hungary

SEMI-FINALS
West Germany **2-1** Soviet Union
England **2-1** Portugal

THIRD-PLACE PLAY-OFF
Portugal **2-1** Soviet Union

FINAL
England **4-2** West Germany (aet)

1970 MEXICO

GROUP 1
Mexico **0-0** Soviet Union
Belgium **3-0** El Salvador
Soviet Union **4-1** Belgium
Mexico **4-0** El Salvador
Soviet Union **2-0** El Salvador
Mexico **1-0** Belgium

	P	W	D	L	F	A	Pts
Soviet Union	3	2	1	0	6	1	5
Mexico	3	2	1	0	5	0	5
Belgium	3	1	0	2	4	5	2
El Salvador	3	0	0	3	0	9	0

GROUP 2
Uruguay **2-0** Israel
Italy **1-0** Sweden
Uruguay **0-0** Italy
Sweden **1-1** Israel
Sweden **1-0** Uruguay
Italy **0-0** Israel

	P	W	D	L	F	A	Pts
Italy	3	1	2	0	1	0	4
Uruguay	3	1	1	1	2	1	3
Sweden	3	1	1	1	2	2	3
Israel	3	0	2	1	1	3	2

GROUP 3
England **1-0** Romania
Brazil **4-1** Czechoslovakia
Romania **2-1** Czechoslovakia
Brazil **1-0** England
Brazil **3-2** Romania
England **1-0** Czechoslovakia

	P	W	D	L	F	A	Pts
Brazil	3	3	0	0	8	3	6
England	3	2	0	1	2	1	4
Romania	3	1	0	2	4	5	2
Czechoslovakia	3	0	0	3	2	7	0

England's Bobby Charlton in full flight against France at Wembley Stadium during the 1966 World Cup.

WORLD CUP RESULTS

Rivelino of Brazil takes the game to Italy in the 1970 final at the Azteca Stadium.

GROUP 4

Peru **3-2** Bulgaria
West Germany **2-1** Morocco
Peru **3-0** Morocco
West Germany **5-2** Bulgaria
West Germany **3-1** Peru
Morocco **1-1** Bulgaria

	P	W	D	L	F	A	Pts
West Germany	3	3	0	0	10	4	6
Peru	3	2	0	1	7	5	4
Bulgaria	3	0	1	2	5	9	1
Morocco	3	0	1	2	2	6	1

QUARTER-FINALS

West Germany **3-2** England
(aet)
Brazil **4-2** Peru
Italy **4-1** Mexico
Uruguay **1-0** Soviet Union
(aet)

SEMI-FINALS

Italy **4-3** West Germany
(aet)
Brazil **3-1** Uruguay

THIRD-PLACE

West Germany **1-0** Uruguay

FINAL

Brazil **4-1** Italy

1974 WEST GERMANY

GROUP 1

West Germany **1-0** Chile
East Germany **2-0** Australia
West Germany **3-0** Australia
East Germany **1-1** Chile
Australia **0-0** Chile
East Germany **1-0** West Germany

	P	W	D	L	F	A	Pts
East Germany	3	2	1	0	4	1	5
West Germany	3	2	0	1	4	1	4
Chile	3	0	2	1	1	2	2
Australia	3	0	1	2	0	5	1

GROUP 2

Brazil **0-0** Yugoslavia
Scotland **2-0** Zaïre
Brazil **0-0** Scotland
Yugoslavia **9-0** Zaïre
Yugoslavia **1-1** Scotland
Brazil **3-0** Zaïre

	P	W	D	L	F	A	Pts
Yugoslavia	3	1	2	0	10	1	4
Brazil	3	1	2	0	3	0	4
Scotland	3	1	2	0	3	1	4
Zaïre	3	0	0	3	0	14	0

GROUP 3

Holland **2-0** Uruguay
Bulgaria **0-0** Sweden
Holland **0-0** Sweden
Bulgaria **1-1** Uruguay
Holland **4-1** Bulgaria
Sweden **3-0** Uruguay

	P	W	D	L	F	A	Pts
Holland	3	2	1	0	6	1	5
Sweden	3	1	2	0	3	0	4
Bulgaria	3	0	2	1	2	5	2
Uruguay	3	0	1	2	1	6	1

GROUP 4

Italy **3-1** Haiti
Poland **3-2** Argentina
Argentina **1-1** Italy
Poland **7-0** Haiti
Argentina **4-1** Haiti
Poland **2-1** Italy

	P	W	D	L	F	A	Pts
Poland	3	3	0	0	12	3	6
Argentina	3	1	1	1	7	5	3
Italy	3	1	1	1	5	4	3
Haiti	3	0	0	3	2	14	0

SECOND ROUND GROUP A

Brazil **1-0** East Germany
Holland **4-0** Argentina
Holland **2-0** East Germany
Brazil **2-1** Argentina
East Germany **1-1** Argentina
Holland **2-0** Brazil

	P	W	D	L	F	A	Pts
Holland	3	3	0	0	8	0	6
Brazil	3	2	0	1	3	3	4
East Germany	3	0	1	2	1	4	1
Argentina	3	0	1	2	2	7	1

SECOND ROUND GROUP B

Poland **1-0** Sweden
West Germany **2-0** Yugoslavia
Poland **2-1** Sweden
West Germany **4-2** Sweden
Sweden **2-1** Yugoslavia
West Germany **1-0** Poland

	P	W	D	L	F	A	Pts
West Germany	3	3	0	0	7	2	6
Poland	3	2	0	1	3	2	4
Sweden	3	1	0	2	4	6	2
Yugoslavia	3	0	0	3	2	6	0

THIRD-PLACE PLAY-OFF

Poland **1-0** Brazil

FINAL

West Germany **2-1** Holland

1978 ARGENTINA

GROUP 1

Argentina **2-1** Hungary
Italy **2-1** France
Argentina **2-1** France
Italy **3-1** Hungary
Italy **1-0** Argentina
France **3-1** Hungary

	P	W	D	L	F	A	Pts
Italy	3	3	0	0	6	2	6
Argentina	3	2	0	1	4	3	4
France	3	1	0	2	5	5	2
Hungary	3	0	0	3	3	8	0

GROUP 2

West Germany **0-0** Poland
Tunisia **3-1** Mexico
Poland **1-0** Tunisia
West Germany **6-0** Mexico
Poland **3-1** Mexico
West Germany **0-0** Tunisia

	P	W	D	L	F	A	Pts
Poland	3	2	1	0	4	1	5
West Germany	3	1	2	0	6	0	4
Tunisia	3	1	1	1	3	2	3
Mexico	3	0	0	3	2	12	0

GROUP 3

Austria **2-1** Spain
Sweden **1-1** Brazil
Austria **1-0** Sweden
Brazil **0-0** Spain
Spain **1-0** Sweden
Brazil **1-0** Austria

	P	W	D	L	F	A	Pts
Austria	3	2	0	1	3	2	4
Brazil	3	1	2	0	2	1	4
Spain	3	1	1	1	2	2	3
Sweden	3	0	1	2	1	3	1

GROUP 4

Peru **3-1** Scotland
Holland **3-0** Iran
Scotland **1-1** Iran
Holland **0-0** Peru
Peru **4-1** Iran
Scotland **3-2** Holland

	P	W	D	L	F	A	Pts
Peru	3	2	1	0	7	2	5
Holland	3	1	1	1	5	3	3
Scotland	3	1	1	1	5	6	3
Iran	3	0	1	2	2	8	1

SECOND ROUND GROUP A

Italy **0-0** West Germany
Holland **5-1** Austria
Italy **1-0** Austria
Holland **2-2** West Germany
Holland **2-1** Italy
Austria **3-2** West Germany

	P	W	D	L	F	A	Pts
Holland	3	2	1	0	9	4	5
Italy	3	1	1	1	2	2	3
West Germany	3	0	2	1	4	5	2
Austria	3	1	0	2	4	8	2

SECOND ROUND GROUP B

Argentina **2-0** Poland
Brazil **3-0** Peru
Argentina **0-0** Brazil
Poland **1-0** Peru
Brazil **3-1** Poland
Argentina **6-0** Peru

	P	W	D	L	F	A	Pts
Argentina	3	2	1	0	8	0	5
Brazil	3	2	1	0	6	1	5
Poland	3	1	0	2	2	5	2
Peru	3	0	0	3	0	10	0

THIRD-PLACE PLAY-OFF

Brazil **2-1** Italy

FINAL

Argentina **3-1** Holland
(aet)

1982 SPAIN

GROUP 1

Italy **0-0** Poland
Peru **0-0** Cameroon
Italy **1-1** Peru
Poland **0-0** Cameroon
Poland **5-1** Peru
Italy **1-1** Cameroon

	P	W	D	L	F	A	Pts
Poland	3	1	2	0	5	1	4
Italy	3	0	3	0	2	2	3
Cameroon	3	0	3	0	1	1	3
Peru	3	0	2	1	2	6	2

GROUP 2

Algeria **2-1** West Germany
Austria **1-0** Chile
West Germany **4-1** Chile
Austria **2-0** Algeria
Algeria **3-2** Chile
West Germany **1-0** Austria

	P	W	D	L	F	A	Pts
West Germany	3	2	0	1	6	3	4
Austria	3	2	0	1	3	1	4
Algeria	3	2	0	1	5	5	4
Chile	3	0	0	3	3	8	0

GROUP 3

Belgium **1-0** Argentina
Hungary **10-1** El Salvador
Argentina **4-1** Hungary
Belgium **1-0** El Salvador
Belgium **1-1** Hungary
Argentina **2-0** El Salvador

	P	W	D	L	F	A	Pts
Belgium	3	2	1	0	3	1	5
Argentina	3	2	0	1	6	2	4
Hungary	3	1	1	1	12	6	3
El Salvador	3	0	0	3	1	13	0

GROUP 4

England **3-1** France
Czechoslovakia **1-1** Kuwait
England **2-0** Czechoslovakia
France **4-1** Kuwait
France **1-1** Czechoslovakia
England **1-0** Kuwait

	P	W	D	L	F	A	Pts
England	3	3	0	0	6	1	6
France	3	1	1	1	6	5	3
Czechoslovakia	3	0	2	1	2	4	2
Kuwait	3	0	1	2	2	6	1

GROUP 5

Spain **1-1** Honduras
Northern Ireland **0-0** Yugoslavia
Spain **2-1** Yugoslavia
Northern Ireland **1-1** Honduras
Yugoslavia **1-0** Honduras
Northern Ireland **1-0** Spain

	P	W	D	L	F	A	Pts
Northern Ireland	3	1	2	0	2	1	4
Spain	3	1	1	1	3	3	3
Yugoslavia	3	1	1	1	2	2	3
Honduras	3	0	2	1	2	3	2

GROUP 6

Brazil **2-1** Soviet Union
Scotland **5-2** New Zealand
Brazil **4-1** Scotland
Soviet Union **3-0** New Zealand
Scotland **2-2** Soviet Union
Brazil **4-0** New Zealand

	P	W	D	L	F	A	Pts
Brazil	3	3	0	0	10	2	6
Soviet Union	3	1	1	1	6	4	3
Scotland	3	1	1	1	8	8	3
New Zealand	3	0	0	3	2	12	0

SECOND ROUND GROUP A

Poland **3-0** Belgium
Soviet Union **1-0** Belgium
Soviet Union **0-0** Poland

	P	W	D	L	F	A	Pts
Poland	2	1	1	0	3	0	3
Soviet Union	2	1	1	0	1	0	3
Belgium	2	0	0	2	0	4	0

SECOND ROUND GROUP B

West Germany **0-0** England
West Germany **2-1** Spain
England **0-0** Spain

	P	W	D	L	F	A	Pts
West Germany	2	1	1	0	2	1	3
England	2	0	2	0	0	0	2
Spain	2	0	1	1	1	2	1

West Germany's Littbarski tackles Urquiaga of Spain during the 1982 World Cup.

Scotland's Graeme Souness on the ball against West Germany at the 1986 finals.

SECOND ROUND GROUP C

Italy **2-1** Argentina
Brazil **3-1** Argentina
Italy **3-2** Brazil

	P	W	D	L	F	A	Pts
Italy	2	2	0	0	5	3	4
Brazil	2	1	0	1	5	4	2
Argentina	2	0	0	2	2	5	0

SECOND ROUND GROUP D

France **1-0** Austria
Northern Ireland **2-2** Austria
France **4-1** Northern Ireland

	P	W	D	L	F	A	Pts
France	2	2	0	0	5	1	4
Austria	2	0	1	1	2	3	1
Northern Ireland	2	0	1	1	3	6	1

SEMI-FINALS

Italy **2-0** Poland
West Germany **3-3** France
(aet)
West Germany won 5-4 on penalties

THIRD PLACE PLAY-OFF

Poland **3-2** France

FINAL

Italy **3-1** West Germany

1986 MEXICO

GROUP A

Bulgaria **1-1** Italy
Argentina **3-1** South Korea
Italy **1-1** Argentina
Bulgaria **1-1** South Korea
Argentina **2-0** Bulgaria
Italy **3-2** South Korea

	P	W	D	L	F	A	Pts
Argentina	3	2	1	0	6	2	5
Italy	3	1	2	0	5	4	4
Bulgaria	3	0	2	1	2	4	2
South Korea	3	0	1	2	4	7	1

GROUP B

Mexico **2-1** Belgium
Paraguay **1-0** Iraq
Mexico **1-1** Paraguay
Belgium **2-1** Iraq
Paraguay **2-2** Belgium
Mexico **1-0** Iraq

	P	W	D	L	F	A	Pts
Morocco	3	1	2	0	3	1	4
England	3	1	1	1	3	1	3
Poland	3	1	1	1	1	3	3
Portugal	3	1	0	2	2	4	2

	P	W	D	L	F	A	Pts
Mexico	3	2	1	0	4	2	5
Paraguay	3	1	2	0	4	3	4
Belgium	3	1	1	1	5	5	3
Iraq	3	0	0	3	1	4	0

GROUP C

Soviet Union **6-0** Hungary
France **1-0** Canada
Soviet Union **1-1** France
Hungary **2-0** Canada
France **3-0** Hungary
Soviet Union **2-0** Canada

	P	W	D	L	F	A	Pts
Soviet Union	3	2	1	0	9	1	5
France	3	2	1	0	5	1	5
Hungary	3	1	0	2	2	9	2
Canada	3	0	0	3	0	5	0

GROUP D

Brazil **1-0** Spain
Northern Ireland **1-1** Algeria
Spain **2-1** Northern Ireland
Brazil **1-0** Algeria
Spain **3-0** Algeria
Brazil **3-0** Northern Ireland

	P	W	D	L	F	A	Pts
Brazil	3	3	0	0	5	0	6
Spain	3	2	0	1	5	2	4
Northern Ireland	3	0	1	2	2	6	1
Algeria	3	0	1	2	1	5	1

GROUP E

West Germany **1-1** Uruguay
Denmark **1-0** Scotland
Denmark **6-1** Uruguay
West Germany **2-1** Scotland
Scotland **0-0** Uruguay
Denmark **2-0** West Germany

	P	W	D	L	F	A	Pts
Denmark	3	3	0	0	9	1	6
West Germany	3	1	1	1	3	4	3
Uruguay	3	0	2	1	2	7	2
Scotland	3	0	1	2	1	3	1

GROUP F

Morocco **0-0** Poland
Portugal **1-0** England
England **0-0** Morocco
Poland **1-0** Portugal
England **3-0** Poland
Morocco **3-1** Portugal

SECOND ROUND

Mexico **2-0** Bulgaria
Belgium **4-3** Soviet Union
(aet)
Brazil **4-0** Poland
Argentina **1-0** Uruguay
France **2-0** Italy
West Germany **1-0** Morocco
England **3-0** Paraguay
Spain **5-1** Denmark

QUARTER-FINALS

France **1-1** Brazil
(aet)
France won 4-3 on penalties
West Germany **0-0** Mexico
(aet)
West Germany won 4-1 on penalties
Argentina **2-1** England
Spain **1-1** Belgium
(aet)
Belgium won 5-4 on penalties

SEMI-FINALS

Argentina **2-0** Belgium
West Germany **2-0** France

THIRD PLACE PLAY-OFF

France **4-2** Belgium

FINAL

Argentina **3-2** West Germany

1990 ITALY

GROUP A

Italy **1-0** Austria
Czechoslovakia **5-1** USA
Italy **1-0** USA
Czechoslovakia **1-0** Austria
Italy **2-0** Czechoslovakia
Austria **2-1** USA

	P	W	D	L	F	A	Pts
Italy	3	3	0	0	4	0	6
Czechoslovakia	3	2	0	1	6	3	4
Austria	3	1	0	2	2	3	2
USA	3	0	0	3	2	8	0

GROUP B

Cameroon **1-0** Argentina
Romania **2-0** Soviet Union
Argentina **2-0** Soviet Union
Cameroon **2-1** Romania
Argentina **1-1** Romania
Soviet Union **4-0** Cameroon

	P	W	D	L	F	A	Pts
Cameroon	3	2	0	1	3	5	4
Romania	3	1	1	1	4	3	3
Argentina	3	1	1	1	3	2	3
Soviet Union	3	1	0	2	4	4	2

GROUP C

Brazil **2-1** Sweden
Costa Rica **1-0** Scotland
Brazil **1-0** Costa Rica
Scotland **2-1** Sweden
Brazil **1-0** Scotland
Costa Rica **2-1** Sweden

	P	W	D	L	F	A	Pts
Brazil	3	3	0	0	4	1	6
Costa Rica	3	2	0	1	3	2	4
Scotland	3	1	0	2	2	3	2
Sweden	3	0	0	3	3	6	0

GROUP D

Colombia **2-0** UAE
West Germany **4-1** Yugoslavia
Yugoslavia **1-0** Colombia
West Germany **5-1** UAE
West Germany **1-1** Colombia
Yugoslavia **4-1** UAE

	P	W	D	L	F	A	Pts
West Germany	3	2	1	0	10	3	5
Yugoslavia	3	2	0	1	6	5	4
Colombia	3	1	1	1	3	2	3
UAE	3	0	0	3	2	11	0

GROUP E

Belgium **2-0** South Korea
Uruguay **0-0** Spain
Belgium **3-1** Uruguay
Spain **3-1** South Korea
Spain **2-1** Belgium
Uruguay **1-0** South Korea

	P	W	D	L	F	A	Pts
Spain	3	2	1	0	5	2	5
Belgium	3	2	0	1	6	3	4
Uruguay	3	1	1	1	2	3	3
South Korea	3	0	0	3	1	6	0

GROUP F

England **1-1** Rep. Of Ireland
Holland **1-1** Egypt
England **0-0** Holland
Egypt **0-0** Rep. Of Ireland
England **1-0** Egypt
Holland **1-1** Rep. Of Ireland

	P	W	D	L	F	A	Pts
England	3	1	2	0	2	1	4
Rep. Of Ireland	3	0	3	0	2	2	3
Holland	3	0	3	0	2	2	3
Egypt	3	0	2	1	1	2	2

Paul Gascoigne takes on Cameroon in the 1990 World Cup quarter-final.

SECOND ROUND

Cameroon **2-1** Colombia
(aet)
Czechoslovakia **4-1** Costa Rica
Argentina **1-0** Brazil
West Germany **2-1** Holland
Rep. Of Ireland **0-0** Romania
(aet)
Rep. Of Ireland won 5-4 on penalties
Italy **2-0** Uruguay
Yugoslavia **2-1** Spain
(aet)
England **1-0** Belgium
(aet)

QUARTER-FINALS

Argentina **0-0** Yugoslavia
(aet)
Argentina won 3-2 on penalties
Italy **1-0** Rep. Of Ireland
West Germany **1-0** Czechoslovakia
England **3-2** Cameroon

SEMI-FINALS

Argentina **1-1** Italy
(aet)
Argentina won 4-3 on penalties
West Germany **1-1** England
(aet)
West Germany won 4-3 on penalties

THIRD-PLACE PLAY-OFF

Italy **2-1** England

FINAL

West Germany **1-0** Argentina

1994 USA

GROUP A

USA **1-1** Switzerland
Colombia **1-3** Romania
USA **2-1** Colombia
Romania **1-4** Switzerland
USA **0-1** Romania
Switzerland **0-2** Colombia

	P	W	D	L	F	A	Pts
Romania	3	2	0	1	5	5	6
Switzerland	3	1	1	1	5	4	4
USA	3	1	1	1	3	3	4
Colombia	3	1	0	2	4	5	3

GROUP B

Cameroon **2-2** Sweden
Brazil **2-0** Russia
Brazil **3-0** Cameroon
Sweden **3-1** Russia
Russia **6-1** Cameroon
Brazil **1-1** Sweden

	P	W	D	L	F	A	Pts
Brazil	3	2	1	0	6	1	7
Sweden	3	1	2	0	6	4	5
Russia	3	1	0	2	7	6	3
Cameroon	3	0	1	2	3	11	1

GROUP C

Germany **1-0** Bolivia
Spain **2-2** South Korea
Germany **1-1** Spain
South Korea **0-0** Bolivia
Bolivia **1-3** Spain
Germany **3-2** South Korea

	P	W	D	L	F	A	Pts
Germany	3	2	1	0	5	3	7
Spain	3	1	2	0	6	4	5
South Korea	3	0	2	1	4	5	2
Bolivia	3	0	1	2	1	4	1

WORLD CUP RESULTS

Hristo Stoichkov of Bulgaria fends of Roberto Mussi of Italy in the 1994 World Cup semi-final in New Jersey.

GROUP D

Argentina **4-0** Greece
Nigeria **3-0** Bulgaria
Argentina **2-1** Nigeria
Bulgaria **4-0** Greece
Greece **0-2** Nigeria
Argentina **0-2** Bulgaria

	P	W	D	L	F	A	Pts
Nigeria	3	2	0	1	6	2	6
Bulgaria	3	2	0	1	6	3	6
Argentina	3	2	0	1	6	3	6
Greece	3	0	0	3	0	10	0

GROUP E

Italy **0-1** Rep. Of Ireland
Norway **1-0** Mexico
Italy **1-0** Norway
Mexico **2-1** Rep. Of Ireland
Rep. Of Ireland **0-0** Norway
Italy **1-1** Mexico

	P	W	D	L	F	A	Pts
Mexico	3	1	1	1	3	3	4
Rep. Of Ireland	3	1	1	1	2	2	4
Italy	3	1	1	1	2	2	4
Norway	3	1	1	1	1	1	4

GROUP F

Belgium **1-0** Morocco
Holland **2-1** Saudi Arabia
Belgium **1-0** Holland
Saudi Arabia **2-1** Morocco
Morocco **1-2** Holland
Belgium **0-1** Saudi Arabia

	P	W	D	L	F	A	Pts
Holland	3	2	0	1	4	3	6
Saudi Arabia	3	2	0	1	4	3	6
Belgium	3	2	0	1	2	1	6
Morocco	3	0	0	3	2	5	0

SECOND ROUND

Germany **3-2** Belgium
Spain **3-0** Switzerland
Saudi Arabia **1-3** Sweden
Romania **3-2** Argentina
Holland **2-0** Rep. Of Ireland
Brazil **1-0** USA
Nigeria **1-2** Italy
(aet)
Mexico **1-1** Bulgaria
(aet)
Bulgaria won 3-1 on penalties

QUARTER-FINALS

Italy **2-1** Spain
Holland **2-3** Brazil
Germany **1-2** Bulgaria
Sweden **2-2** Romania
(aet)
Sweden won 5-4 on penalties

SEMI-FINALS

Brazil **1-0** Sweden
Italy **2-1** Bulgaria

THIRD PLACE PLAY-OFF

Sweden **4-0** Bulgaria

FINAL

Brazil **0-0** Italy
(aet)
Brazil won 3-2 on penalties

1998 FRANCE

GROUP A

Brazil **2-1** Scotland
Morocco **2-2** Norway
Brazil **3-0** Morocco
Scotland **1-1** Norway
Brazil **1-2** Norway
Scotland **0-3** Morocco

	P	W	D	L	F	A	Pts
Brazil	3	2	0	1	6	3	6
Norway	3	1	2	0	5	4	5
Morocco	3	1	1	1	5	5	4
Scotland	3	0	1	2	2	6	1

GROUP B

Italy **2-2** Chile
Austria **1-1** Cameroon
Chile **1-1** Austria
Italy **3-0** Cameroon
Chile **1-1** Cameroon
Italy **2-1** Austria

	P	W	D	L	F	A	Pts
Italy	3	2	1	0	7	3	7
Chile	3	0	3	0	4	4	3
Austria	3	0	2	1	3	4	2
Cameroon	3	0	2	1	2	5	2

GROUP C

Saudi Arabia **0-1** Denmark
France **3-0** South Africa
France **4-0** Saudi Arabia
South Africa **1-1** Denmark
France **2-1** Denmark
South Africa **2-2** Saudi Arabia

	P	W	D	L	F	A	Pts
France	3	3	0	0	9	1	9
Denmark	3	1	1	1	3	3	4
South Africa	3	0	2	1	3	6	2
Saudi Arabia	3	0	1	2	2	7	1

GROUP D

Paraguay **0-0** Bulgaria
Spain **2-3** Nigeria
Nigeria **1-0** Bulgaria
Spain **0-0** Paraguay
Nigeria **1-3** Paraguay
Spain **6-1** Bulgaria

	P	W	D	L	F	A	Pts
Nigeria	3	2	0	1	5	5	6
Paraguay	3	1	2	0	3	1	5
Spain	3	1	1	1	8	4	4
Bulgaria	3	0	1	2	1	7	1

Argentina's Matias Almeyda holds off Dennis Bergkamp of Holland in 1998.

GROUP E

South Korea **1-3** Mexico
Holland **0-0** Belgium
Belgium **2-2** Mexico
Holland **5-0** South Korea
Belgium **1-1** South Korea
Holland **2-2** Mexico

	P	W	D	L	F	A	Pts
Holland	3	1	2	0	7	2	5
Mexico	3	1	2	0	7	5	5
Belgium	3	0	3	0	3	3	3
South Korea	3	0	1	2	2	9	1

GROUP F

Germany **2-0** USA
Yugoslavia **1-0** Iran
Germany **2-2** Yugoslavia
USA **1-2** Iran
Germany **2-0** Iran
USA **0-1** Yugoslavia

	P	W	D	L	F	A	Pts
Germany	3	2	1	0	6	2	7
Yugoslavia	3	2	1	0	4	2	7
Iran	3	1	0	2	2	4	3
USA	3	0	0	3	1	5	0

GROUP G

England **2-0** Tunisia
Romania **1-0** Colombia
Colombia **1-0** Tunisia
Romania **2-1** England
Romania **1-1** Tunisia
Colombia **0-2** England

	P	W	D	L	F	A	Pts
Romania	3	2	1	0	4	2	7
England	3	2	0	1	5	2	6
Colombia	3	1	0	2	1	3	3
Tunisia	3	0	1	2	1	4	1

GROUP H

Argentina **1-0** Japan
Jamaica **1-3** Croatia
Japan **0-1** Croatia
Argentina **5-0** Jamaica
Argentina **1-0** Croatia
Japan **1-2** Jamaica

	P	W	D	L	F	A	Pts
Argentina	3	3	0	0	7	0	9
Croatia	3	2	0	1	4	2	6
Jamaica	3	1	0	2	3	9	3
Japan	3	0	0	3	1	4	0

SECOND ROUND

Italy **1-0** Norway
Brazil **4-1** Chile
France **1-0** Paraguay
(aet)
France won with golden goal
Nigeria **1-4** Denmark
Germany **2-1** Mexico
Holland **2-1** Yugoslavia
Romania **0-1** Croatia
Argentina **2-2** England
(aet)
Argentina won 4-3 on penalties

QUARTER-FINALS

Italy **0-0** France
(aet)
France won 4-3 on penalties
Brazil **3-2** Denmark
Holland **2-1** Argentina
Germany **0-3** Croatia

SEMI-FINALS

Brazil **1-1** Holland
(aet)
Brazil won 4-2 on penalties
France **2-1** Croatia

THIRD-PLACE PLAY-OFF

Holland **1-2** Croatia

FINAL

Brazil **0-3** France

2002 KOREA/JAPAN

GROUP A

France **0-1** Senegal
Uruguay **1-2** Denmark
Denmark **1-1** Senegal
France **0-0** Uruguay
Senegal **3-3** Uruguay
Denmark **2-0** France

	P	W	D	L	F	A	Pts
Denmark	3	2	1	0	5	2	7
Senegal	3	1	2	0	5	4	5
Uruguay	3	0	2	1	4	5	2
France	3	0	1	2	0	3	1

GROUP B

Paraguay **2-2** South Africa
Spain **3-1** Slovenia
Spain **3-1** Paraguay
South Africa **1-0** Slovenia
South Africa **2-3** Spain
Slovenia **1-3** Paraguay

	P	W	D	L	F	A	Pts
Spain	3	3	0	0	9	4	9
Paraguay	3	1	1	1	6	6	4
South Africa	3	1	1	1	5	5	4
Slovenia	3	0	0	3	2	7	0

GROUP C

Brazil **2-1** Turkey
China **0-2** Costa Rica
Brazil **4-0** China
Costa Rica **1-1** Turkey
Costa Rica **2-5** Brazil
Turkey **3-0** China

	P	W	D	L	F	A	Pts
Brazil	3	3	0	0	11	3	9
Turkey	3	1	1	1	5	3	4
Costa Rica	3	1	1	1	5	6	4
China	3	0	0	3	0	9	0

GROUP D

South Korea **2-0** Poland
USA **3-2** Portugal
South Korea **1-1** USA
Portugal **4-0** Poland
Portugal **0-1** South Korea
Poland **3-1** USA

	P	W	D	L	F	A	Pts
South Korea	3	2	1	0	4	1	7
USA	3	1	1	1	5	6	4
Portugal	3	1	0	2	6	4	3
Poland	3	1	0	2	3	7	3

GROUP E

Rep. Of Ireland **1-1** Cameroon
Germany **8-0** Saudi Arabia
Germany **1-1** Rep. Of Ireland
Cameroon **1-0** Saudi Arabia
Cameroon **0-2** Germany
Saudi Arabia **0-3** Rep. Of Ireland

	P	W	D	L	F	A	Pts
Germany	3	2	1	0	11	1	7
Rep. Of Ireland	3	1	2	0	5	2	5
Cameroon	3	1	1	1	2	3	4
Saudi Arabia	3	0	0	3	0	12	0

GROUP F

Argentina **1-0** Nigeria
England **1-1** Sweden
Sweden **2-1** Nigeria
Argentina **0-1** England
Sweden **1-1** Argentina
Nigeria **0-0** England

	P	W	D	L	F	A	Pts
Sweden	3	1	2	0	4	3	5
England	3	1	2	0	2	1	5
Argentina	3	1	1	1	2	2	4
Nigeria	3	0	1	2	1	3	1

GROUP G

Croatia **0-1** Mexico
Italy **2-0** Ecuador
Italy **1-2** Croatia
Mexico **2-1** Ecuador
Mexico **1-1** Italy
Ecuador **1-0** Croatia

	P	W	D	L	F	A	Pts
Mexico	3	2	1	0	4	2	7
Italy	3	1	1	1	4	3	4
Croatia	3	1	0	2	2	3	3
Ecuador	3	1	0	2	2	4	3

GROUP H

Japan **2-2** Belgium
Russia **2-0** Tunisia
Japan **1-0** Russia
Tunisia **1-1** Belgium
Tunisia **0-2** Japan
Belgium **3-2** Russia

	P	W	D	L	F	A	Pts
Japan	3	2	1	0	5	2	7
Belgium	3	1	2	0	6	5	5
Russia	3	1	0	2	4	4	3
Tunisia	3	0	1	2	1	5	1

2ND ROUND

Germany **1-0** Paraguay
Denmark **0-3** England
Sweden **1-2** Senegal
(aet)
Senegal won with golden goal
Spain **1-1** Rep. Of Ireland
(aet)
Spain won 3-2 on penalties
Mexico **0-2** USA
Brazil **2-0** Belgium
Japan **0-1** Turkey
South Korea **2-1** Italy
(aet)
South Korea won with golden goal

QUARTER-FINALS

England **1-2** Brazil
Germany **1-0** USA
Spain **0-0** South Korea
(aet)
South Korea won 5-3 on penalties
Senegal **0-1** Turkey
(aet)
Turkey won with golden goal

SEMI-FINALS

Germany **1-0** South Korea
Brazil **1-0** Turkey

THIRD PLACE MATCH

South Korea **2-3** Turkey

FINAL

Germany **0-2** Brazil

2006 GERMANY

GROUP A

Germany **4-2** Costa Rica
Poland **0-2** Ecuador
Germany **1-0** Poland
Ecuador **3-0** Costa Rica
Costa Rica **1-2** Poland
Ecuador **0-3** Germany

	P	W	D	L	F	A	Pts
Germany	3	3	0	0	8	2	9
Ecuador	3	2	0	1	5	3	6
Poland	3	1	0	2	2	4	3
Costa Rica	3	0	0	3	3	9	0

GROUP B

England **1-0** Paraguay
Trinidad & Tobago **0-0** Sweden
Sweden **1-0** Paraguay
England **2-0** Trinidad & Tobago
Paraguay **2-0** Trinidad & Tobago
Sweden **2-2** England

	P	W	D	L	F	A	Pts
England	3	2	1	0	5	2	7
Sweden	3	1	2	0	3	2	5
Paraguay	3	1	0	2	2	2	3
Trinidad & Tobago	3	0	1	2	0	4	1

GROUP C

Argentina **2-1** Ivory Coast
Serbia & Mont. **0-1** Holland
Holland **2-1** Ivory Coast
Argentina **6-0** Serbia & Mont.
Holland **0-0** Argentina
Ivory Coast **3-2** Serbia & Mont.

	P	W	D	L	F	A	Pts
Argentina	3	2	1	0	8	1	7
Holland	3	2	1	0	3	1	7
Ivory Coast	3	1	0	2	5	6	3
Serbia & Mont.	3	0	0	3	2	10	0

GROUP D

Mexico **3-1** Iran
Angola **0-1** Portugal
Mexico **0-0** Angola
Portugal **2-0** Iran
Portugal **2-1** Mexico
Iran **1-1** Angola

	P	W	D	L	F	A	Pts
Portugal	3	3	0	0	5	1	9
Mexico	3	1	1	1	4	3	4
Angola	3	0	2	1	1	2	2
Iran	3	0	1	2	2	6	1

GROUP E

Italy **2-0** Ghana
United States **0-3** Czech Republic
Italy **1-1** United States
Czech Republic **0-2** Ghana
Czech Republic **0-2** Italy
Ghana **2-1** United States

	P	W	D	L	F	A	Pts
Italy	3	2	1	0	5	1	7
Ghana	3	2	0	1	4	3	6
Czech Republic	3	1	0	2	3	4	3
USA	3	0	1	2	2	6	1

GROUP F

Australia **3-1** Japan
Brazil **1-0** Croatia
Brazil **2-0** Australia
Japan **0-0** Croatia
Croatia **2-2** Australia
Japan **1-4** Brazil

	P	W	D	L	F	A	Pts
Brazil	3	3	0	0	7	1	9
Australia	3	1	1	1	5	5	4
Croatia	3	0	2	1	2	3	2
Japan	3	0	1	2	2	7	1

GROUP G

South Korea **2-1** Togo
France **0-0** Switzerland
France **1-1** South Korea
Togo **0-2** Switzerland
Togo **0-2** France
Switzerland **2-0** South Korea

	P	W	D	L	F	A	Pts
Switzerland	3	2	1	0	4	0	7
France	3	1	2	0	3	1	5
South Korea	3	1	1	1	3	4	4
Togo	3	0	0	3	1	6	0

GROUP H

Spain **4-0** Ukraine
Tunisia **2-2** Saudi Arabia
Spain **3-1** Tunisia
Saudi Arabia **0-4** Ukraine
Saudi Arabia **0-1** Spain
Ukraine **1-0** Tunisia

	P	W	D	L	F	A	Pts
Spain	3	3	0	0	8	1	9
Ukraine	3	2	0	1	5	4	6
Tunisia	3	0	1	2	3	6	1
Saudi Arabia	3	0	1	2	2	7	1

2ND ROUND

Germany **2-0** Sweden
Argentina **2-1** Mexico
England **1-0** Ecuador
Portugal **1-0** Holland
Italy **1-0** Australia
Switzerland **0-0** Ukraine
(aet)
Ukraine won 3-0 on penalties
Brazil **3-0** Ghana
Spain **1-3** France

QUARTER-FINALS

Germany **1-1** Argentina
(aet)
Germany won 4-2 on penalties
Italy **3-0** Ukraine
England **0-0** Portugal
(aet)
Portugal won 3-1 on penalties
Brazil **0-1** France

SEMI-FINALS

Germany **0-2** Italy
Portugal **0-1** France

THIRD PLACE PLAY-OFF

Germany **3-1** Portugal

FINAL

Italy **1-1** France
(aet)
Italy won 5-3 on penalties

Brazil's Ronaldo celebrates scoring the opening goal of the 2002 World Cup final.

Above: Marco Materazzi celebrates equalising for Italy in the 2006 World Cup final.

THE EUROPEAN CHAMPIONSHIP

THE EUROPEAN CHAMPIONSHIP

Above from left to right: France's Sylvain Wiltord kisses the trophy after victory over Italy in 2000; Czechoslovakia enjoy their 1976 win after beating West Germany on penalties; Holland's Adri Van Tiggelen and Frank Rijkaard celebrate in 1988.

The European Championship is the most prestigious European competition for national teams, and falls second in significance only to the World Cup in the football pecking order. It is contested every four years, and the finals are staged two years apart from the World Cup. The championship is open to all members of UEFA.

As early as 1927 Henri Delaunay, head of the French football association, proposed the idea of a championship involving the top European countries – he was also a driving force behind the foundation of the World Cup. However, after the creation of UEFA on June 15, 1954, the idea was raised once again, and two years later the planning got underway for the competition Delaunay had dreamed of. Sadly, he passed away in 1955, but in his honour the trophy played for will forever hold his name.

In 1958, the first qualifying matches for the European Nations Cup were played. The format for the early tournament remained in place until 1980, and consisted of a series of two-legged qualifying rounds, played home and away,

producing four finalists who would contest the semi-finals and final in a host country, with these games to be played over the space of a week.

In the summer of 1960 the first finals of the European Nations Cup were held in Delaunay's native France. Just like the World Cup, the inaugural competition could not remain unspoilt by world politics. The quarter-finals drew the Soviet Union against Spain, whose fascist dictator Franco refused the Communist side entry to his country, and in so doing forfeited the tie. This worked in the Soviet Union's favour, as they finished winners under the inspirational leadership of keeper Lev Yashin, beating Yugoslavia 2-1 in the first final.

By 1968 the tournament had undergone a change of name from the unwieldy European Nations Cup to the European Championship. Hosts Spain and Italy had run out winners in 1964 and 1968 respectively, a sequence that was broken by West Germany in 1972, but even then they were given a scare by hosts Belgium in a close fought semi-final.

In 1976 the tournament was held in an Eastern Bloc country for the first time, with Yugoslavia hosting. Yet another first was created in the final when a spirited Czech side held the holders West Germany to a draw, and the game was decided by a penalty shoot-out. The Czechs held their nerve and ran out 5-3 winners, with Antonin Panenka famously dinking his penalty over a stranded Sepp Maier to claim the trophy.

The 1980 competition saw the final stage format change with the quarter-final and semi-final stages dispensed with, and eight teams competing in two mini-leagues, with the winners of both groups advancing directly to the final. Once again the strength of West Germany saw them through, where they narrowly defeated Belgium with a late goal from match-winner Horst Hrubesch.

Forever tinkering with the format, UEFA reintroduced semi-finals to the tournament in 1984, with the top two teams from each group playing for a place in the final. France,

1904: European-dominated FIFA formed.

1954: UEFA formed to look after European interests.

1956: European Nations Cup launched for the Henri Delaunay Trophy.

1958: Qualifying kicks off in September – the Soviet Union beat Hungary 3-1 in Moscow. 17 teams enter.

1959: Spain withdraw for political reasons giving the Soviet Union a walkover.

1960: France host semi-finals and final in July. The Soviet Union beat Yugoslavia in final.

1962: 26 teams enter. Both England and Yugoslavia suffer shock first round exits.

1964: Spain host closing stages and beat Soviet Union in final.

1966: Qualifying tournament adopted and West Germany and Scotland enter for first time.

1967: Qualifying group winners go to two-legged quarter-final stage. The Soviets come back from 2-0 down to beat Hungary.

1968: Italy win semi-final on toss of a coin and the final after replay. Alan Mullery becomes the first Englishman to be sent-off.

1972: West Germany, with Franz Beckenbauer as attacking sweeper, win the tournament for the first time.

1904   1954   1956   1958   1960   1962   1964   1966   1968   1970   1972

EUROPEAN CHAMPIONSHIP WINNERS & HOST NATIONS

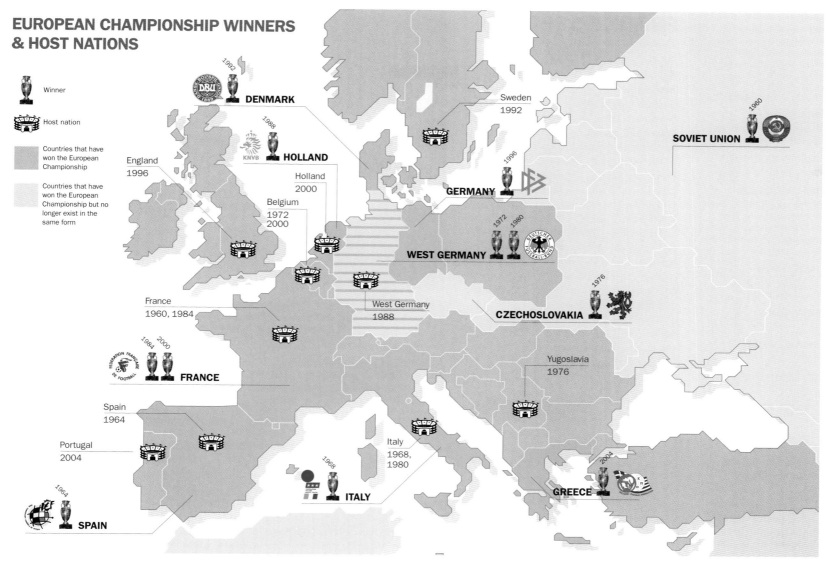

Winner

Host nation

Countries that have won the European Championship

Countries that have won the European Championship but no longer exist in the same form

DENMARK 1992

Sweden 1992

SOVIET UNION 1960

England 1996

HOLLAND 1988

GERMANY 1996

Holland 2000

Belgium 1972 2000

WEST GERMANY 1972 1980

CZECHOSLOVAKIA 1976

France 1960, 1984

West Germany 1988

Yugoslavia 1976

Spain 1964

Portugal 2004

Italy 1968, 1980

FRANCE 1984 2000

ITALY 1968

GREECE 2004

SPAIN 1964

under the inspirational captaincy of Michel Platini, swept all other teams aside, and for the third time in seven tournaments it was the hosts who claimed victory.

The format for the final stages of the 1988 and 1992 competition remained unaltered. The tournaments are best remembered for Dutch master Marco Van Basten's wonderstrike in the final against the Soviet Union in 1988, and for Denmark literally coming from nowhere to defeat the Germans in 1992 final. Having initially failed to qualify, Denmark were only playing as last-minute replacements for the suspended Yugoslavia.

The success of the tournament saw a further expansion in 1996 with 16 teams competing in four leagues to produce eight quarter-finalists. This was the tournament when football came home, as the success of Euro 96 went a long way to rehabilitating the reputation of English football, both on and off the pitch. Despite this, it was still Germany who claimed the trophy. A close final against the Czech Republic was notable for Oliver Bierhoff's 94th minute strike – it was the first time a golden goal winner had decided the outcome of a major international competition. Four years later, and France's David Trezeguet would be

repeating the trick against Italy to conclude another wonderful European final.

The 2004 competition in Portugal provided international football with one of its biggest shocks, as rank outsiders Greece beat the hosts to lift their first major trophy. With Euro 2008 to be split between Austria and Switzerland, the tournament continues to grow in strength and prestige every time it is played. All the football nations of Europe are now not only determined to qualify for the finals, but are also desperate to get their hands on the Henri Delaunay Trophy. But after the victory of Greece in 2004, anything seems possible.

PLAYER RATINGS

In our coverage of European Championship finals over the following pages, all available footage and match reports have been studied by an independent expert, with players awarded marks out of ten for their performance.

Red and yellow card information not available before 1984.

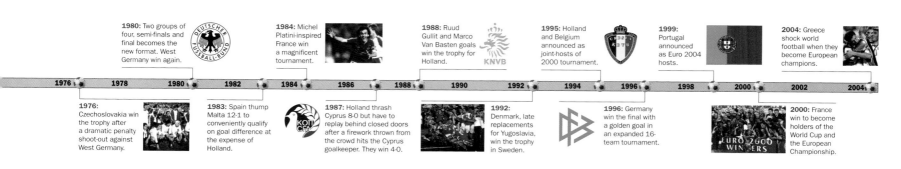

1980: Two groups of four, semi-finals and final becomes the new format. West Germany win again.

1984: Michel Platini-inspired France win a magnificent tournament.

1988: Ruud Gullit and Marco Van Basten goals win the trophy for Holland.

1995: Holland and Belgium announced as joint-hosts of 2000 tournament.

1999: Portugal announced as Euro 2004 hosts.

2004: Greece shock world football when they become European champions.

1976 1978 1980 1982 1984 1986 1988 1990 1992 1994 1996 1998 2000 2002 2004

1976: Czechoslovakia win the trophy after a dramatic penalty shoot-out against West Germany.

1983: Spain thump Malta 12-1 to conveniently qualify on goal difference at the expense of Holland.

1987: Holland thrash Cyprus 8-0 but have to replay behind closed doors after a firework thrown from the crowd hits the Cyprus goalkeeper. They win 4-0.

1992: Denmark, late replacements for Yugoslavia, win the trophy in Sweden.

1996: Germany win the final with a golden goal in an expanded 16-team tournament.

2000: France win to become holders of the World Cup and the European Championship.

FRANCE 1960

As France has provided the game of football with some of its greatest visionaries, it is no real surprise to discover that it was a Frenchman, Henri Delaunay, head of the French Football Federation, who came up with the idea for a tournament between Europe's top nations.

The European Championship, or the European Nations Cup as it was originally called, was finally established at the third UEFA Congress in Stockholm on June 6, 1958, but Delaunay had actually conceived the idea as far back as 1927. At that time, however, getting the World Cup off the ground was the priority. It was Delaunay who chaired the original commission set up by Jules Rimet in 1927 to look into a world football tournament and this took precedence.

When UEFA was created in 1954 Delaunay became its general secretary and rapidly installed two competitions, one for club teams and one for national sides. His aim was to bring into a single competition the three regional tournaments that already existed: the British Home Championship, the Nordic Cup and the Central European Championship. Sadly, Delaunay died in 1955 before he could see his scheme fulfilled, but his son Pierre took over the reins and the trophy was named in his father's honour.

It was agreed to hold the tournament once every four years, in between the World Cups, but UEFA initially struggled to find enough countries who were willing to compete and much behind the scenes negotiating went on to ensure that there was a competitive first tournament. The cause was not helped by the British teams; fearing the end of the Home Internationals, they refused to participate. Also refusing to enter were the 1958 World Cup hosts and runners-up Sweden, along with West Germany and Italy.

In the end 17 out of 33 countries affiliated to UEFA agreed to take part, and after a two-legged eliminator between Ireland and Czechoslovakia had whittled the number of sides down to an even 16 for the qualifiers, the first match in the European Nations Cup was played between the Soviet Union and Hungary.

The remaining 14 nations to enter the qualifying phase were Austria, Bulgaria, Czechoslovakia, Denmark, France, East Germany, Greece, Norway, Poland, Portugal, Romania, Spain, Turkey, and Yugoslavia. The entry fee was £50 and it was agreed gate receipts would be split 50-50 between FIFA and UEFA. The initial structure of the competition was very different from the European Championship as we know it today. Teams played home and away matches, the losing team being eliminated, and the winner proceeding to the next round.

There were further problems, too, when Spain were drawn against the Soviet Union. Under Helenio Herrera, and with stars like Di Stéfano, Suarez and Gento in their squad, the Spanish would have been strong contenders. However, Spain's fascist dictator, General Franco, refused to allow his nation to play against the Communists, Spain losing by default and putting the Soviets through to the semi-finals. Thus four games, the semi-finals, the third place play-off and the final, constituted the tournament proper and were played over five days between July 6 and 10 in Paris and Marseilles.

The hosts had to qualify in the same manner as the other sides, beating Austria convincingly to go through to a semi-final against Yugoslavia, a game which proved to be the most emotionally charged tie of the tournament. The French, third in the 1958 World Cup, were without Raymond Kopa and Golden Boot winner Just Fontaine, but put on a good performance to come back from an early deficit to lead Yugoslavia 4-2 just 15 minutes before the final whistle. However, Tomislav Knez started the comeback and two goals from Drazen Jerkovic were enough to knock France out and stun the host nation.

The Soviet Union proved much too strong for Czechoslovakia in the other semi-final, with Victor Ponedelnik, a poacher in the Jimmy Greaves mould, scoring twice as the USSR eased to a 3-0 win that brought them face to face with Yugoslavia in the final.

The match was a repeat of the 1956 Olympic Games final in Melbourne, which had been won 1-0 by the USSR. Whether this gave them a psychological advantage as the teams lined-up in the early evening at the Parc Des Princes is unclear, but the Soviets were to prove too strong for their opponents once more. They became the first team to lift the Henri Delaunay trophy after coming through in extra-time to win 2-1 and claim their first and only major tournament victory.

SEMI-FINALS

Soviet Union 3-0 Czechoslovakia
Yugoslavia 5-4 France

THIRD PLACE PLAY-OFF

Czechoslovakia 2-0 France

TOP GOALSCORERS

2 goals: François Heutte (France), Valentin Ivanov (Soviet Union), Victor Ponedelnik (Soviet Union), Milan Galic (Yugoslavia), Drazen Jerkovic (Yugoslavia)

FASTEST GOAL

11 minutes: Milan Gallic (Yugoslavia v France)

TOTAL GOALS

17

AVERAGE GOALS

4.25 per game

THE FINAL

SOVIET UNION (0) 2-1 (1) YUGOSLAVIA

(aet; 1-1 at 90 minutes)

Date Sunday July 10, 1960 **Attendance** 18,000

Venue Parc Des Princes, Paris

Played under floodlights in persistent drizzle on a heavy pitch, the inaugural European Nations Cup final was a credit to both sides. The conditions favoured the more technical skills of the Yugoslavs and they started strongly, eventually taking the lead in the 43rd minute as Galic nodded home after a cross by Jerkovic.

The Yugoslavs should have capitalised on several more opportunities, but Lev Yashin made some spectacular saves. Four minutes into the second-half the Soviets equalised through Metreveli and the match became increasingly tactical until the final whistle found both teams locked at 1-1. The Soviets proved stronger in extra-time and in the 113th minute, Ponedelnik headed home from Meshki's cross.

HOW THE TEAMS LINED UP

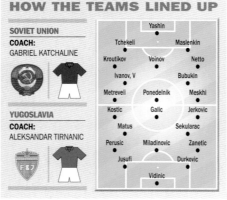

SOVIET UNION
COACH: GABRIEL KATCHALINE

YUGOSLAVIA
COACH: ALEKSANDAR TIRNANIC

SOVIET UNION

YASHIN	*8
TCHEKELI	6
MASLENKIN	6
KROUTIKOV	7
VOINOV	7
NETTO	7
IVANOV, V	7
BUBUKIN	6
METREVELI	7
Goal: 49 mins	
PONEDELNIK	7
Goal: 114 mins	
MESKHI	6

YUGOSLAVIA

VIDINIC	*8
DURKOVIC	6
JUSUFI	7
ZANETIC	5
MILADINOVIC	6
PERUSIC	6
SEKULARAC	5
MATUS	6
JERKOVIC	7
GALIC	7
Goal: 41 mins	
KOSTIC	6

Referee: Ellis (England)

Above: Hosts France took a 4-2 lead in their semi-final with Yugoslavia, only to be undone by three goals in the last 15 minutes. Opposite: The USSR and Yugoslavia battle out the first European Championship final under floodlights.

SEMI-FINALS
Spain 2-1 Hungary
(aet: 1-1 at 90 mins)
Soviet Union 3-0 Denmark

THIRD PLACE PLAY-OFF
Hungary 3-1 Denmark
(aet: 1-1 at 90 mins)

TOP GOALSCORERS
2 goals: Jesus Maria Pereda (Spain), Ferenc Bene (Hungary), Dezso Novák (Hungary)

FASTEST GOAL
6 minutes: Jesus Maria Pereda (Spain v Soviet Union)

TOTAL GOALS
13 goals

AVERAGE GOALS
3.25

SPAIN 1964

The European Championship was still in its infancy and struggling to make its mark in the international calendar. In 1963, however, one result in the qualifying stages captured the headlines and made Europe sit up and take notice. Luxembourg, with a population of just 300,000, produced a remarkable performance over two legs, beating Holland to achieve the greatest victory in their history and the first real upset of the fledgling competition.

Luxembourg's triumph fired the public imagination, but to make matters worse for the humiliated Dutch, both legs were played in their own country. The first, in Amsterdam in September 1963, ended in a 1-1 draw as Nuninga gave the Holland the lead after five minutes, with May equalising half an hour later. The second leg, played in Rotterdam, saw a host of changes in the Dutch line-up but Dimmer gave Luxembourg a shock lead. After Kruiver equalised the outsiders survived an onslaught before Dimmer grabbed an unexpected second 23 minutes from time to seal a famous victory.

Amazingly Luxembourg nearly repeated the feat against Denmark in the quarter-finals, drawing 3-3 and 2-2 before losing the play-off 1-0, a game played, ironically, on neutral territory in Amsterdam. They may have been knocked out but they had created the sensation of the competition and the biggest success in their history. Elsewhere, France crushed England over two legs, while Italy also lost out.

Despite earlier shocks the latter stages had a familiar look, as Spain, Hungary, the Soviet Union and Denmark won through to the last four, with the finals to be played in Spain. The finals took place over four days in June 1964.

While the football was of a decent standard, it failed to grab the attention in the way of the World Cup. Luxembourg's giant-killing acts were entertaining at the time but the spread of matches over a lengthy period did little to concentrate the minds of fans across Europe, and with only four teams making the finals it had little mass appeal.

But there were still players to admire. Spain were favourites thanks to home advantage and the wing skills of Luis Suarez, while the Soviet Union had the best goalkeeper in the world in Lev Yashin, and Hungary's centre-forward Florian Albert, later a European Footballer Of The Year, was a superbly balanced striker who gave hope to his ageing side.

In the semi-final Spain met Hungary in Madrid in front of a crowd of 125,000 that witnessed Jose Villalonga's side make it through to the final in extra-time. Pereda gave them a first-half lead from Suarez's cross, before Bene struck an equaliser six minutes before full-time. It took an Amancio goal in the 115th minute to decide the outcome.

In the other semi-final, the Soviet Union saw off outsiders Denmark with a comfortable 3-0 victory in the Nou Camp to set up a final that would see if Spain could finally match the club achievements of Real Madrid with a national team triumph.

They did, and with it came Spain's first major trophy. It was a fitting tribute to the country that had dominated club football for half a decade – but the national team was not moulded in the same style. They lacked the flair, the grace and the sheer dazzling brilliance of the famous Madrid team in white. Despite offering flashes of skill from Suarez and Amancio, both among the best players in the world at the time, the Spanish generation of 1964 would not go down in history as one of the country's greatest sides.

Above: Spain celebrate winning the European Nations Cup on home soil. Opposite: Soviet Union keeper Lev Yashin concedes the opening goal in the final at the Bernebéu.

THE FINAL

SPAIN (1) **2-1** (1) SOVIET UNION

Date Sunday June 21, 1964 **Attendance** 125,000
Venue Santiago Bernabéu, Madrid

The largest ever crowd to watch a European Championship final turned up to see the home side lift the trophy. They did, but only just. It was a tense affair, although in front of dictator General Franco the Spanish got off to a dream start with a sixth-minute goal from Pereda. Khusainov struck back two minutes later and the Soviets packed their defence, inside-left Kornaev playing as an extra defender.

All the talk in the build-up about Lev Yashin facing the deft skills of the Spanish attack came to little on the big day, although Suarez was in outstanding form. Spain finally found a way through, Zaragoza centre-forward Marcelino scoring the winner with a diving header from Pereda's cross in the 84th minute. The Soviets, with so little time to come back, were beaten.

HOW THE TEAMS LINED UP

SPAIN
COACH: JOSE VILLALONGA

SOVIET UNION
COACH: KONSTANTIN BESKOV

Iribar
Rivilla — Olivella
Calleja — Zoco — Fuste
Pereda — Suarez
Amancio — Marcelino — Lapetra
Khusainov — Ponedelnik — Chislenko
Korneev — Ivanov, V
Anichkin — Voronin — Mudrik
Shesternev — Chustikov
Yashin

SPAIN	
IRIBAR	6
RIVILLA	7
OLIVELLA	7
CALLEJA	6
ZOCO	7
FUSTE	7
PEREDA	7
Goal: 6 mins	
SUAREZ	*9
AMANCIO	7
MARCELINO	8
Goal: 84 mins	
LAPETRA	6

SOVIET UNION	
YASHIN	*8
CHUSTIKOV	6
SHESTERNEV	6
MUDRIK	7
VORONIN	6
ANICHKIN	7
IVANOV, V	6
KORNEEV	7
CHISLENKO	6
PONEDELNIK	6
KHUSAINOV	6
Goal: 8 mins	

Referee: Holland (England)

ITALY 1968

The competition to win the Henri Delaunay Trophy underwent a change of name and format in 1968, as the European Nations Cup became the European Football Championship. The original two-legged knockout tournament was dropped and for the first time replaced with eight qualifying groups totalling a record 31 teams, including newcomers Scotland and West Germany. The eight group winners qualified for the quarter-finals, which were played over two legs.

The big tie of the quarter-finals pitched World Cup-winners England against the defending European champions Spain. Bobby Charlton scored the only goal of the first leg at Wembley, and in the return England won 2-1 in Madrid with goals from Martin Peters and Norman Hunter.

Italy were named as hosts of the latter stages of the tournament after a magnificent 4-3 aggregate win over Bulgaria's best-ever side, featuring the likes of Hristo Bonev and Petar Jekov. It was Jekov who had clinched the winner in a five-goal thriller in Sofia, but in Naples a fortnight later Italy became the first team to qualify for the semi-finals, winning 2-0 with goals from Prati and Domenghini.

Yugoslavia's young and energetic team easily overcame France, after a 1-1 draw in Marseille they thrashed the French 5-1 in Belgrade with two goals each from Petkovic and Musemic, and a single strike from Dzajic.

The best performance in the quarter-finals was by the Soviet Union, who overturned

Above: The Soviets before their play-off with England. Opposite clockwise from top left: Italy dominated the final replay; Facchetti celebrates winning the decisive toss after the USSR semi; England's Bobby Charlton; Italy before the final replay.

a 2-0 defeat by Hungary in Budapest with a magnificent home performance in Moscow, running out 3-2 aggregate winners. It was a tremendous comeback against a team who, later the same year, would be crowned as Olympic champions.

The Soviet Union's reward was a semi-final clash with hosts Italy in Naples. A hard enough challenge in itself, team selection was made even harder by circumstances when winger Igor Chislenko and half-back Murtaz Khurtzilava sustained injuries in an Olympic qualifier against Czechoslovakia just days before. It all meant that team manager Mikhail Yakushin arrived in Italy with an injury-decimated squad.

The 75,000 crowd in the San Paulo Stadium were forced to witness a dreadful game, played in appalling weather conditions, between a makeshift Soviet side and an Italian team with a mortal fear of losing. The Soviets did dominate the first-half, but they squandered the few good chances they created. After the break Rivera returned to the pitch following an enforced first-half absence caused by a collision with the Soviet full-back Afonin, and an impatient Italian crowd saw their team improving to get the better of the second-half. This time, however, it was the turn of the Soviet defence to hold firm. The closing minutes saw Italy produce attack after attack, during which Domenghini hit the post, but even extra-time brought no goals. So a place in the 1968 European Championship final was decided in the dressing room with the spin of a 1916 French ten-franc coin. The hosts won the toss and it was Italy who progressed to the final.

The other semi-final in Florence between favourites England and the gifted young Yugoslav side was equally dismal. Played in a humid, thundery atmosphere, one reporter described the match as a technical dirge. It was a frustrating game involving uncompromising tackling from both sides. After just five minutes England's Norman Hunter had inflicted an ankle injury on Yugoslavian playmaker Ivica Osim, making him a virtual passenger for the rest of the game. It set the tone for the rest of the match and there were a staggering 49 free-kicks awarded.

The decisive action took place in the 85th minute when the excellent Dragan Dzajic beat goalkeeper Gordon Banks with an exquisite volley that proved to be the winning goal. It got worse for England before the final whistle when Alan Mullery, after being ruthlessly brought down by Trivic, retaliated with a blatant kick on his assailant. He became the first England player ever to be sent-off, and that in 96 years of international football.

England, without the suspended Mullery, the injured Alan Ball, and hayfever sufferer Colin Bell, recovered to win an entertaining Third Place Play-Off clash with the Soviet Union. Goals from Bobby Charlton and Geoff Hurst gave an England a deserved 2-0 win.

SEMI-FINALS

Italy **0-0** Soviet Union
(aet: Italy won on toss of coin)
Yugoslavia **1-0** England

THIRD PLACE PLAY-OFF

England **2-0** Soviet Union

TOP GOALSCORER

2 goals: Dragan Dzajic
(Yugoslavia)

FASTEST GOAL

11 mins: Gigi Riva
(Italy v Yugoslavia replay)

TOTAL GOALS

7

AVERAGE GOALS

1.4 per game

FINAL GAME

ITALY

ZOFF	7
BURGNICH	6
FACCHETTI	*8
FERRINI	7
GUARNERI	6
CASTANO	5
DOMENGHINI	7
Goal: 80 mins	
JULIANO	5
LODETTI	7
ANASTASI	7
PRATI	6

YUGOSLAVIA

PANTELIC	*9
FAZLAGIC	8
DAMJANOVIC	7
PAVLOVIC	6
PAUNOVIC	7
HOLCER	8
TRIVIC	7
ACIMOVIC	7
PETKOVIC	6
MUSEMIC	6
DZAJIC	7
Goal: 39 mins	

Referee: Dienst (Switzerland)

THE FINAL

ITALY (0) **1-1** (1) **YUGOSLAVIA** (aet)

Date Saturday June 8, 1968 **Attendance** 69,000
Venue Olympic Stadium, Rome

Italy were favourites but Yugoslavia dominated. Goalkeeper Dino Zoff kept Italy in the game, but was unable to stop Dzajic scoring in the 39th minute. The inability to beat Zoff again proved Yugoslavia's undoing. With ten minutes to go Domenghini's 25-yard free-kick crashed in. Extra-time saw no goals.

REPLAY

ITALY (2) **2-0** (0) **YUGOSLAVIA**

Date Monday June 10, 1968 **Attendance** 50,000
Venue Olympic Stadium, Rome

Italy made five changes and in came Rosato, Salvadore, Mazzola, De Sisti and Riva. The transformed team dominated and Yugoslavia never recovered after Italy's magnificent start. Riva scored with a great left-foot shot early on and after 32 minutes Anastasi fired on the turn to make it 2-0.

REPLAY

ITALY

ZOFF	7
BURGNICH	6
FACCHETTI	6
SALVADORE	7
GUARNERI	7
ROSATO	6
DOMENGHINI	6
MAZZOLA	*9
DE SISTI	7
ANASTASI	8
Goal: 32 mins	
RIVA	7
Goal: 11 mins	

YUGOSLAVIA

PANTELIC	*8
FAZLAGIC	7
DAMJANOVIC	6
PAVLOVIC	6
PAUNOVIC	6
HOLCER	5
TRIVIC	5
ACIMOVIC	5
HOSIC	5
MUSEMIC	6
DZAJIC	7

Referee: Ortiz de Mendibil (Spain)

HOW THE TEAMS LINED UP

Zoff
Burgnich Facchetti Ferrini Guarneri
Castano Domenghini Juliano Lodetti
Anastasi Prati
Dzajic Musemic Petkovic Acimovic
Trivic Holcer
Paunovic Pavlovic Damjanovic Fazlagic
Pantelic

ITALY
COACH: FERRUCCIO VALCAREGGI

YUGOSLAVIA
COACH: RAJKO MITIC

Zoff
Burgnich Facchetti Salvadore Guarneri
Rosato Domenghini Mazzola De Sisti
Anastasi Riva
Dzajic Musemic Hosic Acimovic
Trivic Holcer
Paunovic Pavlovic Damjanovic Fazlagic
Pantelic

Above: The Soviet Union line up before the final. Below right: Paul Van Himst of Belgium on the ball against West Germany. Opposite clockwise from top: Gerd Müller lifts the trophy after West Germany's 3-0 victory; West Germany charge forward; Müller nets one of his two goals; the Germans inspect the trophy.

BELGIUM 1972

It may not be remembered as one of the great international football tournaments of all time, but the 1972 European Championship was significant for one reason: it saw West Germany pick up their first major international trophy since the 1954 World Cup, beginning a golden era of almost 25 years that would see the Germans become arguably the most powerful nation in world football.

To be fair to the Germans, the success had been coming. Finishing a creditable third behind the greatest Brazilian team of all time at the 1970 World Cup had indicated there was something special to come, but 1972 saw the new young team built by coach Helmut Schön truly come of age.

Qualifying for the tournament had begun in 1970, with 32 European nations involved. Italy and West Germany were among the favourites, as both had come into the tournament off the back of promising World Cup campaigns, finishing as runners-up and third respectively. England, meanwhile, were also still considered to be a major football power, despite failing to live up to expectations in Mexico.

In the first qualifying phase, these three each finished top of their groups and remained unbeaten, while the Soviet Union also came through impressively without losing a single game, making them serious contenders for a place in the final.

The quarter-finals saw Hungary eliminate Romania 2-1 in a play-off, the original two-legged encounter finishing 3-3, while the Soviet side cruised through 3-0 against Yugoslavia, their vanquished opponents in the first ever European Championship final. A physical Belgian outfit muscled past Italy, winning 2-1 on aggregate, but the big tie of the round was undoubtedly West Germany against England.

West Germany travelled to Wembley in April 1972 and completed an impressive 3-1 away win in the first leg, the first ever win by Germany on English soil. This result was enough to see them through as the return match ended in a scoreless draw.

Belgium was voted host nation for the final stages and they were drawn against the West Germans, who had now emerged as clear favourites. Home advantage counted for little for the Belgians, as so many German fans made the relatively short trip to Antwerp to cheer on their team. Belgium started well enough, containing the German threat, but a great header from Müller gave the favourites the lead going in at half-time. The Belgians, to their credit, threw men forward in the second period and brought some great saves out of the young German goalkeeper Sepp Maier, but the game turned decisively in West Germany's favour in the 71st minute when Müller put his side two up. Belgium pulled a goal back late on but it was to no avail.

While a crowd of nearly 60,000 had watched the hosts lose the first semi-final, the live televising of the game meant that only 2,000 fans were at the Parc Astrid in Brussels to witness a disappointing display between two of Eastern Europe's top football nations. The skilful Hungarians faced the Soviet Union, a nation with an impressive record in the tournament. But with neither side threatening in the first-half, the game only came to life when Konkov blasted the Soviets in front after the break. Hungary rallied but failed to equalise, even missing a late penalty.

Before the final came the third place play-off. Another disappointing crowd of only 10,000 saw Belgium live up to their physical reputation, grinding out a 2-1 win over the Hungarians.

Three days later at the Heysel Stadium in Brussels, West Germany, playing in front of a largely German crowd, faced the Soviet

THE FINAL

WEST GERMANY (1) **3-0** (0) SOVIET UNION

Date Sunday June 18, 1972 **Attendance** 43,437
Venue Heysel Stadium, Brussels

The West Germans were on the offensive from the start, mounting wave after wave of attack. Netzer controlled the midfield, impressively supported by sweeper Beckenbauer, while Gerd Müller ran the Soviet defence ragged. Heroics early on from the Soviet keeper Rudakov kept the Germans at bay until late in the first-half when Müller met a cross with his chest, brought the ball down and slotted home.

The Germans raised their game after the break, limiting the Soviets to just three shots in the game. The excellent Wimmer played a one-two with Heynckes, before crashing the ball home to put daylight between the two sides. Five minutes later, Müller scored the third goal of the game, wrong-footing the goalkeeper. It made him the tournament's top scorer.

HOW THE TEAMS LINED UP

WEST GERMANY
COACH:
HELMUT SCHÖN

SOVIET UNION
COACH:
ALEKSANDR PONOMAREV

Maier

Höttges Schwarzenbeck Beckenbauer Breitner

Wimmer Hoeness, U Netzer

Heynckes Müller, G Kremers, E

Onishenko Banishevsky Baidachni

Konkov Troshkin Kolotov

Istomin Kaplichny Khurtsilava Dzodzuashvili

Rudakov

Union as clear favourites. Beckenbauer and his team-mates did not disappoint lifting the trophy with a comprehensive 3-0 victory.

The tournament's best team had won and it wouldn't be the last time a German side would return from a major international competition brandishing silverware. Despite it only being the very beginning of a long and successful spell, many critics now believe that this was the best of all the great German sides, even better than the team who went on to lift the World Cup two years later.

WEST GERMANY	
MAIER	7
HÖTTGES	6
BECKENBAUER	8
SCHWARZENBECK	7
BREITNER	7
HOENESS, U	7
WIMMER	8
Goal: 52 mins	
NETZER	*9
HEYNCKES	6
MÜLLER, G	8
Goal: 27 mins, 58 mins	
KREMERS, E	6

SOVIET UNION	
RUDAKOV	*8
DZODZUASHVILI	7
ISTOMIN	6
KHURTSILAVA	7
KAPLICHNY	6
KOLOTOV	6
TROSHKIN	6
BAIDACHNI	7
BANISHEVSKY	5
Subbed: 66 mins (Kozinkevich)	
KONKOV	5
Subbed: 46 mins (Dolmatov)	
ONISHENKO	7
sub: KOZINKEVICH	6
sub: DOLMATOV	6

Referee: Marschall (Austria)

SEMI-FINALS

West Germany 2-1 Belgium
Soviet Union 1-0 Hungary

THIRD PLACE PLAY-OFF

Belgium 2-1 Hungary

TOP GOALSCORER

4 goals: Gerd Müller (West Germany)

FASTEST GOAL

24 mins: Raul Lambert (Belgium v Hungary); Gerd Müller (West Germany v Belgium)

TOTAL GOALS

10

AVERAGE GOALS

2.5 per game

YUGOSLAVIA 1976

If you were to imagine the most unlikely conclusion to a major final, it would probably involve the world champions losing with the last kick of the tournament. But in 1976, that's exactly what happened.

In a brief but exhilarating competition, restricted to only four teams and four days, Czechoslovakia lifted the Henri Delaunay Trophy when the usually nerveless West German team suffered an uncharacteristic outbreak of penalty shoot-out nerves. However, the 1976 championship was about so much more than Uli Hoeness's hoof over the bar. At the peak of a golden era of European football, brilliant, attacking play dominated throughout and the underdog prevailed.

Yugoslavia 76 was one of the most closely fought major tournaments ever staged. Every match, both semi-finals, the final and third-place play-off went into extra-time. The quality of play throughout was both exhilarating and, for those not involved, a chilling reminder of how far the game had moved on, led by Dutch Total Football and the powerful athleticism of West Germany. For some traditional footballing powers,

Above: The victorious Czech team. Opposite clockwise from top left: The final was a close affair between the Czechs and West Germany; the Czechs lift the cup after a penalty shoot-out; an exhausted Franz Beckenbauer; Ivo Viktor celebrates.

SEMI-FINALS
Czechoslovakia 3-1 Holland
(aet: 1-1 at 90 mins)
West Germany 4-2 Yugoslavia
(aet: 2-2 at 90 mins)

THIRD PLACE PLAY-OFF
Holland 3-2 Yugoslavia
(aet: 2-2 at 90 mins)

TOP GOALSCORER
4 goals: Dieter Müller (West Germany)

FASTEST GOAL
8 mins: Jan Svehlík (Czechoslovakia v West Germany)

TOTAL GOALS
19

AVERAGE GOALS
4.75 per game

THE FINAL

CZECHOSLOVAKIA (2) 2-2 (1) WEST GERMANY
(aet: Czechoslovakia won 5-3 on penalties)

Date Sunday June 20, 1976 **Attendance** 35,000

Venue Red Star Stadium, Belgrade

The highly-fancied Germans were stunned by Czechoslovakia's attacking start, and after 25 minutes they were 2-0 down to goals from Svehlík and Dobiás. Müller grabbed one back straight away, but the Czechs looked to be holding on. Wave after wave of West German attacks finally paid off with a dramatic equaliser in the final minute. Now nothing, it appeared, could deny Beckenbauer another trophy in his 100th international appearance. But the Czechs were kept alive in extra-time by keeper Viktor and the game was settled by penalties. When Hoeness blasted over and Panenka slotted home, the trophy was on its way to Prague.

CZECHOSLOVAKIA	
VIKTOR	7
PIVARNÍK	6
ONDRUS	7
CAPKOVIC	7
GÖGH	7
DOBIÁS	8
Goal: 25 mins. Subbed: 94 mins (Vesely)	
MÓDER	8
PANENKA	7
MASNY	*9
SVEHLÍK	7
Goal: 8 mins. Subbed: 79 mins (Jurkemik)	
NEHODA	7
sub: JURKEMIK	7
sub: VESELY	7

WEST GERMANY	
MAIER	7
VÖGTS	7
SCHWARZENBECK	6
BECKENBAUER	*8
DIETZ	6
WIMMER	6
Subbed: 46 mins (Flohe)	
BONHOF	7
BEER	5
Subbed: 80 mins (Bongartz)	
HOENESS, U	5
MÜLLER, D	7
Goal: 28 mins	
HÖLZENBEIN	7
Goal: 89 mins	
sub: FLOHE	5
sub: BONGARTZ	6

Referee: Gonella (Italy)

HOW THE TEAMS LINED UP

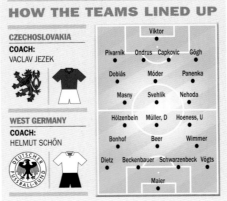

CZECHOSLOVAKIA
COACH: VACLAV JEZEK

Viktor
Pivarník Ondrus Capkovic Gögh
Dobiás Móder Panenka
Masny Svehlík Nehoda

WEST GERMANY
COACH: HELMUT SCHÖN

Hölzenbein Müller, D Hoeness, U
Bonhof Beer Wimmer
Dietz Beckenbauer Schwarzenbeck Vögts
Maier

Yugoslavia 76 rudely showed how far the game had changed and how far they were being left behind. Italy, World Cup finalists just six years earlier, only finished third in their group during qualification.

England, world champions ten years earlier, also failed to progress beyond the group stages, although typically false promise came before the fall. In the opening match of their qualification group, Don Revie's team trounced the eventual winners of the tournament 3-0 at Wembley. Defeat in the return fixture, coupled with an inability to beat Portugal either home or away, spelled elimination as group runners-up one point behind the Czechs.

Qualification for the quarter-finals was a straightforward battle for supremacy across eight groups. Of the British nations, only Wales made it this far after overcoming a group containing Hungary, Austria and Luxembourg. Quarter-finals over two legs then determined which four teams would receive their exclusive invites to the midsummer festival of football.

Yugoslavia made sure they wouldn't miss the party by beating Wales 2-0 at home, then drawing 1-1 in Cardiff. The other bright spot for the British teams was Don Givens, whose eight goals for Northern Ireland in the qualification phase wasn't bettered during the entire tournament.

Joining the hosts in the last four were West Germany, the outrageously talented Holland and the neat but lightly fancied Czechoslovakia. Such a brief tournament needed to catch fire immediately, and in a sensational opening game three players were sent-off as Holland crashed out. For Johan Cruyff and his team-mates, this tournament, sandwiched between their two World Cup final appearances, should have been payback time for their 1974 World Cup final defeat by West Germany. But instead they again paid the price for overconfidence, ending their game against the Czechs with nine men. Their opponents scored two goals in extra-time to run out 3-1 winners.

Holland's exit appeared to pave the way for West Germany. They duly earned their place in the final courtesy of a 4-2 defeat of the hosts, although it was much closer than the score suggests. In one of the competition's classic encounters, watched by 70,000 fans in Belgrade, Yugoslavia raced into a two-goal lead with little more than 30 minutes played. They were still a goal to the good with ten minutes remaining when West Germany brought on Dieter Müller. Within two minutes he had equalised to send the match into extra-time, where he netted twice more to complete his hat-trick and Yugoslavia's misery.

Utterly deflated, the Yugoslavs did well to force the third-place play-off against Holland into extra-time, where Geels scored the winning goal to enable the Dutch to edge the game 3-2 and gain scant consolation in front of a crowd of just 7,000.

All eyes now focused on Belgrade: could the Czechs, a talented but hardly feared football power, possibly match the might of the confident, powerful world champions? Franz Beckenbauer was at the height of his powers and his side contained incredible talent, even by the high standards of the mid-Seventies.

Müller's three goals in the semi-final were enough to retain his place in the German starting line-up, but in Viktor, crowd favourites the Czechs boasted the goalkeeper of the tournament. He was kept busy in a final match that proved worthy of this wonderful tournament, and one that eventually resulted in a surprise win for the Czechs.

ITALY 1980

With the 1976 European Championship in Yugoslavia hailed an unmitigated success of skill, technique and drama, the tournament played out some four years later was nothing short of disastrous.

Negative football, poor refereeing and hooliganism were the abiding memories of Euro 80, while the depressing statistic of just 1.93 goals per game no doubt contributed to attendances that dropped as low as 9,000 for the Czechoslovakia v Greece game. Even the opening fixture between West Germany and the Czechs attracted just 11,000 fans in Rome. In hindsight, staying away was a wise choice considering the fear-riddled game that was settled by a Rummenigge header.

With the competition split into two groups of four teams, and the winners of each group contesting the final, the formula was a disaster waiting to happen. Teams that lost their opening fixture invariably had a mountain to climb and therefore played out meaningless ties, while those in contention for the top spot approached games in a chess-like fashion rather than expressing their true capabilities.

Indeed, it explained why Greece, in their first major tournament, were regarded as the most expressive team in Group One, despite losing their opening games against Holland and the Czechs. A creditable stalemate with West Germany secured their fate, but the fact that a team who ended up with one point were the most talked about of the competition spoke volumes for the entertainment on show.

England, again, flattered to deceive and their opening fixture against Belgium in Turin was shrouded in controversy and disgrace. With 15 minutes to play and the game poised at 1-1, German referee Aldinger disallowed a perfectly valid goal by Woodcock for offside, prompting clashes between fans and riot police on the terraces. The game had already been halted for three minutes in the first-half, following Ceulemans' equaliser, which left England keeper Clemence needing treatment for the effects of tear gas.

With Italy drawing their opening fixture 0-0 against Spain, and all four teams in Group B with a point apiece, the hosts' clash with England was billed as a war of attrition, both on and off the terraces. Yet while the visiting fans remained calm, the players received a battering by an Italian team determined to stay in the competition at all costs. In a game of cat and mouse played out in front of 59,000 supporters, a rare slip by Liverpool full-back Phil Neal proved costly as Tardelli headed home with just 11 minutes remaining.

Although England went on to beat Spain 2-1 in Naples, it was left to Belgium and Italy to fight out a place in the final. Having beaten Spain 2-1, Guy Thys' side knew that a draw

against the Italians would see them progress on goal difference, thus causing one of the all-time tournament shocks. With a vociferous 60,000 crowd behind them in Rome the Italians failed spectacularly in a game riddled with bookings and defensive football. The 0-0 stalemate was enough to see Belgium through. Italy were undone by their defensive instincts, scoring just one goal in three games.

With Holland and West Germany winning their opening games in Group One, it was assumed that both would fight it out for a place in the final, yet with the Cruyff-inspired Total Football conspicuous by its absence, the Dutch were put to the sword in their pivotal second game against the Germans. The 3-2 scoreline flattered the Dutch, and only in their final group game against the Czechs did the real Holland emerge. But by then the 1-1 draw was too little too late and they even lost out on a third place play-off appearance.

West Germany's final points tally of five indicated their dominance in a group that rarely saw them break sweat. Without the likes of Beckenbauer, Bonhof and Müller, they still reached the final by playing only 60 minutes of top-quality football against Holland, where they established a 3-0 lead before taking their foot off the pedal. Safe in the knowledge that a place in the final was assured, West Germany played out a 0-0 draw in their final group game against the Greeks.

The hope was that the final would be the tournament's saving grace, and the omens were good as the third place play-off preamble proved an exciting affair in Naples. With extra-time banished in the hope of more attacking football, Czechoslovakia took the lead against the hosts when Jurkemik scored in the 53rd minute from a Panenka corner. The strike prompted the Italians to emerge from their tournament slumber and they were finally rewarded when a Causio free-kick was headed home by Graziani with 17 minutes remaining.

The Czechs should have wrapped the game up when Nehoda's shot was brilliantly saved by Zoff late in the game, but Barmos silenced the home side with the winner in a 9-8 penalty shoot-out spectacular.

Above: The Italians went out in the semi-finals. Opposite clockwise from top left: Horst Hrubesch scored both goals in West Germany's final win; Karl Heinz Rummenigge clears; Schuster takes on the Belgian defence; West Germany celebrate.

THE FINAL

WEST GERMANY (1) 2-1 (0) BELGIUM

Date Sunday June 22, 1980 **Attendance** 47,864
Venue Olympic Stadium, Rome

Belgium's refusal to play the bridesmaid ensured a lacklustre ten days of football were brought to an exciting climax. The pattern was set as early as the 10th minute, when an inch-perfect pass from Schuster was met by 20-year-old Hamburg striker Horst Hrubesch, who rounded Millecamps before sliding his shot into the corner of the net.

The goal brought Belgium out of their shell, but the West Germans should have doubled their lead when Schuster and Allofs brought fine saves out of goalkeeper Pfaff before the break.

The Belgians drew level with Vandereycken's penalty, awarded for a challenge from Stielike on Van der Elst which was clearly outside the box, but with a minute remaining, Hrubesch met Karl-Heinz Rummenigge's corner to win it for the West Germans.

HOW THE TEAMS LINED UP

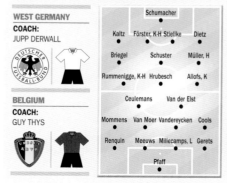

WEST GERMANY
COACH:
JUPP DERWALL

BELGIUM
COACH:
GUY THYS

WEST GERMANY	
SCHUMACHER	6
KALTZ	7
FÖRSTER, K-H	7
STIELIKE	8
DIETZ	6
BRIEGEL	7
Subbed: 55 mins (Cullmann)	
SCHUSTER	*9
MÜLLER, H	6
ALLOFS, K	7
RUMMENIGGE, K-H	7
HRUBESCH ⚽⚽	8
Goal: 10 mins, 88 mins	
sub: **CULLMANN**	6

BELGIUM	
PFAFF	7
GERETS	7
MILLECAMPS, L	6
MEEUWS	*8
RENQUIN	5
COOLS	6
VANDEREYCKEN ⚽	7
Goal: 72 mins (pen)	
VAN MOER	6
MOMMENS	7
VAN DER ELST	7
CEULEMANS	5

Referee: Rainea (Romania)

FRANCE 1984

Above: Michel Platini opens the final scoring from this free kick. Opposite clockwise from top left: Platini on the attack again; Platini gets his hands on the Henri Delaunay Trophy, France's first major honour; the French team greets the final whistle with joy; mixed emotions as Spanish keeper Luis Arconada allows Platini's free-kick to slip through his grasp.

For the French, the 1984 European Championship represented nothing less than a date with destiny. The country was in danger of becoming famous for instigating major football tournaments without ever actually winning them. Two years earlier, at the World Cup, they had exuded quality before being physically battered by West Germany in Seville and losing their nerve in a semi-final they should have won. Now they were desperate to make amends and fulfil their promise. As hosts for the second time, they knew they might never have a better opportunity.

Against this background the 1984 European Championship produced some of the finest football the tournament has ever seen. The final competition was restricted to just eight teams, making qualification a reasonably tight affair, and by the opening game in June 1984 there were some notable absentees, including World Cup holders Italy, who finished a dreadful qualifying campaign second from bottom of their group. Also absent were Holland, Sweden and the Soviet Union, while the failure of England, Scotland, Northern Ireland and Wales to get through to the finals made it a disastrous clean sweep for the British Isles.

England were largely in transition under new manager Bobby Robson. They came second in their group behind Denmark after a 1-0 defeat at home. As the cream of Europe assembled in France that June they went off to play a friendly tournament in South America, ironically throwing up one of the enduring images of English football when John Barnes scored a wonderful solo effort in the Maracanã.

There was no great shame in losing to Denmark as it turned out, because they were an emerging football nation with world class talents like Preben Elkjaer and Michael Laudrup in their ranks. The Danes would go as far as the semi-finals.

In advance of the competition it was clear that the home nation and World Cup runners-up, West Germany, were the favourites. Under Michel Hidalgo Les Bleus were, if anything, an even stronger outfit than they had been two years previous – particularly with the addition of Joel Bats in goal, probably the country's finest ever goalkeeper, and Luis Fernandez in midfield. They also boasted a tight defence that was still being carefully orchestrated by the dependable Maxime Bossis. That, in turn, sat behind possibly the best midfield in the world, even if they were nearly all in their thirties. The only question mark hung over the team's lack of true strike power, which is where Platini's presence was to prove crucial.

Once the tournament got under way France eased through Group A, winning all of their games, which included a 5-0 thumping of neighbours Belgium. Platini was already hitting form, scoring two perfect hat-tricks (left foot, right foot, header) in succession. Denmark qualified for the semi-finals behind them in second place.

The real shock of the competition came in Group B, with holders West Germany failing to make the semi-finals. Even though they were held to a draw by Portugal, the Germans were still tipped to progress to the later stages. However, a last-minute header by Antonio Maceda in their final group showdown with Spain sent them home stunned and cost unpopular coach Jupp Derwall his job. Spain, who also missed a penalty in that match, took their place in the last four, with Portugal completing the semi-final line-up.

The first semi-final, on June 23, paired France with Portugal in the Stade Vélodrome in a match now regarded as a classic. After a slow start to the game France scored first through a Domergue free-kick, before being pegged back to 1-1 by a Jordao header with 16 minutes remaining. The home side then conceded a second goal in extra-time before Domergue, on his 27th birthday, scored again. With the prospect looming of a penalty shoot-out, one that France surely would have lost if recent form was anything to go by, Platini lashed home a Jean Tigana cross to put them through to the final with just 64 seconds remaining on the clock.

The other semi-final between Denmark and Spain was just as tight, if a little less open, and with the two sides locked at 1-1 it was Danish nerves that failed to hold in the penalty shoot-out, Preben Elkjaer knocking the decisive fifth kick over the bar.

Nothing now was going to deny Les Bleus from seizing their moment. The European Championship trophy was named after a Frenchman, and now the name of the French team appeared to be already engraved on it. Despite the weight of expectation, Platini's nerve held and he led his team to victory with his ninth goal in five games. The final proved to be one of his quieter matches, but he was rightly named the player of the tournament.

SEMI-FINALS

France 3-2 Portugal
(aet: 1-1 at 90 mins)

Spain 1-1 Denmark
(aet: Spain won 5-4 on penalties)

THIRD PLACE PLAY-OFF

Did not take place

TOP GOALSCORER

9 goals: Michel Platini (France)

FASTEST GOAL

3 mins: Michel Platini
(France v Belgium)

TOTAL GOALS

41

AVERAGE GOALS

2.73 per game

THE FINAL

FRANCE (0) 2-0 (0) SPAIN

Date Wednesday June 27, 1984 **Attendance** 47,368

Venue Parc Des Princes, Paris

The 1984 final started with some robust play from the Spaniards, designed no doubt to unsettle the hosts, which had the home crowd whistling. The Czech referee, Christov, quickly clamped down and play began to flow from end to end. Giresse had a shot as early as the first minute, but nevertheless there was no score at half-time. When the second-half started the French began to look edgy as they attempted to break the Spanish down, and it took a bad mistake from goalkeeper Arconada to settle Gallic nerves when he let a Platini free-kick squeeze past him. Spain held on and searched for an equaliser, but as they committed more men forward, in the closing moments Bellone was able to break clear and chip over the goalkeeper to seal the game.

FRANCE

BATS	7
BATTISTON	6
Subbed: 72 mins (Amoros)	
LE ROUX	7
Sent-off: 85 mins	
BOSSIS	7
DOMERGUE	6
TIGANA	8
FERNANDEZ	7
PLATINI	*9
Goal: 57 mins	
GIRESSE	8
LACOMBE	6
Subbed: 80 mins (Genghini)	
BELLONE	7
Goal: 90 mins	
sub: AMOROS	6
sub: GENGHINI	5

SPAIN

ARCONADA	5
URQUIAGA	6
SALVA	7
Subbed: 85 mins (Roberto)	
GALLEGO	*8
Booked.	
SENOR	6
FRANCISCO	6
VICTOR	5
CAMACHO	7
JULIO ALBERTO	6
Subbed: 77 mins (Sarabia)	
SANTILLANA	6
CARRASCO	7
Booked.	
sub: ROBERTO	5
sub: SARABIA	5

Referee: Christov (Czechoslovakia)

HOW THE TEAMS LINED UP

FRANCE

COACH:
MICHEL HIDALGO

Bats

Battiston — Le Roux — Bossis — Domergue

Tigana — Fernandez — Platini — Giresse

Lacombe — Bellone

SPAIN

COACH:
MIGUEL MUNOZ

Carrasco — Santillana

Julio Alberto — Camacho — Victor — Francisco

Senor — Gallego — Salva — Urquiaga

Arconada

Above: Holland enjoy collecting the trophy. Opposite clockwise from top left: Goalscorers Gullit and Van Basten celebrate during the final; Lineker of England; Brehme leaps with joy after Germany's semi win; Roberto Mancini takes on Denmark.

WEST GERMANY 1988

A decade after consecutive World Cup finals ended in bitterness and defeat, Holland achieved redemption in one of the most exciting tournaments of the 1980s. Dutch football had been plagued by a sense of unfulfilled potential since the twin losses of 1974 and 1978. In banishing old demons, they closed that chapter and ushered in a new golden era, centred around superstars such as Van Basten, Gullit and Rijkaard.

Holland were undoubtedly the best team of Euro 88, a tournament that produced possibly the finest football in these championships since 1976. Only eight teams qualified again and this time, with all the leading countries except defending champions France booking their places, fireworks were guaranteed.

Group 1, featuring hosts West Germany, Italy, Spain and Denmark, appeared to be the stronger of the two, and few thought that both eventual finalists would emerge from Group 2, made up of Holland, the Soviet Union, the Republic Of Ireland and England. But this group crackled with tension until the final moments when a late goal ended Ireland's adventure and sparked Holland's tournament into life.

By that point the competition had long gone sour for England. Strongly fancied after their World Cup quarter-final appearance in Mexico two years earlier, they suffered a shock 1-0 loss in the opening match against the Irish. The defeat, to a team coached by Englishman Jack Charlton, was a blow Bobby Robson's side never recovered from. They capitulated 3-1 to Holland, in a match remembered for Marco Van Basten's stunning hat-trick, and by the same score to the fast-improving Soviets.

For the Irish, beating England was the catalyst for an unlikely crusade into unknown territory, battering and bettering supposedly superior sides. Denied by a late equaliser in

their next match against the Soviet Union, they headed into their final game against Holland knowing a draw would be enough for a place in the semi-finals. The Soviets, meanwhile, had beaten Holland in their opening match, and having scraped a draw against the Irish they required only a point against a dispirited England in their last game to qualify.

Despite their impressive showing against England, the Dutch were in danger of paying for their opening defeat: they had to beat the Irish. While the improving Soviets cruised past England, Holland struggled to make any impact on the solid, organised Irish, who came closest to scoring when McGrath headed against the post. With Charlton's men eight minutes away from the semi-finals, luck came to Holland's rescue when Koeman miss-hit a shot which Kieft was on hand to guide in.

In Group 1, a draw between West Germany and Italy enabled Spain to steal a march on their rivals by beating Denmark 3-2. However, the old superpowers went on to reassert their dominance; the Germans brushing aside the Danes 2-0 and Italy squeezing past Spain with a single goal. Italy completed their advance with a routine 2-0 defeat of the already-eliminated Danes, while West Germany clinically disposed of Spain by the same scoreline. The group was going according to expectations, with many experts believing the opening encounter between the hosts, World Cup finalists two years earlier, and the Italians, who were building a talented side for Italia 90, had been a dress rehearsal for the final.

The semi-finals threw up arguably the fiercest rivalry in European football as West Germany met Holland. The match inevitably provoked memories of 1974, when West Germany wore down the Cruyff-inspired Dutch. Holland's manager then was Rinus Michels, the man credited with creating Total Football. In a delicious twist of fate, he was back in charge of his national side.

In a match worthy of the final, Holland took the early initiative in Hamburg only for

THE FINAL

HOLLAND (1) **2-0** (0) SOVIET UNION

Date Saturday June 25, 1988 **Attendance** 72,308
Venue Olympic Stadium, Munich

The final will always be remembered for Marco Van Basten's wonder goal ten minutes into the second-half, but until that point the destiny of the trophy was far from certain. The Soviet Union started brightly and had the better of the opening 20 minutes, but gradually the Dutch began to draw their sting. Gullit took control of midfield, the 37-year-old Mühren started hitting probing passes, and Holland, who had the longer period to recover from their semi-final, suddenly looked to be in the ascendancy.

Twelve minutes before half-time Gullit headed Holland in front and Van Basten's vicious volley, which made him the tournament's top scorer with five, doubled the lead in the 54th minute. Van Breukelen saved a late penalty and Holland at last had the silverware they deserved.

HOLLAND		
VAN BREUKELEN		6
VAN AERLE ☐		7
Booked: 49 mins		
KOEMAN, R		7
RIJKAARD		8
VAN TIGGELEN		6
VANENBURG		7
WOUTERS		7
KOEMAN, E		6
MÜHREN, A		7
GULLIT ⚽		8
Goal: 33 mins		
VAN BASTEN ⚽		*9
Goal: 54 mins		

SOVIET UNION		
DASAEV		6
KHIDIATULIN ☐		6
Booked: 42 mins		
DEMIANENKO ☐		7
Booked: 31 mins		
ALEINIKOV		5
RATS		7
LITOVCHENKO ☐		5
Booked: 34 mins		
ZAVAROV		7
MIKHAILICHENKO		*8
GOTSMANOV		6
Subbed: 69 mins (Baltacha)		
PROTASOV		6
Subbed: 72 mins (Pasulko)		
BELANOV		5
sub: BALTACHA		5
sub: PASULKO		5

Referee: Vautrot (France)

HOW THE TEAMS LINED UP

HOLLAND
COACH:
RINUS MICHELS

KNVB

SOVIET UNION
COACH:
VALERY LOBANOVSKY

Van Breukelen
Van Aerle Koeman, R Rijkaard Van Tiggelen
Vanenburg Wouters Koeman, E Mühren, A
Gullit Van Basten

Belanov Protasov
Gotsmanov Mikhailichenko Zavarov Litovchenko
Rats Aleinikov Demianenko Khidiatulin
Dasaev

Matthäus to fire West Germany ahead from the penalty spot in the 53rd minute. The Dutch fell apart, their play growing ragged and the spectre of indiscipline returning to haunt them – until the 73rd minute when the referee levelled the score by awarding them a disputed penalty. Koeman equalised, then in the last minute of normal time Van Basten, out of favour early in the tournament, scored his fourth goal of the competition to derail the hosts and send Holland into the final.

In the other semi-final, the Soviets added a rugged approach to their fast, neat game to beat Italy 2-0 in Stuttgart. Quietly and effectively the Soviet Union had earned the right to contest the final for a fourth time.

Valery Lobanovsky, their manager, was as much a pioneer of the modern game as Dutch coach Michels, the man he would be pitting his wits against in the final. Lobanovsky had led Dynamo Kiev to seven championships before taking over the national side. Would he be the man to end his country's 28-year wait for a second major trophy, or would Michels, 14 years after the disappointment of losing the World Cup final, lead Holland to glory?

SEMI-FINALS
West Germany 1-2 Holland
Soviet Union 2-0 Italy

THIRD PLACE PLAY-OFF
Did not take place

TOP GOALSCORER
5 goals: Marco Van Basten (Holland)

FASTEST GOAL
3 mins: Sergei Aleinikov (England v Soviet Union)

TOTAL GOALS
34

AVERAGE GOALS
2.26 per game

SWEDEN 1992

Euro 92 was an extraordinary tournament for a host of reasons. The redrawing of Europe's political map, following the fall of Communism, had a significant effect on international football, with the former Soviet Union competing as the Commonwealth Of Independent States (CIS), and East and West Germany present as a single unified country. Further political intrigue had seen Yugoslavia disqualified from the tournament in line with United Nations sanctions against Serbia. That meant a last minute call-up for Denmark, runners-up in Yugoslavia's qualifying group by just a single point.

No-one gave Richard Moller Nielsen's team much chance of making an impact as the squad had barely a fortnight to prepare for the competition and many players had been recalled from their summer holidays. In true fairytale style, the Danes went on to prove their doubters spectacularly wrong.

Eight countries, split into two groups of four, contested the finals. Sweden, Denmark, France

Above: John Jensen opens the scoring in the final for Denmark. Below: Hässler and German team-mates enjoy a semi-final goal. Opposite clockwise from top left: Eventual winners Denmark opened with a 0-0 draw against England; Brian Laudrup kisses the trophy; Hosts Sweden equalise against England, they would go on to win; Scotland fell at the first stage.

SEMI-FINALS

Sweden 2-3 Germany
Holland 2-2 Denmark
(aet: Denmark won 5-4 on penalties)

THIRD PLACE PLAY-OFF

Did not take place

TOP GOALSCORERS

3 goals: Dennis Bergkamp (Holland), Tomas Brolin (Sweden), Henrik Larsen (Denmark), Karlheinz Riedle (Germany)

FASTEST GOAL

2 mins: Frank Rijkaard (Holland v Germany)

TOTAL GOALS

32

AVERAGE GOALS

2.13 per game

THE FINAL

DENMARK (1) **2-0** (0) GERMANY

Date Friday June 26, 1992 **Attendance** 37,800

Venue Nya Ullevi Stadium, Gothenburg

Germany started well as Denmark struggled to come to terms with the absence of suspended influential midfielder Henrik Andersen. However, having successfully soaked up the early pressure the Danes went ahead in the 18th minute, when John Jensen rifled the ball past German goalkeeper Bodo Illgner.

Germany tried to reassert themselves but were twice denied by Peter Schmeichel before the interval. The same pattern continued after the break with Vogts' men having the better of the chances. But Germany soon became frustrated at their inability to score and lost their discipline. With 12 minutes left Denmark sealed a famous win when Kim Vilfort made it 2-0, although Germans arguing that he controlled the ball with his hand had a point.

DENMARK

SCHMEICHEL	8
SIVEBAEK	6
Subbed: 65 mins (Christensen)	
NIELSEN, K	6
OLSEN, L	7
CHRISTOFTE	7
JENSEN ⚽	7
Goal: 18 mins	
POVLSEN	*9
LAUDRUP, B	8
PIECHNIK ▯	7
Booked: 32 mins	
LARSEN	6
VILFORT ⚽	7
Goal: 78 mins	
sub: CHRISTENSEN	7

GERMANY

ILLGNER	6
REUTER ▯	6
Booked: 55 mins	
BREHME	*8
KÖHLER	7
BUCHWALD	6
HÄSSLER ▯	6
Booked: 38 mins	
RIEDLE	6
HELMER	5
SAMMER	6
Subbed: 46 mins (Doll)	
EFFENBERG ▯	5
Booked: 35 mins. Subbed: 78 mins (Thom)	
KLINSMANN ▯	6
Booked: 88 mins	
sub: DOLL ▯	6
Booked: 83 mins	
sub: THOM	5

Referee: Galler (Switzerland)

HOW THE TEAMS LINED UP

DENMARK
COACH:
R MOLLER NIELSEN

Schmeichel
Sivebaek Nielsen, K Olsen, L Christofte
Jensen Povlsen Laudrup, B Piechnik
Larsen Vilfort

GERMANY
COACH:
BERTI VOGTS

Klinsmann Effenberg
Sammer Helmer Riedle Hässler
Buchwald Köhler Brehme Reuter
Illgner

and England were in Group A, producing only nine goals between them in six games. Sweden finished top of the group, thanks to wins against Denmark (1-0) and England (2-1, with the prolific Tomas Brolin hitting a terrific winner six minutes from time). The Danes followed them into the semi-finals despite winning only one of their games, 2-1 over France, then managed by the legendary Michel Platini. Injury-ravaged England had once again disappointed on the big stage, returning home with only a single David Platt goal to their name just two years after a penalty shoot-out defeat against West Germany had denied them a place in the World Cup final.

Group B proved a little livelier, although predictably it was Germany and Holland who qualified for the semi-finals at the expense of Scotland and the hodgepodge of nations that made up the CIS. Indeed, the Dutch became red-hot favourites to retain the Henri Delaunay Trophy after squashing Germany 3-1, thanks to goals from Frank Rijkaard, Rob Witschge and Ajax's Dennis Bergkamp, making his first major international tournament appearance. Bergkamp also grabbed Holland's early winner against Scotland in a 1-0 victory. Meanwhile, the Germans lived dangerously, and had Thomas Hässler not struck a last minute equaliser against the CIS in their opening game, it is doubtful they would have made it through to the last four at all.

The tournament really sprang into life at the semi-final stage with two memorable matches. World champions Germany lived up to their prodigious reputation in a tough game with injury-depleted Sweden, Hässler giving Berti Vogts' side an early lead, before Karlheinz Riedle added a second with just over half an hour to go. But the hosts pulled one back when the irrepressible Brolin converted a penalty five minutes later, and even when Riedle added a third two minutes from time after a fine through ball from Thomas Helmer, it failed to kill them off. The Swedes reduced the deficit

immediately, setting up a nail-biting finale, which saw the Germans eventually hold on for the 3-2 win.

The semi-final between Denmark and Holland was even more dramatic, with the still unfancied Danes a goal up through Henrik Larsen after just five minutes following some good work down the right from Brian Laudrup. Bergkamp's equaliser for the Dutch, midway through the first-half, provided short-lived relief as Larsen netted a second just past the half-hour mark. Rinus Michels' side threw everything they had at the Danes in the second-half, and their pressure finally told five minutes from the final whistle when Rijkaard grabbed a second equaliser from a corner.

Somehow the shattered Danes pulled themselves together and kept Holland at bay during extra-time, meaning the tie had to be decided on penalties. It was Marco Van Basten, without a single goal in the tournament, who missed the vital spot-kick as Denmark stunned European fotball by triumphing 5-4 in the lottery of the penalty shoot-out.

The Danes had ridden their luck and eagerly grasped every opportunity that had come their way, but surely they couldn't now win a tournament for which they hadn't even truly qualified. Could they?

ENGLAND 1996

The golden goal rule was to decide the outcome of a successful European Championship, as Germany claimed the trophy from the Czech Republic in a repeat of the 1976 final. But the tournament will be remembered for much more than Oliver Bierhoff's late strike, as a great English summer saw three weeks of fantastic goals, enthusiastic support and penalty shoot-outs.

Held in England for the first time, it was important for the hosts not only to play well, but also to reconstruct their hooligan-tarnished image in front of the eyes of the football world. Under the shrewd management of Terry Venables England opened the tournament against Switzerland, but after a promising start they ran out of ideas and were held 1-1. Group A's other participants were Scotland and Holland, who played out a 0-0 draw.

The so-called Battle of Britain was one of the most eagerly awaited confrontations of the group stages, and the dramatic end-to-end action of the game did not disappoint. England took the lead with Alan Shearer's second goal of the tournament, and then came the passage of play that was to settle the contest. Scotland were awarded a second-half penalty, which David Seaman was fortunate to keep out from Gary McAllister via his elbow and the crossbar. From the resulting corner, England broke down the pitch and, latching on to a through ball, Paul Gascoigne deftly flicked the ball over Colin Hendry's head before volleying home one of the best goals of the tournament, and creating a much-loved moment in English football history in the process.

The team's confidence was high, and in a wonderful display of attacking football they defeated a complacent Dutch side 4-1. The consolation goal was to prove valuable, Patrick Kluivert's strike ensuring qualification for his country ahead of Scotland on goal difference.

Group B saw France finish top and go forward to the quarter-finals along with Spain, at the expense of the Eastern European representatives Bulgaria and Romania. In a low-scoring series of contests, no game was decided by more than one goal. The old war horses of Hristo Stoichkov and Gheorghe Hagi both failed to inspire their teams to get the better of a couple of sides blessed with a new generation of world-class talent.

Every world tournament produces one group packed with a seeming imbalance of strong sides, the so-called Group of Death, and Euro 96 was no exception. Italy, Russia, the Czech Republic and Germany were matched against each other, and something had to give. That something turned out to be Italian participation in the competition, and despite possessing arguably the most talented squad, in many ways they managed to engineer their own departure.

Above left: England's Stuart Pearce after his penalty shoot-out spot-kick in the quarter-final with Spain. Above right: Oliver Bierhoff enjoys scoring in the final. Opposite clockwise from top left: The Czech team celebrate semi-final victory; German goal machine Jurgen Klinsmann; England congratulate Paul Gascoigne on his goal versus Scotland; Italy's Pierluigi Casiraghi.

A confident victory over Russia in the first game saw the Italians make changes to the starting line-up against the underrated Czechs, who snatched a 2-1 victory. In the final game, Italy needed to defeat the already-qualified Germany to go through, but a 0-0 draw and the Czech Republic's point against Russia conspired against them.

Group D saw Portugal and newcomers to the international stage Croatia grab the honours, with Denmark and Turkey knocked out of the tournament. The game of this group was won by Croatia against holders Denmark, and will be remembered for Davor Suker's exquisite chipped finish against Peter Schmeichel.

After the open play of the group stages, the quarter-finals turned out to be tense affairs. England got the better of Spain via a penalty shoot-out, and France eliminated Holland in the same manner. England's shoot-out was notable for the redemption of left-back Stuart Pearce, who laid the ghost of his 1990 World Cup miss to rest after emphatically burying his spot-kick past Zubizarreta in the Spanish goal.

The clash between Germany and Croatia turned out to be the most spiteful of the whole tournament, and despite possessing an array of world-class talent in their side, including Davor Suker and Zvonimir Boban, Croatia temporarily put quality football on hold and attempted to kick lumps out of their German opposition. Jurgen Klinsmann and his side limped out 2-1 winners.

Thanks to mop-top Karel Poborsky's wonderful, improvised lob over Portugal's Vitor Baia, the Czechs continued their impressive run. They secured a place in the final after a 0-0 draw with France at Old Trafford resulted in yet another semi-final penalty shoot-out failure for the French.

The other semi-final between the hosts England and old foes Germany also went to penalties, but not before an epic struggle in the game of the tournament. England made the start they wanted, with the eventual Golden Boot winner Alan Shearer heading them in front in the third minute. But England were unable to press home the advantage and

Germany, through Stefan Kuntz, levelled the score. In extra-time England came agonisingly close to claiming a spot in the final through Darren Anderton and Gascoigne, while Kuntz had a headed goal disallowed. In a repeat of the events of 1990, once again England failed to see off the Germans. It fell to Gareth Southgate to miss the vital penalty and leave the hosts as nothing more than spectators for the final.

THE FINAL

GERMANY (0) 2-1 (0) CZECH REPUBLIC
(aet: 1-1 at 90 mins)

Date Sunday June 30, 1996 **Attendance** 73,611

Venue Wembley Stadium, London

Despite the exit of the hosts, the enthusiastic spirit of Euro 96 continued into the final in front of a full house at Wembley. Germany went into the game as favourites, and coach Berti Vogts' side were determined not to lose back-to-back European Championship finals. The underdog tag didn't deter the fast-improving Czech Republic side, who took the lead in the 59th minute with star player Patrik Berger converting a penalty past goalkeeper Kopke.

Substitute Oliver Bierhoff brought Germany back into the game only four minutes after coming on, and it was the tall striker who made football history by scoring the first ever golden goal in a major tournament final with just four minutes of extra-time on the clock.

HOW THE TEAMS LINED UP

GERMANY
COACH:
BERTI VOGTS

CZECH REPUBLIC
COACH:
DUSAN UHRIN

Kopke
Babbel Sammer Helmer Strunz
Hässler Eilts Scholl Ziege
Klinsmann Kuntz

Berger Nemec Nedved Poborsky
Rada Hornak Kadlec Suchoparek
Kouba

WEST GERMANY		
KOPKE		7
BABBEL		7
SAMMER		7
Booked: 69 mins		
HELMER		6
Booked: 62 mins		
STRUNZ		6
HÄSSLER		6
EILTS		5
Subbed: 46 mins (Bode)		
SCHOLL		5
Subbed: 69 mins (Bierhoff)		
ZIEGE		7
Booked: 91 mins		
KLINSMANN		7
KUNTZ		6
sub: BODE		6
sub: BIERHOFF		*8
Goal: 73 mins, 95 mins		

CZECH REPUBLIC		
KOUBA		6
SUCHOPAREK		6
KADLEC		7
HORNAK		7
Booked: 47 mins		
RADA		5
POBORSKY		*8
Subbed: 88 mins (Smicer)		
NEDVED		7
NEMEC		6
BERGER		7
Goal: 59 mins (pen)		
BEJBL		5
KUKA		7
sub: SMICER		6

Referee: Pairetto (Italy)

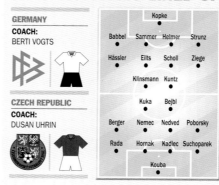

BELGIUM/HOLLAND 2000

Above: Italy clinch a place in the final after a penalty victory over Holland. Opposite clockwise from top left: Alan Shearer wheels away after scoring the winner against Germany; Didier Deschamps holds the cup with the winning French squad; Luis Figo and Nuno Gomez led a talented Portuguese team to the semi-finals; Holland's Patrick Kluivert celebrates.

It was a tournament for purists, full of attacking flair, defensive ingenuity and high drama, most notably in the games played by the Dutch. But Euro 2000 will be remembered for the extension of French footballing dominance, and the grace and guile of Zinédine Zidane. The midfielder, along with Portugal's Luis Figo, was undoubtedly the star of the tournament, entertaining fans with an armoury of tricks, flicks and defence-splitting passes. And while Figo and Portugal were the surprise package of the tournament, it was Zidane's France who extended their superiority following their World Cup win in 1998.

The opening game was indicative of how the tournament was to continue, mixing controversy with exciting football. But that drama would come at a cost, especially for Belgian goalkeeper Filip De Wilde. Eight minutes into the second-half, with Belgium leading Sweden 2-0, he trod on the ball while trying to control a backpass, allowing Swedish striker Johan Mjallby to stroll past him and sweep the ball into the net. Belgium hung on for a deserved win.

England's campaign started with equally catastrophic defensive incidents in Group A. After taking a two-goal lead against Portugal, Kevin Keegan's men were torn apart by Figo and conceded three goals. England went on to defeat arch-rivals Germany 1-0, but a defensive blunder from Phil Neville against Romania led to the penalty which knocked them, along with defending champions Germany, out of the tournament.

Almost immediately Keegan's coaching credentials were criticised by the English press, as well as by a number of his senior players, including first-team defender Martin Keown. The Arsenal centre-half accused the team of being inept tactically and claimed individual and collective errors had prevented England from beating teams they should have swept aside easily. The writing was already on the wall and Keegan's reign as England manager was to be short-lived. Meanwhile, Germany's failure to make it past the first round, almost unthinkable a few years earlier, was seen as indicative of a waning of their power.

Hosts Holland struggled to get out of first gear in their opening Group D game, defeating the Czech Republic by a single penalty, before demolishing Denmark 3-0 to cruise into the quarter-finals. It was here that Patrick Kluivert and his team-mates quickly upped the ante, firing six goals past a bemused Yugoslavian team in a performance that was pure perfection. But in their semi-final clash with Italy, who had defeated a strong Romanian side 2-0 in the quarter-finals, drama struck.

Having been reduced to just ten men after Gianluca Zambrotta was sent-off for a second bookable offence, Italy sat back and defended, with goalkeeper Francesco Toldo commanding his area admirably. Even with two penalty kicks in their favour, Holland, having been unable to convert either, failed to defeat the Italians. Worse was to come and after the golden goal period failed to produce a result, Holland missed the first three penalties of the shoot-out to gift the Italians victory. 'I think they could have played for the whole day shooting at our goal and they would never have scored', said Italian keeper Toldo. Dutch striker Dennis Bergkamp was more damning. 'We only have ourselves to blame,' he said, 'I don't know why Holland can't win a penalty shoot-out.'

Italy, who had infuriated both fans and opponents alike with their ultra-defensive football in Group B, had ground their way to the final. Their qualifying group rivals Turkey were later knocked out of the quarter-finals by the Portuguese 2-0.

The French were ruthless in Group D, easing their way into the quarter-finals without ever looking stretched: a 3-2 defeat at the hands of the Dutch was played at half pace. They dispensed with Spain 2-1 to progress into the semi-finals with goals from Zidane and Djorkaeff; Spain had responded with a converted spot-kick from Mendieta, but minutes before the final whistle Raúl had missed the game's second penalty, and with it the chance to take the game into extra-time. That the Spanish were unable to make it past the quarter-final stage in yet another major competition was proof that the tag of perennial underachievers was hanging heavy.

Still, Spain had provided the game of the tournament when, in their final Group C clash against Yugoslavia, they had come back from 3-2 down to score two goals in stoppage time and win the tie 4-3. At this stage in the competition many felt that the Spanish, with Raúl of Real Madrid and Valencia's Gaizka Mendieta hitting top form in attack, were likely contenders for the title.

The French clearly had other ideas and, after sweeping aside Spain, they defeated the Portuguese in the semi-finals with an extra-time penalty golden goal, slotted home by Zidane after Abel Xavier had controversially been adjudged to have handled in the area. The battle between the tournament's two stars, Zidane and Figo, had gone in favour of the Frenchman. The final set-up a mouth watering battle between the attacking force of France and Italy's defence. But much more drama was to come.

SEMI-FINALS

Portugal 1-2 France
(aet: 1-1 at 90 mins)

Italy 0-0 Netherlands
(aet: Italy won 3-1 on penalties)

THIRD PLACE PLAY-OFF

Did not take place

TOP GOALSCORERS

5 goals: Patrick Kluivert (Holland), Savo Milosevic (Yugoslavia)

4 goals: Nuno Gomes (Portugal)

FASTEST GOAL

3 mins: Paul Scholes
(England v Portugal)

TOTAL GOALS

85 goals

AVERAGE GOALS

2.74 per game

THE FINAL

FRANCE (0) **2-1** (0) **ITALY**
(aet: 1-1 at 90 mins)

Date Sunday July 2, 2000 **Attendance** 50,000

Venue De Kuip Stadium, Rotterdam

Many would have preferred to see the attacking play of Holland against France, rather than the defensive Italians, but nevertheless the climax to Euro 2000 was a fascinating affair.

Having gone a goal down in the 54th minute to Marco Delvecchio, France threw on Sylvain Wiltord and David Trezeguet after 75 minutes. With full-time approaching, fortune favoured the French as Wiltord broke through in injury time to fire the ball beneath the body of goalkeeper Toldo and send the game into extra-time.

The first period was a typically cagey affair until Robert Pires hit a low cross into the Italian penalty area and David Trezeguet fired the ball into the roof of the net for the golden goal that would end the game and hand France victory.

HOW THE TEAMS LINED UP

FRANCE
COACH: ROGER LEMERRE

ITALY
COACH: DINO ZOFF

FRANCE	
BARTHEZ	6
THURAM	6
Booked: 58 mins	
BLANC	*8
DESAILLY	7
LIZARAZU	6
Subbed: 86 mins (Pires)	
DESCHAMPS	6
VIEIRA	6
DJORKAEFF	6
Subbed: 76 mins (Trezeguet)	
ZIDANE	7
DUGARRY	6
Subbed: 57 mins (Wiltord)	
HENRY	7
sub: **WILTORD**	7
Goal: 90 mins	
sub: **TREZEGUET**	7
Goal: 103 mins	

ITALY	
TOLDO	7
CANNAVARO	*8
Booked: 41 mins	
NESTA	7
IULIANO	6
PESSOTTO	7
ALBERTINI	6
DI BIAGIO	6
Booked: 30 mins, Subbed: 66 mins (Ambrosini)	
FIORE	5
Subbed: 53 mins (Del Piero)	
MALDINI	7
TOTTI	6
Booked: 90 mins	
DELVECCHIO	7
Goal: 54 mins, Subbed: 86 mins (Montella)	
sub: **AMBROSINI**	6
sub: **DEL PIERO**	5
sub: **MONTELLA**	5

Referee: Frisk (Sweden)

PORTUGAL 2004

Never has a European Championship victory attracted so much debate. When Greece lifted the famous trophy in front of a largely heartbroken crowd in Lisbon, they had pulled off one of world football's biggest upsets. An Angelos Charisteas header on 57 minutes was enough to put hosts Portugal to the sword, making the Werder Bremen striker a modern-day God in his homeland. Greece had ended the tournament as they had started it, humbling hosts Portugal into submission.

The victory sent shockwaves across Europe. Greece's last venture on to the world stage had been an unmitigated disaster: they lost all three of their 1994 World Cup games, conceding ten goals and scoring none. Even their victorious 2004 team had no star names to speak of, and they were coached by an ageing German who the average Greek fan believed was merely looking for a final payday. But 65-year-old Otto Rehhagel had other ideas. While the brawn of his side fuelled further debate about the merits of Greece's success, his workmanlike system proved to be a winning formula.

Portugal, who came so close to victory in their home country, had started the competition among the favourites. Coached by Luiz Felipe Scolari, who had led Brazil to World Cup success in 2002, the Portuguese went into the tournament with a squad crammed with talent, boasting players of the calibre of Deco and Ricardo Carvalho, the youthful exuberance of Cristiano Ronaldo and the experience of Luis Figo. But as the hosts trudged off the Estadio do Dragao pitch on June 12 after an opening day defeat to Greece, the significance of the result would only become apparent after the tournament was over.

Even with this surprise victory under their belts, Greece only progressed to the next round in second place on goal difference, ahead of group favourites Spain. A 1-1 draw with the Spanish had helped their cause, but a 2-1 defeat to Russia – in which Dmitri Kirichenko scored the fastest goal in European Championship history after just 68 seconds – didn't suggest the glorious performances that lay ahead.

Fate had dealt Rehhagel's men a fortuitous hand, and how they grasped it. Reigning champions France were eliminated in the quarter-finals thanks to a second-half Charisteas header, while the Czech Republic were dispatched in similar style in the semi-finals, the Greeks stifling their technically-gifted opponents before winning the game thanks to a silver goal from defender Traianos Dellas.

While Greece's indomitable style thrust them into the spotlight, there were other highlights to an illuminating competition. England's opening Group B clash with the French had been much vaunted in the international football press. Given the rivalry between the countries

Above: Milan Baros scores for the Czech Republic.
Opposite clockwise from top left: England celebrate a goal from Scholes against Croatia; Henrik Larsson of Sweden after scoring against the Danes; a dejected Christiano Ronaldo following defeat in the final; Greece lift the trophy.

and the number of Gallic players in the English Premiership, it was signposted as the match of the tournament from the moment the draw had taken place. Frank Lampard gave England a deserved 1-0 lead in the 38th minute, while the talents of 18-year-old Wayne Rooney were unveiled to a global audience for the first time. David Beckham missed a 73rd minute penalty but as the game ebbed to its conclusion, England committed football suicide.

With 90 minutes on the clock Emile Heskey gave away a free-kick, which Zinédine Zidane disposed of with ruthless efficiency. Three minutes later a poor back pass from Steven Gerrard was intercepted by Thierry Henry, who was upended by on-rushing keeper David James. Up stepped Zidane to take the resulting penalty kick, and despite twice throwing up while cueing the ball, he slotted home to clinch the most unlikely of victories.

For the neutral observer the most thrilling game saw the Czech Republic come from two down to beat Holland 3-2 in their Group D encounter. Wilfred Bouma and Ruud van Nistelrooy had put the Dutch 2-0 up inside 20 minutes, only for Milan Baros and Jan Koller to turn the game on its head. Dick Advocaat's men were rattled, and to compound their frustration Johnny Heitinga was sent-off with 15 minutes remaining. Vladimir Smicer's 88th minute winner had an inevitable ring to it, the Liverpool man tapping in from close range.

The prequel to this Group D encounter ended 0-0 but was no less captivating as Latvia battled the might of Germany. As surprise qualifiers, the Baltic minnows bowed out with this solitary point, but their celebrations at the final whistle would only be bettered by the Greeks on July 4.

The Germans tumbled out of the 'group of death' following defeat against the Czechs, knowing their decidedly anonymous squad needed much surgery. Holland progressed to the quarter-finals beating Sweden on penalties before crashing out to Portugal. The Czech Republic were emerging as favourites, having dispatched of Denmark 3-0 to set up their semi-

final with Greece. But all eyes were on the hosts, who had battled back from their opening-game debacle to reach a quarter-final clash with England. An early Michael Owen goal should have inspired Sven-Göran Eriksson's men, but following Rooney's departure through injury after 27 minutes it signalled a rearguard action that would prove costly. Postiga equalised on 83 minutes, Sol Campbell had a goal disallowed by ref Urs Meier on the stroke of 90 minutes, before extra-time goals from Rui Costa and Frank Lampard set-up penalties. Inevitably England bowed out, Darius Vassell failing to convert the all-important kick.

The hosts went on to beat the Dutch 2-1 in the semi-final, but there was a consolation for England with the emergence of Rooney. For many, the 18-year-old was the player of the tournament following his four goals, but it was an adversary from across Liverpool's Stanley Park – Milan Baros – who ended up with the Golden Boot. The Greeks, meanwhile, prepared for the Euro 2004 final as the biggest underdogs in the competition's 44 year history, proving that in this wonderful game of football, anything can happen.

SEMI-FINALS

Portugal 2-1 Holland
Greece 1-0 Czech Republic
(aet: 0-0 at 90 mins)

THIRD PLACE PLAY-OFF

Did not take place

TOP GOALSCORERS

5 goals: Milan Baros (Czech Republic)
4 goals: Wayne Rooney (England), Ruud Van Nistelrooy (Holland)

FASTEST GOAL

68 seconds: Dmitri Kirichenko (Russia v Greece)

TOTAL GOALS

77 goals

AVERAGE GOALS

2.48 goals a game

THE FINAL

GREECE (0) **1-0** (0) PORTUGAL

Date Sunday July 4, 2004 **Attendance** 62,865
Venue Estadio da Luz, Lisbon

As they had done for much of the tournament, Greece adopted a safety-first policy, inviting the hosts to break down a rock solid defence. The Portuguese certainly took the early initiative, with Miguel forcing Antonios Nikopolidis into action with a 13th minute drive, while Maniche saw a shot from the edge of the area flash inches wide.

It was not unusual to see the Greeks with ten men behind the ball, and once Angelos Charisteas opened the scoring on 57 minutes with a trademark header from an Angelos Basinas corner, there would be only one winner. Ronaldo passed up a guilt-edged chance, lifting his shot over the bar after being put clean through, and Luis Figo also saw a late shot deflected wide before referee Markus Merk blew time to signal this unlikeliest of victories.

GREECE

NIKOPOLIDIS	7
SEITARIDIS	9
Booked: 64 mins	
KAPSIS	8
DELLAS	8
FISSAS	7
Booked: 66 mins	
ZAGORAKIS	8
KATSOURANIS	7
BASINAS	6
Booked: 45 mins	
GIANNAKOPOULOS	6
Subbed: 76 mins (Venetidis)	
VRYZAS	7
Subbed: 81 mins (Papadopoulos)	
CHARISTEAS	8
Goal: 73 mins	
sub: **VENETIDIS**	5
sub: **PAPADOPOULOS**	5
Booked: 84 mins	

PORTUGAL

RICARDO	5
MIGUEL	7
Subbed: 43 mins (Ferreira)	
ANDRADE	5
RICARDO CARVALHO	6
NUNO VALENTE	6
Booked: 90 mins	
MANICHE	6
COSTINHA	6
Booked: 11 mins. Subbed: 60 mins (Rui Costa)	
RONALDO	6
DECO	5
FIGO	6
PAULETA	6
Subbed: 74 mins (Nuno Gomes)	
sub: **FERREIRA**	5
sub: **RUI COSTA**	6
sub: **NUNO GOMES**	5

Referee: Merk (Germany)

HOW THE TEAMS LINED UP

GREECE
COACH:
OTTO REHHAGEL

Nikopolidis
Seitardis   Dellas   Fissas
Zagorakis   Kapsis   Katsouranis   Basinas
Giannakopoulos   Vryzas   Charisteas

PORTUGAL
COACH:
LUIZ FELIPE SCOLARI

Pauleta
Figo   Deco   Maniche   Ronaldo
Costinha
Nuno Valente   Carvalho   Andrade   Miguel
Ricardo

EUROPEAN CHAMPIONSHIP RESULTS

Above: The England team managed third place in the 1968 European Championship, just two years after their World Cup win.

1960 FRANCE

SEMI-FINALS
Soviet Union **3-0** Czechoslovakia
Yugoslavia **5-4** France

THIRD PLACE PLAY-OFF
Czechoslovakia **2-0** France

FINAL
Soviet Union **2-1** Yugoslavia
(aet)

1964 SPAIN

SEMI-FINALS
Spain **2-1** Hungary
(aet)
Soviet Union **3-0** Denmark

THIRD PLACE PLAY-OFF
Hungary **3-1** Denmark
(aet)

FINAL
Spain **2-1** Soviet Union

1968 ITALY

SEMI-FINALS
Italy **0-0** Soviet Union
(aet)
Italy won on toss of a coin
Yugoslavia **1-0** England

THIRD PLACE PLAY-OFF
England **2-0** Soviet Union

FINAL
Italy **1-1** Yugoslavia
(aet)

REPLAY
Italy **2-0** Yugoslavia

1972 BELGIUM

SEMI-FINALS
West Germany **2-1** Belgium
Soviet Union **1-0** Hungary

THIRD PLACE PLAY-OFF
Belgium **2-1** Hungary

FINAL
West Germany **3-0** Soviet Union

1976 YUGOSLAVIA

SEMI-FINALS
Czechoslovakia **3-1** Holland
(aet)
West Germany **4-2** Yugoslavia
(aet)

THIRD PLACE PLAY-OFF
Holland **3-2** Yugoslavia
(aet)

FINAL
Czechoslovakia **2-2** West Germany
(aet)
Czechoslovakia won 5-3 on penalties

1980 ITALY

GROUP 1
West Germany **1-0** Czechoslovakia
Holland **1-0** Greece
West Germany **3-2** Holland
Czechoslovakia **3-1** Greece
Czechoslovakia **1-1** Holland
West Germany **0-0** Greece

	P	W	D	L	F	A	Pts
West Germany	3	2	1	0	4	2	5
Czechoslovakia	3	1	1	1	4	3	3
Holland	3	1	1	1	4	4	3
Greece	3	0	1	2	1	4	1

GROUP 2
Belgium **1-1** England
Spain **0-0** Italy
Spain **1-2** Belgium
Italy **1-0** England
Spain **1-2** England
Italy **0-0** Belgium

	P	W	D	L	F	A	Pts
Belgium	3	1	2	0	3	2	4
Italy	3	1	2	0	1	0	4
England	3	1	1	1	3	3	3
Spain	3	0	1	2	2	4	1

THIRD PLACE PLAY-OFF
Czechoslovakia **1-1** Italy
(no extra time)
Czechoslovakia won 9-8 on penalties

FINAL
West Germany **2-1** Belgium

1984 FRANCE

GROUP 1
France **1-0** Denmark
Belgium **2-0** Yugoslavia
France **5-0** Belgium
Denmark **5-0** Yugoslavia
France **3-2** Yugoslavia
Denmark **3-2** Belgium

	P	W	D	L	F	A	Pts
France	3	3	0	0	9	2	6
Denmark	3	2	0	1	8	3	4
Belgium	3	1	0	2	4	8	2
Yugoslavia	3	0	0	3	2	10	0

GROUP 2
West Germany **0-0** Portugal
Spain **1-1** Romania
West Germany **2-1** Romania
Portugal **1-1** Spain
West Germany **0-1** Spain
Portugal **1-0** Romania

	P	W	D	L	F	A	Pts
Spain	3	1	2	0	3	2	4
Portugal	3	1	2	0	2	1	4
West Germany	3	1	1	1	2	2	3
Romania	3	0	1	2	2	4	1

SEMI-FINALS
France **3-2** Portugal
(aet)
Spain **1-1** Denmark
(aet)
Spain won 5-4 on penalties

THIRD PLACE PLAY-OFF
Not held

FINAL
France **2-0** Spain

1988 WEST GERMANY

GROUP 1
West Germany **1-1** Italy
Denmark **2-3** Spain
West Germany **2-0** Denmark
Italy **1-0** Spain
West Germany **2-0** Spain
Italy **2-0** Denmark

	P	W	D	L	F	A	Pts
West Germany	3	2	1	0	5	1	5
Italy	3	2	1	0	4	1	5
Spain	3	1	0	2	3	5	2
Denmark	3	0	0	3	2	7	0

GROUP 2
England **0-1** Rep. Of Ireland
Holland **0-1** Soviet Union
England **1-3** Holland
Rep. Of Ireland **1-1** Soviet Union
England **1-3** Soviet Union
Rep. Of Ireland **0-1** Holland

	P	W	D	L	F	A	Pts
Soviet Union	3	2	1	0	5	2	5
Holland	3	2	0	1	4	2	4
Rep. Of Ireland	3	1	1	1	2	2	3
England	3	0	0	3	2	7	0

SEMI-FINALS
West Germany **1-2** Holland
Soviet Union **2-0** Italy

THIRD PLACE PLAY-OFF
Not held

FINAL
Holland **2-0** Soviet Union

1992 SWEDEN

GROUP A
Sweden **1-1** France
Denmark **0-0** England
France **0-0** England
Sweden **1-0** Denmark
Sweden **2-1** England
France **1-2** Denmark

	P	W	D	L	F	A	Pts
Sweden	3	2	1	0	4	2	5
Denmark	3	1	1	1	2	2	3
France	3	0	2	1	2	3	2
England	3	0	2	1	1	2	2

GROUP B
Holland **1-0** Scotland
Germany **1-1** CIS

West Germany's Horst Hrubesch lifts the Henri Delaunay Trophy in 1980.

Above: Holland's victory at Euro 88.

Germany **2-0** Scotland
Holland **0-0** CIS
Scotland **3-0** CIS
Holland **3-1** Germany

	P	W	D	L	F	A	Pts
Holland	3	2	1	0	4	1	5
Germany	3	1	1	1	4	4	3
Scotland	3	1	0	2	3	3	2
CIS	3	0	2	1	1	4	2

SEMI-FINALS

Sweden **2-3** Germany
Holland **2-2** Denmark
(aet)
Denmark won 5-4 on penalties

THIRD PLACE PLAY-OFF

Not held

FINAL

Denmark **2-0** Germany

1996 ENGLAND

GROUP A

England **1-1** Switzerland
Holland **0-0** Scotland
Switzerland **0-2** Holland
Scotland **0-2** England
Scotland **1-0** Switzerland
Holland **1-4** England

	P	W	D	L	F	A	Pts
England	3	2	1	0	7	2	7
Holland	3	1	1	1	3	4	4
Scotland	3	1	1	1	1	2	4
Switzerland	3	0	1	2	1	4	1

Stefan Kuntz celebrates Oliver Bierhoff's winning 'golden goal' in the Euro 96 final.

GROUP B

Spain **1-1** Bulgaria
Romania **0-1** France
Bulgaria **1-0** Romania
France **1-1** Spain
France **3-1** Bulgaria
Romania **1-2** Spain

	P	W	D	L	F	A	Pts
France	3	2	1	0	5	2	7
Spain	3	1	2	0	4	3	5
Bulgaria	3	1	1	1	3	4	4
Romania	3	0	0	3	1	4	0

GROUP C

Germany **2-0** Czech Republic
Italy **2-1** Russia
Czech Republic **2-1** Italy
Russia **0-3** Germany
Russia **3-3** Czech Republic
Italy **0-0** Germany

	P	W	D	L	F	A	Pts
Germany	3	2	1	0	5	0	7
Czech Republic	3	1	1	1	5	6	4
Italy	3	1	1	1	3	3	4
Russia	3	0	1	2	4	8	1

GROUP D

Denmark **1-1** Portugal
Turkey **0-1** Croatia
Portugal **1-0** Turkey
Denmark **0-3** Croatia
Croatia **0-3** Portugal
Denmark **3-0** Turkey

	P	W	D	L	F	A	Pts
Portugal	3	2	1	0	5	1	7
Croatia	3	2	0	1	4	3	6
Denmark	3	1	1	1	4	4	4
Turkey	3	0	0	3	0	5	0

QUARTER-FINALS

England **0-0** Spain
(aet)
England won 4-2 on penalties
France **0-0** Holland
(aet)
France won 5-4 on penalties
Germany **2-1** Croatia
Portugal **0-1** Czech Republic

SEMI-FINALS

France **0-0** Czech Republic
(aet)
Czech Republic won 6-5 on penalties
England **1-1** Germany
(aet)
Germany won 6-5 on penalties

THIRD PLACE PLAY-OFF

Not held

FINAL

Germany **2-1** Czech Republic
(aet)
Germany won with golden goal

2000 BELGIUM/HOLLAND

GROUP A

Germany **1-1** Romania
Portugal **3-2** England
Romania **0-1** Portugal
England **1-0** Germany
England **2-3** Romania
Portugal **3-0** Germany

	P	W	D	L	F	A	Pts
Portugal	3	3	0	0	7	2	9
Romania	3	1	1	1	4	4	4
England	3	1	0	2	5	6	3
Germany	3	0	1	2	1	5	1

GROUP B

Belgium **2-1** Sweden
Turkey **1-2** Italy
Italy **2-0** Belgium
Sweden **0-0** Turkey
Turkey **2-0** Belgium
Italy **2-1** Sweden

	P	W	D	L	F	A	Pts
Italy	3	3	0	0	6	2	9
Turkey	3	1	1	1	3	2	4
Belgium	3	1	0	2	2	5	3
Sweden	3	0	1	2	2	4	1

GROUP C

Spain **0-1** Norway
Yugoslavia **3-3** Slovenia
Slovenia **1-2** Spain
Norway **0-1** Yugoslavia
Yugoslavia **3-4** Spain
Slovenia **0-0** Norway

	P	W	D	L	F	A	Pts
Spain	3	2	0	1	6	5	6
Yugoslavia	3	1	1	1	7	7	4
Norway	3	1	1	1	1	1	4
Slovenia	3	0	2	1	4	5	2

GROUP D

France **3-0** Denmark
Holland **1-0** Czech Republic
Czech Republic **1-2** France
Denmark **0-3** Holland
France **2-3** Holland
Denmark **0-2** Czech Republic

	P	W	D	L	F	A	Pts
Holland	3	3	0	0	7	2	9
France	3	2	0	1	7	4	6
Czech Republic	3	1	0	2	3	3	3
Denmark	3	0	0	3	0	8	0

QUARTER-FINALS

Portugal **2-0** Turkey
Italy **2-0** Romania
Holland **6-1** Yugoslavia
France **2-1** Spain

SEMI-FINALS

Portugal **1-2** France
(aet)
France won with golden goal
Italy **0-0** Holland
(aet)
Italy won 3-1 on penalties

THIRD PLACE PLAY-OFF

Not held

FINAL

France **2-1** Italy
(aet)
France won with golden goal

Didier Deschamps lifts the trophy in Rotterdam after France's triumph at Euro 2000.

2004 PORTUGAL

GROUP A

Portugal **1-2** Greece
Spain **1-0** Russia
Greece **1-1** Spain
Russia **0-2** Portugal
Russia **2-1** Greece
Spain **0-1** Portugal

	P	W	D	L	F	A	Pts
Portugal	3	2	0	1	4	2	6
Greece	3	1	1	1	4	4	4
Spain	3	1	1	1	2	2	4
Russia	3	1	0	2	2	4	3

GROUP B

Switzerland **0-0** Croatia
France **2-1** England
England **3-0** Switzerland
Croatia **2-2** France
Switzerland **1-3** France
Croatia **2-4** England

	P	W	D	L	F	A	Pts
France	3	2	1	0	7	4	7
England	3	2	0	1	8	4	6
Croatia	3	0	2	1	4	6	2
Switzerland	3	0	1	2	1	6	1

GROUP C

Denmark **0-0** Italy
Sweden **5-0** Bulgaria
Bulgaria **0-2** Denmark
Italy **1-1** Sweden
Italy **2-1** Bulgaria
Denmark **2-2** Sweden

	P	W	D	L	F	A	Pts
Sweden	3	1	2	0	8	3	5
Denmark	3	1	2	0	4	2	5
Italy	3	1	2	0	3	2	5
Bulgaria	3	0	0	3	1	9	0

GROUP D

Czech Republic **2-1** Latvia
Germany **1-1** Holland
Latvia **0-0** Germany
Holland **2-3** Czech Republic
Holland **3-0** Latvia
Germany **1-2** Czech Republic

	P	W	D	L	F	A	Pts
Czech Republic	3	3	0	0	7	4	9
Holland	3	1	1	1	6	4	4
Germany	3	0	2	1	2	3	2
Latvia	3	0	1	2	1	5	1

QUARTER-FINALS

Portugal **2-2** England
(aet)
Portugal won 6-5 on penalties
France **0-1** Greece
Sweden **0-0** Holland
(aet)
Holland won 5-4 on penalties
Czech Republic **3-0** Denmark

SEMI-FINALS

Portugal **2-1** Holland
Greece **1-0** Czech Republic
(aet)
Greece won with silver goal

FINAL

Portugal **0-1** Greece

Theodoros Zagorakis celebrates after Greece's shock Euro 2004 victory.

INTERNATIONAL COMPETITIONS

Previous pages: Brazil celebrate
winning the 2004 Copa América.

Right: The Argentinian team,
winners of the 2004 Olympic
football gold medal in Athens.

Below: Cameroon captain Geremi
Njitap Fotso with his Olympic
gold medal in 2000.

OLYMPIC GAMES FINAL RESULTS

1908 LONDON
England **2-0** Denmark

1912 STOCKHOLM
England **4-2** Denmark

1920 ANTWERP
Belgium **2-0** Czechoslovakia
*(Match abandoned after 78 mins.
Czechoslovakia disqualified and
Spain awarded silver)*

1924 PARIS
Uruguay **3-0** Switzerland

1928 AMSTERDAM
Uruguay **1-1** Argentina *(aet)*
Uruguay **2-1** Argentina *Replay*

1932 LOS ANGELES
No Tournament

1936 BERLIN
Italy **2-1** Austria *(aet)*

1948 LONDON
Sweden **3-1** Yugoslavia

1952 HELSINKI
Hungary **2-0** Yugoslavia

1956 MELBOURNE
Soviet Union **1-0** Yugoslavia

1960 ROME
Yugoslavia **3-1** Denmark

1964 TOKYO
Hungary **2-1** Czechoslovakia

1968 MEXICO CITY
Hungary **4-1** Bulgaria

1972 MUNICH
Poland **2-1** Hungary

1976 MONTREAL
East Germany **3-1** Poland

1980 MOSCOW
Czechoslovakia **1-0** East
Germany

1984 LOS ANGELES
France **2 - 0** Brazil

1988 SEOUL
Soviet Union **2-1** Brazil *(aet)*

1992 BARCELONA
Spain **3-2** Poland

1996 ATLANTA
Nigeria **3-2** Argentina

2000 SYDNEY
Cameroon **2-2** Spain *(aet)*
(Cameroon win 5-3 on penalties)

2004 ATHENS
Argentina **1-0** Paraguay

OLYMPIC GAMES

Football at the Olympics has gone through three distinct phases, evolving from a sport that hadn't convinced the International Olympic Committee of its popularity, before eventually becoming an essential ingredient to making any Olympic Games a success. The Olympic football tournament is now watched by more spectators than any other sporting discipline, including athletics. This has led to an uneasy partnership between the IOC and FIFA over the status of the Olympic football tournament.

There were unofficial tournaments at the first three Olympics, although a gold medal was awarded retrospecively at the 1904 games. The first official tournament was at the 1908 London Games. Six purely amateur teams competed, including French 'A' and 'B' teams. The two French sides were knocked out by Denmark, who thrashed the 'B' team 9-0 and, in a game that included a ten-goal haul for Sophus Nielsen, the 'A' team 17-1. After such prolific success, the Danes ultimately lost the final to England 2-0.

The IOC were uncertain as to the popularity of football and actually questioned whether the sport warranted a place in the games in 1912, a competition which was again won by England. From 1920 to 1928, however, the Olympic football tournament was regarded as a world championship and was organised by FIFA, but because they allowed 'broken time' payments to players to compensate for loss of earnings, debate raged between national associations about the definition of amateurism.

Belgium hosted and won the 1920 event held in Antwerp, beating Czechoslovakia 2-0 in the final, but the record books don't always mention the fact that after Larnoe had netted Belgium's second goal in the 78th minute, the Czech team walked off the pitch incensed at what they perceived as refereeing bias.

South American football dominated the Olympics of 1924 and 1928 through the thrilling play of Uruguay, who won both tournaments. The World Cup was finally born two years later and from that point the two events would then rival one another until 1950, when the World Cup established itself as football's premier event.

The post-war years brought the second phase of the Olympic football tournament. The Olympics still held firm to its amateur ethos, which was perfectly circumvented by the rising Eastern European Communist bloc countries. Under communist regimes, football was a leisure activity and the players were paid by, and deemed to work for, whatever national institution or industry their club was affiliated to. Between 1952 and 1980 every Olympic football final was won by an East European team: Hungary (1952, 1964, 1968), USSR (1956), Yugoslavia (1960), Poland (1972), East Germany (1976) and Czechoslovakia (1980). Each final in this period, except for 1960, featured just East European teams.

The sequence was ended when France beat Brazil 2-0 in the 1984 final, but it was only because there had been a Communist bloc boycott of the Los Angeles Olympic Games in retaliation to the Western-led boycott of the Moscow Olympics four years earlier. For that tournament FIFA had already sought to address the problem and had ruled that any European or South American player who had played in a World Cup game became ineligible.

Ironically, it was the the Soviet Union that carefully planned their Olympic ambitions in conjunction with their European and World Cup hopes. The USSR had a hot property in 19-year-old Igor Dobrovolski who had five full caps, all in friendlies. Potentially he could have played at the European Championship in 1988, but he was redirected to the Olympics. It was well worth the gamble as Dobrovolski was excellent, helping the USSR to a gold medal, beating Brazil 2-1 in the final. Brazil were the only non-European side to make it as far as the semi-finals, but in Romario they produced the tournament's star player.

The competition also saw one of the greatest shocks in the history of the Olympics. Italy had been so determined to win the gold medal that they had gone as far as delaying the start of their domestic season to accommodate the Olympic football tournament, but they were comprehensively beaten 4-0 by Zambia, with Kalusha Bwalya scoring a hat-trick.

Professional sport was now an integral part of the Olympics and the IOC wanted the football tournament to reflect that, with big names and big teams. FIFA, on the other hand, did not want a rival to the World Cup. In the third phase of Olympic football, and to the consternation of the IOC, FIFA decreed the tournament could only be an Under-23 event, with teams allowed to include just three overaged players.

Spain hosted and won the event in 1992, beating Poland 3-2 in a thrilling and dramatic final that attracted 95,000 spectators. In 1996

the final was played in Athens, Georgia, some 110 kilometres north west of the Olympic host city of Atlanta where no football matches were staged at all. Nevertheless, a staggering 1.36 million paying spectators witnessed the competition, culminating in Nigeria's 3-2 defeat of Argentina in the final.

Cameroon followed up that African success with victory in Australia in 2000, winning the gold medal in a penalty shoot-out with Spain. It was Cameroon's first Olympic gold medal in any sport, proving that the Olympics needs football, whatever its status.

In 2004 Argentina saw off the threat of Paraguay to win their first Olympic gold medal in 52 years, thanks to an 18th minute Carlos Tevez goal, his eighth of the tournament. The Argentinians did not concede a goal during the tournament and found the going made easier in the second half of the final when Paraguay had both Emilio Martinez and Diego Figueredo sent-off. The most talked about match of the competition, however, was played out for the bronze medal, when Italy had to take to the field against Iraq, the tournament's biggest surprise package. It was an emotional game played just hours after it emerged that a kidnapped Italian journalist had been murdered in Iraq in the aftermath of the war in the country. Alberto Gilardino scored the only goal as Italy won the bronze medal and ended Iraq's spectacular run.

COPA AMÉRICA
(SOUTH AMERICAN CHAMPIONSHIP)

The South American Championship is the oldest continental title in the world, having been staged 42 different times, including eight that are deemed unofficial. It has been played under various names and in varying formats, but since 1975 it has been known as the Copa América. There have been seven different winners of the championship over the years, but for the most part the competition has been dominated by the national sides of Argentina and Uruguay.

Argentina gave birth to the event in 1910, hosting and winning a triangular tournament that also involved Uruguay and Chile. Six years later, as part of the centenary celebrations to mark the country's independence from Spain, a second tournament was organised with the addition of Brazil, but this time the cup was won by Uruguay. Both events were actually unofficial, as the Confederación Sudamericana de Futbol (CONEMBOL) was only founded during the 1916 tournament.

The first official tournament took place in Uruguay just over a year later and was contested by the same four teams with the same outcome, Uruguay winners again. The championships were played on a league basis with all of the games staged in one host city (except 1949) until 1975. During the 1920s the South American Championship was an annual event, but the rise of professionalism led to a hiatus of six years, when an unofficial professional championship was staged in Peru in 1935. The success of this tournament led to a revival in interest and a plethora of sanctioned and unsanctioned tournaments were staged during the Forties and Fifties. These competitions were invariably won by Argentina or Uruguay, except in 1939, 1949 and 1953, when Peru, Brazil and Paraguay triumphed respectively.

By the 1960s the championship began to suffer because of the increased popularity of the international club game, and in particular the Copa Libertadores. Played just twice in the decade, in 1963 and 1967, after being staged 30 times the South American Championship disappeared from the football calendar for eight years. When it did return in 1975, all ten

Right: The victorious Argentinian team after winning the Copa América in 1993.

members of CONEMBOL entered for the first time. The format was revamped and played on a home and away basis. The winners from three groups of three teams joined holders Uruguay in two-legged semi-finals. The final was contested by Peru and Colombia, with each team winning a match before Peru clinched a play-off victory 1-0 in Caracas.

In 1987 the Copa América reverted to being staged by a single host country. This was the ideal logistical solution. However, fans of the various host nations were notoriously fickle and attendances suffered as a consequence. In Argentina that year only 500 fans bothered to turn up to watch Colombia play Bolivia. And in 1995, less than 100 fans watched Paraguay's clash with Venezuela in Uruguay, which at least did have the mitigating circumstances of being played in a torrential downpour.

It also has to be said that most tournaments have not produced good football. The 1987 event was dire and witnessed 14 players sent-off in 13 games. The final between Uruguay and Chile was a foul-riddled affair that saw four players dismissed. Uruguay, as holders, had been given a bye to the semi-finals and, therefore, had successfully defended the title by playing just two games.

The next tournament saw Brazil win their first major honour since the 1970 World Cup victory some 19 years earlier. The competition featured two groups of five teams, leading to a final round of four teams – that meant a schedule of 26 games in 16 days, with teams

playing every other day to bring in the much needed television revenues and gate receipts. CONEMBOL justified this as preparation for the 1990 World Cup, but as one player – Uruguay's Pablo Bengochea – failed a drugs test which revealed more than the permitted amount of caffeine in his urine, it was a schedule too gruelling for some.

The other problem facing teams was that many of the European-based players were absent from the competition, while the best of the talent on display would invariably end up Europe-bound after catching the attention of scouts during the tournament. It was to become a problem that was further aggravated by CONEMBOL's decision to create a fixture-heavy World Cup qualifying programme. To earn the television money, teams played up to 18 qualifying matches. The Copa América became a secondary concern to many teams, who fielded under-strength sides.

A desire to revitalise the event, plus a need for increased TV revenues, led CONEMBOL to invite guest teams from other areas of the world to take part. So far Mexico (finalists in 1993 and 2001), USA, Costa Rica, Japan and Honduras have all participated. Canada was invited in 2001 but when the event in Colombia looked set to be postponed they withdrew, along with Argentina.

Argentina won their 15th title in 1993, beating Mexico 2-1 in the final, while Uruguay's 14th trophy was won in 1995 following a penalty shoot-out win over Brazil. In 1997

Bolivia's Juan Baldivieso scored the Copa América's 2,000th goal, but it was Brazil who lifted the trophy that year, as they did again in 1999. Colombia became the seventh nation to win the Copa América when they hosted the 41st competition in 2001.

The 2004 Copa América competition was a battle between Brazil and Argentina, the two undisputed giants of South American football in recent times. Staged in Peru, the tournament could hardly have come to a more exciting conclusion, Brazil snatching the advantage from Argentina with the last kick of the game, when Adriano's injury-time equaliser resulted in a 2-2 final scoreline and took the game to penalties. The Brazilians converted their first four penalties to win the shoot-out 4-2, leaving the Argentinian team devastated.

GOLD CUP
(CONCACAF CHAMPIONSHIP)

When Jack Warner was elected as President of CONCACAF in April 1990 he insisted on setting up an equivalent to the Nations Cup competitions that existed in Africa, Asia, Europe and South America.

Previous incarnations such as the CCCF Championship, run by the Confederación Centroamericana y del Caribe de Fútbol between 1941 and 1961, and the CONCACAF Championship, which ran from 1963 to 1989 had been limited successes. Mexico did not enter until 1963 and initially did not take the competition that seriously. The United States was another notable absentee.

In 1991 the CONCACAF Gold Cup was born. Twenty-six teams entered chasing the eight final places. The inaugural tournament was hosted by the USA, as have been all subsequent tournaments, although in 1993 and 2003 they co-hosted the event with Mexico.

Under coach Bora Milutinovic, the USA won the first Gold Cup. Recording a 2-0 win over the Mexicans in the semi-final, it was their first victory over their near neighbours in 11 years, which led the Mexico coach Manuel Lapuente to resign. The final against Honduras was played at the Coliseum in Los Angeles and, after a goalless game, the destination of the trophy was decided on penalties. Sixteen penalties were taken in all, during which the USA's goalkeeper Tony Meola, who was voted the tournament's Most Valuable Player, saved three kicks. Spot-kick number 15 saw Clavijo convert to put USA 4-3 ahead, before Espinoza of Honduras fired the ball over the bar to give the Americans victory.

Two years later Mexico got their revenge in a competition of eight teams. Despite being co-hosts, Mexico had originally submitted a 'B' team, but it was rejected by CONCACAF secretary Chuck Blazer. A full strength Mexico blew away most of the opposition, thrashing

Martinique 9-0 (including seven goals for Zaguinho), Canada 8-0, and Jamaica 6-1 in a game that saw keeper Jorge Campos switch to centre-forward when the reserve keeper came on as a substitute in the second-half. In front of 120,000 screaming fans in Mexico City, the Mexicans, under coach Miguel Meija Baron, comprehensively beat USA 4-0 in the final.

A switch of dates from July in odd years to January and February in even years began with the third tournament in 1996. There was a further change with the addition of an invited team, Brazil, who sent their Olympic Under-23 side but still managed to reach the final where they faced Mexico, who were now under ex-USA coach Bora Milutinovic. Backed by the majority of the 88,155 crowd in the Los Angeles Coliseum, and playing in appalling conditions directly after the third place play-off match contested at the same venue, Mexico were cynically determined to win. They committed 38 fouls on the way to a 2-0 victory.

In 1998 the tournament featured ten teams. Brazil were once again invited to take part and allowed to play their games in Miami, despite California being firmly established as the home of the Gold Cup. This was connected to the revenue from television, as Los Angeles was some six hours ahead of Brazil, while Miami offered just a three-hour time difference. In a rain-affected tournament, one tie between Jamaica and El Salvador was postponed because of the weather. There was a low turn-out of 11,234 for the tournament's opening fixture between hosts USA and Cuba (the first meeting between the two countries since 1949), but in the semi-finals USA went on to record their first ever win over Brazil at full international level, thanks to a goal from Preki. The real hero of the

game was goalkeeper Kasey Keller who was magnificent under relentless Brazilian pressure. But it was Mexico, back under the stewardship of Manuel Lapuente, who completed a hat-trick of Gold Cup titles, beating the USA by a single Luis Hernandez goal in the final.

In 2000 there were 12 teams battling for the £100,000 prize money, including guest teams Peru, South Korea and Colombia. It was also the tournament that revealed just how financially dependent the competition was on Mexican success. Mexico were knocked-out at the quarter-final stage by a 'golden goal' from Canada's Richard Hastings, and with hosts USA going out on penalties to Colombia at the

same stage, attendance figures subsequently plummeted. The final between Canada and Colombia attracted just 6,197 spectators inside the Los Angeles Coliseum. Canada, who had earlier progressed through the group stage on the toss of a coin at the expense of South Korea, won 2-0 with a headed goal from Jason De Vos and a Carlo Corazzin penalty.

In 2002 the 12 teams included guests Ecuador, who were knocked-out at the group stage by a draw of lots, which allowed Canada and Haiti through. Mexico sent a 'B' team, under pressure from the clubs back home not to select their best players, but they still managed to increase the disappointing crowds to an average of 18,500 for the event, which climaxed with the USA's 2-0 defeat of Costa Rica with goals from Josh Wolff and Jeff Agoos.

Mexico clinched a record fourth Gold Cup title in 2003. A golden goal from Daniel Osorno in the 97th minute defeated favourites Brazil in the final.

In 2005 the format of the competition's first stage changed from four groups of three teams to three groups of four, with the top two in each group and the two best third-placed teams progressing to the quarter-finals. Again several teams fielded second-string squads, including guests Colombia and South Africa, while the region's strongest teams, Mexico and USA, were missing at least half their usual starting line-ups. Matches in Miami may have had to be postponed because of Hurricane Dennis, but the biggest shock of the competition was Panama's success in reaching the Gold Cup final for the first time. Their path included a penalty shoot-out victory over South Africa in the quarter-finals, but penalties could not save them again in the final. After a scoreless game, the USA won the shoot-out 3-1, Brad Davis slotting home the decisive kick.

Above: The USA's Kasey Keller parades the Gold Cup in 2005. Below: Gold Cup winners Canada in 2000.

THE CONCACAF CHAMPIONSHIP

WINNERS

1941:	Costa Rica
1943:	El Salvador
1946:	Costa Rica
1948:	Costa Rica
1951:	Panama
1953:	Costa Rica
1955:	Costa Rica
1957:	Haiti
1960:	Costa Rica
1961:	Costa Rica
1963:	Costa Rica
1965:	Mexico
1967:	Guatemala
1969:	Costa Rica
1971:	Mexico
1973:	Haiti
1977:	Mexico
1981:	Honduras
1985:	Canada
1989:	Costa Rica

GOLD CUP

WINNERS

1991:	USA
1993:	Mexico
1996:	Mexico
1998:	Mexico
2000:	Canada
2002:	USA
2003:	Mexico
2005:	USA

Above: Japan captain Miyamoto raises the Asian Cup in 2004.

ASIAN CUP

The second oldest continental competition in the world, the Asian Cup is played once every four years and has run uninterrupted since 1956, involving a qualifying competition from the outset. The first three Asian Cups were contested in a four-team league and won by South Korea in both 1956 and 1960, and Israel – who had been runners-up at the first two tournaments – in 1964. The 1964 competition was notable for its lack of skilled football and for its poor sportsmanship.

Iran made their Asian Cup debut in 1968, both hosting and winning the tournament. Iran's success was significant because it boosted the game of football in Arabic countries, where it had previously been banned for religious reasons. The five-team finals marked the last appearance of Israel, while North Korea, the Asian heroes of the 1966 World Cup, bizarrely did not even enter.

Semi-finals and a final were added to the six-team league stage in 1972, Iran dominating the revamped competition and winning the final with a 2-1 victory over South Korea after extra-time, Khalani scoring the 107th minute winner in Bangkok. The Iranians completed a hat-trick of triumphs in 1976 when, as hosts, they beat Kuwait 1-0. Iran went 17 successive Asian Cup games without defeat, with their magnificent run ultimately ended by Kuwait in the semi-finals of the 1980 competition. Kuwait went on to win the trophy in one of the most entertaining tournaments in the history of the Asian Cup: 76 goals were scored in the 24 games.

The number of entrants generally increased as the competition progressed, but in the politically volatile region there were inevitable withdrawals for various reasons. However, the Asian Cup increased in prestige, helped by the gradual rise of professionalism. Saudi Arabia beat China in the 1984 final and successfully defended the title four years later in a Middle East dominated competition, with seven out of the ten finalists from that region.

Japan were victorious at the 1992 Asian Cup, a tournament that was hit by political problems, with only 23 out of the 37 members entering. The finals were marred by violent play on the pitch, with eight players sent-off and 49 booked. Iran were the worst culprits, with three players facing one-year bans and another two receiving match bans.

At the 40th anniversary tournament in 1996 Iran were to win the Fair Play Award, as well as boasting both the highest goalscorer in Ali Daei and the Player Of The Tournament in Khodadad Azizi. The host nation lost a final for the very first time, when Saudi Arabia beat the United Arab Emirates in a penalty shoot-out to win the 12-team tournament. This was a particularly impressive display since three Saudi players had been suspended for breaking Islamic Sharia Law.

Japan beat Saudi Arabia 1-0 in Beirut to win the 2000 tournament, with a goal from Shigeyoshi Mochizuki, only playing in the final because Junichi Inamoto had been suspended. Earlier in the competition Japan had set a goalscoring record when they thrashed Uzbekistan 8-1.

In 2004 China hosted the biggest Asian Cup tournament yet, with 16 teams competing. The hosts reached their first final in 20 years, inspiring a home television audience of 250 million to tune in to the deciding game with Japan, making it the most watched sporting event in Chinese TV history. The hosts made the better start, but in the 22nd minute they found themselves behind to a Takashi Fukunishi goal scored against the run of play. Despite a first-half equaliser from China's Li Ming, Japan went on to win 3-1 through goals from Koji Nakata and Keiji Tamada. The home fans, who had booed the Japanese national anthem before the game, demonstrated their anger at the final whistle while Japan picked up the trophy.

To avoid clashes with the Olympics and the European Championships, the next Asian Cup will be held in 2007. The competition will be co-hosted by four nations: Indonesia, Malaysia, Thailand and Vietnam.

ASIAN GAMES

Football has always been part of the multi-sport Asian Games since the inaugural event was held in India in 1951. Six teams entered the first tournament, playing matches of 80 minutes in duration, but the standard was not particularly high with the hosts beating Iran 1-0 in the final.

From such humble beginnings the football tournament has increased in size, with Taiwan, mainly represented by players from Hong Kong, winning the finals in 1954 and 1958, beating South Korea on both occasions. The latter competition was marred by accusations of biased and incompetent refereeing.

In political terms the participation of both Taiwan and Israel were a problem in 1962 and hosts Indonesia rescinded the invitation to both teams. In 1974 both North Korea and Kuwait refused to play Israel, so after a 3-0 win over Burma, the Israelis found themselves in the final, where they lost to Iran by an own-goal.

On two occasions the gold medal has been shared. In both 1970 and 1978 South Korea were held to 0-0 draws, firstly by Burma and then by North Korea. South Korea finally won the gold medal outright in 1986, a competition noted for a quarter-final round decided entirely by penalty shoot-outs.

Iran has dominated the Asian Games since 1990, winning three out of four tournaments. Goalkeeper Ahmadreza Abedzadeh was the hero in Beijing in 1990, saving two penalties in a 4-1 shoot-out victory over North Korea. That tournament was played in the shadow of the Iraqi invasion of Kuwait. The Kuwaiti team went on to reach the quarter-finals, while Iraq was banned from the competition and both India and Indonesia withdrew.

Iran won the gold medal again in 1998, beating Kuwait 2-0 in the first final between West Asian sides. Despite having Mehdi Mahdavikia sent-off late in the game, Iran outplayed a depleted Kuwait, with first-half goals from Ahmed Karimi and Karim Bagheri. By this point, the tournament had become a 24-team event (although Saudi Arabia withdrew) and was played over three weeks.

By the 2002 Asian Games, the football tournament had been revamped and turned into an Under-23 competition, with each team allowed to field up to three over-age players. The idea was to prepare Asian teams for the Olympics. However, this revamp seemed to have a detrimental effect on attendances.

Held in South Korea after the World Cup, the cream of Asian youth seemed a massive turn-off to Korean fans now accustomed to the big names of world football, and many of the games were played in half-empty stadiums. When South Korea were knocked out by Iran in the semi-finals, fans attempted to get refunds for their final tickets. Dissatisfied with their team's performance, the South Korean football association immediately sacked coach Park Hang-Seo for delivering just the bronze medal. He had been assistant to Guus Hiddink at the World Cup just months earlier and he managed to last just two months in the top job after the Dutchman's departure.

Iran became the first team to retain the title outright, beating Japan 2-1 with goals from Kazemeyan and Bayatiniya. The tournament marked the return of Afghanistan after an 18-year absence, but they lost all three games, conceding 32 goals.

THE ASIAN CUP
WINNERS

1956: South Korea
1960: South Korea
1964: Israel
1968: Iran
1972: Iran
1976: Iran
1980: Kuwait
1984: Saudi Arabia
1988: Saudi Arabia
1992: Japan
1996: Saudi Arabia
2000: Japan
2004: Japan

THE ASIAN GAMES
WINNERS

1951: India
1954: Taiwan
1958: Taiwan
1962: India
1966: Burma
1970: Burma & South Korea *(title shared)*
1974: Iran
1978: South Korea & North Korea *(title shared)*
1982: Iraq
1986: South Korea
1990: Iran
1994: Uzbekistan
1998: Iran
2002: Iran

AFRICAN NATIONS CUP

The first African Nations Cup was held in Sudan in 1957 between Egypt, Ethiopia, South Africa and Sudan, the founder members of the Confédération Africaine de Football (CAF). However, South Africa were forced to withdraw when they refused to send a multi-racial team. They offered only an all-white or an all-black team, neither of which was acceptable to the other CAF members. South Africa did not return to the African Nations Cup until they hosted and won the 1996 tournament.

In the Khartoum Stadium on February 16, 1957, the first African Nations Cup was decided when Egypt easily defeated Ethiopia 4-0, with all four goals scored by El Diba. It was appropriate that Egypt should be the first winners, since the trophy itself had been donated by General Abdel Aziz Mustapha, a former president of CAF and an Egyptian. Since then the African Nations Cup has developed from a small three-team tournament to a 16-team event that is televised all over the world.

The 1960s saw the rise of Ghana, winners of the tournament in 1963 and 1965, runners-up in 1968 and 1970. Ghana had drawn on the experience of a number of European coaches and even embarked on a European tour in 1962, proving themselves to be far and away the best team in Africa at the time. Although successive Nations Cup triumphs were just 23 months apart, only one player, Odametey, played in both finals. Ghana finally won the Abdel Aziz Abdallah Salem Cup – as the original African Nations Cup trophy was officially known – outright in 1978.

For the 1968 tournament there was a qualifying round for the first time – and that year's final, when Zaire beat favourites Ghana 1-0 with a goal from Kalala, was the first African Nations Cup match to be televised. In 1970 Sudan beat Ghana in the final, but it was Ivory Coast who broke the record for the biggest win in the finals with a 6-1 thrashing of Ethiopia, Pokou scoring a record haul of five goals in that game.

The African Nations Cup finally came of age in the Eighties. Nigeria, buoyant through oil money, staged a magnificent tournament in 1980, with state-of-the-art facilities and enormous spectator support. A total of 735,000 fans attended the 16 games, including an 80,000 capacity crowd in the Surulere in Lagos for a final that saw Nigeria beat Algeria 3-0.

A new dimension was brought to the African Nations Cup in 1982 when all the games, staged in Libya, were played on artificial pitches. Technically it was a good tournament but goals were at a premium. The final itself was resolved by a penalty shoot-out, with Ghana overcoming the hosts 7-6 on penalties after a 1-1 draw.

Ivory Coast was consumed by football fever when they staged the tournament in 1984, but

national pride – and local interest in the competition – was severely dented when the hosts went out in the first round. The crowds stayed away from the latter stages and the organisers were forced to give tickets away to get a capacity crowd for the final, in which Cameroon came from a goal down to beat Nigeria 3-1. This tournament was the first to seriously arouse the interest of European scouts following the impressive performance of the African nations at the 1982 World Cup. This proved the start of the plundering of African talent by the leading clubs of Europe, a problem for the tournament in later years.

The refusal of European clubs to release their players in 1990 contributed to a poor tournament. In 1992 CAF responded by switching the event to January and increasing the number of finalists to 12. Of the 263 players on call, some 83 were professionals from the European leagues. It was nations from western Africa that dominated the tournament, which for the first time had comprehensive television coverage. Sadly it was not a great tournament, although the final produced a dramatic climax. After a goalless draw, the match was settled with a 20-minute penalty shoot-out involving 24 spot-kicks. Ivory Coast ultimately won the shoot-out 11-10 when Ghana's Tony Baffoe saw his kick saved after Kouame Ake had converted with his second penalty of the shoot-out.

The 1994 final was one of the best in the history of the African Nations Cup. Zambia faced Nigeria, just a year after the air crash that had wiped out the Zambian national team. Litana put Zambia ahead after just three

minutes, but Emmanuel Amunike equalised two minutes later and then scored the winner in the 47th minute. Amazingly it had been his first appearance in the tournament, making him the 19th squad player used by Nigeria in the finals.

In the following tournament, Mahmoud Al-Gohari became the first man to win the African Nations Cup as both a player (1959) and a coach, when he guided Egypt to glory in Burkina Faso in 1998. It was Cameroon, however, who became the dominant side of the first tournaments of the 21st Century. They became the first team in 37 years to retain the title when they lifted the trophy in 2000 and 2002.

In 2004, under the direction of legendary French coach Roger Lemerre, Tunisia won the cup for the very first time. They had taken the lead in the final after just four minutes through Dos Santos, but Youssef Mokhtari equalised for Morocco with a header shortly before half-time. It was a mistake by Morocco keeper Khalid Fouhami that gifted striker Ziad Jaziri the winner six minutes into the second-half, enabling the hosts to lift the trophy.

In 2006 Egypt won the competition for a record fifth time after beating Ivory Coast 4-2 on penalties. Although the match had finished goalless in front of a crowd of 75,000 in Cairo, hosts Egypt had their chances during the match, including a disallowed goal with seven minutes of normal time remaining and a missed penalty in extra-time. But Egypt's hero was keeper Essam Al Hadary, who saved spot-kicks from Ivory Coast captain Didier Drogba and Bakary Kone in the deciding shoot-out.

Above: Egypt get their hands on the African Nations Cup in 2006.

AFRICAN NATIONS CUP
WINNERS
1957: Egypt
1959: Egypt
1962: Ethiopia
1963: Ghana
1965: Ghana
1968: Congo-Kinshasa
1970: Sudan
1972: Congo
1974: Zaïre
1976: Morocco
1978: Ghana
1980: Nigeria
1982: Ghana
1984: Cameroon
1986: Egypt
1988: Cameroon
1990: Algeria
1992: Ivory Coast
1994: Nigeria
1996: South Africa
1998: Egypt
2000: Cameroon
2002: Cameroon
2004: Tunisia
2006: Egypt

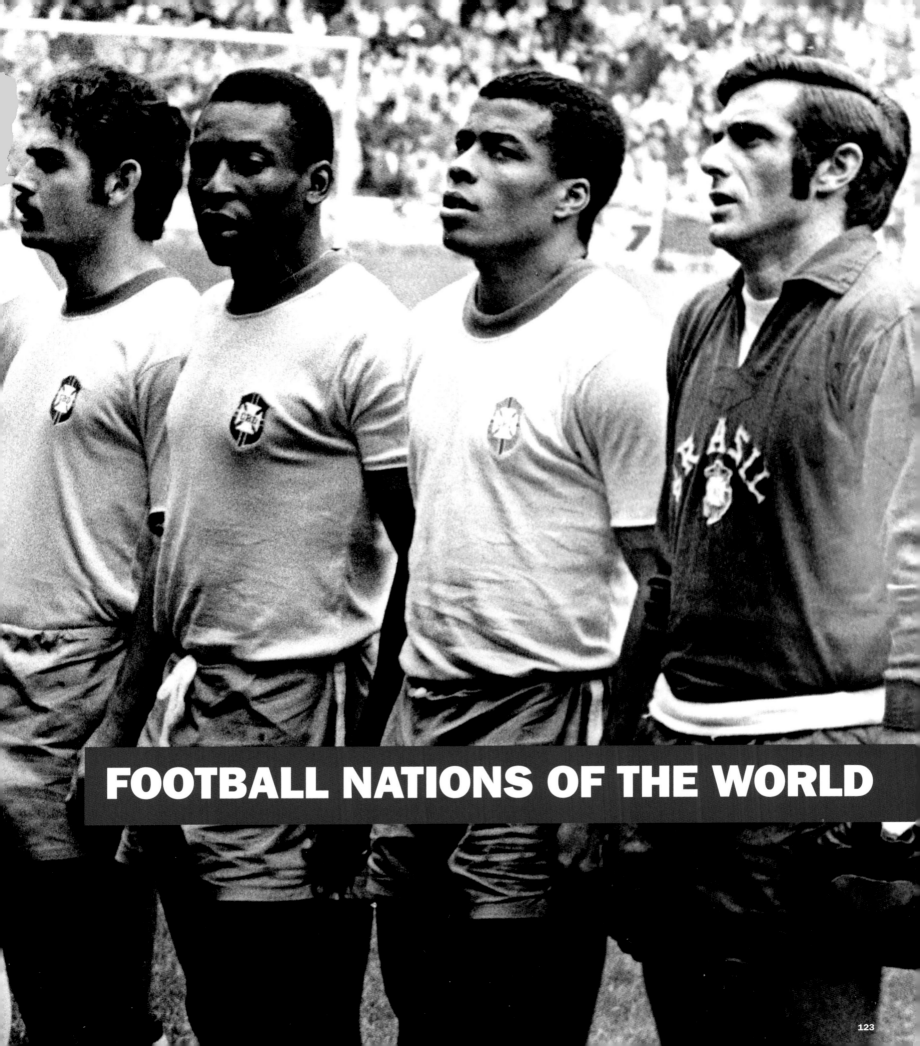

FOOTBALL NATIONS OF THE WORLD

THE COUNTRIES AND CONFEDERATIONS OF WORLD FOOTBALL

FIFA FÉDÉRATION INTERNATIONALE DE FOOTBALL ASSOCIATION

Founded: 1904 **Headquarters:** Zurich, Switzerland **Members:** 207

Competitions: World Cup, Women's World Cup, Under-17 World Championship, World Youth Championship, World Club Championship, Confederations Cup

The FIFA World rankings listed for each country in this chapter are as they stood in July 2006.

CONCACAF

CONFEDERATION OF NORTH, CENTRAL AMERICAN AND CARIBBEAN ASSOCIATION FOOTBALL

Founded: 1961

Headquarters: New York, USA

Members: 35

Competitions: Gold Cup, Women's Gold Cup, Champions Cup, Copa Pan-Americana

Seats On FIFA Executive

UEFA	🧍🧍🧍🧍🧍🧍🧍🧍
AFC	🧍🧍🧍🧍
CAF	🧍🧍🧍🧍
CONMEBOL	🧍🧍🧍
CONCACAF	🧍🧍🧍
FIFA	🧍🧍
OFC	🧍

CONMEBOL

CONFEDERACIÓN SUDAMERICANA DE FÚTBOL

Founded: 1916

Headquarters: Asunción, Paraguay

Members: 10

Competitions: Copa América, Copa Libertadores, Copa Pan-Americana

UEFA
UNION OF EUROPEAN FOOTBALL ASSOCIATIONS

Founded: 1954

Headquarters: Nyon, Switzerland

Members: 52

Competitions: European Championship, European Champions League, UEFA Cup, Intertoto Cup, European Supercup, European Women's Championship

OFC
OCEANIA FOOTBALL CONFEDERATION

Founded: 1966

Headquarters: Auckland, New Zealand

Members: 11

Competitions: Oceania Nations Cup, OFC Club Championship, Oceania Women's Tournament

AFC
ASIAN FOOTBALL CONFEDERATION

Founded: 1954

Headquarters: Kuala Lumpur, Malaysia

Members: 46

Competitions: Asian Cup, Asian Games, Asian Super League, Asian Women's Championship, Asian Champions League, AFC Cup, AFC President's Cup

CAF
CONFÉDÉRATION AFRICAINE DE FOOTBALL

Founded: 1957

Headquarters: Cairo, Egypt

Members: 53

Competitions: African Cup Of Nations, CAF Cup, African Champions League, African Cup Winners' Cup, CAF Super Cup

AFGHANISTAN

Federation: Afghanistan Football Federation
Founded: 1933
Joined FIFA: 1948
Confederation: AFC
FIFA world ranking: 173

ALBANIA

Federation: Federata Shqiptare e Futbolit
Founded: 1930
Joined FIFA: 1932
Confederation: UEFA
FIFA world ranking: 65

Football arrived in Albania at the turn of the century but the ruling Turks actively prevented the locals playing the game. Independence in 1912 saw the game flourish and in 1930 the Football Association of Albania (FSF) was formed, along with the Albanian league championship. However, between 1938 and 1944 football activities ceased, with the country first under the control of Mussolini's Fascists and then the Soviet-backed Communists.

Football returned after World War II and Albania claimed their only title as Balkan Cup winners in 1946. A period of self-imposed isolation followed and between 1954 and 1963 Albania played just one international. In the 1960s Albania began to compete at both club and national level for the first time. They remain one of Europe's football minnows, with a poor record. During the 1980s, for example, the national team won just two matches. On the domestic scene in Albania, the game is dominated by the Tirana clubs.

ALGERIA

Federation: Fédération Algérienne de Football
Founded: 1962
Joined FIFA: 1963
Confederation: CAF
FIFA world ranking: 93
Honours: African Nations Cup 1990

Arguably the greatest moment in Algerian football history was the shock 2-1 defeat of the mighty West Germany at the 1982 World Cup. Algeria, under coach Mahieddine Khalef, gave

a resolute defensive performance against the attacking Germans, with goals from Rabah Madjer and Lakhdar Belloumi earning the landmark victory. However, Algeria were cheated out of a second round place by 'The Great Gijón Swindle', when a convenient 1-0 win for West Germany over Austria sent both those nations through at Algeria's expense. In 1990 Algeria finally experienced success when they hosted and won the African Nations Cup for the first time, an Oudjani goal beating Nigeria 1-0 in the final.

It was the French who introduced the game to Algeria at the turn of the century. By the 1920s the Muslim Algerians embraced the game and football quickly became the focus of a rising nationalist sentiment that was to lead to the country's independence from France in 1962. The first Algerian national league culminated in 1963 with USM Algeria winning the title. JS Kabylie (aka JE Tizi-Ouzou), the Berber region team, have been the most successful Algerian side both at home and in the modern African game, having recently won a hat-trick of CAF Cups in 2000, 2001 and 2002.

AMERICAN SAMOA

Federation: American Samoa Football Association
Founded: 1984
Joined FIFA: 1998
Confederation: OFC
FIFA world ranking: 196 (joint)

ANDORRA

Federation: Federació Andorrana de Fútbol
Founded: 1994
Joined FIFA: 1996
Confederation: UEFA
FIFA world ranking: 131 (joint)

In October 2004 Andorra recorded their first competitive win after eight years, beating Macedonia 1-0 in a World Cup qualifier. Their previous two victories were friendly wins over Belarus in 2000 and Albania in 2002. The Principality of Andorra boasts an open eight-club top division vying for a fan-base from its 70,000 inhabitants.

ANGOLA

Federation: Federação Angolana de Futebol
Founded: 1977
Joined FIFA: 1980
Confederation: CAF
FIFA world ranking: 55

For a country that has been blighted by over 30 years of bloody civil war, Angola's first World Cup qualification in 2006, under coach Luís Oliveira Gonçalves who took over in 2003, was nothing short of incredible. The 'Palancas Negras' (the Black Impalas) had only previously appeared in three African Nations Cup tournaments, winning just one match and never getting past the first phase, but they had won the regional COSAFA Cup on three occasions in 1999, 2001 and 2004. Many Angolan-born players have been raised in Portugal and the Federação Angolana de Futebol searches for European-based players for the national team. The domestic Angolan league is dominated by club sides AS Aviacao and Petro Atletico.

ANGUILLA

Federation: Anguilla Football Association
Founded: 1990
Joined FIFA: 1996
Confederation: CONCACAF
FIFA world ranking: –

ANTIGUA AND BARBUDA

Federation: Antigua and Barbuda Football Association
Founded: 1928
Joined FIFA: 1970
Confederation: CONCACAF
FIFA world ranking: 145

THE COUNTRIES OF UEFA

ARGENTINA

Federation: Asociación del Fútbol Argentina
Founded: 1893
Joined FIFA: 1912
Confederation: CONMEBOL
FIFA world ranking: 3
Honours: World Cup 1978, 1986; Copa América 1910, 1921, 1925, 1927, 1929, 1937, 1941, 1945, 1946, 1947, 1955, 1957, 1959, 1991, 1993; Olympics 2004

Argentina's football history can be traced back to 1867, when immigrant English and Italian rail workers and sailors introduced the game to the South American country. The English High School put together a club that captured ten of the 12 league titles following the formation of the Argentinian league in 1891 and although they were the most successful team, Buenos Aires FC claim to be the first formed in the country and the first outside of the British Isles and the USA.

The first international played outside of England also involved Argentina, who beat Uruguay 3-1 in 1901. The first South American championship was also hosted and won by the country some nine years later, although the tournament consisted of just two other teams, Uruguay and Chile.

The early years of the 20th Century saw the league's reputation grow in stature with the formation of the Buenos Aires 'Big Five': River Plate (founded by the English), Racing Club (the French and European descendants born in Argentina), Boca Juniors, Independiente and San Lorenzo, clubs that dominate the championship to this day.

The years either side of World War I saw the number of clubs rise to 20 and in the 1920s the league was at its most expansive, with 36 clubs. On the world stage Argentina had a good showing in the inaugural World Cup, losing to hosts and old foes Uruguay 4-2 in the final. This success led to the beginning of the professional era in 1931, with Boca Juniors setting the pace following three championship victories in the first five seasons. River Plate and Independiente would also enjoy extended spells of dominance, with the former enjoying a purple patch of five championships in six years during the 1950s.

It was within the first three decades of the formation of its professional league that Argentina established itself as a super power in world football. Attendances grew, stadiums improved and the international team won eight of its record 15 Copa América titles.

The ultimate prize of winning the World Cup had eluded the nation thus far. However, a league-restructuring programme in 1967

Above: The Argentina players celebrate winning the Copa América after their victory over Mexico in Ecuador in 1993.
Opposite: Diego Maradona capped a series of fine performances in the tournament by lifting the World Cup in 1986.

had a positive effect. The formation of two regional competitions, the Metropolitano and the Nacional, cut down on travelling times and expenses, leaving clubs to flourish and this was reflected with Racing Club, Estudiantes, Independiente and Boca Juniors all winning the World Club Cup within the next ten years.

Boca's victory against West German side Borussia Mönchengladbach in 1977 also proved to be the catalyst to World Cup success the following year. As hosts, César Luis Menotti saw his team sweep all before them, including pre-tournament favourites Holland 3-1 in the final. Played out to a ticker tape welcome in the Monumental Stadium, Buenos Aires, Mario Kempes's two goals made him more popular than the country's president and as soon as the tournament ended, a statue was erected in the capital in the striker's honour.

Yet while Kempes had secured a place in Argentinian football history, his star would soon be cast into the shadows by the emerging talent of Diego Armando Maradona. Having started his career with Argentinos Juniors, where he scored 116 goals in 166 games, a move to Boca Juniors proved equally fruitful and the 20-year-old's performances secured his team the 1981 Metropolitano title.

Maradona's undoubted talents were thrust onto the world stage at the 1982 World Cup finals in Spain and although he made an impression with his silky skills, unrivalled ball control and wonderful dribbles, his suspect temperament was also on show as a rash kick at Brazil substitute Batista brought an end to his participation with a red card.

Bowing out in round two proved to be a temporary blip for Argentinian football and having reverted to a single national league in

1985, Independiente's World Club Cup victory against Liverpool in 1984 and River Plate's success against Steaua Bucharest two years later only emphasised the buoyancy which carried itself through to the 1986 World Cup finals, where Maradona reigned supreme.

Fans of Pelé might argue otherwise, but never in a World Cup had one player made such an impact. Although Real Madrid striker Jorge Valdano's contribution can't be underestimated, Maradona literally took teams apart single-handedly, as both Belgium and England – the 'Hand of God' goal apart – would confirm. His second goal against Bobby Robson's side is regarded as one of the all-time great strikes, and although the skipper did not reach his usual dizzy heights in the 3-2 final win against West Germany, few would argue that he deserved to lift the trophy at the very peak of his career.

Argentina again reached the final in 1990, when the Germans gained revenge – but their unsightly mix of roughhouse tactics and safety-first approach won them few friends. Diego Maradona's positive drugs test at the 1994 World Cup further blemished Argentina's reputation as arch-rivals Brazil gained the ascendancy.

The new century has seen a resurgence, bringing success for club side Boca Juniors, who have contested four Copa Libertadores finals, winning three since 2000. The national team won the 2004 Olympic title, featuring Carlos Tevez who was voted South American Player Of The Year in 2003, 2004 and 2005. They lost both the 2004 Copa América, on penalties, and the 2005 Confederation Cup to Brazil. With Lionel Messi in the team they also won the World Youth Championship for the fourth time in ten years in 2005, but lost to Germany on penalties in the quarter-finals of the 2006 World Cup.

1860

1867: The first football matches in Argentina are played between immigrant English and Italian rail workers and Argentinians.

1870

1870s: English High School build a team that captures ten of 12 titles in the early stages of Argentine football.

1890

1893: The Argentine Association Football League is founded.

1901: Argentina and Uruguay contest the first international game outside England, while club side River Plate are formed.

1900

1905: Boca Juniors are founded.

1910

1910: The first South American Championship is hosted and won by Argentina.

1920

1929 to 1959: Argentina win nine of their 14 Copa América titles during this period.

1930

1930: Argentina reach the final of the first World Cup, losing 4-2 to hosts Uruguay.

1965

1966: Antonio Rattin is sent off in an aggressive World Cup quarter-final with England, whose manager Alf Ramsey calls the Argentines 'animals'.

1970

1970: Argentina fail to qualify for the Mexico World Cup.

1975

1978: As hosts, Argentina reach their second World Cup final, beating Holland 3-1. Mario Kempes is the star of the side.

1980

1986: Inspired by Diego Maradona, Argentina win their second World Cup, beating West Germany in the final in Mexico.

1985

1990

1990: Argentina lose the World Cup final to West Germany. Monzon becomes the first player to be sent-off in a World Cup final, followed by Dezotti.

1995

1998: Argentina are knocked out of the World Cup in the quarter-finals by Holland.

2000

2004: Argentina win the Olympic title beating Paraguay in an all-South American final.

2005

THE COUNTRIES OF CONCACAF

CANADA

UNITED STATES OF AMERICA

BERMUDA

US VIRGIN ISLANDS

PUERTO RICO

BRITISH VIRGIN ISLANDS

HAITI

ANGUILLA

DOMINICAN REPUBLIC

CUBA

ST KITTS AND NEVIS

TURKS AND CAICOS ISLANDS

ANTIGUA AND BARBUDA

MONTSERRAT

CAYMAN ISLANDS

BAHAMAS

DOMINICA

MEXICO

ST LUCIA

JAMAICA

ST VINCENT AND THE GRENADINES

BELIZE

BARBADOS

ARUBA

GUATEMALA

COLOMBIA

GRENADA

EL SALVADOR

TRINIDAD AND TOBAGO

HONDURAS

PANAMA

NETHERLANDS ANTILLES

NICARAGUA

VENEZUELA

SURINAM

COSTA RICA

ECUADOR

GUYANA

BRAZIL

PERU

PARAGUAY

BOLIVIA

URUGUAY

CHILE

ARGENTINA

THE COUNTRIES OF CONMEBOL

ARMENIA

Federation: Football Federation of Armenia
Founded: 1992
Joined FIFA: 1992
Confederation: UEFA
FIFA world ranking: 105

Ararat Yerevan are Armenia's leading side, forming the nucleus of the national team. In 1973 they won the Soviet league and cup double. The Armenian league rarely goes through a season without at least one team failing to complete the programme of fixtures.

ARUBA

Federation: Arubaanse Voetbal Bond
Founded: 1932
Joined FIFA: 1988
Confederation: CONCACAF
FIFA world ranking: 196 (joint)

AUSTRALIA

Federation: Football Federation Australia Limited
Founded: 1961
Joined FIFA: 1963
Confederation: AFC
FIFA world ranking: 33
Honours: Oceania Nations Cup 1980, 1996, 2000, 2004

Football in Australia has been completely overhauled with the instigation of the Hyundai A-League in 2005 (a league of eight club franchises). The switching of confederations from the Oceania Football Confederation to the Asian Football Confederation in 2006, and a Federation revamp and name change that dropped the word 'soccer' in favour of football have help to rebrand the sport in Australia.

The inaugural A-League Championship was won by Sydney FC, coached by Pierre Littbarski and inspired on the field by Dwight Yorke and in the boardroom by Hollywood star Anthony LaPaglia. Attendances doubled but all the clubs suffered financial problems when television and sponsorship revenues were not realised.

From the 2007-8 season the champions can participate in the Asian Champions League and Australia have entered the Asian Cup from the 2007 competition. Previously as members of the OFC they had dominated the Oceania Cup, winning it four times, while their clubs – Adelaide City in 1987, South Melbourne 1999, Wollongong Wolves 2001 and Sydney FC in 2005 – made a clean sweep of the Oceania Champions Cup.

Australia's last role as a member of the OFC was to represent the region at the 2006 World Cup for only the second time in their history. The national team is dependent on players who mostly ply their trade in Europe. Of the 23-man squad for Germany 2006 only two players were with Australian clubs, compared with the 1974 World Cup squad that was exclusively Australian-based.

AUSTRIA

Federation: Österreichischer Fussball-Bund
Founded: 1904
Joined FIFA: 1905
Confederation: UEFA
FIFA world ranking: 60

On October 12, 1902, the first international football match between European nations outside of Britain was staged when Austria defeated Hungary 5-0 in Vienna, a city that became the centre of football excellence in central Europe. In Vienna, the emphasis was placed on the kind of skill, short passing and innovative tactics that had the rest of Europe astounded. In 1911 the Austrian league was formed (albeit exclusively with Vienna-based clubs), followed eight years later by the Austrian Cup, with both competitions dominated by FK Austria Vienna and SK Rapid Vienna.

The 1930s saw the arrival of Austria's 'Wunderteam', including the celebrated player Matthias Sindelar who scored 27 international goals in his career. Between February 1931 and June 1934 Austria were defeated just twice in a 30-game run that saw them score 101 goals.

They were also World Cup semi-finalists in 1934, losing to Italy 1-0, and Olympic Games runners-up in 1936. Austria looked set to dominate the European game, but when the country was absorbed by Hitler's Germany, Austrian football ceased to exist.

In the Fifties the Austrian game experienced a brief renaissance under Walter Nausch that saw them reach the semi-finals of the 1954 World Cup. The side included Ernst Ocwirk and Gerhard Hanappi and will be remembered for the incredible 7-5 quarter-final victory over hosts Switzerland.

Austrian football influence then began to fade and the national team did not qualify for the World Cup again until 1978. At both club and international level the game had became quite ordinary, and despite unearthing such individual talents as Hans Krankl and Herbert Prohaska, the nadir was reached with a 1-0 defeat by the Faeroe Islands in 1990.

AZERBAIJAN

Federation: Azerbaycan Futbol Federasiyalari Assosiasiyasi
Founded: 1992
Joined FIFA: 1994
Confederation: UEFA
FIFA world ranking: 109

Four clubs dominate Azeri football: Neftchi Baku, Karabakh Agdam, Turan Taz and Kepez Ganca. In 1994-5 Turan became the first club from Azerbaijan to play in a European competition, and the national side, enforced to play all their home games in Turkey, entered the European Championship. Since then home games have been played in Baku.

Left: Armenia's Artur Petrosyan in action against Wales.

Below: Australia's Harry Kewell attacks in a friendly international against Norway in 2004.

BAHAMAS

Federation: Bahamas Football Association
Founded: 1967
Joined FIFA: 1968
Confederation: CONCACAF
FIFA world ranking: 193

BANGLADESH

Federation: Bangladesh Football Federation
Founded: 1972
Joined FIFA: 1974
Confederation: AFC
FIFA world ranking: 143 (joint)

BELARUS

Federation: Football Federation of the Republic of Belarus
Founded: 1992
Joined FIFA: 1992
Confederation: UEFA
FIFA world ranking: 73

BAHRAIN

Federation: Bahrain Football Association
Founded: 1957
Joined FIFA: 1966
Confederation: AFC
FIFA world ranking: 94

BARBADOS

Federation: Barbados Football Association
Founded: 1910
Joined FIFA: 1968
Confederation: CONCACAF
FIFA world ranking: 152

Dinamo Minsk, the leading Belorussian side in the old Soviet Supreme League, dominated the early years of the Belarus championship and the national team. Since then sides such as Slavia Mozyr, BATE Borisov and Belshina have all made their mark, while the national team have had highs (beating Holland) and lows (losing to Andorra). Among the nation's successful exports in recent years is Alexander Gleb, who plies his trade with Arsenal in the English Premiership, and was voted Belarus Player Of The Year in 2002.

Opposite centre: Van Himst of Belgium in action in 1972.

Below: Belgium's Eric Gerets gets the better of West Germany's Franz Beckenbauer in the 1980 European Championship final.

BELGIUM

Federation: Union Royale des Sociétiés de Football Association
Formed: 1895
Joined FIFA: 1904
Confederation: UEFA
FIFA world ranking: 57
Honours: Olympics 1920

Belgians loved football from the beginning and their contribution and promotion of the game is too often overlooked. The Royal Antwerp club was formed in 1880, the Belgian league began in 1896, and the national team played their first game against France in 1904.

Belgium were founder members of FIFA and heavily promoted the World Cup to the extent they were one of only four European sides to travel to Uruguay in 1930 for the first tournament. Indeed the first World Cup final referee was a Belgian, Jean Langenus. This unfettered enthusiasm saw the amateur game flourish. Semi-professionalism was reluctantly accepted later but it was not until 1972 that club football turned professional.

Anderlecht, after another round of the club mergers that have littered Belgian football history, took the domestic game up a level in 1973. Belgium's most successful club went on to lift the European Cup Winners' Cup in both 1976 and 1978, and the UEFA Cup in 1983.

Between 1982 and 2002 Belgium qualified for every World Cup, reaching the semi-final

BELIZE

Federation: Football Federation of Belize
Founded: 1980
Joined FIFA: 1986
Confederation: CONCACAF
FIFA world ranking: 196 (joint)

BENIN

Federation: Fédération Béninoise de Football
Founded: 1968
Joined FIFA: 1969
Confederation: CAF
FIFA world ranking: 106

in 1986 and losing to a Maradona-inspired Argentina. In the European Championship they were runners-up in 1980 and have twice hosted the tournament (in 1972 and as co-hosts in 2000).

The most profound influence on the modern game was caused by a Belgian, when the Bosman Ruling shook football to its roots. Jean-Marc Bosman brought a court case that ultimately led to freedom of movement of foreign players within Europe and gained legal rights for players, allowing them to leave a club once their contract expires without the need for a transfer fee.

BERMUDA

Federation: Bermuda Football Association
Founded: 1928
Joined FIFA: 1962
Confederation: CONCACAF
FIFA world ranking: 160

BHUTAN

Federation: Bhutan Football Federation
Founded: 1983
Joined FIFA: 2000
Confederation: AFC
FIFA world ranking: 187

BOLIVIA

Federation: Federación Boliviana de Fútbol
Founded: 1925
Joined FIFA: 1926
Confederation: CONMEBOL
FIFA world ranking: 85
Honours: Copa América 1963

Bolivia is a modest football nation, but on the international stage they have enormous home advantage due to the altitude at La Paz, which is 12,000 feet above sea level. Away from home they have not been so reliable. Their only Copa

América success was in 1963 when they hosted the tournament. Bolivia have reached the World Cup finals just three times: in 1930 (invited), 1950 (walk-over) and 1994. Down the years the domestic game in all its incarnations – La Paz League (1914), National Championship (1926) and the National League (1977) – has been dominated by three clubs: The Strongest, Jorge Wilsterman and Bolivar.

BOSNIA-HERZEGOVINA

Federation: Football Federation of Bosnia-Herzegovina
Founded: 1992
Joined FIFA: 1996
Confederation: UEFA
FIFA world ranking: 43

Bosnia's independence didn't provide a unified football scene. Initially there were three separate leagues for the Muslim, Croat and Serbian entities, but in 2002-3 Bosnia's national division was extended to 20 teams, coming from all areas of the country. Similarly, non-Muslim players have only been selected for the national team since 1999.

BOTSWANA

Federation: Botswana Football Association
Founded: 1970
Joined FIFA: 1976
Confederation: CAF
FIFA world ranking: 104

Above right: Erwin Sanchez of Bolivia fends of Germany's Thomas Berthold at the 1994 World Cup.

Above left: Benin's Ogounbiyi Mouitala tries to intercept the ball in a World Cup qualifier against Egypt in Cairo in 2005.

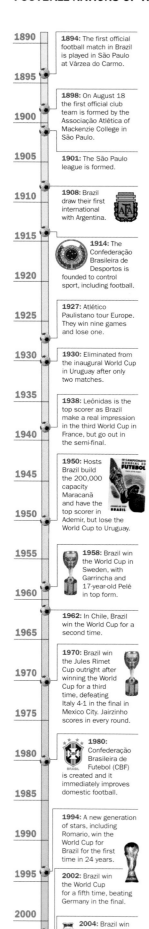

BRAZIL

Federation: Confederação Brasileira de Futebol

Founded: 1914

Joined FIFA: 1923

Confederation: CONMEBOL

FIFA world ranking: 1

Honours: World Cup 1958, 1962, 1970, 1994, 2002; Copa América 1919, 1922, 1949, 1989, 1997, 1999, 2004; Confederations Cup 2005

Some quarters believe that football was brought to Brazil by British and Dutch sailors in the second half of the 19th Century. Yet the accepted consensus is that Charles Miller, who was born in Brazil but educated in Southampton, returned to his birthplace in 1894 with two footballs, a rule book and a set of playing kit to teach the locals of São Paulo the laws of the beautiful game.

The first recorded football match in Brazil took place that year between the employees of the local gas company and the São Paulo railway, which the latter side won 4-2. The game created fervent interest in the sport and within just four years the first club side – Mackenzie Athletic Association – had been formed, creating a snowball effect throughout São Paulo and beyond.

In 1901 the São Paulo League was formally established, Río de Janeiro following suit and in 1914 the Brazilian national team played its first official international fixture, losing 3-0 to neighbours Argentina.

The Brazilian Confederation of Sport was formed in 1914 and football became far more organised, yet competitions were still only staged within individual states and the game did not begin to resemble a professional sport until 1933. With many teams touring Europe, there was a real danger of a player exodus. Certainly Leônidas da Silva had achieved international acclaim by showing off his famed bicycle kick, while Friedenreich, a prolific striker, was said to have scored more than a thousand goals. It was imperative that suitable financial incentives were put in place to keep such players in Brazil, but this originally met with stiff resistance from clubs who wished to remain amateur. As a result it was an under-strength Brazil that participated in the first two World Cups of 1930 and 1934.

The internal bickering among the regions continued and it wasn't until 1960 and the birth of the Copa Libertadores (a South American competition for the best team in each country) that Brazil were prompted into forming the nationwide Taca do Brazil cup competition, while the national league (the Brasileiro) was created as late as 1971.

Above: Pelé celebrates scoring for Brazil in the 1970 World Cup final against Italy. Opposite clockwise from top right: Junior Roque and Ronaldinho celebrates Brazil's 2002 World Cup win; Jairzinho playing against West Germany in 1973; Romario lifting the 1994 World Cup; Brazil celebrate at the 2004 Copa América; Ronaldo after the Brazil's fourth World Cup triumph in 1994; the legendary Zico. Centre: Robinho and Kaká celebrate at the 2005 Confederations Cup.

Both competitions were formed during a purple period in the history of Brazilian international football. Having hosted the 1950 World Cup finals and built the famous Maracanã Stadium, defeat in the final by Uruguay was an indication that the country was fast emerging as a major force in world football. Within eight years Brazil were hailed world champions in a tournament that saw the arrival of 17-year-old Pelé in a team that also included such esteemed names as Garrincha, Zagalo and Gilmar. In 1962, with the majority of the same team, Brazil lifted the World Cup again, as Czechoslovakia were defeated 3-1 in the final.

Dominance at international level was also reflected on the domestic front, as Pelé's team, Santos, won the World Club Cup in 1962 and 1963, defeating Benfica and AC Milan respectively. It would be another 18 years, however, until a Brazilian team, the Zico-inspired Flamengo, would again emerge victorious in the competition.

However you look at the history of Brazilian football, thoughts inevitably turn to the World Cup winning side of 1970, regarded by many as the greatest team in the history of the sport. With Pelé at his peak, his team-mates Rivelino, Tostão, Gérson, Jairzinho and Carlos Alberto also became household names as the team swept all before them. The finals, held in Mexico, were also the first to be televised in colour, bringing another dimension to the samba flair on offer. Certainly Carlos Alberto's emphatic strike in the 4-1 final win against Italy remains an enduring image.

Pelé's retirement from the international fold led to an extended lull, and although the country continued to be a source of great talent, yielding the likes of Paulo Cesar, Zico, Falção, Socrates and Cerezo, the country remained dormant on the world stage for 24 years.

So highly regarded had Brazilian players become that a player drain to Europe was inevitable. What remained was a weak national league that saw teams with ever-changing sides, and the first 20 seasons saw 13 different champions – to this day the national league remains a fragile organisation and attendances reflect the entertainment on offer. Flamengo, arguably Brazil's most famous side, had an average attendance of less than 14,000 in 2002.

Yet there were signs of a renaissance with the national team; silver medals at the 1984 and 1988 Olympics provided the foundation for the 1994 World Cup winning team. Goalkeeper Taffarel, captain Dunga and star striker Romario formed the backbone of the Olympic sides and their potential finally came to fruition with World Cup victory against Italy, in a game that was settled on penalties.

A new belief had been restored to the national team and with the emerging young players Ronaldo, Denilson and Rivaldo added to the side, they made their intentions known with an appearance in the 1998 final, this time against hosts France. A mysterious illness to Ronaldo on the morning of the game put paid to any chances of victory, but four years on the Inter Milan forward was determined to make amends. Brazil swept all before them, their brand of free-flowing, attacking football made them worthy champions. An inspired Ronaldo, who scored eight goals in the competition, helped to restore their standing as the world's leading football nation, and in 2006, despite Brazil's surprise exit in the quarter-finals, he became the World Cup's all-time top goalscorer

BRITISH VIRGIN ISLANDS

Federation: British Virgin Islands Football Association
Founded: 1974
Joined FIFA: 1996
Confederation: CONCACAF
FIFA world ranking: 168

BRUNEI DARUSSALAM

Federation: Football Association of Brunei Darussalam
Founded: 1959
Joined FIFA: 1969
Confederation: AFC
FIFA world ranking: 178

BULGARIA

Federation: Bulgarski Futbolen Soius
Founded: 1923
Joined FIFA: 1924
Confederation: UEFA
FIFA world ranking: 37

Communism was good for football in Bulgaria. Prior to 1944, although football was played, it was not being played or organised very well – there was an aborted attempt at a national league and the national team failed to win a game in its first six years. The arrival of Soviet troops brought wholesale changes to Bulgarian life, and football was completely overhauled. A new national league with a pyramid feeder system was put in place, with promotion and relegation throughout. Clubs became affiliated to an official organisation: CSKA (Army), Levski (Interior Ministry) and Lokomotiv Sofia (railways). Players were professionals in all but name: while working for a power company or a government department, these workers embarked on a full-time regime of football training known and used throughout the Communist bloc as 'The System'.

The quality of Bulgarian football improved immeasurably, none more so than CSKA (then known as CDNA). Inspired by the goals of Ivan Kolev, between 1951 and 1962 CDNA were champions 11 times, a trend that ultimately made club football predictable. The army side provided much of the national team and Bulgaria were regarded as one of Europe's top teams, becoming World Cup regulars from 1962 (although they failed to win a single game at the finals). CSKA were unpopular despite their success, mainly because the army club could pick players by simply drafting them.

The fall of communism forced clubs to become financially independent, which led to the selling of players. Ironically, this has helped the national team, as their top stars have gained experience abroad. In 1994 Bulgaria reached the World Cup semi-finals, with Barcelona's Hristo Stoichkov the tournament's joint top scorer. Together with Levski, CSKA remain one of Bulgaria's strongest sides.

BURKINA FASO

Federation: Fédération Burkinabé de Foot-Ball
Founded: 1960
Joined FIFA: 1964
Confederation: CAF
FIFA world ranking: 74

BURUNDI

Federation: Fédération de Football du Burundi
Founded: 1948
Joined FIFA: 1972
Confederation: CAF
FIFA world ranking: 157

CAMBODIA

Federation: Cambodian Football Federation
Founded: 1933
Joined FIFA: 1953
Confederation: AFC
FIFA world ranking: 183 (joint)

Below: Hristo Stoichkov of Bulgaria celebrates qualification for the 1998 World Cup after victory over Russia.

CAMEROON

Federation: Fedération Camérounaise de Football
Founded: 1960
Joined FIFA: 1962
Confederation: CAF
FIFA world ranking: 12
Honours: African Nations Cup 1984, 1988, 2000, 2002; Olympics 2000

Cameroon are known as the 'Indomitable Lions' and their roar was first heard on the world stage in 1982, when they boosted black African soccer with an unbeaten appearance at the World Cup, drawing their three group games against Peru, Poland and Italy. But it was eight years later in Italy that Cameroon took African soccer to the next level. A Roger Milla-inspired Cameroon defeated world champions Argentina 1-0 in their opening match and then went on a run that took them to within ten minutes of a semi-final place before they were defeated 3-2 by England.

Although Cameroon's subsequent World ·Cup appearances have not reached the same giddy heights there has been success in the African Nations Cup where they became the first side in 37 years to win successive cups in 2000 and 2002. They also won at the 2000 Olympics, beating Spain in the final. All three wins came after penalty shoot-outs.

Football had been played in both British and French protectorate regions of the pre-independence country, but did not really thrive until business began running the clubs in the 1940s. Independence from Britain and France saw the latter protectorate become Cameroon and the formation of a national league and cup soon followed in 1960. These competitions have been dominated by the two Yaoundé clubs, Canon and Tonnerre, with Union Douala providing the third force. In recent years they have been joined by Cotonsport, who have also made an impact.

Oryx Doula were the first African Cup winners in 1964, an achievement later matched by Canon Yaoundé and Union Doula. A number of Cameroonian players have been voted African Player Of The Year: Roger Milla (1976 and 1990), Thomas N'Kono (1979 and 1982), Jean Manga Onguene (1980), Theophile Abega (1984) and Samuel Eto'o (2003, 2004 and 2005) with many more players playing in Europe.

Above: Roger Milla on the ball against England in the quarter-final of the 1990 World Cup. At 38 years of age, he was one of the stars of the Italia 90.

Above left: Cameroon's Lauren Etame Mayer, Geremi Njitap Fotso and Daniel Ngom Kome celebrate their winning the Olympic gold medal in 2000.

CANADA

Federation: The Canadian Soccer Association
Founded: 1912
Joined FIFA: 1913
Confederation: CONCACAF
FIFA world ranking: 54
Honours: Olympics 1904; CONCACAF Championship 2000

In a land where ice hockey dominates, football has struggled to make any kind of impact, despite Olympic Games glory in 1904 courtesy of Galt FC. It had been hoped that Canada's 1986 World Cup appearance would finally inspire a permanent league but it was not to be. Leading Canadian clubs such as Montreal Impact, Toronto Lynx and Vancouver Whitecaps compete in the USA's First Division A-League, the division below the Major Soccer League (MSL), although Toronto, with its new football specific stadium, was awarded the 13th franchise to play in the USA's MSL from 2007.

CAPE VERDE ISLANDS

Federation: Federação Cabo-Verdiana de Futebol
Founded: 1982
Joined FIFA: 1986
Confederation: CAF
FIFA world ranking: 102

CAYMAN ISLANDS

Federation: Cayman Islands Football Association
Founded: 1966
Joined FIFA: 1992
Confederation: CONCACAF
FIFA world ranking: 175

CENTRAL AFRICAN REP

Federation: Fédération Centrafricaine de Football
Founded: 1961
Joined FIFA: 1963
Confederation: CAF
FIFA world ranking: 172

Centre: The Cayman Islands defend their goal as it comes under attack by Cuba's Ariel Alvarez.

CHAD

Federation: Fédération Tchadienne de Football
Founded: 1962
Joined FIFA: 1988
Confederation: CAF
FIFA world ranking: 128

CHILE

Federation: Federación de Fútbol de Chile
Founded: 1895
Joined FIFA: 1912
Confederation: CONMEBOL
FIFA world ranking: 46

Valaparaiso FC became Chile's first club in 1889 and others, mainly British in origin, followed. In 1895 the second oldest football federation in South America was founded. The Chilean national team played its first international in 1910, although it did not win a game until 1926. Chilean football took a turn for the better in 1925 when David Arellano founded the country's most successful and popular club, Colo Colo. Arellano and Colo Colo became the driving force behind the new professional national league in 1933. Through the years the league has been an open competition but from the 1970s it was Colo Colo who dominated.

On the international stage Chilean football has made little impact, although in 1991 Colo Colo did win the country's first international club honour when they lifted the Copa Libertadores. Chile have occasionally appeared in the World Cup but without success, save for the 1962 competition, when as hosts they reached the semi-finals. The performance was marred by the appalling spectacle against Italy known as 'the Battle of Santiago'.

Chile were handed a ban in 1989 when goalkeeper Roberto Rojas faked an injury in a World Cup qualifier against Brazil.

CHINA

Federation: Football Association of the People's Republic of China
Founded: 1924
Joined FIFA: 1931-58, 1976
Confederation: AFC
FIFA world ranking: 89

China played in the first international match in Asia at the Far Eastern Games in Manila in February 1913, losing 2-1 to hosts the Philippines. China joined FIFA in 1931 and took part at the Munich and London Olympics in 1936 and 1948 respectively, but they did not enter the World Cup. In 1958 China withdrew from FIFA in protest at the membership of Taiwan. This self-imposed exile did little for the domestic game, even though the national league ran from 1953 to 1966. It was not until 1976 that China rejoined FIFA – the National League had been resurrected and cultural and

sporting ties were brokered. The quality of football was very poor, although there were occasional highlights, such as eight-time champions Lioaning winning the Asian Champions Cup in 1990, and China finishing runners-up in the Asian Cup in 1984 and the Asian Games in 1994.

The advent of professionalism, with its foreign player imports and sponsorship (from online gambling companies and breweries, amongst others) gave the Chinese Super League a boost. The league was enlarged from 12 to 14 clubs in 2005 and to 16 clubs in 2006 (then reduced to 15 when one club went bust). Dalian Shide have won the title in eight of the first 12 years that the Super League has been running. The 2006 season introduced promotion and relegation for the first time.

In 2002 China qualified for the World Cup and hosted the 2004 Asian Cup, losing to Japan in the final, much to the displeasure of the home fans. The game has improved, with several leading Chinese players making careers abroad.

CHINESE TAIPEI

Federation: Chinese Taipei Football Association
Founded: 1936
Joined FIFA: 1954
Confederation: AFC
FIFA world ranking: 149

COLOMBIA

Federation: Federación Colombiana de Fútbol
Founded: 1924
Joined FIFA: 1936-50, 1954
Confederation: CONMEBOL
FIFA world ranking: 21
Honours: Copa América 2001

Colombia has had a dark and controversial football history, but illuminating the darkness are flamboyant players who have produced breathtaking moments, ranging from the spectacular goals of Carlos Valderrama to the astonishing 'scorpion' save of goalkeeper Rene Higuita in a friendly against England.

In 1948 a wealthy independent professional league (the DiMayor) was born in Colombia, and among the 18 wealthy clubs was Deportivo Municipal, who became known as 'Los Millonarios', because they were bankrolled by two extremely rich Bogotá businessmen.

In its four-year existence, this new league became known as the 'El Dorado' period – as

Opposite: Carlos Valderrama of Colombia in 1998.

Below: China celebrate after winning the East Asian Football Championship in 2005.

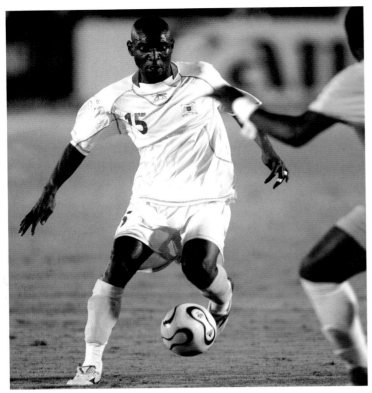

Above: Herita Ilunga of the Democratic Republic of Congo, at the African Nations Cup in 2006.

Croatia's Igor Stimac, Zvonimir Boban and Davor Suker celebrate their victory over the Holland after the World Cup third place play-off match in 1998.

COMOROS ISLANDS

Federation: Federation Comorienne de Football
Founded: 1979
Joined FIFA: 2005
Confederation: CAF
FIFA world ranking: –

CONGO

Federation: Fédération Congolaise de Football
Founded: 1962
Joined FIFA: 1962
Confederation: CAF
FIFA world ranking: 108
Honours: African Nations Cup 1972

CONGO DR

Federation: Fédération Congolaise de Football Association
Founded: 1919
Joined FIFA: 1962
Confederation: CAF
FIFA world ranking: 67
Honours: African Nations Cup 1968, 1974

In 1974, when known as Zaïre, the Democratic Republic of Congo became the first sub-Saharan (and black African) team to qualify for the World Cup. Heavily influenced by Europe – and Belgium in particular who had introduced the game to the country – Zaïre were a major force in African football from the mid-Sixties to the mid-Seventies, winning the African Nations Cup twice.

COOK ISLANDS

Federation: Cook Islands Football Association
Founded: 1971
Joined FIFA: 1994
Confederation: OFC
FIFA world ranking: 194 (joint)

COSTA RICA

Federation: Federación Costarricense de Fútbol
Founded: 1921
Joined FIFA: 1927
Confederation: CONCACAF
FIFA world ranking: 45
Honours: CONCACAF Championship 1941, 1946, 1948, 1953, 1955, 1960, 1961, 1963, 1969, 1989

The formal birth of Costa Rican football was in 1921, the year their federation was founded and the inaugural league championship kicked-off. CS Herediano were the dominant club before the war, while Deportivo Saprissa were the runaway team of the Sixties and Seventies, a period when the Costa Rican national team were the strongest in the region, winning seven of ten CCCF Championships and three of the subsequent CONCACAF titles before the tournament was again revamped in 1991. Despite such an impressive record Costa Rica shunned the World Cup until 1958. They have since qualified three times, in 1990, when they beat Scotland, 2002 and 2006.

CROATIA

Federation: Croatian Football Federation
Founded: 1912, 1991
Joined FIFA: 1992
Confederation: UEFA
FIFA world ranking: 23

During the Second World War Croatia, under German occupation, did have its own league and national team until Tito's Communists took over the Balkan region. Croatian players and clubs were among the powerhouses of Yugoslav football prior to real independence in 1991 and official FIFA recognition in 1992. Clubs such as Dinamo Zagreb and Hajduk Split were regular challengers to the Belgrade-

it existed outside of FIFA jurisdiction, Colombian clubs refused to pay transfer fees and were able to lure star players from all over South America and Europe with offers of lucrative wages and signing-on fees. They attracted players of the calibre of Alfred Di Stéfano and Nestor Rossi, but by the time Colombia was readmitted to FIFA in 1954, the huge fees had smashed the Colombian game.

In the mid-Sixties a rival organisation challenged the incumbent football association and this political infighting led to FIFA taking on the running of Colombian football until the current FCF was formed. Colombia was due to host the 1986 World Cup but was forced to withdraw after being unable to provide sufficient facilities and communications for a 24-team tournament.

In the Eighties and Nineties Colombian league football was an exciting spectator sport, but off the pitch it had become unpleasant, with allegations of money-laundering by drug cartels and of high stake bets and bribes. Players, officials and investigators have all been brutally murdered during this period. In one of the more notorious incidents, international defender Andres Escobar was shot dead after returning from the 1994 World Cup, having inadvertently scored an own-goal against the USA during the tournament.

The state of Colombian football has been so bad that there have been times when the league has been suspended and the national side has refused to play at home, but in 2001 Colombian football had a chance to celebrate once more when the national team won the Copa América for the first time, beating Mexico in the final.

based clubs, while in 1967 Dinamo Zagreb became the first Croatian (and Yugoslav) club to lift a European trophy when they won the Fairs Cup, defeating Leeds.

Great players such as Zvonimir Boban, Robert Jarni and Robert Prosinecki (half-Croat) were part of the Yugoslav national team that qualified for the European Championship in 1992, but by then Croatia had declared independence, their clubs had withdrawn from the Yugoslav league and Croatian players were forbidden from playing for Yugoslavia. The team were forced to withdraw from Euro 92.

In the shadow of civil war and grave economic problems, the Croatian league kicked-off in the 1992-3 season without the country's biggest stars, many having chosen to play their club football abroad. However, the Croatian game has gained in popularity because of the exploits of the national side, who made a startling impact at the 1996 European Championship by reaching the quarter-finals, and later going on to finish third at the 1998 World Cup in France.

CUBA

Federation: Asociación de Fútbol de Cuba
Founded: 1924
Joined FIFA: 1932
Confederation: CONCACAF
FIFA world ranking: 96 (joint)

CYPRUS

Federation: Cyprus Football Association
Founded: 1934
Joined FIFA: 1948
Confederation: UEFA
FIFA world ranking: 92

Football was introduced to Cyprus by British servicemen in the late 1870s, although it wasn't until 1934 that an association was formed. A league and cup campaign was launched a year later, with Trast AC winning both titles. With a population of mainly Greek Cypriots, the most successful teams were of Greek origin and only one Turkish Cypriot side, Cetinkaya TSK, has ever taken the national title. Following the division of the island in 1974, teams from both communities found themselves displaced and although the so-called Turkish Republic of Northern Cyprus has a league, it is not recognised by FIFA. Throughout the 1990s, the Cypriot league

grew stronger, with Anorthosis Famagusta becoming the most prominent side. The national team took its biggest scalp in 1998, beating Spain 3-2 in a Euro 2000 qualifier.

CZECH REPUBLIC

Federation: Ceskomoravsky Fotbalovy Svaz
Founded: 1901
Joined FIFA: 1907-18, 1994
Confederation: UEFA
FIFA world ranking: 10
Honours: European Championship 1976; Olympics 1980 (both as Czechoslovakia)

From the 1993-4 season, Czechoslovakia split into two: the Czech Republic and Slovakia. It is fair to say that in footballing terms the Czech Republic was the stronger of the two. This was proved almost instantly when the Czech Republic not only qualified for the 1996 European Championship (Slovakia didn't), but reached the final at Wembley, losing to Germany through a golden goal. The country's biggest names, like Patrik Berger and Pavel Nedved, have performed at the highest level, following in the tradition of former Czech greats like Masopust, Novak and Planicka.

Football had been played in the region since the 1890s. In Bohemia, a province of the Austro-Hungarian empire, both Slavia and

Sparta clubs were formed in 1893, while a Bohemian league and a football association were founded, and a national team existed until Czechoslovakia declared independence in 1918. Seven years later the regions of Bohemia, Monravia and Slovakia formed a new professional Czech league.

Czechoslovakia became a strong football nation. They reached the 1920 Olympic final but stormed off during the second-half of the game, complaining that the referee was biased against them. They were also the 1934 World Cup runners-up, losing to Italy in the final.

On the domestic front it was Slavia and Sparta who dominated both league and cup. In 1945 Communist rule led to both clubs becoming affiliated to state organisations. Slavia and Sparta lost their stranglehold of the Czech game and were eclipsed by the army team, Dukla Prague. Dukla, in turn, became the core of the national side in the Sixties, when Czechoslovakia often came close without ever winning the final prize – they finished third in the 1960 European Championship, and were runners-up in the 1962 World Cup (to Brazil) and 1964 Olympics (to Hungary).

The late Seventies saw another resurgence with Czechoslovakia winning the 1976 European Championship in Yugoslavia, beating West Germany in a dramatic 5-3 penalty shoot-out. Four years later they were Olympic champions. At home Dukla's star began to fade even before independence and Sparta and Slavia re-emerged as dominant teams again in a free market economy.

Below: Vladimir Smicer of the Czech Republic celebrate scoring against Holland at Euro 2004.

Above: Last-minute entrants, Denmark surprised everyone by taking the 1992 European Championship in Sweden.

DENMARK

Federation: Dansk Boldspil-Union
Founded: 1889
Joined FIFA: 1904
Confederation: UEFA
FIFA world ranking: 17
Honours: European Championship 1992

Denmark caused the biggest football shock of the Nineties. They had failed to qualify for the 1992 European Championship and just a week before the tournament many of their players were already sunning themselves on the beach when the call came that offered them the chance to become last-minute replacements for Yugoslavia. With no preparation the squad

went on to win the trophy, beating Germany 2-0 in the final with goals from John Jensen and Kim Vilfort. This was undoubtedly the finest hour in Denmark's football history.

The triumph followed a period in the 1980s when the Danish game had gained recognition and plaudits for its thrilling style, with the development of a talented crop of players, most notably the Laudrup brothers, Brian and Michael, Jesper Olsen, Jan Molby, John Sivebaek and Soren Lerby. These players took Denmark to their first World Cup in 1986, where they reached the second round only to meet an in-form Spain, who beat them 5-1. For the European Championship triumph, the squad also boasted Peter Schmeichel, Henrik Larsen and Flemming Povlsen.

The first truly great Danish player was Allan Simonsen, who was voted European Player Of The Year in 1977. He played for two great European sides, Barcelona and Borussia

Mönchengladbach, and his success as a professional led the DBU to allow professional players to be selected for the national team in 1976. The introduction of professionalism into the Danish game came in 1978.

Before 1978 Danish football had been strictly an amateur game ever since the first club KB Copenhagen was formed in 1876. Among the great amateur players of the early years was Niels Bohr, who later won the Nobel Prize for Physics. The first professional club was Brondby, who led the way in turning Danish football from a pastime into a national success story. The other significant move came in 1991 when the Superliga switched from a summer season to a winter season in line with the major leagues of Europe.

Though they missed out in 1994, Denmark recaptured some form in the 1998 World Cup, reaching the quarter-final, where they lost narrowly to Brazil.

DJIBOUTI

Federation: Fédération Djiboutienne de Football
Founded: 1979
Joined FIFA: 1994
Confederation: CAF
FIFA world ranking: 196 (joint)

DOMINICA

Federation: Dominica Football Association
Founded: 1970
Joined FIFA: 1994
Confederation: CONCACAF
FIFA world ranking: 183 (joint)

DOMINICAN REPUBLIC

Federation: Federación Dominicana de Fútbol
Founded: 1953
Joined FIFA: 1958
Confederation: CONCACAF
FIFA world ranking: 186

EAST TIMOR

Federation: Federação Futebol Timor Leste
Founded: 2002
Joined FIFA: 2005
Confederation: AFC
FIFA world ranking: –

ECUADOR

Federation: Federación Ecuatoriana De Fútbol
Founded: 1925
Joined FIFA: 1926
Confederation: CONMEBOL
FIFA world ranking: 28

Ecuador, under Hernan Dario Gomez, qualified for the World Cup for the first time in 11 attempts in 2002, finishing runners-up to Argentina in the ten-strong CONMEBOL group. Notably, this magnificent achievement also included their first-win over Brazil. Luis Fernando Suarez repeated the feat, including another win over Brazil, and guided Ecuador to the finals in Germany in 2006. In the Copa América Ecuador have not done quite as well, and prior to 2006 the national team had played just three matches in Europe.

Barcelona and El Nacional are Ecuador's most successful clubs, sharing 25 titles between them since 1957. Barcelona are the only Ecuadorean club to appear in the Copa Libertadores final, in 1990 and 1998. For the ten clubs of the top flight, in February 2005 Ecuador adopted the Opening (Apertura) and Closing (Clausura) Season format for the league, a popular system in South America that splits the championship into two campaigns. The Opening Season runs from February to July and the Closing Season from July to December. The Apertura climaxes with a knockout phase for the top eight sides while the Clausura finishes with the top six playing in a home and away mini league. The top three teams from the Clausura kick-off with three, two or one bonus points.

EGYPT

Federation: Egyptian Football Association
Founded: 1921
Joined FIFA: 1923
Confederation: CAF
FIFA world ranking: 29
Honours: African Nations Cup 1957, 1959, 1986, 1998, 2006

Egypt are Africa's most successful football nation, even though they have appeared in only two World Cups. The 'Pharoahs' have won the African Nations Cup a record five times and have made 20 appearances at the finals, hosting the tournament four times. In Cairo-based Al Ahly they have Africa's best club side of recent years. Having won the African Champions League in 2001 and 2006 (adding to their triumphs of 1982 and 1987), they won seven successive Egyptian championships between 1994 and 2000, and added the 2005 title with a 26-game unbeaten season, winning by a staggering 31-point margin. Al Ahly's nearest rivals are five times African Champions League winners Zamalek, who went 52 league games without defeat between December 2002 and November 2004.

Egypt were the initial trail-blazers for African football: they were the first team to play in the Olympics in 1928 and the World Cup finals in 1934. A founder member of the Confederation Africaine de Football (CAF) in 1957, Egypt provided the organisation's first president in Abdel Aziz Abdullah Salem. Another leading Egyptian, General Abdel Aziz Mustapha, donated

the original African Nations Cup trophy in the same year, while the national team won the first two African Nations Cup tournaments.

Ever since football arrived in the country at the turn of the century it had been a popular pastime. In 1907 native Egyptians got behind the newly-formed Al Ahly, an exclusive all-Egyptian sporting club and a beacon for nationalist pride. Al Ahly developed into Egypt's most popular and successful club, dominating the Farouk Cup (1922-48) and, from 1949, the league championship and Cup of Egypt. The presence in the country of allied forces during World War II boosted the already well-organised domestic game and inspired the championship and cup competitions.

Above: Egypt celebrate winning the African Nations Cup in 2006 after victory over Ivory Coast.

EL SALVADOR

Federation: Federacion Salvadorena de Futbol
Founded: 1935
Joined FIFA: 1938
Confederation: CONCACAF
FIFA world ranking: 147
Honours: CONCACAF Championship 1943

El Salvador have qualified for the World Cup just twice, causing a war and suffering the worst defeat in World Cup finals history. In 1969 the team were involved in a controversial three-game second round qualifying clash with neighbouring Honduras. Border infractions and rioting followed the first two games, and when El Salvador finally defeated Honduras 3-2 in neutral Mexico, the result inflamed an already tense border situation, causing the El Salvadorian Army to invade Honduras to protect its citizens (migrant workers) from persecution. The action sparked all out war between the two countries.

Back on the football field, in 1982 El Salvador were thrashed 10-1 by Hungary – the biggest ever defeat in a World Cup finals – and crashed out without a point.

ENGLAND

Federation: Football Association
Founded: 1863
Joined FIFA: 1905-28, 1946
Confederation: UEFA
FIFA world ranking: 5
Honours: World Cup winners 1966

England enjoys a lofty status as the home of football. The modern game was fashioned here in the mid 19th Century and rapidly exported all over the world. Its clubs are enshrined in the local community, have powerful historical roots and provide a focus for millions of people each week. The basic structure of English football was pretty much in place by 1888 when the 12-member Football League was installed. The first FA Cup final had been won by Wanderers 16 years before and the Football Association had been founded back in 1863.

Developing the game inevitably gave England a headstart in terms of the world game. Its teams played 2-3-5, that led to the classic WM formation that served English football to the 1950s. England regularly drubbed foreign opposition – whenever they deigned to play them, that is.

However, this classically insular island approach, together with an overbearing sense of superiority, meant that England's Football Association repeatedly stood apart from the game's most significant developments. When FIFA pioneered a world tournament in the 1920s the FA declined to take part. It then resigned from the federation in 1928 and did not rejoin until 1946 or enter a World Cup until 1950. As its insularity deepened, the English game remained oblivious to any thought of modernisation.

The myth of English superiority was rocked in 1953 when Hungary took the national side apart, winning 6-3 at Wembley. Yet when UEFA launched the European Nations Cup (later the European Championship) England initially refused to take part on the basis that it would undermine the all-important British Home International Championship. For this reason a talented generation of players, including Billy Wright, Stanley Matthews and Tom Finney, were held back from the kind of competition that would have elevated their game further.

Still, justification for the FA's stance finally arrived in 1966 when England, led by one of its great ambassadors, Bobby Moore, hosted the World Cup finals and won in front of a passionate Wembley crowd, beating West Germany 4-2 with Geoff Hurst's hat-trick.

Yet English football failed to capitalise on the resultant euphoria. Four years later, with with arguably a better squad, they lost narrowly

Above: England's Duncan Edwards makes goal line clearance against Scotland in 1957. Opposite top: England's stars of 1966 celebrate with the World Cup. Opposite bottom from left to right: Stanley Matthews in action against Scotland at Hampden Park in 1961; England's second-highest goalscorer Gary Lineker; future legend Wayne Rooney in 2005.

to eventual champions Brazil in a group game seen as a potential warm-up for the final. They then crashed out in a disastrous quarter-final confrontation with West Germany that signified a period of upheaval from which it took years to recover.

England failed to qualify for two successive World Cups in the Seventies and were then hamstrung by technical shortcomings through the following decade. A semi-final appearance at Italia 90 with a side that included Paul Gascoigne, arguably the country's greatest talent ever, hardly heralded a new era given the failure to qualify for the World Cup again in 1994, or progress beyond the quarter-final stages since.

The nation's uneven international history is belied by the achievements of its clubs in Europe. Typically of the period, the Football League advised champions Chelsea not to take part in the inaugural European Cup competition created in 1955. However, Manchester United forged ahead a year later and would surely have won a trophy long before their eventual breakthrough in 1968 but for the tragedy of the 1958 Munich air disaster.

The late Seventies and early Eighties represented a golden era for English clubs in Europe, with four European Cup wins for Liverpool, one for Aston Villa and a brace of back-to-back trophies for Nottingham Forest. UEFA Cups and Cup Winners' Cups also arrived with regularity. But the dominance was ended abruptly in the wake of the 1985 Heysel tragedy, in which a pitched battle between Liverpool fans and Juventus supporters resulted in 39 deaths and a six-year ban from European competition for English clubs.

Domestically, English football has thrived and continues to support four professional divisions. In the modern era four clubs have largely held sway. Liverpool remain the all-time most successful club in the country with 18

league championships and six FA Cups, having regularly built upon the revival overseen by Bill Shankly in the Sixties. Manchester United are the country's richest and most successful club of recent times, winning eight Premiership titles between 1993 and 2003, including three league and cup doubles. They also won a European Cup, with homegrown talents like David Beckham and Paul Scholes at the core of a team built by Alex Ferguson. Arsenal have maintained a consistent challenge, with two league and cup doubles under Frenchman Arsène Wenger in the past decade. Latterly Roman Abramovich's money has helped Chelsea compete at the highest level, with back-to-back Premiership titles in 2005 and 2006. On The European stage, both Arsenal and Liverpool have featured in recent Champions League finals.

Hooliganism has been an unpleasant feature of English football and it took a heavy toll in the Eighties. Gate receipts declined and further disasters – the 1985 Bradford fire and the 1989 Hillsborough tragedy – only served to underline the fact that the game's structure needed a radical overhauling. The 1990 Taylor Report and the consequent move to all-seater stadia helped usher in a new era for English football in the Nineties. Money flooded in via television and corporate sponsorship, and the advent of the Premier League in 1992 further revamped the game's image.

The buoyancy of the Premiership is now dependent on record-breaking television and sponsorship deals. The deserved reputation that the Premiership maintains for exciting, fast-paced, attacking football is built on the talents of many top quality foreign imports, not on homegrown players. Until significant grassroots adjustments are made, England will always be seen as a nation forced to elevate work-rate over technique and suffer the consequences internationally.

EQUATORIAL GUINEA

Federation: Fédération Ecuatoguineana de Fútbol
Founded: 1976
Joined FIFA: 1986
Confederation: CAF
FIFA world ranking: 95

ETHIOPIA

Federation: Ethiopian Football Federation
Founded: 1943
Joined FIFA: 1953
Confederation: CAF
FIFA world ranking: 101
Honours: African Nations Cup 1962

FIJI

Federation: Fiji Football Association
Founded: 1938
Joined FIFA: 1963
Confederation: OFC
FIFA world ranking: 134

ERITREA

Federation: Eritrean National Football Federation
Founded: 1996
Joined FIFA: 1998
Confederation: CAF
FIFA world ranking: 177

FAEROE ISLANDS

Federation: Fotboltssamband Føroya
Founded: 1979
Joined FIFA: 1988
Confederation: UEFA
FIFA world ranking: 169 (joint)

The Faeroe Islands had a sensational debut on the international football stage. In their first competitive match in September 1990, the part-time players of the Faeroe Islands beat Austria 1-0 in Sweden, thanks to goalscorer Allan Morkore and bobble-hatted goalkeeper Martin Knudsen. Football has been played on the islands for more than a century with a league (since 1942) and cup competition (1967), and unofficial international matches against Iceland, Greenland and the Shetlands. Local weather conditions and a lack of pitches had hindered their ability to host matches, but a grass pitch was laid in Tórshavn to allow the Faeroes to play their internationals at home. The leading sides are the Tórshavn clubs – HB, B36 and Fram, as well as KI Klaksvik and GÍ Gotu. The league has also attracted imported Brazilian players in recent years.

FINLAND

Federation: Suomen Palloliito Finlands Bollförbund
Founded: 1907
Joined FIFA: 1908
Confederation: UEFA
FIFA world ranking: 70 (joint)

Sami Hyppia and Jari Litmanen are probably Finland's most famous footballers, having both won the European Cup. A prolific goalscorer who played for Barcelona, Liverpool and Ajax, Litmanen won it with the Dutch side in 1995, while defender Hyppia lifted the trophy with Liverpool in 2005. Many Finnish footballers have made a living abroad but not with the same impact as Hyppia and Litmanen.

A Finnish league has been in existence since 1908 and in recent years has been dominated by HJK Helsinki and Haka Valkeakoski. On the international stage Finland, unlike their Scandinavian neighbours, have made little impact. Finnish clubs provide early round fodder in the European competitions, but Kuusysi Lahti did reach the European Cup quarter-finals in 1986.

ESTONIA

Federation: Eesti Jalgpalli Liit
Founded: 1921, 1992
Joined FIFA: 1923, 1992
Confederation: UEFA
FIFA world ranking: 82 (joint)

Estonia was the first Baltic side to play a full international, when they were thrashed 6-0 by Finland in 1920. The game marked the start of a largely undistinguished 121-match record (including a failed qualification attempt for the 1938 World Cup) that ran until Estonia became a part of the Soviet Union. The return to independence in the early Nineties saw the revival of both the national team and league competition. Estonia's strongest team is Flora Tallinn, who also form the backbone of the national side. Some players have had careers abroad, most notably goalkeeper Mart Poom.

Above: One of Finland's few football legends, Sami Hyypia, in action in 2003.

Right: Faroe Islands defender Hans Froo Hansen celebrates with team-mates after scoring against Scotland.

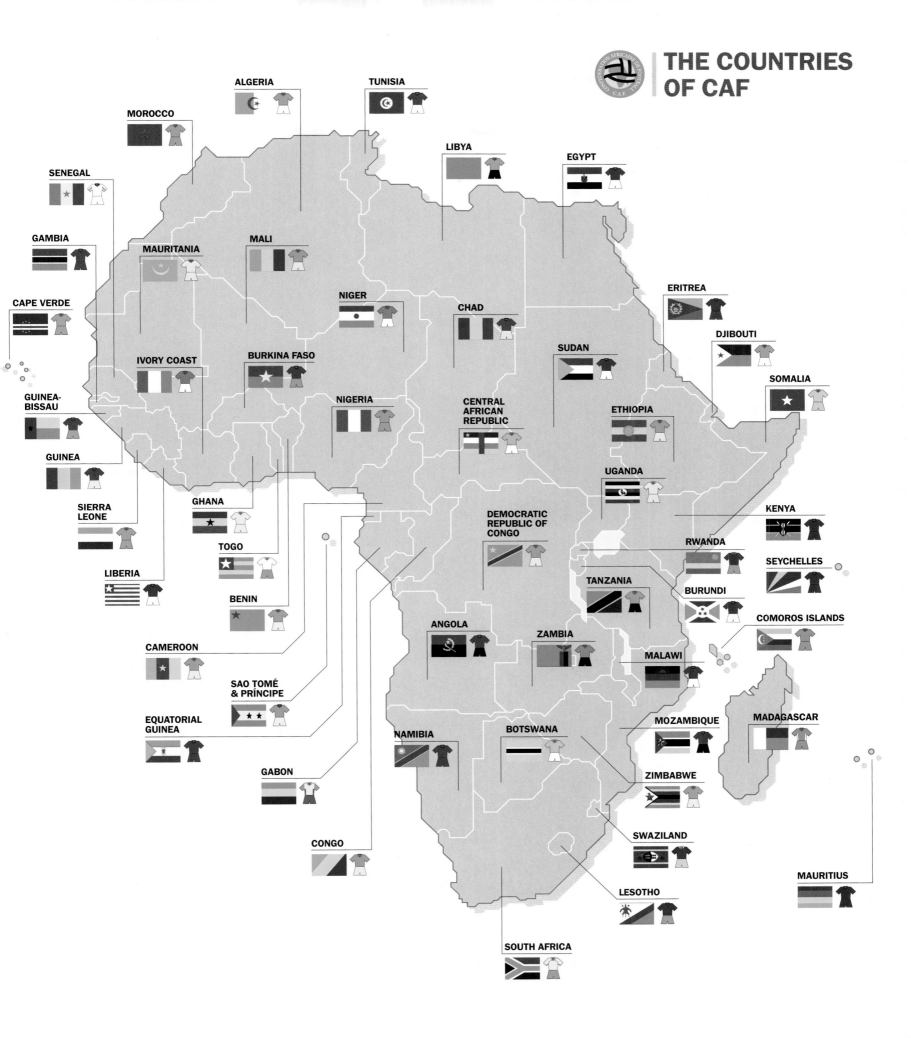

THE COUNTRIES OF CAF

ALGERIA

TUNISIA

MOROCCO

LIBYA

EGYPT

SENEGAL

GAMBIA

MALI

MAURITANIA

NIGER

CHAD

ERITREA

CAPE VERDE

SUDAN

DJIBOUTI

BURKINA FASO

IVORY COAST

SOMALIA

GUINEA-BISSAU

NIGERIA

CENTRAL AFRICAN REPUBLIC

ETHIOPIA

GUINEA

UGANDA

SIERRA LEONE

GHANA

DEMOCRATIC REPUBLIC OF CONGO

KENYA

TOGO

RWANDA

LIBERIA

SEYCHELLES

BENIN

TANZANIA

BURUNDI

CAMEROON

ANGOLA

ZAMBIA

COMOROS ISLANDS

SAO TOMÉ & PRÍNCIPE

MALAWI

EQUATORIAL GUINEA

MOZAMBIQUE

MADAGASCAR

GABON

NAMIBIA

BOTSWANA

ZIMBABWE

CONGO

SWAZILAND

MAURITIUS

LESOTHO

SOUTH AFRICA

FRANCE

Federation: Fédération Française de Football
Founded: 1919
Joined FIFA: 1904
Confederation: UEFA
FIFA world ranking: 4
Honours: World Cup 1998; European Championship 1984, 2000; Olympics 1984

France have played a key role in football development: inventing major competitions, pioneering youth training policies, and belatedly enjoying the success on the pitch that their input off it deserved.

FIFA president Jules Rimet launched the World Cup in 1930; Gabriel Hanot, a former international and editor of sports paper *L'Equipe*, was the driving force behind the European Cup; and the name of the European Championship trophy is that of its founder, Henri Delaunay. Yet in the early days France were seen as outsiders, struggling to break through despite their involvement in the game. Poor domestic attendances in comparison to the English, Spanish and Italian leagues undermined attempts to make an impact.

Lille won the first professional league title in 1932, although Sochaux, backed by Peugeot, were the most prominent team of the era. France hosted the World Cup in 1938 and the tournament was considered a success, despite the home team going down 3-1 in a quarter-final defeat to eventual winners Italy.

After World War II the introduction of international club competitions gave France an opportunity to flourish. They did so thanks to Reims, who became the first of three dominant French club sides. Reims reached the final of the first European Champions Cup, losing 4-3 to Real Madrid in Paris in 1956. The sides met three years later, with the same outcome, by which time Reims had become France's greatest team of the era.

Raymond Kopa was the French star of the time, playing for Reims before switching to Real Madrid to play alongside the likes of Ferenc Puskás and Alfredo Di Stéfano. An outside-right or centre-forward, he had a leading role at the 1958 World Cup finals. France reached the semi-finals as Kopa formed a brilliant partnership with Just Fontaine, who scored a record 13 goals, a tournament tally unlikely ever to be beaten. But the Sixties saw a decline and to improve football standards the FFF introduced a national youth training programme with the aim of producing better-skilled professional players.

This training system would later bear fruit remarkably. In the meantime St Etienne filled the void. In the 1970s they became France's

Above: Michel Platini at the World Cup in 1986. His time in the national team coincided with a golden period for France.
Opposite top: Captain Didier Deschamps lifts the Henri Delaunay Trophy after France's victory over Italy at Euro 2000.
Opposite bottom: The French team celebrate World Cup success on home soil in 1998.

premier side and challenged for major honours but lost 1-0 in the European Cup final to Bayern Munich in Glasgow in 1976.

Their success barely hinted at even more exciting times to come. In the 1980s a French generation of such talent and flair emerged that they were dubbed the 'Blue Brazil' and finally won France's first major international trophy. Michel Platini was the leading player as France reached the semi-finals of the 1982 World Cup, beaten on penalties by West Germany after a thrilling 3-3 draw made infamous by German goalkeeper Harald Schumacher's brutal foul on French defender Patrick Battiston.

The side was skilful and devastating to watch. Two years later, under manager Michel Hidalgo, France finally got their reward by becoming European champions on home soil. Platini scored nine goals in five matches and, aided by the likes of Jean Tigana and Alain Giresse, he led Hidalgo's champions as they beat Spain 2-0 in the final to earn their place among the tournament greats.

Platini's retirement in 1987 led to a slump for the national side but Marseille came along as the new heroes of French football. Run by businessman Bernard Tapie, they were a dazzling side that left the rest trailing in France and became a genuine European superpower.

Marseille won four league titles from 1989 to 1992 and played a superb style of open, attacking football with a side boasting Chris Waddle, Abedi Pele and Jean-Pierre Papin. After near misses in 1990 and 1991 they became the first French side to lift the European Cup with a 1-0 win over AC Milan in Munich in 1993. Triumph, however, turned to scandal when it emerged Marseille had fixed a league match against Valenciennes before

the final. It tainted their European triumph and plunged French football into misery.

In the 1990s French players moved abroad in greater numbers because of the Bosman ruling and the national team improved dramatically as key players gained confidence from other leagues. Coach Aimé Jacquet built a superb side for the 1998 World Cup around the sublime skills of playmaker Zinédine Zidane. The side had not been expected to win but went from strength to strength to reach the final, deservedly beating Brazil 3-0 at the Stade de France in Paris to achieve their greatest-ever success. Zidane scored twice on the big day and the nation celebrated with more than one million supporters pouring on to the Champs-Elysées.

France had found a winning formula and triumphed at the European Championship two years later with an even higher standard of play. Thierry Henry led a more potent attack, and Zidane produced some majestic midfield displays. After failing to show the same flair at subsequent tournaments, this golden generation of French stars, inspired again by Zidane who had been talked out of his earlier international retirement, surprised fans when they reached the final of the 2006 World Cup. They lost on penalties and Zidane, playing his last ever game, was red-carded for butting Marco Materazzi.

Since the beginning of the 21st Century the French league has been dominated by Lyon, who won five successive league titles between 2001 and 2006 and became part of the coveted and influential G-14 group of clubs. The French league, however, loses its best talents to the more attractive Italian Serie A and the English Premiership. Nevertheless, France still has a thriving youth academy programme which augurs well for the future of the national team.

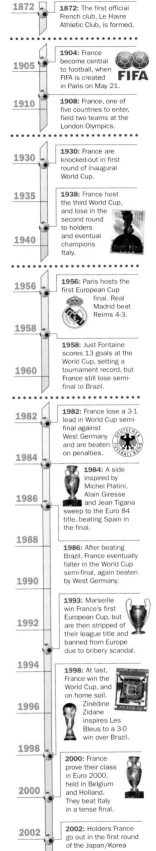

1872: The first official French club, Le Havre Athletic Club, is formed.

1904: France become central to football, when FIFA is created in Paris on May 21.

1908: France, one of five countries to enter, field two teams at the London Olympics.

1930: France are knocked-out in first round of inaugural World Cup.

1938: France host the third World Cup, and lose in the second round to holders and eventual champions Italy.

1956: Paris hosts the first European Cup final. Real Madrid beat Reims 4-3.

1958: Just Fontaine scores 13 goals at the World Cup, setting a tournament record, but France still lose semi-final to Brazil.

1982: France lose a 3-1 lead in World Cup semi-final against West Germany and are beaten on penalties.

1984: A side inspired by Michel Platini, Alain Giresse and Jean Tigana sweep to the Euro 84 title, beating Spain in the final.

1986: After beating Brazil, France eventually falter in the World Cup semi-final, again beaten by West Germany.

1993: Marseille win France's first European Cup, but are then stripped of their league title and banned from Europe due to bribery scandal.

1998: At last, France win the World Cup, and on home soil. Zinédine Zidane inspires Les Bleus to a 3-0 win over Brazil.

2000: France prove their class in Euro 2000, held in Belgium and Holland. They beat Italy in a tense final.

2002: Holders France go out in the first round of the Japan/Korea World Cup without scoring a goal.

2006: Zidane inspires France to the World Cup final, but is sent-off before Italy win the trophy on penalties.

GABON

Federation: Fédération Gabonaise de Football
Founded: 1962
Joined FIFA: 1963
Confederation: CAF
FIFA world ranking: 96 (joint)

GAMBIA

Federation: Gambia Football Association
Founded: 1952
Joined FIFA: 1966
Confederation: CAF
FIFA world ranking: 158

GEORGIA

Federation: Georgian Football Federation
Founded: 1990
Joined FIFA: 1992
Confederation: UEFA
FIFA world ranking: 87

Dinamo Tblisi were Georgia's leading force in the former Soviet Supreme League, winning the championship in 1964 and 1978, and lifting the European Cup Winners' Cup in 1981. In the Georgian league Tblisi dominated, winning eight successive titles (including six successive league and cup doubles) until Torpedo Kutaisi mounted a serious challenge with a hat-trick of titles themselves.

Below: Mounbounga Roaurgue of Gabon is challenged by Nigeria's Agahowa in their World Cup qualifier in 2005.

GERMANY

Federation: Deutscher Fussball-Bund
Founded: 1900
Joined FIFA: 1904
Confederation: UEFA
FIFA world ranking: 9
Honours: World Cup 1954, 1974, 1990; European Championship 1972, 1980, 1996 [*all except 1996 won as West Germany]

Germany's outstanding tournament record is all the more remarkable given their late start in the game. They enjoyed barely any success before the Second World War, and until 1950 had virtually no international relations. It was, indeed, a modest beginning for one of football's superpowers. Yet since those difficult early days Germany have become a standard-bearers, winning trophies at every level and earning a reputation as one of the authentic masters of the modern era.

The nation has produced an array of great players over the past five decades, including arguably the world's greatest defender, Franz Beckenbauer, and deadliest goalscorer, Gerd Müller. Three times World Cup winners, finalists on three further occasions, and three times European champions, the nation's record is unequalled in Europe.

While success at national team level runs deep, their domestic clubs have also made a lasting impact. Bayern Munich have lifted the European Cup four times, their most recent success coming in 2001, and they have reached nine major continental finals. They are one of the richest and most successful clubs in the world. Other German sides, such as Borussia Mönchengladbach and Borussia Dortmund, have also triumphed on the European stage, and the quality of league sides has been consistently high during the growth of club competitions.

German teams have developed a well-documented ability to rise to the occasion, no matter what the circumstances. They are noted – and envied – for making the most of their talents, and on occasion becoming greater than the sum of their parts. The German mix of skill, tactical nous and unshakeable self-belief goes beyond levels other nations attain. They have found a winning formula, yet their humble origins mean success is not taken for granted.

The start of the Bundesliga in 1963 saw standards improve following more than half a century of regionalised leagues. West Germany had emerged from the post-war doldrums to score their first major triumph when they won the 1954 World Cup, despite Hungary being the outstanding team of the era. They beat Ferenc Puskás's side 3-2 in the final and during the Sixties became a force to be reckoned with, losing 4-2 in extra-time to hosts England in the 1966 World Cup final.

The pattern for success was set. In 1972 they became European champions for the first time, beating the Soviet Union in the final, and two years later, on home soil, ran out World Cup winners for a second time when Müller, in typical fashion, scored the winner in a 2-1 victory over Holland in the newly-built Olympiastadion in Munich.

Beckenbauer was the star of his era, thanks to his revolutionary style of play. Originally a midfielder at the 1966 World Cup finals, in the Seventies he became a free-moving defender who operated behind the markers and attacked from deep positions. The man nicknamed 'Der Kaiser' wooed crowds with his elegance on the ball and counter-attacking instincts.

Müller, the ultimate poacher, was equally important, creating little outside the box but scoring an astonishing total of 68 goals in 62 internationals. His stocky build and deceptive pace made him a nightmare for defenders to handle and, alongside Beckenbauer, he also inspired Bayern Munich to a hat-trick of European Champions Cup victories from 1974 to 1976, as both players deservedly picked up European Footballer Of The Year awards.

German football was built around the sweeper system, with the 3-5-2 formation using wing-backs and central strikers favoured by both club and country. In 1980, Bernd Schuster helped West Germany become European champions, with Karl-Heinz Rummenigge as a centre-forward of pace and power.

West Germany's last triumph prior to reunification came in 1990, when they won a third World Cup. Lothar Matthäus was the driving force behind their success in midfield, with Jürgen Klinsmann forming a potent attacking duo with Rudi Völler. They beat Argentina 1-0 in the final with an Andreas Brehme penalty, gaining revenge for defeat to the same opponents in the 1986 final.

Their next success came thanks to a former East Germany star, Matthias Sammer, who was player of the tournament when a united Germany won Euro 96. He was the best example of a sweeper since Beckenbauer and inspired Borussia Dortmund to an unlikely European Cup triumph 12 months later, before retiring prematurely because of injury.

Yet German football struggled by its own high standards in the 1990s, failing to meet expectations at a series of tournaments. Bayern Munich won a fourth European Cup in 2001, on penalties over Valencia, yet the 5-1 defeat to England in a World Cup qualifier in Munich in 2001 marked arguably the lowest point in the history of the national team. However, they bounced back at the 2002 World Cup and reached the final, thanks to the extraordinary goalkeeping of Oliver Kahn. They lost to Brazil 2-0, but Kahn was voted Player Of The Tournament and Völler's side defied the critics.

Four years later Germany hosted the World Cup. Jurgen Klinsmann brought his progressive coaching techniqies and love of attacking football to the national team and defied expectations by reaching the semi-finals. Miroslav Klose ended the tournament as its highest scorer but the team proved unlucky to be knocked out by Italy with two goals in the last two minutes of extra-time. After over 50 years of success, though, it seems that Germany can never be written off.

German success stories, clockwise from top left: Fritz Walter clutches the Jules Rimet Cup after West Germany's shock win over Hungary at the 1954 World Cup final in Berne; Andreas Brehme and Lothar Matthaus celebrate with the World Cup Trophy in 1990; Franz Beckenbauer in action; victory over the Czech Republic at Euro 96 was the first triumph after German reunification.

1900: The Deutscher Fussball Bund is founded in 1900.

1904: The DFB becomes an official member of FIFA.

1934: Germany make their World Cup finals debut, finishing in third place.

1938: Germany lose a first round World Cup replay to Switzerland.

1954: West Germany shock the world by defeating the invincible Hungarians to win the World Cup.

1960: Eintracht Frankfurt lose 7-3 to Real Madrid in the greatest ever European Cup final.

1966: West Germany reach the World Cup final, but lose to hosts England after a disputed goal.

1972: One of the greatest West German sides wins the European Championship.

1974: After defeat in the first round to the East Germans, West Germany win the World Cup as hosts, beating Holland in the final.

1980: Inspired by Bernd Schuster, West Germany collect another European Championship.

1990: West Germany win the World Cup in a poor final with Argentina.

1996: Now known as Germany, the newly-unified national team win Euro 96, Bierhoff's goal beating the Czechs.

1997: Borussia Dortmund win the Champions League.

2001: Bayern beat Valencia to win the Champions League.

2002: Germany reach the final of the World Cup, losing to Brazil.

2006: Hosts Germany finish third at the World Cup after losing the semi-final to Italy.

GHANA

Federation: Ghana Football Association
Founded: 1957
Joined FIFA: 1958
Confederation: CAF
FIFA world ranking: 25
Honours: African Nations Cup 1963, 1965, 1978, 1982

The 'Black Stars' of Ghana were the first team to win the African Nations Cup four times. By the late Seventies and early Eighties they looked like the African team destined to make an impact on the football stage, but Ghana's first World Cup was not to come until 2006.

Ghana have always produced great players, including Ibrahim Sunday and Karim Abdul Razak, who were voted African Player Of The Year in 1971 and 1978 respectively. Abedi Pele also won that honour in three successive seasons in 1991, 1992 and 1993. The first two were while he was with French side Marseille, with whom he won the European Cup. The new century has seen Ghana develop another grand collection of players, such as Stephen Appiah, Samuel Kuffour and Michael Essien, all of whom helped Ghana to the 2006 World Cup, where they reached the second round before losing to Brazil.

Ghana's top clubs are Hearts Of Oak and Asante Kotoko who have dominated the domestic game. Both contested the inaugural African Confederation Cup in 2004, with Hearts Of Oak winning the all-Ghanaian affair 8-7 on penalties. The two sides have also won the African Champions Cup, with Asante triumphing in 1970 and 1983, while Hearts lifted the trophy in 2000. The Ghanaian League has two divisions of eight teams and the winners of each division contest a play-off to determine the champions. Football was introduced to Ghana by the British and influenced to the extent that the great Stanley Matthews guested for Hearts Of Oak in 1957.

GREECE

Federation: Elliniki Podosferiki Omospondia
Founded: 1926
Joined FIFA: 1927
Confederation: UEFA
FIFA world ranking: 32
Honours: European Championship 2004

Greece's European Championship triumph in 2004 was one of the biggest shocks in the competition's history. Under German coach Otto Rehhagel the Greeks had been instilled with a self-belief that had been lacking in previous sides. They amazingly defeated hosts Portugal 2-1 in their opening game and next drew with Spain, despite having a player sent-off in each. Those results were enough to send them through to the quarter-finals, where an Angelos Haristeas goal knocked out the holders and then an extra-time goal from Traianos Dellas put out the Czech Republic. In the final Greece faced the hosts Portugal as underdogs, but a 57th minute header from Haristeas was enough for them to be crowned European champions, with captain Theo Zagorakis lifting the trophy.

Greek sport, including football, was for a long time dominated by the amateur ethos. Despite the massive popularity of the game, full-time professionalism did not arrive until 1979, making Panthinaikos's 1971 European Cup final appearance against Ajax at Wembley an even greater achievement – the game remains the only occasion that a Greek club has reached a major European final.

A national league kicked-off in the Sixties and it has since been dominated mainly by three teams: Olympiakos Piraeus, Panathiniakos and AEK Athens. The previous Greek league, founded in 1928, was restricted to clubs from just Athens and Salonica and it was one of the same big three clubs who topped the league in all but two seasons.

Aside from the all-embracing amateur ethos, in the first half of the 20th Century Greek football development also stalled in the face of great

Below: Greece pulled off one of the biggest shocks in world football when they won the 2004 European Championship.

adversity: civil war, Balkan conflict, political instability and the Second World War have all played their part in preventing the growth of the sport. After professionalism was introduced in 1979, hooliganism blighted Greek football through the 1980s, but the game survived and the hooligan problem has lessened over the years, although it has not completely disappeared.

Greece's European victory has rewarded fans who have always kept the game popular. Before 2004 Greece were a disappointment, managing only one previous appearance in the finals in 1980 and a single World Cup appearance in 1994. Even as European champions they did not qualify for the 2006 World Cup.

GRENADA

Federation: Grenada Football Association
Founded: 1924
Joined FIFA: 1978
Confederation: CONCACAF
FIFA world ranking: 159

GUAM

Federation: Guam Football Association
Founded: 1975
Joined FIFA: 1996
Confederation: AFC
FIFA world ranking: 196

GUATEMALA

Federation: Federación Nacional de Fútbol de Guatemala
Founded: 1919
Joined FIFA: 1946
Confederation: CONCACAF
FIFA world ranking: 53
Honours: CONCACAF Championship 1967

GUINEA

Federation: Fédération Guinéenne de Football
Founded: 1959
Joined FIFA: 1961
Confederation: CAF
FIFA world ranking: 24

GUINEA-BISSAU

Federation: Federação de Futebol da Guiné-Bissau
Founded: 1974
Joined FIFA: 1986
Confederation: CAF
FIFA world ranking: 179 (joint)

GUYANA

Federation: Guyana Football Federation
Founded: 1902
Joined FIFA: 1968
Confederation: CONCACAF
FIFA world ranking: 131 (joint)

HAITI

Federation: Fédération Haïtienne de Football
Founded: 1904
Joined FIFA: 1933
Confederation: CONCACAF
FIFA world ranking: 123
Honours: CONCACAF Championship 1957, 1973

Haiti were the first Caribbean side to play in the World Cup finals, reaching the tournament in West Germany in 1974 a year after winning their second and last CONCACAF Championship. Forward Sanon put Haiti ahead against Italy but they eventually lost 3-1. Disturbingly, Ernst Jean-Joseph failed a drug test, was beaten up by his own officials and sent back to Haiti. Heavy defeats by Poland (0-7) and Argentina (1-4) followed. Since then they have been eclipsed by the rise of the USA and the dominance of Mexico. Haiti have their own league, with clubs such as Don Bosco and Roulado Gônaïves picking up the title in recent years.

Above: Guinea players celebrate after their match with Tunisia at the 2006 African Nations Cup.

Above left: Fredy Thompson of Guatemala makes a sliding tackle as Andrew Williams of Jamaica heads for goal in 2005.

HOLLAND

Federation: Koninklijke Nederlandse Voetbal Bond (KNVB)

Founded: 1889

Joined FIFA: 1904

Confederation: UEFA

FIFA world ranking: 6

Honours: European Championship 1988

Architects of 'Total Football' and birthplace of some of the game's finest talents, Holland remains one of the most innovative and exciting footballing cultures in the world – yet it was also one of its later developers.

Holland was one of the first countries outside of Britain to pick up on the appeal of football. The country's first club, Haarlemse FC, was founded in 1879 and its football association was set up ten years later. But while the Dutch football association's insistence on adhering to amateur, Calvinist principles yielded some return at the Olympics in the 1920s, it eventually proved to be a barrier to progress. In the post-war era it was evident that Holland lagged behind tactically and they regularly failed to make it through qualification for major championships.

Eventually the exodus of top players, like Ajax's Cor Van Der Hart and Xerxes' Faas Wilkes, to foreign clubs forced the KNVB to usher in professionalism in 1954. Ten years later the decision began to pay dividends as Dutch football accelerated into a new era, uncluttered by old traditions.

The breakthrough came in the mid-Sixties when the concept of Total Football took hold at Ajax with coach Rinus Michels and the young Johan Cruyff, Holland's most talented footballer ever. Their game plan relied on every player being comfortable on the ball, willing to play fluidly and move into space constantly. It has characterised the nation's football ever since – and influenced many other teams.

Ajax served notice that Dutch football had emerged from the dark ages with a memorable 5-1 thrashing of Bill Shankly's Liverpool in 1966. Three years later the club made their first appearance in the European Champions Cup final, losing to AC Milan, before winning the trophy on three successive occasions between 1971 and 1973 beating Panathiniakos 2-0 at Wembley, Inter Milan 2-0 in Rotterdam and Juventus 1-0 in Belgrade.

At the 1974 World Cup Holland began to emerge as a real force on the international stage, but despite going 1-0 up in the first two minutes of the final against West Germany with a penalty from Neeskens, the team's over-confidence proved to be its downfall and they eventually lost to the hosts 2-1.

Above: Dutch captain Johan Cruyff, the master of 'Total Football'. Opposite clockwise from top left, the stars of Holland. Ruud Van Nistelrooy in action in 2005; Johnny Rep at the 1978 World Cup; Ruud Gullit picks up the 1988 European Championship trophy; and Frank Rijkaard at the 1992 European Championship.

The psychological blow inflicted by that defeat then hung over Dutch football for a generation. Four years later in the final in Argentina they were again undone by the hosts, on this occasion in extra-time.

The ghost was partially laid to rest in 1988 when the most talented Dutch team since the mid-Seventies, a side built around Ruud Gullit, Frank Rijkaard and Marco Van Basten, won the European Championship playing thrilling, attacking football – they also had the added satisfaction of gaining revenge over their German hosts in the semi-final.

Domestically the Dutch Eredivisie only came into existence in 1956 and has been totally dominated by three clubs ever since. Ajax (who won the inaugural title), PSV and Feyenoord annually turn the championship into a three-horse race. The lack of competition is another reason for the country's best (and most heavily-taxed) players regularly to seek more challenging climes. In 1973 Cruyff headed for Barcelona, while Rijkaard, Gullit and Van Basten became the bedrock for AC Milan's success in the early Nineties.

Ajax remain one of the most famous clubs in the world. Founded in 1900 the team began their early domination of Dutch football under Englishman Jack Reynolds, who enshrined their reputation for attacking play. Ajax have won the league on 29 occasions, most recently in 2004. In 1995 the club won the Champions League, thanks to a solitary goal from an 18-year-old Patrick Kluivert. A year later they moved to a state of the art stadium, the Amsterdam Arena, which is also a venue for internationals.

Amsterdam is effectively a one-club city and its bitterest rivals can be found in the port of

Rotterdam at Feyenoord, the team that first put Dutch football on the map when they lifted the European Cup in 1970. While Feyenoord fans still harbour an inferiority complex about the Amsterdamers, the club has had its fair share of success, not least in 14 championships and, in the Nineties, dominance in the cup competition, the KNVB Beker. Feyenoord's stadium, De Kuip, annually hosts the competition's final, and European glory also returned to De Kuip in May 2002 with a UEFA Cup win over Borussia Dortmund.

The third player in Holland's 'big three' is based in Eindhoven, home to industrial giant Philips, which also bankrolls PSV (Philips Sport Vereniging), the football club founded in 1913. Unsurprisingly PSV are the richest club in the Netherlands, though only the second most successful with 18 championship wins. The club's greatest era arrived with Ruud Gullit in the mid-Eighties, a period capped by a European Cup win in 1988. On a general note, hooliganism became an unpleasant feature of Dutch football in the Nineties and a compulsory membership scheme for fans was introduced in 1996.

Financially Dutch Clubs have suffered in recent years. By 2002 the 36 professional clubs had accumulated debts of £16 million. The annual league battle between Ajax and PSV has not helped. Never before has the Ajax youth policy been so valued for club and country, as new talent is unearthed regularly. Holland were semi-finalists at Euro 2004 under Dick Advocaat, and qualified for their eighth World Cup in 2006 under coach Marco Van Basten, introducing many new young players who point to a new era for Holland.

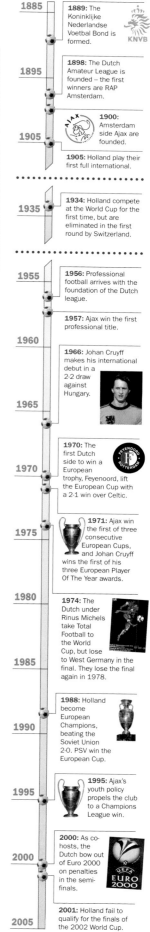

1885

1889: The Koninklijke Nederlandse Voetbal Bond is formed.

1895

1898: The Dutch Amateur League is founded – the first winners are RAP Amsterdam.

1905

1900: Amsterdam side Ajax are founded.

1905: Holland play their first full international.

1935

1934: Holland compete at the World Cup for the first time, but are eliminated in the first round by Switzerland.

1955

1956: Professional football arrives with the foundation of the Dutch league.

1957: Ajax win the first professional title.

1960

1966: Johan Cruyff makes his international debut in a 2-2 draw against Hungary.

1965

1970: The first Dutch side to win a European trophy, Feyenoord, lift the European Cup with a 2-1 win over Celtic.

1970

1971: Ajax win the first of three consecutive European Cups, and Johan Cruyff wins the first of his three European Player Of The Year awards.

1975

1974: The Dutch under Rinus Michels take Total Football to the World Cup, but lose to West Germany in the final. They lose the final again in 1978.

1980

1985

1988: Holland become European Champions, beating the Soviet Union 2-0. PSV win the European Cup.

1990

1995: Ajax's youth policy propels the club to a Champions League win.

1995

2000: As co-hosts, the Dutch bow out of Euro 2000 on penalties in the semi-finals.

2000

2001: Holland fail to qualify for the finals of the 2002 World Cup.

2005

HONDURAS

Federation: Federación National Autónoma de Fútbol de Honduras
Founded: 1951
Joined FIFA: 1951
Confederation: CONCACAF
FIFA world ranking: 38
Honours: CONCACAF Championship 1981

The early 1980s saw the heyday of football in Honduras – the nation won the CONCACAF Championship in 1981 and also qualified for the World Cup in Spain. Honduras, who drew with hosts Spain and Northern Ireland, could have qualified for the second stage but they lost to a Petrovic penalty against Yugoslavia.

Below: Hungary captain Ferenc Puskás congratulates Fritz Walter, holding the Jules Rimet Cup, on West Germany's victory in the 1954 World Cup final.

HONG KONG

Federation: The Hong Kong Football Association
Founded: 1914
Joined FIFA: 1954
Confederation: AFC
FIFA world ranking: 117 (joint)

The former British colony of Hong Kong was at the forefront of football development on the Asian continent. They were founder members of the Asian Football Confederation in 1954 and hosted the inaugural Asian Cup in 1956. The Hong Kong league was the first professional league on the continent, drawing players from abroad, especially British players. The league began in 1946 and was first won by the Royal Air Force team. Hong Kong's leading clubs are Happy Valley and Sun Hei, who won all four domestic trophies (league, FA Cup, League Cup and Shield) in 2005, the first club since South China in 1991.

HUNGARY

Federation: Magyar Labdarúgó Szövetség
Founded: 1901
Joined FIFA: 1906
Confederation: UEFA
FIFA world ranking: 84
Honours: Olympics 1952, 1964, 1968

Once numbered among the game's most innovative footballing cultures, Hungary are a shadow of their former selves. Great promise failed to yield major trophies, talent drained away and socio-political decline has now left the country financially crippled.

The Hungarian football association was founded more than 100 years ago, but a professional league did not arise until the Twenties. Jewish-based club MTK (Magyar Testgyakorlók Köre) became a dominant force under the coaching of Scotsman Jimmy Hogan and it made clear the need for some kind of organised league-based competition.

Pre-World War II Hungary began to display the ability and cohesion to challenge the hegemony of established footballing giants like England and Italy. The national side reached the 1938 World Cup final before ushering in the era of the 'Magical Magyars', rewriting the way the game was played in the Fifties with a clutch of legends including Bózsik, Kocsis, Hidegkuti and Puskás. Their impact was vividly underlined in 1953 when they became the first

non-British team to beat England at Wembley with a resounding 6-3 victory.

In 50 games played between 1950 and 1955, Hungary lost just once – agonisingly it was the 1954 World Cup final, where they threw away an early 2-0 lead to end up losing 3-2 to West Germany. The team's promise ended abruptly with the Soviet invasion of their country in 1956. Many of the players were on tour with Honvéd and chose not to return. Kocsis and Czibor headed for Barcelona, while Puskás opted for Real Madrid.

Within six years, a talented new side had emerged, with the likes of striker Florian Albert taking Hungary to the quarter-finals of both the 1962 and 1966 World Cups. It was to be their last hurrah. Despite Olympic golds in 1964 and 1968, Hungary failed to qualify for the 1970 World Cup finals and have not been present since 1986, where they managed a first-round victory against Canada, but went out after heavy defeats to the Soviet Union and France. A fourth place finish in the 1972 European Championship remains their best showing in the modern era, where the team lost to a solitary goal in the semi-final against the Soviet Union.

At club level Hungarian football has rarely looked like capitalising on the brilliance of its national teams. Budapest-based Ferencváros dominated domestic football in the Nineties, but their only European success came as long ago as 1965 when they won the UEFA Cup, beating Juventus. They made one appearance in the Champions League in 1995-6. Local rivals Honvéd, once the army side which provided the core of the Golden Squad, Ujpesti TE, and 2002 winners Zalaegerszegi TE make up the running.

In 1999 the Hungarian Football Federation took drastic action to halt the alarming decline in quality footballers, revamping the entire grassroots structure of the game in an initiative known as the Bózsik Programme.

The financial strictures on clubs, however, continue to undermine the domestic game. In February 2003 First Division side Dunaferr SE parted company with almost their entire playing and coaching staff because of financial problems. The revival of the Magical Magyars remains a long way off.

ICELAND

Federation: Knattspyrnumsamband Island
Founded: 1947
Joined FIFA: 1947
Confederation: UEFA
FIFA world ranking: 107

The Icelandic league, played between April and October, is dominated by the Reykjavik clubs – KR, Valur, Fram and Vikingur have been the big winners, but IA Akranes and FH Hafnarfjördur have also risen to prominence in recent years. Iceland is regarded as a minor football nation but they rarely suffer heavy defeats and at home are very difficult to beat.

INDIA

Federation: All India Football Federation
Founded: 1937
Joined FIFA: 1948
Confederation: AFC
FIFA world ranking: 130

Like so many sports in India, football was introduced by the British. However, the Indian population has shown little interest in the game, instead preferring cricket and hockey. The early Calcutta league was strictly a British affair, but Indian teams such as Mohammedan Sporting, East Bengal and Mohon Bagan did spring up to challenge the British dominance. Mohon Bagan, to mark the club's centenary, were officially named 'The National Football Team of India'. Indian players have included Jumma Khan, the first Indian to play in boots, and Syed Abdus Sumad, 'the Indian Stanley Matthews', who played until he was 52.

INDONESIA

Federation: Persatuan Sepakbola Seluruh Indonesia
Founded: 1930
Joined FIFA: 1952
Confederation: AFC
FIFA world ranking: 139

IRAN

Federation: Islamic Republic of Iran Football Federation
Founded: 1920
Joined FIFA: 1945
Confederation: AFC
FIFA world ranking: 47
Honours: Asian Cup 1968, 1972, 1976

Iranian football rose to prominence in the Sixties and Seventies with the national team winning a hat-trick of Asian Cups and making the

Olympic quarter-finals in 1976. The highlight was a deserved 1-1 draw with Scotland at the 1978 World Cup, influenced in no small way by the contribution of British and Yugoslav coaches. In the Nineties Iran re-emerged from a period of instability, qualifying for the 1998 World Cup and recording their first win at the finals. Germany 2006 was their third World Cup.

In the modern era Iran has a reputation of playing good football and is one of Asia's leading lights. Forward Ali Daei became the first man to score 100 international goals in November 2004, while Ali Karimi was voted the Asian Player Of The Year in 2005. They are two of a handful of players who have had successful careers playing in Germany's Bundesliga.

Only three Iranian clubs have achieved success in the Asian Champions Cup: Taj Club (1970), Esteghlal (1991) and Pas (1993). There is a healthy, openly-fought, 16-team Iranian league that is played between September and May, where no one team has dominated since Pirouzi in the late 1990s.

IRAQ

Federation: Iraqi Football Association
Founded: 1948
Joined FIFA: 1950
Confederation: AFC
FIFA world ranking: 88

One of the top six sides on the Asian continent, more often than not it is Iraq who misses out on World Cup qualification and fail to make the final step in the Asian Cup. They did qualify for the 1986 World Cup under Brazilian coach Evaristo de Macedo, but they lost all three of

their group games. In the post-Saddam Hussein era the national team, who incredibly reached the 2004 Olympic semi-finals, cannot play at home for security reasons.

Domestic competitive football resumed in 2004-5 with four divisions of nine teams leading to a 12-team play-off phase that was finally won by Al Quwa Al Jawia.

ISRAEL

Federation: Israel Football Association
Founded: 1928
Joined FIFA: 1929
Confederation: UEFA
FIFA world ranking: 51
Honours: Asian Cup 1964

Israel were a strong force in the Asian Football Confederation, runners-up twice in the first two Asian Cups of 1956 and 1960, before lifting the trophy in 1964. They also qualified for the World Cup finals in 1970, drawing with Italy and Sweden and losing to Uruguay.

However, Israel's national team were a political hot potato in Asian football. The AFC contrived that Israel avoided their Arab neighbours and grouped them with Far East opposition, such as Japan and South Korea. Arab disquiet was brought to a head and Israel were thrown out of the AFC in 1976, being shunted first into Europe and then Oceania, even facing South American opposition in World Cup play-offs. As a consequence Israel have had the distinction of having played World Cup qualifiers on every continent.

Israel were given a permanent football home in Europe when UEFA accepted them in 1991.

Above: Iran celebrate victory over Japan in the 2002 Asian Cup final.

1895

1898: Formation of the Federazione Italiana Giuoco Calcio. The first championship is played in just one day and won by Genoa.

1905

1910: The national team debuts in the Milan Arena, beating France 6-2.

1915

1913: The first national championship takes place. Pro Vercelli win the title, beating Lazio in the final 6-0.

1930

1930: Italy decide against entering the first World Cup.

1935

1934: The beginning of a golden period, as Italy win the World Cup. They lift the trophy again in 1938 and win Olympic gold in 1936.

1940

1944: The Italian title doesn't take place for two seasons. Torino dominate the decade, winning all five titles contested between 1943 and 1948.

1945

1950

1949: Torino's plane crashes in the fog, decimating the greatest Italian club side, and killing eight of the national team a year before the World Cup.

1955

1957: Fiorentina make it to the second European Cup final, but lose 2-0 to Real Madrid.

1960

1963: AC Milan become the first Italian side to win the European Cup, beating Benfica 2-1.

1965

1968: Italy become champions of Europe.

1970

1970: Italy lose the World Cup final to Brazil.

1975

1980: A bribery scandal is revealed in Italy involving top players and officials. Paolo Rossi is banned for two years.

1980

1982: The head of Italy's football federation resigns on the eve of the World Cup after a betting scandal. Paolo Rossi returns to help Italy win third World Cup, beating West Germany.

1985

1990

1990: Italy host the World Cup, but Azeglio Vicini's team only manage to finish third.

1995

1994: Italy finish runners-up to Brazil in the World Cup.

2000

2006: After a shaky start to the tournament, Italy win the World Cup after beating France in a penalty shoot-out.

2005

ITALY

Federation: Federazione Italiana Giuoco Calcio
Founded: 1898
Joined FIFA: 1905
Confederation: UEFA
FIFA world ranking: 2
Honours: World Cup 1934, 1938, 1982, 2006; European Championship 1968; Olympics 1936

The Italian league, Serie A, wasn't founded until the 1929-30 season, but there had been a football association operating in the country since 1898. Italy's biggest club sides – Juventus, AC Milan and Internazionale – were established in a period stretching from 1897 to 1908, but they are all a dominant influence on European football to this day. In the 1980s and 1990s, Italian club football lavished money on expensive foreign players and consequently ruled European competition, AC Milan winning the European Champions Cup in 1989, 1990 and 1994, and Juventus doing likewise in 1996. Furthermore, eight out of 11 UEFA Cup finals between 1989 and 1999 were won by Italian sides, with four of them being all-Italian affairs.

The country's national side enjoyed similar dominance in the 1930s. Italy hadn't competed in the first finals in Uruguay in 1930, but were named hosts of the second, four years later. Their arrival on the world stage, under legendary manager Vittorio Pozzo, was marked with a crushing 7-1 win over the United States. Pozzo's side found Spain, their quarter-final opponents, a much tougher nut to crack, and they had a controversial equaliser to thank for taking what had already been a bruising tie to a replay, which they duly won. Italy defeated Austria 1-0 in the semi-final and, cheered on by Fascist dictator Benito Mussolini, came from behind to overcome Czechoslovakia with two late goals in the final.

To underline their superiority, Italy went on to win the gold medal at the Berlin Olympics in 1936 – they defeated Austria 2-1 in the final and were no doubt glad to put to rest conspiracy theories about the nature of their World Cup victory two years earlier (some had suggested that Italy had unfairly benefited from their status as hosts, with Mussolini accused of engineering his team's victory in the tournament).

The first European team to win the Jules Rimet trophy soon became the first nation to retain it, the Italians travelling to France in 1938 with a much remodelled side. Strangely enough it was Norway rather than hosts France or Brazil who caused the Italians the most problems on their way to the final, but a fine display from goalkeeper Aldo Olivieri and an

Above: Coach Vittorio Pozzo and his World Cup winning team of 1934. Opposite clockwise from top left, Sandro Mazzola in 1974; coach Marcello Lippi and the victorious Italian World Cup team of 2006; Paolo Rossi, the man who won Italy the World Cup in 1982; Roberto Baggio in action at France 98.

extra-time winner saw Pozzo's attack-minded side win 2-1 to progress to the quarter-finals.

France were duly dispatched 3-1 and two second-half goals put paid to the Brazilians in the semi-finals (one, a penalty from Giuseppe Meazza, was scored as he struggled to hold up his shorts in which the elastic had snapped). Italy met Hungary in the final in Paris, running out 4-2 winners, with Silvio Piola and Luigi Colaussi bagging two each. It was a historic win not just for Italy, but with World War II just over a year away, for fascism also.

Post-war, Italy had to endure many years in the international wilderness. In 1949, the entire first team squad of reigning champions Torino were killed in a plane crash, effectively ripping the heart out of the national side a little over a year before they were expected to defend their world title in Brazil. Italy failed to make it past the first round in the finals and subsequently missed out altogether in 1958. They also had to endure the humiliation of losing to North Korea in 1966.

Just two years later, however, Italian football got itself back on track when the country hosted – and won – the 1968 European Championship. Although they had to rely on the toss of a coin to defeat the Soviet Union in the semi-finals (the game had finished 0-0 after extra-time), and it had taken a replay to see off Yugoslavia in the final, coach Ferrucio Valcareggi built on that success, taking his side all the way to the final of the 1970 World Cup, where they were heavily defeated by Brazil.

Under coach Enzo Bearzot, Italy finished fourth at the Argentina finals in 1978, but won the World Cup for a third time in 1982. They did it the hard way too, drawing all three of their first round games, before beating reigning champions Argentina and favourites Brazil in the second group phase. The latter match – a 3-2 win – was memorable thanks to an astonishing hat-trick from 25-year-old Paolo Rossi, who'd only recently returned to football following a two-year ban for match-fixing.

Rossi hit two more in the semi-final against Poland and was the scorer of Italy's first goal in a 3-1 final triumph over West Germany.

Italy finished third when hosting the World Cup in 1990, losing to Argentina on penalties in the semi-final. They were beaten on penalties again in the 1994 final by Brazil, but finally claimed their fourth title in 2006. Captained by Fabio Cannavaro and coached by Marcello Lippi, they beat France 5-3 on penalties after at 1-1 draw at Berlin's Olympic Stadium to become Europe's most successful nation in the World Cup.

Their record at the European Championship has been less impressive. Their appearance in the final in 2000, where they were undone by a last-minute equaliser and a golden goal by France, was their first since winning it in 1968. In 2004 they were eliminated in the group stages, and they have yet to score more than two goals in a game in the competition.

While Italian club sides remain some of the strongest in Europe, domestically the Italian league is still living in the wake of its spending spree in the 1990s. Many of the clubs who failed to deliver glory in exchange for unrealistic spending plans are now paying the price for over-ambition in a market that has seen attendances stagnating and uncertainties over TV revenues.

While Fiorentina, Napoli, Sampdoria and Genoa have struggled, Lazio opted to restructure their finances in 1998 with a partial flotation on the Italian stock exchange. The decision paid dividends two years later when they claimed their first title in 26 seasons. Roma and Juventus followed suit and both won the title in the subsequent campaigns. But scandal is never far from Italian football. In 2002 Lazio's future was put in jeopardy by a financial scandal involving owner Sergio Cragnotti that left the club in the hands of financial caretakers, and in 2006 they were implicated in Italy's biggest ever match-fixing scandal, that saw Juventus punished with relegation to Serie B, and Fiorentina, Lazio and Milan deducted points. Juventus were also stripped of their two most recent league titles.

IVORY COAST

Federation: Fédération Ivoirienne de Football
Founded: 1960
Joined FIFA: 1960
Confederation: CAF
FIFA world ranking: 20
Honours: African Nations Cup 1992

It was the French that introduced the sport of football to the Ivory Coast. The West African nation has one of the best-organised and richest leagues on the continent, but its strength at home has not often been turned into success in the international arena. Stade Abidjan won the African Champions Cup in 1966 and ASEC Mimosas won the African Champions League in 1998.

The national team, under coach Yeo Martial, won the African Nations Cup in 1992, beating Ghana in a dramatic 11-10 penalty shoot-out. Kouame Aka scored the decisive kick before legendary goalkeeper Alain Gouamene, who was to play in a record seven African Nations Cups, made a save. The victorious squad included two of the most famous Ivory Coast players, French league stars Youssef Fofana and Abdoulaye Traore.

It was not until 2006 that the 'Elephants' reached the World Cup finals for the first time, thanks to French coach Henri Michel and a new group of African stars such as Didier Drogba and Kolo Toure. The side were also runners-up at the African Nations Cup in 2006, losing out to hosts Egypt on penalties in the final. En route to the final they triumphed over Cameroon in a shoot-out that took 24 spot-kicks to decide.

ASEC Mimosas are the Ivory Coast's most successful club. They have developed a very successful youth academy that attracts all the best young talent, not only for the club but for the French League. Since 1990 the club have only failed to win the championship twice.

JAMAICA

Federation: Jamaica Football Federation
Founded: 1910
Joined FIFA: 1962
FIFA world ranking: 78
Confederation: CONCACAF

Jamaica has had a football federation, care of its former British colonial rulers, since 1910, although it does not have much history as an organised sport. The rise of the 'Reggae Boyz'

in the late Nineties saw Jamaica qualify for their first World Cup in France under Brazilian coach Rene Simoes. For the first time Jamaica raided players from the English league and 'imported' players of Jamaican descent, such as Frank Sinclair, Fitzroy Simpson, Robbie Earle, Marcus Gayle, Paul Hall and Deon Burton, beating Japan 2-1 in their final group game following defeats by Croatia and Argentina. Jamaica were the inaugural winners of the Caribbean Cup in 1991, lifting the trophy again in 1998 and 2005.

JAPAN

Federation: The Football Association of Japan
Founded: 1921
Joined FIFA: 1929-45, 1950
Confederation: AFC
FIFA world ranking: 49
Honours: Asian Cup 1992, 2000, 2004

Since co-hosting the 2002 World Cup the Japanese domestic game has thrived. By 2005 the J.League had grown to a record 30 clubs comprising of an 18-club top league and a 12-club second division. The previous season had seen attendances break the seven million barrier for the first time, with all but a handful of clubs making a profit. The emphasis has been on developing community ties, vital youth schemes and, most importantly, a restrained financial budget so overspending should not happen.

It is a much-needed boost in popularity after the trough of poor attendances in the latter 1990s, when the existence of some clubs was seriously under threat. The J.League has managed to retain many of its leading players, although some still ply their trade in Europe. Their experience has helped the national side who are such a vital component of success for football in Japan.

Japan, under Brazilian legend and former J.League player and coach Zico, won the Asian Cup for the third time in 2004, beating China 3-1 in Beijing with goals from Takashi Fukunishi, Koji Nakata and Keiji Tamada. Despite being knocked out in the groups stages, qualification for the 2006 World Cup maintained the popularity of the game, reaffirming the country's status as one of Asia's football powerhouses.

The J.League had its origins in 1993 when, in a major commercial revamp of the domestic game, there was a $20 million of investment in a fully-fledged professional league. The early years attracted players from abroad, including England's Gary Lineker and Brazil's Zico, who was to stay at Kashima Antlers as player and coach for 15 years.

The importance of imported talent from Europe and South America has lessened, which

has allowed young Japanese players to thrive. A case in point was 16-year-old Takayuki Moromoto who was voted the J.League's 2004 Young Player Of The Year.

JORDAN

Federation: Jordan Football Association
Founded: 1949
Joined FIFA: 1958
FIFA world ranking: 98
Confederation: AFC

KAZAKHSTAN

Federation: Football Union of Kazakhstan
Founded: 1914
Joined FIFA: 1994
FIFA world ranking: 140
Confederation: UEFA

KENYA

Federation: Kenya Football Federation
Founded: 1960
Joined FIFA: 1960
FIFA world ranking: 117 (joint)
Confederation: CAF

KUWAIT

Federation: Kuwait Football Association
Founded: 1952
Joined FIFA: 1962
Confederation: AFC
FIFA world ranking: 100
Honours: Asian Cup 1980

Prince Fahid calling his Kuwaiti national team off the field after France had 'scored' a fourth goal at the 1982 World Cup is the abiding memory of Kuwaiti football. They did manage to secure a draw with Czechoslovakia at the same tournament. Two years earlier Kuwait had hosted and won the Asian Cup, beating South Korea 3-0.

Opposite: Ivory Coast's Didier Drogba misses a penalty in the decisive shoot-out in the 2006 African Nations Cup final.

Above: Libya's Marei Mohamed Suliman celebrates scoring against Ivory Coast at the 2006 African Nations Cup.

KYRGYZSTAN

Federation: Football Federation of Kyrgyz Republic
Founded: 1992
Joined FIFA: 1994
Confederation: AFC
FIFA world ranking: 121

LAOS

Federation: Fédération Lao de Football
Founded: 1951
Joined FIFA: 1952
Confederation: AFC
FIFA world ranking: 182

LATVIA

Federation: Latvijas Futbola Federacija
Founded: 1921
Joined FIFA: 1922, 1991
Confederation: UEFA
FIFA world ranking: 82 (joint)

Between 1922 and 1949 Latvia were the strongest of the Baltic states but remained a minnow in football terms. They came within a whisker of qualifying for the 1938 World Cup but lost 2-1 to Austria in a play-off. Soviet occupation in 1940 eventually led to the demise of the Latvian national team, but after independence they took part in the qualifying stages for the 1994 World Cup and 1996 European Championship. Since their return to

Right: Liberian football legend, George Weah in 2002.

international football, Latvia have yet to make any impression on either competition. Latvia's leading club is Skonto Riga, who have won the revived Latvian championship a world record 14 successive times.

LEBANON

Federation: Fédération Libanaise de Football Association
Founded: 1933
Joined FIFA: 1935
Confederation: AFC
FIFA world ranking: 112

LESOTHO

Federation: Lesotho Football Association
Founded: 1932
Joined FIFA: 1964
Confederation: CAF
FIFA world ranking: 133

LIBERIA

Federation: Liberia Football Association
Founded: 1936
Joined FIFA: 1962
Confederation: CAF
FIFA world ranking: 136 (joint)

Liberian football has never been very strong but in striker George Weah, the country has produced one truly great player. Weah has been African, European and World Player Of The Year, plying his trade at a number of top European clubs and has provided enormous support to the game in his native country.

LIBYA

Federation: Libyan Football Federation
Founded: 1962
Joined FIFA: 1963
Confederation: CAF
FIFA world ranking: 79

LIECHTENSTEIN

Federation: Liechtensteiner Fussball-Verband
Founded: 1934
Joined FIFA: 1974
Confederation: UEFA
FIFA world ranking: 124

Liechtenstein earned their first ever World Cup qualifying point by drawing 2-2 at home to Portugal and then recorded their first ever competitive wins with 4-0 and 3-0 victories over Luxembourg in the same 2006 World Cup qualifying group. There is no national league in Liechtenstein, with clubs playing in the lower divisions of the Swiss league.

LITHUANIA

Federation: Lietuvos Futbolo Federacija
Founded: 1922
Joined FIFA: 1923, 1992
Confederation: UEFA
FIFA world ranking: 69

Despite the Soviet take-over of Lithuania, the football federation never actually cancelled its membership of FIFA and, following the country's independence, it was reactivated in 1992. Lithuania was the worst performing of the Baltic states, its clubs barely making an impact on the Soviet league until Zhalgiris

Vilnius won promotion to the Supreme Soviet League in 1982, finishing third in 1987. Sigitas Jakabauskas was the first Lithuanian to play for the Soviet Union in 1985, while Viacheslav Sukristovas and Valdas Ivanauskas were Soviet Olympic gold medal winners in 1988. FBK Kaunas have been the dominant team in a Lithuanian league that lost many of its best players after independence.

LUXEMBOURG

Federation: Federation Luxembourgeoise de Football
Founded: 1908
Joined FIFA: 1910
Confederation: UEFA
FIFA world ranking: 194 (joint)

The part-time footballers of Luxembourg have one of the most dire records in Europe. Their clubs have suffered the worst aggregate defeats in European football, Dudelange losing 18-0 over two legs to Benfica, Jeunesse Hautcharage defeated 21-0 by Chelsea, and US Rumelange conceding 21 goals at the hands of Feyenoord. A European Championship quarter-final place in 1964 was the country's finest moment.

MACAO

Federation: Associacao de Futebol de Macau
Founded: 1939
Joined FIFA: 1976
Confederation: AFC
FIFA world ranking: 183 (joint)

MACEDONIA FYR

Federation: Football Federation of Macedonia
Founded: 1908
Joined FIFA: 1994
Confederation: UEFA
FIFA world ranking: 70 (joint)

In 2003, the country's leading clubs formed UPC – a union of premiership clubs – to take over the running of the Macedonian league from the federation. Leading club Vardar Skopje have gone down in history as the only Macedonian side to have won a national Yugoslav trophy, the Yugoslav Cup, in 1961.

MADAGASCAR

Federation: Fédération Malagasy de Football
Founded: 1961
Joined FIFA: 1962
Confederation: CAF
FIFA world ranking: 156

MALAWI

Federation: Football Association of Malawi
Founded: 1966
Joined FIFA: 1967
Confederation: CAF
FIFA world ranking: 80

MALAYSIA

Federation: Persatuan Bolasepak Malaysia
Founded: 1933
Joined FIFA: 1956
Confederation: AFC
FIFA world ranking: 146

MALDIVES

Federation: Football Association of Maldives
Founded: 1982
Joined FIFA: 1986
Confederation: AFC
FIFA world ranking: 126 (joint)

MALI

Federation: Fédération Malienne de Football
Founded: 1960
Joined FIFA: 1962
Confederation: CAF
FIFA world ranking: 63

MALTA

Federation: Malta Football Association
Founded: 1900
Joined FIFA: 1959
Confederation: UEFA
FIFA world ranking: 122

Malta has a special place in footballing history as it was on the Mediterranean island that the first referee's whistle was heard, in a 1-1 draw between soldiers of the Shropshire Regiment and locals from Cospicua St Andrew's, in 1886. Malta did not join FIFA until 1959 and only then with the permission of the English FA, to whom they had been affiliated since 1900. They did not enter the World Cup until 1974 and have since had very limited success. One of Europe's smallest football nations, the Maltese league is dominated by Sliema Wanderers and Valletta, with Birkirkara a third force.

MAURITANIA

Federation: Fédération de Football de la République de Mauritanie
Founded: 1961
Joined FIFA: 1964
Confederation: CAF
FIFA world ranking: 166

MAURITIUS

Federation: Mauritius Football Association
Founded: 1952
Joined FIFA: 1962
Confederation: CAF
FIFA world ranking: 135

Left: Daniel Huss of Luxembourg pressures Yugoslavia's Ljubinko Drulovic in 2000.

Above: Mexico's Pavel Pardo holds the Gold Cup trophy after victory over Brazil at the Azteca Stadium in 2003.

MEXICO

Federation: Federación Mexicana De Fútbol Asociación

Founded: 1927

Joined FIFA: 1929

Confederation: CONCACAF

FIFA world ranking: 18

Honours: CONCACAF Championship 1965, 1971, 1993, 1996, 1998, 2003

Mexico commands a special place in the hearts of international football fans worldwide for hosting the 1970 World Cup finals, which provided the canvas on which the great Brazilians of that era could let their artistry flow.

Mexico have regularly appeared at the World Cup, having taken part 13 times, their strongest showings coming in 1970 and 1986 where, as hosts, they progressed to the quarter-finals. In 1986, it took a penalty shoot-out with eventual finalists West Germany to eliminate the team led by the great Hugo Sanchez, the most famous Mexican player of recent years. Sanchez, known for his extravagant and often over-the-top goal

celebrations, was a familiar figure in Europe, having plied his trade very successfully for many years in Spain with Real Madrid.

Some critics argue that Mexican football has suffered internationally over the years due to a lack of meaningful competition in the Central American region. Only in recent years, with the rise of the United States as a credible footballing force, have Mexico experienced a serious rival in a geographical neighbour. Many had argued that the nation, six times the CONCACAF championship winners, would benefit from joining the South American championship (the Copa América) and in 1993, together with the USA, they were invited to do so.

Mexico reached the Copa América final at the first attempt, losing to Argentina 2-1 after a late Gabriel Batistuta strike. Since then they have continued to take part in the competition and have become one of the strongest nations, finishing third in 1997 and 1999, and reaching the final again in 2001.

After the near miss of the 1986 World Cup, Mexico qualified for the 1990 tournament in Italy but did not attend because they were banned after fielding over-age players in an international youth tournament. In 1999 further controversy surrounded the Mexican side when, following the team's impressive

third place in the Copa América, accusations were made of drug-taking among the players.

Of the 18 top flight clubs in the Mexican league all, apart from one, are subsidiaries of larger non-football companies. That one club is the unfashionable, and not very successful, Atlas of Guadalajara. Money remains the dominant force in Mexican football to the extent that allegations of corruption are constantly made, a result of all the vested interests of all of these outside businesses. The league itself has undergone significant changes since it began, most recently in 1993 when it split the season into a winter and summer league, a system also popular in many countries in South America.

The glamour club in Mexico is América from Mexico City. Bought by broadcasting company Televisa and heavily promoted through the purchase of overseas stars and widespread television exposure, the club quickly developed a nationwide following. América became the strongest force in Mexican football in the Eighties and since then Televisas has also added Atlante and Necaxa to its stable. All three clubs play in the world famous Azteca national stadium in Mexico City, itself owned by the company. Since then, broadcasting rivals TV Azteca have followed suit, and bought into the Veracruz and Moriela clubs.

MOLDOVA

Federation: Federatia Moldoveneasca de Fotbal
Founded: 1990
Joined FIFA: 1994
Confederation: UEFA
FIFA world ranking: 77

When Nistru Kishinev (later renamed Zimbru Chisinau) finished sixth in the Soviet league in 1957, it was the best ever performance by a Moldovan club. Zimbru have subsequently proved the strongest team in a poor Moldovan league and, along with Sheriff, they provide most of the playing staff to a poor national side.

MONGOLIA

Federation: Mongolian Football Federation
Founded: 1959
Joined FIFA: 1998
Confederation: AFC
FIFA world ranking: 181

MONTSERRAT

Federation: Montserrat Football Association
Founded: 1994
Joined FIFA: 1996
Confederation: CONCACAF
FIFA world ranking: 196 (joint)

MOROCCO

Federation: Fédération Royale Marocaine de Football
Founded: 1955
Joined FIFA: 1959
Confederation: CAF
FIFA world ranking: 40
Honours: African Nations Cup 1976

Morocco became the first African team to progress to the second round of the World Cup in 1986. They topped the group after 0-0 draws with England and Poland, and a 3-1 win over Portugal. They faced West Germany, but were beaten by a last minute goal. When Morocco made their very first World Cup appearance in 1970, the team was captained by Idriss Bamouss, who later became president of the Moroccan football association, and they shocked their German opponents by taking the lead before losing 2-1. They later drew 1-1 with Bulgaria. At the World Cup in 1994, Morocco lost all three group games by a single goal, while four years later, a 2-2 draw with Norway and an emphatic 3-0 win over Scotland was impressive enough but it still failed to take them through.

It was the French who introduced football to Morocco and several Moroccan-born players have featured for the French national team, including Larbi Ben Barek. Independence from France in 1956 brought a remarkably robust and open league (started in 1916). Three Moroccan sides – FAR Rabat in 1985, Raja Casablanca in 1989, 1997, 1999 and Wydad Casablanca in 1992 – have won the African Champions Cup, while Ahmed Faras (1975), Mohamed Timoumi (1985), Badou Zaki (1986) have been voted African Player Of The Year.

MOZAMBIQUE

Federation: Federação Mocambicana de Futebol
Founded: 1976
Joined FIFA: 1980
Confederation: CAF
FIFA world ranking: 126 (joint)

MYANMAR

Federation: Myanmar Football Federation
Founded: 1947
Joined FIFA: 1957
Confederation: AFC
FIFA world ranking: 163

NAMIBIA

Federation: Namibia Football Association
Founded: 1990
Joined FIFA: 1992
Confederation: CAF
FIFA world ranking: 167

NEPAL

Federation: All Nepal Football Federation
Founded: 1951
Joined FIFA: 1970
Confederation: AFC
FIFA world ranking: 164 (joint)

NETHERLANDS ANTILLES

Federation: Nederlands Antilliaanse Voetbal Unie
Founded: 1921
Joined FIFA: 1932
Confederation: CONCACAF
FIFA world ranking: 176

NEW CALEDONIA

Federation: Fédération Calédonienne de Football
Founded: 1928
Joined FIFA: 2004
Confederation: OFC
FIFA world ranking: 171

Below: Morocco's Mohammed El Yaagoubi fends off an Egyptian challenge in 2006.

Above: North Korea celebrate their amazing victory over Italy in the 1966 World Cup finals.

NEW ZEALAND

Federation: Soccer New Zealand
Founded: 1891
Joined FIFA: 1948
Confederation: OFC
FIFA world ranking: 117 (joint)
Honours: Oceania Nations Cup 1973, 1998, 2002

New Zealand's football team are known as the 'All Whites' to distinguish themselves from the dominant Rugby Union 'All Blacks'. They are now the leading force in the Oceania region following Australia's defection to the AFC. Their only World Cup appearance was in 1982, 12 years after the national league kicked-off.

NICARAGUA

Federation: Federación Nicaraguense de Fútbol
Founded: 1931
Joined FIFA: 1950
Confederation: CONCACAF
FIFA world ranking: 161 (joint)

NIGER

Federation: Fédération Nigerienne de Football
Founded: 1967
Joined FIFA: 1967
Confederation: CAF
FIFA world ranking: 169 (joint)

Right: George Best in action for Northern Ireland in 1967.

NIGERIA

Federation: Nigeria Football Association
Founded: 1945
Joined FIFA: 1959
Confederation: CAF
FIFA world ranking: 11
Honours: African Nations Cup 1980, 1994; Olympics 1996

The formation of a football association and the launching of the Governor's Cup (later renamed the FA Challenge Cup in 1954) saw the formal birth of football in Nigeria after it had been introduced by the British. However, it was not until the 1970s that Nigerian football, despite its popularity, began to develop thanks to huge investment from petrol dollars.

A national league was quickly formed and the ever-popular FA Challenge Cup became strictly a club competition after previously accepting representative sides from outside the capital of Lagos. A combination of stability and investment began to reap rewards, most notably when Nigeria hosted and won the 1980 African Nations Cup, beating Algeria 3-0 in the final. More significant was the 1985 FIFA Under-16 World Cup victory which saw Nigeria beat West Germany 2-1, with goals from Sanni Adamu and Victor Igbinoba. It was the first world title won by an African nation.

This was to provide the springboard that helped Nigeria's 'Super Eagles' to qualify for three successive World Cups in 1994, 1998 and 2002, lift the African Nations Cup a second time in 1994, and win the football tournament at the 1996 Olympics. In addition, Rashidi Yekini (1993), Emmanuel Amunike (1994), Nwankwo Kanu (1996) and Victor Ikpeba (1997) have all been voted African Footballer Of The Year.

Nigerian players are in demand all over the world and these days a player from a Nigeria-based club is a rarity in the national squad. Players are often snapped up by European clubs at a young age and this experience of professionalism has helped the national team fulfil its potential.

NORTH KOREA

Federation: Football Association of the Democratic People's Republic of Korea
Founded: 1945
Joined FIFA: 1958
Confederation: AFC
FIFA world ranking: 91

Prior to the 1960s, North Korean football was strictly a domestic sport, with any contact at the international level limited to just the Communist countries. In 1966, however, North Korea entered the World Cup for the first time, qualifying for the finals after beating Australia in a play-off. The country astounded the world with their skill and sportsmanship, with Pak Doo Ik making history with a winning goal against the mighty Italy to take the Koreans into the quarter-finals against Portugal. Amazingly, North Korea then stormed into a 3-0 lead through Pak Seung Jin, Li Dong Woon and Yang Sung Kook but, equally astonishingly, ended up losing 5-3.

NORTHERN IRELAND

Federation: Irish Football Association
Founded: 1880
Joined FIFA: 1911
Confederation: UEFA
FIFA world ranking: 75

The Irish FA is the fourth oldest football federation in the world and, until 1923, controlled football throughout Ireland. Their main opposition were England, Scotland and Wales in the annual Home International Championship that ran from 1884 to 1984, although they were far from successful in the competition – winning it outright just three times (in 1914, 1980 and 1984).

Northern Ireland did not meet non-British opposition until 1951 – three years after they stopped picking players from southern Ireland. Successive World Cup qualification in 1982 and 1986 showcased the country's best team, featuring the likes of Martin O'Neill, Sammy McIlroy, Gerry Armstrong, Norman Whiteside and Pat Jennings. Northern Ireland's best World Cup performance, however, was in 1958 when a Danny Blanchflower-led team reached the quarter-finals in their first appearance.

George Best, the greatest Irish player, never got to play in a World Cup but won every other honour with his club Manchester United. There has been a league championship

THE COUNTRIES OF AFC

AFC — Asian Football Confederation

MONGOLIA
LEBANON
KYRGYSTAN
TURKMENISTAN
UZBEKISTAN
SYRIA
NORTH KOREA
SOUTH KOREA
TAJIKISTAN
IRAN
BANGLADESH
CHINA
AFGHANISTAN
IRAQ
NEPAL
BHUTAN
MACAO
KUWAIT
JORDAN
PAKISTAN
LAOS
CHINESE TAIPEI
INDIA
JAPAN
PALESTINE
CAMBODIA
HONG KONG
BAHRAIN
GUAM
SAUDI ARABIA
QATAR
VIETNAM
MYANMAR
YEMEN
UAE
SRI LANKA
BRUNEI
PHILIPPINES
OMAN
THAILAND
MALDIVES
INDONESIA
SINGAPORE
MALAYSIA
EAST TIMOR

AUSTRALIA

THE COUNTRIES OF OFC

VANUATU
SAMOA
AMERICAN SAMOA
SOLOMON ISLANDS
PAPUA NEW GUINEA
FIJI
TONGA
COOK ISLANDS
TAHITI
NEW CALEDONIA
NEW ZEALAND

contested since 1891 but Northern Ireland's club football is semi-professional, with the best players often poached by the professional clubs of England and Scotland. There is also a sectarian element to Irish football with teams such as Linfield and Cliftonville regarded as Protestant and Catholic clubs respectively.

NORWAY

Federation: Norges Fotballforbund
Founded: 1902
Joined FIFA: 1908
Confederation: UEFA
FIFA world ranking: 52

It has taken Norway a long time to achieve the breakthrough on the international stage after years merely making up the numbers. After watching Scandinavian neighbours Denmark and Sweden make waves in world football, Norway finally broke through in the 1990s and qualification for two successive World Cups in 1994 and 1998 has given Norwegian football a great impetus. They even managed a 2-1 win over Brazil in the group stages of the 1998 World Cup in France, before losing to Italy in the second round.

The improvement has coincided with an increasing number of Norwegian players making their name abroad. This was largely because Norwegian players were proving cheaper to sign than other players across Europe in the Eighties and Nineties. Players such as Erik Thorstvedt, Stig Inge Bjornebye, Tore Andre Flo and Ole Gunnar Solksjaer have not only succeeded in the English Premiership, but have also won a host of honours.

Ironically, the domestic game in Norway has shifted from an open championship to being largely dominated by one club – Rosenborg. The Trondheim club won the Norwegian title on a record 13 successive occasions between 1992 and 2004 and have regularly featured in the Champions League.

Below: Paraguay's Cesar Ramirez on the ball against Wales.

Football has been played in Norway since the 1890s and the oldest club, Odds BK of Skein, was formed in 1894. A federation and cup competition were started in 1902, with the national team debuting in 1908 with an 11-3 defeat by Sweden. Norway did not win a game for ten years but they did win bronze at the 1936 Berlin Olympics, during which, in front of Hitler, they beat Germany 2-0.

OMAN

Federation: Oman Football Association
Founded: 1978
Joined FIFA: 1980
Confederation: AFC
FIFA world ranking: 86

PAKISTAN

Federation: Pakistan Football Federation
Founded: 1947
Joined FIFA: 1948
Confederation: AFC
FIFA world ranking: 153 (joint)

PALESTINE

Federation: Palestine Football Federation
Founded: 1928, 1962
Joined FIFA: 1998
Confederation: AFC
FIFA world ranking: 120

PANAMA

Federation: Federación Nacional de Fútbol de Panamá
Founded: 1937
Joined FIFA: 1938
Confederation: CONCACAF
FIFA world ranking: 59
Honours: CONCACAF Championship 1951

Panama, under coach Jose Hernandez, lost 3-1 on penalties to the USA after a 0-0 draw in the

2005 CONCACAF Gold Cup final and also, for the first time, reached the final group stage of the 2006 World Cup qualifiers. Not since the 1951 CCCF Championship win have Panama done so well.

PAPUA NEW GUINEA

Federation: Papua New Guinea Football Association
Founded: 1962
Joined FIFA: 1963
Confederation: OFC
FIFA world ranking: 174

PARAGUAY

Federation: Asociacion Paraguaya de Futbol
Founded: 1906
Joined FIFA: 1921
Confederation: CONMEBOL
FIFA world ranking: 19
Honours: Copa América 1953, 1979

Of the great footballing nations of South America, Paraguay remain one of the poorest and least glamorous. But for a small country it can be proud of several of its international achievements: the national team has been twice winners of the South American Championship, in 1953 and 1979, and has made seven World Cup appearances, including the 2006 finals in Germany. Leading club Olimpia, meanwhile, have three Copa Libertadores triumphs – 1979, 1990 and 2002 – to add to their 38 Paraguayan league titles. There have been four Paraguayan footballers who have been South American Player Of The Year: Julio Cesar Romero (1985), Raul Amarilla (1990), Jose Luis Chilavert (1996) and Jose Cardozo (2002), who is the nations all-time top goalscorer.

The Paraguayan League with its ten-team Apertura and Clasura Championships is played between February and December with a month hiatus during July. It is dominated by the Asuncion-based clubs, with Cerro Porteño, Guarani, Libertad, Nacional and Olimpia all hailing from the capital. Usually the winners of each Championship play-off determine the overall national title winners and Asuncion is always represented.

In recent years Argentine Gerardo Martino has been the most influential coach winning four successive titles between 2002 and 2005. The first two were with Libertad and the others were with Cerro Porteño. Most of Paraguay's leading players, however, play their football abroad in the more lucrative European and South American leagues, but they still return to play for their country. Carlos Gamarra, who has played in three World Cups, became the first Paraguayan to win 100 caps in 2005.

PERU

Federation: Federacion Peruana De Futbol
Founded: 1922
Joined FIFA: 1926
Confederation: CONMEBOL
FIFA world ranking: 42
Honours: Copa América 1939, 1975

Peru entered the international arena in the 1927 South American Championship – the Copa América – with a 4-0 defeat to Uruguay. It was to be a forgettable start for the Peruvians who went on to concede 26 goals in their first seven games. They did go on to win the

tournament in 1939 though, and again in 1975.

On the world stage Peru have only really been a strong force in one era, qualifying for the World Cups of 1970, 1978 and 1982. Coached by former Brazilian star Didi, the team reached the quarter-finals in 1970. The 1978 side included several memorable players, such as the eccentric goalkeeper Ramon Quiroga, Hector Chumpitaz, and the real star of the side, Teófilo Cubillas. He inspired the team through to the second phase of the tournament, successfully negotiating a group which included Iran, a talented Scotland side, and eventual runners-up Holland. Cubillas

was particularly impressive in his side's 3-1 defeat of the Scots, scoring a memorable goal.

The Peruvian capital Lima has always been the heart of the nation's club football. The Lima-based league was traditionally the strongest in the country until the national championship was set up in 1966. Club football today continues to be dominated by three teams, who are all from Lima: Alianza, Universitario and Sporting Crystal, though a Peruvian club side has still to achieve success beyond its national borders and pursue a successful Copa Libertadores campaign.

Left: Peru line-up for the 1978 World Cup.

PHILIPPINES

Federation: Philippine Football Federation
Founded: 1907
Joined FIFA: 1928
Confederation: AFC
FIFA world ranking: 192

POLAND

Federation: Polski Zwiazek Pilki Noznej
Founded: 1919
Joined FIFA: 1923
Confederation: UEFA
FIFA world ranking: 30
Honours: Olympics 1972

Poland played their first international against Hungary in 1921 but had to wait 50 years for the game to come of age. In fact, Polish football effectively peaked in the 1970s, with a stylish brand of attacking play that produced a tournament victory at the 1972 Olympics and three excellent World Cup campaigns.

The Poles registered third place in West Germany in 1974 after famously eliminating England along the way to qualification. During this golden era, the team featured its finest talents ever, including Grzegorz Lato (who went on to win 95 caps and become an MP), Kazimierz Deyna, and the nation's top goalscorer, Wlodzimierz Lubanski.

The Poles were further strengthened by the addition of forward Zbigniew Boniek, who went on to play for Juventus and Roma and was later appointed national coach in August 2002. The side were unlucky not to progress further than the semi-finals in 1982, but by the mid-Eighties Polish football had slid into rapid decline, the game blighted by corruption, hooliganism and dwindling crowds.

The national side subsequently failed to qualify for a single World Cup or European Championship in the Nineties and, after successfully qualifying for the 2002 and 2006 World Cups, the team performed poorly. Their results in 2002 so enraged one fan that he attempted to sue Edyta Gorniak for singing the national anthem too slowly and making the team tired prior to the game with South Korea.

The Polish domestic game took off in the mining regions of Silesia in the early 20th Century. Three teams, Cracovia (famous for being Pope John Paul II's side), Wisla Krakow and LKS Lodz formed in 1906, though the league has largely been dominated by the army side Legia Warsaw and Widzew Lodz. Both of those teams have reached the semi-finals of the European Cup but have never progressed further. Lodz, meanwhile, made just one solitary appearance in the 1996-7 Champions League stage of the competition.

Match-fixing and crowd trouble continue to plague the Polish game. Both Lodz and Legia had their stadiums closed in 1997, and in 1998 the government suspended the domestic league campaign in the face of a FIFA ban because of internal wrangling.

Further match-rigging scandals caused the league to be completely restructured for the 2001-2 season, but internal problems meant the format had to be altered a year later. Wisla Krakow are the country's most successful club of recent times, having finished no lower that second since 1999 and winning the title six times in that period. But despite domestic success, they have made no headway in the European Champions League.

Below: Polish football legend, Grzegorz Lato

PORTUGAL

Federation: Federação Portuguesa de Futebol
Founded: 1914
Joined FIFA: 1923
Confederation: UEFA
FIFA world ranking: 8

It is a close call as to which of the Iberian nations is the greatest underachiever. On reflection, given their ability to fall consistently short of expectation at both club and international level, Portugal must accept that unwanted accolade ahead of Spain.

In fact, for a nation with such a passionate footballing culture, a record of just four World Cup finals appearances is abysmal. A belated start in 1966 saw a side featuring Eusébio, 'the Black Pearl', unfortunate to be eliminated by hosts England. They finished third in the tournament but, rather than push on, it took Portugal 20 years to make another appearance, only to fail at the first round stage. A dispute between the federation and players at that tournament soured the late Eighties and resulted in Portugal attempting to qualify for the 1988 European Championship with their youth side.

At the same time, however, back-to-back World Youth Championship wins in 1989 and 1991 ushered in a group of young players including Luis Figo, Rui Costa and Paulo Sousa, who were rapidly hailed as 'the Golden Generation'. Figo would later become World Player Of The Year and the most expensive signing in the game's history.

Once again, though, performance failed to outstrip expectation, though at the European Championship in 2000 the team did progress to the semi-finals. However, a handball decision in sudden-death extra-time went against them and prompted acrimonious scenes. When the team finally qualified for another World Cup, in 2002 , inconsistency saw elimination by hosts South Korea and further displays of bad sportsmanship.

The 2004 European Championship offered the Golden Generation a chance for redemption. For the first time Portugal were hosting the competition and recognising the opportunity, the FPF appointed Brazilian World Cup winner Luiz Felipe Scolari to the position of national team coach in 2002. Portugal had a great tournament and went all the way to the final where they were hot favourites but they were beaten by surprise winners Greece. Two years later Scolari took the team to the semi-finals of the World Cup, where they lost to France.

At club level, the Portuguese league is a tale of two cities: Lisbon and the northern port of Oporto. No club outside of these two centres has ever won the league. In the capital, it is

Benfica who figure largest in the game's history. Founded in 1904, The Eagles have won the championship on more than 30 occasions. The club also won two European Champions Cups in succession in 1961 and 1962, inspired in the second final by the country's greatest player, Eusébio, whose statue stands outside the club's Stadium Of Light.

While Sporting Lisbon won their first championship for 20 years in 2000, it was a minor blip since FC Porto have dominated domestically for the past decade, culminating in their second European Cup success in 2004 (they had also won it in 1987).

Porto also won the final of the UEFA Cup in 2003 and, to underline the city's new found status, even smaller rivals Boavista managed a first ever championship win in 2001.

PUERTO RICO

Federation: Federación Puertorriqueña de Fútbol
Founded: 1940
Joined FIFA: 1960
Confederation: CONCACAF
FIFA world ranking: 190

QATAR

Federation: Qatar Football Association
Founded: 1960
Joined FIFA: 1970
Confederation: AFC
FIFA world ranking: 76

REPUBLIC OF IRELAND

Federation: Football Association Of Ireland
Founded: 1921
Joined FIFA: 1923
Confederation: UEFA
FIFA world ranking: 39

The Football Association Of Ireland was founded in 1921, following the division of the country into two separate entities. The Republic played their first proper internationals at the 1924 Olympics in Paris, and in 1949 became the first foreign country to defeat England on home soil – a 2-0 win at Goodison

Above: Roy Keane urges his Republic Of Ireland team-mates onward in 2005.

Opposite: One of the greatest players in the history of the game, Portugal's Eusébio, takes on the Hungarian goalkeeper during the 1966 World Cup finals.

Park. Although Ireland had entered all but the inaugural World Cup competition, they had never qualified for the finals, despite going close on at least a couple of occasions. Their record in the European Championship was similarly anaemic, although they had made it to the quarter-finals in 1964.

Ireland's fortunes changed for the better with the appointment, in February 1986, of Jack Charlton as coach. Charlton had been a member of England's World Cup-winning side, had enjoyed a long and distinguished career as a player at Leeds United, and had managed several English league clubs with varying degrees of success. Charlton scoured the English divisions looking for players who hadn't been picked for England, Scotland or Wales with a family link strong enough to qualify them to play for the Republic (at least one grandparent of Irish extraction). Soon he had recruited the likes of John Aldridge, Kevin Sheedy and Ray Houghton, and had steered Ireland to the finals of 1988's European Championship in West Germany. Although they failed to reach the semi-final stage, Ireland did beat England 1-0, thanks to a goal after five minutes from Houghton and some inspired goalkeeping from Celtic's 'Packie' Bonner.

Ireland qualified for their first ever World Cup finals two years later and, having beaten Romania in a heart-stopping penalty shoot-out in the second round, made it to the quarter-finals. There it took a winner from the tournament's top scorer, Italy's Toto Schillaci,

Below: Romania's best known football export, Gheorghe Hagi.

to halt their ambitions. Despite remaining unbeaten during the qualifiers, Ireland didn't make it to the European Championship in 1992, but got their 1994 World Cup campaign off to an incredible start by beating eventual finalists Italy 1-0. Charlton's team were beaten 2-0 in the second round by Holland.

Charlton stepped down as manager in 1996 (the Republic had failed to qualify for that year's European Championship in England), to be replaced by former Ireland international Mick McCarthy. Having negotiated a difficult qualification group that included both Portugal and Holland, Ireland overcame Iran following a two-legged play-off to book their place at the 2002 World Cup. Unfortunately, their tournament was completely overshadowed by the ill-tempered spat that erupted between McCarthy and his captain, Roy Keane, who then walked out on the team.

Following a heated row about the poor quality of the team's preparation for the tournament, Keane returned home and announced his retirement from international football. Ireland went on to reach the tournament's second round, before being eliminated in a penalty shoot-out by Spain. Since then the Irish have failed to qualify for a major tournament.

In 2003 the Irish league switched to a spring to autumn (March to November) football season. Bohemians and Shelbourne have been the two powerhouses since 2000, sharing out the last six titles between them until Cork City broke the duopoly in 2005.

RUSSIA

Federation: Russian Football Union
Founded: 1912
Joined FIFA: 1912, 1992
Confederation: UEFA
FIFA world ranking: 34
Honours: European Championship 1960; Olympics 1956, 1988

The Soviet Union, before its break-up, produced some of the finest football teams that Europe has ever seen. Often written off as too rigid in their tactical approach to the game, their teams' real legacy is revealed by a glance at the history books. Soviet sides in their heyday played thrilling, effective football that was successful at the highest level. The Soviet Union won the Olympic gold medal in 1956 and 1988, the inaugural European Championship in 1960, and produced teams in other decades ranked among the finest in the world. The 1980s generation under Valery Lobanovsky was the most exciting national side in recent memory.

Russia had great players too, such as Lev Yashin, considered by many to be the finest goalkeeper of all time. Oleg Blokhin was also an outstanding left-winger, while Igor Belanov deservedly won the European Footballer Of The Year award in 1986.

ROMANIA

Federation: Federatia Romana de Fotbal
Founded: 1909
Joined FIFA: 1923
Confederation: UEFA
FIFA world ranking: 26

Romania played at the first three World Cups from 1930 onwards but subsequently missed out on qualifying for the world's premier competition until 1970. In the last three decades, however, Romanian football has become a potent force, notably through Steaua Bucharest, their leading club, and Gheorghe Hagi, their most outstanding player.

Steaua, the army team, were founded in 1948 as CCA Bucharest, and earned the right to be placed among the European greats in the 1980s when they produced a series of superb line-ups. They took the biggest prize of all in 1986 when they lifted the European Cup by beating Barcelona on penalties. The game, however, is widely regarded as a dour, goalless affair – not that Steaua cared.

Steaua went on to reach the final again in 1989, with Hagi added to the team, but lost heavily (4-0) to an AC Milan team that cruised to victory following their opponents' poor show. A host of Romanian players moved abroad in the 1990s after the fall of dictator Nicolae Ceausescu, including Gheorghe Popescu, an elegant defender who starred for Barcelona among others, and striker Florin Raducioiu, who played in all five major European leagues. But the star was Hagi, a wonderfully gifted midfielder with a wicked left foot. He, more than anybody, was the driving force behind Romania's development.

The Romanian game has waned since then. The national team failed to qualify for the 2002 and 2006 World Cups, as well as Euro 2004. The Bucharest-centric game offers little real contest with the championship spoils shared between Steaua, Dinamo and, occasionally, Rapid since 1991 when Universitatea Craiova won the title on goal difference from Steaua.

Romanian club football has suffered from an exodus of its best players, while the big three mop up the rest of the local talent, just like they did in the communist era. With no indication of a breakthrough in the Champions League, Romanian football fans await the resurgence of the national side.

ST LUCIA

Federation: St Lucia Football Association
Founded: 1979
Joined FIFA: 1988
Confederation: CONCACAF
FIFA world ranking: 115

ST VINCENT AND THE GRENADINES

Federation: Saint Vincent and The Grenadines Football Federation
Founded: 1979
Joined FIFA: 1988
Confederation: CONCACAF
FIFA world ranking: 129

SAMOA

Federation: Samoa Football (Soccer) Federation
Founded: 1968
Joined FIFA: 1986
Confederation: OFC
FIFA world ranking: 188

SAN MARINO

Federation: Federazione Sammarinese Giouco Calcio
Founded: 1931
Joined FIFA: 1988
Confederation: UEFA
FIFA world ranking: 191

Left: Aleksandr Zavarov shoots for the Soviet Union in the 1988 Euro Championship final. Since the break up of the Soviet Union, Russia have struggled to make the same impact.

In the domestic league, Moscow dominated the game in the first half of the century and it was not until 1961 that a team from outside the capital won the title (Dynamo Kiev). But fittingly, Dynamo Moscow became the first Soviet side to reach a European final, losing 3-2 to Glasgow Rangers in the European Cup Winners' Cup in 1972.

The Soviet Union had really established a formidable reputation by that stage. Their 1960 European Championship triumph did not go unnoticed, even though the competition was low-key at the time. In the final, they beat Yugoslavia 2-1 after extra-time in Paris.

They also reached the World Cup quarter-finals in 1962 and the semi-finals in England four years later. Yashin was the star of that side and was the first Soviet player to attract worldwide recognition.

In 1975 Blokhin, at his peak, inspired Dynamo Kiev to beat Ferencváros 3-0 in the European Cup Winners' Cup final to earn Soviet club football its first major trophy. He also collected the European Footballer Of The Year award, becoming the second winner after Yashin in 1963. He was an exciting talent who would have been a success abroad if allowed to leave his homeland.

Dinamo Tblisi also won the Cup Winners' Cup in 1981 and it was this generation that caught the eye in brilliant fashion at club and international level. Belanov starred for both Dynamo Kiev and the Soviet Union in 1986, helping his club win the Cup Winners' Cup with an emphatic 3-0 victory over Atletico Madrid and inspiring the Soviets to impressive displays at the World Cup finals – scoring a hat-trick in the 4-3 second round defeat to Belgium. Alexander Zavarov was his able midfield deputy who later played for Juventus, and Rinat Dassayev a worthy successor to Yashin in goal.

Lobanovsky, the godfather of Soviet football,

was coach of their greatest triumphs in the Seventies and Eighties and continued to oversee the development of the most talented players and the structure of the national team until his death in 2002. However, since the break-up of the Soviet Union, Russia have struggled to make any impact on the world stage, with Ukraine seen as a bigger footballing power. Yet exports such as Victor Onopko and Valery Karpin excelled in Spain, while Vladimir Beschastnykh boasted an impressive scoring record for his country. In a bold move to improve Russia's international standing Guus Hiddink was appointed coach of the national side in 2006.

RWANDA

Federation: Fédération Rwandaise de Football Amateur
Founded: 1972
Joined FIFA: 1978
Confederation: CAF
FIFA world ranking: 103

ST KITTS & NEVIS

Federation: St Kitts and Nevis Football Association
Founded: 1932
Joined FIFA: 1992
Confederation: CONCACAF
FIFA world ranking: 136 (joint)

Davide Gualteri holds the record for the quickest goal in international football, scoring for San Marino after just 8.3 seconds against Graham Taylor's England in a World Cup qualifying defeat in November 1993. The Most Serene Republic of San Marino, located within Northern Italy, has run a national amateur league and cup since 1986, featuring teams such as Tre Fiori and Domagnano, yet it is Gualteri's goal against England which remains the nation's highlight to date.

Opposite: Scotland striker Joe Jordan surges past a Wales defender during a World Cup qualifier in 1977.

SAO TOMÉ AND PRINCIPE

Federation: Federação Santomense de Futebol
Founded: 1975
Joined FIFA: 1986
Confederation: CAF
FIFA world ranking: 196 (joint)

SAUDI ARABIA

Federation: Saudi Arabia Football Federation
Founded: 1959
Joined FIFA: 1959
Confederation: AFC
FIFA world ranking: 81
Honours: Asian Cup 1984, 1988, 1996

Saudi Arabia is the greatest exporter of oil in the world and it is from this influx of wealth that football got the kick-start it needed in the 1970s. Millions of dollars were invested in state-of-the-art facilities and clubs such as Al Hilal, Al Nasr and Al Ahli began to thrive.

Foreign coaches were lured to the country by the large salaries and in 1979 the Saudi Arabian league championship kicked-off. This investment and patience began to pay off as the Saudis won the Asian Cup in 1984 and 1988 – they beat China 2-0 in Singapore with goals from Shaye Nafisah and Majed Abdullah and retained the trophy four years later by beating South Korea 4-3 on penalties after a goalless draw in Qatar.

Below: Mohammad Haidar of Saudi Arabia in action against South Korea in 2005.

One year on and the World Under-17 Cup was won in Scotland. This Saudi Arabian side formed the basis of the country's future success, as four successive World Cup appearances followed. Their first appearance, in 1994, saw Saudi Arabia play Morocco in the first-ever all-Arab World Cup clash, while Saeed Owairan scored the goal of the tournament against Belgium. After the 2006 World Cup finals, Asia's best goalkeeper Mohammed Al-Deayea retired from international football after making a record 181 appearances.

SCOTLAND

Federation: Scottish Football Association
Founded: 1873
Joined FIFA: 1910, 1924, 1946
Confederation: UEFA
FIFA world ranking: 41

Scotland were involved in the first ever international football match. It was at home against England on November 30, 1872, and it began one of the world's great sporting rivalries. That first game ended in a goalless draw but, unlike England, the Scots never went on to taste glory at the highest level.

Despite being consistent qualifiers for the World Cup finals, Scotland have often under-performed against teams they really should have comfortably beaten, while performing heroically against far mightier opposition.

The Scots qualified for their first ever World Cup in 1950 after finishing runners-up in the British Home Internationals tournament, but they chose not to attend, insisting they would only want to go to Brazil as winners.

Perhaps the Scotland team that should have had most impact on the greatest footballing stage was the one that went to the World Cup in Argentina under Ally MacLeod in 1978. A decent outside bet, this Scotland side were packed with talented players, many based in the English top flight, such as Kenny Dalglish, Graeme Souness, Archie Gemmill, Joe Jordan, Don Masson and Bruce Rioch.

Ally MacCleod recklessly promised the nation that Scotland would bring the World Cup home, a bold claim he would live to regret. Scotland disappointed, both on and off the field, losing to Peru and only scraping a draw with lowly Iran before, in typically Scottish fashion, beating well-fancied Holland and almost, but not quite, qualifying for stage two. The Dutch were the eventual tournament runners-up. Meanwhile, winger Willie Johnston was sent home in disgrace after failing a dope test.

Perhaps the most celebrated Scottish international win though, came not in a major tournament but in 1967 against the 'Auld Enemy', England. The world champions, undefeated since lifting the trophy the previous year at Wembley, were beaten 3-2 by the skill, spirit and guile of Scottish legends Jim Baxter, Billy Bremner and Denis Law.

Recent times have seen the rapid demise of Scottish football at international level, with too many foreign players preventing young local talent from getting top-flight club football often being cited as the main reason for the decline.

At club level, Scottish football has historically been dominated by the 'Old Firm' of Celtic and Rangers, possibly the fiercest rivalry in club football anywhere in the world. Celtic can claim 40 league titles and 33 Scottish Cups to Rangers' 51 titles and 31 Scottish Cups. Other clubs have had brief stays at the top, notably Edinburgh sides Hibernian and Hearts in the Fifties and Sixties, and for quite a while in the early Eighties it seemed that the 'new firm' of Aberdeen and Dundee United had broken the stranglehold, the former being quite dominant for a spell, winning three league titles, four Scottish Cups and a European Cup Winners' Cup in a six year period. Normal service was resumed by the middle of the decade though, and once again today it is Celtic or Rangers carving up the trophies between them.

In Europe both sides have struggled to really have an impact on the major competitions. Rangers' only European triumph came in the 1972 Cup Winners' Cup, but Celtic made history in 1967 when they became the first Scottish side to lift the European Cup, beating Inter Milan in the final. They were runners up in 1970 and they also reached the final of the UEFA Cup in 2003.

SENEGAL

Federation: Fédération Sénégalaise de Football
Founded: 1960
Joined FIFA: 1962
Confederation: CAF
FIFA world ranking: 35

Senegal, under French coach Bruno Metsu, caused a sensation with their first appearance at the World Cup finals in 2002 by reaching the quarter-finals, making a star of striker El Hadji Diouf along the way. They also beat defending world champions France 1-0, drew 1-1 with Denmark, led Uruguay 3-0 before being held to a draw, and then beat Sweden 2-1. The success owed much to Metsu's predecessor Peter Schnittiger – the German had been involved with Senegalese football since 1968, but in 1995 he had been appointed to structure a development programme for both the national team and the club game.

SERBIA & MONTENEGRO

Federation: Football Association of Serbia and Montenegro
Founded: 1919
Joined FIFA: 1919
Confederation: UEFA
FIFA world ranking: 36
Honours: Olympics 1960 [*as Yugoslavia]

Since 2003, the team previously known as Yugoslavia has been renamed Serbia and Montenegro, the latest step of a disintegration that has seen the former Yugoslavia break-up in 1991 after a bloody civil war. In football terms at least, the split was heart-breaking because Yugoslavia had one of the most exciting teams in Europe. They were serious contenders to win the European Championship in 1992, but by the time the finals were due to kick-off most of the non-Serbian players had refused to take part and UEFA took the decision to expel them from the competition. Their replacements Denmark went on to win the tournament.

Yugoslavia did not exist until after the First World War, but several clubs in Serbia did. A Yugoslav championship began in 1923 but it was not until after the Second World War, under the rule of the communist Tito, that the league began to take real shape. It was the Serbian clubs that dominated, such as Red Star Belgrade and Partizan Belgrade. In 1991, Red Star became the first and only Yugoslav side to win the European Cup when they beat Marseille 5-3 on penalties after a goalless draw.

Yugoslavia were one of only four European sides to play in the first World Cup. They contested the football final at the Olympic Games on four successive occasions but won only once, in 1960, when they beat Denmark 3-1. They reached the World Cup semi-final twice (1930 and 1962), the quarter-finals on three occasions (1954, 1958 and 1990), and in 1968 they also reached the European Championship final, but lost to hosts Italy after a replay.

Yugoslavia have always produced some excellent individual footballers – Bobek, Dzajic, Prosinecki, Savicevic, Sekularec – but have never quite combined for the final step to glory. Serbia and Montenegro have been in the doldrums since the break-up but finally emerged with qualification for their first major tournament. Under coach Ilija Petkovic, they qualified for the 2006 World Cup by topping their group ahead of Spain through solid teamwork rather than flamboyant star players of the Yugoslav era. They have had to endure seeing Croatia and Slovenia take part in previous tournaments. At home, the league is still dominated by Red Star and Partizan.

In May 2006 Montenegro held a referendum and voted for independence from Serbia. The two football associations split in July 2006 but they will play the Euro 2008 qualifiers together.

SEYCHELLES

Federation: Seychelles Football Federation
Founded: 1979
Joined FIFA: 1986
Confederation: CAF
FIFA world ranking: 141 (joint)

SIERRA LEONE

Federation: Sierra Leone Football Association
Founded: 1967
Joined FIFA: 1967
Confederation: CAF
FIFA world ranking: 155

SINGAPORE

Federation: Football Association of Singapore
Founded: 1892
Joined FIFA: 1952
Confederation: AFC
FIFA world ranking: 111

SLOVAKIA

Federation: Slovak Football Association
Founded: 1993
Joined FIFA: 1907, 1994
Confederation: UEFA
FIFA world ranking: 44

Between 1939 and 1944 there was a short-lived Slovak league which was won four times by SK Slovan Bratislava, who were one of Slovakia's strongest teams in the subsequent Czechoslovakian league up until 1992. Since then the old order has been swept away, with teams such as Kosice, MSK Zilina and Artmedia Bratislava taking the honours too.

SLOVENIA

Federation: Football Association of Slovenia
Founded: 1920
Joined FIFA: 1992
Confederation: UEFA
FIFA world ranking: 61

Slovenian clubs made no impact on the Yugoslav league. Since independence Maribor Branik, with seven successive titles, dominated until HIT Gorica ended their reign in 2003. The national team played at Euro 2000 and World Cup 2002 but have made little progress since.

Below: Serbia and Montenegro celebrate qualifying for the World Cup after victory over Bosnia-Herzegovina in 2005.

SOLOMON ISLANDS

Federation: Solomon Islands Football Federation
Founded: 1978
Joined FIFA: 1988
Confederation: OFC
FIFA world ranking: 151

SOMALIA

Federation: Somalia Football Federation
Founded: 1951
Joined FIFA: 1960
Confederation: CAF
FIFA world ranking: 179 (joint)

SOUTH AFRICA

Federation: South African Football Association
Founded: 1892, 1991
Joined FIFA: 1952-76, 1992
Confederation: CAF
FIFA world ranking: 72
Honours: African Nations Cup 1996

Football has been played in South Africa since the 1870s but the progress of the game was hindered for many years by the existence of apartheid. The all-white National Professional League initially kicked-off in 1959, while a rival, but highly successful and non-white National Professional Soccer League was formed in

1972. The two leagues merged in 1978, but South Africa's apartheid policy had seen its FIFA membership suspended in 1952 and cancelled in 1976. In 1991, South Africa returned to international competition and they have subsequently won the African Nations Cup in 1996 and qualified for the 1998 and 2002 World Cup finals. They are scheduled to host the 2010 tournament.

SOUTH KOREA

Federation: Korea Football Association
Founded: 1928
Joined FIFA: 1948
Confederation: AFC
FIFA world ranking: 56
Honours: Asian Cup 1956, 1960

South Korea gave Asian football a huge boost by reaching the semi-finals of the 2002 World Cup, a competition that they co-hosted with Japan. This was an amazing feat for a country who had failed to win a single match in their five previous World Cup tournaments.

Backed by stunning home support, and coached by Dutchman Guus Hiddink, the

Koreans overcame their inferiority complex and all of the pre-tournament predictions: they beat Poland 2-0, drew 1-1 with USA and defeated Portugal 1-0. The last group game was estimated to have been watched on television by 75 per cent of Korean households.

A sensational 2-1 second round win over Italy followed, while a tense 5-3 penalty shoot-out overcame Spain. It was Germany who put paid to the dream with a single goal victory.

South Korea have long been a consistent force in Asian football, although not always as winners. They produce many talented young players and have won the Asian Under-20 title on 11 occasions. The creation of a professional league in 1983 (later becoming the K-League) lifted Korean football and accounted for a development of the game that resulted in qualification for six successive World Cups from 1986 onwards.

Investment from big business has helped clubs and it is evident in team names such as Suwon Bluewings, Pusan Icons, Ulsan Hyundai and Pohang Steelers. This financial backing, however, does not necessarily translate into high wages for Korean players and several star names have moved abroad, with Japan a popular destination. South Korea's greatest player was Hong Myung-bo, who played in four successive World Cups and won a host of domestic honours.

Above: South Africa's winning team celebrate victory in the African Nations Cup with Nelson Mandela in 1996.

Left: South Korea's Young Pyo Lee and Ki Hyeon Seol celebrate victory over Spain at the 2002 World Cup.

1898: The first club side, Recreativo Huelva, are founded, followed by Athletic Bilbao, Madrid, Atlético Madrid and Barcelona.

1900

1902: The Spanish Cup is established.

1905

1904: Spain become a founding member of FIFA.

1910

1913: The Real Federacion Española de Futbol is formed, with King Alfonso XIII as honorary president.

1928: The modern league championship emerges with ten teams competing.

1930

1929: Barcelona win the first-ever Spanish league title, Real Madrid are runners-up.

1935

1936-39: La Liga is suspended during the Spanish Civil War.

1950

1950: Spanish football grows more powerful. In the Brazil World Cup, Spain finish a best-ever fourth.

1955

1956: Real Madrid win the first European Cup. They go on to win it for the next four years too.

1960

1960: In the European Championship, Spain draw the Soviet Union, but General Franco withdraws his side for political reasons.

1965

1964: Spain win the final of the European Championship in front of 125,000 at Madrid's Estadio Bernabéu.

1980

1982: A talented Spanish side host the World Cup, but fail to get past the second round.

1985

1984: Spain reach the final of the European Championship, but lose to France.

1990

1992: Barcelona win their first European Cup, beating Sampdoria 1-0 at Wembley.

1995

1994: Spain reach the World Cup quarter-final, going out to favourites Italy. After that game they go on a run of 31 unbeaten internationals.

2000

2002: Spain are controversially knocked out of the quarter-finals of the World Cup on penalties by South Korea.

2005

2006: Barcelona win the Champions League final in Paris.

SPAIN

Federation: Real Federación Española de Fútbol
Founded: 1913
Joined FIFA: 1904
Confederation: UEFA
FIFA world ranking: 7
Honours: European Championship 1964; Olympics 1992

Football came to Spain in the latter part of the 19th Century, a result of British businessmen operating throughout the country's northern ports. A relative latecomer to a game that had already grown throughout Europe, Bilbao – the industrial port closest to England – became the first city associated with the game, and the city's flagship side, Athletic Bilbao, display their English roots to this day in the club's colours.

The game spread quickly among students in the port towns and, as had been seen in England, throughout the industrial cities. Irun, Gijon, Seville, La Coruna and Valencia all boasted teams, but Recreativo Huelva hold the honour of being the first club formed, in 1898.

The more revered football names of Real Madrid, Atlético Madrid and Barcelona soon followed, but with the exception of Real (then known simply as Madrid FC), the game never reached the highest level in the interior of the country. It was as late as 1913, under the honorary presidency of King Alfonso XIII, that a number of regional unions consolidated to form the nationwide Real Federación Española de Fútbol.

Yet thanks to the representatives of Madrid FC, the dominant club side in the country, Spain had already become a founding member of FIFA, while the Spanish Cup, formed some 11 years earlier, was thriving and is now regarded as one of the oldest, if not most prestigious, cup competitions in Europe.

Indeed, it was predicted that the cup would have greater longevity than its league counterpart following a very inauspicious start. From its inception, the championship was a professional establishment but it took some time for it to become a truly countrywide competition, and it did not emerge in its modern form until the 1928-9 season, when just ten clubs competed for the main prize.

Madrid FC were given the name 'Real' (royal) as a gift by King Alfonso prior to the league's inception, and they continued their dominance, signing goalkeeper Zamora for £2,000 which, at the time, was a price tag more commonplace in the financially buoyant English league.

The Spanish Civil War between 1936 and 1939 saw its political overtones spread into the football arena and highlighted the bitter rivalry

Above: Spain's Fernando Hierro in action at the 2002 World Cup. Opposite clockwise from top left, the stars of Spain: the country's greatest strikers Emilio Butragueno; Fernando Torres on the ball at the 2006 World Cup in Germany; a Real Madrid legend, Raul at the 2002 World Cup; Jose Alesanco in action in 1982.

that had grown between Barcelona and Real Madrid. As the flagship side of Catalonia, a region seeking independence from Spain, Barcelona associated their rivals with fascist dictator General Franco and once the league campaign resumed, matches between the two sides proved to be bruising affairs. To further fuel the antipathy, teams from the Basque provinces also had their own agenda, and to this day Athletic Bilbao will only employ players who were born in the region.

The distain between clubs only served to establish La Liga Española as one of the most competitive in Europe, and by the 1950s, Barcelona and Real were leading the way with seven titles in the decade between them, while both regularly boasting crowds approaching the 100,000 mark. Their dominance was unrivalled and the next logical step for both sides was to test themselves against the continent's finest clubs.

Following the inception of the European Champions Cup in 1956, Real Madrid won five finals in succession, the first being an exciting 4-3 victory against French side Stade de Reims. Leading the line for Real was Alfredo Di Stéfano, who scored the team's opening goal and who proceeded to score in each of the next four finals. His feats are now legendary, likewise the Real team who took their fifth European Cup success with an emphatic 7-3 victory against Eintracht Frankfurt. Di Stéfano netted a hat-trick while Hungarian wing wonder, Ferenc Puskás, scored four.

It took Barcelona 36 years to win their first European Cup, when a Ronald Koeman free-kick defeated Sampdoria 1-0 at Wembley in 1992, and it was a further 14 years until they won it again. Indeed, they have lived in the shadow of their fierce rivals for longer than their fans care to remember, despite winning 18 Spanish league titles and 11 European trophies by 2006. Although lagging behind Real both on the continent and in terms of domestic title wins, they do have the edge in Spanish Cups (24 to 17). Their wonderful Nou Camp stadium has also been the home to such legendary players as Johan Cruyff, Diego Maradona, Hristo Stoichkov, Romario and Ronaldo.

Today, the Spanish league is widely regarded as one of the best in Europe, not only reflected by the exciting football displayed but also in terms of the contributions made to the Champions League by its teams. Real Madrid won three of the five finals between 1998 and 2002, Barcelona won it in 2006, while the widely underrated force of Valencia finished runners-up in both the 2000 and 2001 finals.

Yet despite a flourishing domestic league, a frustration for all Spanish football fans is their underachieving national team. Some point to the intense regionalism as the root cause of Spain's underachievement but, whatever the reason, their 1964 European Championship victory against the Soviet Union, in front of 125,000 fans in Madrid's Bernabéu Stadium, remains their most significant success on the international stage.

SRI LANKA

Federation: The Football Federation of Sri Lanka
Founded: 1939
Joined FIFA: 1950
Confederation: AFC
FIFA world ranking: 138

SUDAN

Federation: Sudan Football Association
Founded: 1936
Joined FIFA: 1948
Confederation: CAF
FIFA world ranking: 113 (joint)

SURINAM

Federation: Surinaamse Voetbal Bond
Founded: 1920
Joined FIFA: 1929
Confederation: CONCACAF
FIFA world ranking: 150

SWAZILAND

Federation: National Football Association of Swaziland
Founded: 1968
Joined FIFA: 1978
Confederation: CAF
FIFA world ranking: 153 (joint)

SWEDEN

Federation: Svenska Fotbollförbundet
Founded: 1904
Joined FIFA: 1904
Confederation: UEFA
FIFA world ranking: 22
Honours: Olympics 1948

There's no doubt that in football terms, Sweden – with a population in 2006 of around nine million and a domestic game that isn't even fully professional – have always punched above their weight on the international stage. The Swedish FA was founded in 1904 and its national team qualified for their first World Cup tournament in 1934. The Scandinavians shocked the mighty Argentina 3-2 during a run that took them all the way to the quarter-finals, where they were edged out 2-1 by Germany. They went one better in 1938, reaching the semi-finals (where they were defeated 5-1 by Hungary) before going down 4-2 to Brazil in the third-place play-off.

In 1948, Englishman George Raynor was appointed national team coach, and he led them to a gold medal at the 1948 Olympic Games in London. However, Sweden's success at the Olympics had its downside as AC Milan, impressed by the form of several of the country's top players, wasted no time in signing them to professional contracts in Italy's lucrative Serie A. With strict rules barring players from the national team if they made their living abroad, Raynor had access to only two of his Olympic gold medal-winning side for the 1950 World Cup finals in Brazil. Despite such limitations, the remodelled Swedish team pulled off a major surprise in the tournament's first round by beating Italy's professional stars 3-2. Despite a crushing 7-1 defeat by Brazil, they went on to pip Spain to third place.

A bronze medal at the 1952 Olympics in Helsinki was achieved despite major injury problems, and in time for the 1958 World Cup finals, held on home turf, the Swedish FA finally rescinded its rule that only home-based players could appear for the national side.

As a result, Sweden fielded what many claim was their best ever team, with previously barred veterans such as Gunnar Gren and Nils Liedholm returning to international action. Buoyed by home advantage, Sweden made it all the way to the final, defeating the likes of West Germany and Hungary, before being cut down to size 5-2 by Brazil.

Since then Sweden's World Cup adventures have been less successful although, under highly-regarded coach Tommy Svensson, they did shock many observers by finishing third in 1994, losing out to eventual winners Brazil in the semi-finals by a single goal.

Below: Sweden's 'greatest player of the last 50 years', Henrik Larsson celebrates scoring against Bulgaria at Euro 2004.

Sweden have only qualified for three European Championship finals in 1992, 2000 and 2004. They were quarter-finalists in 2004, losing to Holland on penalties, and, as hosts, semi-finalists in 1992, losing 3-2 to Germany. The Swedes also reached the last eight of the 1964 competition losing 4-2 on aggregate to the Soviet Union.

SWITZERLAND

Federation: Schweizerischer Fussballverband
Founded: 1895
Joined FIFA: 1904
Confederation: UEFA
FIFA world ranking: 13

Switzerland is the home to both the European and world governing bodies of football, UEFA and FIFA, and was instrumental in each organisation's formation. They had plenty of experience, having been introduced to football by the English in the 1860s. British influence was enormous and is reflected in the club names, such as Grasshoppers, the country's most successful side, and Young Boys. The first club to be formed was St Gallen in 1879.

A Swiss championship was contested as early as 1898, although a national league did not kick-off until 1934. Switzerland played internationals from 1903, and in the first half of the century they had a strong team, winning an Olympic silver medal in 1924 and reaching the World Cup quarter-finals in 1934 and 1938.

Karl Rappan, Switzerland's Austrian coach, revolutionised tactics when he devised the 'Swiss Bolt' in the 1930s, a forerunner of the sweeper system. Switzerland's star began to fade after the war and the club game never elevated itself. The national side was not helped by the rivalry between the French, German and Italian communities of the country, who down the years have accused various coaches of bias towards one another making the job a difficult one.

SYRIA

Federation: Association Arabe Syrienne de Football
Founded: 1936
Joined FIFA: 1937
Confederation: AFC
FIFA world ranking: 110

TAHITI

Federation: Fédération Tahitienne de Football
Founded: 1989
Joined FIFA: 1990
Confederation: OFC
FIFA world ranking: 164 (joint)

TAJIKISTAN

Federation: Tajikistan National Football Federation
Founded: 1936
Joined FIFA: 1994
Confederation: AFC
FIFA world ranking: 116

Left: Switzerland's best player of the 1990s, Stephane Chapuisat.

TANZANIA

Federation: Football Association of Tanzania
Founded: 1930
Joined FIFA: 1964
Confederation: CAF
FIFA world ranking: 143 (joint)

THAILAND

Federation: Football Association of Thailand
Founded: 1916
Joined FIFA: 1925
Confederation: AFC
FIFA world ranking: 113 (joint)

Below: Syria's Ali Dyab and Majid Al-Haj celebrate their team's semi-final win against Iran in the West Asian Games.

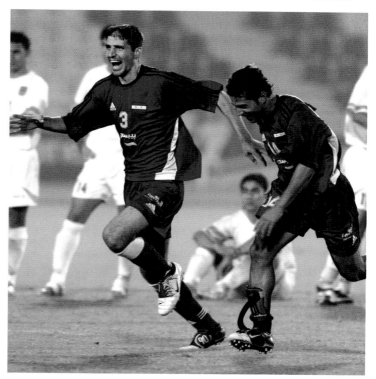

Above: Togo's Abdel Coubadja in action in 2006.

TONGA

Federation: Tonga Football Association
Founded: 1965
Joined FIFA: 1994
Confederation: OFC
FIFA world ranking: 189

TRINIDAD AND TOBAGO

Federation: Trinidad and Tobago Football Federation
Founded: 1908
Joined FIFA: 1963
Confederation: CONCACAF
FIFA world ranking: 64

Trinidad and Tobago, population 1.2 million, became the smallest country to qualify for the World Cup in 2006. The Trinbagonians had been close before in 1974, 1990 and 2002. The 'Soca Warriors' have won the Caribbean Cup on nine occasions, while club side Defence Force have won the CONCACAF Champions Cup twice, in 1978 (shared) and 1985. Football was amateur on the islands until 1996 when a semi-pro league was created, but in 1999 the Professional Football League came into being, with 14 teams competing over a 26-match season. The title has been won by Defence Force, Williams Connection, San Juan Jabloteh and North East Stars.

TUNISIA

Federation: Fédération Tunisienne de Football
Founded: 1956
Joined FIFA: 1960
Confederation: CAF
FIFA world ranking: 31
Honours: African Nations Cup 2004

Tunisia won the African Nations Cup for the first time in 2004, beating Morocco 2-1 in the final. They had previously been losing finalists in 1965 and 1996. Under coach Roger Lemerre, who guided France to the European Championship in 2000, Tunisia maintained their position as one of Africa's leading football nations and also qualified for their third successive World Cup (fourth in all) in 2006. Tunisia were the first African team to win a

TOGO

Federation: Fédération Togolaise de Football
Founded: 1960
Joined FIFA: 1962
Confederation: CAF
FIFA world ranking: 48

A national holiday was called when Togo qualified for the 2006 World Cup. The West African nation were a shock qualifier from a continent where they were not even considered a major player. 'Les Eperviers' (the Sparrow Hawks) had previously qualified for just six African Nations Cup tournaments and had never gone beyond the first round. Qualifying for the World Cup was by far Togo's biggest-ever football success, with the 1987 African Youth Cup final appearance and Emmanuel Adebayor's fifth place in the 2004 African Player Of The Year poll the closest other achievements. At home Togo's league is dominated by two clubs, AS Dounaes and Dynamic Togolais.

match at the finals of the World Cup when they beat Mexico 3-1 in 1978.

Tunisian clubs Club Africain and Esperance have both won the African Champions League, in 1991 and 1994 respectively. Esperance is Tunisia's most successful club side, with Etoile Sahel and Club Africain their main rivals. In recent years Tunisian teams have managed regular appearances in the continent's club competitions winning three Cup Winners' Cups and four CAF Cups between 1995 and 2004.

The Ligue Nationale is played between August and May and is well-organised and of a high standard, while many players have established careers in Europe, particularly in France. Despite the reputation of producing talented players, only one Tunisian has ever been voted African Player Of The Year, Tarak Dhiab in 1977.

TURKEY

Federation: Turkiye Futbol Federasyonu
Founded: 1923
Joined FIFA: 1923
Confederation: UEFA
FIFA world ranking: 27

Football had a hard time in establishing itself in Turkey. The rulers of the Ottoman Empire disliked a game that had been introduced by the British. Football was not seen as a priority at a time of the Balkan Wars, World War I, Civil War and war with Greece. However, once Turkey was declared a republic in 1923, a football federation was formed, regional competition got underway, and the national team made its first forays into the international arena.

A professional league was launched in 1959 and the national team began to get some serious attention, however it was not until the 1990s that Turkey began to make an impact. In 2000, Galatasaray, Turkey's leading club alongside Besiktas and Fenerbahçe, won the UEFA Cup, beating Arsenal on penalties. The Turkish league has also been boosted by importing players and coaches from around the world.

The national team managed to qualify for their first European Championship in 1996. In 2002 they also made it to their first World Cup finals in 48 years, finishing third, but they have subsequently failed to build on this success.

Turkish fans are among the most passionate in the game, creating one of the noisiest and most intimidating atmospheres in international football, and this sometimes spills over into tensions on the field, as it did after play-off defeat to Switzerland ended the team's 2006 World Cup ambitions. As a result Turkey were ordered to play all of their home Euro 2008 qualifiers behind closed doors.

TURKS & CAICOS ISLANDS

Federation: Turks and Caicos Islands Football Association
Founded: 1996
Joined FIFA: 1998
Confederation: CONCACAF
FIFA world ranking: 196 (joint)

TURKMENISTAN

Federation: Football Federation of Turkmenistan
Founded: 1992
Joined FIFA: 1994
Confederation: AFC
FIFA world ranking: 148

UGANDA

Federation: Uganda Football Association
Founded: 1924
Joined FIFA: 1959
Confederation: CAF
FIFA world ranking: 99

UKRAINE

Federation: Football Federation of Ukraine
Founded: 1991
Joined FIFA: 1992
Confederation: UEFA
FIFA world ranking: 15

Dynamo Kiev are, without doubt, Ukraine's most successful club, having won 16 Soviet league titles, the European Cup Winners' Cup in 1975 and 1986 – and dominated the Ukrainian league since its inception in 1992. Only Shakhtar Donetsk have provided a serious challenge, breaking Dynamo's domination with league wins in 2002, 2005 and 2006.

The national team missed out on three successive major competitions at the play-off stage until they finally qualified for the 2006 World Cup. Ironically, Kiev had formed the backbone to the successful Soviet Union team before its dissolution in 1992.

Oleg Blokhin, the coach who took Ukraine to the 2006 World Cup, was voted European Footballer Of The Year in 1975 and fellow Ukrainian Igor Belanov repeated the feat in 1986. In the modern game national team captain Andriy Shevchenko, a European Champions League winner with AC Milan in 2003, was voted European Footballer Of The Year in 2004.

UNITED ARAB EMIRATES

Federation: United Arab Emirates Football Association
Founded: 1971
Joined FIFA: 1972
Confederation: AFC
FIFA world ranking: 90

Football, disliked by the region's religious leaders, took time to gain popularity. When the UAE was formed in 1971, football began to be taken seriously. Leading coaches were enticed to the country, including England boss Don Revie and Brazil's Carlos Alberto Parreira. It was the Brazilian ethos that was adopted and UAE qualified for the World Cup in 1990.

UNITED STATES

Federation: United States Soccer Federation
Founded: 1913
Joined FIFA: 1913
Confederation: CONCACAF
FIFA world ranking: 16
Honours: CONCACAF Championship 1991, 2002, 2005

'Soccer', as football is affectionately known in America, was introduced in the USA in Boston as early as 1862. In its formative years it resembled rugby, but in 1884 the American Football Association was formed, in affiliation with the FA in England, to bring the game in line with that played across the Atlantic. European immigrants filled most teams, mainly on the eastern seaboard, and leagues appeared and disappeared with regularity.

The formation of the American Amateur Football Association (later to become the US Soccer Federation) in 1913 saw affiliation to FIFA and the beginnings of an American Soccer League. This professional attitude led, in 1930, to the national team reaching the semi-finals of the inaugural World Cup finals.

Soccer, however, failed to capture the imagination of a country brought up on 'American football' and baseball and few eyebrows were raised when the ASL folded in 1933. Regional leagues continued, but three silent decades followed and even the famous 1-0 victory against England in the 1950 World Cup failed to stir the passions.

The formation of the North American Soccer League in 1968 brought the game to the mainstream, in the Seventies attracting such football giants as Pelé, who played for the New York Cosmos, Franz Beckenbauer and Johan Cruyff. Attendances boomed, yet when these great names hung up their boots, crowds tailed-off and the league was disbanded in 1984. The NASL did, however, succeed in making football one of most popular youth sports in the country.

FIFA awarded the USA the 1994 World Cup and from that the Major League Soccer was born. Since hosting the 1994 World Cup, football in the United States has thrived. The national team has qualified for every World Cup since, lifted CONCACAF Gold Cup twice (adding to their 1991 Championship win) and hovered around the top ten of FIFA's official world rankings. The Major League Soccer has been running for 11 seasons and has sanctioned an increased number of franchises. By 2008, the MSL should boost 14 teams, including one from Toronto in Canada. By 2007 five soccer specific stadiums were scheduled to be built. Sponsorship and television revenues have been increasing and the champions of MLS league qualify for the CONCACAF Champions Cup. DC United have been the most successful club to date, winning four championships with the MLS title also going to Chicago Fire, Kansas

Below: USA's Kasey Keller and Frankie Hejduk hold up the Gold Cup in 2005.

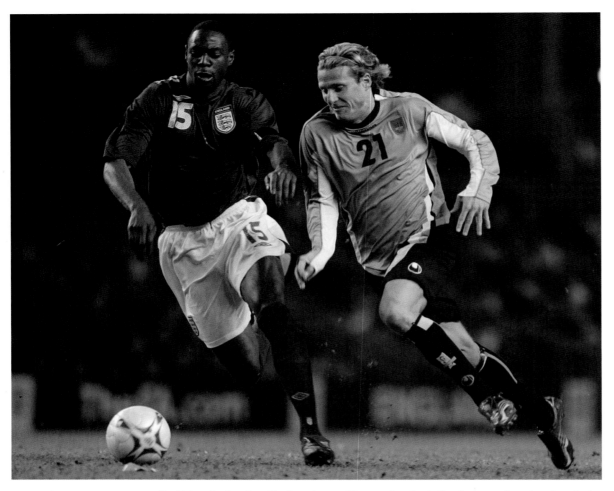

Above: Uruguay's Diego Forlan harries England defender Ledley King in 2006.

of interest in the tournament, Uruguay turned down the chance to defend their world title in 1934. They didn't compete in the finals again until 1950, when the first post-World War II tournament was held in Brazil. As it turned out, the wait proved more than worth it for Uruguay. They thumped Bolivia 8-0, with Omar Miguez scoring a hat-trick, before joining Brazil, Spain and Sweden in a 'mini league' to decide the champions. It ended up in an all-or-nothing showdown with the hotly fancied hosts in front of more than 205,000 fans packed into the Maracanã stadium. Despite falling behind in the second-half, Uruguay clinched their second World Cup victory in 20 years with goals from Juan Schiaffino and Alcide Ghiggia.

They made the semi-finals in 1954 and the quarter-finals in 1966, but there was no doubting Uruguay's World Cup star was seriously on the wane. After beating Australia in a two-legged play-off, they qualified for the 2002 World Cup finals, something they hadn't managed since 1990, but coach Victor Pua's side failed to win any of their group games and were soon heading home to South America. They failed to qualify for the 2006 finals, losing to Australia on penalties in a play-off.

Uruguay have an excellent record in the South American Championship (the Copa América) and even contested the tournament's very first match, in 1910, chalking up a 3-0 win over Chile in Buenos Aires. They went on to win eight of the first 18 tournaments up to 1942, an astonishing run. Their last appearance in a Copa América final came in 1999, when they were humbled 3-0 by Brazil. They finished fourth in 2001's tournament after losing a third-place play-off to Honduras on penalties.

City Wizards, San Jose Earthquakes and Los Angeles Galaxy since its inception.

Every CONCACAF Gold Cup has been hosted or co-hosted by the USA since 1991. They finally won the trophy in 2002, beating Costa Rica 2-0 in the final, and they won it again in 2005, beating Panama 3-1 on penalties.

URUGUAY

Federation: Asociación Uruguaya de Fútbol
Founded: 1900
Joined FIFA: 1923
Confederation: CONMEBOL
FIFA world ranking: 14
Honours: World Cup 1930, 1950; Copa América 1916, 1917, 1920, 1923, 1924, 1926, 1935, 1942, 1956, 1959, 1967,1983, 1987,1995; Olympics 1924, 1928

The tiny South American nation was arguably the biggest force in world football in the first half of the 20th Century, winning Olympic gold medals in 1924 and 1928, and being crowned world champion in both 1930 and 1950. Not only were they very successful, the Uruguayans were also stylish, playing imaginative pass-and-move football which stood in stark contrast to

the physicality then prevalent elsewhere in the world game.

Uruguay were the first South American country to enter the football tournament at the Olympic Games and made an immediate impact in 1924 in Paris. Europeans had rarely encountered skills such as those displayed by team captain Jose Nasazzi and strikers such as Hector Castro, Pedro Cea and Hector Scarone. The South Americans cantered along to the final, where goals from Pedro Petrone, Cea and Angel Romano gave them an easy 3-0 victory over Switzerland.

Four years later Uruguay returned to the Olympics – this time held in Amsterdam – to defend their title. They beat fellow South Americans, Argentina, 2-1 to win gold after a replay. Uruguay's success in the Olympics led to the country being offered the chance to host the first World Cup in 1930. Because of the distance, many European countries stayed away from the tournament and as a result the Uruguayan hosts had to make do with only 13 entrants, including themselves. However, the low turnout didn't seem to distract the South Americans from the matter at hand: they repeated their excellent Olympic form and won the competition. Again it was neighbours and rivals Argentina who Uruguay put to the sword in the final, this time 4-2, with one of their goals coming from the one-armed Hector Castro.

Apparently upset at Europe's seeming lack

US VIRGIN ISLANDS

Federation: US Virgin Islands Soccer Federation
Founded: 1992
Joined FIFA: 1998
Confederation: CONCACAF
FIFA world ranking: 196 (joint)

UZBEKISTAN

Federation: Uzbekistan Football Federation
Founded: 1946
Joined FIFA: 1994
Confederation: AFC
FIFA world ranking: 50

VANUATU

Federation: Vanuatu Football Federation
Founded: 1934
Joined FIFA: 1988
Confederation: OFC
FIFA world ranking: 161 (joint)

VENEZUELA

Federation: Federación Venezolana de Fútbol
Founded: 1926
Joined FIFA: 1952
Confederation: CONMEBOL
FIFA world ranking: 68

Venezuela is the weakest football nation in South America, where the sport ranks behind both baseball and basketball in popularity. Professional football arrived in 1957 and Caracas FC is the country's leading team. The national team has never won a match in the Copa América and will host the tournament for the first time in 2007.

VIETNAM

Federation: Vietnam Football Federation
Founded: 1962
Joined FIFA: 1964
Confederation: AFC
FIFA world ranking: 141 (joint)

WALES

Federation: Football Association of Wales
Founded: 1876
Joined FIFA: 1910-20, 1924-28, 1946
Confederation: UEFA
FIFA world ranking: 58

Football in Wales has always been a poor second to Rugby Union, despite the existence of a national team since March 1876 and a national FAW Cup competition since 1878. What Wales lacked was a national league, which did not arrive until 1993, although its semi-professional status did not attract the country's strongest sides – Cardiff City, Swansea City and Wrexham – who have been playing in the English league since the 1920s.

Cardiff actually won the English FA Cup in 1927, while other clubs such as Colwyn Bay and Merthyr Tydfil also ply their trade in England. This situation, along with English clubs plundering the best of Welsh talent, leaves domestic Welsh football a poor product. Nevertheless, the national side qualified for the 1958 World Cup, reached the 1976 European Championship quarter-finals – at the time only the semis and finals were played as one tournament – and lifted the British Championship outright on seven occasions.

Wales have produced a host of great players, including Ivor Allchurch, John Charles, Ryan Giggs, Ian Rush and Mark Hughes. In 2002 Hughes, as coach, also guided Wales through their best unbeaten sequence in the country's history. His successor was John Toshack.

YEMEN

Federation: Yemen Football Association
Founded: 1962
Joined FIFA: 1980
Confederation: AFC
FIFA world ranking: 125

ZAMBIA

Federation: Football Association of Zambia
Founded: 1929
Joined FIFA: 1964
Confederation: CAF
FIFA world ranking: 62

On April 28, 1993 tragedy struck Zambian football when a plane carrying the national team crashed into the Atlantic, killing 18 players and five officials. The loss was devastating at a time when Zambia looked set to qualify for the 1994 World Cup. The team had finished third at the 1990 African Nations Cup and were quarter-finalists in 1992. In 1988 they had reached the quarter-finals of the Olympic tournament after thrashing Italy 4-0, a game which saw African Player Of The Year Kalusha Bwalya (not on the plane) score a hat-trick. Power Dynamos had won the African Cup Winners' Cup in 1991 – the first Zambian club team to win an international trophy – but since the disaster, the country has failed to hit such heady heights.

ZIMBABWE

Federation: Zimbabwe Football Association
Founded: 1965
Joined FIFA: 1965
Confederation: CAF
FIFA world ranking: 66

Apartheid policies of the former Rhodesia kept the country out of the international arena until the 1970 World Cup. However, CAF did not accept the renamed Zimbabwe until 1980 after the instigation of black majority rule. Despite producing players of the calibre of Bruce Grobbelaar and Peter Ndlovu, Zimbabwe have yet to make an impact on the international stage, although they came within one game of reaching the 1994 World Cup finals.

Above: Gentle giant John Charles (left) leads Wales on to the pitch to face Scotland in 1962.

185

CLUB COMPETITIONS OF THE WORLD

EUROPEAN CUP & CHAMPIONS LEAGUE

The Champions League is the world's foremost club cup competition, but the origins of the European Cup, or the European Champions Clubs' Cup to give its more precise name, came into being following a boast by the English press that champions Wolverhampton Wanderers were the best club side in world football. The outlandish claim was the result of a 3-2 friendly victory in 1954 against Hungarian side Honvéd under the new Molineux floodlights. It was also a knee-jerk reaction from Fleet Street journalists, who had witnessed the England national team comprehensively beaten the previous year by Hungary's 'Magical Magyars' – 6-3 at Wembley and then 7-1 in Budapest six months later.

With the Hungarians inspired by the skill and tactical awareness of Puskás, Czibor and Kocsis, both results finally buried the myth that England remained the best exponents of the beautiful game. The pride of a nation had been dented, yet the result at Molineux – and the subsequent 4-0 victory by Wolves against Spartak Moscow – saw some pride restored to a bruised ego.

The boast, however, fell on deaf ears on the continent. Gabriel Hanot, editor of French sports newspaper *L'Equipe* and a former French international, was particularly aggrieved by the claims from England. In response to the *Daily Mail*'s comment that Wolves were 'the best team in the world', Hanot suggested that a new European tournament – devised for teams from nominated countries played on a home-and-away basis – should be implemented to determine the best team on the continent.

His observations received a somewhat lukewarm reaction from a number of football associations, with the English FA particularly concerned at the impact that a new competition would have on their own domestic campaign. Yet, following a meeting in Paris on April 2, attended by 15 of Europe's leading clubs, it was decided that Hanot's format should be presented to FIFA for it to receive international recognition.

Within four weeks, the world's governing body gave the competition its seal of approval and handed responsibility for its smooth running to UEFA. The European Champions Clubs Cup saw its very first match kick-off between Sporting Lisbon and Partizan Belgrade on September 4, 1955. In total, 16 countries had teams represented in the inaugural competition, but English league champions Chelsea were conspicuous by their absence. Pressured into withdrawing from the competition by Alan Hardaker, the anti-European secretary of the Football League, Chelsea's place went instead to Polish side Gwardia Warsaw.

Although these were humble beginnings, 38,000 fans attended the first final between Real Madrid and Stade de Reims, and so was born a tournament that has thrilled and excited for over 50 years. The amazing final of 1960, which saw Real Madrid run out 7-3 victors against Eintracht Frankfurt, is now widely regarded as the greatest spectacle of club football ever seen.

Other highlights include Celtic's shock win against Inter Milan in Lisbon in 1967, the dominance of the Johan Cruyff-inspired Ajax sides of the early 1970s, and the stranglehold that English clubs seemed to have on the

competition towards the end of that decade and into the early Eighties. If England had little to do with the competition upon its inception, the nation has been intrinsically linked with the European Cup ever since, and not always for the happiest of reasons. For Manchester United, February 6, 1958 marks the darkest day in the club's illustrious history after eight of the fabled 'Busby Babes' were tragically killed on a Munich runway on the way back from their 5-4 aggregate quarter-final win against Red Star Belgrade.

Having stopped to refuel, the freezing conditions caused two aborted take-offs and on the third attempt the plane failed to gain altitude, hit a house and burst into flames. Roger Byrne, Geoff Bent, Mark Jones, David Pegg, Liam Whelan, Eddie Colman and Tommy Taylor died instantly, while the game's biggest rising star – Duncan Edwards – passed away two weeks later. Manager Sir Matt Busby survived, but it took him another ten years to rebuild his team into European champions.

Yet the darkest moment in the competition's history came on May 29, 1985, when drunken Liverpool 'fans' went on the rampage inside the Heysel Stadium, Brussels, prior to the club's appearance in the final against Juventus. Italian supporters came under a hail of missiles and were faced with a spontaneous charge behind the goal. As they cowered in the corner of Terrace Z, a wall gave way under the pressure and 39 people were crushed to death while hundreds were injured. This wanton act of barbarism brought shame on English football and, more importantly, prompted UEFA to

Above from left to right: Real Madrid's Fernando Hierro lifts the trophy in 2002; Nottingham Forest celebrate after victory over Malmö in 1979; Manchester United's Peter Schmeichel holds the trophy in 1999.

EUROPEAN CUP & CHAMPIONS LEAGUE WINNERS

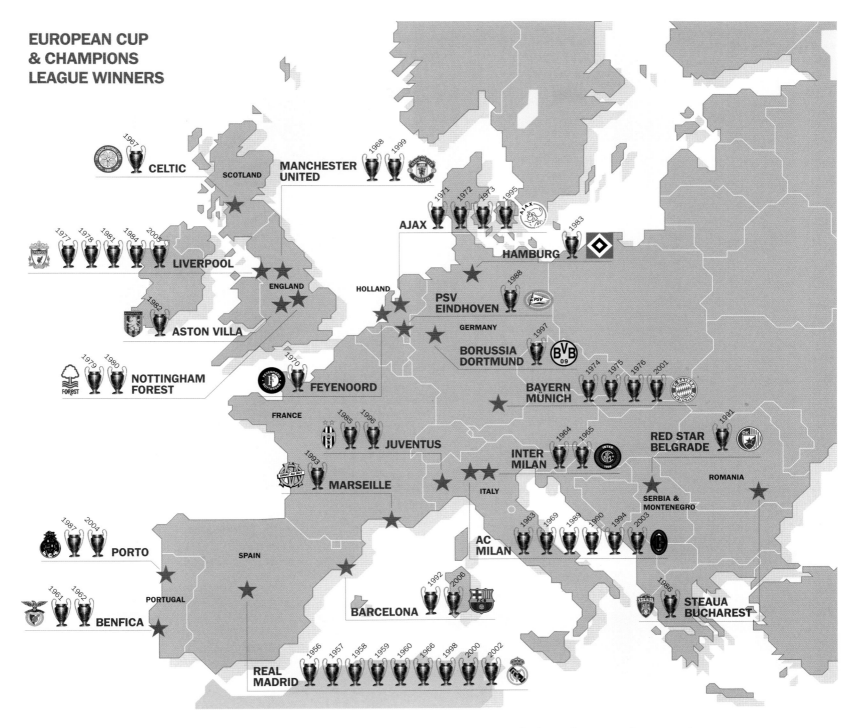

CELTIC 1967

MANCHESTER UNITED 1968 1999

AJAX 1971 1972 1973 1995

HAMBURG 1983

LIVERPOOL 1977 1978 1981 1984 2005

ASTON VILLA 1982

PSV EINDHOVEN 1988

NOTTINGHAM FOREST 1979 1980

BORUSSIA DORTMUND 1997

FEYENOORD 1970

BAYERN MUNICH 1974 1975 1976 2001

JUVENTUS 1985 1996

INTER MILAN 1964 1965

RED STAR BELGRADE 1991

MARSEILLE 1993

PORTO 1987 2004

AC MILAN 1963 1969 1989 1990 1994 2003

BARCELONA 1992 2006

STEAUA BUCHAREST 1986

BENFICA 1961 1962

REAL MADRID 1956 1957 1958 1959 1960 1966 1998 2000 2002

ban English clubs 'indefinitely' from all European club competitions. It would be another six years before the country would be represented in the European Cup.

On their return English teams would find a very different competition. With commercialism beginning to exert a much stronger influence on the sport, the bigger clubs were looking for more financial revenue from the competition, while the breakdown of the Eastern Bloc meant more quality teams and therefore a more exploitable overall package had been created.

In 1991-2 the format changed. The first and second rounds continued as normal, but the third round consisted of two mini leagues of four teams, with the winners meeting in the final. The league format met with widespread approval and guaranteed a cash windfall for those teams participating in the latter stages. The following season UEFA formalised the changes, rebranding the competiton as the Champions League.

In 1993-4 UEFA revamped the competition again, adding a semi-final phase for the top two teams in each group. The following season the tournament grew in size even further, the first two rounds replaced by a larger group phase: the holders and the seven top seeded teams would progress to four league groups, each containing four clubs, with the other clubs coming from a round of preliminary ties. The top two teams in each group progressed to the

quarter-finals. As the seasons have passed further changes have been implemented so that several of the highest-placed finishers in certain domestic leagues are now guaranteed a place in the competition, and such is the windfall that many teams now bank on qualification to ensure financial stability.

The model is now in place for a European Super League to evolve, consisting of only the most elite. While these big name clubs ultimately aspire to take control of the competition, for the time being it remains in the hands of UEFA. But whoever runs Europe's premier club competition in the future, the likelihood is that a Wolves or Honvéd will never again claim to be the continent's dominant club.

Right: AC Milan won Italy's first European Cup, beating Benfica at Wembley in 1963.

1956: REAL MADRID

PARC DES PRINCES, PARIS June 13

Real Madrid **4-3** Stade de Reims
(Spain)　　　　(France)

With a vociferous crowd behind them, Reims took a 2-0 lead through Leblond and Templin, but favourites Real Madrid soon found their composure and stamped their mark on the game. Alfredo Di Stéfano scored from the edge of the box and Rial's headed equaliser set up a storming second-half. A goal from Real winger Joseito was disallowed shortly after the break and Reims took advantage when Michel Hidalgo headed in Kopa's free-kick to edge them back in front. Madrid's 67th minute equaliser came when a Marquitos shot was deflected home, and with ten minutes remaining Rial scored his second to win the game.

1957: REAL MADRID

BERNABÉU STADIUM, MADRID May 30

Real Madrid **2-0** Fiorentina
(Spain)　　　(Italy)

Real Madrid's second final was played in front of a partisan 124,000 crowd, and although the Italians possessed skilful Brazilian Julinho and Argentine striker Miguel Montuori, they were no match for the Spaniards. The game was a stale affair until the 70th minute when Real winger Enrique Mateos was fouled and Alfredo Di Stéfano converted the kick. Six minutes later Gento found himself with the goalkeeper to beat and held his nerve to secure victory.

Below: Real Madrid's 1960 win over Eintracht Frankfurt was perhaps the greatest game ever.

1958: REAL MADRID

HEYSEL STADIUM, BRUSSELS May 28

Real Madrid **3-2** AC Milan (aet)
(Spain)　　　(Italy)
2-2 at 90 minutes

With Milan marshalled by Cesare Maldini, in an edgy match the Italians kept Di Stéfano and Kopa at bay until the 59th minute when Schiaffino put Milan into the lead. Di Stéfano equalised in the 74th minute, only for Grillo to put Milan back in front minutes later. Within 60 seconds Rial levelled the game, and although Liedholm came close for the Italians, hitting the bar in the dying moments, the match went to extra-time and Madrid made it three successive wins when Gento scored at the second attempt.

1959: REAL MADRID

NECKAR STADIUM, STUTTGART June 3

Real Madrid **2-0** Stade de Reims
(Spain)　　　(France)

In a dour affair, the French were criticised for a lack of adventure as Real won at a canter. The pattern was set as early as the second minute when Mateos shot past Colonna and, shortly after the restart, Di Stéfano scored the second to continue his record of scoring in every final. After the game, Real's Raymond Kopa moved back to Reims. French football would not see another team in the final until 1976.

1960: REAL MADRID

HAMPDEN PARK, GLASGOW May 18

Real Madrid **7-3** Eintracht Frankfurt
(Spain)　　　(West Germany)

Quite possibly the greatest attacking game of football ever staged, Frankfurt were blown away by the flair and imagination of Real. A near post volley from Kress put the Germans into the lead, but Di Stéfano netted twice before Puskás crashed in a left-foot shot to make it 3-1 at half-time. Ten minutes after the break Puskás scored a penalty, then followed up with a header from Gento's cross. He scored his fourth with a shot on the turn, before a Stein goal 15 minutes from time gave the Germans some respectability. Yet almost immediately, a Puskás pass set up Di Stéfano for his hat-trick before Stein scored again following a Madrid defensive blunder.

1961: BENFICA

WANKDORF STADIUM, BERNE May 31

Benfica **3-2** Barcelona
(Portugal)　　(Spain)

Barcelona's attack of Kubala, Kocsis and Czibor was rightly feared, but opponents Benfica, with the likes of Augusto, Coluna and Germano, were fast becoming the best team on the continent. The Spaniards took the lead through a Kocsis header on 19 minutes but found themselves on the back foot as Benfica scored twice in two minutes through Aguas and a Ramellets own-goal. In the 55th minute Benfica scored their third with a Coluna volley before a Barça onslaught saw Czibor get one back and he, Kocsis and Kubala all hit the post.

1962: BENFICA

OLYMPIC STADIUM, AMSTERDAM May 2

Benfica **5-3** Real Madrid
(Portugal)　　(Spain)

Another classic encounter saw Puskás score three times inside 38 minutes for Madrid, becoming the only player to have scored hat-tricks in two European Cup finals. Benfica cut back the deficit by half-time through Aguas and Cavern, but with Di Stéfano pulling the strings changes were made. He was man-marked by Cavern in the second-half and the game swung in Benfica's favour. Coluna pounced on a slip by Puskás to level and the stage was set for 19-year-old Eusébio to weave his magic. Having won a penalty, he slammed the kick past Araquistain in the 65th minute, and three minutes later connected with a pass from Coluna to secure victory.

1963: AC MILAN

WEMBLEY STADIUM, LONDON May 22

AC Milan **2-1** Benfica
(Italy)　　(Portugal)

A half-full Wembley witnessed a no-nonsense display by Milan. The plan was to stifle Coluna, but the strategy played into Eusébio's hands as he left Trapattoni in his wake to score after 18 minutes. Milan's determination shone through in the second-half and when Rivera found Altafini, the centre-forward fired home. With Coluna a passenger following Pivatelli's crude challenge, there would be only one winner and that came via Altafini who, having picked up the ball on the halfway line, ran half the length of the pitch before firing past Costa Pereira at the second attempt.

1964: INTER MILAN

PRATER STADIUM, VIENNA May 27

Inter Milan **3-1** Real Madrid
(Italy)　　(Spain)

Having conceded just four goals in the tournament, Inter were favourites to win in Vienna, and when Sandro Mazzola scored from 25 yards in the 43rd minute, he had dealt a fatal blow. A 61st minute mistake by keeper Vicente let in Milani to put the Italians 2-0 ahead, and although Puskás hit a post, the writing was on the wall for Real. Felo cut the deficit with a 70th minute header but normality was resumed just six minutes later when Mazzola pounced on a bad clearance to secure victory.

1965: INTER MILAN

SAN SIRO, MILAN May 27

Inter Milan **1-0** Benfica
(Italy)　　(Portugal)

Prior to the final Benfica complained to UEFA that hosting the game at Inter's ground gave the Italians an unfair advantage and threatened to field their youth team. They finally backed down when made fully aware of the financial benefits, but in hindsight their youngsters might have made a better job of it. Played in pouring rain, the players struggled with their footing and the match was settled when Jair's shot slithered through the hands of Costa Pereira in the 42nd minute.

1966: REAL MADRID

HEYSEL STADIUM, BRUSSELS May 11

Real Madrid **2-1** Partizan Belgrade
(Spain)　　(Yugoslavia)

Although the club was in its eighth final, it was an inexperienced Real side that faced the Yugoslavs and victory looked to be slipping away when Vasovic headed in Pirmajer's cross in the 56th minute. Real's response was to launch an all-out attack and in the 70th minute Amancio met a through pass from Grosso to shoot past Soskic. With their tails up, and Partizan's star striker Galic struggling with injury, Serena curled home from 25 yards to wrap the game up some six minutes later.

1967: CELTIC

ESTÁDIO NACIONAL, LISBON May 25

Celtic **2-1** Inter Milan
(Scotland)　　(Italy)

Celtic turned the Portuguese stadium into a sea of green and white, a sight that spurred Jock Stein's side into action against their much-fancied and defensively-organised opponents. A good start was a necessity but when Craig felled Cappellini after six minutes, referee Tschenscher pointed to the spot and Mazzola sent Simpson the wrong way.

Lesser teams could have crumbled, but Celtic went for broke and when Auld and Gemmell hit the bar, it gave an indication of the Scots' dominance. They were finally

rewarded in the 62nd minute when left-back Gemmell hit a 20-yard rocket into the corner of Sarti's net. The Inter defence was rattled and in the 83rd minute a Murdoch shot appeared to be going wide before Chalmers intercepted to guide the ball home.

1968: MANCHESTER UNITED

WEMBLEY STADIUM, LONDON May 29

Manchester United **4-1** Benfica (aet)
(England)　　(Portugal)
1-1 at 90 minutes

The first-half was a scrappy affair with chances at a premium, playmaker George Best being tightly marked by Cruz and Humberto. Sadler came closest to breaking the deadlock with two half-chances but it wasn't until the second-half, when Ashton began to cause problems down the left flank, that United looked dangerous. They were finally rewarded when Bobby Charlton headed home a Dunne cross in the 52nd minute, but 1-0 never looked a scoreline that would be enough to secure victory.

When Jaime Graça equalised with nine minutes to go, Benfica proved that the match was anything but over. Eusébio had a great chance to win the game in the dying seconds and it proved to be the defining moment as Best waltzed round two defenders to put United back in the lead early in extra-time. The goal demoralised Benfica and further strikes from Kidd and Charlton finally laid to rest the ghost of 1958.

Above: Archie Gemmell turns away after scoring Celtic's first goal in the 1967 European Cup final in Lisbon.

Above: Allan Clarke is fouled by Bayern's Franz Beckenbauer in the 1975 European Cup final – but to the anger of Leeds United no penalty is given.

1969: AC MILAN

BERNABÉU STADIUM, MADRID May 28

AC Milan **4-1** Ajax
(Italy)   (Holland)

In a move rarely associated with Italian sides, Milan attacked from the start against an inexperienced Ajax, Prati hitting the post in the first minute. They opened the scoring as early as the sixth minute when Prati's looping header sailed over Bals' goal, and despite Ajax's best intentions, the lead was doubled when Prati's shot flew in from the edge of the box. After Keizer was fouled by Lodetti just inside the penalty area, Vasovic's spot-kick gave Ajax hope on the hour. But Sormani put away Milan's third just five minutes later and Prati completed his hat-trick after 74 minutes to seal the win.

1970: FEYENOORD

SAN SIRO, MILAN May 6

Feyenoord **2-1** Celtic (aet)
(Holland)   (Scotland)
1-1 at 90 minutes

With Feyenoord underdogs, Celtic reverted to a 4-2-4 formation, believing an offensive action would win them the game. That assumption appeared to be correct when, in the 29th minute, Gemmell swept home from 25 yards. But within three minutes the Dutch equalised when Hasil's free-kick was lofted over a static Celtic defence for captain Israel to head home. Feyenoord completely dominated the second-half but somehow Celtic made it to extra-time

and goalkeeper Williams kept them in the game with fine saves from Kindvall and Wery. He could do nothing, however, when Kindvall took advantage of McNeill's slip to steer home the winner with four minutes remaining.

1971: AJAX

WEMBLEY STADIUM, LONDON June 2

Ajax **2-0** Panathinaikos
(Holland)   (Greece)

Puskás's love affair with the European Cup continued as he guided the Greeks to their solitary final appearance as manager. They started as big underdogs against the Total Football of Ajax, who took a grip on the game as early as the fifth minute when Keizer whipped in a left-wing cross for Van Dijk to head clinically past Oeconomopoulos. The Greek keeper then pulled off a number of fine saves, most notably from the impressive Cruyff, and although the Dutch seemed content to sit on their one goal advantage, Panathinaikos failed to seize the initiative. The game was won in the 87th minute when Haan finished off Cruyff's mazy run.

1972: AJAX

DE KUIP STADIUM, ROTTERDAM May 31

Ajax **2-0** Inter Milan
(Holland)   (Italy)

The Italians adopted their defensive 'catenaccio' tactics in an attempt to overcome the Dutch masters, however it was clear from kick-off that

they were fighting a losing battle as Ajax played with the flair and imagination that had won them a domestic double back in Holland.

The loss of centre-half Giubertoni after 12 minutes did not help Inter's cause, but the deadlock wasn't breached until the 47th minute when Cruyff pounced on a mix-up between Bordon and Burgnich to stroke home. The goal forced the Italians to attack and Mazzola had a good chance to equalise before European Footballer Of The Year, Johan Cruyff, made the game safe in the 77th minute.

1973: AJAX

RED STAR STADIUM, BELGRADE May 30

Ajax **1-0** Juventus
(Holland)   (Italy)

In a mirror image of the previous year's final, Dutch artistry overcame Italian stubbornness as Ajax became only the second team in history to win the cup three years in succession. On a humid night in Yugoslavia, Ajax went for an early kill and were rewarded when a deep Blankenburg cross was met by wonderkid Johnny Rep, who rose above Marchetti to head home. Again Cruyff teased the opposition and, although his team-mates couldn't take advantage, the result was never in doubt as the masters nonchalantly played possession football as the game drew to a close.

1974: BAYERN MUNICH

HEYSEL STADIUM, BRUSSELS May 15

Bayern Munich **1-1** Atlético Madrid (aet)
(West Germany)   (Spain)
0-0 at 90 minutes

In a closely-fought encounter Atlético had the better of the early exchanges, their flair and passing catching the Germans offguard. Bayern upped the tempo in the second-half but, although Müller and Hoeness looked dangerous, the game went to extra-time. The deadlock was broken when a delightful Aragones free-kick beat Maier, and with seven minutes remaining the cup appeared to be heading to Spain. Yet, in typical fashion, the Germans rose from the ashes and with just seconds remaining, Schwarzenbeck unleashed a shot from 35 yards that flew past Reina. The title would be decided by a replay.

REPLAY

HEYSEL STADIUM, BRUSSELS May 17

Bayern Munich **4-0** Atlético Madrid

With playmaker Irureta suspended and centre-half skipper Adelardo later substituted through injury, Madrid were on the back foot and the match proved to be a one-sided affair. Although the score was just 1-0 at half-time, thanks to Hoeness's 28th minute strike, the Germans turned the screw after the break and doubled their lead when Müller volleyed home

Kapellmann's cross. A delicate lob from Müller made it three, and with eight minutes remaining Hoeness scored his second by rounding the goalkeeper.

1975: BAYERN MUNICH

PARC DES PRINCES, PARIS May 28;

Bayern Munich **2-0** Leeds United
(West Germany)   (England)

With their physical, no-nonsense approach, United bossed the game in the opening half and had two legitimate appeals for a penalty turned down when Beckenbauer appeared to intercept a pass to Lorimer with his hand and later tripped Clarke inside the box. It simply wasn't going to be United's night, which was confirmed when Lorimer volleyed into the roof of the net after 67 minutes, only for the goal to be disallowed for offside. This decision caused rioting by a section of the Leeds fans and they were further riled when Roth scored in the 72nd minute following good work from Müller. Although Leeds continued to throw men forward, the Germans wrapped the game up with eight minutes remaining as Müller ghosted past Madeley and beat Stewart at his near post.

1976: BAYERN MUNICH

HAMPDEN PARK, GLASGOW May 12

Bayern Munich **1-0** St Etienne
(West Germany)   (France)

Although the scoreline suggests a tight game, it was anything but as St Etienne's imagination was matched with Bayern's counter-attacking football. The Germans were denied a goal in the second minute when Müller was deemed offside as he slotted the ball past Curkovic, but television replays proved he had been onside. The decision galvanised the French, who saw Bathenay and Santini hit the woodwork, but 12 minutes into the second-half Bayern landed the killer blow when a Beckenbauer free-kick was lashed home by Roth.

1977: LIVERPOOL

OLYMPIC STADIUM, ROME May 25

Liverpool **3-1** Borussia
                    Mönchengladbach
(England)   (West Germany)

Liverpool's creativity was rewarded in the 27th minute when Heighway's cross was met by McDermott and his shot flew past Borussia goalkeeper Kneib. Yet within six minutes of the restart, Simonsen intercepted a poor Case back-pass and his left-foot shot beat Clemence emphatically. The goal lifted the Germans, and the England goalkeeper was called into action on a number of occasions after that.

Having ridden the storm, Liverpool imposed themselves again and another Heighway cross was met by Smith, who rose quickest to make

it 2-1. With Kevin Keegan – in his last game for the club – running rings round the Germans, defender Vogts scythed him down and Neal converted the resulting spot-kick.

1978: LIVERPOOL

WEMBLEY STADIUM, LONDON May 10

Liverpool **1-0** Club Brugge
(England)   (Belgium)

In total contrast to the previous year's final, Liverpool retained their crown in a totally uninspiring game. With the influential Lambert and Courant both absent through injury, Brugge's defence-first policy stifled Liverpool, themselves below par after another intense domestic season. A Case free-kick was the closest either side came to scoring in the first-half, but The Reds finally broke the deadlock in the 66th minute when Dalglish latched on to a through ball from Souness to delightfully chip over advancing goalkeeper Jensen. Liverpool became the first English team to win the European Cup twice, ample consolation for losing the championship and League Cup to Nottingham Forest.

1979: NOTTINGHAM FOREST

OLYMPIC STADIUM, MUNICH May 30

Nottingham Forest **1-0** Malmö
(England)   (Sweden)

Another poor final, as Malmö were missing their influential defenders Larsson, Andersson and skipper Tapper, while Forest were without Gemmill and O'Neill. They did, however, have £1 million man Trevor Francis in their ranks, and he scored the only goal of the game on the stroke of half-time when he met Robertson's cross with a far post header. Robertson also hit the post himself after the break, and Birtles

missed a sitter with just goalkeeper Moller to beat. A Ljungberg free-kick proved to be Malmö's only clear attempt at goal.

1980: NOTTINGHAM FOREST

BERNABÉU STADIUM, MADRID May 28

Nottingham Forest **1-0** Hamburg
(England)   (West Germany)

With Trevor Francis absent with an Achilles injury and goalkeeper Peter Shilton struggling with a calf problem, Hamburg took the game to Forest, with full-back Kaltz and midfielder Memering keen to feed Kevin Keegan whenever possible. Yet as they pushed forward, Forest broke on the counter-attack, a move which worked to perfection in the 19th minute when Robertson played a neat one-two with Birtles before striking home from the edge of the box. Reimann had a goal disallowed for offside on the half-hour mark and although Keegan and Nogly went close, Forest held on.

1981: LIVERPOOL

PARC DES PRINCES, PARIS May 27

Liverpool **1-0** Real Madrid
(England)   (Spain)

With Camacho and Cortes shadowing Souness and Dalglish, and Real playmaker Stielike hustled off his game by Lee, an extremely tense first-half saw chances at a premium. Yet as the second-half got underway, Real skipper Camacho was clean through only to see his shot sail over the bar. It would act as a wake-up call to Liverpool, who then took a hold of the game, and a Ray Kennedy throw-in was chested down by Alan Kennedy who skipped past a tackle from Cortes before driving home from an acute angle. Liverpool held on and Bob Paisley became the first coach to win the European Cup three times.

Left: Trevor Francis enjoys Nottingham Forest's first European Cup win in 1979.

Below: Phil Neal and Alan Kennedy celebrate their third European Cup success, this time in 1981 against Real Madrid.

Above: Tony Morley lifts the cup after Aston Villa defeat Bayern Munich in 1982.

inspiring his team-mates to fight back. In the 67th minute, Tony Morley's bobbling cross was met by Peter Withe, who spooned the ball home past Müller.

1983: HAMBURG

OLYMPIC STADIUM, ATHENS May 25

Hamburg **1-0** Juventus
(West Germany)   (Italy)

With six of Italy's World Cup-winning team in their ranks, including Paolo Rossi, plus French midfield maestro Michel Platini, a Juve victory was seen as a formality. Yet it was West German industry that reigned supreme, and within eight minutes Hamburg were ahead, as captain Magath's looping shot fooled the 41-year-old keeper Dino Zoff. Platini and Rossi were poor throughout and the only Juventus player to emerge with any credit was Boniek, whose runs were a constant torment. But there was no denying Hamburg their victory, while Juventus were left to rue the hype that had surrounded the team in the build-up to the game.

1984: LIVERPOOL

OLYMPIC STADIUM, ROME May 30

Liverpool **1-1** Roma (aet)
(England)   (Italy)
1-1 at 90 minutes; Liverpool won 4-2 on penalties

The Italians may have been spurred on by a vociferous home crowd, but Liverpool managed to silence them after just 15 minutes when Tancredi lost the ball under pressure and Phil Neal gratefully stroked it home. Within seconds Souness scored but was ruled offside, and the Reds were left to rue the decision as Pruzzo headed home Conti's cross on 38 minutes. Liverpool goalkeeper Grobbelaar made key saves from Falção and Tancredi, and after extra-time stalemate the game went to penalties. In front of the Roma fans Nicol missed the opening kick, while Di Bartolomei scored. Neal then scored while Conti, distracted by the leg-wobbling antics of Grobbelaar, missed. Souness, Righetti and Rush all scored before Graziani hit the crossbar. It was left to Alan Kennedy to wrap the game up and he converted with consummate ease.

1982: ASTON VILLA

DE KUIP STADIUM, ROTTERDAM May 26

Aston Villa **1-0** Bayern Munich
(England)   (West Germany)

With a strong team that included German internationals Rummenigge and Hoeness, Bayern were clear favourites to lift the trophy in 1982. But it was Villa who started brightest, going close through both Withe and Evans. The early promise threatened to be undone, however, when goalkeeper Rimmer was taken off with an injured neck and replaced by 23-year-old Nigel Spink after just nine minutes. Any nerves that the youngster might have been experiencing were settled with two fantastic saves from Durnberger and Rummenigge,

1985: JUVENTUS

HEYSEL STADIUM, BRUSSELS May 29

Juventus **1-0** Liverpool
(Italy)   (England)

The on-field events at Heysel were completely overshadowed by rioting on the terraces, which resulted in the deaths of 39 Juventus fans. Prior to kick-off, a group of Liverpool fans charged at their Italian rivals behind the goal and, as the Juve fans fled the barrage of missiles being aimed in their direction, a wall collapsed under the pressure. The enormity of the disaster became apparent as kick-off approached, with

many fans being pulled out unconscious or dead. There is little doubt the crumbling stadium and lack of organisation was partly to blame, but it was at the ugly face of English hooliganism that UEFA vented their fury. As a result English club sides were banned from all European competition for five years, while Liverpool were banned for six. Juventus won the game thanks to Platini's penalty.

1986: STEAUA BUCHAREST

SÁNCHEZ PIZJUÁN STADIUM, SEVILLE May 7

Steaua Bucharest **0-0** Barcelona (aet)
(Romania)   (Spain)
Steaua won 2-0 on penalties

After a manic start that saw referee Vautrot hand out cards like confetti, the game settled down and Steaua Bucharest took control through their playmakers Balint and Balan. Yet it was Terry Venables' Barcelona who went closest to breaking the deadlock with a Bernd Schuster header on the half-hour. With the match goalless at half-time, the Romanian rearguard shone in the second-half and Barça's closest effort came from Steve Archibald, who headed over the crossbar. Extra-time failed to separate the sides and the game went to penalties. The first four were saved, but as Lacatus and Balint converted, Barcelona's next two were saved, handing Steaua success.

1987: PORTO

PRATER STADIUM, VIENNA May 27

Porto **2-1** Bayern Munich
(Portugal)   (West Germany)

The Germans took a controversial lead when Porto's Magalhaes was illegally ordered back from a Bayern throw-in. As he retreated the ball was deflected off his head to Kögl, who headed home himself. The injustice unsettled Porto as Rummenigge and Matthäus also went close, but the second-half was a contrasting affair as Sousa began pulling the strings in midfield. The equaliser came in the 77th minute when Madjer cheekily backheeled the ball past Pfaff, and two minutes later Juary connected with Madjer's cross to seal victory.

1988: PSV EINDHOVEN

NECKAR STADIUM, STUTTGART May 25

PSV Eindhoven **0-0** Benfica (aet)
(Holland)   (Portugal)
PSV won 6-5 on penalties

With PSV boasting four players from the Dutch national team that would win the European Championship that summer, they were clear favourites. Their chances were further boosted when Benfica skipper Diamantino was ruled out with injury. But as the Portuguese side launched a damage limitation exercise, the game petered out to a boring spectacle. Vanenburg and Gillhaus went close for PSV

after the break, while Nielsen missed an open goal, but extra-time proved equally dreary and only penalties lifted the gloom that had descended around the stadium. All penalties were expertly taken until PSV keeper Van Breukelen pushed out Veloso's weak effort.

1989: AC MILAN

NOU CAMP, BARCELONA May 24

AC Milan **4-0** Steaua Bucharest
(Italy)   (Romania)

With the likes of Gullit, Van Basten, Rijkaard and Maldini in their ranks, Milan confirmed their status as Europe's top side with a total demolition of Steaua Bucharest. The passing and movement was a joy to behold and, although Lacatus and Hagi were early threats, the Romanians were soon under pressure. Milan took the lead after 18 minutes when Bumbescu fluffed a clearance and Gullit was on hand to tuck the ball home. Eight minutes later Van Basten rose to head home Tassotti's cross. As the half drew to a close, Gullit received a pass from Donadoni and in one movement swivelled to volley past Lung. It would have been easy to shut up shop but within 60 seconds of the restart Van Basten received Rijkaard's through ball to score the fourth.

1990: AC MILAN

PRATER STADIUM, VIENNA May 23

AC Milan **1-0** Benfica
(Italy)   (Portugal)

Milan adopted a more defensive approach than the previous year, due in part to Benfica's very lively forward line of Magnusson and Valdo. Indeed, the Portuguese made most of the running in the first-half, but it was Milan who came closest to breaking the deadlock when Marco Van Basten's shot was well-saved by Silvino. The match was settled by the best move of the game involving Costacurta, Filippo Galli and Van Basten, whose through ball was coolly tucked home by Frank Rijkaard. Ruud Gullit had a chance to make the final 15 minutes more comfortable, but despite a scare from Carlos, Milan held on.

1991: RED STAR BELGRADE

SAN NICOLA STADIUM, BARI May 29

Red Star Belgrade **0-0** Marseille (aet)
(Yugoslavia)   (France)
Red Star won 5-3 on penalties

With both sides famous for their attacking instincts, it was somehow inevitable that the game would become a tedious affair. Red Star played with a lone striker in Pancev, a defensive midfield and an uncompromising defence, which meant the flair of Marseille's Jean-Pierre Papin and Chris Waddle were given little space or time to shine. The first half was forgettable, but at least the French side took the game to their opponents after the break and Waddle went close in the 75th minute with a header that flashed wide. Papin also went close but it was Prosinecki who almost won the game for Red Star, his late free-kick shaving the post. Waddle passed on the penalty shoot-out, unable to shake the memory of his World Cup semi-final miss of the previous year. Instead it was Amoros who handed Red Star victory after his kick was saved.

1992: BARCELONA

WEMBLEY STADIUM, LONDON May 20

Barcelona **1-0** Sampdoria (aet)
(Spain)   (Italy)
0-0 at 90 minutes

Barça took to the field in an unfamiliar orange kit and, although they showed more attacking instincts than their edgy opponents, Cruyff's side were nearly caught on the break when Lombardo's shot was well held by Zubizarretta.

The pace picked up in the second-half, with Vialli missing two guilt-edged chances, while Barça striker Stoichkov saw his shot rebound off a post. As the clock ticked, anxiety set in and a melee followed Baquero's poor tackle on Cerezo. Mancini had a chance to win with the ensuing free-kick, but the game went into extra-time. In the 110th minute, Barcelona controversially took the lead after referee Schmidhuber wrongly judged that Invernezzi had fouled Eusebio on the edge of the box. From the resulting free-kick, Ronald Koeman's ferocious strike beat Pagliuca to secure victory.

1993: MARSEILLE

OLYMPIC STADIUM, MUNICH May 26

Marseille **1-0** AC Milan
(France)   (Italy)

It was all change for Milan, who left Ruud Gullit on the bench while Jean-Pierre Papin was sacrificed for Marco Van Basten, making only his third appearance following ankle

surgery. Marseille, on the other hand, had their own problems with rumours of match-fixing threatening to overshadow their very existence.

Milan dominated the opening half-hour and could have been 2-0 up if Massaro had shown more composure, but the French gradually clawed their way back into the game. Völler went close with a shot that rebounded off goalkeeper Rossi's legs, while Boksic also saw an effort shave the bar. But the breakthrough finally came on the stroke of half-time when Boli rose to powerfully head home Pele's corner for the Frenchmen.

The second-half was one-way traffic as Milan pushed for an equaliser, but although Papin and Massaro both went close, they were left to rue Van Basten's shocking 48th minute miss from just eight yards out. Following the game, Marseille were found guilty of match fixing, banned from European football and relegated to the French Second Division.

1994: AC MILAN

OLYMPIC STADIUM, ATHENS May 18

AC Milan **4-0** Barcelona
(Italy)   (Spain)

With Barça displaying the attacking prowess of Stoichkov, Romario and Sergi, it was anticipated that the Italians would implement 'catenaccio' to the highest degree, yet the game was turned on its head as Milan displayed their own brand of breathtaking, offensive football.

They showed their intentions from the start when Panucci's header was disallowed in the ninth minute, and although Romario forced a good save from Rossi, Massaro broke the deadlock from Savicevic's cross in the 22nd minute. He added a second on the stroke of half-time following good work from Donadoni, and the game was all but sealed in the 47th minute when Savicevic chipped the ball over Zubizarretta from 20 yards. Desailly, playing in midfield, scored a fourth and Savicevic had time to hit the post twice before the final whistle put Barcelona out of their misery.

1995: AJAX

ERNST HAPPEL STADIUM, VIENNA May 24

Ajax **1-0** AC Milan
(Holland)   (Italy)

Although Van Gaal's young side had beaten Milan twice earlier in the competition, by the time of the final Milan had not conceded a goal for five European matches and were clear favourites. As the first-half progressed, Milan took a hold of the game, and although they hadn't created much, they were bossing the midfield. In defence Desailly, Baresi and Paolo Maldini were comfortably dealing with the threat of Ajax forwards Litmanen, George and Overmars.

The first real chance of the game came via a Desailly shot on 41 minutes, while Van der Sar saved from Simone on the stroke of half-time. Ajax were happy to return to the dressing room

on level terms and Van Gaal then played a masterstroke by bringing on young strikers Kanu and Kluivert, who helped turn the game around with their pace and trickery. The winner came in the 85th minute when Rijkaard's through ball found Kluivert and, at 18 years and 327 days, he became the youngest ever European Cup final goalscorer.

1996: JUVENTUS

OLYMPIC STADIUM, ROME May 22

Juventus **1-1** Ajax (aet)
(Italy)   (Holland)
1-1 at 90 minutes; Juventus won 4-2 on penalties

Although missing the injured Overmars, Ajax were everybody's tip to retain the trophy. But a defensive mix up between Frank De Boer and goalkeeper Van der Sar on 12 minutes let in Juventus striker Fabrizio Ravanelli to score from the acutest of angles. Both sides had chances as the half progressed – most notably from Musampa and Del Piero – and in the 41st minute a foul by Vierchowod on Kanu resulted in a De Boer free-kick being turned home by Litmanen. Vialli and Del Piero had chances to win the game for Juventus in the second-half, but extra-time was required. Del Piero had a great chance at the death but shot straight at Van der Sar. There was a feeling that it wasn't to be for the Italians, but they held their nerve in the shoot-out with Peruzzi saving from Edgar Davids and Sonny Silooy.

Below: Milan celebrate putting four goals past Barcelona in the 1994 European Cup final.

1997: BORUSSIA DORTMUND

OLYMPIC STADIUM, MUNICH May 28

Borussia Dortmund **3-1** Juventus
(Germany)   (Italy)

With the Germans containing four ex-Juve players – Kohler, Möller, Paulo Sousa and Reuter – Dortmund had an added incentive to do well, but what followed was one of the biggest upsets in European Cup history.

For the first half-hour Juventus attacked with purpose through Boksic and Vieri, but it was the Germans who struck first when Lambert's chip was met by Riedle, who rifled the ball home. Within five minutes, Riedle had doubled Dortmund's lead, heading home Möller's cross. But the game was far from over for Juve, who saw Zidane hit the post and Vieri have a goal disallowed before half-time.

Throwing caution to the wind, Lippi replaced defender Porrini with Del Piero and it was a move that appeared to pay off when the substitute scored after 64 minutes. Far from perturbed, Borussia scored a third when Ricken spotted Peruzzi off his line and lobbed the goalkeeper from 35 yards.

1998: REAL MADRID

AMSTERDAM ARENA, AMSTERDAM May 20

Real Madrid **1-0** Juventus
(Spain)   (Italy)

With 21 internationals on the pitch and a further six on the bench, this game was billed as a clash of the giants. But although both teams started brightly enough, neither side could make their pressure pay. Edgar Davids and Roberto Carlos were both booked as frustrations grew and Mijatovic, causing constant problems down the left, was a target of some uncompromising Juventus defending.

Raúl missed a golden opportunity to open the scoring on the stroke of half-time, while Inzaghi repeated the feat for Juventus soon after the restart, following good work from Davids. But just as fans were beginning to consider the possibility of extra-time, Real Madrid took the lead with less than 20 minutes remaining. Seedorf crossed from the right and although Carlos's shot was saved, Mijatovic was on hand to slot the ball home from a tight angle.

1999: MANCHESTER UNITED

NOU CAMP, BARCELONA May 26

Manchester United **2-1** Bayern Munich
(England)   (Germany)

With Keane and Scholes suspended, the odds were against United lifting the trophy for the first time in 31 years and their chances looked even more remote after a shaky start. As early as the sixth minute Johnsen fouled Jancker, and from the resulting free-kick Basler fired the ball over Schmeichel and into the net. United's creative force of Giggs and Blomqvist

were contained, Effenberg and Jeremies had control of the midfield, while Andy Cole and Dwight Yorke were given little opportunity to show their obvious talent. Indeed, as the game wore on and United became more desperate, they left themselves open and Effenberg went close while Scholl hit the bar.

As the game entered its 90th minute, with the Bayern fans already celebrating their team's success, United keeper Peter Schmeichel went up for a last-gasp Beckham corner. He failed to connect but the ball fell to Giggs, whose shot was intercepted by substitute Teddy Sheringham who fired the ball into the back of the net. The Bayern Munich players were clearly distraught and before they had managed to rediscover their composure, Beckham sent in another corner, which was flicked on by Sheringham and diverted home by substitute Solskjaer.

2000: REAL MADRID

STADE DE FRANCE, PARIS May 24

Real Madrid **3-0** Valencia
(Spain)   (Spain)

In the first final between two teams from the same country, Madrid completely dominated with their brand of attacking football and breathtaking skill. With Steve McManaman pulling the strings in midfield, wing-backs Carlos and Salgado marauding forward at every opportunity, and Raúl a constant threat in attack, there was only ever going to be one winner. The only surprise was that it took 39 minutes for Real to open the scoring. A Carlos free-kick was deflected into the path of Anelka, whose ball found Morientes unmarked at the far post.

In the 63rd minute McManaman was rewarded as he crashed home through a pack of players to put the game beyond Valencia's reach, but the best was saved until last as Raúl ran 70 yards before rounding Canizares and tucking the ball home.

2001: BAYERN MUNICH

SAN SIRO, MILAN May 23

Bayern Munich **1-1** Valencia (aet)
(Germany)   (Spain)
1-1 at 90 minutes; Bayern won 5-4 on penalties

In a game of penalties, Valencia opened the scoring as early as the second minute when Mendieta's shot was adjudged to have hit Andersson on the arm and the Spanish playmaker stepped up to convert the penalty kick himself. Incredibly, referee Jol awarded another spot-kick just five minutes later when Angloma scythed Effenberg down, but Scholl's kick was saved by the legs of Canizares.

The early edge, both psychological and in

Above: The celebrations start for Bayern Munich in 2001.

Below: Real Madrid's Karembeu, Morientes and Raúl parade the trophy in 1998.

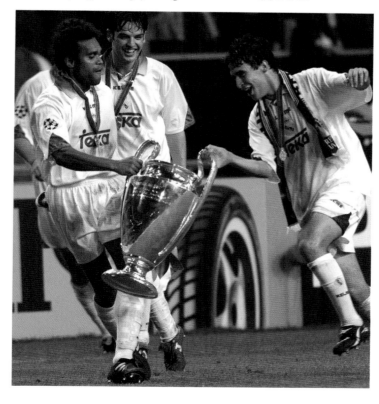

Above: A celebration charge from the players of AC Milan in 2003.

Opposite top: Arsenal goalkeeper Jens Lehmann sees red in 2006. He became the first player to be sent-off in a European Cup final.

Opposite bottom: Steven Gerrard inspired Liverpool's fantastic comeback from 3-0 down to win the Champions League in 2005.

Right: José Mourinho's Porto get their hands on the cup in 2004.

terms of goals, would not last for the Spaniards as Bayern enjoyed plenty of possession, with Lizarazu and Salihamidzic causing problems down the left. Scholl went close with a free-kick and Carew could have made it 2-0 to Valencia with a header that flashed wide, but it was the introduction of Jancker that proved crucial.

Within five minutes of coming on, the big striker's challenge on Carboni forced the Italian defender to handle the ball and Effenberg stepped up to send Canizares the wrong way. In extra-time Canizares blocked a close range shot from Elber, Scholl fired a free-kick tamely wide, and the Valencia keeper kept out an angled drive by Salihamidzic, but the Germans held their nerve to win a tense penalty shoot-out.

2002: REAL MADRID

HAMPDEN PARK, GLASGOW May 15

Real Madrid **2-1** Bayer Leverkusen
(Spain)   (Germany)

Zidane's breathtaking volley in the final minute of the first-half is the enduring image of a game that saw Real's class overcome Leverkusen's stubbornness. The French star, who had contributed little in the previous 44 minutes, met a left-wing cross from Carlos and let fly from the edge of the area with a waist-high volley that flew past goalkeeper Butt.

Earlier Raúl had struck in the ninth minute from a move that began with a long throw by Carlos, and Brazilian defender Lucio had headed the leveller in the 14th minute from a Schneider free-kick. But Zidane apart, the star of the show was young Real goalkeeper Casillas, who replaced the injured Sanchez in the 67th minute before making fine saves from a Basturk header and Berbatov's injury-time strike. The result meant that Madrid,

beaten in the league and Spanish Cup final after being on course for the treble, finally won the biggest prize of all in their centenary year.

2003: AC MILAN

OLD TRAFFORD, MANCHESTER May 28

AC Milan **0-0** Juventus (aet)
(Italy)   (Italy)
Milan won 3-2 on penalties

In the first all-Italian final in the 48-year history of the competition, Juventus faced Milan minus suspended Czech midfielder Nedved. Without him the team lacked midfield urgency as Milan had three good scoring chances in the first 45 minutes. Shevchenko had the ball in the Juventus net in the eighth minute, but Rui Costa was adjudged offside, while Inzaghi went close with a diving header that was

spectacularly saved by Buffon. Six minutes before the break another chance fell to Rui Costa when Pirlo found him in front of goal, but the Portuguese midfielder pulled his shot wide of Buffon's right-hand post. An effort from Trezeguet and a Del Piero shot on the stroke of half-time were Juve's best of the half and, indeed, the game.

The second-half degenerated into a game of defensive mastery. Extra-time and penalties were inevitable, but even the shoot-out proved disappointing, and it was left to Shevchenko to score the winner and make up for his earlier disappointment.

2004: PORTO

ARENA AUFSCHALKE, GELSENKIRCHEN May 26

Porto **3-0** AS Monaco
(Portugal)   (France)

José Mourinho's disciplined Porto side ended their surprising campaign by becoming European champions for the first time since 1987. Monaco started brightly and looked the better of the two sides, but after injury robbed them of their captain and playmaker, Ludovic Giuly, midway through a sterile first-half, Porto took the initiative. A 38th minute volley from Brazilian teenager Carlos Alberto put the Portuguese champions in the lead, but Monaco continued to press forward and constantly looked the more threatening of the two sides.

Porto proved dangerous on the counter-attack, Brazilian playmaker Deco breaking from the halfway line and receiving a return pass from substitute Dmitri Alenitchev before scoring a delightful chipped goal with 20 minutes left. Four minutes later the veteran Russian star Alenitchev scored Porto's third, firing home a deflected pass from Derlei Silva. Monaco had been punished ruthlessly on the break, enabling Porto to add the Champions League trophy to the UEFA Cup they had won the previous year.

2005: LIVERPOOL

ATATÜRK STADIUM, ISTANBUL May 25

Liverpool **3-3** AC Milan (aet)
(England)   (Italy)

3-3 at 90 mins; Liverpool won 3-2 on penalties

In an unprecedented comeback at this level, Liverpool became champions of Europe for a fifth time with three goals in six incredible second-half minutes. Outclassed before the break, the Reds found themselves 3-0 down by half-time, Paolo Maldini putting Milan in front inside the first minute. Liverpool's Harry Kewell limped off injured after just 22 minutes, and two goals from Hernan Crespo at the close of the first-half compounded Liverpool's problems.

Steven Gerrard threw Liverpool a lifeline in the 54th minute, heading home a John Arne Riise's cross, and within six minutes the scores were level, the tie taken into extra-time thanks to goals from Smicer and Alonso, who had followed up his own saved penalty to score. After extra-time the game was settled by a dramatic penalty shoot-out. Andriy Shevchenko, scorer of the winning penalty in the 2003 final, was this time denied by Jerzy Dudek, whose goal-line antics conjured up memories of Bruce Grobbelaar in 1984.

2006: BARCELONA

STADE DE FRANCE, PARIS May 17

Barcelona **2-1** Arsenal
(Spain)   (England)

A final that had all the potential to be the most exciting in years, the match exploded in to life from the kick-off, with Arsenal's Thierry Henry coming close twice in the opening exchanges. But after just 18 minutes of free-flowing, end-to-end football, the game took a sensational turn that altered the flavour of the tie and settled the destination of the trophy. Ronaldinho played a ball through to Samuel Eto'o, but the Cameroon forward was caught on the edge of the box by onrushing Jens Lehmann. The ball fell to Giuly, who tapped it home, but the referee disallowed the goal, awarded a free-kick to Barcelona and red-carded the Arsenal keeper, the first player ever to be sent-off in a European Cup final.

Playing with just ten men, Almunia replacing Lehmann, Arsenal absorbed the pressure and snatched the lead through a 37th minute Sol Campbell header. Arsenal held their own, Henry spurning his fair share of chances before Eto'o scored with just 14 minutes remaining. While the Gunners tired in the heavy rain, Barcelona surged forward and Belletti scored the winner in the 80th minute.

INTER-CITIES FAIRS CUP & UEFA CUP

Above from left to right: The 1992 Ajax side celebrate after beating Torino on away goals; Mick Mills of Ipswich lifts the trophy in 1981; Porto beat Celtic to win the UEFA Cup in 2003.

Opposite clockwise from top left: Albelda and Baraja of Valencia raise the UEFA Cup in 2004; Parma start the celebrations after defeating Marseille; Billy Bremner and the Leeds United team party in the dressing room in 1971; CSKA Moscow's big moment in 2005.

Europe's second most prestigious international cup competition began life as something of an anomaly. Known originally as the Inter Cities Fairs Cup, it was thought up in 1955 shortly after the inception of the European Cup by the future president of FIFA, Sir Stanley Rous, and two future FIFA vice-presidents, Switzerland's Ernst Thommen and Italy's Ottorino Barrasi. Their idea was to hold a tournament for European cities which regularly organised trade fairs. Entry was unrelated to final league placings, which threw up some insignificant teams early on like DOS of Utrecht, as well as some peculiar representative sides featuring players from several clubs, like the London Select XI that starred in the first campaign.

The first Fairs Cup involved teams from Barcelona, Basle, Birmingham, Copenhagen, Frankfurt, Lausanne, Leipzig, London, Milan and Zagreb. Originally conceived as a two-year tournament, it actually lasted for three, during which time 23 games were played in a clumsy group system complicated by withdrawals. The final was contested over two legs by Barcelona, using players exclusively from FC Barcelona, and the London Select XI which included Arsenal goalkeeper Jack Kelsey, Tottenham's Danny Blanchflower, Fulham's Johnny Haynes and Jimmy Greaves of Chelsea. London, who had played several games under floodlights at Wembley, held Barcelona 2-2 in front of 45,000 fans at Stamford Bridge on March 5, 1958, but were routed 6-0 in the return two months later.

Two years on the format was altered, limiting participation to 16 professional club sides from cities that held trade fairs. Barcelona held on to the trophy, beating Birmingham City who went on to lose two finals in a row, defeated the following year by AS Roma, the only Italian club to lift the 'Coppa Delle Fiere'.

Following this brief Italian interlude, Spanish clubs returned to their position of predominance in the competition. Between 1962 and 1964 the final was an all Spanish affair, Valencia winning twice in succession before losing in the third consecutive year to Real Zaragoza in a one-legged confrontation at Barcelona's Nou Camp stadium. The Mediterranean hegemony was finally broken by Hungarians Ferencváros in 1965, before Barcelona reclaimed the title again a year later.

There were more changes in 1967 when the competition was renamed the European Fairs Cup and increased to 48 entrants, the first of a succession of expansions that saw 64 sides competing in the 1969-70 season, by which time it was unofficially known as the 'Runners-Up Cup'. Never was a title more merited than in 1968 when Don Revie's Leeds United lifted the trophy. They had earned the status of 'nearly men' in English football and were the beaten Fairs Cup finalists the previous season, losing to Dinamo Zagreb. However, they shook off their 'bridesmaid' image, progressing smoothly past AC Spora, Partizan Belgrade, Hibernian, Rangers and Dundee, before holding on to a narrow 1-0 first leg lead against Ferencváros.

Leeds United's first victory opened the door for English clubs to dominate the competition for six years, with Newcastle picking up the trophy the following season. The Magpies had finished tenth in the First Division the previous season but qualified thanks to a one-city, one-team rule. They demonstrated their worth by seeing off the challenge of Sporting Lisbon, Real Zaragoza and Glasgow Rangers before a 6-2 victory over an Újpest Dozsa side that featured six Hungarian internationals.

In 1970 Arsenal beat Anderlecht to win their first European trophy despite finishing 12th in the league that season, the lowest position ever for the competition's winners. Facing a 3-1 deficit from the away leg, Arsenal looked set to notch up an unenviable record of three final defeats in succession (they had lost the two previous League Cup finals) but romped to a 3-0 win at Highbury, ending a run of 17 years without a trophy.

Leeds returned to prominence in 1971, taking what proved to be the last ever Fairs Cup by beating Juventus on away goals, a rule used for the first time in the competition's history, after the original match was abandoned due to an unplayable pitch.

With the competition being turned over to UEFA the following season, Leeds and Barcelona, as the two sides with the best overall playing record in the competition, contested a specially organised play-off on September 22, 1971. Barcelona won 2-1 and the trophy now resides permanently at the Nou Camp.

The first winners of the new 1972 trophy, a silver cup on a yellow marble plinth designed and crafted by the Bertoni workshops in Milan, were Tottenham, who won an all English affair

with Wolverhampton Wanderers on aggregate.

Liverpool's first UEFA Cup win the following year was the culmination of eight consecutive seasons of continental action, including a Fairs Cup semi-final – a record no other English club could boast. Their two-legged final with Borussia Mönchengladbach was an epic that included a first leg abandoned at Anfield due to a waterlogged pitch. Bill Shankly used those 27 minutes of wasted play to rejig his side, replacing Brian Hall with John Toshack the following evening – a move that saw them post a 3-0 win that Borussia could not quite pull back in the return.

The 1974 competition was notable for the outbreak of crowd trouble at the final after Spurs fans went on the rampage following a 2-0 defeat to Feyenoord in Rotterdam, a display which led to the club being banned from the competition for two years. However, ten years later a fan died in rioting and 200 arrests were made after the Londoners beat Anderlecht in the competition's first penalty shoot-out, goalkeeper Tony Parks writing his name in the club's history.

After Liverpool's 1976 victory over the Belgian side Club Brugge, it would be another five years before an English side again lifted the UEFA Cup, with Juventus, PSV Eindhoven, Borussia Mönchengladbach and Eintracht Frankfurt passing the trophy around in the intervening period. Bobby Robson's Ipswich Town restored English pride in 1981, with Frans Thijssen and Arnold Muhren squaring up to fellow Dutchmen AZ 67 Alkmaar and emerging 5-4 aggregate winners. One year on the cup went to a Scandinavian side for the first time with IFK Gothenberg overcoming West German club Hamburg. The Swedes would lift the trophy again in 1987.

Tottenham's 1984 triumph effectively saw the end of English dominance as the Heysel

disaster in the European Cup final a year later led to English clubs being banned from European competition for five years (Liverpool were banned for six). No English side would compete in the competition again until Aston Villa were allowed to enter in September 1990, beating the Czechs Banik Ostrava. It was 11 years before an English team actually lifted the cup again, when Liverpool beat Spanish side Alaves in a 5-4 thriller decided by an own golden goal, though Arsenal did reach the final against Galatasaray in 2000, an occasion that resulted in further violence and the first ever UEFA Cup win for a Turkish team.

The late Eighties saw Italy belatedly make a mark on the competition. Maradona's Napoli broke the drought, beating Stuttgart in 1989, opening the door for Serie A clubs to dominate in a six-year run broken only by Ajax in 1992. Juventus and Inter were the main beneficiaries with three of the finals all-Italian affairs.

After two wins for German clubs the 1998 final again featured two Italian sides in the competition's first one-legged final, Milan beating Lazio 3-0 in Paris. By then the expansion of the Champions League had resulted in a further raft of changes: those clubs failing to qualify for the Champions League group stages received a bye in to the next round of the UEFA Cup. In the 1999-2000 season the trophy was effectively merged with the European Cup Winners' Cup and further qualification routes were opened up to the three 'winners' of the Intertoto Cup and three clubs from UEFA's Fair Play League.

In 2003 Porto became Portugal's first winners of the competition, beating Celtic in Seville. The following year Valencia secured their first European trophy since 1980, beating Marseille 2-0 in Gothenburg; they were helped when the French had keeper Fabien Barthez sent-off just before half-time.

The format of the competition was given a significant overhaul for the 2004-5 season. After the first round, the 40 surviving teams entered a group phase, featuring eight pools of five. Unlike the group phase of the Champions League, where teams play each other home and away, in the UEFA Cup each club plays just two home and two away games. The top three teams in each group progress to the next round, where they are joined by the eight third-placed teams from the Champions League group phase. From this point, the UEFA Cup returns to its traditional format: a two-legged knockout competition with a one-off final.

The first winners of the new look UEFA Cup were CSKA Moscow. With the final played in Lisbon, home advantage helped Sporting to an early lead, but CSKA won 3-1 to take the UEFA Cup to Russia for the first time. Seville were also first-time winners in 2006, beating Middlesbrough 4-0 to celebrate the club's centenary in real style. Nevertheless, the continual aggrandisement of the Champions League only serves to diminish the status of UEFA Cup further, to the point that the original 'Runners-Up Cup' is now viewed by major clubs as merely a consolation prize.

THE WINNERS OF THE FAIRS CUP/UEFA CUP

1958: BARCELONA

1ST LEG March 5

London Select XI **2-2** Barcelona
(England) (Spain)

2ND LEG May 1

Barcelona **6-0** London Select XI
Barcelona won 8-2 on aggregate

1960: BARCELONA

1ST LEG March 29

Birmingham City **0-0** Barcelona
(England) (Spain)

2ND LEG May 4

Barcelona **4-1** Birmingham City
Barcelona won 4-1 on aggregate

1961: AS ROMA

1ST LEG September 27

Birmingham City **2-2** AS Roma
(England) (Italy)

2ND LEG October 11

AS Roma **2-0** Birmingham City
AS Roma won 4-2 on aggregate

1962: VALENCIA

1ST LEG September 8

Valencia **6-2** Barcelona
(Spain) (Spain)

2ND LEG September 12

Barcelona **1-1** Valencia
Valencia won 7-3 on aggregate

1963: VALENCIA

1ST LEG June 12

Dynamo Zagreb **1-2** Valencia
(Yugoslavia) (Spain)

2ND LEG June 26

Valencia **2-0** Dynamo Zagreb
Valencia won 4-1 on aggregate

1964: REAL ZARAGOZA

NOU CAMP, BARCELONA June 25

Real Zaragoza **2-1** Valencia
(Spain) (Spain)

1965: FERENCVÁROS

COMUNALE, TURIN June 23

Ferencváros **1-0** Juventus
(Hungary) (Italy)

1966: BARCELONA

1ST LEG September 14

Barcelona **0-1** Real Zaragoza
(Spain) (Spain)

2ND LEG September 21

Real Zaragoza **2-4** Barcelona (aet)
Barcelona won 4-3 on aggregate

1967: DYNAMO ZAGREB

1ST LEG August 30

Dynamo Zagreb **2-0** Leeds United
(Yugoslavia) (England)

2ND LEG September 6

Leeds United **0-0** Dynamo Zagreb
Dynamo Zagreb won 2-0 on aggregate

1968: LEEDS UNITED

1ST LEG August 7

Leeds United **1-0** Ferencváros
(England) (Hungary)

2ND LEG September 11

Ferencváros **0-0** Leeds United
Leeds United won 1-0 on aggregate

1969: NEWCASTLE UNITED

1ST LEG May 29

Newcastle United **3-0** Újpest Dozsa
(England) (Hungary)

2ND LEG June 11

Újpest Dozsa **2-3** Newcastle United
Newcastle United won 6-2 on aggregate

1970: ARSENAL

1ST LEG April 22

Anderlecht **3-1** Arsenal
(Belgium) (England)

2ND LEG April 28

Arsenal **3-0** Anderlecht
Arsenal won 4-3 on aggregate

1971: LEEDS UNITED

1ST LEG May 26

Juventus **0-0** Leeds United
(Italy) (England)
Match abandoned after 51 mins waterlogged pitch

1ST LEG REPLAY May 28

Juventus **2-2** Leeds United

2ND LEG June 3

Leeds United **1-1** Juventus
Leeds United won on away goals rule

The Fairs Cup was replaced by The UEFA Cup in the 1971-72 season

1972: TOTTENHAM HOTSPUR

1ST LEG May 3

Wolverhampton **1-2** Tottenham
Wanderers Hotspur
(England) (England)

2ND LEG May 17

Tottenham **1-1** Wolverhampton
Hotspur Wanderers
Tottenham Hotspur won 3-2 on aggregate

1973: LIVERPOOL

1ST LEG May 9

Liverpool **0-0** Borussia
Mönchengladbach
(England) (West Germany)
Match abandoned after 27 mins waterlogged pitch

1ST LEG REPLAY May 10

Liverpool **3-0** Borussia
Mönchengladbach

2ND LEG May 23

Borussia **2-0** Liverpool
Mönchengladbach
Liverpool won 3-2 on aggregate

1974: FEYENOORD

1ST LEG May 21

Tottenham **2-2** Feyenoord
Hotspur
(England) (Holland)

2ND LEG May 29

Feyenoord **2-0** Tottenham
Hotspur
Feyenoord won 4-2 on aggregate

1975: B. MÖNCHENGLADBACH

1ST LEG May 7

Borussia **0-0** FC Twente
Mönchengladbach
(West Germany) (Holland)

2ND LEG May 21

FC Twente **1-5** Borussia
Mönchengladbach
Borussia Mönchengladbach won 5-1 on aggregate

1976: LIVERPOOL

1ST LEG April 28

Liverpool **3-2** Club Brugge
(England) (Belgium)

2ND LEG May 19

Club Brugge **1-1** Liverpool
Liverpool won 4-3 on aggregate

1977: JUVENTUS

1ST LEG May 4

Juventus **1-0** Athletic Bilbao
(Italy) (Spain)

2ND LEG May 18

Athletic Bilbao **2-1** Juventus
Juventus won on away goal rule

1978: PSV EINDHOVEN

1ST LEG April 26

SC Bastia **0-0** PSV Eindhoven
(France) (Holland)

2ND LEG May 9

PSV Eindhoven **3-0** SC Bastia
PSV Eindhoven won 3-0 on aggregate

1979: B. MÖNCHENGLADBACH

1ST LEG May 9

Red Star Belgrade **1-1** Borussia
Mönchengladbach
(Yugoslavia) (West Germany)

2ND LEG May 23

Borussia **1-0** Red Star Belgrade
Mönchengladbach
Borussia Mönchengladbach won 2-1 on aggregate

1980: EINTRACHT FRANKFURT

1ST LEG May 7

Borussia **3-2** Eintracht
Mönchengladbach Frankfurt
(West Germany) (West Germany)

2ND LEG May 21

Eintracht **1-0** Borussia
Frankfurt Mönchengladbach
Eintracht Frankfurt won on away goal rule

1981: IPSWICH TOWN

1ST LEG May 6

Ipswich Town **3-0** AZ 67 Alkmaar
(England) (Holland)

2ND LEG May 20

AZ 67 Alkmaar **4-2** Ipswich Town
Ipswich Town won 5-4 on aggregate

1982: IFK GOTHENBURG

1ST LEG May 5

IFK Gothenburg **1-0** Hamburg
(Sweden) (West Germany)

2ND LEG May 19

Hamburg **0-3** IFK Gothenburg
IFK Gothenburg won 4-0 on aggregate

1983: RSC ANDERLECHT

1ST LEG May 4

Anderlecht **1-0** Benfica
(Belgium) (Portugal)

2ND LEG May 18

Benfica **1-1** Anderlecht
RSC Anderlecht won 2-1 on aggregate

1984: TOTTENHAM HOTSPUR

1ST LEG May 9

Anderlecht **1-1** Tottenham
Hotspur
(Belgium) (England)

2ND LEG May 23

Tottenham **1-1** Anderlecht (aet)
Hotspur
Tottenham Hotspur won 4-3 on penalties

1985: REAL MADRID

1ST LEG May 8

Videoton **0-3** Real Madrid
(Hungary) (Spain)

2ND LEG May 22

Real Madrid **0-1** Videoton
Real Madrid won 3-1 on aggregate

1986: REAL MADRID

1ST LEG April 30

Real Madrid **5-1** Köln
(Spain) (West Germany)

2ND LEG May 6

Köln **2-0** Real Madrid
Real Madrid won 5-3 on aggregate

1987: IFK GOTHENBURG

1ST LEG May 6

IFK Gothenburg **1-0** Dundee United
(Sweden) (Scotland)

2ND LEG May 20

Dundee United **1-1** IFK Gothenburg
IFK Gothenburg won 2-1 on aggregate

1988: BAYER LEVERKUSEN

1ST LEG May 4

Espanyol **3-0** Bayer Leverkusen
(Spain) (West Germany)

2ND LEG May 18

Bayer Leverkusen **3-0** Espanyol (aet)
Beyer Leverkusen won 3-2 on penalties

1989: NAPOLI

1ST LEG May 3

Napoli **2-1** Vfb Stuttgart
(Italy) (West Germany)

2ND LEG May 17

Vfb Stuttgart **3-3** Napoli
Napoli won 5-4 on aggregate

1990: JUVENTUS

1ST LEG May 2

Juventus **3-1** Fiorentina
(Italy) (Italy)

2ND LEG May 16

Fiorentina **0-0** Juventus
Juventus won 3-1 on aggregate

1991: INTER MILAN

1ST LEG May 8

Inter Milan **2-0** AS Roma
(Italy) (Italy)

2ND LEG May 22

AS Roma **1-0** Inter Milan
Inter Milan won 2-1 on aggregate

1992: AJAX

1ST LEG April 29

Torino **2-2** Ajax
(Italy) (Holland)

2ND LEG May 13

Ajax **0-0** Torino
Ajax won on away goals rule

1993: JUVENTUS

1ST LEG May 5

Borussia **1-3** Juventus
Dortmund
(Germany) (Italy)

2ND LEG May 19

Juventus **3-0** Borussia
Dortmund
Juventus won 6-1 on aggregate

1994: INTER MILAN

1ST LEG April 26

Austria Salzburg **0-1** Inter Milan
(Austria) (Italy)

2ND LEG May 11

Inter Milan **1-0** Austria Salzburg
Inter Milan won 2-0 on aggregate

1995: PARMA

1ST LEG May 3

Parma **1-0** Juventus
(Italy) (Italy)

2ND LEG May 17

Juventus **1-1** Parma
Parma won 2-1 on aggregate

1996: BAYERN MUNICH

1ST LEG May 1

Bayern Munich **2-0** Bordeaux
(Germany) (France)

2ND LEG May 15

Bordeaux **1-3** Bayern Munich
Bayern Munich won 5-1 on aggregate

1997: FC SCHALKE 04

1ST LEG May 7

FC Schalke 04 **1-0** Inter Milan
(Germany) (Italy)

2ND LEG May 21

Inter Milan **1-0** FC Schalke 04
(aet)
FC Schalke 04 won 4-1 on penalties

1998: INTER MILAN

PARC DES PRINCES, PARIS May 6

Inter Milan **3-0** Lazio
(Italy) (Italy)

1999: PARMA

LUZHNIKI, MOSCOW May 12

Parma **3-0** Marseille
(Italy) (France)

2000: GALATASARAY

PARKEN, COPENHAGEN May 17

Galatasaray **0-0** Arsenal (aet)
(Turkey) (England)
Galatasaray won 4-1 on penalties

2001: LIVERPOOL

WESTFALEN, DORTMUND May 16

Liverpool **5-4** Alavés (aet)
(England) (Spain)

2002: FEYENOORD

DE KUIP, ROTTERDAM May 8

Feyenoord **3-2** Borussia
Dortmund
(Holland) (Germany)

2003: FC PORTO

OLIMPICO, SEVILLE May 21

Porto **3-2** Celtic (aet)
(Portugal) (Scotland)

2004: VALENCIA

NYA ULLEVI, GOTHENBURG May 19

Valencia **2-0** Marseille
(Spain) (France)

2005: CSKA MOSCOW

JOSÉ ALVALADE, LISBON May 18

CSKA Moscow **3-1** Sporting Lisbon
(Russia) (Portugal)

2006: SEVILLE

PSV STADIUM, EINDHOVEN May 10

Seville **4-0** Middlesbrough
(Spain) (England)

EUROPEAN CUP WINNERS' CUP

Above from left to right: Willie Miller leads Aberdeen's parade in 1983; Arsenal keeper David Seaman lifts the cup in 1994; Real Zaragoza celebrate after victory over Arsenal in 1995.

Opposite clockwise from top left: Dinamo Tbilisi celebrate in 1981; Lazio, winners of the last ever final in 1999; Ron Harris and the Chelsea team bring the cup home to their fans in 1971; Barcelona striker Gary Lineker holds the cup in 1989.

When Lazio's Pavel Nedved struck home the winning goal against Mallorca in the 81st minute of the 1999 European Cup Winners' Cup final at Villa Park, he was not only ensuring the win for the Rome side, he was also entering the history books as the last ever player to score in the tournament. After 39 years the competition was discontinued, and swallowed up by the expanded UEFA Cup. This was due in the most part to the increased importance of the Champions League, and pressure on UEFA to streamline its European club fixtures. The final nail in the competition's coffin could be said to be Barcelona's decision to play in the Champions League rather than defend their title in 1998.

The European Cup Winners' Cup was launched in 1960, and organised to run in parallel with the UEFA Cup. Based on the same format as the European Cup, with home and away knockout ties up to the final, the participants in the competition were generally the winners of their domestic cup, as well as the previous season's holders. However, if the cup winners were identical to the winners of the national championship (who would therefore be competing in the European Cup), the runners-up in the cup competition would take part. At the time the tournament was established many European countries didn't possess a domestic cup competition, but the promise of qualification and extra revenue meant they soon acquired one.

The first Cup Winners' Cup tournament attracted teams from ten countries. Inspired by legendary Swedish winger Kurt Hamrin, the trophy was won by Fiorentina – the first piece of European silverware to be won by an Italian side. They overcame Rangers 4-1 on aggregate in a final played over two legs (the format changed to a one-off game the following year). Rangers themselves reached the final after disposing of Wolverhampton Wanderers in a keenly contested all-British semi-final.

With the competition deemed a success, the following year saw a far larger pool of entrants, with some 23 countries now taking part. The final again saw Fiorentina involved, but this time they were deprived of the distinction of retaining their title by Atlético Madrid, who lifted the cup after a 3-0 replay win. Curiously, the replay was played nearly four months after the original game.

In 1963 the holders once again had the opportunity to retain their trophy by making it to the final, but this time Atlético fell at the last hurdle. Their conquerors were Bill Nicholson's double-winning Tottenham side, and the result was an emphatic 5-1 win, with the prolific Jimmy Greaves and Terry Dyson both getting on the scoresheet twice. The victory made Tottenham the first English club to get their hands on a European trophy. Over the course of its 39 years the Cup Winners' Cup saw many British clubs making it to the final. In 1965, in front of a 100,000 capacity Wembley crowd, West Ham United brought the trophy back to London with their 2-0 defeat of TSV 1860 Munich. Neighbours Chelsea made it a hat-trick for sides from the English

capital in 1971 with their stunning Peter Osgood-inspired replay victory over the mighty Real Madrid. The year before, northern pride had been restored with Manchester City's victory over Górnik Zabrze of Poland. The silverware headed to Maine Road thanks to goals by Neil Young and Francis Lee.

Rangers also had success in the competition, and over the course of the 1972 final they narrowly got the better of Dinamo Moscow, coming out of the game 3-2 winners after leading 3-0 for much of the game. This was third time lucky for the Glasgow side, who were on the wrong end of two final defeats in 1960 and 1967. It wasn't always plain sailing for the English clubs that made the final either. In the 1966 final Liverpool were unlucky to lose out to Borussia Dortmund after extra-time, and a similar fate befell Leeds United (1973), West Ham (1976) and Arsenal (1980 and 1995) in subsequent finals. Arsenal's 1980 defeat was against Valencia, and after a 0-0 draw it was the first European club final to be decided on penalties. It was former England midfielder Graham Rix's failure from the spot that gave the Spaniards the trophy.

After an 11 year gap without any British success it was left to Alex Ferguson's Aberdeen to heroically recapture the Cup Winners' Cup in 1983, and they achieved it at the expense of Real Madrid. Played in atrocious weather conditions, the match was settled by substitute John Hewitt's diving header in extra-time and was a famous victory for the Scottish side. Since Aberdeen's triumph there have been four

Top left: Parma's Lorenzo Minotti at Wembley in 1993.

Top right: West Ham's Bobby Moore shows the cup to the fans outside the Town Hall in 1965.

Opposite top: Youri Djorkaeff of Paris Sant-Germain in action in the 1996 final.

Opposite bottom: Rangers keeper Billy Ritchie saves a shot from Fiorentina's Kurt Hamrin in the first leg of the final in 1961.

Below: Terry Dyson and Jimmy Greaves of Tottenham give a victory thumbs-up. They scored two goals each in the 1963 final.

other British successes. In 1985 Howard Kendall's Everton disposed of Rapid Vienna with a clinical 3-1 win, with goals from Andy Gray, Trevor Steven and Kevin Sheedy. It was to be the last time English clubs participated in European competition until 1991, following their ban in the wake of the Heysel tragedy. This was the year that saw Manchester United take the honours from Barcelona with Mark Hughes starring in a 2-1 win.

In 1994 Arsenal finally got their name on the trophy with a 1-0 victory, courtesy of an Alan Smith goal against the much-fancied Parma. The following year they were to suffer heartache as former Tottenham midfielder Nayim, now playing for Real Zaragoza, famously chipped David Seaman from nearly the half-way line. The last English side to win the trophy were Chelsea, who secured the title for a second time in 1998 with their narrow win against Stuttgart in Stockholm, thanks to an opportunistic strike from Gianfranco Zola. The Italian had only come on a minute earlier as a substitute and found the roof of the net with his first touch.

Other teams to win the Cup Winners' Cup on more than one occasion were AC Milan (1968 and 1973), Anderlecht (1976 and 1978), and Dynamo Kiev (1975 and 1986). However, if there was one team who could lay claim to being the team of the tournament over its entire history, then it would have to be Barcelona. The Catalan side have lifted the trophy four times – ironic then, that their refusal to play in the tournament in 1998 would (indirectly) lead to the discontinuance of the competition.

Their first success was in the 1979 final when they edged out Fortuna Düsseldorf 4-3 in extra-time in one of the great finals of the competition's history. The 1982 final saw them storm to victory over Standard Liege in front of 100,000 fans in their own stadium, while a 2-0 victory over Italian side Sampdoria in 1989 at the Wankdorf Stadium in Berne, Switzerland, saw them complete a hat-trick of victories. The string of successes was rounded off in the 1997 final when Ronaldo's 37th minute penalty was enough to defeat Paris Saint-Germain. The French side were the holders of the trophy, and with no side ever managing to retain the Cup Winners' Cup,

history, as well as the referee's whistle, was clearly against them.

Throughout the history of the tournament many high-profile sides, such as Barcelona, had laid claim to the trophy. However, part of the event's charm lay in the fact that some of the lesser known clubs were also able to compete against the major teams of European football, something that rarely happened in the UEFA Cup, and was even scarcer in the European Cup. In 1981, arguably the greatest ever shock of the Cup Winners' Cup came about when Welsh Cup winners Newport County somehow managed to reach the quarter-finals, one round further than the holders Valencia. Newport were in the English Division Four at the time.

Smaller clubs to go all the way to the final have included Slovan Bratislava, who in 1969 saw off the challenge of Barcelona to lift the trophy in a famous 3-2 victory for the Slovak side. In 1974 FC Magdeburg of East Germany held the trophy aloft after beating a star-studded AC Milan side 2-0 in Rotterdam. Georgia's Dynamo Tbilisi ran out winners in 1981, and Belgium's Mechelen also added their name to the roll of honour in 1988 with a win over Dutch giants Ajax.

Always the third tournament behind the European Cup and the UEFA Cup in terms of prestige in the European club calendar, nevertheless the Cup Winners' Cup packed a lot of passion, spectacle and great football into its 39 year history. Nedved's goal ensures that Lazio will be the holders of the trophy in perpetuity, but such giants of the game as Barcelona, AC Milan, Manchester United and Juventus all have fond memories of a trophy that for a period of time proudly sat in a special place in their trophy cabinet.

THE WINNERS OF THE EUROPEAN CUP WINNERS' CUP

1961: FIORENTINA
1ST LEG May 17

Rangers **0-2** Fiorentina
(Scotland) (Italy)

2ND LEG May 27

Fiorentina **2-1** Rangers
Fiorentina won 4-1 on aggregate

1962: ATLÉTICO MADRID
HAMPDEN PARK, GLASGOW May 10

Atlético Madrid **1-1** Fiorentina
(Spain) (Italy)

REPLAY: NECKAR, STUTTGART
September 5

Atlético Madrid **3-0** Fiorentina

1963: TOTTENHAM HOTSPUR
DE KUIP, ROTTERDAM May 15

Tottenham **5-1** Atlético Madrid
Hotspur
(England) (Spain)

1964: SPORTING LISBON
HEYSEL, BRUSSELS May 13

Sporting Lisbon **3-3** MTK Budapest (aet)
(Portugal) (Hungary)

REPLAY: BOSUIL, ANTWERP
May 15

Sporting Lisbon **1-0** MTK Budapest

1965: WEST HAM UNITED
WEMBLEY, LONDON May 19

West Ham United **2-0** 1860 Munich
(England) (West Germany)

1966: BORUSSIA DORTMUND
HAMPDEN PARK, GLASGOW May 5

Borussia **2-1** Liverpool (aet)
Dortmund
(West Germany) (England)

1967: BAYERN MUNICH
FRANKEN, NÜREMBERG May 31

Bayern Munich **1-0** Rangers (aet)
(West Germany) (Scotland)

1968: AC MILAN
DE KUIP, ROTTERDAM May 23

AC Milan **2-0** Hamburg
(Italy) (West Germany)

1969: SLOVAN BRATISLAVA
ST JAKOB, BASLE May 21

Slovan Bratislava **3-2** Barcelona
(Czechoslovakia) (Spain)

1970: MANCHESTER CITY
PRATER, VIENNA May 29

Manchester City **2-1** Górnik Zabrze
(England) (Poland)

1971: CHELSEA
KARAISKAKIS, PIRAEUS May 19

Chelsea **1-1** Real Madrid (aet)
(England) (Spain)

REPLAY: KARAISKAKIS, PIRAEUS May 21

Chelsea **2-1** Real Madrid

1972: RANGERS
NOU CAMP, BARCELONA May 24

Rangers **3-2** Dinamo Moscow
(Scotland) (Soviet Union)

1973: AC MILAN
KAFTANTZOGLIO SALONICA May 16

AC Milan **1-0** Leeds United
(Italy) (England)

1974: FC MAGDEBURG
DE KUIP, ROTTERDAM May 8

FC Magdeburg **2-0** AC Milan
(East Germany) (Italy)

1975: DYNAMO KIEV
ST JAKOB, BASLE May 14

Dynamo Kiev **3-0** Ferencváros
(Soviet Union) (Hungary)

1976: RSC ANDERLECHT
HEYSEL, BRUSSELS May 5

Anderlecht **4-2** West Ham United
(Belgium) (England)

1977: HAMBURG
OLYMPISCH, AMSTERDAM May 11

Hamburg **2-0** RSC Anderlecht
(West Germany) (Belgium)

1978: RSC ANDERLECHT
PARC DES PRINCES, PARIS May 3

Anderlecht **4-0** Austria Vienna
(Belgium) (Austria)

1979: BARCELONA
ST JAKOB, BASLE May 16

Barcelona **4-3** Fortuna
Düsseldorf (aet)
(Spain) (West Germany)

1980: VALENCIA
HEYSEL, BRUSSELS May 14

Valencia **0-0** Arsenal (aet)
(Spain) (England)
Valencia won 5-4 on penalties

1981: DYNAMO TBILISI
RHEIN, DÜSSELDORF May 13

Dynamo Tbilisi **2-1** FC Carl-Zeiss
Jena
(Soviet Union) (East Germany)

1982: BARCELONA
NOU CAMP, BARCELONA May 12

Barcelona **2-1** Standard Liège
(Spain) (Belgium)

1983: ABERDEEN
NYA ULLEVI, GOTHENBURG May 11

Aberdeen **2-1** Real Madrid (aet)
(Scotland) (Spain)

1984: JUVENTUS
ST JAKOB, BASLE May 16

Juventus **2-1** FC Porto
(Italy) (Portugal)

1985: EVERTON
DE KUIP, ROTTERDAM May 15

Everton **3-1** Rapid Vienna
(England) (Austria)

1986: DYNAMO KIEV
GERLAND, LYON May 2

Dynamo Kiev **3-0** Atlético Madrid
(Soviet Union) (Spain)

1987: AJAX
OLYMPIC, ATHENS May 13

Ajax **1-0** Lokomotive
Leipzig
(Holland) (East Germany)

1988: KV MECHELEN
MEINAU, STRASBOURG May 11

KV Mechelen **1-0** Ajax
(Belgium) (Holland)

1989: BARCELONA
WANKDORF, BERNE May 10

Barcelona **2-0** Sampdoria
(Spain) (Italy)

1990: SAMPDORIA
NYA ULLEVI, GOTHENBURG May 9

Sampdoria **2-0** Anderlecht (aet)
(Italy) (Belgium)

1991: MANCHESTER UNITED
DE KUIP, ROTTERDAM May 15

Manchester **2-1** Barcelona
United
(England) (Spain)

1992: WERDER BREMEN
ESTADIO DA LUZ, LISBON May 6

Werder Bremen **2-0** Monaco
(Germany) (France)

1993: PARMA
WEMBLEY, LONDON May 12

Parma **3-1** Royal Antwerp
(Italy) (Belgium)

1994: ARSENAL
PARKEN, COPENHAGEN May 4

Arsenal **1-0** Parma
(England) (Italy)

1995: REAL ZARAGOZA
PARC DES PRINCES, PARIS May 10

Real Zaragoza **2-1** Arsenal (aet)
(Spain) (England)

1996: PARIS SAINT-GERMAIN
KING BAUDOUIN, BRUSSELS May 8

Paris Saint- **1-0** Rapid Vienna
Germain
(France) (Austria)

1997: BARCELONA
DE KUIP, ROTTERDAM May 14

Barcelona **1-0** Paris Saint-
Germain
(Spain) (France)

1998: CHELSEA
RASUNDA, STOCKHOLM May 13

Chelsea **1-0** Stuttgart
(England) (Germany)

1999: LAZIO
VILLA PARK, BIRMINGHAM May 19

Lazio **2-1** Mallorca
(Italy) (Spain)

COPA LIBERTADORES
(THE SOUTH AMERICAN CLUB CUP)

The Copa Libertadores is the premier club event in South America, and has been played between the continent's top sides on an annual basis since its inception in 1960. Very much the equivalent of the European Cup, the competition was sparked into life when UEFA proposed that the champions of Europe should play against the South American champions for a world title (the World Club Cup). Seven national league winners competed home and away on a knockout basis. In the inaugural tournament it was Uruguay's Peñarol who were first to lift the trophy, beating Olimpia of Paraguay 1-0 in the first leg and drawing 1-1 in the second. Rather than winning on goal aggregate they were deemed to have won on points, having a win and a draw to Olimpia's one draw and a defeat. This system continued until 1988 when goal aggregate was introduced.

The competition was not without historical precedent, as in 1948 a similar tournament was held in Chile, staged by Santiago's leading club, Colo Colo. The event was won by Brazil's Vasco Da Gama, but proved to be such a financial disaster for all involved that it was not staged again. It was with such an uncertain legacy that the current Copa Libertadores was launched. However, the tournament has not only survived but flourished, despite format changes and many moments of controversy, to become the most important date in the South American football calendar, far exceeding the Copa América in terms of popularity.

In 1962 Pelé, by then a star on the global stage, gave the competition's profile a much needed image boost as his Santos side got the better of Peñarol (still the champions after having retained their title in 1961). Although the first leg in Montevideo had been played out without incident, resulting in a 2-1 win for Santos, the second leg was far more unsavoury, the game suspended shortly after half-time as the referee was knocked unconscious by a stone thrown from the crowd. After a lengthy delay the game was restarted with Peñarol ahead 3-2, only for a linesman to endure the same fate, just as Peñarol were on the verge of adding to their lead. The game was abandoned and awarded to the Uruguayans, forcing a play-off which saw Santos come out 3-0 winners. The following year they retained the trophy, beating Boca Juniors convincingly both home and away with Pelé at the fore.

It was to be the last time a Brazilian side won the Copa Libertadores for 13 years. This was due, in part, to the strong Argentinian teams taking the event more seriously, but also to a four-year Brazilian boycott from 1966 to 1970, after an amendment to the competition's format allowed the entry of league runners-up. The extra fixtures not only caused disruption to the Brazilian national league, but reduced the tournament's financial rewards.

The boycott opened the door for Peñarol to claim another title, this time snatching victory from River Plate with 4-2 win after a replay. Two of the goals were scored by Alberto Spencer, one of the tournament's most prolific marksmen. Sadly, the event was again spoilt by controversy, as two former Peñarol players in the River Plate side, Cubilla and Matosas, were accused of deliberately 'throwing' the game.

In 1969, two of the strongest Argentine clubs, Velez Sarsfield and River Plate, followed Brazil's example and played no part in the tournament in protest over fixture congestion. This action inevitably lead to CONMEBOL streamlining the competition by reducing the number of group matches and the following year the teams of both countries joined as normal.

In the early Seventies it was Buenos Aires club Independiente, who dominated the competition with a remarkable run of four consecutive titles. In 1972 The Red Devils got the better of Universitario de Deportes of Peru, while Colo Colo were their victims the following year in a close fought play-off game. Once again the 1974 final couldn't be decided over two legs, but Independiente held their nerve to claim a 1-0 victory over São Paulo. Their fantastic run culminated with a win over Chile's Unión Española in 1975. Again the tournament was won as a result of a play-off game, with the Argentine side winning 2-0, with goals from Ruiz Moreno and Bertoni. Independiente still hold the record for the most titles with seven.

Independiente's run of unparalleled success was finally brought to an end by Cruzeiro of Brazil, who included veteran Jairzinho in their side. However, with the notable exception of a Zico-inspired Flamengo in 1981, it was to be teams from Argentina and Uruguay that continued to dominate the Copa Libertadores in the late Seventies and through the Eighties. Boca Juniors won the trophy in 1977 and 1978,

Above from left to right: Arnulfo Valentierra raises the trophy for Once Caldas in 2004; a River Plate players kisses the trophy in 1996; Cruzeiro of Brazil after their triumph in 1997.

Opposite clockwise from top left: Carlos Tevez of Boca Juniors in 2003; São Paulo keeper Rogerio in 2005; Grêmio celebrate in 1995; Palmeiras in 1999.

Above: Juan Riquelme is carried by his Boca Juniors team-mates after victory in 2001.

Below right: Olimpia of Paraguay kiss the trophy in 2002.

Opposite: São Paulo's Marcio Amoroso celebrates his goal in the second leg of the 2005 final.

with Argentinian sides River Plate, Argentinos Juniors and Independiente also savouring victory during a rich period for the nation. For Uruguay, both Peñarol (1982 and 1987) and Nacional (1980 and 1988) completed a brace of victories. The latter's 1988 win was to be the last time a Uruguayan side picked up the cup.

The smaller nations were at last beginning to challenge the long-established monopoly of South America's major football nations. The first team from outside Brazil, Argentina or Uruguay to succeed were Olimpia of Paraguay in 1979; they defeated the mighty Boca Juniors 2-0 in their home leg, and managed to secure a 0-0 draw in Buenos Aires to claim the trophy.

From 1985 through to 1987, Colombian side America de Cali competed in three consecutive finals, but were unfortunate to be runners-up each time. A similar fate was suffered by Cobreloa of Chile, who finished on the losing end in both 1981 and 1982. But the less celebrated nations were not to be denied: Colombia's Atletico Nacional narrowly defeated Olimpia in 1989, and the following year the Paraguayan side made it to the final again, this time defeating Ecuador's Barcelona. In 1991 the pattern continued and major sides were once again frozen out when Colo Colo of Chile claiming the trophy for the first time. These successes coincided with a format change in 1988: two-legged knockouts for the quarter-finals and semi-finals, and extra-time and penalties to decide the final instead of a play-off.

Considering the country's dominance on the international stage, the record of Brazilian sides was a relatively poor one coming into the Nineties. This was all set to change, however. In 1992, with talented midfielder Raí pulling the strings in midfield, São Paulo beat Newell's

Old Boys 3-2 on penalties. The following year, with a team including international players such as Cafu, Paulinha and Muller among their ranks, they defeated Chile's Universidad Catolica 5-3 on aggregate. The competition, always reflecting the shift in power of South American club football, then saw Brazilian sides win a further four of the next six titles, with separate wins for Gremio, Cruzeiro, Vasco da Gama and Palmeiras.

Trends never last in the South American Club Cup though, and the new millennium saw a resurgence from Argentine giants, Boca Juniors. A talented side, under coach Carlos Bianchi they claimed back-to-back titles in 2000 and 2001 with penalty shoot-out victories

against Palmeiras and Cruz Azul (clubs from Mexico were first invited to play in 1998). Indeed, 2001 saw the competition relaunched with another new format, plus a lucrative TV deal and sponsorship. Where only five sides had previously been eliminated at the group stages, now 16 dropped out. This has helped to discourage negative play, and the more attacking style of football has made the Copa Libertadores much more entertaining.

Olimpia won the cup for the second time in 2002, while Boca Juniors beat Santos in both legs the following year. In 2004 the underdog triumphed as tiny Colombian side Once Caldas put Brazilian giants Santos and São Paulo to the sword on the way to the final. Waiting for them would be Boca Juniors, who had scraped through two violent semi-final clashes with local rivals River Plate. The Colombians defended well in Buenos Aires to come away from the first leg of the final with a draw, but River Plate lost their nerve in the return leg, missing four penalties in a row in the shoot-out to allow Once Caldas to lift the Copa Libertadores trophy for the first time.

Due to a change to the rules the previous year, the 2005 final was the first final contested between teams from the same country. It was also the first time the 'away goals' rule could be employed to decide games. After a 1-1 draw with Atlético Paranaense is the first leg, São Paulo won the cup with a 4-0 home win in the return, Atlético blowing their chance to score from the penalty spot when only one goal down.

The competition has now become more popular than ever. Despite its many problems in the past, and the current dire financial plight of many of South America's high-profile club sides, the ever-improving Copa Libertadores has the strength and will to keep evolving, and is now truly established as one of the great international club competitions.

THE WINNERS OF THE COPA LIBERTADORES

1960: PEÑAROL
1ST LEG June 12
Peñarol **1-0** Olimpia
(Uruguay) (Paraguay)
2ND LEG June 19
Olimpia **1-1** Peñarol
Peñarol won on points aggregate

1961: PEÑAROL
1ST LEG June 4
Peñarol **1-0** Palmeiras
(Uruguay) (Brazil)
2ND LEG June 11
Palmeiras **1-1** Peñarol
Peñarol won on points aggregate

1962: SANTOS
1ST LEG July 28
Peñarol **1-2** Santos
(Uruguay) (Brazil)
2ND LEG August 2
Santos **2-3** Peñarol
PLAY-OFF August 30
Santos **3-0** Peñarol

1963: SANTOS
1ST LEG September 3
Santos **3-2** Boca Juniors
(Brazil) (Argentina)
2ND LEG September 11
Boca Juniors **1-2** Santos
Santos won on points aggregate

1964: INDEPENDIENTE
1ST LEG August 6
Nacional **0-0** Independiente
(Uruguay) (Argentina)
2ND LEG August 12
Independiente **1-0** Nacional
Independiente won on points aggregate

1965: INDEPENDIENTE
1ST LEG April 9
Independiente **1-0** Peñarol
(Argentina) (Uruguay)
2ND LEG April 12
Peñarol **3-1** Independiente
PLAY-OFF April 15
Independiente **4-1** Peñarol

1966: PEÑAROL
1ST LEG May 12
Peñarol **2-0** River Plate
(Uruguay) (Argentina)
2ND LEG May 18
River Plate **3-2** Peñarol
PLAY-OFF May 20
Peñarol **4-2** River Plate (aet)

1967: RACING CLUB
1ST LEG August 15
Racing Club **0-0** Nacional
(Argentina) (Uruguay)
2ND LEG August 25
Nacional **0-0** Racing Club
(aet)
PLAY-OFF August 29
Racing Club **2-1** Nacional

1968: ESTUDIANTES DE LA PLATA
1ST LEG May 2
Estudiantes **2-1** Palmeiras
de La Plata
(Argentina) (Brazil)
2ND LEG May 7
Palmeiras **3-1** Estudiantes
de La Plata
PLAY-OFF May 15
Estudiantes **2-0** Palmeiras
de La Plata

1969: ESTUDIANTES DE LA PLATA
1ST LEG May 15
Nacional **0-1** Estudiantes
de La Plata
(Uruguay) (Argentina)
2ND LEG May 22
Estudiantes **2-0** Nacional
de La Plata
Estudiantes de La Plata on points aggregate

1970: ESTUDIANTES DE LA PLATA
1ST LEG May 21
Estudiantes **1-0** Peñarol
de La Plata
(Argentina) (Uruguay)
2ND LEG May 27
Peñarol **0-0** Estudiantes
de La Plata
Estudiantes de La Plata on points aggregate

1971: NACIONAL
1ST LEG May 26
Estudiantes **1-0** Nacional
de La Plata
(Argentina) (Uruguay)
2ND LEG June 2
Nacional **1-0** Estudiantes
de La Plata
PLAY-OFF June 9
Nacional **2-0** Estudiantes
de La Plata

1972: INDEPENDIENTE
1ST LEG May 17
Universitario **0-0** Independiente
de Deportes
(Peru) (Argentina)
2ND LEG May 24
Independiente **2-1** Universitario
de Deportes
Independiente won on points aggregate

1973: INDEPENDIENTE
1ST LEG May 22
Independiente **1-1** Colo Colo
(Argentina) (Chile)
2ND LEG May 29
Colo Colo **0-0** Independiente
PLAY-OFF June 6
Independiente **2-1** Colo Colo (aet)

1974: INDEPENDIENTE
1ST LEG October 12
São Paulo **2-1** Independiente
(Brazil) (Argentina)
2ND LEG October 16
Independiente **2-0** São Paulo
PLAY-OFF October 19
Independiente **1-0** São Paulo

1975: INDEPENDIENTE
1ST LEG June 18
Unión Española **1-0** Independiente
(Chile) (Argentina)
2ND LEG June 25
Independiente **3-1** Unión Española
PLAY-OFF June 29
Independiente **2-0** Unión Española

1976: CRUZEIRO
1ST LEG July 21
Cruzeiro **4-1** River Plate
(Brazil) (Argentina)
2ND LEG July 28
River Plate **2-1** Cruzeiro
PLAY-OFF July 30
Cruzeiro **3-2** River Plate

1977: BOCA JUNIORS
1ST LEG September 6
Boca Juniors **1-0** Cruzeiro
(Argentina) (Brazil)
2ND LEG September 11
Cruzeiro **1-0** Boca Juniors
PLAY-OFF September 14
Boca Juniors **0-0** Cruzeiro (aet)
Boca Juniors won 5-4 on penalties

1978: BOCA JUNIORS
1ST LEG November 23
Deportivo Cali **0-0** Boca Juniors
(Colombia) (Argentina)
2ND LEG November 28
Boca Juniors **4-0** Deportivo Cali
Boco Juniors won on points aggregate

1979: OLIMPIA
1ST LEG July 22
Olimpia **2-0** Boca Juniors
(Paraguay) (Argentina)
2ND LEG July 27
Boca Juniors **0-0** Olimpia
Olimpia won on points aggregate

1980: NACIONAL
1ST LEG July 30
Internacional **0-0** Nacional
Porto Alegre
(Brazil) (Uruguay)
2ND LEG August 6
Nacional **1-0** Internacional
Porto Alegre
Nacional won on points aggregate

1981: FLAMENGO
1ST LEG November 13
Flamengo **2-1** Cobreloa
(Brazil) (Chile)
2ND LEG November 20
Cobreloa **1-0** Flamengo
PLAY-OFF November 23
Flamengo **2-0** Cobreloa

1982: PEÑAROL
1ST LEG November 26
Peñarol **0-0** Cobreloa
(Uruguay) (Chile)
2ND LEG November 30
Cobreloa **0-1** Peñarol
Peñarol won on points aggregate

1983: GRÊMIO
1ST LEG July 22
Peñarol **1-1** Grêmio
(Uruguay) (Brazil)
2ND LEG July 28
Grêmio **2-1** Peñarol
Grêmio won on points aggregate

1984: INDEPENDIENTE
1ST LEG July 24
Grêmio **0-1** Independiente
(Brazil) (Argentina)
2ND LEG July 27
Independiente **0-0** Grêmio
Independiente won on points aggregate

1985: ARGENTINOS JUNIORS
1ST LEG October 17
Argentinos **1-0** América Cali
Juniors
(Argentina) (Colombia)
2ND LEG October 22
América Cali **1-0** Argentinos
Juniors
PLAY-OFF October 24
Argentinos **1-1** América Cali (aet)
Juniors
Argentinos Juniors won 5-4 penalties

1986: RIVER PLATE
1ST LEG October 22
América Cali **1-2** River Plate
(Colombia) (Argentina)
2ND LEG October 29
River Plate **1-0** América Cali
River Plate won on points aggregate

1987: PEÑAROL
1ST LEG October 21
América Cali **2-0** Peñarol
(Colombia) (Uruguay)
2ND LEG October 28
Peñarol **2-1** América Cali
PLAY-OFF October 31
Peñarol **1-0** América Cali (aet)

1988: NACIONAL
1ST LEG October 19
Newell's Old Boys **1-0** Nacional
(Argentina) (Uruguay)
2ND LEG October 26
(aet) Nacional **3-0** Newell's Old Boys
Nacional won 3-1 on aggregate

1989: ATLÉTICO NACIONAL
1ST LEG May 24
Olimpia **2-0** Atlético Nacional
(Paraguay) (Colombia)
2ND LEG May 31
Atlético Nacional **2-0** Olimpia (aet)
Atlético Nacional won 5-4 on penalties

1990: OLIMPIA
1ST LEG Oct 3
Olimpia **2-0** Barcelona
(Paraguay) (Ecuador)
2ND LEG October 10
Barcelona **1-1** Olimpia
Olimpia won 3-1 on aggregate

1991: COLO COLO
1ST LEG May 29
Olimpia **0-0** Colo Colo
(Paraguay) (Chile)
2ND LEG June 5
Colo Colo **3-0** Olimpia
Colo Colo won 3-0 on aggregate

1992: SÃO PAULO
1ST LEG June 10
Newell's Old Boys **1-0** São Paulo
(Argentina) (Brazil)
2ND LEG June 17
São Paulo **1-0** Newell's Old Boys
(aet)
São Paulo won 3-2 on penalties

1993: SÃO PAULO
1ST LEG May 19
São Paulo **5-1** Universidad
Católica
(Brazil) (Chile)
2ND LEG May 26
Universidad **2-0** São Paulo
Católica
São Paulo won 5-3 on aggregate

1994: VÉLEZ SARSFIELD
1ST LEG August 24
Vélez Sarsfield **1-0** São Paulo
(Argentina) (Brazil)
2ND LEG August 31
São Paulo **1-0** Vélez Sarsfield
(aet)
Vélez Sarsfield won 5-3 on penalties

1995: GRÊMIO
1ST LEG August 24
Grêmio **3-1** Atlético Nacional
(Brazil) (Colombia)
2ND LEG August 30
Atlético Nacional **1-1** Grêmio
Grêmio won 4-2 on aggregate

1996: RIVER PLATE
1ST LEG June 19
América Cali **1-0** River Plate
(Colombia) (Argentina)
2ND LEG June 26
River Plate **2-0** América Cali
River Plate won 2-1 on aggregate

1997: CRUZEIRO
1ST LEG August 6
Sporting Cristal **0-0** Cruzeiro
(Peru) (Brazil)
2ND LEG August 13
Cruzeiro **1-0** Sporting Cristal
Cruzeiro won 1-0 on aggregate

1998: VASCO DA GAMA
1ST LEG August 12
Vasco da Gama **2-0** Barcelona
(Brazil) (Ecuador)
2ND LEG August 26
Barcelona **1-2** Vasco da Gama
Vasco da Gama won 4-1 on aggregate

1999: PALMEIRAS
1ST LEG June 2
Deportivo Cali **1-0** Palmeiras
(Colombia) (Brazil)
2ND LEG June 16
Palmeiras **2-1** Deportivo Cali
(aet)
Palmeiras won 4-3 on penalties

2000: BOCA JUNIORS
1ST LEG June 14
Boca Juniors **2-2** Palmeiras
(Argentina) (Brazil)
2ND LEG June 21
Palmeiras **0-0** Boca Juniors (aet)
Boca Juniors won 4-2 on penalties

2001: BOCA JUNIORS
1ST LEG June 20
Cruz Azul **0-1** Boca Juniors
(Mexico) (Argentina)
2ND LEG June 28
Boca Juniors **0-1** Cruz Azul (aet)
Boca Juniors won 3-1 on penalties

2002: OLIMPIA
1ST LEG July 24
Olimpia **0-1** São Caetano
(Paraguay) (Brazil)
2ND LEG July 31
São Caetano **1-2** Olimpia (aet)
Olimpia won 4-2 on penalties

2003: BOCA JUNIORS
1ST LEG June 25
Boca Juniors **2-0** Santos
(Argentina) (Brazil)
2ND LEG July 2
Santos **1-3** Boca Juniors
Boca Juniors won 5-1 on aggregate

2004: ONCE CALDAS
1ST LEG June 23
Once Caldas **0-0** Boca Juniors
(Colombia) (Argentina)
2ND LEG June 30
Boca Juniors **1-1** Once Caldas
Once Caldas won 2-0 on penalties

2005: SÃO PAULO
1ST LEG July 6
Atlético **1-1** São Paulo
Paranaense
(Brazil) (Brazil)
2ND LEG July 14
São Paulo **4-0** Atlético
Paranaense
São Paulo won 5-1 on aggregate

WORLD CLUB CUP & WORLD CLUB CHAMPIONSHIP

Above from left to right: Hernan Bermudez of Boca Juniors raises the cup after victory over Real Madrid in the 2000 World Club Cup; Ajax, winners in 1995; Bayern Munich in 2001.

Opposite clockwise from top left: Real Madrid with the World Club Cup in 2002; Corinthians celebrate the first World Club Championship in 2000; São Paulo after the 2005 World Club Championship; Manchester United enjoy their success in the 1999 World Club Cup.

Despite its grandiloquent title, the World Club Cup is widely regarded as an annual sideshow by all but the holders and their fans. Since the first contest – held between the winners of the European Cup and the Copa Libertadores – in 1960, it has enjoyed a chequered history, marred by violent encounters and withdrawals. If anything, its legacy has been a magnification of the cultural divide between Europe and South America.

The Intercontinental Cup, as it was first known, was a logical progression from the European Cup for UEFA general secretary Henri Delaunay, though it took several more years to organise. Played over two legs, home and away, the inaugural trophy was won by Real Madrid who had enjoyed an unbroken run of success in the European Cup since it commenced five years earlier. Just two months after their legendary 7-3 victory over Eintracht Frankfurt, Madrid travelled to Montevideo to face the Uruguayans, Peñarol. The encounter, a 0-0 draw, was played in monsoon conditions, but Real romped to a 5-1 win in the return with Puskás scoring twice.

Peñarol were back the following year and this time they struck the first blow for South America, beating Portugal's Benfica in a play-off, as aggregate goals did not count at the time. Eusébio made his debut in the deciding match after being flown in especially.

The cup was to reside in South America for three years with Pelé's awesome Santos winning it twice in succession. However, their second match against Milan began the trend towards foul play, with two players sent-off in the bad-tempered play-off game. The cup did eventually arrive in the city of Milan after the ultra-defensive Inter side triumphed twice in succession, conceding only one goal in two dour encounters with Argentinian team Independiente between 1964 and 1965.

The competition's descent into bad feeling plumbed new depths as the decade came to an end. In 1966 the Spanish press had rubbished the quality of the Uruguayan pitch, but it was the introduction of British teams that led to the descent into anarchy. In 1967 Celtic's 'Lisbon Lions' had become the first British side to lift the European Cup. Five months later they faced Argentina's Racing Club in a series of matches memorable only for the violence of the encounters. Anti-English feeling in Argentina was still running high after the 1966 World Cup encounter, which provoked England manager Ramsey to describe them as 'animals', and the Scots took the brunt of this sentiment.

Celtic won a bad-tempered first leg 1-0, but in the return tie, at the Avellaneda Stadium, goalkeeper Ronnie Simpson was struck by a brick before the kick-off and John Fallon had to take his place. The deciding game, staged in Montevideo, degenerated into war as Celtic had four players sent-off and Racing two. By the final whistle the 1-0 scoreline in the South Americans' favour was of little consequence. 'We should have stuck to our guns and refused to play a third match,' lamented Celtic chairman Bob Kelly after the event. 'We couldn't have expected it to be anything but a disgrace.'

If at all possible the spirit of competition worsened still further the following year when Manchester United met Estudiantes. Upon landing in Buenos Aires for the first leg, the English team were greeted with a polo match in their honour, but when their opponents boycotted the official reception the tone was set. The game descended into hostility with Nobby Stiles, described in the programme as 'brutal, badly intentioned and a bad sportsman', a target for ill-treatment. The aggression of Estudiantes was led by Carlos Bilardo, who was later to become Argentina's national team coach, lifting the World Cup in 1986.

Kicked and punched regularly, Stiles was eventually dismissed, not for retaliating, but for gesturing at a linesman over an offside call. George Best later recalled objects raining down on him every time he got the ball and decided he was better off not calling for it. In the equally bad-tempered return leg at Old Trafford he was dismissed for thumping his tormentor while the referee was in the process of booking him. Matt Busby later declared: 'Holding the ball out there put you in danger.'

Paddy Crerand's conclusion that 'the whole thing was a total waste of time' began to take seed with many European sides. The travelling was demanding, especially mid-season, and clubs were not willing to risk injury.

The Seventies were marked by a succession of withdrawals. Ajax declined to take part in 1971 and 1973 and were replaced by defeated finalists Panathinaikos and Juventus, both losing out to their South American opposition.

Above: Celtic's John Hughes in action against Racing Club in the 1967 final.

Opposite top: European defeat in 1994 as Velez Sarsfield beat AC Milan.

Opposite bottom: Vasco da Gama's Edmundo is brought down by Rincon of Corinthians during the World Club Championship in 2000.

Below left to right: Juan Veron scores against Manchester United as Estudiantes de La Plata win the 1968 World Club Cup; Liverpool defenders surround São Paulo forward Amoroso during the 2005 World Club Championship.

The withdrawals continued. In 1975 Bayern Munich's decision to opt out led to the cancellation of the match, but when they held on to their European crown the following season they were rewarded with the title 'world club champions' after beating Brazilians Cruzeiro. However, two years later the event was cancelled again when Liverpool declined to travel. Nottingham Forest followed suit in 1979 to be replaced by Swedes Malmö.

The competition was clearly doomed unless action was taken. The solution arrived in 1980 when Japanese vehicle manufacturers Toyota offered to sponsor the trophy if it was held in Tokyo. On February 11, 1981, 62,000 fans packed into the city's national stadium to witness the first Toyota Cup match between Nacional Montevideo and Brian Clough's Nottingham Forest. The Uruguayans won the tie 1-0 in a tight defensive encounter that saw them shut up shop after Victorino scored the only goal in the tenth minute.

With English clubs dominating Europe they contested the trophy for the next two seasons, but both Liverpool and Aston Villa lost out. In fact an English side would not lift the cup until 1999, when Manchester United capped their unique treble when Roy Keane volleyed home the only goal against Brazilians Palmeiras.

The competition's farcical side was again demonstrated when Cruzeiro of Brazil signed several players on loan, including Bebeto, for their 1997 encounter with Borussia Dortmund. Fortunately they were defeated.

The impact of Manchester United's 1999 win was undermined by the knowledge that the trophy was to be superseded by the World Club Championship just a few months later. After ten years in which the competition had degenerated into a pleasant sideshow, FIFA decided a revamp was necessary, allowing it to flex its muscles over rivals UEFA in the process. Architect Sepp Blatter decreed the trophy was now to be decided by a mini-tournament, something not greeted with much warmth by European leagues already suffering from fixture congestion. Manchester United and Real Madrid were selected to represent Europe against sides from South America, Oceania, Africa and Central America.

In England there was controversy over the withdrawal of the holders from the FA Cup to take part in the tournament, the club being put under pressure to go by a government wanting to secure the 2006 World Cup.

In the end the European sides failed to progress and the final was contested between Brazilian sides Corinthians and Vasco da Gama. The São Paulo club duly became first World Club Champions after a penalty shoot-out, pocketing a purse of $6 million.

Having rejigged the template once, FIFA attempted to expand the competition to 12 teams the following year, adding Japan's Jubilo Iwata as compensation for the curtailment of the Toyota Cup. But the 2001 tournament, scheduled to be played in Spain, had to be cancelled due to the bankruptcy of ISMM-ISL, FIFA's former marketing partner. All teams and Spain's government were compensated.

The World Club Cup continued in its usual format in Tokyo in November 2000, with Boca Juniors, Bayern Munich and Real Madrid lifting the trophy one after the other. The following two finals were both settled by penalty shoot-outs, Boca Juniors beating AC Milan in 2003, while Porto's game with Once Caldas of Colombia in 2004 needed 18 spot-kicks to settle the tie in favour of the Portuguese team.

Porto proved to be the final winners as it was decided to merge the competition with the World Club Championship in 2005, resulting in a six-team inter-continental tournament between the winners of the Copa Libertadores (São Paulo), the CONCACAF Champions Cup (Saprissa), and the Champions Leagues of Europe (Liverpool), Asia (Al Ittihad), Africa (Al-Ahly) and Oceania (Sydney). Against the run of play, São Paulo beat Liverpool 1-0 in Yokohama to win the cup.

While the World Club Championship proved a success, the future of the World Club Cup looks as uncertain as its past, as there have been rumours of bringing it back between the winners of the Recopa Sudamericana and the European Super Cup.

THE WINNERS OF THE WORLD CLUB CUP (THE INTERCONTINENTAL CUP)

1960: REAL MADRID
1ST LEG July 3
Peñarol **0-0** Real Madrid
(Uruguay)   (Spain)
2ND LEG September 4
Real Madrid **5-1** Peñarol
Real Madrid won 5-1 aggregate

1961: PEÑAROL
1ST LEG September 4
Benfica **1-0** Peñarol
(Portugal)   (Uruguay)
2ND LEG September 17
Peñarol **5-0** Benfica
PLAY-OFF September 19
Peñarol **2-1** Benfica

1962: SANTOS
1ST LEG September 19
Santos **3-2** Benfica
(Brazil)   (Portugal)
2ND LEG October 11
Benfica **2-5** Santos
Santos won 8-4 on aggregate

1963: SANTOS
1ST LEG October 16
AC Milan **4-2** Santos
(Italy)   (Brazil)
2ND LEG November 14
Santos **4-2** AC Milan
PLAY-OFF November 16
Santos **1-0** AC Milan

1964: INTER MILAN
1ST LEG September 9
Independiente **1-0** Inter Milan
(Argentina)   (Italy)
2ND LEG September 23
Inter Milan **2-0** Independiente
PLAY-OFF September 26
Inter Milan **1-0** Independiente
(aet)

1965: INTER MILAN
1ST LEG September 8
Inter Milan **3-0** Independiente
(Italy)   (Argentina)
2ND LEG September 15
Independiente **0-0** Inter Milan
Inter Milan won 3-0 on aggregate

1966: PEÑAROL
1ST LEG October 12
Peñarol **2-0** Real Madrid
(Uruguay)   (Spain)
2ND LEG October 26
Real Madrid **0-2** Peñarol
Peñarol won 4-0 on aggregate

1967: RACING CLUB
1ST LEG October 18
Celtic **1-0** Racing Club
(Scotland)   (Argentina)
2ND LEG November 1
Racing Club **2-1** Celtic
PLAY-OFF November 4
Racing Club **1-0** Celtic

1968: ESTUDIANTES DE LA PLATA
1ST LEG September 25
Estudiantes **1-0** Manchester
de la Plata   United
(Argentina)   (England)
2ND LEG October 16
Manchester **1-1** Estudiantes
United   de la Plata
Estudiantes de la Plata won 2-1 on aggregate

1969: AC MILAN
1ST LEG September 8
AC Milan **3-0** Estudiantes
de la Plata
(Italy)   (Argentina)
2ND LEG October 22
Estudiantes **2-1** AC Milan
de la Plata
AC Milan won 4-2 on aggregate

1970: FEYENOORD
1ST LEG August 26
Estudiantes **2-2** Feyenoord
de la Plata
(Argentina)   (Holland)
2ND LEG September 9
Feyenoord **1-0** Estudiantes
de la Plata
Feyenoord won 3-2 on aggregate

1971: NACIONAL MONTEVIDEO
1ST LEG December 15
Panathinaikos **1-1** Nacional
Montevideo
(Greece)   (Uruguay)
2ND LEG December 29
Nacional **2-1** Panathinaikos
Montevideo
Nacional Montevideo won 3-2 on aggregate

1972: AJAX
1ST LEG September 6
Independiente **1-1** Ajax
(Argentina)   (Holland)
2ND LEG September 28
Ajax **3-0** Independiente
Ajax won 4-1 on aggregate

1973: INDEPENDIENTE
OLYMPIC STADIUM, ROME November 28
Independiente **1-0** Juventus
(Argentina)   (Italy)

1974: ATLÉTICO MADRID
1ST LEG March 12
Independiente **1-0** Atlético Madrid
(Argentina)   (Spain)
2ND LEG April 10
Atlético Madrid **2-0** Independiente
Atlético Madrid won 2-1 on aggregate

1975
Bayern Munich **v** Independiente
(West Germany)   (Argentina)
Not contested

1976: BAYERN MUNICH
1ST LEG November 23
Bayern Munich **2-0** Cruzeiro
(West Germany)   (Brazil)
2ND LEG December 21
Cruzeiro **0-0** Bayern Munich
Bayern Munich won 2-0 on aggregate

1977: BOCA JUNIORS
1ST LEG March 21, 1978
Boca Juniors **2-2** Borussia
Mönchengladbach
(Argentina)   (West Germany)
2ND LEG August 1, 1978
Borussia **0-3** Boca Juniors
Mönchengladbach
Boca Juniors won 5-2 on aggregate

1978
Liverpool **v** Boca Juniors
(England)   (Argentina)
Not contested

1979: OLIMPIA
1ST LEG November 18, 1979
Malmö **0-1** Olimpia
(Sweden)   (Paraguay)
2ND LEG March 2, 1980
Olimpia **2-1** Malmö
Olimpia won 3-1 on aggregate

1980: NACIONAL
NATIONAL STADIUM, TOKYO February 11
Nacional **1-0** Nottingham
Forest
(Uruguay)   (England)

1981: FLAMENGO
NATIONAL STADIUM, TOKYO December 13
Flamengo **3-0** Liverpool
(Brazil)   (England)

1982: PEÑAROL
NATIONAL STADIUM, TOKYO December 12
Peñarol **2-0** Aston Villa
(Uruguay)   (England)

1983: GRÊMIO
NATIONAL STADIUM, TOKYO December 11
Grêmio **2-1** Hamburg
(Brazil)   (West Germany)

1984: INDEPENDIENTE
NATIONAL STADIUM, TOKYO December 9
Independiente **1-0** Liverpool
(Argentina)   (England)

1985: JUVENTUS
NATIONAL STADIUM, TOKYO December 8
Juventus **2-2** Argentinos
Juniors (aet)
(Italy)   (Argentina)
Juventus won 4-2 on penalties

1986: RIVER PLATE
NATIONAL STADIUM, TOKYO December 14
River Plate **1-0** Steaua
Bucharest
(Argentina)   (Romania)

1987: FC PORTO
NATIONAL STADIUM, TOKYO December 13
FC Porto **2-1** Peñarol (aet)
(Portugal)   (Uruguay)

1988: NACIONAL
NATIONAL STADIUM, TOKYO December 11
Nacional **2-2** PSV Eindhoven
(aet)
(Uruguay)   (Holland)
Nacional won 7-6 on penalties

1989: AC MILAN
NATIONAL STADIUM, TOKYO December 17
AC Milan **1-0** Atlético Nacional
(aet)
(Italy)   (Columbia)

1990: AC MILAN
NATIONAL STADIUM, TOKYO December 9
AC Milan **3-0** Olimpia
(Italy)   (Paraguay)

1991: RED STAR BELGRADE
NATIONAL STADIUM, TOKYO December 8
Red Star Belgrade **3-0** Colo Colo
(Yugoslavia)   (Chile)

1992: SÃO PAULO
NATIONAL STADIUM, TOKYO December 13
São Paulo **2-1** Barcelona
(Brazil)   (Spain)

1993: SÃO PAULO
NATIONAL STADIUM, TOKYO December 12
São Paulo **3-2** Milan
(Brazil)   (Italy)

1994: VÉLEZ SARSFIELD
NATIONAL STADIUM, TOKYO December 1
Vélez Sarsfield **2-0** AC Milan
(Argentina)   (Italy)

1995: AJAX
NATIONAL STADIUM, TOKYO November 28
Ajax **0-0** Grêmio (aet)
(Holland)   (Brazil)
Ajax won 4-3 on penalties

1996: JUVENTUS
NATIONAL STADIUM, TOKYO November 26
Juventus **1-0** River Plate
(Italy)   (Argentina)

1997: BORUSSIA DORTMUND
NATIONAL STADIUM, TOKYO December 2
Borussia **2-0** Cruzeiro
Dortmund
(Germany)   (Brazil)

1998: REAL MADRID
NATIONAL STADIUM, TOKYO December 1
Real Madrid **2-1** Vasco da Gama
(Spain)   (Brazil)

1999: MANCHESTER UNITED
NATIONAL STADIUM, TOKYO November 30
Manchester **1-0** Palmeiras
United
(England)   (Brazil)

2000: BOCA JUNIORS
NATIONAL STADIUM, TOKYO November 28
Boca Juniors **2-1** Real Madrid
(Argentina)   (Spain)

2001: BAYERN MUNICH
NATIONAL STADIUM, TOKYO November 27
Bayern Munich **1-0** Boca Juniors (aet)
(Germany)   (Argentina)

2002: REAL MADRID
YOKOHAMA STADIUM December 3
Real Madrid **2-0** Olimpia
(Spain)   (Paraguay)

2003: BOCA JUNIORS
YOKOHAMA STADIUM December 14
Boca Juniors **1-1** AC Milan (aet)
(Argentina)   (Italy)
Boca Juniors won 3-1 on penalties

2004: PORTO
YOKOHAMA STADIUM December 12
Porto **0-0** Once Caldas (aet)
(Portugal)   (Colombia)
Porto won 8-7 on penalties

WORLD CLUB CHAMPIONSHIP

2000: CORINTHIANS
MARACANÃ, RIO DE JANEIRO January 14
Corinthians **0-0** Vasco da Gama
(aet)
(Brazil)   (Brazil)
Corinthians won 4-3 on penalties

2005: SÃO PAULO
YOKOHAMA STADIUM December 18
São Paulo **1-0** Liverpool
(Brazil)   (England)

OTHER INTERNATIONAL CLUB COMPETITIONS

EUROPEAN SUPER CUP

The Super Cup was originally conceived by UEFA as a celebration match between the winners of the European Cup and the Cup Winners' Cup. The latter competition is now defunct and the place is taken up by the UEFA Cup winners.

AFC CHAMPIONS LEAGUE

In 2002 the AFC launched the Asian Champions League and replaced both the Asian Champions Cup, Asian Cup Winners' Cup and the Asian Super Cup in the process. The competition is open to the top 14 countries. The top two teams from each country are drawn into seven groups of four. The group winners qualify for the quarter-finals and are joined by the existing holders. Ties are played over two legs, as are the semi-finals and final. The competition runs from February to November each year.

Al Ain of the United Arab Emirates were the inaugural winners in 2003. Subsequent winners have been Al Ittihad of Saudi Arabia who beat Songnam IIhwa 6-3 on aggregate in 2004 and Al Ain 5-3 on aggregate in 2005.

There had been a fledgling Asian Champions Team Cup between 1967 and 1971 that was dominated by the Israelis. Maccabi Tel Aviv won it twice, in 1968 and 1971, while Hapoel Tel Aviv won the inaugural competition and lost the 1970 final to Iran's defunct Taj Club.

The Champions Cup was revived in the mid-Eighties with increasing success. The last years saw the competition dominated by South Korea. Between 1996 and 2002 Korean clubs won the event five times. On two occasions the cup climaxed with an all-Korean final, in 1997 and 2002. Suwon Samsung Bluewings won it in 2001 and 2002 and were preceded by Pohang Steelers in 1997 and 1998 and Ilhwa Chunwa in 1996. Japan's Jubilo Iwata broke the Korean stranglehold in 1999.

AFC CUP

The AFC Cup was launched in 2004 and is contested by representatives of the next 14 developing countries that are not represented in the Asian Champions League. Six nations did not take part or withdrew teams from the first competition, but the prize is worthwhile as success in this tournament earns elevation to the Champions League the following season. The competition kicks off with five groups of four teams, with the group winners and the three best runners-up qualifying for the quarter-finals. The rest of the competition is played out with two-legged knockout ties.

The first final in 2004 was an all-Syrian affair between Al Jaish and Al Wahda. Al Jaish won on the away goals rule after a 3-3 aggregate draw, despite both matches being played in the same stadium in Damascus. Al Jaish became the first Syrian side to win a major Asian trophy and elevated the Syrians to the Champions League the following season. The result justified the AFC's policy of creating club competitions between nations who are at the same level.

In 2005, when four nations were excluded for their refusal to take part in the inaugural tournament, leaving three groups of four and two groups of three in the first phase, Jordan's Al-Faysali beat Lebanon's Al-Nijmeh 6-2 on aggregate in the final.

AFC PRESIDENT'S CUP

The remaining 17 nations not deemed 'mature' enough for the Champions League or 'developing' for the AFC Cup were allowed to enter the inaugural AFC President's Cup in May 2005. However, nine of the countries declined to take part. The event was held as an eight-team tournament hosted by Nepal. The first phase saw two groups of four, with the top two teams qualifying for the semi-finals. The winners of the semi-finals contested the final. Tajikistan's Regar-TadAZ Tursunzade beat Kyrgyzstan's Dordoy-Dinamo Naryn 3-0 in the final to become the competition's first winners but there was no elevation to the AFC Cup.

AFRICAN CHAMPIONS LEAGUE

The African Champions League succeeded the African Champions' Cup in 1997. The two events have produced the most open competition of any confederation tournament, having produced 19 different winners from 13 different nations down the years. The African Champions' Cup was born in 1964 when an international club competition on the continent became feasible. Many nations had become independent

Above from left to right: Saudi Arabia's Al-Ittihad after their AFC Champions League win in 2004; Egypt's Al-Ahli lift the African Champions League trophy in 2001; Valencia celebrate winning the European Super Cup in 2004.

from their former colonial rulers and formed their own leagues. With the exception of the first tournament the competition was based on the format of Europe's established club competitions. Ties were to be played home and away, including the final. Zaïre's TP Englebert were a leading force early on, appearing in four successive finals between 1967 and 1970, winning the first two and losing the second pair.

Guinea's Hafia Conakry were the team to beat in the 1970s as they reached the final on five occasions, winning in 1972, 1975 and 1977. Hafia's presence confirmed the early dominance of west and central Africa. This was largely because the north of the continent showed little interest until the 1980s. Then the countries of the north – Algeria, Egypt, Morocco and Tunisia – put a stranglehold on the African Champions' Cup. Egyptian clubs have won ten times, with Zamalek the most successful side, earning the title on five occasions. In 2005 fellow Egyptian outfit Al Ahly were crowned Asian Champions for the third time.

The Champions League format replaced the traditional knockout format in 1997. The competition, which kicks off in March, goes through a preliminary, first and second round knockout stage until the eight remaining teams play home and away in two league groups of four. The top two sides from each group contest the two-legged semi-finals and the winners of those ties play a two-legged final.

CAF CONFEDERATION CUP

The CAF Confederation Cup replaced the African Cup Winners' Cup and CAF Cup in 2004 and was a result of allowing more than one team from a country to take part in the Champions League. As with the European competition, teams knocked out of the early stages of the African Champions League have a second attempt at international club glory in the Confederation Cup.

After the preliminary, first and second rounds there is an intermediate round where the unlucky teams knocked out from the second round of the Champions League join the remaining eight teams in the Confederation Cup. From this intermediate round the eight winners form two groups of four and the group

Above: Boca Juniors of Argentina start to party after beating Mexico's Pumas UNAM in the Copa Sudamericana in 2005.

winners qualify for the two-legged final. In 2004 Hearts Of Oak beat Asante Kotoko in an all-Ghanian final. Both matches finished 1-1 and Hearts Of Oak won the first Confederation Cup 8-7 on penalties. In 2005 it was Morocco's FAR Rabat who were successful, beating Nigeria's Dolphins 3-1 on aggregate in the final.

CONCACAF CHAMPIONS CUP

The CONCACAF Champions Cup has been around since 1962 and was initially contested by the clubs of latin and central America. In the late 1990s clubs from USA's Major Soccer League also joined the fray. The competition has experimented with tournament and league formats and has settled on a bizarre mixture of the two. The quarter-finalists are made up of two teams each from Mexico and the United States, who are given automatic byes. The top three teams from the UNCAF Cup also qualify for the last eight, leaving one side to win through the first and second rounds by simply winning their matches over two legs. Then a semblance of normality is assumed with the remaining fixtures played over two legs to determine the winner. Mexico has dominated the competition with Club América recording the country's 22nd win in 2006. Fellow Mexican outfit Cruz Azul are the most successful in the competition with five wins, in 1969, 1970, 1971, 1996 and 1997.

UNCAF CLUB CHAMPIONSHIPS

The UNCAF Cup is played between the nations of Central America and, since 1999, acts as qualifier for the CONCACAF Champions Cup where the top three teams qualify for the quarter-finals. The 2003 third-place Alajuelense went on to win the Champions Cup in 2004 and Saprissa won it in 2005. The competition was first played between 1971 and 1983 as the Torneo

Fraternidad. In 1996 it was revived for three years as the Tourneo Grandes de Centroamerica, but the final in 1998 between Muncipal and Saprissa was never played. Alajuelense of Costa Rica won the 2005 competition beating Olimpia of Honduras 4-2 on penalties after a 1-1 aggregate draw. In the 23 times the competition has been contested since its inception, Saprissa, Municipal and Olimpia have all won it four times.

COPA SUDAMERICANA

A knockout competition with ties played over two legs in South America. It is sponsored by a sports marketing firm in Argentina and entry is by invitation only. Brazilian clubs were notable by their absence, citing their own fixture congestion. It was brought in to replace the Copa Mercosur and Copa Merconorte, which in turn had displaced the Supercopa in 1997. It is, in effect, South America's UEFA Cup. Argentina's San Lorenzo were the inaugural winners in 2002. Peru's Cienciano won it the following year, only for Boca Juniors to reclaim the trophy for Argentina in 2004 and 2005. The second win was over Mexico's Pumas UNAM after a penalty shoot-out in which goalkeeper Roberto Abbondanzieri saved two kicks and scored the decisive penalty himself.

OCEANIA CHAMPIONS CUP

This competition has an ad hoc existence and is only played, except the inaugural event in 1987, when Oceania needs to supply a representative to the FIFA World Championship. Played as a tournament, it was dominated by Australia, until they joined the Asian Football Confederation. All four competitions have been won by Australian clubs: Adelaide City (1987), South Melbourne (1999), Wollongong City Wolves (2001) and Sydney FC (2005).

Left: Costa Rica's Saprissa lift the trophy after winning CONCACAF Champions Cup final in 2005.

GREAT CLUBS OF THE WORLD

AJAX

AMSTERDAM, HOLLAND
Stadium: Amsterdam Arena
(50,200)

Founded: 1900 **Honours:** World Club Cup 1972, 1995; European Cup 1971, 1972, 1973, 1995; Cup Winners' Cup 1987; UEFA Cup 1992; Super Cup 1972, 1973, 1995; League 29; Cup 16

The name Ajax is synonymous with the term 'Total Football'. This was a concept of play that saw footballers of supreme technical ability able to interchange positions during a game in a way that had never previously been seen on the European stage. Not only was it magnificent to watch, it was also highly successful. At the height of their powers in the early Seventies, Ajax not only lifted the European Cup on three successive occasions but they also enjoyed back-to-back Super Cup wins and a World Club Cup.

This Ajax side had talent in abundance, with the likes of Johan Neeskens, Arie Haan and Ruud Krol, but the star of the side was Johan Cruyff. These names were products of the revered Ajax youth system and it has continued to produce talent, unearthing such players as Frank Rijkaard, Marco Van Basten, Dennis Bergkamp, Marc Overmars and Patrick Kluivert.

While the relaxation of overseas signings saw Ajax lose many of their young stars, with the club fielding a more international line-up, it was fitting that their last major success on the European stage, a 1-0 Champions League victory over Milan in 1995, saw Louis Van Gaal's side fielding the backbone of the Dutch team – Van Der Sar, Reiziger, the De Boers, Blind, Davids, Seedorf and Overmars, and the win was sealed by homegrown Patrick Kluivert. Since then Ajax's successes have been mainly domestic. Their last league title was in 2004 and they won the Dutch Cup in 2006.

ANDERLECHT

BRUSSELS, BELGIUM
Stadium: Constant Vanden Stock (28,063)

Founded: 1908 **Honours:** Cup Winners' Cup 1976, 1978; UEFA Cup 1983; Super Cup 1976, 1978; League 28; Cup 8

Anderlecht are Belgium's most successful club. Formed in Brussels on May 27, 1908, it wasn't until 1947 that they won their first league title. However, a further 27 league championships, a national record by some margin, illustrates the Mauves' willingness to make up for lost time, and the level of their domestic dominance.

Success on the European stage came in the late Seventies, a golden period when the club reached three consecutive Cup Winners' Cup finals. In 1976 they got the better of West Ham,

winning 4-2 to claim their first European title. The following campaign they lost to Hamburg, but a year later they again lifted the cup, beating FK Austria 4-0. The club added the UEFA Cup to their honours list in 1983 with a 2-1 aggregate victory over Benfica. The following season saw them reach the final again, this time losing out to Tottenham after a penalty shoot-out.

The following decade saw a decline in the club's fortunes, with the occasional relegation scare and numerous managerial changes, but with league title wins in 2000, 2001, 2004 and 2006, Anderlecht have once again risen to the top of the Belgian ladder and are enjoying playing Champions League football.

ARSENAL

LONDON, ENGLAND
Stadium: Emirates Stadium
(60,000)

Founded: 1886 **Honours:** Cup Winners' Cup 1994; Fairs Cup 1970; League 13; Cup 10; League Cup 2

Arsenal were formed as Dial Square by workers at the Woolwich armaments factory in south London, before turning professional in 1891 as Woolwich Arsenal. The club gained election to Division Two in 1893 and promotion followed 11 years later. Relegation in 1913 was tempered by the club's move to Highbury, when they dropped the 'Woolwich' prefix. The move was the work of chairman Sir Henry Norris, who saw great potential in the north London catchment area. Despite finishing in just fifth place in Division Two in 1915, promotion to the top division was 'engineered' by Norris in somewhat strange circumstances when the league resumed after World War I and his appointment of manager Herbert Chapman in 1925 transformed the club into one of the greatest in world football.

Not only did Arsenal get white sleeves and their own tube station after Chapman rebuilt the team, they also won five championships in the 1930s and two FA Cups. Chapman died before he could see all of these achievements, and after the Second World War the club were not the same force. Although they went on to win the

title in 1948, 1953 and the 'double' of 1971, it wasn't until the appointment of George Graham in 1986 that the team emerged as a consistent force. Graham's disciplinarian style, shrewd buying and faith in the club's youth system yielded the championship within three years. As the team matured, they won the title again in 1991, the League Cup and FA Cup double in 1993 and enjoyed Cup Winners' Cup success against Parma a year later.

Arsenal's one-dimensional play won them few friends, but the appointment of Arsene Wenger in 1996 changed the club's image emphatically. The Frenchman has championed a stylish approach on the pitch and forward-thinking preparation off it. His team won the 'double' in 1998 and 2002, the Premiership in 2004 without losing a game, and the FA Cup in 2003 and 2005. After stuttering form in the Champions League, he took the club to their first European Cup final in 2006. At the start of the 2006-7 season, Arsenal relocated to the Emirates Stadium, their new 60,000-seater home.

ASTON VILLA

BIRMINGHAM, ENGLAND
Stadium: Villa Park
(39,217)

Founded: 1874 **Honours:** European Cup 1982; European Super Cup 1982; League 7; Cup 7; League Cup 5

A founding member of the Football League, Aston Villa are one of the oldest clubs in the world. Five of their seven titles and three of six FA Cups were won by 1900. Between the turn of the century and the club's first relegation in 1936, Villa remained powerful: champions in 1910, runners-up on seven occasions, and FA Cup winners three times. Although return to the top flight on this occasion was swift, after relegation the club were never the same force, sinking as far as the Third Division in 1970.

Controversially, Villa won the FA Cup in 1957 against Manchester United's 'Busby Babes' (United played some of the match with ten men

Opposite clockwise from top: The legends of Ajax: celebrating victory in the 1995 Champions League final; Johan Cruyff, the master of Total Football in 1972; Michael Laudrup raises the Dutch Cup after beating PSV Eindhoven 5-0 in 1998.

Left: Arsenal goalscoring legend Cliff Bastin.

Below: Aston Villa's Johnny Dixon lifts the FA Cup after victory over Manchester United in 1957.

Above: Nacional coach Santiago Escobar celebrates with his team afer winning the Colombian championship in 2002.

after their keeper was injured), and they also triumphed in the League Cup in 1961. They were finalists again as a Third Division team ten years later, but promotion under Vic Crowe in 1972 proved the impetus the club needed. Ron Saunders continued the revival after his arrival in 1974, taking them to the top flight the following year and winning the title in 1981. Midway through the next season Saunders resigned, leaving his assistant Tony Barton to take over the team just three months before Villa's greatest ever night: Peter Withe's single goal beating Bayern Munich in Rotterdam to win the 1982 European Cup.

Relegation came in the late 1980s, but Graham Taylor soon reversed the fortunes of the club. They finished runners-up in the title race in 1990, and again in 1993 under Ron Atkinson. But while now seen as secure in the Premiership, Villa are rarely considered as contenders. League Cup victories in 1994 and 1996, and an FA Cup final appearance in 2000, at least give their fans a case for arguing that Villa remain a major force in English football. But the extent of the club's future success may depend on its owner, as long-time chairman Doug Ellis has made it clear that he is prepared to sell if the price is right.

ATHLETIC BILBAO

  BILBAO, SPAIN
Stadium: San Mamés
(46,223)

Founded: 1898 **Honours:** League 8; Cup 24

Among the oldest clubs in Spain, Athletic Bilbao share the honour of having never been relegated from Spain's top flight with Real Madrid and Barcelona. This Basque club's English name originally stems both from British influence in the region, and local suspicion of anything Spanish. Engineers from the UK brought football to the quarry-workers of this area of northern Spain in the late 1800s, and the club still sticks to the selection policy of 'la cantera' or 'the quarry': only picking players of Basque origin. The most famous of these was Rafael Moreno Aranzadi, or 'Pitxitxi' (the top goalscorer in La Liga still wins a trophy named after him).

Bilbao also employed English coaches. Freddy Pentland won two league titles and five cups in the 1920s and 1930s and, despite their lack of impact on the European stage, at home Bilbao are second only to Barcelona as winners of the Spanish Cup. These glory days were recaptured in the 1980s when Javier Clemente's fearsome team, including notorious defender Goikoetxea, 'The Butcher Of Bilbao', won the league in 1983 and the treble in 1984.

Bilbao's magnificent stadium, nicknamed 'La Catedral', has been home to many legends: striker Zarraonandia, goalkeepers Iríbar and Zubizarreta, and modern heroes Guerrero and Exteberría. The club's domestic achievements – though their last good season was as runners-up in 1998, their centenary year – are incredible given their stubborn loyalty to 'la cantera'.

ATLÉTICO MADRID

  MADRID, SPAIN
Stadium: Vicente Calderón
(57,500)

Founded: 1903 **Honours:** World Club Cup 1974; Cup Winners' Cup 1962; League 9; Cup 9

Formed in 1903 by three Basque students based in Madrid, the club performed poorly in its early years. Indeed, it wasn't until after the Civil War and a merger with the Spanish air force's side,

Atlético Aviacion, that success came to the club.

Although Atlético Madrid have spent a large part of their history in the shadow of neighbours Real Madrid, the club has regularly won Spanish domestic competitions. Nicknamed 'Los Colchoneros' (The Mattressmakers, due to the club's kit), they have also performed credibly on the European stage. In 1959 they reached the semi-finals of the European Cup but, ironically, were beaten to a place in the final by Real. They did, however, manage to win the European Cup Winners' Cup with victory against Fiorentina in 1962, and the World Club Cup in 1974.

In the late 1980s the club was taken over by the flamboyant Jesus Gil, and it has been his erratic and often dubious financial behaviour that has defined the club in the decades that followed. In his first ten years at the club he managed to hire and fire more than 25 coaches. However, his unique approach was vindicated in 1996 when Atlético won the Spanish league and cup double, and for just a short while crept out of the shadow of Real. However relegation in 2000 saw Atlético spend two years out of the top flight before promotion back the Primera Liga in 2002, where they have remained a mid-table club ever since.

ATLETICO NACIONAL

  MEDELLIN, COLOMBIA
Stadium: Atanasio Girardot
(52,000)

Founded: 1936 **Honours:** Copa Libertadores 1989; Copa Interamericana 1989; Copa Merconorte 1998, 2000; League 8

Atletico Nacional's first league title in 1954 coincided with the Colombian FA rejoining FIFA after a four-year dispute over transfer payments. The club have subsequently added a further seven league titles to their honours list, the latest full title in 1999 when they pipped America De Cali in a close-run race. However, it was ten years earlier in 1989 that the club experienced its best period by becoming the first Colombian team to win the Copa Libertadores. Future Colombia coach Francisco Maturana led Nacional to the trophy with a win over Olimpia of Paraguay. This was followed by an appearance in the final of the World Club Cup, a 1-0 defeat to Milan in Tokyo.

Medellin is an area at the centre of Colombia's drug industry and, as a result, controversy has never been far away from the club. Indeed, Pablo Escobar, the leader of the biggest drug cartel, was a lifelong Nacional fan, and the club flag was draped over the coffin at his funeral in 1993. Recent players to wear the green and white include flamboyant keeper Jose Luis Chilavert, and Medellin-born striker Juan Pablo Angel.

After 2002, Colombian football switched back to a two-part season, the Apertura (opening) and the Clausura (closing), but without a deciding play-off. Nacional won the Apertura in 2005.

BARCELONA

SPAIN

Stadium: Nou Camp
(98,600)

Founded: 1899 **Honours:** European Cup 1992, 2006; Cup Winners' Cup 1979, 1982, 1989, 1997; Fairs Cup 1958, 1960, 1966; European Super Cup 1992, 1997; League 18; Cup 24

One of the biggest and best-supported clubs in world football, FC Barcelona have only won the ultimate prize – the European Cup – on two occasions. By the standards of almost any football club, 18 national titles, 24 domestic cups and 11 European trophies would be seen as an incredible record, but Barcelona's achievements have always been judged by the yardstick set by bitter rivals Real Madrid, who dominated the European Cup for much of its first ten years.

With a club history mired in the politics of mid-20th Century Spain, Barcelona were, for many, a symbol of Catalan defiance in a country oppressed by Franco's centralist government in Madrid. But ironically for a club synonymous with the spirit of Catalonia, its roots were originally in the expatriate communities of the city. In October 1899 Swiss football enthusiast Hans Gamper placed an advert in the local sports newspaper *Los Deportes* and recruited a team largely drawn from the various English businesses of the city, the club's famous strip inspired by the school colours of one of the English players, Arthur Witty. FC Barcelona played their first game on Christmas Eve 1899, fielding a team comprised largely of foreigners to beat local side FC Catala 3-1, with Arthur Witty scoring to seal the win.

Swift progress was made in the early years of the century, with Barcelona reaching the first final of the Spanish Cup (the Copa Del Rey) in 1902, although by the time they finally won the competition in 1910, Real Madrid had already lifted the trophy four times.

When the first Spanish national league came into being in the 1928-9 season, Barcelona beat Real Madrid to the title by just two points, and since then, along with Real and Athletic Bilbao, they share the honour of having never been relegated. But although Barça continued to win domestic honours for the next 20 years, it was really in the period between 1948 and 1960 that the club built a team of substance and a stadium to house it, the Nou Camp, which opened in 1957.

Barcelona's greatest period of achievement was under the management of Argentinian Helenio Herrera, who arrived at the club in 1958, shortly after their first European triumph in the Fairs Cup. During his two-year spell at Barça, Herrera shook the club at its roots, placing his faith in both young Catalan players nurtured through the youth team and his 'tricky

Above: Under Johan Cruyff Barcelona finally won the European Cup for the first time, beating Sampdoria at Wembley in 1992. Playing in their orange away strip, the team changed into their famous Blaugrana shirts to collect the trophy.

foreigners', Hungarians Sandor Kocsis and Zoltan Czibor. In Herrera's first season in charge, Barça eclipsed the Real Madrid of Di Stéfano and Puskás to take the league title with a record haul of points.

Victory over Birmingham City in the 1960 Fairs Cup was followed by another league title, but no amount of success could ease the pain caused by the end of that season's European Cup campaign when, despite recording significant aggregate victories over CNDA Sofia (8-4), AC Milan (7-1) and Wolves (9-2), semi-final humiliation by Real Madrid was deemed disastrous. Before the clash Herrera had fallen out with his star Ladislao Kubala over bonus payments. Zoltan Czibor backed his fellow Hungarian and both were dropped. Barcelona lost both legs 3-1. Herrera took the blame and was forced to resign.

The following season saw a 3-2 defeat to Benfica in the European Cup final, despite having dumped Real Madrid from the competition en route. In La Liga it was the onset of a decade of dominance by Madrid, who won eight of the remaining nine titles during the Sixties (Atlético Madrid interrupting this run in 1966). Triumphs in the Copa Del Rey in 1963 and 1968 were scant consolation, and while Barcelona again won the Fairs Cup

in 1966, they would not retake the league until 1974, after securing the services of Johan Cruyff. In the mid-Sixties Spain had banned imported players, but the ban was lifted in 1973 in time for the club to spend a world record fee of £922,000 on Cruyff, who took them from the relegation zone to the title for the first time in 14 years. Better than that, the season also included a 5-0 away thrashing of Real Madrid.

Although success in La Liga would evade the club for another 11 years, when Terry Venables secured the title, it was Cruyff who would again prove saviour, returning as coach to deliver Barça their first triumph in the European Cup, a single Ronald Koeman goal at Wembley in the 1992 final beating Sampdoria to the prize. However, a 4-0 defeat to Milan in the final two years later did little to endear Cruyff to the Barcelona board, and despite having taken the club to four league titles in a row, failure to win a trophy in 1995 and 1996 led to his acrimonious departure.

Dutchman Louis Van Gaal brought back-to-back titles to the Nou Camp in 1998 and 1999, but by filling the side with so many of his countrymen – Kluivert, Reiziger, Cocu, Zenden, Overmars and the De Boers – he proved unpopular and was forced to resign. A second spell at the club for Van Gaal just a year later was unsuccessful and he was replaced midway through his second season, but under Radomir Antic the club finished sixth in La Liga in 2003, their worst position since 1942.

In recent seasons under enthusiastic young president Joan Laporta, and coach Frank Rijkaard, the club has once again started to dominate Spanish football. With players of the calibre of Henrik Larsson, Ronaldinho and Samuel Eto'o, Barcelona won back-to-back league titles in 2005 and 2006, and triumphed in the 2006 Champions League final, beating ten-man Arsenal 2-1 in Paris.

The Nou Camp: one of the great venue of world football.

1895

1899: Barcelona play their first game at Bonanova Racetrack on Christmas Eve against FC Catala.

1900

1902: Barça are losing finalists in the first Copa Del Rey to Vizcaya Bilbao. They also play Madrid for the first time, winning 3-2.

1905

1910

1905: The club play Madrid for the first time in Barcelona, winning 3-2.

1915

1920

1922: Barça move to a new stadium at Les Corts.

1925

1930

1929: The club wins the first ever Spanish league title.

1935

1937-39: The national league is abandoned during Spanish Civil War.

1940

1945

1950: The club sign Hungarian legend Ladislao Kubala.

1950

1955

1957: The first game is played at the Nou Camp

1960

1958: Barça win their first European trophy, the Fairs Cup.

1965

1961: Despite beating Real Madrid on the way, the club lose the European Cup final to Benfica.

1970

1974: Johan Cruyff is signed from Ajax.

1975

1980

1979: Barça lift the Cup Winners' Cup for first time.

1985

1982: After four years of chasing, the club finally sign Maradona.

1990

1988: Johan Cruyff returns as manager.

1995

1992: Barça win the European Cup for the first time, beating Sampdoria 1-0 at Wembley. They win it again in 2006, beating Arsenal.

2000

2005

BAYERN MUNICH

MUNICH, GERMANY
Stadium: Allianz Arena
(66,000)

Founded: 1900 **Honours:** World Club Cup 1976;
European Cup 1974, 1975, 1976, 2001; Cup
Winners' Cup 1967; UEFA Cup 1996; League 20;
Cup 13

Bayern celebrated their centenary year winning the Bundesliga and DFB Cup double for the third time, and followed it up in 2001 with their seventh appearance – and fourth victory – in the European Cup final. Yet, incredibly, they weren't even their city's representative in the initial Bundesliga of 1963. That honour fell to TSV Munich 1860. Bayern had triumphed only once in the regional play-offs which previously decided the German championship – back in 1932. It wasn't until attack-minded Yugoslav coach Tschik Cajkovski took over in 1963 that Bayern started their climb to the top.

In the 1965 Bundesliga promotion play-offs, Cajkovski included three promising youngsters in his team: Sepp Maier in goal, Gerd Müller in attack, and Franz Beckenbauer in midfield. Maier holds Bayern's appearances record, including 422 consecutive games; Müller, 'Der Bomber', netted an astonishing 365 goals in 427 games; and Beckenbauer, 'Der Kaiser', is, quite simply, one of the greatest footballers ever.

This trio helped Bayern to cup wins in 1966 and 1967, and a Cup Winners' Cup victory in 1967 against Rangers. They completed their first league and cup double in 1969 under new boss Branko Zebec. With the addition of three more world-class players, Paul Breitner, Uli Hoeness and Georg Schwarzenbeck, Bayern saw the dawn of a golden era. Zebec's replacement, Udo Lattek, led them on a four-year unbeaten home run. They won three titles in a row, and notched-up the first of three consecutive European Cup wins

Bayern Munich's Bixente Lizarazu and Willy Sagnol parade the European Cup in front of their fans after the 2001 Champions League final.

in 1974, with a 4-0 victory over Atlético Madrid, following it with wins over Leeds and St Etienne.

Domestically their triumphs dried up as the old guard left or retired, but the club were revitalised by the emergence of striker Karl-Heinz Rummenigge and the return of Breitner. The arrival of the influential Lothar Matthäus in 1984 prompted another trio of league wins. In the early 1990s, however, Bayern struggled and 'Der Kaiser' returned as club president in 1994 to reverse their fortunes, overseeing the team's UEFA Cup win in 1996 as coach.

A new breed of Bayern stalwarts emerged under Ottmar Hitzfeld, the most successful Bayern coach ever, with players such as Kahn, Effenberg and Linke. They put their last minute defeat by Manchester United in the 1999 Champions League final behind them to win in 2001 against Valencia, while pocketing another string of German titles, including the league and cup double in 2000 and 2003. After a poor season where Bayern were defeated in the quarter-final of the German Cup by second division Alemannia Aachen, Hitzfeld lost his job. He was replaced by Felix Magath, who won the league and cup double in 2005 and 2006.

In 2005 Bayern moved from the Olympic Stadium to the new Allianz Arena, which the club owns jointly with TSV 1860.

BENFICA

LISBON, PORTUGAL
Stadium: Estadio da Luz
(45,000)

Founded: 1904 **Honours:** European Cup 1961, 1962; League 31; Cup 24

After a decade of underachievement for Benfica ended when they won the title for the first time in 11 years in 2005, the club has at last started to look like a true contender once again. Few sides in history could compare with the Benfica side

of the 1960s, yet while they swept all before them on home soil, an amazing six European Cup final appearances in that decade alone brought just two victories. Spanish opposition was beaten in both 1961 and 1962 in the shape of Barcelona and Real Madrid – the 1962 final ending in a remarkable 5-3 victory as the great Eusébio (a statue of whom now stands outside Benfica's ground) scored twice after Ferenc Puskás fired a first half hat-trick for Real. The Italian clubs were not quite so charitable, with both Inter Milan and AC Milan foiling Benfica in the three finals that followed. And in 1968 it was Manchester United's turn to heap further final misery on the Lisbon giants.

In 1978 the club scrapped its policy of fielding only Portuguese citizens (and those from the colonies – Eusébio was born in Mozambique) in an effort to compete with Europe's best sides once again. The policy seemed to work as the club returned to European final action. However, as before, the club fell at the final hurdle on each occasion, finishing runners-up in the UEFA Cup in 1983 and in the European Cup in 1988 and 1990. The most galling defeat of all was losing 6-5 on penalties to PSV Eindhoven in 1988.

Despite going eight years without a major trophy from the mid-1990s, Benfica managed to remain Portugal's best known club. Success in the Portuguese Cup in 2004, with a 2-1 victory over Porto, kickstarted a mini revival, and the following season they won their first league title in 11 years. In 2003 they moved from their world famous Estádio da Luz – Stadium Of Light – in order to take residence in a newly constructed Estádio da Luz, built just yards away especially for Euro 2004.

BOCA JUNIORS

BUENOS AIRES, ARGENTINA
Stadium: La Bombonera
(58,750)

Founded: 1905 **Honours:** World Club Cup 1977, 2000, 2003; Copa Libertadores 1977, 1978, 2000, 2001, 2003; Supercopa 1989; Recopa Sudamericana 1990, 2005; Copa Sudamericana 2004, 2005; League 22

Boca Juniors will be forever associated with former player and fervent fan Diego Maradona, but, in truth, the great man has only played a bit part in the club's long and eventful history. They were founded in 1905 by Irishman Patrick MacCarthy, together with a group of Italian immigrants, in the poor docklands of Buenos Aires, the neighbourhood that gave birth to the tango. To this day the club's humble roots have not been forgotten, and Boca Juniors will forever represent working class Argentina.

Six titles in the national amateur league signalled the club's arrival as a domestic force, and there hasn't been a decade since that the club hasn't got its hands on silverware. In

1931 they were the first winners of the inaugural Argentine Professional League. A decade later Boca moved to the Estadio Dr Camilo Cichero, or as it is commonly known, 'La Bombonera' (The Chocolate Box).

Despite a flurry of domestic titles it was only with the arrival of disciplinarian coach Juan Carlos Lorenzo in 1976 that Boca emerged as a force outside of Argentina. During his five-year tenure, Boca won the South American Club Cup (the Copa Libertadores) for the first time in 1977. A year later the title was defended with victory over Colombia's Deportivo Cali. While Boca's physical style of play under Lorenzo didn't win them too many friends among football purists, a 5-2 aggregate victory against Borussia Mönchengladbach in 1977's World Club Cup kept their fans in a satisfied state of frenzy.

In 1980 Boca Juniors paid £1 million for Diego Maradona, but he was quickly sold on to Spanish club Barcelona in a £3 million world record deal two seasons later. After his departure Boca's dominance waned, and it wasn't until the club's back-to-back successes in the Copa Libertadores in 2000 and 2001, under Carlos Bianchi, that status as a genuine intercontinental superpower was reaffirmed.

They won the competition again in 2003 and recent wins in the World Club Cup have helped cement this reputation, with victory over Real Madrid in 2000, and a penalty shoot-out win against AC Milan in 2003.

BORUSSIA DORTMUND

DORTMUND, GERMANY
Stadium: Westfalen Stadium (81,264)

Founded: 1909 **Honours:** World Club Cup 1997; European Cup 1997; Cup Winners' Cup 1966; League 6; Cup 2

Borussia Dortmund's history has seen success in two distinct eras separated by a barren period stretching more than 30 years. The first taste of silverware occurred in the 1956-7 campaign when the club gained its first West German league title, a feat that was repeated the following season. This heralded the start of what was to be the first golden era for the club: another title in 1963 was followed by the German Cup in 1965 and triumph in the European Cup Winners' Cup a year later. The 2-1 extra-time victory over Liverpool at Hampden Park gave Dortmund a special place in the record books, as the first German side to win a European trophy.

With the exception of a second German Cup in 1989, nothing but dust was added to the trophy cabinet at the Westfalenstadion until 1995, when a Matthias Sammer-inspired Dortmund pipped Werder Bremen to the Bundesliga title. The following year they ran out league winners again, but better was to come. The 1997 Champions League final in Munich's Olympic

Stadium saw Dortmund, with two goals by Karl-Heinz Riedle and one by Lars Ricken, defeat a strong Juventus side 3-1. A subsequent 2-0 victory over Brazil's Cruzeiro in the World Club Cup final that year established the club's position as a force on the global football stage. At the turn of the millennium they became the first publicly traded football club on the German stock market

In recent years, however, Dortmund have struggled. Poor financial management forced the club to sell their stadium, and although they continue to lease it back, it was renamed Signal Iduna Park in 2006. Their average attendances remain over 70,000 a game (the highest in Germany), but the club came close to bankruptcy in 2005. Measures to steady the ship have included the players taking a 20 per cent pay cut.

CELTIC

GLASGOW, SCOTLAND
Stadium: Celtic Park (61,000)

Founded: 1888 **Honours:** European Cup 1967; League 40; Cup 33; League Cup 13

Celtic's crowning moment was the 1967 European Cup final in Lisbon, when they beat Inter Milan 2-1 to become the first British side to win the competition. They nearly repeated the feat in 1970 when, skippered again by Billy McNeill, they lost 2-1 to Feyenoord. The achievement of 'The Lions Of Lisbon' was especially heartening because all their players came from within a 30-mile radius of Celtic Park.

Celtic were very much the team of Glasgow's

Irish immigrant community. A Catholic priest founded them as a charity, but they were never charitable to opponents and their ongoing rivalry with the Protestants of Rangers started early.

Under long-serving manager Willie Maley, their superb pre-First World War team won six consecutive championships. Between the wars Maley introduced such legends as Patsy Gallagher and Jimmy McGrory, still the club's leading goalscorer. After World War II Celtic faltered until the appointment of ex-player Jock Stein in 1965. He soon moulded a great side from the likes of Tommy Gemmell, Bertie Auld and tricky winger Jimmy Johnstone and in 1967 the team won every competition they entered, including the European Cup. Joined along the way by the likes of Kenny Dalglish and Lou Macari, Celtic won nine league titles in a row.

In the years that followed, league glory was shared between Celtic, 'Old Firm' adversaries Rangers, and new force Aberdeen. The 1990s, however, belonged to Rangers. Celtic underwent a transformation to be able to compete, and new owner Fergus McCann rebuilt the club and stadium. Following the example set by Rangers, Celtic imported foreign players, including goal machine Henrik Larsson. The strategy paid off as it prevented Rangers from breaking Celtic's own record of successive title wins.

Martin O'Neill arrived at the helm in 2000 and won the treble in his first season and the double in 2004. He took Celtic to their first European final in 33 years in 2003, but they lost the UEFA Cup to Porto. He left the club in May 2005, to be replaced by Gordon Strachan, who clinched the 2006 league title and League Cup in his first season.

Above: Boca Juniors celebrate with the Copa América trophy in 2005.

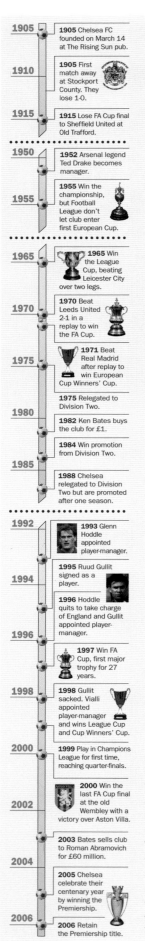

1905 Chelsea FC founded on March 14 at The Rising Sun pub.

1905 First match away at Stockport County. They lose 1-0.

1915 Lose FA Cup final to Sheffield United at Old Trafford.

1952 Arsenal legend Ted Drake becomes manager.

1955 Win the championship, but Football League don't let club enter first European Cup.

1965 Win the League Cup, beating Leicester City over two legs.

1970 Beat Leeds United 2-1 in a replay to win the FA Cup.

1971 Beat Real Madrid after replay to win European Cup Winners' Cup.

1975 Relegated to Division Two.

1982 Ken Bates buys the club for £1.

1984 Win promotion from Division Two.

1988 Chelsea relegated to Division Two but are promoted after one season.

1993 Glenn Hoddle appointed player-manager.

1995 Ruud Gullit signed as a player.

1996 Hoddle quits to take charge of England and Gullit appointed player-manager.

1997 Win FA Cup, first major trophy for 27 years.

1998 Gullit sacked. Vialli appointed player-manager and wins League Cup and Cup Winners' Cup.

1999 Play in Champions League for first time, reaching quarter-finals.

2000 Win the last FA Cup final at the old Wembley with a victory over Aston Villa.

2003 Bates sells club to Roman Abramovich for £60 million.

2005 Chelsea celebrate their centenary year by winning the Premiership.

2006 Retain the Premiership title.

CHELSEA

LONDON, ENGLAND
Stadium: Stamford Bridge
(42,360)

Founded: 1905 **Honours:** European Cup Winners' Cup 1971, 1998; European Super Cup 1998; League 3; FA Cup 3; League Cup 3

The history of Chelsea Football Club begins with their home ground, Stamford Bridge. Opened in 1877, for the best part of 30 years it was used only for athletics meetings. Then, in 1904, football enthusiast Gus Mears and his brother bought the deeds to the ground and had Scottish architect Archibald Leitch build a football stadium on it. The new arena was initially offered to Fulham FC but they declined to move from their Craven Cottage home nearby, leaving Mears little choice but to form his own club. Although based in the London borough of Fulham, the new team took its name from a neighbouring borough and on March 14, 1905, in a Fulham Road pub called The Rising Sun, Chelsea FC were born.

The club were elected to the Second Division of the Football League on May 29, 1905 and played their first competitive match in September of the same year (an away defeat to Stockport County). After two seasons the club enjoyed promotion to Division One in 1907. The highlight of the club's early years, though, was their first appearance in an FA Cup final, in 1915. Chelsea lost 3-0 to Sheffield United at Old Trafford in a match that has become known as 'The Khaki Final' because of the number of army uniforms on display in the crowd.

Chelsea made their first major impact on English football under manager Ted Drake, who had taken charge of the club in 1952. Drake had a no-nonsense style and was determined to reshape the club in his image. Out went Chelsea's rather fusty nickname 'The Pensioners' and in came a host of young players hungry for success, the so-called 'Drake's Ducklings'. Chelsea won their first league title in 1955, clinching victory in the season's penultimate game against Sheffield Wednesday.

Drake's side couldn't repeat those heroics in the following seasons and the manager left the club in 1962 with Chelsea briefly relegated. Things got slightly better for the club as the decade progressed, winning the League Cup for the first time in 1965 and reaching the final of the FA Cup in 1967 (only to lose to Tottenham). Dave Sexton arrived as manager that year and with the likes of striker Peter Osgood and young midfield wizard Charlie Cooke, Chelsea were getting rave notices for their brand of free-flowing football. But there was grit in this side, too, evidenced when they beat Don Revie's uncompromising Leeds

Above: Two league titles in a row for Chelsea as captain John Terry lifts the 2006 Premiership trophy.

United after a hard-fought replay to lift the FA Cup in 1970. The following year they had to roll up their sleeves again, this time to win the European Cup Winners' Cup in extra-time against mighty Real Madrid.

The success was short-lived and Chelsea spent seven of the nine seasons between 1976 and 1984 in the Second Division. In 1983 they were almost relegated to Division Three. There were other problems for new owner Ken Bates, who had taken on the club for the nominal sum of £1 in 1982: attendances at Stamford Bridge were poor, hooliganism was rife and the club was sinking under a mountain of debt (the result of over-ambitious ground improvements begun in the 1970s). Worst of all, Chelsea no longer owned Stamford Bridge, which had been sold in the late Seventies by the Mears family to property developers. It wasn't until 1994 that the irascible Bates was able to buy it back.

After the famine of the 1980s, the following decade proved something of a feast. Glenn Hoddle (1993-6), Ruud Gullit (1996-8) and Gianluca Vialli (1998-2000) were recruited as managers and each took their multinational Chelsea team on just a little bit further than his predecessor. Hoddle's Chelsea reached an FA Cup final in only his first season in charge, while Gullit's side won the trophy for the first time in 26 years. Vialli, meanwhile, won an FA Cup, a League Cup, a European Cup Winners' Cup and the European Super Cup all in the space of two years. The Cup Winners' Cup success was particularly sweet, Italian maestro Gianfranco Zola hitting the winner against Stuttgart just moments after coming on as a second-half substitute.

Chelsea's success on the pitch had come at a price, as had the ambitious Chelsea Village hotel and business project built at Stamford

Bridge. The club's borrowing had raged out of control and they were close to financial collapse in 2004, as huge loan repayments to banks became due. Luckily, a financial saviour was found, Roman Abramovich bringing to an end Ken Bates' 22-year reign as Chelsea supremo.

The Russian oil billionaire bought the club for £60 million and bankrolled a spending spree on players unprecedented in world football, of which the £48.4 million spent on just two players – striker Didier Drogba (£24 million) and club record signing Michael Essien (£24.4 million) – was just the tip of the iceberg. Abramovich's cash injection into the team reaped quick dividends as Claudio Ranieri's side made the semi-finals of the Champions League for the first time and came second to Arsenal in the Premiership, their highest league finish for nearly half a century.

However, for Roman Abramovich this wasn't deemed good enough and amiable 'Tinkerman' Ranieri was soon replaced as manager by José Mourinho, the methodical and controversial Portuguese coach who had guided little-fancied Porto to Champions League success in 2004.

Mourinho's impact on football in England was immediate, Chelsea winning their first league title in 50 years in 2005. They repeated that success the following year in a campaign that saw them leading the title race by 18 points with just two months to play, but a late surge by Manchester United gave the season some belated excitement. After clinching the title playing against rivals United, José Mourinho threw his winners' medal into the Stamford Bridge crowd.

Despite this league success, European glory continues to elude Chelsea, with another semi-final appearance in 2005 all they have to show in the Champions League for Abramovich's massive financial outlay.

COLO COLO

SANTIAGO, CHILE
Stadium: David Arellano
(62,500)

Founded: 1925 **Honours:** Copa Libertadores 1991;
League 23; Recopa Sudamericana 1992; Copa
Interamericana 1991; Cup 10

Chile's most successful club side gained their exotic name from the local slang term for a 'wildcat'. Based in the capital, Santiago, they were one of the first South American teams to tour Europe and visited both Spain and Portugal in 1927. Founder members of the Chilean league in 1933, Colo Colo have tasted victory in the championship on an unprecedented 23 occasions. Their record in the haphazardly scheduled Chilean Cup – established in 1958, but not played between 1962 and 1973 or since 2001 – is also peerless, with ten wins.

In 1973 they became the first Chilean side to reach the final of the South American Club Cup, but lost 2-1 to Independiente of Argentina in a a play-off. However, with a 3-0 aggregate win in 1991 over Olimpia of Paraguay, Colo Colo finally became the first (and only) Chilean club to lift the trophy. The triumph was made all the greater for a well-deserved victory over the might of Boca Juniors in the semi-final. Their subsequent appearance in the World Club Cup ended in a heavy 3-0 defeat against Red Star Belgrade.

In recent years, like many other South American teams, the club have experienced significant money problems, but they have now bounced back from bankruptcy in 2002.

CORINTHIANS

SÃO PAULO, BRAZIL
Stadium: Alfredo Schurig,
Parque São Jorge (14,000)

Founded: 1910 **Honours:** World Club Championship
2000; São Paulo State League 25; League 4; Cup 2

In 1910 the famed Corinthians, one of English football's pioneering clubs, toured Brazil, winning all their games. Such was their influence that a group of students from the Tatuapé area of São Paulo were inspired to set up their own club, adopting the English team's name in their honour. São Paulo expanded rapidly to become one of the world's biggest cities and the club grew with it to become one of the best supported clubs in Brazil, regularly switching matches from its modest home ground, the Parque São Jorge, to the council-owned Pacaembu stadium with its 40,000 capacity.

Their fans, known as the 'Fiel' – the 'faithful' – are also among the country's most fervent, so much so that when the team was flirting with relegation during the mid-Nineties a group of them ambushed the Corinthians team bus.

Despite their mass popularity Corinthians failed to win a national title until 1990 and then had to wait until the end of the decade to repeat the feat. The team cashed in on that success by winning the first World Club Championship, beating rivals Vasco De Gama on penalties in the Maracanã in January 2000.

Poor management of the club's affairs has caused Corinthians to struggle in recent years, but after signing a ten-year deal that gave Media Sports Investments control of the finances of the club, quality players were signed, such as Argentine striker Carlos Tevez. In December 2005, under coach Antônio Lopes, they were crowned champions for the fourth time.

Among the famous players to have worn the Corinthians shirt in the past are Rivelino, Socrates, Dunga and Rivaldo.

DYNAMO KIEV

KIEV, UKRAINE
Stadium: Valeri Lobanovsky
Dynamo Stadium (82,000)

Founded: 1927 **Honours:** Cup Winners' Cup 1975,
1986; European Super Cup 1975; Ukrainian League
11, Soviet League 13; Ukrainian Cup 7, Soviet Cup 8

Founder members of the Soviet Union league in 1936, Dynamo Kiev had to wait until 1961 for their first championship. After this landmark was reached, the club established itself as a major force in Soviet football, and Kiev's final total of 13 Soviet League titles, beating the 12 of their rivals Spartak Moscow, will forever remain a record following the dissolution of the Soviet Union in 1991.

In 1975, under the guidance of legendary coach Valeri Lobanovsky, Kiev became the first team from the Soviet Union to win a European trophy, demolishing Ferencváros 3-0 in the final of the Cup Winners' Cup. Indeed, the history of the club cannot be separated from that of Lobanovsky, who guided them to success in the same competition in 1986. His death in May 2002 cast a great shadow over Ukrainian football, and as a mark of respect Dynamo re-named their stadium after him.

Above: Dynamo Kiev celebrate victory over Spartak Moscow in the Commonwealth Champions Cup in Moscow in 2002.

Since the formation of the post-Communist Vischcha Liga in Ukraine few clubs can boast such a stranglehold over domestic football. With the aid of former luminaries such as Andrei Shevchenko and Sergei Rebrov, Dynamo Kiev have won 11 of the 14 championships contested. The exceptions occurred in 2002, 2005 and 2006, when Shaktar Donetsk consigned Kiev to second place. Dynamo bounced back, winning the Ukrainian Cup in 2006 but were runners-up in the league after finishing level on points with Shaktar Donetsk.

DYNAMO MOSCOW

MOSCOW, RUSSIA
Stadium: Dynamo
(36,800)

Founded: 1923 **Honours:** Soviet League 11; Soviet
Cup 7; Russian Cup 1

Dynamo Moscow will always be known for their association with goalkeeping legend, Lev Yashin. The 'Black Panther' played 326 times for the club, winning the league title six times and the Soviet Cup twice. It was during his tenure between the sticks that the club experienced its most successful era. Since his departure Dynamo have for the great part lived in the shadow of their great rivals, Spartak Moscow, though they can lay claim to being the first Soviet team to reach a European final, when in 1972 they went down 3-2 to Rangers in the Cup Winners' Cup.

In 1923 Dynamo Moscow were ominously taken under the control of Felix Dzerzhinsky, the leader of the Russian secret police and future head of the KGB. The club is more famed, however, for an historic four-match tour of Britain in 1945. Helping to feed the appetite of a public starved of competitive football due to the Second World War, the Russians greatly impressed with their ball skills and progressive play, beating a strong Arsenal side, demolishing Cardiff 10-1, and gaining creditable draws against Chelsea and Rangers.

Since the formation of the post-Communist Vysshaya Liga in 1991 Dynamo have largely disappointed, with only a Russian Cup victory

Left: Corinthians enjoy the moment after their victory in the World Club Championship final in 2000.

The early 1930s were the club's most famous years and corresponded with the Austrian national team's domination of European football. It was no coincidence as the so-called Austrian 'Wunderteam' contained many players from FK Austria, including the legendary Matthias Sindelar. Club success came not only in the form of domestic league titles, but also with victories in the Mitropa Cup. FK Austria claimed this prestigious trophy in 1933 and 1936.

In 1977 a new sponsor changed the club's name to the unwieldy FK Austria Memphis, and the modern side have failed to live up to the Violets' glorious past. An appearance in the 1978 Cup Winners' Cup final led to a heavy 4-0 defeat at the hands of Anderlecht. There are signs, however, that the glory years are returning. After changing ownership in 1999, the club received a significant increase in their budget to buy players. Consequently the club won the league and cup double in 2003 and 2006.

Champions League football has led the club to make plans to increase the capacity of the Franz Horr Stadium.

FEYENOORD

ROTTERDAM, HOLLAND
Stadium: Feyenoord Stadium (51,000)

Founded: 1908 **Honours:** World Club Cup 1970; European Cup 1970; UEFA Cup 1974, 2002; League 14; Cup 10

Feyenoord became the first Dutch side to land a European trophy when they won the European Cup in 1970. Amsterdam-based rivals Ajax had missed out in the final the previous year to Milan, but the Rotterdam side's 2-1 victory over Celtic at the San Siro stadium in Milan began a four-year monopoly of Europe's top prize for Dutch clubs. Sadly for Feyenoord, whose defence of their trophy ended in the ignominy of going out to Romanian minnows UT Arad, their 1970 victory was just the forerunner to an Ajax hat-trick of successes.

More European glory followed in 1974 with victory over Tottenham in the UEFA Cup final, but the Eighties and Nineties saw Feyenoord eclipsed by both Ajax and PSV Eindhoven in the Dutch league. Domestic cup triumph proved to be their biggest area of success during this period, as problems off the pitch took more of the headlines, with financial difficulties for the club and a disturbing hooligan element among their support mirroring the decline in fortunes on the field.

Leo Beenhakker helped Feyenoord to their most recent league title in 1999, but subsequent managers have failed to match this achievement, including Ruud Gullit in his one season at the club. Current coach, Erwin Koeman, has brought some much needed stability to the team and has signed a contract until 2009.

Above: Feyenoord players take the trophy to their fans at the San Siro after beating Celtic in the 1970 European Cup final.

in 1995 to add to the roll of honour. To add insult to injury, in 1998 Dynamo's undersoil heating malfunctioned and managed to scorch the playing surface rendering it unplayable.

In 2005 the club broke Russian transfer records when they signed Portuguese stars Maniche and Costinha from Porto, but both players failed to settle and Maniche transferred to Chelsea within six months, leaving Dynamo to continue to struggle in the Russian league.

EINTRACHT FRANKFURT

FRANKFURT, GERMANY
Stadium: Waldstadion (48,000)

Founded: 1899 **Honours:** UEFA Cup 1980; League 1; Cup 4

Eintracht Frankfurt may have been formed more than 100 years ago, and were founder members of the Bundesliga in 1963, but to most people the club's reputation is based on just one game. The 90 minutes in question is the 1960 European Cup final at Hampden, when they were on the wrong end of a 7-3 scoreline dished out by a Real Madrid side inspired by the combined genius of Ferenc Puskás and Alfredo Di Stéfano. Many football pundits still look back on the match as the finest ever played.

This is of scant consolation to Frankfurt, as the club has perpetually struggled to escape the shadow of that game. That's not to say there haven't been successes, with 1980's UEFA Cup triumph over fellow German side Borussia Mönchengladbach being an obvious one. Inspired by such world-class stars as German midfielder Andy Möller and Ghanaian striker Tony Yeboah, the club underwent a brief renaissance in the early Nineties with a series of impressive tilts at the domestic league title.

In recent years, however, Frankfurt have bounced between the two top divisions in the Bundesliga, and have been beset by crippling financial problems, so much so that they were very nearly expelled to the amateur leagues in 2002, eventually managing to retain their status after appeal. Their only success has been reaching the German Cup final in 2006, and although losing to Bayern Munich, it was enough to assure them of a place in the UEFA Cup.

FK AUSTRIA VIENNA

VIENNA, AUSTRIA
Stadium: Franz Horr Stadion (11,800)

Founded: 1911 **Honours:** League 23; Cup 25

Founded in the Austrian capital on March 12, 1911, by members of the Vienna Cricket and Football Club, the team were initially known as SV Amateure Vienna, and won their first league title under this name in 1924. With the onset of a professional league the name changed to FK Austria two years later.

FLAMENGO

RÍO DE JANEIRO, BRAZIL
Stadium: Gavea (8,000)
Maracanã (95,095)

Founded: 1911 **Honours:** World Club Cup 1981; Copa Libertadores 1981; Mercosur Cup 1999; Río State League 28; League 5; Cup 2

Football in Río still reflects the divisions of race and class in the city, and while rivals Fluminense are seen to represent the middle class, Flamengo have always been the club of the people. This appeal makes them by far the most popular club in Brazil, and 'Fla's' support is garnered not just from the favellas of Río itself, but from districts throughout the country. Ironically enough, the club was formed when disaffected members of Fluminense joined the Flamengo rowing club in 1911 to create a football team.

Despite enormous popularity within their own country it wasn't until the early 1980s that the club established themselves as a force to be reckoned with on the world stage. Under the influence of Zico, one of the club's greatest players, Flamengo finally lifted the Copa Libertadores in 1981 by beating Cobreloa of Chile in an ill-tempered game. In doing so they fielded what is still regarded as one of the strongest ever Brazilian club sides. To cap the achievement, later in the same year they produced another great performance in Tokyo, with Zico again to the fore, to dismiss a strong Liverpool team 3-0 in the World Club Cup final.

The club's home is the Gávea Stadium but all of the team's games are played at the much bigger Maracanã. Financial problems have meant the club has struggled to challenge for honours in recent years.

FLUMINENSE

RÍO DE JANEIRO, BRAZIL
Stadium: Laranjeiras (8,000)
Maracana (95,095)

Founded: 1902 **Honours:** Río State League 30; League 1

Fluminense were founded in 1902 by the wealthy expat British community, and those privileged origins continue to define the club. 'Flu' are still regarded as the club of Río's elite middle classes, in direct contrast to the 'everyman' appeal of bitter rivals Flamengo. The club were founder members of the Río de Janeiro Amateur League, and trophies came early with four successive titles spanning 1906 to 1909. Further domestic trophies have been captured, including five consecutive Río State League titles between 1936 to 1941, but since the national championship was first staged in 1971, they have only won the Brazilian league once, in 1984.

For all their success in Brazil, Fluminense have amazingly yet to win an international tournament. Flu's overall record in the Copa Libertadores – not reaching a single final – is a poor one. This comes as more of a surprise when you consider the list of great players that the club has had to call upon over the years. The magical Didi played for the club in the early 1950s, pulling the strings in the club's midfield as much as he did for Brazil's World Cup winning sides of 1958 and 1962. Carlos Alberto, Brazil's 1970 World Cup-winning captain, is another club legend.

GALATASARAY

ISTANBUL, TURKEY
Stadium: Ali Sami Yen Stadium (40,000)

Founded: 1905 **Honours:** UEFA Cup 2000; Super Cup 2000; League 15; Turkish Cup 14

Galatasaray are Turkey's most successful club side, with a long and distinguished history that has passion written through it at every stage. Founded by Ali Sami Yen and a group of friends from the Galatasaray Lycée school, the club's stated aim was 'to play together like Englishmen, to have a colour and a name, and to beat the non-Turkish teams'.

Winners of the Istanbul league nine times between 1924 and 1958, it took the club four seasons before they won the national Turkish league after its establishment in 1959, lifting a first championship trophy in 1962 after having been eclipsed in preceding campaigns by their Istanbul rivals Fenerbahçe (twice) and Besiktas.

Their greatest triumph came in 2000 when they beat Arsenal on penalties to win their first UEFA Cup, having already won the domestic league. A few months later they beat Real Madrid in the Super Cup final with a golden goal from Mario Jardel. The manager at the time, Fatih Terim, was already a club legend, having played 327 times for the team, but UEFA Cup success raised him above other Galatasaray greats like Metin Oktay, Turgay Seren and Gheorghe Hagi.

The intimidating atmosphere created by their supporters led to the Ali Sami Yen Stadium being dubbed 'Hell'. The ground has undergone a significant renovation recently but plans to relocate the club to a brand new, purpose-built stadium have also been discussed.

HAMBURG SV

HAMBURG, GERMANY
Stadium: Volksparkstadion (55,000)

Founded: 1887 **Honours:** European Cup 1983; Cup Winners' Cup 1977; League 6; Cup 3

On paper Hamburg are the oldest club in Germany. Having been formed in 1887 as SC Germania, in June 1919 the club merged with Hamburg FC and FC Falke to create Hamburg SV, with the red and white strip picked as a compromise that was suitable for all parties.

National champions twice in the 1920s when the title was decided in a play-off format between the winners of the various regional leagues, Hamburg would not win the title again until they clinched the West German championship in 1960 under the leadership of legendary centre-forward Uwe Seeler. This Hamburg side took Barcleona close in the semi-final of the 1961 European Cup, losing in a play-off, and seven years later finished as runners-up to Milan in the Cup Winners' Cup. But by the time of Seeler's retirement in 1972, the club had yet to

Below: Hamburg's Horst Hrubesch celebrates after the 1983 European Cup final.

taste European glory. That changed in 1977 with a 2-0 Cup Winners' Cup win over Anderlecht, with goals from Georg Volkert and Felix Magath.

Spearheaded in the late Seventies by Kevin Keegan – his performances for the club saw him voted European Player Of The Year for both 1978 and 1979 – Hamburg clinched their first Bundesliga title in 1979, ushering in a truly golden period for the club. The magic of Keegan couldn't help Hamburg avoid a 1-0 defeat to Nottingham Forest in the European Cup final of 1980, but without him they went on to win the Bundesliga in 1982 and 1983 (finishing runners-up four times in the decade too) and the German Cup in 1987.

In 1983 Felix Magath was the Hamburg hero once again as he scored the only goal of the 1983 European Cup final against a Juventus team that boasted Platini, Zoff, Gentile, Tardelli and Rossi. But since the Eighties, Hamburg fans haven't had too much to cheer about, the side too often settling for mid-table mediocrity.

In August 2004 the club was knocked out of the German Cup 4-2 by regional league side Paderborn in one of the most infamous games in recent football history. It was discovered that referee Robert Hoyzer had accepted money from a Croatian gambling syndicate to fix the match. The resulting scandal sent shockwaves through German football. The club have recovered to finish third in the title race in 2006.

INDEPENDIENTE

BUENOS AIRES, ARGENTINA
Stadium: Doble Visera De Cemente (57,901)

Founded: 1905 **Honours:** World Club Cup 1973, 1984; Copa Libertadores 1964, 1965, 1972, 1973, 1974, 1975, 1984; Copa Interamericana 1973, 1974, 1975; Recopa Sudamericana 1995; League 14

Formed in the Avellaneda suburb of Buenos Aires, Independiente were founded, strangely enough, by employees of the City Of London department store. The club may not possess the global glamour of River Plate or Boca Juniors, but can boast far greater success in the Copa Libertadores than either of their higher-profile city rivals. Indeed, they were the first Argentine side to claim the trophy in 1964, getting the better of Uruguay's Nacional. A record-breaking seven Copa Libertadores titles, including an unlikely-to-be-equalled run of four successive triumphs from 1972 to 1975, has earned the club the deserved nickname of 'The King of Cups'.

The silverware spree didn't end there, and a brace of World Club Cups have also competed for space in the crowded trophy cabinet. The first of these wins was by a single goal against Juventus in Rome in 1973, followed 11 years later by victory over Liverpool by the same scoreline in Tokyo. Since the glory days, Independiente's fortunes have declined, with mounting debts,

bad management, and declining crowds forcing the club to sell top players. The joint sale of Diego Forlan to Manchester United (£7.5 million) and Vincente Vuoso (£3.5 million) to Manchester City proved absolutely vital to the club's survival in 2002.

INTER MILAN

MILAN, ITALY
Stadium: Giuseppe Meazza (85,700)

Founded: 1908 **Honours:** World Club Cup 1964, 1965; European Cup 1964, 1965; UEFA Cup 1991, 1994, 1998; League 14* *(including 2006 title stripped from Juventus)*; Cup 5

Giovani Paramithotti founded Football Club Internazionale Milano on March 9, 1908, after he and a group of his supporters broke away from AC Milan following a major policy disagreement with the club's owners. The name Internazionale was chosen because the club was to be open to players of all nationalities, unlike AC Milan who only allowed Italians to join them. To underline the club's commitment to internationalism, their first captain hailed from Switzerland. All things considered, it comes as no surprise that the rivalry between Milan's two teams remains one of the fiercest in world football almost a century after the split.

Inter won their first Italian championship in 1910, picked up another in 1920, and were one of the founders of Serie A in 1929. They became the only club never to have lost top-flight status after Juventus were demoted in 2006 for involvement in a match-fixing scandal. Along the way they have boasted many world-class players, including Brazilians such as Ronaldo and Jair, Germans Jürgen Klinsmann, Andreas Brehme and Lothar Matthäus, Portugal's Luis Figo, and from Italy, goal-scoring defender Giacinto Facchetti, who became the club's chairman in 2004, and Giuseppe Meazza, the prodigious striker after whom the San Siro stadium is now formally named – a stadium, incidentally, that they share with AC Milan.

When the fascists under Benito Mussolini came to power in Italy Inter Milan were forced to take on a less cosmopolitan name: in 1929 they became Ambrosiana, after the patron saint of the city of Milan. The name switch didn't do Inter any harm on the pitch and they won three Serie A titles – in 1930, 1938 and 1940 – as well as the Coppa Italia in 1939. They were also successful in the Mitropa Cup, a prototype of today's UEFA Cup and European Cup, making the semi-finals twice (1930 and 1936) and the final once (1933).

After the Second World War and the defeat of fascism, Inter reverted to their original name, appointing Alfredo Foni as coach and continuing to add trophies to their cabinet, winning back-to-back titles in 1953 and 1954.

It wasn't until the 1960s under another coach – Helenio Herrera – that they were able to enjoy domestic, European and international success at the same time. Serie A winners in 1963, Inter were crowned European champions for the first time the following season, comfortably beating Real Madrid 3-1 in the final in Vienna with two goals from striker Sandro Mazzola. They then beat Independiente of Argentina in the same year's World Club Cup, before pulling off an even more impressive trophy haul in 1965.

Having already been crowned Italian title winners and eliminating Liverpool in the semi-finals of the European Cup, Inter retained the trophy with a 1-0 win in Milan over mighty Benfica. They then beat Independiente 3-0 over two legs to keep their world crown intact. Inter retained their league title the following season and made it to the final of the European Cup in 1967, only to lose to Celtic 2-1 after initially taking the lead through a Mazzola penalty.

A title win in 1971 and a European Cup final appearance the following season (they lost 2-0 to Ajax) couldn't disguise the fact that without their massively influential coach Herrera, who had joined Roma, Inter's time as one of the world's biggest clubs had come to an end.

The rest of Seventies and Eighties were hardly unkind to the club – they won Serie A in 1980 and 1989, and the Coppa Italia in 1978 and 1982, but it wasn't until the Nineties that the Milan club once again made significant waves in Europe. In 1991 they won the UEFA Cup for the first time, beating AS Roma 2-1 in a two-legged all-Italian final, and repeated the feat three years later with a 2-0 aggregate victory over Austria Salzburg.

Another UEFA Cup final appearance followed in 1997, but having battled out a draw over two legs with German side Schalke, they lost 4-1 on penalties in Milan. Inter returned to put matters right in 1998 in their fourth final appearance in eight years, beating Lazio 3-0 in the competition's first one-off final.

In a concerted attempt to re-establish Inter as a force in both the Italian league and the much-coveted Champions League, the club appointed Argentinian Hector Cúper as coach in 2001. Cúper had taken his previous side, Valencia of Spain, to successive European Cup finals, and it didn't take long for him to make an impact at Inter. The club were involved in the fight for the 2001-2 domestic title right up until the last day of the season. Inter eventually finished third behind Juventus and Roma, with just two points separating the top three.

Roberto Mancini took over as coach in 2004 and in his first two seasons Inter won the Coppa Italia twice and the Supercoppa Italiana. In 2006 they finished the title race third behind Juventus and Milan, but after Juventus were relegated and stripped of the title for their part in a major match-fixing scandal, and Milan were deducted 30 points, the title has been retrospectively awarded to Inter, their 14th championship win.

JUVENTUS

TURIN, ITALY
Stadium: Delle Alpi
(69,000)

Founded: 1897 **Honours:** World Club Cup 1985, 1996; European Cup 1985, 1996; Cup Winners' Cup 1984; UEFA Cup 1977, 1990, 1993; League 27* *(stripped of 2005 & 2006 titles)*; Cup 9

Famously founded on a Turin park bench by a group of students in November 1897, Juventus have become the most successful Italian club of all time. Never out of Serie A since its formation in 1929, and crowned champions 29 times between 1905 and 2006 (although they have been stripped of two of these), they have also featured some of the world's most celebrated players, including Michel Platini, Zinédine Zidane, Dino Zoff and Giampiero Boniperti, whose name is still revered in Turin more than 50 years after he first made his mark in the team. Indeed, his scoring record for the club was only broken on January 10, 2006, when Alessandro Del Piero scored three times in a match against Fiorentina to pass Boniperti's record of 182.

Originally playing in pink, Juventus adopted their famous black-and-white stripes in 1903 after a club official visited England and liked Notts County's shirts so much that he took a bundle of them back home with him.

It wasn't until the 1930s that Juventus truly emerged as a superpower in the Italian league. They won five consecutive championship titles between 1931 and 1935 under coach Carlo Carcano, a feat that remains unrepeated. Players such as goalkeeper Gianpiero Combi, centre-half Monti, winger Raimondo Orsi and striker Giovanni Ferrari went on to help Italy win the World Cup in 1934 – Orsi even scored the equaliser against Czechoslovakia in the final. During this time Juventus also reached the semi-final of the Mitropa Cup on four consecutive occasions. Unfortunately, they never made it to

Above: Juventus captain Gaetano Scirea greets Liverpool's Phil Neal before the 1985 European Cup final. Opposite top: Torricelli, Padovano and Del Piero with the European Cup in 1996. Opposite bottom left to right: Vialli, Baggio and Zidane.

the final and on one occasion were actually disqualified from the tournament after a brutal semi-final against Slavia (who were also banned).

Intermittent success in the league and cup continued throughout the Fifties and Sixties (they won back-to-back cups in 1959 and 1960 and league titles in 1960 and 1961), but it wasn't until the Seventies that the club translated their domestic success into European progress. They made it to the final of the Fairs Cup in 1971, but after three drawn games with Leeds (one a replay of the abandoned first leg), they lost out on the away goals rule. In 1977 they won the UEFA Cup on the same rule against Athletic Bilbao, although they came close to throwing the tie away having led 2-0 on aggregate before being pegged back by the determined Spaniards. Juventus added the Cup Winners' Cup to their trophy cabinet in 1984 with a 2-1 victory over Porto.

The European Champions Cup continued to elude them: their first final came in 1973 but they were defeated 1-0 by Ajax, and history repeated itself in 1983 when they lost to Hamburg by the same scoreline. Juventus were finally crowned European champions for the first time in the Heysel Stadium in 1985, when a team featuring Italy's 1982 World Cup hero Paolo Rossi defeated Liverpool 1-0. Sadly their moment of glory was overshadowed by the deaths of 39 Italian fans during pre-match violence between supporters.

The 1990s promised much for Juventus. Massive sums of money were spent on securing the services of Roberto Baggio from Fiorentina and Gianluca Vialli from Sampdoria, and the club won the UEFA Cup twice, in 1990 and 1993. It was only when Marcello Lippi joined as coach from Napoli, though, that the Juventus success story moved up a gear. The Turin side claimed their first league title in nine years in 1995 (also claiming the Coppa Italia) and won back-to-back championships in 1997 and 1998. Even more impressively, Lippi's side beat Ajax on penalties to lift the European Cup for a second

time in 1996, following it with a crushing 9-2 aggregate win over Paris Saint-Germain in the same year's European Super Cup. Juventus also reached the final of the European Cup in 1997 and 1998, but despite starting the games as favourites, lost on both occasions – 3-1 to Borussia Dortmund and then 1-0 to Real Madrid.

Lippi left for Inter Milan in 1999 after a final trophy-free season at the Delle Alpi, but returned after only a year at the San Siro. He won the Serie A title in dramatic fashion in his first season back, pipping Lazio and Inter to the title on the final day. After winning the title again in 2003, Juventus were within reach of the trophy they most wanted, the European Cup. They had reached the final after dispensing with Barcelona and Real Madrid, but after a scoreless match at Old Trafford, Italian rivals AC Milan won the game on penalties after five of the first seven spot-kicks had been missed.

The following season proved disappointing and Marcello Lippi quit to take over the national team. Juventus shocked everyone when they announced Roma coach Fabio Capello as his replacement. Capello guided them to the 2005 title but has been unable to make any further progress for the club in the Champions League.

After sharing a ground with Torino for many years, Juventus will soon have a home of their own. Their rivals moved to the Stadio Grande Torino at the end of the 2005-6 season. Juventus will also move to the stadium for one season, while the Delle Alpi is being redeveloped. The Stadio Grande Torino was originally built for the 1934 World Cup finals and was named the Stadio Mussolini (later the Stadio Comunale) and it played home to Juventus from 1933 to 1990, providing the venue for 18 of their league titles.

The club won the 2006 championship but their involvement in the biggest match-fixing scandal in Italian football history resulted in Juventus being relegated to Serie B, where they will start with a 17 points deduction. They have also been stripped of their last two league titles.

STADIO DELLE ALPI

The Stadio Delle Alpi was built to host the 1990 World Cup, but has never been popular. Juve will leave the stadium for the 2006-7 season while the Delle Alpi is being rebuilt: the running track is being removed and the capacity reduced. The hope is that it will become more intimate and live down its 'stadium without a soul' tag. The new stadium will be renamed when it reopens.

Timeline

1897: Students from Turin's Liceo D'Azeglio form a sports club. The team play in pink shirts.

1903: Juve adopt the famous black and white shirt, inspired by the strip of Notts County.

1905: Juventus beat more experienced teams from Genoa and Milan to win their first Italian title.

1923: Edoardo Agnelli, son of Fiat's founder, is elected club president. The club moves to a new stadium.

1926: Juventus win their second title.

1931: Juve win the title for five years in a row, from 1931-5.

1933: Juve move home again. A stadium is built for the World University Games and the team play here until 1990.

1947: Giovanni Agnelli becomes president of Juventus.

1955: Umberto Agnelli takes over the presidency from his older brother Giovanni.

1957: John Charles is bought for £70,000 from Leeds, doubling the British transfer record.

1961: Juve become the first Italian club entitled to wear the star after winning ten titles.

1972 to 1986: Juve win nine titles and all major European and Intercontinental tournaments.

1985: Juventus defeat Liverpool to win the European Cup, but it is a game remembered for the deaths of fans in the Heysel Stadium.

1990: Juve win the UEFA Cup and Italian Cup. They move to the 69,041-capacity Stadio Delle Alpi.

1994: Coach Marcello Lippi guides the team to their first title in nine years.

1996: Juve beat Ajax on penalties to win the Champions League.

2006: Win Serie A, but are stripped of title and relegated to Serie B for involvement in a match-fixing scandal.

KASHIMA ANTLERS

KASHIMA, JAPAN
Stadium: Kashima Soccer Stadium (41,800)

Founded: 1991 **Honours:** League 4; League Cup 3; Emperor's Cup 2

Formerly the factory team of Sumitomo Metals, the club transformed into Kashima Antlers in 1991, taking their name and logo from the town's literal translation as Deer Island. Kashima began J.League life by winning the first ever stage of the two-stage race, but the club had to wait until 1996 for a first full title. In the following five years the club overtook more traditional sides like Verdy Kawasaki to become Japan's dominant team, winning an unprecedented treble (league title, Nabisco Cup and Emperor's Cup) in 2000.

This dominance was built on the presence of Brazilian imports such as Jorginho, Alcindo and the legendary Zico, who joined at the club's foundation in 1991 and eventually became their general manager. Zico retired before the club won their first title but is so revered in Kashima he has had two statues dedicated to him. He became Japan national coach in 2002.

Although based in a modest-sized town, Kashima Antlers are one of the best supported sides in the league, averaging 17,000 fans per game. After five years without a title, the club parted company with manager Toninho Cerezo and appointed yet another Brazilian coach (their sixth), Paulo Autuori, who was prised away from São Paulo early in 2006 after winning the World Club Championship with the Brazilian club.

LAZIO

ROME, ITALY
Stadium: Olimpico (82,000)

Founded: 1900 **Honours:** Cup Winners' Cup 1999; European Super Cup 1999; League 2; Cup 4

Until the arrival of Sven-Göran Eriksson as coach at the start of the 1997-8 season, it's safe to say that Lazio had been one of Italian football's great underachievers. Founded on January 9, 1900, by Luigi Bigiarelli and eight friends, the club had endured decades waiting in the wings while Juventus and AC Milan paraded centre stage. However, Lazio's threadbare trophy cabinet – containing an Italian Cup (1958) and a single league title (1974) – was soon filled to bursting as the Rome side took seven trophies in three heady seasons of achievement.

With a team that included Marcelo Salas, Juan Sebástian Verón and Christian Vieri, Eriksson won two Italian Cups, two domestic Super Cups (played between the Italian league champions and cup winners), the UEFA Super Cup and a European Cup Winners' Cup. He also steered Lazio to a second league title in 2000, before leaving the club the following season.

In 2002 a financial scandal forced owner Sergio Cragnotti to leave the club, leaving Lazio in the hands of financial caretakers until it was sold in 2004. Despite this the club managed to win the Italian Cup in 2004 but it had to lower overheads by losing many veteran players. With modest ambitions at the start of 2005-6, the team punched above its weight, coach Delio Rossi galvanising a squad short on quality but rich in spirit. But after being caught up in Italy's match-fixing scandal in 2006 they received a 19 point deduction for the 2006-7 season.

LEEDS UNITED

LEEDS, ENGLAND
Stadium: Elland Road (40,204)

Founded: 1919 **Honours:** Fairs Cup 1968, 1971; League 3; Cup 1; League Cup 1

Following allegations of illegal payments to players, Second Division Leeds City were wound-up by the FA in October 1919. Leeds United were formed the following month. With Port Vale having taken over Leeds City's remaining fixtures, the new United began in the Midland League, before entering the Second Division after turning professional in 1920.

In the 1930s, in Edwards, Hart and Copping, Leeds United boasted one of the great half-back lines in English football, while in 1957 the club made headlines by selling John Charles to Juventus for a British-record of £67,000. For much of their first 40 years, however, Leeds merely bounced between the top two divisions. It wasn't until the mid-Sixties that the team really became a force in English football, mainly as a result of the appointment in 1961 of Don Revie as player-manager.

Although relegated in 1960, over the next five years Revie would transform the club, changing

the team colours from blue and gold to their now famous all-white (inspired by the European triumphs of Real Madrid), and rebuilding the team around a talented group of young players that included Jack Charlton, Billy Bremner, Peter Lorimer, Norman Hunter, Paul Reaney, Paul Madeley, Eddie Gray and Johnny Giles.

Promoted to Division One as champions in 1964, in their first year back in the top flight they narrowly lost the title on goal average to Manchester United and the FA Cup final to Liverpool, helping to establish a reputation that would haunt the club for the next decade. Under Revie they would be known as the greatest runners-up in English football: five times they would finish second in the league, three times in the FA Cup, and once each in all three European competitions.

That's not to say that success eluded them. In 1968 they first beat Arsenal to win the League Cup, before lifting the Fairs Cup with a 1-0 aggregate win over Ferencváros. The following year they won their first league title, and in 1971 they beat Juventus to again lift the Fairs Cup. In 1972 a single Allan Clarke goal beat Arsenal to win the centenary FA Cup, and in 1974, at the end of the Revie era, they won their second league championship.

Following this success, Revie left Elland Road to take charge of the national team. Brian Clough was the nominated successor, but his tenure in the Leeds hotseat lasted days rather than months, leaving Jimmy Armfield to complete the season and take the team to the 1975 European Cup final. The match proved pivotal in the history of Leeds United – not only did they lose 2-0 to an understrength Bayern Munich, but after a riot by their fans, the club were banned from all European competition for the next five years.

Leeds were relegated in 1982, their glory days seemingly behind them. Managed in turn by former legends Allan Clarke, Eddie Gray and Billy Bremner, Leeds United turned to Howard Wilkinson, poached from nearby Sheffield Wednesday, who finally brought the good times back to Elland Road after joining the club in 1988. Achieving promotion in 1990, he took Leeds back to the very top of the English game two years later when, inspired by the mercurial Frenchman Eric Cantona, the club clinched the final Football League title before the onset of the Premier League.

Building on that revival, at the turn of the century Leeds, under David O'Leary, were once again regarded as a force to be reckoned with, reaching the semi-finals of the Champions League in 2001. But in attempting to reach those heady heights, the club financially overstretched themselves, and they are still paying the price for their ambition today, relegated in 2004 after coming perilously close to going out of business. Bought by former Chelsea chairman Ken Bates in January 2005, manager Kevin Blackwell took the team to the play-off final in 2006.

Right: Lazio's were the winners of the last ever European Cup Winners' Cup in 1999.

LIVERPOOL

LIVERPOOL, ENGLAND
Stadium: Anfield
(46,000)

Founded: 1892 **Honours:** European Cup 1977, 1978, 1981, 1984, 2005; UEFA Cup 1973, 1976, 2001; European Super Cup 1977, 2001, 2005; League 18; Cup 7; League Cup 7

Liverpool have their city neighbours and great rivals, Everton, to thank for their existence. Then residents at Anfield, Everton became embroiled in an argument with the stadium's owner, John Houlding, over rent payments, and, unable to find an acceptable solution, left to set up a new home at Goodison Park. In possession of a football ground but no team to play in it, Houlding formed Liverpool FC on March 15, 1892, and soon saw them rise from the local Lancashire League to Division Two, and then gain promotion to the top-flight in 1894.

The first of 18 league championships came in 1901, with four more titles arriving over the course of the next 50 years. However, Liverpool returned to the Second Division in 1954 and it wasn't until the arrival of charismatic Scotsman, Bill Shankly, as manager in late 1959 that the foundations were laid for the huge success enjoyed by the club in the Seventies and Eighties.

Shankly's approach combined great tactical acumen with infectious enthusiasm, and his ability to instill self-belief in his players was second to none. Liverpool finally returned to Division One in 1962 and claimed a sixth championship two years later. But Shankly was only just getting started: two more league titles (1966 and 1973) and two FA Cups (1965 and 1974) followed, before his retirement in 1974. Most significant of all Shankly's achievements though was the club's first European trophy: they beat Borussia Mönchengladbach 3-2 over two legs to lift the UEFA Cup in 1973.

Shankly's successor was Bob Paisley, a quietly spoken Geordie, who had been first team coach and a vital member of the legendary Anfield 'boot room'. Paisley's achievements at Liverpool

Above: The legendary Liverpool manager, Bill Shankly.

Above: Liverpool's champions of Europe in 1978: Case, Neal, Clemence, Kennedy, Hughes, Souness and Dalglish.

have never been matched in the English game. In nine extraordinary years he took The Reds to six league titles, three League Cups, one UEFA Cup and three European Cups, the first of which came in 1977 with a 3-1 win against Borussia Mönchengladbach. Liverpool retained the trophy in 1978 with a 1-0 win over Club Brugge and lifted it again in 1981, beating Real Madrid 1-0.

When Paisley stepped down as manager in 1983 he was replaced by another member of the Anfield backroom staff, Joe Fagan. Any notions that the Liverpool success story was about to come to a halt were dispatched in his first season, as Liverpool claimed an impressive treble: league title, League Cup and European Cup (won on penalties against AS Roma).

Liverpool reached the European Cup final the following year but lost 1-0 to Juventus in the Heysel Stadium in Brussels. The game itself was overshadowed by the terrible events that occurred as supporters of the two sides rioted. Thirty-nine Italian fans lost their lives when a wall collapsed, leading to a ban that kept English clubs, including Liverpool, out of European competition for the next five years.

Fagan's reign at Anfield was surprisingly short and when he stepped down at the end of the 1984-5 season he was replaced by Kenny Dalglish, the first player-manager in the club's history. The Scottish international guided The Reds to a league and FA Cup double in his first season in charge (1985-6) and further league titles in 1988 and 1990. Dalglish's side also won the FA Cup in 1989, but their triumph was tinged with tragedy: on April 15 of that year

96 Liverpool fans were crushed to death at Sheffield Wednesday's Hillsborough ground before kick-off in an FA Cup semi-final tie between The Reds and Nottingham Forest.

Dalglish quit suddenly at the end of the 1991 season to be replaced by Graeme Souness. In his three seasons in charge, Souness won the FA Cup (1992) but Liverpool's primacy in the league started to slip. He was replaced in 1994 by veteran Anfield coach Roy Evans, an appointment that suggested Liverpool were trying to recapture the old 'boot room' philosophy of promoting from within. When Evans failed to recapture the glory days, Gerard Houllier was brought in to work alongside him, eventually taking over the role.

Houllier returned the club to winning ways, with triumphs in the FA Cup, UEFA Cup, Super Cup and League Cup in 2001, and the League Cup again in 2003, but a 19th league title and success in the Champions League continued to elude Liverpool, and at the end of the 2003-4 season, he became the first manager in the club's history to be sacked.

It was his replacement Rafael Benítez who finally delivered what this great club wanted. At the end of his first rather lacklustre season, Liverpool reached the Champions League final, and despite going 3-0 down before half-time, a comeback inspired by captain Steven Gerrard saw The Reds push the game to extra-time, and a penalty shoot-out brought the club their fifth European Cup. Gerrard inpsired a similar victory in the 2006 FA Cup final, coming back from 2-0 down to win the game on penalties.

Timeline

1890

1892: Liverpool FC are founded on March 15. They win their first game 7-1, a friendly against Rotherham played on September 1.

1900

1901: Liverpool clinch their first league title.

1910

1906: The club wins a second title and builds the Spion Kop.

1945

1947: The club win their fifth league title, 24 years after the previous one.

1950

1954: After finishing 22nd in the league, Liverpool are relegated to Division Two.

1955

1959: Bill Shankly is appointed manager.

1960

1964: A title win sparks a golden era for the club, with further titles in 1966 and 1973, and the FA Cup in 1965 and 1974.

1965

1973: Kevin Keegan scores two goals to win the UEFA Cup.

1970

1974: Bill Shankly retires and is replaced by coach Bob Paisley.

1975

1977: Liverpool beat Mönchengladbach to win the European Cup.

1980

1981: Alan Kennedy's goal is enough to defeat Real Madrid and win the European Cup.

1984: New manager Joe Fagan wins a title, a European Cup and a League Cup in his first season.

1985

1986: Kenny Dalglish is appointed manager and guides the club to the double.

1990

1989: During an FA Cup semi-final 96 Liverpool fans die.

1995

2001: Liverpool win the League Cup, the FA Cup and the UEFA Cup.

2000

2004: Rafael Benítez joins Liverpool.

2005: Coming back from 3-0 down, Liverpool win European Cup.

THE CHAMPIONS CUP WITH FIVE WINS, LIVERPOOL HAVE THE BEST RECORD OF ANY ENGLISH CLUB IN THE EUROPEAN CUP.

1977
Liverpool 3
B. Mönchengladbach 1
Olympic Stadium, Rome

1978
Liverpool 1
Club Brugge 0
Wembley Stadium, London

1981
Liverpool 1
Real Madrid 0
Parc Des Princes, Paris

1984
Liverpool 1
Roma 1
Liverpool won 4-2 on penalties
Olympic Stadium, Rome

2005
Liverpool 3
AC Milan 3
Liverpool won 3-2 on penalties
Atatürk Stadium, Istanbul

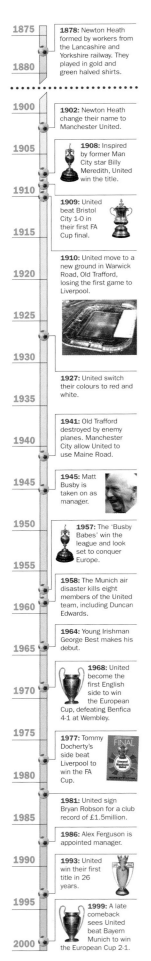

MANCHESTER UNITED

ENGLAND
Stadium: Old Trafford
(69,000)

Founded: 1878 **Honours:** World Club Cup 1999; European Cup 1968, 1999; Cup Winners' Cup 1991; European Super Cup 1991; League 15; Cup 11; League Cup 2

The story of Manchester United is a rags-to-riches tale. Now a commercial giant across the world, United have come a long way from their humble beginnings. Formed as Newton Heath by employees of the Lancashire and Yorkshire Railway Company, the club had severe financial problems and were saved from bankruptcy in 1902 by a local brewery owner. The club took on the name Manchester United and almost immediately a period of success followed with a first league championship in 1908, followed 12 months later with victory in the FA Cup final.

To cope with growing attendances United left their Bank Street home, moving to Old Trafford in 1910, losing the first game at their new ground 4-3 to Liverpool. The 1920s and 1930s saw United bounce between the top two Divisions, and in 1934 relegation to Division Three was only avoided on the final day of the season. Financial difficulties again struck the club as attendances fell and during the Second World War the main stand at Old Trafford was destroyed during a German bombing raid. But United's fortunes were to change forever when the club appointed Matt Busby as manager in 1945.

Claiming his first silverware with the 1948 FA Cup victory over Blackpool, Busby made the club a force in English football once again, giving youth its chance by promoting players like Jackie Blanchflower and Roger Byrne to the first team. His policy paid dividends in 1952 when the club finally won the league.

Rising star Duncan Edwards was thrown into the first team as a 16-year-old and further

OLD TRAFFORD

Constructed in 1909, Old Trafford was rebuilt after Second World War bomb damage. In the 1970s it became the first English stadium to erect perimeter fencing. With the rebuilding of the Stretford End in 1994, it became a perfect bowl. Known as 'The Theatre Of Dreams', the stadium features a memorial clock outside, commemorating the Munich air disaster.

Above: Bobby Charlton, Shay Brennan and Alex Stepney celebrate with the European Cup in 1968. Opposite from top left: George Best takes on Norman Hunter of Leeds in 1970; Roy Keane kisses the Premiership trophy in 2003; the United team after winning the 1963 FA Cup final; the class of 1999 lift the Champions League trophy.

league success followed in 1956 and 1957. But the club were rocked by tragedy the following year when a plane carrying the team back from a European match against Red Star Belgrade crashed after refuelling in Munich, killing 22 people, including seven players. Fifteen days later Edwards also died, failing to recover from his injuries in a German hospital.

United still managed to reach the FA Cup final that year but Busby had to rebuild the side and he did so with the likes of Nobby Stiles, Denis Law and George Best, combining brilliantly with players such as Bobby Charlton, a survivor of the Munich crash.

The title was won again in 1965 and 1967 and this time United made sure they left their mark on Europe. Extra-time goals at Wembley from Best, Kidd and Charlton gave United a 4-1 victory over Benfica to lift the 1968 European Cup, a remarkable achievement just ten years after the Munich air crash. Busby was knighted but he bowed out at the top, retiring in 1969, and United found he was a difficult man to replace.

Briefly out of the top flight in the mid-Seventies, United fans were becoming starved of the kind of success that they had become accustomed to, despite FA Cup victories in 1977, 1983 and 1985. Alex Ferguson was appointed manager in November 1986 and soon the balance of football power in England began to shift from Merseyside to Manchester.

The Nineties began with Ferguson guiding the club to success in the FA Cup, the European Cup Winners' Cup and the League Cup in three

consecutive years, but the championship still eluded them. The wait, having now stretched to 25 years, looked certain to come to an end in 1992, but United somehow contrived to hand the title to Leeds.

Leeds repaid the favour by selling Eric Cantona to Old Trafford and he provided the missing link for Ferguson's side. Inspired by the Frenchman, United won the title in 1993 and 1994, and were crowned champions five times in the Nineties.

Cantona retired in 1997 at the age of 30, but by now Ferguson, like Busby, had built his side around the products of the club's youth system, with players like Ryan Giggs, David Beckham, Paul Scholes and the Neville brothers, Gary and Phil. United's crowning year came in 1999, when their all-conquering side added the European Cup and World Club Cup to their domestic double. Not only was the manner of the European Cup victory amazing (substitutes Sheringham and Solskjaer each scored in injury-time to beat Bayern Munich 2-1), it enabled Ferguson to emulate the achievements of Busby.

Ferguson too was knighted as the league domination continued in 2000 and 2001. He reneged on his promise to retire, bringing the title back again in 2003, but more recently times have been a bit harder for United fans as the club have struggle to keep pace with the huge financial clout of Chelsea. They have also had to come to terms with the hostile £800 million takeover of the club in 2005 by American businessman Malcolm Glazer, a bid financed largely by borrowing.

MARSEILLE

MARSEILLE, FRANCE
Stadium: Vélodrome
(60,000)

Founded: 1898 **Honours:** European Cup 1993;
League 9 (inc. 1993 revoked); Cup 10

Olympique Marseille have cut a swathe through the history of French football to become the most famous club from France across the world. Winning their first French league title in 1937, they added a second in 1948 during the early days of professional football. Known as 'l'OM', they enjoyed huge popular support in their native south of France. Further success was difficult to come by, but they enjoyed another period of glory in the early Seventies, winning back-to-back titles in 1971 and 1972, Yugoslav striker Josip Skoblar setting a record of 44 goals in a season in the 1970-1 campaign.

Marseille failed to build on their triumphs but returned to prominence in glorious fashion in 1986 when businessman Bernard Tapie became chairman, triggering the club's most successful spell. He spent lavishly on star players such as Jean-Pierre Papin, Chris Waddle and Enzo Francescoli, and guided them to four consecutive league titles from 1989 to 1992.

Tapie established Marseille as a force to be reckoned with at home and abroad. Papin was the league's top scorer five seasons in a row, and Waddle became a cult hero in France. Others, such as Brazilian Carlos Mozer and Ghanaian midfielder Abedi Pele added touches of class.

Marseille reached the European Cup semi-finals in 1990, losing to a controversial Benfica goal, and the final in 1991, when they lost on penalties to Red Star Belgrade in Bari. In 1993 they finally realised their dream by beating Milan thanks to a headed goal from Basile Boli.

Joy turned to agony when the club was found guilty of fixing a league match with Valenciennes. Tapie was forced out, the club was relegated and headed for financial ruin. They started the long comeback with promotion in 1996 and battled to the UEFA Cup final in 1999, before losing 3-0 to Parma. Inspired by Didier Drogba, they reached the final again in 2004, losing this time to Valencia. Their only trophy in recent years has been the little regarded Intertoto Cup in 2005.

Below: Marseille's Franck Sauzée enjoys the moment after winning the European Cup in 1993.

MILAN

MILAN, ITALY
Stadium: Giuseppe Meazza
(85,700)

Founded: 1899 **Honours:** World Club Cup 1969, 1989, 1990; European Cup 1963, 1969, 1989, 1990, 1994, 2003; Cup Winners' Cup 1968, 1973; European Super Cup 1989, 1990, 1994, 2003; League 17; Cup 5

Although Juventus can lay claim to being Italy's most successful club in domestic football, on the European stage they run a distant second to AC Milan, six-time winners of the European Cup, a record only bettered by Spanish giants Real Madrid. The Milan Cricket And Football Club was founded on December 16, 1899, by Englishman Albert Edwards, and over the last century it has become one of the world's richest clubs: first bankrolled by tyre magnate Piero Pirelli, but in more recent times by Silvio Berlusconi, former Prime Minister and Italy's richest man.

Milan won their first Italian title in 1901, with two more added in 1906 and 1907. They finished third in 1929-30, Serie A's first season, and contested their first Coppa Italia final in 1942, losing to Juventus after a replay. It wasn't until the 1950s, however, that Milan really found their feet, winning four titles in nine years. Their success initially stemmed from the purchase of Gunnar Gren, Nils Liedholm and Gunnar Nordahl, the stars of Sweden's Olympic gold medal-winning team of 1948. Nordahl went on to score 210 goals in 257 games for the club, while Liedholm later became club coach in the early 1980s.

Milan's first serious foray into European competition was in 1956 when they reached the semi-final of the first European Cup. They lost to Real Madrid 5-4 on aggregate and were beaten again by the Spanish giants in the 1958 final, 3-2 after extra-time. Starting the 1960s in impressive form, Milan notched their fifth Serie A title in 1962 and won their first European Cup the following year at Wembley against holders Benfica. The Italians won 2-1, despite falling behind to a Eusébio goal.

In 1965 they claimed another European title after beating German side Hamburg 2-0 in the final of the Cup Winners' Cup. A second European Cup followed in 1969, when Milan put out holders Manchester United in the semi-finals, before thumping Ajax 4-1 in the final itself – Pierino Prati scoring a hat-trick. In the same year Milan won their first World Club Cup, beating Estudiantes de la Plata of Argentina 4-2 on aggregate, despite their opponents' inexcusably violent behaviour in the second leg.

Milan started the Seventies brightly with appearances in two consecutive Cup Winners'

Cup finals. In 1973 they beat Leeds 1-0, but they lost the second 2-0 to FC Magdeburg. With that defeat European success dried-up for Milan and they had to rely on domestic honours to assuage the ambitions of their fans. The club won the Italian title in 1979 and the Coppa Italia three times between 1972 and 1977, but dark days were just around the corner. In 1980 a betting scandal broke, implicating the club's goalkeeper, Enrico Albertosi, and president, Felice Colombo. Milan were relegated to Serie B as punishment and nearly went out of business altogether, before Berlusconi stepped in to save them from bankruptcy in 1986.

Much rejuvenated by Berlusconi's millions and the inspired management of Arrigo Sacchi,

THE SAN SIRO

The home of both AC Milan and Inter Milan, the Stadio Giuseppe Meazza is still largely known as the San Siro, the original name it took from the district in which it is located. Built in 1926, a £50 million overhaul for the 1990 World Cup included the addition of a third tier built on impressive cylindrical towers at the corners of the stadium.

the club dominated European football in the late 1980s and early 1990s. They beat Steaua Bucharest 4-0 in the 1989 European Cup final, with Dutch superstars Ruud Gullit and Marco Van Basten both scoring twice. Milan retained the trophy the following year, a single Frank Rijkaard goal this time giving them victory over Benfica. Defeat in the 1993 final to Marseille was a momentary blip as the Milan giants triumphed once again the following year with a solid 4-0 demolition of Barcelona. A further European Cup final appearance came in 1995 when Patrick Kluivert, who would go on to play for Milan, scored a late winner for Ajax.

Milan were equally impressive domestically, winning their first league title for nine seasons in 1988 and three more consecutively between 1992 and 1994. The trio of titles coincided with an extraordinary 58-match unbeaten streak between 1991 and 1993. A fifth title in nine years came in 1996, with George Weah providing the firepower up front, and three years later they won their final seven games to pip Lazio to the title by just a point. The club's last championship came in 2004.

The dearth of recent success on the European stage was addressed by a Champions League win in 2003, when they beat Juventus on penalties at Old Trafford, Andriy Shevchenko scoring the winning spot-kick. But two years later, after leading Liverpool 3-0 at half-time in the 2005 final, Milan somehow managed to surrender their lead to a Steven Gerrard-inspired comeback, this time Shevchenko failing to convert the penalty that handed the Champions League trophy to Liverpool.

Top left: Ruud Gullit lifts the European Cup in 1989. Top right: the Milan team after the 2003 Champions League final. Above: Cesare Maldini holds up the European Cup in 1963.

MILLONARIOS

BOGOTA, COLOMBIA
Stadium: Estadio Nemesio Camacho (56,000)

Founded: 1938 **Honours:** Copa Merconorte 2001; League 13

Millonarios are the most successful club in Colombia in terms of domestic titles, but they have never managed to consistently translate this dominance into silverware outside of their own country and they have a poor record in the Copa Libertadores for a club of their stature.

The bulk of the club's major triumphs were achieved in the Fifties, an era known as 'El Dorado', when Millonarios were at the centre of a worldwide transfer controversy. Along with Independiente Santa Fe, the Bogota club refused to pay transfer fees to overseas clubs, and a rebel league was formed. This coincided with a player strike in Argentina, and lured by the massive signing-on fees and wages on offer, Millonarios were able to attract their most famous player, Alfredo Di Stéfano. Along with his fellow Argentines, Nestor Rossi and Adolfo Perderna, the team won four league titles in five years. In the process they earned the nickname the 'Blue Ballet' for their artistry on the pitch. Di Stéfano scored a remarkable 267 goals in 292 games for Millonarios before swapping Colombia for further fame and fortune with Real Madrid.

Below left: Carlos Castro of Millonarios holds the Copa Merconorte trophy in 2001.

Below right: Luis Islas celebrates with the trophy after Nacional won Uruguay's league title.

They have not been without their problems. It has been closely associated with the Medellin drug cartel, a situation hindering performances on the pitch in recent years, and the club's financial problems in 2005 led them to cancel plans to move to their own stadium.

NACIONAL

MONTEVIDEO, URUGUAY
Stadium: Parque Central (16,000), Centenario (73,609)

Founded: 1899 **Honours:** World Club Cup 1971, 1980, 1988; Copa Libertadores 1971, 1980, 1988; Recopa Sudamericana 1989; Copa Interamericana 1972, 1979; League 41

Fans of Nacional proudly lay claim to being the first South American club formed by its citizens rather than the expatriot community. In 1903 the entire Nacional team to a man was selected to play for Uruguay in an international against Argentina – they won 3-2 and the date continues to be part of the club's annual celebrations. Along with city rivals Peñarol, they have remained a controlling force in Uruguayan football ever since – there have only been eight occasions since the Uruguayan league turned professional in 1932, when neither of the teams have won the title.

Triumphs have not only been confined to home soil, and a trio of victories in the Copa Libertadores is matched by the same number of successes in the World Club Cup, the most eye-catching of which was a 1-0 victory against Brian Clough's Nottingham Forest in 1980, when the trophy was contested in Tokyo.

Famous footballers to play in Nacional's colours include Hèctor Scarone, one of Uruguay's greatest ever forwards and the inspiration behind his country's World Cup triumph in 1930. After years plying his trade abroad with Barcelona and Inter Milan, he returned to Nacional and finally retired as a player at the age of 55.

NOTTINGHAM FOREST

NOTTINGHAM, ENGLAND
Stadium: City Ground (30,602)

Founded: 1865 **Honours:** European Cup 1979, 1980; European Super Cup 1979; League 1; Cup 2; League Cup 4

Before Brian Clough took charge of Second Division Nottingham Forest in 1975 they had never won the league and had won the FA Cup just twice, in 1898 and 1959. Five years later they had become champions of Europe twice over.

Promoted to Division One in 1977, Forest clinched the title in their first season back in the top flight. To consolidate the club's bid for European glory the following season Clough signed Trevor Francis from Midlands rivals Birmingham City, making him English football's first million-pound player. In his first European game Francis's single goal brought victory against Malmo in the European Cup final, helping Forest to become only the third club in the competition's history to lift the trophy at the first attempt. One year later they repeated the feat, beating Hamburg – complete with their European Footballer Of The Year, Kevin Keegan – 1-0 to lift the trophy in the Bernabéu Stadium.

Under Clough's stewardship Forest went on to appear in six League Cup finals in 12 years, running out winners four times. Their one appearance in the FA Cup final in this period resulted in defeat to Tottenham in 1991, and two years later Forest were relegated in Clough's last game before retirement.

Bouncing between divisions with very little impact, Forest's subsequent progress has been hampered by the financial problems besetting the club. Powered by the goals of striker Stan Collymore they secured promotion to the top flight under Frank Clark in 1994, and returned again as Division One champions in 1998, but relegation the following year signalled that this once-great club's glory days may be well and truly behind them. Relegation to the third tier of English football in 2005 may make it hard for them to come back, although their unsuccessful battle for a play-off place went down to the last game of the season in 2006.

PALMEIRAS

SÃO PAULO, BRAZIL
Stadium: Estádio Palestra Itália (35,000)

Founded: 1914 **Honours:** Copa Libertadores: 1999; Copa Mercosur 1998; São Paulo State League 21; League 4; Cup 1

For all the great players to have come through the ranks at Palmeiras – Oberdan, Ademir da Guia, Djalma Santos, Edmundo – perhaps the most recognisable name recently linked with the São Paulo club is a manager who went on to make a mark on the world stage. Despite success in the early 1970s and 1990s, it was at the end of the century when Luiz Felipe Scolari guided them to victory in the Copa Mercosur (1998) and the Copa Libertadores (1999).

Palmeiras were founded after Italian sides Torino and Pro Vercelli visited Brazil in 1914, and a group of Italians who lived in São Paulo decided to create an Italian club, Palestra Italia. That visit inspired one of the fiercest local derbies in the world, as the creators of the club were former members of Corinthians. From that moment they were branded 'the betrayers'. After Palestra (subsequently becoming Palmeiras, and known locally as 'O Verdao', the Greens) split from Corinthians, the first São Paulo derby was played on May 6, 1917, and the intensity and passion has remained for the club ever since. Derbies between the two teams often have to be played in São Paulo's Morumbi Stadium, which has a capacity of 80,000. The club were relegated to the Second Division in 2002 but bounced back as champions at their first attempt.

PARIS SAINT-GERMAIN

PARIS, FRANCE
Stadium: Parc des Princes (48,712)

Founded: 1970 **Honours:** European Cup Winners' Cup 1996; League 2; Cup 7

Paris Saint-Germain were founded in 1970 after the demise of some of the capital's major clubs. An amalgamation of FC Paris and Stade Saint-Germain, they played their first campaign in France's second division and were promoted at the first attempt. The following season they finished 16th but, under pressure from the city council, were forced to split, creating Paris FC and Saint-Germain. FC continued to play in the top division whereas PSG began in the third. In the 1972-3 season PSG were promoted after the disqualification of Quevilly. The following campaign ended with PSG in second and they were promoted to the top flight (ironically, Paris FC were relegated).

PSG have won the title twice and the Coupe de France seven times, most recently in 2006. In Europe, the club have won the Cup Winners' Cup and reached European semi-finals in five consecutive years between 1993 and 1997. PSG were bought in 1994 by media company Canal+ and in April 2006 were sold to a consortium of US firms for £34 million.

The club have had two players on their books who have gone on to win the World Player Of The Year accolade: George Weah was European and World Footballer Of The Year in 1995, while Ronaldinho left PSG in 2003 and became FIFA World Footballer Of The Year in 2004 and 2005 after an £18 million transfer to Barcelona.

Above: Nottingham Forest's John McGovern with the European Cup in 1980.

PEÑAROL

MONTEVIDEO, URUGUAY
Stadium: Estadio Charrúa
(12,000), Centenario (73,609)

Founded: 1893 **Honours:** World Club Cup 1961,
1966, 1982; Copa Libertadores 1960, 1961,
1966, 1982, 1987; League 47

Peñarol were founded in 1893 by the large British expatriate community in Montevideo under the rather cumbersome name of Central Uruguayan Railways District Club, and were inaugural winners of the league in 1900. As British influence waned, the club officially changed its name to the more acceptable Peñarol on December 13, 1913, after the poor, rural area of the city from where they emerged. To this day, the club's support is associated with the working class element of the nation's capital.

Along with bitter rivals, Nacional, the two clubs have dominated Uruguayan football with more than 80 league titles shared between them.

However, Peñarol have also been fantastic ambassadors for the Uruguayan game outside of its borders, and won the first ever Copa Libertadores in 1960 against Olimpia of Paraguay, and successfully defended the crown a year later against Brazil's Palmeiras. Three more South American Club Cup titles have come their way, the last being a play-off victory against America de Cali of Colombia in 1987.

In 1997 Peñarol won five titles in a row – the quinquenio – for the second time. Further proof of Peñarol's durability, and a defining achievement in world football, is that they were the first club to win the World Club Cup three times. This feat was achieved with victory over a Eusébio-inspired Benfica in 1961, a 4-0 aggregate win over Real Madrid in 1966, and a 2-0 victory against Aston Villa in 1982.

PORTO

OPORTO, PORTUGAL
Stadium: Estadio das Antas
(50,000)

Founded: 1893 **Honours:** World Club Cup 1987,
2004; European Cup 1987, 2004; UEFA Cup 2003;
European Super Cup 1987, 2003, 2004; League
21; Cup 13

It was in the mid-1970s that Porto really came of age and began to threaten the Lisbon monopoly of Sporting and Benfica. That they have succeeded in shifting the balance of power owes much to the presidency at that time of Pinto da Costa and the management of Jose Maria Pedroto. Porto assumed almost total dominance of the league, and despite a rotation of managers and high profile players, they won nine titles in the 12 years up until the end of the Nineties, the pinnacle of that glory period coming in 1987.

While it may have been a year when they enjoyed no domestic success, they did complete a memorable international treble, winning the European Cup, European Super Cup and World Club Cup. The European Cup came at the expense of Bayern Munich in Vienna with two late goals clinching a 2-1 victory. It made up for their disappointment three years earlier, when the club lost the final of the Cup Winners' Cup.

Porto won eight of the ten league titles in the 1990s, and in 2003 they further asserted their dominance by adding the UEFA Cup to their domestic league and cup double. This proved to be just the start as the following season, under José Mourinho, Porto won the Champions League with a victory over Seville. They won the World Club Cup same year, and completed back-to-back victories in the European Super Cup. In 2006 they won the league and cup double.

PSV EINDHOVEN

EINDHOVEN, HOLLAND
Stadium: Philips Stadion
(36,000)

Founded: 1913 **Honours:** European Cup 1988;
UEFA Cup 1978; League 19; Cup 8

Funded by electronics giants Philips, PSV were champions just 15 years after joining the Dutch league and have overtaken Feyenoord to offer the greatest challenge to Ajax's domination of Dutch football. PSV have housed some of the top Dutch and international players of recent times. Ronald Koeman, Ruud Gullit and Ruud Van Nistelrooy all had spells in Eindhoven, while Brazilian stars Romario and Ronaldo each preceded their Barcelona careers with spells at the Philips Stadium.

The late Eighties and early Nineties saw Eindhoven at the height of their powers, capped with a penalty shootout victory over Benfica in

Below: Porto lift the Champions League trophy in 2004.

the 1988 European Cup final. On the domestic front the club were almost unstoppable, with six league titles in seven seasons between 1986 and 1992. The final two came under Bobby Robson, who had joined Eindhoven for two seasons straight after leading England to the semi-finals of the 1990 World Cup.

The millennium began with PSV back in dominant form in Holland, with former player Eric Gerets leading them to the league title in 2000 and 2001. Guus Hiddink brought the trophy back in 2003, 2005 and 2006. He then won the Dutch Cup in 2005 and reached the final again in 2006, losing 2-1 to Ajax. But with star players often lured to other European leagues, the club has been unable to make an impact in the Champions League. Nevertheless Hiddink took them to the semi-finals in 2005, when they were beaten by AC Milan. After taking Australia to the World Cup finals in 2006, Hiddink left PSV to take control of the Russian national team. He was replaced by Ronald Koeman.

RANGERS

	GLASGOW, SCOTLAND
	Stadium: Ibrox Park
	(50,500)

Founded: 1873 **Honours:** Cup Winners' Cup 1972; League 51; Cup 31; League Cup 24

Rangers are the historically Protestant half of perhaps the most passionate rivalry in all football: the 'Old Firm' battle with Catholic club Celtic. The Gers have the edge in domestic triumphs, due largely to three sustained periods of dominance. The first came in the inter-war years (1918-39) under manager William Struth, when Alan 'Wee Blue Devil' Morton and Bob McPhail terrorised defences. The second great Rangers team emerged after the Second World War, built around George Young in their 'Iron

Curtain' defence, and schemer Willie Waddell.

The third era of success arrived with the appointment of ex-Liverpool player Graeme Souness as player-manager in 1986. With the lavish financial backing of the club's new owner, David Murray, he brought in English players like Terry Butcher and Trevor Steven, and to the horror of the more bigoted fans, signed Mo Johnston, a Catholic and a former Celtic player!

Walter Smith continued the modernisation through the 1990s, bringing Paul Gascoigne to the club and equalling Celtic's record of nine consecutive titles. Rangers stopped a Celtic hat-trick in 2003, retaking the league title.

Other players who have contributed to the club's success over the years include midfield genius Jim Baxter and record goalscorer Ally McCoist, while the Rangers team of 1972 won the club their only European trophy, with

skipper John Greig lifting the Cup Winners' Cup before going on to manage one of the two treble-winning sides of the Seventies.

RAPID VIENNA

	VIENNA, AUSTRIA
	Stadium: Hanappi
	(19,600)

Founded: 1899 **Honours:** League 31; Cup 14

One of Austria's oldest teams, Rapid Vienna possess a long and eventful history. The Viennese side captured the inaugural Austrian League title in 1911-2, and matched this achievement by reclaiming the title on eight more occasions in the following 12-year period. An overall total of 32 championships is a record on the European mainland. After the 1938 annexation by Germany they competed in the German National Championship, and even managed to win the 1941 German league title and the German Cup.

The club won the Mitropa Cup in 1930 and 1951 and have produced a great many famous players over the years, including master goal poacher Franz 'Bimbo' Binder, who scored more than 1,000 club goals in a remarkable career. Midfielder Gerhard Hanappi not only played 93 times for Austria, but also designed the club stadium (now named after him). Other legends include Karl Rappan, Walter Zeman, Ernst Happel, Franz Hasil and the prolific marksman Hans Krankl, who won the European Golden Boot in 1978 after scoring 41 goals.

Despite success at home, Rapid Vienna have never won a European trophy, and the closest they have come is finishing runners-up in the Cup Winners' Cup in 1985 and 1996, losing to Everton and Paris Saint-Germain respectively.

Above: PSV Eindhoven celebrate with the European Cup in 1988.

Left: It was Rangers' turn to lift the Scottish Cup in 1969, a feat they have managed on 31 occasions.

REAL MADRID

MADRID, SPAIN
Stadium: Santiágo Bernabéu
(106,000)

Founded: 1902 **Honours:** World Club Cup 1960, 1998, 2002; European Cup 1956, 1957, 1958, 1959, 1960, 1966, 1998, 2000, 2002; UEFA Cup 1985, 1986; League 29; Cup 17

In the ongoing debate to decide the greatest club of all time it's hard to make a case for anyone other than Real Madrid. In 104 years of existence the club have won the Spanish championship 29 times and the European Cup, the toughest test in club football, a record nine times.

Madrid Football Club was officially born in 1902 but did not take the regal prefix 'Real' until 1920 when King Alfonso XIII granted the title in recognition of their role in founding the tournament that eventually became the Copa Del Rey, the Spanish Cup. The club's first chairman Julian Palacios was aided – with some irony, given their bitter rivalry with Barcelona – by two Catalans, the Padrós brothers, Carlos and Juan. The former went on to become club president and Spain's representative at the inaugural meeting of FIFA in 1904, a gesture symbolic of the club's status at the centre of the national game.

While Madrid's founding fathers were all Spaniards its first player-manager was an Englishman, former Corinthians player Arthur Johnson, and it was he who also instigated the famous all-white strip. In their early years the club struggled to make a mark on the fledgling football scene in Spain, with Athletic Bilbao and Barcelona holding sway. The most significant

ESTADIO SANTIAGO BERNABÉU

The home of Real Madrid, the Bernabéu was built between 1943 and 1947 to replace the Charmartín ground, which was all but destroyed in the war. Initially financed by a membership scheme, at one time the ground boasted a capacity of 125,000. Overhauled for the 1982 World Cup, it was the venue for that year's World Cup final.

Above: Alfredo Di Stefano scores in the 1960 European Cup final. Opposite clockwise from top: European Cup victory in 2002; Savio and Roberto Carlos kiss the World Club Cup in 1998; David Beckham celebrates scoring at the Bernebéu.

development at this time was the arrival at the club of the young Santiágo Bernabéu, the single most important individual in Real's history. Bernabéu joined the club as a junior in 1909, helped erect its first purpose-built ground, the O'Donnell Stadium, went on to captain the side and be associated with the fortunes of the club for nearly 70 years until his death in 1978.

By the 1920s the newly-titled Real Madrid had embarked on a strategy designed to install it as Spain's most prestigious club. It demonstrated its intention, as it has done on many occasions since, with a string of big-name signings, an act which accelerated the growth of professionalism in the Spanish league. However, when the first national league began in 1929 Real were runners-up to Barcelona. It took them three more years to win the first of two back-to-back titles, but by the time they won the league again in 1954, the capital had been destroyed by civil war, rebuilt, and Bernabéu was the club's president.

His presence at the helm ushered the club into an era of dominance. It was he who brokered a bold new stadium in the city's richest district in 1947, eventually named after him, and it was he who financed deals to bring in a string of impressive talents including Gento, Puskás, Kopa and, the biggest of all, Alfredo Di Stéfano, 'the Blond Arrow'.

It was Di Stéfano, more than any other player, who propelled Real to glory, scoring 228 league goals between 1953 and 1964. More importantly, his 49 goals in Europe established the club's name outside Spain as Real drove on to improbable heights by winning the newly-created European Cup for five years in succession, an unparalleled feat. Di Stéfano scored in all five finals, crowning his efforts with a hat-trick in the 7-3 victory over Eintracht

Frankfurt at Hampden Park in 1960, a game regarded as one of the finest ever.

League titles continued at regular intervals, but while there was one more European Cup triumph in 1966 over Partizan Belgrade – making an astonishing six winners medals for their outstanding winger Gento – Real could not maintain their high standards.

The next 29 years became known as 'The Wilderness Years' as the team strived in vain to rekindle the chemistry that had made it so unbeatable. Two successive UEFA Cup wins in the mid-Eighties would have satisfied most fans, but not those of Real. Significantly the club refused to even enter the competition until 1972. Nevertheless, that squad – which featured the striker Emilio Butragueño, Michel and Martin Vásquez (dubbed 'the Vulture Squadron') and the backflipping Mexican goal machine Hugo Sanchez – revived memories.

The glory days finally returned in 1998 with Predrag Mijatovic's strike against Juventus that won the European Cup. That victory began a fresh golden era as Real embarked on a huge spending spree financed by the sale of their training ground. Signings of superstars like Zidane and Figo smashed the transfer barrier and embellished a team already packed with stars like Raúl and Iker Casillas.

Real have won the European Cup three times since the beginning of the Champions League format, the most special win coming in their centenary year in Glasgow, 42 years on from the legendary 7-3 victory. But although FIFA rapidly declared Real 'The Best Club Of The 20th Century', the pressure to constantly deliver success on the biggest stage has led to a succession of coaches in recent years and a lack of silverware since their last title win in 2003.

KINGS OF EUROPE

REAL MADRID'S VICTORIES IN THE CHAMPIONS CUP FINAL

1956 | Real Madrid | 4
Stade De Reims | 3
Parc Des Princes, Paris

1957 | Real Madrid | 2
Fiorentina | 0
Bernabéu, Madrid

1958 | Real Madrid | 3
AC Milan | 2
Heysel, Brussels

| Real Madrid | 2
Stade De Reims | 0
Neckar, Stuttgart — **1959**

1960 | Real Madrid | 7
Eintracht Frankfurt | 3
Hampden Park, Glasgow

1966 | Real Madrid | 2
Partizan Belgrade | 1
Heysel, Brussels

1998 | Real Madrid | 1
Juventus | 0
Arena, Amsterdam

2000 | Real Madrid | 3
Valencia | 0
Stade De France, Paris

2002 | Real Madrid | 2
Bayer Leverkusen | 1
Hampden Park, Glasgow

1902: Founded as Madrid Football Club on March 6, the team takes its all-white strip from English club, Corinthians. Their first coach is Englishman Arthur Johnson.

1912: Santiago Bernabéu debuts in the first team.

1920: The club's name is changed to Real Madrid in June 1920 after King Alfonso XIII gives his official blessing to the team.

1924: The opening of Chamartín Stadium is celebrated with a match between Madrid and Newcastle United.

1932: Real win their first Spanish title.

1943 Santiago Bernabéu is appointed club president.

1947: A new stadium is built and will be named after the club president.

1953: Argentine legend Alfredo Di Stéfano is signed.

1956: Real win the first European Cup with a 4-3 victory over Reims.

1958: Hungarian star Ferenc Puskás signs for Madrid.

1960: Real Madrid defeat Eintracht Frankfurt 7-3 to claim their fifth successive European Cup title.

1971: Paco Gento winds up an 18-year career with the club in a Cup Winners' Cup final defeat.

1986: The UEFA Cup is won for a second consecutive year with a victory over Köln.

1990: Real win fifth consecutive Spanish title, setting scoring record of 107 goals in 38 games.

1998: Named by FIFA as best club in football history, they also win the Champions League, beating Juventus 1-0.

2001: One year after signing Figo for £37.5m Real spend £45.8m on Zinédine Zidane.

2003: Sign England captain David Beckham.

RED STAR BELGRADE

BELGRADE, SERBIA
Stadium: Red Star
(56,000)

Founded: 1945 **Honours:** World Club Cup 1991; European Cup 1991; League 24; Cup 20

Known as Crvena Zvezda in their native Serbia (formerly Yugoslavia), it was students of the city's university who founded Red Star Belgrade in March 1945. The first football team to be created in Yugoslavia after liberation, they won their first league title in 1951. Since then they have dominated their country's domestic game, outstripping bitter rivals Partisan to record successes in both league and cup.

Red Star have always been associated with playing precise, technical football, and of producing a constant stream of home-grown talent. The club have a strong reputation in European competitions, establishing it early when they reached the semi-final of the second European Cup in 1957, losing to Fiorentina. The Red Star Stadium was the first ground in the old Eastern bloc to host a major European final, and is known affectionately to home fans as 'the Marakana'.

The club's finest moment was achieved in Bari in 1991 when they captured the European Cup, winning a penalty shoot-out after a negative performance in a 0-0 draw against Marseille. There may have been many more successes in European competitions, had it not been for the fact that Red Star have always struggled to hold on to their best players. The exit door at the Marakana has seen such world-class talent as Dragan Stojkovic, Robert Prosinecki, Dejan Stankovic and Darko Pancev walk through it.

RIVER PLATE

BUENOS AIRES, ARGENTINA
Stadium: Monumental
(56,449)

Founded: 1901 **Honours:** World Club Cup 1986; Copa Libertadores 1986, 1996; Copa Interamericana 1987; League 32

Founded in 1901, the side was originally formed in the poor Boca district of Buenos Aires, but later migrated north to the altogether more affluent Retiro area of the city. The move led to the nickname of the 'Millionaires', and established with their erstwhile neighbours, the equally-celebrated Boca Juniors, one of the fiercest rivalries in world football.

A major force in the foundation of the first Argentine professional league, River Plate have enjoyed two distinct golden eras. From 1936 to 1957 they swept all before them, winning a total of 12 national titles, and in the late 1940s producing the much-admired forward line of Jose Manuel Moreno, Omar Labruna, and Adolfo Padernera – known to the fans as 'La Maquina' (The Machine).

The 1960s was a lean decade for the club, but since winning the league title in 1975 River have re-established themselves as one of the giants of the game in Argentina, adding a seemingly endless stream of championship triumphs. In 1986, inspired by Uruguayan playmaker Enzo Francescoli and Norberto Alonso, River Plate finally won the Copa Libertadores, beating América of Colombia, and went on to get the better of Steaua Bucharest to gain the club's only World Club Cup trophy. A decade later, River once again beat América to capture a second South American Club Cup title. This time they were denied a second World Club Cup by a single Alessandro Del Piero strike in a close fought match with Juventus.

While Boca Juniors can name Diego Maradona as their most famous former player, the roll call of River Plate old boys reads like a who's who of goalscoring greats. Alfredo Di Stéfano scored 27 league goals for River during the 1946-7 season, while prolific marksmen such as Omar Sivori, Luis Artime, Mario Kempes, Marcelo Salas, Hernan Crespo and, more recently, Javier Saviola have all played for the Buenos Aires club with distinction.

ROMA

ROME, ITALY
Stadium: Olimpico
(82,000)

Founded: 1927 **Honours:** Fairs Cup 1961; League 3; Cup 7

Founded in 1927 when four local clubs merged (Roman, Pro Patria, Alba and Fortitudo), Associazone Sportiva Roma were members of Serie A when it was inaugurated in 1929. Their record since has been one of occasional highs and rather more frequent lows.

A first Serie A title didn't arrive until 1942, although they did finish as runners-up in both 1931 and 1936. Relegated from Serie A at the start of the 1950s, Roma bounced back a decade later to become one of the first Italian teams to win a European trophy, defeating Birmingham City in the Fairs Cup final in 1961, winning 4-2 on aggregate.

Domestic cup wins in 1964 and 1969 couldn't disguise the fact that Roma spent much of the next two decades in the football wilderness, but things improved dramatically in the 1980s. They won the Coppa Italia four times in seven seasons, added a second Serie A title in 1983 and reached the European Cup final the following season, eventually losing to Liverpool 4-2 on penalties after a 1-1 draw in their home stadium.

Under former AC Milan coach Fabio Capello, Roma won their first Serie A title for 18 years in 2001, helped by the enormous firepower of Gabriel Batistuta, Vincenzo Montella and Francesco Totti. The following season they only missed out on the title on the season's last day in a terrific three-way tussle with Juventus and Inter, with just two points separating the three teams. They have been runners-up twice since, in 2002 and 2004, and in 2006 they reached the final of the Italian Cup.

SANTOS

SÃO PAULO, BRAZIL
Stadium: Vila Belmiro
(22,000)

Founded: 1912 **Honours**: World Club Cup 1962, 1963; Copa Libertadores 1962, 1963; São Paulo State League 16; League 2

There are very few clubs in the world game whose reputation is based so solely on the exploits of just one player. However, when that player is Pelé, the synonymous relationship becomes all the more understandable. The great man joined Santos as a 15-year-old in 1956, and made his final appearance in the famous all-white kit in 1974. During his tenure the São Paulo side won five times in the Taça Brasil, the Brazilian cup competition that held sway before the start of the Brazilian League in 1971. With Pelé, they also achieved back-to-back Copa Libertadores wins in 1962 and 1963 and two World Club Cups with victories over AC Milan and Benfica, the latter featuring a hat-trick from Pelé in the Stadium Of Light.

Of course, it would be unjust to label Santos as a one-man team during this era, and the club provided the Brazilian national side with many other players who took part in the victorious World Cup campaigns of 1958, 1962 and 1970, including goalkeeper Gilmar, centre-back Mauro and midfielder Zito. In demand and in the glare of the global spotlight, the club took to the world stage with a stream of friendly match tours, and subsequently reaped the financial benefits.

Not unsurprisingly Pelé was a difficult act to follow, and with his retirement the club saw fortunes both on and off the pitch take a severe dip. Debts mounted and the lack of silverware gradually took the club away from the elite group in Brazilian football.

Victory in the Río-São Paulo Tournament in 1997 was the exception rather than the rule. Supporters seemed to have lost the faith and even the appointment of Pelé as the club's youth academy director in 1999 was regarded more as a promotional tool rather than an effective measure. Nonetheless it proved to be something of a turning point, and against the odds Santos revived the glory days by adding the 2002 and 2004 Brazilian championship to their long list of silverware success.

Opposite: Pelé, the young rising star of Santos.

Above: São Paulo parade the Paulista championship trophy at the Morumbi Stadium in 2005.

SÃO PAULO

SÃO PAULO, BRAZIL
Stadium: Morumbi (67,800)

Founded: 1935 **Honours:** World Club Championship 2005; World Club Cup 1992, 1993; Copa Libertadores 1992, 1993, 2005; Recopa Sudamericana 1993, 1994; São Paulo State League 21; League 3

The youngest of the five São Paulo-based clubs that participate in the National Championships, São Paulo FC were founded in 1935, the result of a coming together of two clubs, CA Paulistino and AA de Palmeiras. A convincing five São Paulo titles between 1943 and 1949 soon signalled the arrival of a new major force in the industrial city. As a result of this success, the massive 140,000 capacity Morumbi Stadium was built in 1960 (now reduced to 67,800). However, the club spent much of this decade in the shadow of their crosstown rivals Santos.

Under the attack-minded guidance of the legendary Brazilian coach Telê Santana, São Paulo's very own glory days were to arrive in the early 1990s, when they were arguably the strongest club side in the world. Two consecutive Copa Libertadores titles, with victories over Paraguay's Olimpia and Newell's Old Boys of Argentina, were followed up by back-to-back triumphs in the World Club Cup. The first saw São Paulo defeat Barcelona 2-1 with both goals from Raí, while the 1993 final witnessed them overcome the much-heralded masters of Europe, AC Milan, with full-back Cafu at the centre of

everything good that the team produced.

São Paulo's position as the major power in the city from which they take their name suffered a blow after Telê Santana quit the club in 1996, allowing Corinthians and Palmeiras to become the dominant clubs. São Paulo were back in the news in 1998, however, when they sold Denilson for a then world record £22 million to Spanish club Real Betis.

In 2005, under former Peru coach, Paulo Autuori, São Paulo became the first Brazilian team to win the Copa Libertadores three times, and later the same year they clinched the World Club Championship beating Liverpool in Tokyo.

SPARTA PRAGUE

PRAGUE, CZECH REPUBLIC
Stadium: Stadion Letná (21,000)

Founded: 1893 **Honours:** League 30; Cup 22

Sparta are the most successful Czech club ever, and that's in spite of several periods when their fortunes have faltered. During the 1970s they even suffered the indignity of relegation. Established as Kralovske Vinohrady (King's Vineyard) in 1893, it wasn't until after the First World War that their reputation as 'Iron Sparta' really grew, when they competed under the name of AC Sparta.

In the inter-war years they vied constantly with neighbours Slavia Prague, winning numerous trophies and achieving the league and cup double in 1936. They also proved a dominant force in Europe, winning the Mitropa Cup – a prestigious forerunner of the European Cup – in both 1927 and 1934. Their star player, Oldrich Nejedly, finished top scorer in the 1934 World Cup, playing in a Czechoslovakia team who lost out in the final to Italy (Sparta and rivals Slavia provided all 11 Czech players for the match). Another World Cup hero, Andrej Kvasnak – who played in the 1962 final – was the playmaker of the fine Sparta team of the mid-1960s.

The club finally settled on their current moniker in 1965. After the Second World War they had suffered several name changes, becoming for a time Sparta Bratrstvi and Spartak Praha Sokolovo, but fans always called them Sparta. After the relatively dark days of the Seventies, the club started to win trophies again, including the double in 1988 and 1989. Players like Skuhravy, who shone at the World Cup in 1990, and Hasek were followed by Frydek and Kouba, and the club continued to succeed despite seeing much of their talent travel abroad.

Throughout the post-Communist era – and despite some financial and managerial upheavals – Sparta have dominated Czech football, and have even ruffled the feathers of bigger clubs in European competition.

SPARTAK MOSCOW

MOSCOW, RUSSIA
Stadium: Lokomotiv (29,300)

Founded: 1922 **Honours:** Soviet League 12; Russian League 9; Soviet Cup 10, Russian Cup 3

Spartak Moscow formed in 1922 and were initially linked to the Moscow food producers' co-operative. It wasn't until the Spartak name was adopted in 1935 that the club began to prosper. The first Soviet league title was won in 1936, and the club triumphed again in 1938 and 1939. Always leading lights in the Soviet Union, a stage they shared with Dynamo Kiev, they were champions four more times in the 1950s, and inspired the founding of the European Cup with their friendly matches against Wolverhampton Wanderers in 1954 and 1955.

Completely dominating domestic football in the early years of the post-Communist era, they won nine of the first ten titles in the Vysshaya Liga since its formation in 1991. They also achieved a hat-trick of league and cup doubles in this fruitful period. But after oil magnate Andrei Chervichhenko bought the club in 2000, Spartak's grip on Russian football has loosened. Chervichhenko sold his interest in the club in 2004 and the following season Spartak finished runners-up in the league, their best performance since their last title win in 2001.

Despite regularly appearing in the Champions League and enjoying several encouraging campaigns, European silverware has remained elusive. Spartak's best ever performance came in 1995-6, when they walked their qualification group with a 100 per cent record, only to fall at the quarter-final hurdle to Nantes.

SPORTING LISBON

LISBON, PORTUGAL
Stadium: Estadio José de Alvalade (52,411)

Founded: 1906 **Honours:** Cup Winners' Cup 1964; League 18; Cup 13

Sporting have always been in the difficult position of competing for Lisbon domination with local rivals Benfica, and while achieving a league and cup double in 2002, they have been unable to prevent the balance of power in Portugal from switching to Porto.

In the Forties and Fifties Sporting could lay claim to having the upper hand over Benfica, with championships in each decade, but only six more titles were to follow between the beginning of the Sixties and the end of the millennium. There was European success in Antwerp, with a 1-0 replay victory over MTK Budapest in the Cup Winners' Cup in 1964, but the club flattered to deceive over a long period of time.

Their cause was not aided by the fact that a number of top players had to be sold due to financial problems, among them Luis Figo, who left for Barcelona after helping the club to Portuguese Cup success in 1995. The departures on the field have been mirrored by the changes off it, with the likes of Bobby Robson and Carlos Queiroz paying the ultimate price for the dearth of league success, as the club spent 18 years trying to follow up the title success of 1982. Winning the championship in 2000 and 2002 has at least reminded Portuguese football fans that Sporting can compete at the top of the table.

STEAUA BUCHAREST

BUCHAREST, ROMANIA
Stadium: Ghencea
(30,000)

Founded: 1947 **Honours:** European Cup 1986;
League 22; Cup 20

Unlike most Eastern bloc army teams since the dissolution of the Soviet Union, Steaua continue to be their nation's most powerful and successful team, but in the new millenium, other clubs have started to challenge their dominance.

Initially formed as Armata in 1947, they adopted the name CCA Bucharest two years later, and won the national league three times in a row in the early 1950s. The Steaua name – the word means 'star' – wasn't adopted until 1962, and silverware under this name wasn't long in coming, with the capture of numerous league and cup titles in the late Sixties and early Seventies. However, the 1980s proved to be a golden decade, and the league and cup double in 1985 was followed by European Cup triumph the following year. Disposing of Rangers and Anderlecht on the way to the final, Steaua pulled off the improbable to beat Barcelona 2-0 in a penalty shoot-out. A remarkable achievement in itself, it was also the first time a Communist country had lifted the European Cup.

Buoyed by this success, the talented Gheorghe Hagi was added to the squad a year later, and the result was a hat-trick of doubles from 1987 to 1989. This era also produced another European Cup final appearance, but this time Steaua were defeated 4-0 by an AC Milan side inspired by Ruud Gullit and Marco Van Basten.

TOTTENHAM HOTSPUR

LONDON, ENGLAND
Stadium: White Hart Lane
(36,240)

Founded: 1882 **Honours:** UEFA Cup 1972, 1984;
European Cup Winners' Cup 1963; League 2;
FA Cup 8; League Cup 3

Hotspur FC, as the club were originally known, were formed in 1882 by boys from the Hotspur cricket club and the local North London grammar school. They were renamed Tottenham Hotspur Football and Athletic Club two years later, turned professional in 1895, and became the first non-league club to win the FA Cup in 1901. They gained entry to the second tier of the Football League in 1908.

A further FA Cup win (1921) and their first league championship (1951) followed, but it wasn't until the early Sixties that Tottenham enjoyed a period of sustained success. In 1961, under coach Bill Nicholson (manager from 1958 to 1974) and captain Danny Blanchflower, Tottenham became the first English club to complete a league and cup double since Preston North End in 1889. They followed it up with further FA Cup triumphs in 1962 and 1967, and European Cup Winners' Cup success in 1963.

Tottenham started the 1970s in fine fettle, winning two League Cups and appearing in the final of the UEFA Cup twice (winning against Wolves in 1972, losing to Feyenoord in 1974). However, after a poor start to the 1974-5 season, Nicholson quit. Tottenham have since struggled to recapture their glory days, although they came close in the 1980s when a stylish team featuring the silky skills of Glenn Hoddle won back-to-back FA Cups (1981 and 1982) and the UEFA Cup (1984). In 2006, under Martin Jol, Spurs finished fourth in the Premiership, their highest league position since 1990.

VALENCIA

VALENCIA, SPAIN
Stadium: La Mestalla
(55,000)

Founded: 1919 **Honours:** UEFA Cup 1962, 1963, 2004; Cup Winners' Cup 1980; European Super Cup 2; League 6; Cup 6

Valencia's defeats in consecutive Champions League finals – to Real Madrid in 2000, and to Bayern Munich in 2001 – were more than just a disappointment to fans. Neutrals everywhere admired the underdogs and their style of play. To make matters worse, they hadn't even won their league to qualify. But the team eventually got their reward when they won their first title in La Liga for more than 20 years in 2002, having been coached to their previous title in 1971 by the great Alfredo Di Stéfano.

Nevertheless, 'Los Chés' – nicknamed after a local greeting, roughly translated as 'mate' – have always had a tradition for silky play. They won three titles in the 1940s, with goal-getting wizard Edmundo 'Mundo' Suárez twice lifting the 'Pichichi' – or Pitxitxi – award as the league's top-scorer. In the early Sixties another classy incarnation of the team played in the style of a junior Real Madrid, appearing in three consecutive Fairs Cup finals, winning two.

Argentinian World Cup giant Mario Kempes helped the club to their Cup Winners' Cup final

triumph over Arsenal in 1980 (although he missed his spot-kick in the penalty shoot-out), and lately, under the astute guidance of Hector Cúper and then Rafael Benítez, players such as Claudio López, Gaizka Mendieta and Kily González, have kept up the club's reputation for fiesta football. Under Benítez the club won the title in 2002, and a league and UEFA Cup double in 2004.

VASCO DA GAMA

RÍO DE JANEIRO, BRAZIL
Stadium: São Januario
(35,000)

Founded: 1915 **Honours:** Copa Libertadores 1998; Copa Mercosur 2000; Río State League 22; League 4

The club of Rio's Portuguese community, Vasco were named after the celebrated explorer. Football in Río had been the preserve of the elite until Vasco broke the mould by winning the 1923 championship with a team that included mixed-race and working class players. Outraged, Río's leading teams launched a breakaway league, and were only persuaded back with the agreement that players would have to complete a registration form, a task deemed beyond most of Brazil's illiterate poor. The literacy test was eventually abolished in 1929, but the club will always be revered for paving the way for democracy in Brazilian football.

With Flamengo and Fluminense's history inexorably entwined, Vasco are regarded as the perpetual outsiders in the battle for footballing superiority in Río. That's not to say they haven't brought home a number of trophies. The club's greatest triumph was capturing the Copa Libertadores in 1998 with a 4-1 aggregate win over Barcelona of Ecuador. Following on from this success, Vasco were invited to play in the inaugural World Club Championships in 1999, where they beat Manchester United 3-1 on the way to the final. But after contesting a 0-0 draw with Corinthians, they lost on penalties.

Below: The Tottenham double-winning team of 1960-1.

LEGENDS OF FOOTBALL

Above: Brazil captain Carlos Alberto with England's Bobby Moore at the 1970 World Cup.

ADEMIR

Country: Brazil
Born: November 8, 1922
Position: Centre-forward
Clubs: Recife, Vasco da Gama, Fluminense, Vasco Da Gama

Son of the famous 1938 World Cup defender Domingos, goalscorer Ademir Marques de Menezes went a long way in establishing Brazil as a post-war footballing power. He made his international debut in 1945 and went on to score 32 goals in 37 games. His finest hour came in the 1950 World Cup when he fully deserved the Golden Boot for his total of nine goals, including four against Sweden. The forward line trio of Ademir, Zizinho and Jair is still considered one of Brazil's finest ever. Ademir's presence necessitated opponents to field an extra full-back which was the seed for Brazil's famed 4-2-4 formation. A prolific goalscorer at club level in the Rio State League, he was a five times league winner with Vasco da Gama, and he continued his success with a further title at city neighbours Fluminense.

MOHAMED AL-DEAYEA

Country: Saudi Arabia
Born: August 2, 1972
Position: Goalkeeper
Clubs: Al Tae, Al Hilal

Mohamed Al-Deayea is the greatest goalkeeper that Asia has ever produced. He played 181 times for his country after succeeding his elder brother, who had been part of the Asian Cup winning teams of 1984 and 1988. His international career began against Bangladesh at the Asian Games in Beijing in 1990, and ended, through retirement, in June 2006 at Al-Deayea's fourth successive World Cup, although in Germany he was a non-playing squad member. His 100th appearance had been at the 1998 World Cup finals against South Africa. By then he was team captain. He continued to play his club football for Al Hilal after his international retirement.

FLORIAN ALBERT

Country: Hungary
Born: September 15, 1941
Position: Centre-forward
Club: Ferencváros

Florian Albert was an elegant and gifted striker who enjoyed a long and successful career at club and international level. He was difficult to mark and had an ability to bring others into play. At the 1966 World Cup he shone as Hungary beat holders Brazil 3-1 at Goodison Park and was impressive during their run to the quarter-finals with his guile and skill.

Albert appeared for Hungary at the 1960 Olympic Games when they finished third, and he also turned out at the 1962 World Cup finals in Chile. At that tournament he scored a superb solo goal against England and struck a hat-trick against Bulgaria. Tall and slender, he was different from previous Hungarian strikers but equally effective and had shown his promise while still at school, making his international debut at the age of 17.

Albert spent his career with Ferencváros, picking up four titles. He helped them become the first Hungarian club to win a continental trophy when they lifted the Fairs Cup in 1965 and he was voted European Footballer Of The Year in 1967. He played 75 times for Hungary, scoring 31 goals. He retired in 1974.

DEMETRIO ALBERTINI

Country: Italy
Born: August 23, 1971
Position: Midfield
Clubs: AC Milan, Padova, Atlético Madrid, Lazio, Atalanta, Barcelona

Albertini brought down the curtain on his illustrious career in December 2005 while a Barcelona player, but it is the 14 seasons between 1988 and 2002 when he played for AC Milan for which the cultured midfielder will be most fondly remembered. A product of the club's youth system, he made his Milan debut as a 17-year-old in 1989, and after a period on loan at Padova, he established himself as a first team regular at the San Siro in the 1991-92 season. He went on to play nearly 300 games for the club, winning five Serie A titles (including three in a row between 1992 and 1994) and a European Cup (1994). His association with Milan ended in 2002 following a season on loan at Spanish side Atlético Madrid. Moves to Atalanta and Lazio followed before he joined Barcelona in January 2005 at the age of 33. He was capped by Italy 79 times.

CARLOS ALBERTO

Country: Brazil
Born: July 17, 1944
Position: Defender
Clubs: Fluminense, Santos, Flamengo, New York Cosmos, California Surf

Carlos Alberto's career can be summed up in one sublime moment – the goal he scored in the 1970 World Cup final for Brazil against Italy. Charging on to a pass from Pelé 25 yards out, the right-back – and team captain – hammered the ball past hapless Italian goalkeeper Enrico Albertosi, proving the Brazilians had power to match their silky skills. Alberto's goal came four minutes from time and sealed a 4-1 victory for Brazil. At club level, Alberto won league titles in both Brazil (in his second spell with Fluminense) and in the United States (playing with Pelé at New York Cosmos). He moved into management in the early 1980s, bossing clubs in Brazil (including Flamengo and Fluminense) and Egypt (Zamalek), as well as the Azerbaijan and Nigerian national teams.

IVOR ALLCHURCH

Country: Wales
Born: October 16, 1929
Position: Inside-forward
Clubs: Swansea City, Newcastle United, Cardiff City, Swansea City

Grace and elegance were the watchwords of Ivor Allchurch, an inside-forward who still stands second in the record books in his country's goalscoring charts – just behind Ian Rush. Tall and blond, inevitably he was known as the 'Golden Boy', but he sadly failed to gain just reward for his ample talents as he spent his entire career playing for clubs at the wrong end of the table. Only at the 1958 World Cup in Sweden did a wider audience get to appreciate his sublime talents, when he was part of a talented Welsh team that narrowly went down Pelé's Brazil in the quarter-finals.

The 251 goals that he scored in 694 league appearances attest to both the quality of his finishing and his durability, while eight of his 68 Welsh caps were gained partnering his brother Len, who also played for Swansea.

LUIGI ALLEMANDI

Country: Italy
Born: November 8, 1903
Position: Left-Back
Clubs: Juventus, Inter Milan, Roma

An ever-present member of Italy's triumphant 1934 World Cup-winning team, including the 2-1 extra-time win over Czechoslovakia in the final. Between 1925 and 1936 he played 24 times for his country and occasionally he captained the side. However, while at Inter Milan in 1927 he was accused of match-fixing the Turin derby while he was at Juventus. The accusation was unfounded but the subsequent suspension kept him from playing for club and country. He later captained Inter Milan to the Serie A championship.

JOSÉ ALTAFINI

Country: Brazil, Italy
Born: August 27, 1938
Position: Centre-forward
Clubs: Palmeiras, São Paulo, AC Milan, Napoli, Juventus, Chiasso

José Altafini's career spanned three decades, two international careers and a change of name. In the unique nickname tradition of his native Brazil he was known as 'Mazzola' for his resemblance to the Torino captain killed in the Superga air crash, and he represented his country with distinction in the 1958 World Cup.

The re-adoption of his birth name came with a move to AC Milan, and four years later he represented Italy at the World Cup in Chile, making him one of only five World Cup players to have turned-out for two countries. His finest hour came in Milan's 1963 European Cup campaign when he scored 14 goals, including both goals in a 2-1 win over Benfica in the final.

ANTONIO ALZAMENDI

Country: Uruguay
Born: June 7, 1956
Position: Forward
Clubs: Sud America, Independiente, River Plate, Nacional, UNAM, Peñarol, Logrones, Deportivo Mandiyú, Corrientes, Rampla Juniors

Antonio Alzamendi was the 1986 South American Player Of The Year when the continent may have thought the year belonged to Diego Maradona. Alzamendi helped River Plate to the Argentinian championship and the Copa Libertadores, and rounded off his year off by scoring the decisive goal in the World Club Cup final in Tokyo against Steaua Bucharest. He had also featured in the 1986 World Cup finals, and later at Italia 90. He helped Uruguay win the Copa América in Argentina where he had spent ten successful years in club football as a prolific striker, scoring 105 goals in 204 games. He also played club football in Spain, Mexico and Uruguay.

AMARO AMANCIO

Country: Spain
Born: October 12, 1939
Position: Inside-right/Outside-right
Clubs: Deportivo La Coruna, Real Madrid

Amancio was one of Spain's most exciting players of the 1960s. He was groomed by the great Real Madrid, winning the European Cup in an all-Spanish side in 1966. Two years earlier, he had helped Spain to their 1964 European Championship triumph. He scored 11 goals in 42 appearances for his country. The brilliance of the player was in his ability to play primarily as an inside or outside-right but with equal aplomb switch to the other flank. A leg injury in a Spanish Cup game looked to have ended his career but he recovered to feature in the resurgence of Real Madrid in the 1970s.

JOSE LEANDRO ANDRADE

Country: Uruguay
Born: November 20, 1898
Position: Wing-half
Clubs: Bella Vista, Nacional

Jose Leandro Andrade was one of the mainstays of the great Uruguayan side of the late 1920s and early 1930s, and helped his country to gain Olympic gold medals in Paris in 1924 and Amsterdam in 1928. His career

Left: Ivor Allchurch in action for Newcastle, October 1958.

Below: Jose Altafini, scorer of both AC Milan goals, leaves the Wembley pitch following 2-1 victory over Benfica in the 1963 European Cup final.

looked as though it was to finish prematurely when injury struck in 1929, but he battled back and his experience was a vital factor when his Uruguayan side lifted the inaugural World Cup in 1930 on home soil. Andrade is regarded as one of the greats of the golden generation of Uruguayan football, alongside defender Jose Nasazzi and influential striker Hector Scarone. An old fashioned wing-half, Andrade played 41 times for his country before hanging up his international boots in 1933.

VICTOR ANDRADE

Country: Uruguay
Born: February 14, 1927
Position: Left-half
Clubs: Wanderers, Peñarol

Victor Andrade emulated the triumph of his uncle, the great Jose Leandro Andrade, by winning the World Cup with Uruguay in 1950. The diminutive Andrade was a tenacious left-half who was an excellent ball winner, which was perfectly epitomised in the decisive 1950 World Cup match against Brazil in which he often frustrated the hosts. Four years later in an injury-hit Uruguayan side he played as an attacking centre-half and was captain in the semi-finals. He was part of the Peñarol side that never finished lower than runners-up in the national league in the 1940s and 1950s.

OSVALDO ARDÍLES

Country: Argentina
Born: August 3, 1952
Position: Midfield
Clubs: Huracán, Tottenham Hotspur, Paris Saint-Germain, Blackburn Rovers, Queens Park Rangers, Swindon Town

After making his name with Argentine club side Huracán, and despite weighing in at only ten stone and 5ft 6ins in height, Osvaldo 'Ossie' Ardíles forged a reputation as a creative midfield force in the Argentinian national team under coach César Luis Menotti. Despite impressive displays picking up a World Cup winner's medal for Argentina in 1978, many believed Ardíles would struggle with the rigours of the English Football League when he signed for Tottenham. The reality couldn't have been more different and Ardíles settled into midfield alongside the muscle of Graham Roberts and the grace of Glenn Hoddle, spraying passes around the pitch at will as Spurs picked up two FA Cups in 1981 and 1982 and a UEFA Cup in 1984. Sadly, when Argentina invaded the Falklands in 1982 Ardíles was on World Cup duty and it was decided that he should go out on loan to Paris Saint-Germain after the conflict. On his return he enjoyed five more seasons at White Hart Lane, moving to Blackburn on loan before ending his playing career as player-coach at Swindon.

ROBERTO BAGGIO

Country: Italy
Born: February 18, 1967
Position: Centre-forward
Clubs: Vicenza, Fiorentina, Juventus, AC Milan, Bologna, Inter Milan, Brescia

One of eight children and born in the small town of Caldogno, Baggio first made his name as a 15-year-old winger in Italy's Serie C1 (or third division) with local club side Lanerossi Vicenza. When he was 18, Baggio was signed by Fiorentina, then in Italy's top flight, and became a regular in their first team during the 1987-8 season. He stayed with the Florence side for five seasons, in that time becoming one of Italian football's hottest properties and making his international debut against Holland on November 16, 1988. His last two seasons in Florence saw Baggio score 32 league goals in 62 appearances, and in the 1989-90 season, his final year with the club, Fiorentina made it to the final of the UEFA Cup, only to lose out 3-1 on aggregate to Juventus.

Astonishingly, just a week after losing to Juventus, Fiorentina sold Baggio to them for a then world record £8 million. The news provoked such fury amongst fans in Florence that riot police had to be called in to quell two days of violent disturbances.

Aged 23 and a recent convert to Buddhism, Baggio made his World Cup debut for Italy in 1990. He started the tournament on the bench but, against Czechoslovakia, scored one of the best goals that the tournament had ever seen: a powerful run from the halfway line that left defenders for dead. Italy still only managed to finish third though.

Baggio's time at Juventus was extremely successful. The Turin club won the UEFA Cup in 1993, finished runners-up in 1995, and under coach Marcello Lippi, claimed the league title in 1995. Baggio himself was named European and World Footballer Of The Year in 1993, and continued to score regularly for Juventus (78 goals in 99 league appearances spread over five seasons). However, with the precociously talented Alessandro Del Piero waiting in the wings, and a wealth of strike talent elsewhere in the squad, Baggio was finding it harder to hold down a first team place. He joined AC Milan in 1995 and won the title in his first year.

By 1994, Baggio had arguably become the most famous, if not the most popular, player in Italy, and it was these talismanic qualities that made him the focus of his country's World Cup campaign the same year. Italy had barely qualified for the second round stage and, as the tournament wore on, seemed to rely more and more on 'the Divine Ponytail' (as Baggio was nicknamed). He scored a last-minute equaliser and an extra-time penalty winner to eliminate Nigeria in the second round, before snatching the decider in the quarter-final against Spain. Another brace of goals dispatched Bulgaria in the semi-finals and when it came down to penalties against Brazil in the final, even though he had been carrying an injury, it seemed certain that Baggio would net the deciding spot-kick and keep Italy's World Cup hopes alive. But he scooped his penalty – Italy's fifth and last – over the bar, handing victory to Brazil.

With a record of 27 goals in 56 games for Italy, Baggio was recalled to the national team for the 1998 World Cup finals in France where he was able to atone for the penalty miss of four years before, converting a vital spot-kick against Chile to give Italy a 2-2 draw.

Baggio signed for Bologna in 1998 and then played for Inter Milan before settling at Brescia, where he played until retiring in 2004.

GORDON BANKS

Country: England
Born: December 30, 1937
Position: Goalkeeper
Clubs: Chesterfield, Leicester City, Stoke City, Fort Lauderdale Strikers

Only one Englishman can lay claim to the title World's Greatest Goalkeeper. Gordon Banks became a legend for his composure, his agility, consistency and all-round technique, yet never played for a major club.

Banks was born the son of a foundryman in Tinsley, Sheffield, in December 1937 and developed his physical strength hauling bags of coal and hod-carrying when he left school. He took up goalkeeping as an amateur and was picked up by Third Division Chesterfield at the age of 15, making his league debut against Colchester on November 29, 1958. Leicester City spotted his potential and Banks moved to Filbert Street in July 1959 for £7,000, making his Division One debut that September in a 1-1 draw with Blackpool.

Banks is today credited with developing many of the facets of modern goalkeeping. He would stay behind for hours after training, concentrating on technique, learning angles and inventing specialised routines designed to improve his strength and agility. However, he did not adopt gloves regularly until 1970, preferring to spit sticky saliva from chewing gum on to his hands and let it dry.

In May 1961, in his second season, Banks made his first Wembley appearance, picking up a loser's medal in the FA Cup final against double-winners Tottenham Hotspur. Two years later he picked-up another runners-up medal against Manchester United.

Banks was called into the England squad by Walter Winterbottom for a 1962 friendly against Portugal while at Leicester, but it was Alf Ramsey who awarded him his first cap on April 6, 1963. Though the game ended in a defeat to Scotland, Banks rapidly became a fixture in the England side.

He was the rock of the 1966 World Cup-winning team, conceding just one goal before the final against West Germany, a penalty to Eusébio. But his finest performance came at Mexico 70, the day after he was awarded an OBE. Facing Pelé for the first time in his career in the titanic clash between the holders and the tournament favourites, he managed to scoop the Brazilian's sharp, downward header up and over the bar. It became the most replayed save of all time. But when it came to the most crucial game of the tournament Banks was unfortunately absent through illness, felled by 'Montezuma's revenge'. Peter Bonetti took his place and conceded three goals against West Germany in the quarter-final, ending England's dream of retaining the Jules Rimet trophy in Mexico.

A year after lifting the World Cup, Stoke City expressed an interest in Banks, and Leicester, knowing they had the promising Peter Shilton in reserve, let him go for £52,000 in April 1967. Banks won the League Cup with Stoke in 1972 but never achieved FA Cup or league honours. He was FIFA Goalkeeper Of The Year on six occasions and the Football Writers' Player Of The Year in 1972. He would undoubtedly have played at the top for much longer had a car crash that summer not cost him the sight in one eye.

He kept 35 clean sheets in 73 games for England and lost just nine games. He enjoyed a short spell in the North American Soccer League playing for Fort Lauderdale Stikers, before returning to England in 1979 for an unsuccessful stint in management in charge of Telford United.

Above: Gordon Banks won the World Cup with England, the League Cup with Stoke City and was voted FIFA Goalkeeper Of The Year six times.

1955

1955: Signs professional forms with Third Division North side, Chesterfield.

1956

1957

1958

1959: Transferred to Leicester City for £7,000.

1959

1960

1961: Losing FA Cup finalist against Bill Nicholson's double-winning Tottenham.

1961

1962

1963: Losing FA Cup finalist again, this time on the receiving end of a 3-1 reverse against Manchester United. In this year 'Banks of England' also makes his international debut in a 2-1 defeat by a Jim Baxter-inspired Scotland.

1963

1964

1965

1966: A member of England's World Cup-winning side, Banks didn't concede a goal in the tournament until the semi-finals.

1966

1967

1968

1967: Joins Stoke City ahead of Liverpool in £52,000 move.

1969

1970: Pulls off wonder save against Pelé in the World Cup finals, but misses quarter-final defeat by West Germany due to illness. Awarded the OBE.

1970

1971

1972

1972: Helps Stoke win League Cup, and is named Footballer Of The Year. Disaster strikes as he loses an eye in a serious car crash.

1973

1974

1975

1977: Plays for Fort Lauderdale Strikers in the NASL. Despite his handicap, Banks is voted the league's most valuable goalkeeper in his first season.

1976

1977

1978

FRANCO BARESI

Country: Italy
Born: May 8, 1960
Position: Sweeper
Club: AC Milan

Born near Brescia, in the Lombardy region of Italy, Baresi enjoyed two decades of football with his only club, AC Milan. Making his professional debut in an away game against Verona on April 23, 1978, Baresi went on to establish himself as the finest sweeper in the world during Milan's glory years of the late Eighties and early Nineties.

The consummate modern defender, Baresi was nicknamed 'The Steel Man' – he was a formidable stopper but was also comfortable bringing the ball out of defence and joining in with attacking moves. He captained Milan to numerous league titles (the last in 1996), World Club Cups and Italian Cups, as well as to European Cup glory in 1989 and 1990. Sadly, he missed his club's 4-0 demolition of Barcelona in the European Cup final of 1994 as he was suspended.

Baresi made his international debut for Italy against Romania in December 1982, although he had been a non-playing member of the squad that had won the World Cup in Spain a few months earlier. He went on to play for his country 81 times, 31 of them as captain, but suffered heartbreak in the World Cup final of 1994, Italy losing to Brazil in a game where he missed a penalty in the climactic shoot-out. When Baresi retired from the game in 1997, Milan retired his famous Number 6 shirt.

Below: AC Milan's Franco Baresi lifts the European Cup at the Nou Camp in 1989.

CLIFF BASTIN

Country: England
Born: March 14, 1912
Position: Left-winger
Clubs: Exeter City, Arsenal

'Boy Bastin' started his career with hometown club Exeter but joined Arsenal as a raw 16-year-old in 1929. He was not just a great left-winger, but also a talented inside-forward, the position he preferred. He helped The Gunners to their first trophy, the FA Cup, in his debut season, and four goals on the way to the final against Huddersfield set the tone for his career. An incredible turn of pace and uncanny dribbling ability made Bastin the pivotal figure in an Arsenal team that yielded five league titles and two FA Cup win in the 1930s, while he became a mainstay of the England squad from the age of 19. A cartilage operation in 1934 shortened his career, but his tally of 178 goals in 396 games remained an Arsenal record until Ian Wright passed the barrier in 1997.

GABRIEL BATISTUTA

Country: Argentina
Born: February 1, 1969
Position: Forward
Clubs: Newell's Old Boys, River Plate, Boca Juniors, Fiorentina, Roma, Inter Milan, Al Arabi

Born in Avellaneda, north of Buenos Aires, Gabriel Batistuta idolised Mario Kempes but outstripped his hero to become Argentina's all-time top scorer with 56 goals in 78 appearances. His exploits in front of goal earned him the nickname 'Bati-Gol' and he starred in three successive World Cups in 1994, 1998 and 2002.

He made his league debut for Newell's Old Boys in 1988. He built his reputation with Boca Juniors in their championship-winning season of 1991, before moving to Fiorentina. There he became a club legend and was Serie A's top scorer in 1994-5, before switching to Roma and finally winning the Scudetto in 2001.

Retiring from international football after Argentina's early exit from the World Cup in 2002, he joined Inter Milan on loan, and then played for Qatar side Al Arabi, before retiring in March 2005 after a series of injuries. In 2004 he was named in FIFA's centenary list of the 125 Greatest Living Footballers.

VLADIMIR BEARA

Country: Yugoslavia
Born: August 28, 1928
Position: Goalkeeper
Clubs: Hajduk Split, Red Star Belgrade, Alemania Aachen, Victoria Cologne

The 'Great Vladimir' was the outstanding Yugoslav goalkeeper during the 1950s, when he played at the 1950, 1954 and 1958 World Cup tournaments, as well as earning a silver medal at the 1952 Olympics. He represented his country on 60 occasions. With Hajduk Split he won the Yugoslav league title on three occasions between 1950 and 1955. A move to Red Star gave him four more titles by 1960 and successive Yugoslav Cup triumphs in 1958 and 1959 .

BEBETO

Country: Brazil
Born: February 16, 1964
Position: Centre-forward
Clubs: Vitória, Flamengo, Vasco da Gama, Deportivo De La Coruna, Seville, Flamengo, Cruzeiro, Vitória, Botafogo, Toros Neza, Kashima Antlers, Vasco da Gama, Al-Ittihad

The fresh-faced striker was best known outside of Brazil for his 'cradling the baby' celebration during the 1994 World Cup, but it was his unfailing ability to find the back of the net that established his pedigree. He rarely won headlines when partnering Romario, though his 39 goals in 75 internationals leaves him fifth on Brazil's all-time scoring list. He was controversially transferred in 1989 from Flamengo, where he was a fans' favourite, to rivals Vasco da Gama. A move to Europe followed, where he won the Spanish Cup with Deportivo De La Coruna. He was a member of Brazil's losing World Cup finalists in 1998, and he continued to play around the world until retirement in 2002.

FRANZ BECKENBAUER

Country: West Germany
Born: September 11, 1945
Position: Midfield/Sweeper
Clubs: Bayern Munich, New York Cosmos, Hamburg

What Franz Beckenbauer touches invariably turns to gold. Both as player and manager, at club and international level, he is a winner. Beckenbauer picked up his nickname – 'Der Kaiser' – for his imperious style. As a footballer he was utterly in control, a chess player who read the game in his head, but was also blessed with an excellent touch, a good change of pace and flawless distribution.

Beckenbauer joined Bayern as a junior in 1959 playing on the left but gradually moved inside, making his debut at 18 years of age. The club were promoted to the top division of the Bundesliga in 1965, finishing third in their first season behind city rivals TSV 1860 Munich. In the following two seasons Bayern won the German Cup twice, then a European Cup Winners' Cup in 1967.

His classy performances led to a rapid call-up to the West German squad and he made his international debut in a 2-1 victory over Sweden on September 26, 1965. At the 1966 World Cup he established himself at the heart of the German side, scoring four goals, including the winner in the semi-final with Russia, but he was unable to stop England from lifting the trophy.

Four years later in Mexico he had a measure of revenge in the quarter-finals. When manager Alf Ramsey withdrew Bobby Charlton from the game while England were leading, it freed up Beckenbauer in midfield and he scored the first goal that propelled West Germany's comeback. The Germans lost the semi-final with Italy and Beckenbauer finished the game with a dislocated shoulder, playing on with his arm strapped across his chest.

A year later he took over as captain of the national team and led them to a European Championship final win over the Soviet Union in 1972, having redefined the sweeper's role by gliding out of defence with mazy runs to set up devastating counter-attacks. Two years later he experienced his crowning moment as a player, captaining the national side to World Cup victory on home soil in a game that saw Holland threaten to overrun the Germans. Beckenbauer remained unfazed and when the Dutch flagged he marshalled his forces and pushed his side to victory. He retired from international football in 1977 with 103 caps.

On the domestic front he helped Bayern Munich to dominate the mid-Seventies, leading them to an impressive hat-trick of European Cups between 1974 and 1976. He finished his Bayern career with three league titles and four German Cups, twice being voted European Footballer Of The Year, in 1972 and 1976. He played for three years with New York Cosmos, winning the NASL Soccer Bowl three times before returning to West Germany with Hamburg. After one final season with the Cosmos he retired.

His cerebral style and ability to lift others made him a natural for management and, without experience of coaching a club side, he took over his country in 1984, pushing his players to two World Cup finals. At Italia 90 he became the first person to captain and manage a World Cup-winning side. After a spell with Marseille he returned to Bayern as manager in 1994, winning the Bundesliga in his first season before becoming the club president, and then the vice president of the German Football Federation. He was president of the German World Cup 2006 Organising Committee.

IGOR BELANOV

Country: Soviet Union
Born: September 25, 1960
Position: Forward
Clubs: SKA Odessa, Chernomerets, Dynamo Kiev, Borussia Mönchengladbach

Igor Belanov was voted European Footballer Of The Year in 1986 after a sensational period when he topped the goalscoring charts in

Dynamo Kiev's title-winning season, won the European Cup Winners' Cup and, just three weeks before the Mexico World Cup, found himself catapulted into the Soviet squad along with 11 other Kiev team-mates, thanks to new Soviet coach and former Kiev manager Valeri Lobanovski. He went on to score a hat-trick against Belgium in the second round, but the Soviets lost 4-3. After 1986 Belanov was plagued by injuries, although he did earn a move to West Germany and played in the 1988 European Championship final, missing a penalty in the 2-0 defeat by Holland.

MIODRAG BELODEDICI

Country: Romania, Yugoslavia
Born: May 20, 1964
Position: Sweeper
Clubs: Steaua Bucharest, Real Star Belgrade, Valencia, Real Valladolid, Villarreal

Miodrag Belodedici was the first player to win the European Cup with two different clubs, Steaua Bucharest in 1986 and Red Star Belgrade in 1991. On both occasions the final was decided on penalties, with Steaua beating Barcelona 2-0 and Red Star defeating Marseille 5-3 after goalless draws. Belodedici was born in Serbia but raised in Romania, and played for them 20 times between 1984 and 1988, when to escape the Ceausescu regime he sought asylum in Yugoslavia. In his absence he was convicted of treason and sentenced to ten years in prison, declining to play for Romania again until 1992, long after the collapse of the Ceausescu regime. He went on to feature in the 1994 World Cup and Euro 2000.

FERENC BENE

Country: Hungary
Born: December 17, 1944
Position: Centre-forward
Clubs: Ujpest Dozsa, Volan SC, Sepsi 78, Soroksari, Kecskemeti

An iconic figure in his homeland, Bene is best remembered for his 12 goals – including six against Morocco – in the 1964 Olympics, which helped Hungary to the gold medal. He joined Ujpest as a teenager before inspiring the club to eight championship victories and three cup successes. Five times the Hungarian league's top marksman, he was forced to play outside-right for his country, due to the presence of Florian Albert, but he still managed 36 goals in 76 games for Hungary, the highlight being a tremendous individual effort in a shock 3-1 victory over Brazil at Goodison Park during the 1966 World Cup finals.

DENNIS BERGKAMP

Country: Holland
Born: May 10, 1969
Position: Centre-forward
Clubs: Ajax, Inter Milan, Arsenal

Dennis Bergkamp is one of the most famous products of the Ajax youth system. Having made his debut against Roda JC in 1986, he went on to become the pivotal figure in a side that won the Dutch title, the UEFA Cup and the Cup Winners' Cup. He was the Dutch league's top scorer between 1991 and 1993, and his 103 goals in 185 games made him a most wanted striker.

Above: 'Der Kaiser', Franz Beckenbauer slides in on England's Colin Bell during the 1970 World Cup quarter-final.

Above: Germany's Oliver Bierhoff celebrates scoring the goal that won the 1996 European Championship.

He joined Inter Milan in a £12 million deal in 1993 but his 11 goals in two seasons – despite another UEFA Cup success – was regarded as a failure. A £7.5 million transfer to Arsenal in the summer of 1995 shocked the football world, but it proved to be a shrewd move. Bergkamp soon began to weave his magic as both provider and scorer following Arsene Wenger's arrival.

Under Arsene Wenger Bergkamp played an instrumental part in Arsenal's league and cup double of 1998, and he capped the season by winning the PFA and Footballer Writers' Player Of The Year awards. He also played a prominent role in the Dutch side that reached the semi-finals of the World Cup. Although many argue he failed to recapture his form in the ensuing seasons, Bergkamp was back to his best as Arsenal secured their second double in 2002.

Famously scared of flying, Bergkamp drove to many of Arsenal's European away games and quit international football in 2000 rather than face the long flight to Japan for the 2002 World Cup. He retired at the end of the 2005-6 season.

GEORGE BEST

Country: Northern Ireland
Born: May 22, 1946
Position: Centre-forward
Clubs: Manchester United, Stockport County, Fulham, Los Angeles Aztecs, Motherwell, Hibernian, Bournemouth, Brisbane Lions

The name George Best became a byword for 'booze' and 'birds' in an era when footballers broke the superstar barrier, but the image overshadowed the talent of a man who was arguably the greatest player to have emerged from the British Isles.

Best was the complete all-round player. Blessed with quick feet and even quicker intelligence he would toy with defenders like a cat with a mouse. He could pass and finish but he never forgot to work for the team. For all his razzmatazz a Best goal was generally celebrated with a hand half raised, perhaps a finger pointing upwards. Gordon Banks cites a dazzling run which left him lying on his

Opposite: A legend in his own lifetime and an icon of his age, George Best was dubbed 'the fifth Beatle'.

backside as the best goal ever scored against him. Not long after that encounter the two met again in an international. As Banks prepared to kick the ball upfield, Best flipped it out of the keeper's hands and headed it in the back of the net. It was typical of Best's impudence but the referee mistakenly disallowed it.

Best arrived in Manchester from Belfast in 1961 aged just 15 years and made his Old Trafford debut two years later against West Bromwich Albion. Sharp, quick-witted and stylish, he launched the club into a new era that helped it overcome the loss of the 'Busby Babes' and, teamed with Bobby Charlton and Denis Law, brought two league titles in 1965 and 1967. In six seasons he scored 190 goals in 290 games, but his crowning moment was lifting the European Cup at Wembley in 1968 after characteristically rounding the goalkeeper to score in the 4-1 win over Benfica.

Best was named European Player Of The Year but his taste for the game was diminishing. With the retirement of the patrician Sir Matt Busby, his behaviour became increasingly rebellious. Managers came and went in an awkward period of transition at the club and when Tommy Docherty dropped Best, the Irishman responded by walking out. FIFA became involved, issuing a ban, but it was rescinded allowing Best to join Stockport County in 1975. It was to be the first stationing post in a spiralling career.

Living the life of a pop star (he was dubbed 'the fifth Beatle') Best played in the USA before returning home to join Fulham in September 1976. There he rediscovered a taste for the game, forming an entertaining partnership with another wayward genius, Rodney Marsh. Fulham's gate doubled for their first home game together and Best put them one up with barely a minute on the clock. At Fulham he also became the first player in the Football League to be shown a red card after the introduction of the new card system. The great tragedy of his career was that despite winning 37 caps for Northern Ireland he was never able to perform on the world stage.

Best succumbed to alcoholism and received a liver transplant in July 2002, but on November 25, 2005, aged just 59, he died suffering multiple organ failure. He was buried alongside his mother, with an estimated crowd of 100,000 lining the streets of Belfast in the pouring rain, to say a final farewell to the 'Belfast Boy'.

JOSEF 'PEPI' BICAN

Country: Austria, Czechoslovakia
Born: September 25, 1913
Position: Centre-forward
Clubs: Hertha Vienna, SK Rapid, Admira, SK Slavia Prague, Vitkovice ZKG, Dynamo Prague

Josef Bican was born in Vienna to Czech parents and grew up to be a free-scoring centre-forward

for both Austria and Czechoslovakia. He was elevated into Austria's Wunderteam after playing with Rapid. He played 19 times for Austria including the 1934 World Cup semi-final. Bican then moved to Prague and went on to score 14 international goals in 17 appearances for the Czechs but he missed out on playing at the 1938 World Cup because of a clerical error over his citizenship.

OLIVER BIERHOFF

Country: Germany
Born: May 1, 1968
Position: Forward
Clubs: Bayer Uerdingen, Hamburg, Borussia Mönchengladbach, Casino Salzburg, Ascoli, Udinese, AC Milan, Monaco, Chievo

A prolific striker for both club and country, Oliver Bierhoff often confounded his critics. A brilliant header of the ball, he consistently added to his game and eventually reached the heights of Italy's Serie A, where he scored 103 goals. Born in Karlsruhe, Bierhoff struggled to shine in the German Bundesliga before ressurecting his career in Austria with Casino Salzburg. A loan move to Italy took him to Ascoli, where he stayed for four years, most of which was spent in Serie B. He moved on to Udinese in 1995 and became top scorer in the Italian league with 27 goals in 1998, earning a transfer to AC Milan, where he won the Serie A title in 1999.

He won 70 caps for Germany, scoring 37 goals, and is best remembered for his 'Golden Goal' at Wembley in the final of the 1996 European Championship, the first such sudden death decider in a major tournament. He is also remembered for a six-minute hat-trick against Northern Ireland. He retired from international football after spending much of the 2002 World Cup on the bench, playing just 81 minutes. He ended his career at Chievo in May 2003.

FRANZ 'BIMBO' BINDER

Country: Austria, Germany
Born: December 1, 1911
Position: Centre-forward/Inside-left
Clubs: St Polten, Rapid Vienna

Franz 'Bimbo' Binder is credited as being the first European player to score a thousand goals in his career with clubs St Polten and Rapid Vienna, as well playing internationally for Austria (20 times) and Germany (9 times). Binder is purported to have scored 1,006 goals in 756 games before hanging up his boots in 1950, when he turned to management with Rapid Vienna. He later took charge of Austria's national team. He was certainly the greatest Austrian player of the 1930s, gaining success with Rapid both in the Austrian league and, after the Anschluss of 1938, the Greater Germany championship.

Right: Between 1892 and 1914 Steve Bloomer scored 353 goals in the English football league.

LAURENT BLANC

Country: France
Born: November 19, 1965
Position: Defender
Clubs: Montpellier, Napoli, Nimes, Saint-Etienne, Auxerre, Barcelona, Marseille, Inter Milan, Manchester United

A graceful defender, Laurent Blanc began as an attacking midfielder but converted to defence early in his career. He enjoyed a nomadic time, switching regularly from one club and league to another and winning few trophies, but made his name at international level playing for France for more than a decade. He impressed at three European Championships, particularly in 2000 when France emerged as winners, and he starred at the 1998 World Cup but missed the final through suspension. Confident on the ball and a calming influence in the team, he won 97 caps and scored 16 goals in becoming one of France's greatest players. He may have retired from international football in September 2000, but he signed for Manchester United the following year and won the English Premier League in 2003, his final season as a player.

Below: Danny Blanchflower lifts the 1962 FA Cup after Tottenham's victory over Burnley at Wembley.

DANNY BLANCHFLOWER

Country: Northern Ireland
Born: February 10, 1926
Position: Half-back
Clubs: Glentoran, Barnsley, Aston Villa, Tottenham Hotspur

Having started his career at the end of World War II with Belfast side Glentoran, Robert Dennis Blanchflower signed for Barnsley for £6,000 in 1949, but his annoyance at the Yorkshire club's lack of ambition prompted a £15,000 move to Aston Villa in 1951. He made 155 appearances for Villa, but he was unhappy at a training regime that foccused on physical exercise rather than ball work, and it was at Tottenham where Blanchflower emerged as one of the most astute defenders of his generation. When Arsenal pulled out of a proposed transfer in 1954, the White Hart Lane club stepped into the breach, signing Blanchflower for £30,000 – then a record fee for a half-back.

His outspoken ways did not go down well initially, but the appointment of Bill Nicholson as manager in 1958 proved to be a defining moment in the Irishman's career. He was the manager's voice on the pitch, while his cultured yet steadfast defending became the foundation on which the club's 1961 'double' success was built. Twice voted Footballer Of The Year, he also skippered Tottenham to FA Cup success in 1962 and the European Cup Winners' Cup in 1963.

Between 1949 and and 1963 he made 56 appearances for Northern Ireland, often alongside his brother Jackie. He captained his country to the quarter-finals of the World Cup in 1958. He died in December 1993.

OLEG BLOKHIN

Country: Soviet Union
Born: November 5, 1952
Position: Centre-forward
Clubs: Dynamo Kiev, Vorwärts Steyr

Oleg Blokhin was one of the quickest players to play the game, a claim that becomes all the more creditable when it is revealed that his personal trainer was Olympic sprint champion Valeri Borzov. But you don't become the Soviet Union's most-capped player through pace alone, and after moving inside from the left-wing to centre-forward, Blokhin became a reliable and prolific goalscorer. His 39 goals in 101 international appearances is a national record, and he was crowned European Footballer Of The Year in 1975 for leading Dynamo Kiev to their European Cup Winners' Cup triumph. As a reward for his services to Soviet football Blokhin was allowed to move to Western Europe, and played out the rest of his career with Vorwärts Steyr in Austria. He later coached the Ukranian national team and in 2002 was elected as an MP for the Ukraine parliament.

STEVE BLOOMER

Country: England
Born: January 20, 1874
Position: Centre-forward/Inside-right
Clubs: Derby Swifts, Derby County, Middlesbrough, Derby County

Steve Bloomer was a Victorian football superstar. His image was used to sell products as diverse as football boots and tonics. The reason was his prolific goalscoring prowess: between 1892 and 1914 he scored a staggering 353 league goals in 598 games. He also had a phenomenal record for his country, netting 28 goals in 23 games, a record that stood until the 1950s. He also helped England to six British Championships. After retiring from the game in 1914 he took a coaching job in Germany but was interned at the beginning of World War I.

ZBIGNIEW BONIEK

Country: Poland
Born: March 3, 1956
Position: Forward
Clubs: Zawisza Bydgoszcz, Widzew Lodz, Juventus, Roma

Zbigniew Boniek made his name in Poland's magnificent team that played at the 1978 and 1982 World Cups. After the latter tournament, in which he missed the crucial semi-final against Italy through suspension, he was snapped-up by Juventus and featured in a star-studded team alongside Michel Platini and Paolo Rossi. With Juventus Boniek won both the European Cup Winners' Cup in 1984, scoring the winner against Porto in the final, and the European Champions Cup in 1985. He also won a number of Italian domestic trophies with Juventus and Roma. He scored 24 goals in 80 appearances for Poland.

JEAN-MARC BOSMAN

Country: Belgium
Born: October 30, 1964
Position: Midfield
Clubs: Standard Liege, FC Liege

The Belgian midfielder won't be remembered for his skills as a journeyman footballer, but rather the court ruling which bears his name. In December 1995, the European Court of Justice found in Bosman's favour in a case he had brought against his former club FC Liege. In 1990, Liege had prevented Bosman from joining French club Dunkirk, despite the fact his contract with them had expired and their new offer to him demanded he take a pay cut. The 'Bosman ruling', as it quickly became known, allowed professional players within the European Union to move freely to another club at the end of their term of contract with their current team. Despite his win in court, Bosman reaped none of the rewards that the ruling should have made his. Instead he finished his playing days in the Belgian fourth division, eventually retiring from the game aged 31.

JÓZSEF BÓZSIK

Country: Hungary
Born: September 28, 1929
Position: Right-half
Club: Kispest Honvéd

József Bózsik was a member of the 'Magical Magyars' side that inflicted a humiliating 6-3 defeat on England at Wembley in 1953. One of the goals was a stunning 30-yard effort from Bózsik. His 15-year international career began with a debut in the 9-0 thrashing of Bulgaria in August 1947 and ended with his 100th appearance in April 1962, a 1-1 draw with Uruguay in which he scored. In that period, Bózsik went to two World Cups with Hungary and made an appearance in the final against West Germany in 1954. He also won a gold medal at the Olympic Games in 1952. At club level he was a star player alongside the likes of Ferenc Puskás at Kispest (later Honvéd).

LIAM BRADY

Country: Republic Of Ireland
Born: February 13, 1956
Position: Midfield
Clubs: Arsenal, Juventus, Sampdoria, Inter Milan, Ascoli, West Ham United

In an era where cultured footballers at Arsenal had become a rarity, Brady's ball skills and sweet left foot made him shine like a beacon. Given the nickname 'Chippy', for his love of fast food rather than his football ability, he made his debut in 1973 for a team in transition. As The Gunners continually struggled in the lower reaches of Division One, the Irish international's skilful performances were worthy of a higher stage – his swirling 25-yard effort against Tottenham in 1978 remains one of Arsenal's greatest goals.

Despite their inconsistencies, the club did reach three successive FA Cup finals and it was following the 1980 defeat against West Ham that Brady decided to try his luck abroad. His emphatic performances against Juventus in the European Cup Winners' Cup that season – Arsenal lost the final to Valencia on penalties – made him a target for the Italian giants and it was no surprise when he moved to Turin for £600,000 that summer.

Brady's skills were custom-made for life in Serie A, and as a fundamental component of Giovanni Trapattoni's side he helped Juventus to successive Scudetto titles. Shockwaves were created when he was then sold to make way for Michel Platini, and following two seasons at Sampdoria and spells at Inter and Ascoli, he ended his career back in England. He played 89 games in three seasons for West Ham before retiring in 1990.

RAYMOND BRAINE

Country: Belgium
Born: April 28, 1907
Position: Centre-forward
Clubs: Beerschot, Sparta Prague, Vorst

One of Belgium's greatest-ever players who won the Belgian championship four times with Beerschot in the 1920s. In 1931 he was suspended by the Belgian FA having violated the country's strict amateur rules. Sparta Prague, under Englishman Harry Dick, signed Braine as a professional where he was a huge hit to the extent that the Czech authorities tried to convince him to become a Czech citizen so he could play in the 1934 World Cup. The Belgium FA relented their suspension and he played for his native Belgium in the 1938 tournament. Including Olympic appearances, Braine played 54 times over 14 years and scored 26 goals.

ANDREAS BREHME

Country: West Germany
Born: November 9, 1960
Position: Left-back
Clubs: Kaiserslautern, Bayern Munich, Inter Milan, Real Zaragoza, Kaiserslautern

Andreas Brehme started and finished his career at Kaiserslautern but was most famous for winning the 1990 World Cup for West Germany, putting an end to one of the most disappointing finals of all time. West Germany were making hard work of beating an ill-disciplined Argentina side when Brehme converted an 85th minute penalty to win the game 1-0. That was a richly deserved personal

Above: West Germany's Andreas Brehme celebrates scoring in the 1990 World Cup semi-final.

triumph for Brehme, who was acknowledged as one of the world's best left-backs during the Eighties and Nineties. Typically German in style, Brehme was all about determination, strength, endeavour and uncompromising tackling, though in the German tradition he was always willing to thunder forward too. He had a successful club career, notably with Inter Milan. Along with Lothar Matthäus and Jurgen Klinsmann, Brehme was one of a trio of high-profile German internationals in the Inter Milan side which won the 1989 Serie A title and 1991 UEFA Cup.

PAUL BREITNER

Country: West Germany
Born: September 5, 1951
Position: Left-back
Clubs: Bayern Munich, Real Madrid, Eintracht Braunschweig, Bayern Munich

Nicknamed 'Der Afro' for his distinctive curly hairstyle, Paul Breitner has won everything there is to win in the game. A member of the all-conquering West Germany team of the 1970s, he enjoyed success in the 1972 European Championship, two years later adding a World Cup winners' medal to his collection. The 1974 tournament saw left-back Breitner adding attacking flair to West Germany's play. He converted the penalty in the final against Holland that put the Germans back in contention. The same year also saw 'Der Afro' claim the European Cup with Bayern Munich, and seal a move to Real Madrid. A falling out with the national coaching staff saw him miss the 1978 World Cup, but he returned in 1982 and again scored in the final.

Above: Emilio Butragueño leaves France's Jean Tigana in his wake.

BILLY BREMNER

Country: Scotland
Born: December 9, 1942
Position: Midfield
Clubs: Leeds United, Hull City, Doncaster Rovers

Bremner was Leeds United's midfield general during the club's glory years of the 1960s and 1970s and the perfect leader for Don Revie's ruthlessly single-minded side. He signed for Leeds as a 15-year-old and broke into the first team during the 1959-60 season. They were relegated that year, but returned to Division One in 1964 with a formidable team – and Bremner was the heartbeat of it.

By the time he left Leeds in September 1976 he had won two league titles, an FA Cup, a League Cup, and narrowly missed out on so much more – Leeds were title runners-up five times, beaten FA Cup finalists three times, and European Cup runners-up once. The winner of 54 Scotland caps, Bremner's fiery temper was never far from the surface and his career was littered with flashpoints, most famously in the 1974 Charity Shield when he squared up to Liverpool's Kevin Keegan, resulting in both players being sent-off. But incidents like that didn't detract from the fact that Bremner was a supremely talented footballer.

He later managed Leeds for a spell in the 1980s, and was hugely mourned when he died of a heart attack in 1997.

EMILIO BUTRAGUEÑO

Country: Spain
Born: July 22, 1963
Position: Centre-forward
Clubs: Real Madrid, Celaya

Right: Mexico keeper Antonio Carbajal is floored as Sweden's Agne Simonsson scores at the 1958 World Cup.

Throughout the Eighties and Nineties defences lived in fear of 'The Vulture'. That was Butragueño's nickname and he lived up to it well. Save for a final hurrah at Mexican club Celaya, Butragueño spent his career at Real Madrid, where his avalanche of goals brought trophies galore. Graduating from Real's youth ranks and the club's second team, Castilla, Emilio established himself as a penalty-box poacher, inspiring Madrid to consecutive UEFA Cups in 1985 and 1986. He is best remembered for an extraordinary four-goal display for Spain against Denmark at the 1986 World Cup. He was a Real legend by the time he left in 1995 and he also served as vice-president at the club.

KALUSHA BWALYA

Country: Zambia
Born: August 16, 1963
Position: Midfield
Clubs: Mufulira Blackpool, Mufulira Wanderers, Cercle Brugge, PSV Eindhoven, América, Necaxa, Leon, Al Wahda, Irapuato, Vera Cruz, Correcaminos

Kalusha Bwalya, a player of exciting promise with enthralling dribbling skills and a powerful shot, was the star of Zambian football. He initially came to prominence at the African Nations Cup in 1986, but it was a sensational performance at the 1988 Olympics – his hat-trick inspiring Zambia to a shock 4-0 thrashing of the mighty Italy – that made his name. By then he had been transferred to Belgian club Cercle Brugge. Not surprisingly that year he was also voted Zambia's Player Of The Year and Africa's Player Of The Year.

ERIC CANTONA

Country: France
Born: May 24, 1966
Position: Striker
Clubs: Martigues, Auxerre, Marseille, Bordeaux, Montpellier, Marseille, Nimes, Leeds United, Manchester United

Eric Cantona became a legend in English football for helping Manchester United win their first league title for 26 years. He began his career at Auxerre and became the most expensive player in France when he joined hometown club Marseille for £2.2 million in 1988. A gifted but temperamental striker, he struggled to make an impact in France despite winning the French Cup at Montpellier, and came to life only when he moved to England at the age of 25.

At Leeds United he inspired the team to the league title in 1992, before controversially joining rivals Manchester United – much to the consternation of the fans at Elland Road. His skill and leadership lifted Manchester United back to the top of the English game as he claimed four more league titles, two FA Cups and the PFA Player Of The Year award, but he was unable to inspire them to a Champions League triumph.

His biggest headlines were made when he leapt studs first into the crowd after a fan had abused him from the terraces. He made just 45 appearances for his country, scoring 19 goals. He retired from the game in 1997.

ANTONIO CARBAJAL

Country: Mexico
Born: June 7, 1929
Position: Goalkeeper
Clubs: Espana, Leon

Antonio Carbajal was awarded FIFA's gold award for services to football, recognising his achievement as a player and coach. He carved out his legendary status by becoming the first player to appear in five World Cups, playing in each tournament between 1950 and 1966. He was only once on the winning side, against Czechoslovakia in 1962. In the same game he conceded the then quickest goal in World Cup history, after just 15 seconds. He gained his first and only clean sheet at the finals in his 11th and last appearance. He had made his international debut at the 1948 Olympics.

CARECA

Country: Brazil
Born: October 5, 1960
Position: Centre-forward
Clubs: Guarani, São Paulo, Napoli, Hitachi

Adored equally in Brazil and Naples, Careca was one of the main supporting players in the Diego Maradona era that brought such unprecedented success to the Italian club. He forged his name at unfashionable Guarani, who he helped to the Brazilian championship. Careca's powerful shot and pace constantly unnerved defenders, but injury denied him a place in the 1982 World Cup. He made amends, however, in both 1986 and 1990, scoring seven goals in nine games. He teamed up with Maradona and compatriot Alemao at Napoli in 1987 for his greatest years, winning the Italian league title and the UEFA Cup.

JAN CEULEMANS

Country: Belgium
Born: February 28, 1957
Position: Centre-forward/Midfield
Clubs: Lierse, Club Brugge

Arguably the greatest player that Belgium has produced, Jan Ceulemans had an impressive

international career that spanned almost 14 years and saw him score 23 goals in 96 games for his country. For a nation of its size, Belgium overachieved on the international stage throughout the 1980s, and Ceulemans was the team's driving force. Peaking in fourth place at the Mexico World Cup of 1986, Belgium lost out in the semi-finals to the eventual winners, Argentina.

Ceulemans resisted the lure of the more wealthy leagues, and appeared happy to stay in his native country despite being courted by some of Europe's top clubs – most notably AC Milan, who were reportedly close to signing him at one point. He was the Belgian league's record signing when he moved from Lierse to Brugge in 1978 for £250,000.

JOHN CHARLES

Country: Wales
Born: December 27, 1931
Position: Centre-forward/Centre-half
Clubs: Leeds United, Juventus, Roma, Cardiff City

Charles started his career as an apprentice with his local club Swansea City aged 15 years old, before a lack of playing opportunities forced him to sign for Leeds United in 1949. It was at Elland Road that Charles made his name,

before signing for Juventus for a world record transfer fee of £67,000 in 1957. He became arguably Britain's most successful European export and during his first season in Turin he scored an incredible 29 goals. He helped Juve to three Italian titles in five years, scoring 93 goals in 155 games. Nicknamed 'Il Buono Gigante' – 'the Gentle Giant' – he was later voted the best foreign player ever to represent the club during a fan poll in 1997.

Part of the Wales side that progressed to the quarter-finals of the World Cup in 1958 , injury ruled Charles out of the decisive game with Brazil that saw them knocked out of the competition. John Charles was a strong centre-forward who was equally proficient in the centre-back role. It has been said that the legendary Nat Lofthouse was once asked to name the best centre-half that he had played against and he answered 'John Charles'. The same week Billy Wright was asked to name the greatest centre-forward he had faced, and he too answered 'John Charles'.

After five years in Italy, Charles, returned to a Leeds United side under the stewardship of Don Revie. He found it difficult to adjust, however, and after 91 days he was back in Italy, this time with Roma. But after scoring on his debut against Bologna, he felt uncomfortable back in Italy and returned home to Cardiff City for £20,000.

Above: John Charles scores for Wales against England at Wembley in 1954.

BOBBY CHARLTON

1956: Scores twice on debut for Manchester United and wins first league championship medal.

1958: Survives Munich air disaster, then scores on England debut against Scotland.

1963: Manchester United win FA Cup final against Leicester.

1965: Wins his second championship with Manchester United

1966: Inspires England to World Cup victory and is voted European Footballer Of The Year.

1967: Wins the championship with United again

1968: Scores twice in United's European Cup final victory over Benfica at Wembley.

1970: Plays last game for England, substituted in 3-2 defeat by West Germany in the World Cup.

1973: Leaves Manchester United to manage Preston North End.

1984: Returns to Manchester United to take up a place on the board.

1994: Receives a knighthood from the Queen in her Birthday Honours List.

Born: October 11, 1937
Country: England
Position: Inside left/Outside-left/Centre-forward
Clubs: Manchester United, Preston North End

'There has never been a more popular footballer,' remarked former Manchester United manager Sir Matt Busby of Bobby Charlton. 'He was as near perfection as man and player as it is possible to be.' Certainly Charlton had his fans as part of a rejuvenated Manchester United side and an England World Cup-winning team in the 1960s (Jimmy Hill once claimed that at the peak of his powers Charlton was the most famous living Englishman), but fate so nearly cut short a wonderful career at an early age.

On February 8, 1958, Charlton was caught up in the Munich air disaster that killed eight of the 'Busby Babes' – a name given to Sir Matt Busby's Manchester United side because of their youth. Charlton was thrown 40 yards from the wreckage as the plane skidded across the runway and ploughed into the airport's perimeter fence. He escaped with a head wound, but it so easily could have been worse: 23 people died in the crash, including the exciting United player Duncan Edwards.

Charlton recovered that year to make it to the FA Cup final and despite the growing clamour for him to be selected for the starting line-up of England's team for the World Cup in Sweden, he was happy with his role as a non-playing squad member.

At club level, Charlton had impressed early on, scoring ten goals in his first 14 games and he became central to Busby's plans. With his quick thinking, powerful shooting boots and dipping, fizzing crosses, Charlton was used to devastating effect by Busby, first as an inside-forward, then as a left-winger and centre-forward, and later in central midfield. He

Above: The young Manchester United star Bobby Charlton in his 1957 FA Cup final shirt. Below: Keeping a watchful eye on Brazil's Clodoaldo at the 1970 World Cup finals.

helped United to FA Cup victory in 1963, and two league titles in 1965 and 1967, as well as a famous European Cup victory in 1968, beating Benfica 4-1 in the final at Wembley.

He was equally explosive for England. Geoff

Hurst might have stolen the headlines after his World Cup-winning hat-trick in 1966, but it was Charlton who steered England to the final, kickstarting their campaign with a dazzling goal against Mexico. Running 30 yards from midfield, he blasted a drive from outside the penalty area that flew into the net, helping England to a 2-0 win. It was one of the more spectacular efforts of his 49 goals scored in an England shirt, a record that still stands. England swept aside France, Argentina, Portugal, and West Germany to become world champions in a year that Charlton was voted Footballer Of The Year, European Footballer Of The Year and Player Of The World Cup.

After a disappointing World Cup in 1970, when Charlton was controversially substituted during England's defeat to West Germany, he played out his final years at United before retiring in 1973 (on the same day as his brother, Leeds United's Jack Charlton). He turned out for Preston as player/manager the following season, but after one year in charge he decided that management was not for him.

HECTOR CHUMPITAZ

Country: Peru
Born: April 12, 1944
Position: Centre-back
Club: Unidad Vecinal, Deportivo Municipal, Universitario, Atlas, Sporting Cristal

Hector Chumpitaz was, for much of his international career, Peru's inspirational captain. The Peruvian authorities recognised him as playing for the national team on 147 occasions, of which only 105 were officially recognised by FIFA. Chumpitaz had made his international debut in 1965 and went on to appear in two World Cups, in 1970 and 1978. The latter was the most significant as the 34-year-old captain helped Peru through to the second phase. Three years earlier he was part of Peru's Copa América triumph in Colombia. For a decade he played for Universitario in the Peruvian league and finished his career in 1984 with Sporting Cristal.

CLODOALDO

Country: Brazil
Born: September 26, 1949
Position: Midfield
Club: Santos

Clodoaldo played in every game of Brazil's successful 1970 World Cup campaign at the age of just 20. He scored the equaliser in their 3-1 semi-final win over Uruguay, launching their comeback for victory. A defensive midfielder, he was the baby of Mario Zagalo's team and provided a platform for the likes of Jairzinho and Rivelino to launch attacks. Yet despite the rock-like security he supplied, he never played at a World Cup again.

At club level, Clodoaldo spent his entire career at Santos, making over 500 appearances and winning the Paulista state championship five times, in 1967, 1968, 1969, 1973 and 1978.

MARIO ESTEVES COLUNA

Country: Portugal
Born: August 6, 1935
Position: Centre-forward/Inside-right/Left-half
Clubs: Deportivo Lourenço Marques, Benfica, Lyon

Mario Coluna was a member of the great Benfica side of the 1950s and 1960s. He began as a lethal centre-forward, but after the arrival of the legendary Eusébio he turned into a formidable midfielder. Born in Mozambique, Coluna was to make 57 appearances for Portugal and he captained the side that reached the 1966 World Cup semi-finals. His greatest achievements were with Benfica, winning 19 honours and scoring in the 1961 and 1962 European Cup victories, as well as making three other European Cup final appearances in 1963, 1965 and 1968. Coluna also played in Mozambique with Marques, and later became the country's Sports Minister.

GIANPIERO COMBI

Country: Italy
Born: December 18, 1902
Position: Goalkeeper
Club: Juventus

Gianpiero Combi was the first of the truly great Italian goalkeepers. He captained Italy to triumph in the 1934 World Cup, beating Czechoslovakia 2-1 after extra-time. The final was Combi's 47th and last appearance for his country, a career that had started dauntingly ten years earlier with a 7-1 defeat by Hungary. He also retired from club football in 1934, going out on a high with Juventus, winning a fourth successive Italian league championship. Combi also won a bronze medal at the 1928 Amsterdam Olympics when Italy finished third, beating Egypt 11-3 in the third place play-off game.

ALESSANDRO COSTACURTA

Country: Italy
Born: April 24, 1966
Position: Defender
Club: AC Milan

If success is measured by the number of medals a player has won then this imposing Italian defender is one of the most successful footballers of recent times. In over 20 years with Milan, his haul of silverware has included seven Serie A titles, four European Cups and two European Super Cups. Indeed, his career's only major disappointments both came in 1994 when suspensions ruled him out of the World Cup final and the Champions League final.

He didn't make his debut for Italy until 1991 (aged 25) but went on to play 59 times. Before retiring from international football in 1998, Costacurta had played for Italy at Euro 96 and in two World Cups (1994 and 1998).

Left: Benfica's Mario Coluna talks to former Manchester United star Charlie Mitten in 1962. His team-mate Eusébio looks on.

Below left: Clodoaldo is watched by England's Terry Cooper at the 1970 World Cup.

Below: Alessandro Costacurta of AC Milan.

Above: Teófilo Cubillas in action at the 1978 World Cup, where he scored five goals.

JOHAN CRUYFF

Country: Holland
Born: April 25, 1947
Position: Forward
Clubs: Ajax, Barcelona, Los Angeles Aztecs, Washington Diplomats, Levante, Ajax, Feyenoord

Hugely talented, wilful and unpredictable, Johan Cruyff symbolises the golden era of Dutch football and remains inextricably linked with the concept of Total Football. Brought up just around the corner from Ajax's ground where his mother was a cleaner, Cruyff joined the club in 1959 and made his debut on November 1964, aged 17, scoring the only Ajax goal in a 3-1 defeat to Groningen. With the arrival of Rinus Michels, the architect of Total Football, the club accelerated into the modern era with breathtaking style.

Lightweight but blessed with superb balance and huge stamina, Cruyff could cover acres of space and dictate the play. Ajax won five league titles in his first spell with the club but it was three consecutive European Cups between 1971 and 1973 that helped define the legend of the 'Flying Dutchman', resulting in a hat-trick of European Footballer Of The Year awards. Scoring both his side's goals in the 2-0 win over Inter Milan in 1972 capped one of his finest performances.

Making his first international appearance on September 7, 1966, Cruyff scored on his debut in a 2-2 draw with Hungary. He also became the first Dutchman to be dismissed in an international two months later. By the time of the 1974 World Cup Cruyff was captain and the Dutch team had gone from perennial outsiders to hot favourites. Cruyff played in a custom-made Dutch strip with two stripes on his sleeve, rather than the three stripes worn by his team-mates, insisting that as he was sponsored by a rival company he would not wear a shirt with

Opposite: A majestic Johan Cruyff rounds the floored Argentinian goalkeeper to score for Holland during the 1974 World Cup.

the famous Adidas branding. He orchestrated play with teasing skills and dazzling surges, unveiling the celebrated 'Cruyff turn' to the watching millions. The shift in the balance of power was vividly demonstrated when the Dutch beat a physical Brazil 2-0 in a game notable for a sublime volley from the captain. Losing the final to West Germany did nothing to diminish Cruyff's stature, even though he was shackled by Berti Vogts during its most crucial phase. Four years later he refused to join the Dutch squad for the 1978 World Cup, a gesture typical of his rebellious personality. He had won 48 caps and scored 33 goals.

By the summer of 1974 he had moved to Barcelona for a record fee of £922,300. The Catalan side were struggling but Cruyff scored twice on his debut and led them to their first championship since 1960.

In 1978 he announced his retirement to go into business but returned to playing in the North American Soccer League a year later. He eventually rejoined Ajax in December 1981, taking them to two more championships, but his swansong came with bitter rivals Feyenoord, whom he guided to a league and cup double in 1984. In his last season, at 37, he was voted Dutch Player Of The Year.

Cruyff inevitably went into management with Ajax in 1985, winning a European Cup Winners' Cup, but quit three years later after another dispute. In May 1988 he took over at Barcelona, guiding the club to four consecutive league titles between 1991 and 1994. He brought them the European Cup for the first time in 1992, but four years later he was sacked.

A heavy smoker with a congenital heart condition, he had a bypass operation in 1991, but his health does not stop him from being linked with Barcelona and Holland every time there is a vacancy. From his record it is not hard to fathom why.

TEÓFILO CUBILLAS

Country: Peru
Born: March 8, 1949
Position: Midfield
Clubs: Alianza, Basel, FC Porto, Alianza, Fort Lauderdale Strikers

Teófilo Cubillas is easily Peru's greatest ever player. At 21 years old he was the third highest goalscorer at the 1970 World Cup finals, behind Gerd Müller and Jairzinho. He starred again in 1978 when he shot down Scotland's World Cup hopes with two goals in a surprise 3-1 win. He went on to score a hat-trick against Iran, taking his tally in the World Cup to ten. He was named South American Footballer Of The Year in 1972 and helped Peru to the 1975 Copa América. In contrast to his very impressive international achievements – 81 caps and 26 goals – his club career was modest, but he eventually became the Peruvian Minister for Sport.

ZOLTÁN CZIBOR

Country: Hungary
Born: August 23, 1929
Position: Left-winger
Clubs: Komarom, Ferencváros, Csepel, Honvéd, Barcelona, Espanyol

Czibor was the talented left-footer who supplied much of the ammunition for the great Hungarian forward line of Puskás and Kocsis in the 1950s. Between 1949 and 1956 he played 42 times for the 'Magical Magyars' and scored 17 goals. Having won the Olympic title in 1952, Czibor's talents helped Hungary to the World Cup final in Switzerland in 1954. He was outstanding in the 4-2 semi-final success over Uruguay, but the Hungarians surrendered a two goal lead to lose the final to West Germany. At the time of the Hungarian revolution in 1956, Czibor – like Puskás and Kocsis – took advantage of a Honvéd tour to settle in Spain, where he was to win back-to-back league titles with Barcelona.

ALI DAEI

Country: Iran
Born: March 21, 1969
Position: Forward
Clubs: Javanan Ardabil, Esteghlal Ardabil, Tahirani Tehran, Tejarat Tehran, Pirouzi Tehran, Alasad, Arminia Bielefeld, Bayern Munich, Hertha Berlin, Al Shabab, Persepolis, Saba Battery

Ali Daei was one of Iran's most popular and famous players. He was the first Iranian (along with Karim Bagheri) to play professional football in Europe. In 1998, after he was dropped from the national team for criticising tactics, fans organised a poll calling for (and getting) his reinstatement. Daei made his international debut in June 1993 against Oman and went on to become one of Asia's most dangerous strikers, forming an excellent partnership with Khodadad Azizi. In 1996 he scored 22 goals for his country, including eight at the Asian Cup. He was voted the 1999 Asian Player Of The Year and became the first player to score 100 international goals.

KENNY DALGLISH

Country: Scotland
Born: March 4, 1951
Position: Centre-forward
Clubs: Celtic, Liverpool

Alan Shearer tells a story about trying to mark his then manager at Newcastle in a practice game. Dalglish kept spinning off him and racing away with the ball. 'How did you know where I was?' Shearer asked. 'I could see your shadow,' was the reply from his boss. With a football at his feet Kenny Dalglish had the instincts of a gunslinger.

Above: Everton's Dixie Dean (right) is introduced to Spanish goalkeeper Zamora in 1931.

Possessed of quickfire reflexes, an acute awareness of opponents and team-mates, exquisite touch, and the ability to shield the ball seemingly forever, Dalglish ranks among the finest players Scotland has ever produced.

He joined Celtic as a junior in 1967 and might have gone straight to Liverpool at 15 but for a failed trial. Instead Celtic farmed him out to Cumbernauld to toughen him up. Jock Stein's Celtic were a top European side and though he made his league debut against Raith Rovers on October 4, 1969, it took time to establish himself. However, in seven seasons there he was to make 204 appearances, score 112 goals and win four league championships and four Scottish Cups.

In August 1977 he made the move to Liverpool for a UK record fee of £440,000. Bought to replace the departing Kevin Keegan, he won the European Cup in his first season. The trophies continued to come: three European Cups, a hat-trick of league titles between 1982 and 1984, and two Footballer Of the Year awards.

Dalglish also played for Scotland at every level, making his debut as a substitute against

Belgium on November 10, 1971. He was part of the 1974 Scotland World Cup squad, but despite not losing, and holding Brazil to a draw, they crashed out on goal difference. In Argentina four years later Dalglish opened the scoring against Holland in the superb 3-2 win, but the team were again on a plane home after the first round. No matter how Scotland performed in the World Cup, the 'Tartan Army' idolised Dalglish just for scoring in the 1977 2-1 victory over England at Wembley.

He travelled to a third World Cup in 1982, and scored in the opening game against New Zealand, and would have appeared at a fourth tournament under Alex Ferguson but for injury. He made his last international appearance against Luxembourg in November 1986, retiring with 102 caps, having equalled Denis Law's scoring record of 30 goals.

In 1985 Dalglish succeeded Joe Fagan when he became player-manager of Liverpool, winning the elusive league and cup double in his first season in charge, and going on to win a total of three league titles as manager.

When the Hillsborough disaster struck the city in 1989, Dalglish conducted himself

impeccably, but following on as it did from the deaths at Heysel four years earlier it was a significant added pressure and he quit the club unexpectedly in February 1991.

Eight months later he surprised everyone by coming out of retirement to manage Blackburn Rovers, taking the dormant club into the Premier League and then to a championship in 1995. He was unable to repeat the trick when he moved to Newcastle United in February 1997 but still took the club to their first major cup final in 20 years.

WILLIAM 'DIXIE' DEAN

Country: England
Born: 21 January, 1907
Position: Centre-forward
Clubs: Tranmere Rovers, Everton, Notts County

Things could have worked out so differently had William 'Dixie' Dean not recovered from the motorcycle accident that nearly ended his career in 1926. But one year on from a 36-hour coma, Dean had scored twice on his England debut as a teenager. It was a miraculous

Left: Didier Deschamps and Marcel Desailly celebrate winning Euro 2000.

rehabilitation. Dean's career had started promisingly at Tranmere Rovers but in 1925 he moved to Goodison Park. It was here that Dean earned a reputation as a quick striker with devastating aerial strength, and during the 1927-8 season he scored 60 league goals, with a further 22 strikes in other competitions as Everton went on to take the title. 'People ask me if that 60-goal record will ever be beaten,' he once said. 'I think it will, but there's only one man who will do it and that's the fella who walks on water.'

Dean continued to score regularly at both club and international level, notching up a total of 379 goals for Everton and 18 international goals despite only representing England 16 times, but by the time he was transferred to Notts County in 1938 he was past his best. Sadly he passed away in 1980, but the venue was fitting: Goodison Park for a clash between Everton and Liverpool. Dean had died in his spiritual home.

JIMMY DELANEY

Country: Scotland
Born: September 3, 1914
Position: Outside-right
Clubs: Celtic, Manchester United, Aberdeen, Falkirk, Derry City, Cork Athletic, Elgin City

Jimmy Delaney's career spanned both sides of the Second World War and he made a unique mark on the game by becoming the only player to have won the Scottish Cup, the FA Cup and the Irish Cup. He won the Scottish Cup with Celtic in 1937, beating Aberdeen 2-1 in the final. He also won two league titles with the club. He lifted the FA Cup with Manchester United in 1948 in a thrilling 4-2 win over Blackpool, and in 1954, at the age of 39 and as the Irish league's most expensive player at £1,500, he finally won the Irish Cup with Derry City after two replays with Glentoran.

MARCEL DESAILLY

County: France
Born: September 7, 1968
Position: Defender
Clubs: Nantes, Marseille, AC Milan, Chelsea, Al Gharafa

A colossal player at club and international level, Marcel Desailly is one of the greatest defenders in the history of the game. He started his career alongside Didier Deschamps at Nantes, moved to Marseille, winning the European Cup in 1993, and scored in the final when AC Milan clinched the trophy the following year. Immensely strong and powerful, he was a midfielder during five years at Milan but always played in defence for France and was a key figure as they won the World Cup in 1998 (despite being sent-off in the final) and the European Championship in 2000. He became France's most capped player of all time in April 2003 before retiring from international football after Euro 2004. During his playing career with Chelsea, Desailly became captain after the departure of Dennis Wise and was so solid in defence that he became known as 'The Rock', winning the FA Cup and UEFA Super Cup with the club, leaving in July 2004 to finish his playing career with Al Gharafa in Qatar. He ended the 2005 season as the club's top scorer.

DIDIER DESCHAMPS

Country: France
Born: October 15, 1968
Position: Midfield
Clubs: Nantes, Marseille, Bordeaux, Marseille, Juventus, Chelsea, Valencia

A hugely successful footballer, Deschamps started out at Nantes and captained Marseille to a European Cup triumph aged just 24 in 1993. He joined Juventus and became a key figure in the side, winning the European Cup and World Club Cup in 1996, and Italian titles in 1995, 1997 and 1998. Deschamps captained France to World Cup victory on home soil in 1998 and led the side's winning European Championship campaign in 2000 before quitting international football. A prodigious worker, he read the game well and provided a platform for more creative players. He won 103 caps, retiring in 2001.

KAZIMIERZ DEYNA

Country: Poland
Born: October 23, 1947
Position: Midfield
Clubs: Wlokniarz Starogard Gdanski, LKS Lodz, Legia Warsaw, Manchester City, San Diego Sockers

Kazimierz Deyna was the creative midfield driving force of Poland's greatest ever team during the 1970s. The Legia Warsaw player had shot to prominence at the 1972 Olympics, scoring both goals in the 2-1 victory over Hungary in the final. He went on to win 102 caps and was captain of Poland at two successive World Cups. In 1974 Deyna helped a free-scoring Poland to third place, and in 1978 helped them to the second round group stage. During this period he figured in the top ten of Europe's Footballer Of The Year award on three occasions. He also appeared in the film *Escape To Victory*. He died in a car crash in 1989.

Above: Polish midfielder Kaimierz Deyna wearing the colours of Manchester City.

1943: Makes his debut for River Plate at the age of 17.

1947: Copa América winner with Argentina. He is capped seven times by his country.

1949: During players' strike in Argentina, he moves to Millonarios of Bogota to play in pirate league. Capped three times by Colombia.

1953: Joins Real Madrid for $70,000.

1956: Wins first of five consecutive European Cups and makes the first of 31 appearances for Spain.

1959: The Blond Arrow is named European Footballer Of The Year for a second time.

1960: Scores a hat-trick in Real's incredible 7-3 defeat of Eintracht Frankfurt in European Cup final.

1963: Kidnapped by the Venezuelan Liberation Front while on tour of the country with Real, he is released unharmed.

1964: Leaves Real to join Espanyol, before retiring to take up coaching.

1971: Guides Valencia to Spanish championship.

1981: He coaches River Plate to Argentine National League title.

1983: Returns to Real Madrid as first team coach.

2000: Appointed Honourary President at Real Madrid.

ALFREDO DI STÉFANO

Country: Argentina, Colombia, Spain
Born: July 4, 1926
Position: Centre-forward
Clubs: River Plate, Huracán, Millonarios, Real Madrid, Espanyol

Born in Argentina of Italian parentage, Alfredo Di Stéfano was just 15 years of age when he joined the famous River Plate side of the 1940s and within a year he had made his debut in a team that included Adolfo Pedernera and Labruna, two of Argentina's greatest ever players.

Unable to make an immediate impression in an attack that included such players, he was loaned to Huracán to hone his skills, and some 10 goals in 25 games saw his return following Pedernera's departure to Atalanta. Now 20 years of age, his impact on the team was immediate as he led River Plate to the 1947 championship with 27 goals in 30 games. His elevation to the Argentinian national team was inevitable, and six goals helped his country retain the Copa América championship that year.

A players strike in 1949, the result of a poor wage structure, led to an exodus of players into the pirate 'Di Mayor' league in Colombia. As this league was outside of the jurisdiction of FIFA, no transfer fees were paid, therefore the clubs could afford to tempt players with higher wages. Alongside Pedernera, Di Stéfano joined Millonarios of Bogota and became the club's second highest goalscorer of all time, scoring 267 goals as they won four titles in five seasons.

With his place in the country's football history assured, Di Stéfano represented the Colombian national team, regardless of the fact that he had already played for Argentina. But with so few fixtures arranged, he made just four appearances for his adopted nation.

Di Stéfano was regarded as the best player in South America and when he was lured to join Real Madrid in 1953, the opportunity

Above: Di Stéfano heads wide against Barcelona in 1960. Below left: Di Stéfano scores the first goal in a 5-3 victory over their rivals in the Spanish League in 1960. Below right: Posing for Barcelona's other team, Espanyol in 1964.

came late in his career. Santiago Bernabéu, president of the Spanish club, orchestrated the move after the 27-year-old impressed in a friendly between Real and Millonarios. For a while they were involved in a tug-of war with Barcelona for his services, but he signed for Madrid that summer for $70,000.

The next ten seasons would see him revered as one of the greatest players on the planet and he became the most popular player in Real's history. His first season delivered the Spanish title, and within three years his opening goal inspired the club to an inaugural European Cup final victory against Stade de Reims. Di Stéfano would score in each of the next four finals as Real made the trophy their own.

The second triumph against Fiorentina was significant as it capped a tremendous season in which he not only topped the scoring in the competition, but also in the Spanish league,

where Real reigned supreme. His exploits made him a household figure across the continent and it was little surprise when he was named European Player Of The Year.

It was the fifth European Cup success that highlighted both Di Stéfano's standing in the game and Real's dominance. Having finished the previous campaign as Spain's top scorer for the fourth consecutive season, he led the club to a 7-3 drubbing of Eintracht Frankfurt in the final. His hat-trick, allied to the four goals of Ferenc Puskás, saw Di Stéfano at his peak, and although he would reach two more finals, Di Stéfano's star was on the wane.

A 3-1 European Cup defeat by Inter Milan in 1964 proved to be his last major game for the club, and although he scored 19 goals in two seasons for Barcelona-based Espanyol, a back injury forced him to hang up his boots at the ripe old age of 40.

DIDI

Country: Brazil
Born: October 8, 1928
Position: Midfield
Clubs: Americano of Campos, FC Rio Branco, FC Lencoes, Madureiro, Fluminense, Botafogo, Real Madrid, Valencia, Botafogo

Waldyr Pereira, more famously known as Didi, represented his country on 85 occasions and was the inspiration behind Brazil's successive World Cup triumphs of 1958 and 1962. Indeed, Brazil's free-flowing 4-2-4 system owed much to Didi's speed, thoughtful play and extraordinary technique. He was the first of the great free-kick specialists, scoring 12 of his 31 international goals from dead ball situations. He forged his playing reputation with Fluminense and Botofogo, but a dream move to Real Madrid did not work out. He later became coach of Peru and shocked South American football when he guided them to the 1970 World Cup.

IGOR DOBROVOLSKI

Country: Soviet Union, CIS, Russia
Born: August 27, 1967
Position: Midfielder
Clubs: Dinamo Moscow, CD Castellon, Servette, Genoa, Marseille, Dinamo Moscow, Atlético Madrid, Fortuna Dusseldorf, Dinamo Moscow, Tiligul-Tiraspol

Igor Dobrovolski was the star of the Soviet Union's 1988 Olympic Games gold medal-winning team in Seoul . When the Soviet Union subsequently fell apart Dobrovolski, a Moldovan by birth, went on to play for CIS and Russia. However, although he refused to play for coach Pavel Sadyrin at the 1994 World Cup he did play at Euro 96 without being at a club. He made several attempts to be a success abroad but always returned to Dinamo. In all he played 47 international matches.

DOMINGOS

Country: Brazil
Born: November 19, 1912
Position: Centre-back
Clubs: Bangu, Vasco da Gama, Nacional, Boca Juniors, Flamengo, Corinthians

Domingos da Guia is regarded as one of the all-time great Brazilian defenders. He played at the 1938 World Cup, where they reached the semi-finals, and enjoyed a club career across South America. He started at Bangu and starred for Vasco da Gama and Flamengo. He also played abroad and won the Uruguayan league at Nacional and the Argentine title at Boca Juniors.

Nicknamed 'The Divine Master', Domingos was a highly skilled player, introducing a refined technique at the back. He often dribbled the ball out of the penalty area, something rarely seen at the time. He made 30 appearances for Brazil and died in 2000.

TED DRAKE

Country: England
Born: August 16, 1912
Position: Centre-forward
Clubs: Southampton, Arsenal

Edward Joseph Drake is part of Arsenal folklore, having scored all seven goals in the 7-1 thrashing of Aston Villa on December 14, 1935. The Villa Park slaying showed Drake at his fearless best in a Highbury career that yielded two league championships, an FA Cup winners medal and five England caps. Drake signed from Southampton in March 1934 and although his seven goals in ten games helped wrap up the title, he hadn't played enough games to secure a medal. He made up for the disappointment by netting 42 goals in 41 league appearances the following season as the Gunners cruised to a third successive title. After retiring, Drake managed Chelsea to the First Division title in 1955.

DRAGAN DZAJIC

Country: Yugoslavia
Born: May 30, 1946
Position: Outside-left
Clubs: Red Star Belgrade, SEC Bastia

Dragan Dzagic is regarded as the greatest Yugoslav player of all time. After making his international debut at the age of 18, the Red Star Belgrade winger scored 23 goals in 85 appearances for his country. He helped Yugoslavia to the European Championship final of 1968 and the semi-finals in 1976, as well the 1974 World Cup finals. A winger who truly mesmerised defenders with his speed and agility when carving out chances, his power also made him a direct threat to any goalkeeper. With Red Star he won five Yugoslav championships and four Yugoslav Cups between 1961 and 1975, scoring 287 goals in 590 appearances.

DUNCAN EDWARDS

Country: England
Born: October 1, 1936
Position: Midfield
Club: Manchester United

Even today, some people still rate Duncan Edwards as the greatest player to have worn the Manchester United shirt. For someone who played only 151 matches for his club and 18 for his country before his death following the Munich air disaster at the age of 21, that

appears difficult to believe, but not to those lucky fans who saw him play.

Unusually strong and quick, he played his first game for Manchester United aged 16. Comfortable anywhere on the pitch, he could play in defence, midfield or attack. His all round game, speed and power meant he was the brightest of the 'Busby Babes' who won back-to-back championships before the heart of the side was lost on an icy runway. After the crash, Edwards clung to survival for 15 days before slipping away. He would have been 29 at the 1966 World Cup. Had he lived, many believe he, rather than Bobby Moore, would have been the man who lifted the World Cup.

Above: Manchester United's Duncan Edwards takes to the field in Belgrade in 1958. On the way back from the match he died from injuries sustained in the Munich air disaster at just 21.

STEFAN EFFENBERG

Country: Germany
Born: August 2, 1968
Position: Midfield
Clubs: Borussia Mönchengladbach, Bayern Munich, Fiorentina, Borussia Mönchengladbach, Bayern Munich, Wolfsburg, Al-Arabi

Stefan Effenberg has graced some of Europe's top teams and at his peak was one of Europe's top players, but he will probably be best remembered for being sent home from the 1994 World Cup for making obscene gestures to the German fans. It was a rash act that more or less ended his international career as he only added two more German caps to his collection afterwards, bringing his overall tally up to 35. A German Cup winner in 1995 with Mönchengladbach, he had two spells at the club, as he did with Bayern Munich, with whom he won three German league titles and the Champions League in 2001. He also had

a spell with Fiorentina in the early 1990s, finishing his career in 2004 after one season with Qatari side Al-Arabi.

PREBEN ELKJAER-LARSEN

Country: Denmark
Born: September 11, 1957
Position: Striker
Clubs: Vanlose, Köln, Lokeren, Hellas Verona, Vejle BK

Denmark matured as a football nation in the 1980s when they boasted three players of world class: the Laudrup brothers and Elkjaer-Larsen. Explosive on and off the field, Elkjaer-Larsen was the kind of player who made things happen. First capped in 1977, he starred in the 1984 European Championship and was voted third best player of the 1986 World Cup, in which he scored a hat-trick in Denmark's 6-1 rout of Uruguay. His 25 goals in 66 matches helped Hellas Verona to the Italian title in 1985. He had retired by the time of his country's greatest triumph, the 1992 European Championship.

ARSENIO ERICO

Country: Paraguay
Born: March 30, 1915
Position: Centre-forward
Clubs: Club Nacional, Independiente, Huracán

In 1937 the Argentine league witnessed a goalscoring sensation when Independiente's Arsenio Erico netted a record 47 goals in 34 games during the league season. It was a record that epitomised Erico as a prolific goalscorer, and on numerous occasions he managed to find the net five times in a game. He was discovered at the age of 17 when he played in a charity match for the Paraguay Red Cross in Buenos Aires. He was spotted by the directors of Independiente and immediately signed in exchange for a donation to the Red Cross. His career was blighted by injury though and he retired in 1947 while playing for Huracán.

EUSÉBIO

Country: Portugal
Born: January 25, 1942
Position: Centre-forward
Clubs: Sporting Lourenço Marques, Benfica, Boston Minutemen, Toronto Metros, Las Vegas Quicksilver, Beira Mar, Monterrey

Eusébio Da Silva Ferreira was born in the Portuguese colony of Mozambique in 1942 and although he excelled at basketball and athletics, he made his name as a footballer with local club Sporting Lourenço Marques, a feeder for Portuguese side Sporting Lisbon.

In 1960, he was deemed ready for the Portuguese league, but having successfully arrived at Lisbon airport, en-route to Sporting's headquarters he was 'kidnapped' by rival club Benfica and hidden in an Algarve fishing village until a deal was struck in the best interests of all parties.

Benfica were prompted to take such evasive action after their coach, Bela Guttmann, heard about Eusébio in a hairdresser's salon. Having flown out to Mozambique to witness his talent at first hand, Guttmann made it his mission to sign 'The Black Panther' as soon as the opportunity presented itself.

As a fresh-faced 18-year-old, it took Eusébio a little time to adapt to his new surroundings, but within two years he had managed to secure a place in Benfica folklore as a member of the triumphant European Cup side that beat Spanish giants and five-times winners, Real Madrid. Eusébio scored twice in the 5-3 victory and the following year was selected to play for a Rest Of The World side against England at Wembley, as part of the Football Association's centenary celebrations.

He endeared himself to the British public in the game and the bond was further cemented three years later when he became a star of the 1966 World Cup finals as a member of the Portuguese team. Having reached the quarter-finals, Portugal were shocked when North Korea took a 3-0 lead, but Eusébio inspired his team-mates into one of the greatest ever World Cup comebacks. He scored four goals as Portugal won the game 5-3, and although he left the tournament in tears following semi-final defeat against England, he was the competition's top-scorer with nine goals. Such was his impact, he even had a waxwork model erected in his honour at Madame Tussauds in London.

Goals were certainly Eusébio's forte and from 1964 to 1968, and again in 1970 and 1973, he was Portugal's top league scorer. He was also the continent's top scorer in 1968 and 1973, with 42 and 40 goals respectively, and in his 15 years at Benfica there were just two seasons in which he did not win a domestic or European honour.

With a European Cup winners' medal already to his name, when Benfica faced Manchester United at Wembley in 1968 he again had an opportunity to go one better than the runner-up medals he had picked up in 1963 and 1965. With the scores at 1-1, he was denied a late winner by a fine save from Alex Stepney and United went on to win in extra-time. Eusébio again left Wembley in tears again but the bittersweet experience of the competition was tempered by his total tally of 46 cup goals, second only to the great Alfredo Di Stéfano.

A knee injury forced Eusébio to end his top-flight career at 32 and he saw out his playing days in the NASL with the Boston Minutemen, Toronto Metros and Las Vegas Quicksilver. He returned to Benfica as coach in 1977, but having scored 38 goals in 46 games for Portugal, and 727 goals in 715 games in total, it is undoubtedly as a scorer of goals that he will be best remembered.

GIACINTO FACCHETTI

Country: Italy
Born: July 18, 1942
Position: Left-back
Clubs: Trevigliese, Inter Milan

Starting out as a striker at his first club Trevigliese, Facchetti was converted into a left-back by team coach Helenio Herrera when he joined Inter Milan. Encouraged to attack as well as taking care of his defensive duties – something unique at the time in Italian football – Facchetti netted 60 league goals in an Inter career lasting 17 years. His most celebrated goal came in 1965 in a European Cup semi-final second-leg match against Liverpool, when despite being 3-1 down from the first leg at Anfield, Inter defeated the English side 3-0 in the return match, with Facchetti netting the decider. He made 94 appearances for Italy and was team captain when his country made the World Cup final in 1970.

FALÇÃO

Country: Brazil
Born: October 16, 1953
Position: Midfield
Clubs: Internacional, Roma, São Paulo

Paulo Roberto Falção was an elegant and graceful midfielder who sprang to prominence as part of the outstanding Brazil side at the 1982 World Cup. He played alongside Zico, Socrates and Toninho Cerezo in a wonderfully creative midfield and brought his own flair and style to the team. At club level Falção played in Brazil for Internacional and was their greatest-ever player. With excellent passing vision and an eye for goal – he often scored

Opposite: 'The Black Panther', Eusébio of Benfica.

Below: Paulo Falção celebrates scoring against New Zealand at the 1982 World Cup.

from long range – he led the side to three national titles in 1975, 1976 and 1979.

He moved to Italy in 1980, and in 1983 led Roma to their first title triumph in over 50 years. Roma reached the European Cup final the following year, where they lost to Liverpool on penalties in their own Stadio Olimpico. Falção returned to Brazil in 1985 and played a final season at São Paulo. He won 38 caps for his country, scoring nine goals.

ATTILIO FERRARIS IV

Country: Italy
Born: March 26, 1904
Position: Right-half/Centre-half
Clubs: Roma-Fortitude, Roma, Lazio, Bari

Attilio Ferraris got the attention of Italy coach Vittorio Pozzo when injury to Roma's centre-half in an Italian league match saw Ferraris switch from right-half to centre-half. He displayed such unwavering commitment to the position and the Roma cause that Pozzo elevated him to the national side. Between 1926 and 1935 Ferraris played 31 times for Italy including the 1934 World Cup. Getting Ferraris to the World Cup took some work by Pozzo, as the player was a heavy smoker, owned his own bar and was incredibly unfit, but the Italian coach turned him around to great effect for Italy's first World Cup win.

BERNABE FERREYRA

Country: Argentina
Born: February 12, 1909
Position: Inside-forward
Clubs: Tigre, River Plate

Ferreyra was the first legendary player of Argentine football, although he only played four times for his country. His name was made in the domestic game, firstly with Tigre and then River Plate. He joined River Plate in 1932, and during his debut season with the club he scored a record 43 goals. No-one, it seems, could stop the player, causing one Buenos Aires newspaper to offer a gold medal to any goalkeeper who could keep a clean sheet against him. Ferreyra though was not fêted with honours, winning the Argentine title just twice in 1936 and 1937.

ELIAS FIGUEROA

Country: Chile
Born: March 25, 1946
Position: Left-back
Clubs: Unón La Calera, Santiago Wanderers, Peñarol, Internacional, Club Palestino, Fort Lauderdale Strikers, Colo Colo

Elias Figueroa Brander is the greatest Chilean player ever, having won consecutive South American Footballer Of The Year titles in 1974,

1975 and 1976. No other player has achieved such a feat. His talent was recognised early on and he was captain of Chile's Under-17 team. Born in Valpariso, Figueroa quickly established himself as a player of elegance, earning himself the respected nickname 'Don Elias'. At the 1974 World Cup he was voted the tournament's best defender, while at club level he won the national titles in three countries: twice in Uruguay with Peñarol in 1967 and 1968, twice in Brazil with Internacional in 1975 and 1976, and once in Chile with Palestino in 1978.

TOM FINNEY

Country: England
Born: April 5, 1922
Position: Winger
Club: Preston North End

Tom Finney started his love affair with Preston North End in the summer of 1940 when he signed as a part-time professional. Slight of build and with a quick turn of pace, he made an immediate impression by scoring on his debut in a 2-1 defeat at Liverpool that August. He continued to impress his hometown club but the Second World War interrupted his career and he was shipped off to the Middle East before he could sign on as a full professional. On his return at the start of the 1946-7 season, Finney scored in a 3-2 win against Leeds United and his flourishing reputation was soon rewarded with an England call-up for a match against Northern Ireland. His debut goal in a 7-2 victory was the first of 30 he would score in 76 appearances for his country, and with 18 of them coming in his first 24 appearances he was vying with Stanley Matthews for the title of the greatest England player of his generation.

A host of clubs tried to prise Tom Finney away from Preston's grasp, including Italian club Palermo, who reportedly offered him £10,000, a car, a villa and huge salary, but he stayed fiercely loyal and spent his entire career at Deepdale. Although he failed to win a major honour in his career with the club, he was twice voted England's Footballer Of The Year in 1954 and 1957 and his 187 league goals remain a club record.

JUST FONTAINE

Country: France
Born: August 18, 1933
Position: Centre-forward
Clubs: AC Marrakesh, US Marocaine Casablanca, Nice, Stade de Reims

Just Fontaine made history when he scored 13 goals at the World Cup finals in 1958 to set a record that looks unlikely ever to be beaten. It stands as the highest number of goals scored by one player in a single tournament, yet he was not even France's first-choice centre-forward before the World Cup began. Only an injury to René Bliard gave him the chance to make football history.

Fontaine was born in Morocco and won his first cap for France in 1953. He was left out for nearly three years and returned to the international fold to play just four times before the World Cup in 1958.

At the finals held in Sweden he formed a wonderful partnership with Raymond Kopa. Fontaine's assets were pace and a potent left foot, and he couldn't stop scoring. He was a star in the French league with Nice and Stade de Reims, with whom he lost in the 1959 European Cup final. To prove his World Cup exploits were no fluke, he finished as the European Cup's leading scorer in the 1958-59 season with ten goals. A broken leg ended his career and he went on to briefly manage France. He won 21 caps and scored 30 goals.

Right: Just Fontaine, scorer of a record 13 goals in the 1958 World Cup, is chaired off after the third-place play-off.

ENZO FRANCESCOLI

Country: Uruguay
Born: November 12, 1961
Position: Forward/Midfield
Clubs: Wanderers, River Plate, Racing Club Paris, Marseille, Cagliari, Torino, River Plate

When a footballer of the stature of Zinédine Zidane names his first born son after his hero, you know the player receiving such a tribute is exceptionally special. Enzo Francescoli certainly was. He graced Latin and European football for two decades in a career that yielded almost 200 club goals. He was voted South American Footballer Of The Year in 1984, and again when he returned from Europe for one final season in 1995. Nicknamed 'El Principe' (The Prince), he combined silky movement with great attacking play from midfield, and he was as adept at creating chances as he was converting them. He was top scorer in the Argentine league in 1984, 1986 and 1995.

ARTHUR FRIEDENREICH

Country: Brazil
Born: July 18, 1892
Position: Striker
Clubs: Germania, Ipiranga, Americao, Paulistano, São Paulo, Flamengo

Few players can claim to be better than Pelé, but in sheer volume of goals scored, Arthur Friedenreich can. In a 26-year career, 'The Tiger' scored a world record 1,329 goals – 49 more than Pelé. Of German and Brazilian parentage, his significance extends far beyond the playing field. An Englishman had originally introduced football to Brazil in the late 19th century, and for the first two decades of the 20th century it remained the preserve of white people. Friedenreich helped to change that. He played for the first Brazilian national side in a friendly against Exeter City in 1914 and went on to win 17 caps, scoring eight goals, until his final international appearance in 1930.

GARRINCHA

Country: Brazil
Born: October 28, 1933
Position: Right-wing
Clubs: Pau Grande, Botafogo, Corinthians, Flamengo, Bangu, Portuguesa Santista, Olaria, Atletico Junior Barranquilla, Red Star Paris

It was a miracle that Garrincha became one of Brazil's greatest players because a childhood illness had left one leg curved and the other slightly shorter. The nickname Garrincha meant 'Little Bird' or 'wren', and he was an outstanding dribbler with the ball, possessing a wonderful swerving 'banana' shot. Garrincha was part of the Brazil side which lifted the 1958 World Cup

but, although he might have been overshadowed by the exciting young Pelé on that occasion, in the 1962 finals he was Brazil's inspiration. He scored twice in the quarter-final win over England and then twice again in the semi-finals against hosts Chile, fully deserving his second winners' medal. His last game for Brazil was against Hungary at the 1966 World Cup; it was the first time in his 60 international matches that Brazil had lost with Garrincha in the side. Sadly, his wild off-the-field lifestyle caught up with him in 1983, when he died aged 49.

PAUL GASCOIGNE

Country: England
Born: May 27, 1967
Position: Midfield
Clubs: Newcastle United, Tottenham Hotspur, Lazio, Rangers, Middlesbrough, Everton, Burnley, Gansu Tianmu Boston United

The English game has produced legends like Bobby Moore, Bobby Charlton and Stanley Matthews, but none more talented than Paul Gascoigne. At his best Gascoigne could do things with a football beyond the scope of those men. He could run with it at pace, dance through tackles, see a pass no-one else could, strike the ball with power or caress it. Yet he proved incapable of handling his talent.

Born in Gateshead, Gascoigne joined nearby Newcastle United as a boy and made his senior debut at just 17 years of age, coming on as a substitute against QPR on April 13, 1985. He went on to make 106 league and cup appearances for the club, scoring 22 goals, but he never truly won over the Geordie crowd.

He moved south to Tottenham in July 1988 for £2 million and rapidly flowered under manager Terry Venables in a stylish attacking side. England manager Bobby Robson gave him his international debut as a substitute against Denmark on September 14, 1988, and he forced his way into the World Cup squad for Italia 90. England rode their luck to the semi-finals, losing on penalties to Germany. As the dream of World Cup glory ebbed away, Gazza lifted his shirt to wipe away the tears, creating one of the game's most iconic images.

Above: The majestic Garrincha in full flight against Sweden in the 1958 World Cup final.

In May 1991 Spurs agreed an £8 million move to Lazio after that season's FA Cup final against Nottingham Forest, but Gascoigne ruptured a cruciate ligament in a wild challenge on Gary Charles. Four months later he fell down outside a nightclub, smashing the same kneecap and delaying his comeback by three months. In subsequent years 27 operations would take their toll on his body.

He made a belated debut appearance for Lazio in a friendly with Spurs on September 23, 1992, and two months later scored his first goal in Serie A, an 87th minute headed equaliser in the Rome derby that forever endeared him to the Lazio fans.

Gascoigne's career in Italy proceeded in stops and starts as he drifted in and out of games. Then, in April 1994, a wild training ground tackle on Alessandro Nesta shattered his shin in two places. It was a year before he managed to return to the game, but within a month of the season ending he joined Rangers, where he won the Scottish Player Of The Year award in 1996, two Scottish Cups, and two championship medals. Terry Venables, now England coach, brought him back for Euro 96, where he demonstrated flashes of his old brilliance, not least with a delicious goal against Scotland.

A £3.5 million move to Middlesbrough in March 1998 failed to convince critics he was anything but a shadow of the player he once was. He made his debut in the League Cup final but could not wrench the game from Chelsea's grasp. Glenn Hoddle subsequently omitted him from England's 1998 World Cup squad.

Former Rangers boss Walter Smith took him to Everton in July 2000 and the move initially worked for Gascoigne, but he was also plagued by injury niggles exacerbated by years of heavy drinking. Following Smith's dismissal he headed for Burnley, a stint that lasted just four months. Attempts to find a suitable British club the following season foundered and he moved to Gansu Tianmu in the Chinese B League, marking another bizarre downward turn in the Gazza soap opera. He had a brief foray into management with Kettering Town in 2005, but he lasted just 39 days at the club.

FRANCISCO GENTO

Country: Spain
Born: October 22, 1933
Position: Left-wing
Clubs: Rayo Cantabria, Real Santander, Real Madrid

Supporters love to see wingers in full flight and none came more dazzling or decorated than outside-left Francisco 'Paco' Gento. Blessed with electric pace and intricate dribbling ability, he provided the ammunition to Puskás and Di Stéfano in Real's heyday. Gento joined Real from Santander in 1953 and played 800 games for the club, scoring 256 goals and winning 11 championship medals. He was capped 43 times for Spain and featured in the 1960 European Championship winning squad, but his greatest achievement was to appear in all eight of Real Madrid's European Cup finals between 1956 and 1966, picking up a winner's medal in six of them and scoring the extra-time winner in the 1958 game against AC Milan.

ERIC GERETS

Country: Belgium
Born: May 18, 1954
Position: Right-back
Clubs: Standard Liège, AC Milan, MVV Maastricht, PSV Eindhoven

The Belgian defender is one of his country's most celebrated players, picking up 86 caps in an international career that stretched between 1975 and 1991. Gerets was also part of the Belgian team which reached the final of the 1980 European Championship in Italy, where they ultimately lost out to a West Germany winner only two minutes from time. At club level, Gerets' greatest achievement came with Dutch side PSV Eindhoven, who he captained to victory in the 1988 European Cup final against Benfica on penalties. Now a coach, Gerets guided Lierse and Club Brugge to the Belgian title, and won back-to-back championships with PSV in 2000 and 2001.

GÉRSON

Country: Brazil
Born: January 1, 1941
Position: Midfield
Clubs: Flamengo, Botafogo, São Paolo, Fluminense

Gérson was the successor to Didi as Brazil's midfield general in the 1966 World Cup, but his country's ageing team were eliminated early. Four years later, however, it was a very different story. Gérson had a superb World Cup in 1970 where he orchestrated most of Brazil's attacking moves. In the first round, against Romania, he provided a trademark 40-yard pass from midfield for Pelé to score, and his range of distribution, together with his midfield scheming, was a consistent delight for all. In the final against Italy, Gérson was arguably the man of the match and scored Brazil's second goal in the memorable 4-1 rout. He will be forever remembered as an integral part of Mario Zagalo's Brazil 1970 side.

JOHNNY GILES

Country: Republic of Ireland
Born: January 6, 1940
Position: Midfield
Clubs: Manchester United, Leeds United, West Bromwich Albion, Vancouver Whitecaps, Shamrock Rovers

When Leeds recruited Giles in 1963 it proved a brilliant bit of business and a crucial move in manager Don Revie's team-building plans. The Irishman became one of the key players in Revie's superb side of the Sixties and Seventies, forming a lengthy partnership in central midfield with Billy Bremner. It was Bremner who supplied the fire and Giles the coolness of passing, though he wasn't shy of a strong challenge himself when it was needed.

His period at Elland Road would be filled with honours. Leeds won the title in 1969 and 1974, and the FA Cup in 1972, but while Giles twice picked up Fairs Cup winners' medals, the closest he came to success in the European Cup was defeat to Bayern Munich in the 1975 final. After leaving Leeds, Giles became player-manager at West Brom and later managed the Republic Of Ireland, stepping down in 1980.

GILMAR

Country: Brazil
Born: August 22, 1930
Position: Goalkeeper
Clubs: Jabaquara São Paulo, Corinthians, Santos

Gilmar is regarded as the finest goalkeeper Brazil has ever produced. He played in goal when they became world champions for the first time in 1958 and retained the title four years later. In 1958 he let in only three goals in six matches and was equally impressive at the 1962 World Cup in Chile. Agile and brave, he proved a formidable last line of defence.

Gilmar played for Corinthians, and after a decade joined Santos, where he enjoyed his greatest moments at club level, clinching the World Club Cup in 1962 and 1963. He won 94 caps and retired in 1969.

Below: Gerson avoids being swept away by the crowd after the 1970 World Cup final.

FERNANDO GOMES

Country: Portugal
Born: November 22, 1956
Position: Centre-forward
Clubs: FC Porto, Sporting Gijon, Sporting Lisbon

Fernando Mendes Soares Gomes was Portugal's legendary striker who twice won Europe's Golden Boot, in 1983 and 1985. On both occasions he was captaining Porto, his hometown club, scoring 36 and 39 league goals respectively. Both Porto, with whom he signed at the age of the 17, and Gomes were at the height of their powers. Gomes, however, missed out on the highlight of the 1987 European Cup final with a broken leg. He was the Portuguese league's top goalscorer six times in all and won five titles and three Portuguese Cups. During a 17-year career Gomes also played 46 times for Portugal.

ALAIN GOUAMENE

Country: Ivory Coast
Born: June 15, 1966
Position: Goalkeeper
Clubs: ASEC Mimosas, Raja Casablanca, ASEC Abidjan, Toulouse, SCO Angers, FC Lorient, Deauville, Toulouse

Alain Gouamene became the first ever player to appear in seven African Nations Cup tournaments, representing Ivory Coast between 1988 and 2000. The highlight was the 1992 tournament in which Gouamene saved three penalties in the semi-final shoot-out with Cameroon and then, in the final, he was the hero in an incredible penalty shoot-out which ended 11-10 in Ivory Coast's favour. Gouamene scored from the spot himself to make it 10-9 before making the trophy-winning save.

JIMMY GREAVES

Country: England
Born: February 20, 1940
Position: Centre forward
Clubs: Chelsea, AC Milan, Tottenham Hotspur, West Ham United

Jimmy Greaves always knew how to make an impression, scoring on every debut he made. But then he had a habit of scoring goals, his guile and pace helping him to notch up 357 of them throughout his career.

After working his way through the Chelsea youth ranks in the late Fifties, he soon entertained management and fans alike with his quick feet and imaginative individualism. After four seasons at Stamford Bridge (including two seasons as the league's top scorer), Greaves moved to AC Milan in search of higher wages but found it difficult to settle

and returned home to Spurs only six months later for a then record £99,999. He settled at White Hart Lane quickly, helping Spurs to two FA Cups and European glory in the Cup Winners' Cup, a first for any British club.

An England favourite throughout his career, the disappointment of sitting out the World Cup final in 1966 took its toll (injured early in the tournament, he was fit enough to return to the starting line-up but Ramsey persevered with a winning team). Greaves slipped into alcoholism and by the time he signed for West Ham as part of a cash/player exchange with Martin Peters in 1969, his talents were in decline. During the latter stages of his career, and then in his retirement years, Greaves struggled with the bottle and became a shadow of his former self. He later recovered and resurrected his career as a football pundit on the popular British television show *Saint And Greavsie*.

GUNNAR GREN

Country: Sweden
Born: October 31, 1920
Position: Inside-right
Clubs: Garda, IFK Gothenburg, AC Milan, Fiorentina, Genoa, Orgryte, GAIS Gothenburg, Skogens

Gunnar Gren was the inside-right of AC Milan's famous 'Grenoli' Swedish midfield triumvirate – alongside Nordahl and Liedholm. Gren had been spotted by the Italian club at the 1948 London Olympics, where he had

captained Sweden to the gold medal, scoring twice in the 3-1 victory over Yugoslavia in the final. The lure of a professional career – as opposed to the strictly amateur one in Sweden – took him to Milan and later Fiorentina and Genoa. When his native Sweden opened the doors to professionalism, Gren returned and was instrumental in helping hosts Sweden reach the 1958 World Cup final.

GYULA GROSICS

Country: Hungary
Born: February 4, 1926
Position: Goalkeeper
Clubs: Dorog, Honvéd, Tatabanya

A member of the 'Magical Magyars' team of the 1950s, Grosics was Hungary's greatest ever goalkeeper. Spectacular and assured in equal measure, he was a resilient last line of defence, dominating his penalty area and directing the play. He represented his country 86 times from 1947 onwards, winning a gold medal at the 1952 Helsinki Olympics, as well as playing at the World Cups of 1954, 1958 and 1962.

Grosics was turned from hero to villain in 1954 after ending up on the losing side in the World Cup final. On his return to Hungary, he was falsely accused of spying and was kept under house arrest for 13 months and exiled from army club Honvéd, eventually being allowed to play for Second Division Tatabanya. He was recalled to the national team in August 1956, but later lived in exile after the Soviet invasion, before returning to play for Hungary once again.

Above: Jimmy Greaves scores for Chelsea against Tottenham at Stamford Bridge in 1961.

RUUD GULLIT

Country: Holland
Born: September 1, 1962
Position: Centre-forward/sweeper/midfield
Clubs: Haarlem, Feyenoord, PSV Eindhoven, AC Milan, Sampdoria, AC Milan, Sampdoria, Chelsea

Ruud Gullit (who changed his birth name from 'Rudi Dil') is one of the most versatile and intelligent players the European game has yet produced, comfortable in a number of positions and enormously successful with clubs from three different countries, as well as at international level.

He made his professional debut in 1978, aged 16, for Haarlem, who were then managed by former West Bromwich Albion player Barry Hughes. His confident appearances at sweeper for the Dutch minnows led to Gullit's debut for Holland on his 19th birthday in 1981, in a 2-1 win over Switzerland. Successful moves to Feyenoord (1982 for £300,000) and PSV Eindhoven (1985 for £400,000) followed, but when the Dutchman became unhappy at PSV he was snapped up by Italian giants AC Milan in 1987 for a world record fee of £5.5 million.

The following year was truly extraordinary for Gullit, as Milan won their first league title for a decade and Holland became European champions for the first time. Gullit captained the Dutch side that day and scored one of their goals in the 2-0 win over the Soviet Union. To cap a fantastic year, he was named European and World Player Of The Year. Gullit's success story continued the following season as AC

Below: Ruud Gullit celebrates scoring in the 1989 European Cup final.

Milan thumped Steaua Bucharest 4-0 in the European Cup final, with the Dutchman recovering from a serious knee injury in time to not only play in the match, but to also score two of the goals. Milan retained their European crown the following season but Gullit's year was again disrupted by knee problems, causing doubts to arise about the future of his career.

Frustrated by injuries and after failing to make the side for Milan's European Cup final loss to Marseille in 1993, Gullit joined Sampdoria on a free transfer. But his form there was so good that his former club quickly swooped to re-sign him. Around the same time Gullit called time on an international career that had seen him grace just one World Cup, despite the fact that he was regarded as one of the best players on the planet.

After quitting Holland in 1992 for 'personal reasons' Gullit had a change of heart and returned to the fold. However, it was a short-lived affair and after a spat with national team coach Dick Advocaat, he walked out on the Holland squad just three weeks before the 1994 World Cup finals. It took Dutch fans a long time to forgive him.

After one last season with Sampdoria, Gullit finally left Italian football for good in 1995 to join Chelsea on a free transfer. And when the man who signed him, Glenn Hoddle, quit the club to become England coach, the Dutchman took over as player-manager.

In 1997 Chelsea beat Middlesbrough 2-0 in the FA Cup final, but Gullit's time at Stamford Bridge turned sour following disputes with both players and the club's hierarchy. He was sacked in February 1998, only to resurface as manager of Newcastle later the same year, another relationship that was to end in his dismissal.

GHEORGHE HAGI

Country: Romania
Born: February 5, 1965
Position: Midfield
Clubs: FC Constanta, Sportul Studentesc, Steaua Bucharest, Real Madrid, Brescia, Barcelona, Galatasaray

Known as the 'Maradona of the Carpathians', Gheorghe Hagi arrived on the world stage as the inspirational goalscoring flair behind the Steaua Bucharest team of the 1980s. Upon his controversial arrival in 1986 (with government approval, he was all but kidnapped from his previous team, Sportul Studentesc), they won three consecutive national league titles and also reached the final of the European Cup.

Such performances didn't go unnoticed and a big money move to Real Madrid followed. But despite glimpses of his trademark magic he failed to fulfil his enormous potential and moved on to Italy to play for Brescia.

Hagi has never been anything less than a talismanic figure for his country, inspiring them to great things over the course of three World Cups. In 1990, his Romanian side were eliminated in the second round after doing well to qualify from a tough group. The following tournament saw them perform fantastically well, winning their group and getting the better of a strong Argentina 3-2 in the second round. At the World Cup in 1998 his ageing side played admirably, beating England in the group stage, before narrowly losing to Croatia. He retired from international football after Euro 2000, having made 125 appearances, scoring 35 goals.

Towards the end of his playing career Hagi joined Galatasaray, where his famed creative qualities had a significant impact, and he led the Turkish side to their first ever piece of European silverware when they beat Arsenal in 2000 to lift the UEFA Cup.

KURT 'KURRE' HAMRIN

Country: Sweden
Born: November 19, 1934
Position: Forward/Outside-right
Clubs: Huvudsta IS, AIK Stockholm, Juventus, Padova, Fiorentina, AC Milan, AS Napoli, IFK Stockholm

Kurre Hamrin was a gifted attacker who made his name in Italy, winning several European club trophies, with Fiorentina (Cup Winners' Cup 1961) and AC Milan (Cup Winners' Cup 1968 and European Cup 1969). He scored both goals in the 1968 final against Hamburg in Rotterdam. Hamrin was also a World Cup runner-up in 1958, scoring four times in the tournament, including one sensational semi-final goal which typified his skill as he dribbled past several West German players before netting.

HOSSAM HASSAN

Country: Egypt
Born: August 10, 1966
Position: Striker
Clubs: Al Ahly, PAOK Salonica, Neuchatel Xamax, El Ain, Zamalek, Al Masry

A squad member of Egypt's 2006 African Nations Cup win, Hossam Hassan played in all matches except in the final. In so doing he set a new African record by making his 168th appearance for his country, at his seventh tournament. Not bad for a player who had retired four years earlier, after winning the African Champions League for the second time. He had lifted the cup with Al Alhy in 1987 and Zamalek in 2002. He made his international debut for Egypt in September 1985 in a friendly against Norway in Oslo. He quickly established himself as captain of the national team, his performances earning him a move to Europe, the first of several Egyptian players to do so. He played for Egypt at the 1990 World Cup.

JOHNNY HAYNES

Country: England
Born: October 17, 1934
Position: Inside-forward
Clubs: Fulham, Durban City

For two decades, Johnny Haynes was Fulham's star and even now, over 50 years since his 1952 debut, he is still considered the best player in the club's history. Renowned for his superb passing, Haynes became the first British player to earn £100 a week and repaid Fulham's faith in him by staying loyal to the club. For England, he won 56 caps, scoring 18 goals, and captained the side 22 times. He also played in the 1958 and 1962 World Cups and scored twice in the 9-3 win over Scotland in 1961. He joined South African side Durban in 1970 after 594 league appearances for Fulham – still a club record. He died after a car crash in Scotland in 2005.

NANDOR HIDEGKUTI

Country: Hungary
Born: March 3, 1922
Position: Outside-right/Centre-forward
Clubs: Herminamezo, MTK Budapest

Nandor Hidegkuti was the first foreign player to score a hat-trick against England at Wembley in Hungary's historic 6-3 win in 1953. A star of MTK Budapest, he scored 39 international goals in 68 appearances, but it was more than his statistics that made him special, it was also the way he played. Hidegkuti was not an out-and-out striker but a deep-lying centre-forward. It was this role that contributed to Hungary's free-scoring reputation. It created space for others and opportunities for himself in equal measure. Appearances at two Worlds Cups (1954 and 1958) and an Olympic gold in 1952 underlined Hidegkuti's reputation in the 1950s.

FERNANDO HIERRO

Country: Spain
Born: March 23, 1968
Position: Centre-back/Midfield
Clubs: Real Valladolid, Real Madrid, Al Rayyan, Bolton Wanderers

Fernando Hierro, Spain's most-capped outfield player, was justifiably described by coach Fabio Capello as 'the Spanish Baresi'. Malaga-born Hierro was a tough-tackling ball-winner who broke the record for the most bookings and sendings-off in the history of the Spanish league. He was also a skilful player, comfortable as a centre-back with Real Madrid or in a midfield holding role with Spain. He featured in four World Cup squads, evolving from non-playing member in 1990 to captain in 2002. He also won the European Cup three times, the Spanish league five times, as well as the Spanish Cup and World Club Cup. He retired in 2005 after a sterling season with Bolton and became coach of Malaga.

JOSE RENE HIGUITA

Country: Colombia
Born: August 27, 1966
Position: Goalkeeper
Clubs: Millonarios, Real Cartegena, Junior Barranquilla, Deportivo Pereira

Eccentric on the pitch and troubled off it, there has never been a keeper quite like Colombia's 'El Loco'. Renowned for dribbling the ball out of his area, taking on opposition players and even getting on the scoresheet, his defining moment came at Wembley in 1995 against England: to save a lob from Jamie Redknapp, Higuita flipped in midair, his feet above his head, and flicked the ball away with the bottom of his boots. The move became known as the 'scorpion kick' and the fame it bought Higuita marked an upturn in his fortunes. His earlier mistake at the World Cup finals in 1990 had seen Colombia eliminated, and he had also spent six months in jail in 1993 for involvement in a kidnapping case.

GEOFF HURST

Country: England
Born: December 8, 1941
Position: Forward
Clubs: West Ham United, Stoke City, West Bromwich Albion, Seattle Sounders, Cork Celtic

Though not England's most prolific ever goalscorer, Geoff Hurst will always be his nation's most celebrated for scoring the first hat-trick in a World Cup final: the three goals which secured England the Jules Rimet trophy for the first and only time. The son of a pre-war centre-half, Hurst was born in Ashton-Under-Lyme but moved to Essex as a boy. He joined West Ham as a junior, making his league debut in February 1960 against Nottingham Forest. Manager Ron Greenwood fashioned The Hammers into an exciting, stylish unit and Hurst, a fierce striker of the ball and powerful in the air, became its cutting edge. He won the FA Cup in 1964 and the European Cup Winners' Cup a year later, scoring 180 goals in 410 appearances before moving to Stoke City in August 1972 and West Brom three years later.

Hurst scored 24 goals in 49 appearances for his country but was only a fringe member of the England squad in the early stages of the 1966 World Cup. He would not have played in the final but for an injury to Jimmy Greaves earlier in the tournament. Hurst seized the opportunity, and even when Greaves was declared fit before the final, Hurst held on to

his place in the line-up. He became player-manager of Telford in 1976, coached with England for five years and had an unsuccessful six-month spell as manager of Chelsea. He was knighted in 1998.

Above: England's Geoff Hurst, the only player to score a hat-trick in a World Cup final.

VALENTIN IVANOV

Country: Soviet Union
Born: November 19, 1934
Position: Inside-forward/Midfield
Club: Torpedo Moscow

Soviet football enjoyed a purple patch in the early 1960s: the national team won the inaugural European Championship in 1960, and two years later they reached the quarter-finals of the World Cup, thanks largely to Ivanov's lethal finishing. He had been on target once in the 1958 finals but in 1962 he scored four goals, finishing the tournament as joint top scorer. It was an accolade he shared with five other players, including the Brazilians Garrincha and Vavá. Scoring in the opening match against Yugoslavia, he was on target twice in the 4-4 draw with Colombia, and again against Uruguay before the Soviets bowed out 2-1 to Chile in the quarter-final. He scored 26 international goals between 1955 and 1966 and was Russian Player Of The Year in 1957.

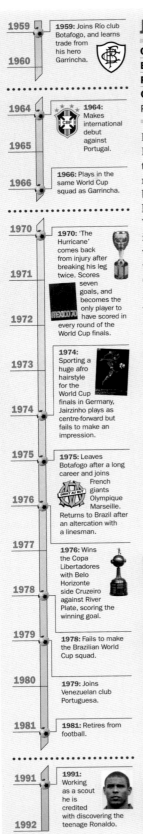

1959: Joins Río club Botafogo, and learns trade from his hero Garrincha.

1964: Makes international debut against Portugal.

1966: Plays in the same World Cup squad as Garrincha.

1970: 'The Hurricane' comes back from injury after breaking his leg twice. Scores seven goals, and becomes the only player to have scored in every round of the World Cup finals.

1974: Sporting a huge afro hairstyle for the World Cup finals in Germany, Jairzinho plays as centre-forward but fails to make an impression.

1975: Leaves Botafogo after a long career and joins French giants Olympique Marseille. Returns to Brazil after an altercation with a linesman.

1976: Wins the Copa Libertadores with Belo Horizonte side Cruzeiro against River Plate, scoring the winning goal.

1978: Fails to make the Brazilian World Cup squad.

1979: Joins Venezuelan club Portuguesa.

1981: Retires from football.

1991: Working as a scout he is credited with discovering the teenage Ronaldo.

JAIRZINHO

Country: Brazil

Born: December 25, 1944

Position: Winger/centre-forward

Clubs: Botafogo, Marseille, Cruzeiro, Portuguesa

If Pelé was the greatest player ever to play for Brazil, then there's a long list of legends not too far behind him battling it out to be recognised as the next best. Jairzinho would be close to the top of that list, essentially for his fantastic performances in the team's 1970 World Cup triumph. He had already played in the 1966 finals in England, though there was little evidence then that he would take the tournament by storm four years later. With Garrincha still in the side, Jairzinho, then just 21 years old, made do with a role on the left wing of Brazil's attack and wasn't at his best. He played in all three of his team's matches, but Brazil were poor and went home after the group stages.

Four years later it was another story. Jairzinho arrived in Mexico as a member of a very different Brazil side indeed and, with Garrincha retired, was able to play in his natural position as an attacking right-winger. Blessed with a direct style, scorching pace and a fierce shot, he was simply too much for opposing defenders to handle, and by the end of the tournament he had collected a winners' medal and made history by scoring in every round of the competition.

Jairzinho started off with a double in his first match, a 4-2 win over Czechoslovakia, and then

Above: Jairzinho was a star of the 1970 World Cup final against Italy, a game Brazil won 4-1. Below: Jairzinho takes on Romania, on the way to scoring a goal in every round of the 1970 World Cup tournament.

scored the winning goal in the victory over England, lauded as one of the most memorable matches of all time. The outstanding incident from that encounter has always been Gordon Banks' gravity-defying save from Pelé's downward header, but it's often forgotten that it was Jairzinho's run and cross which provided the chance. And that it was the winger who

settled a tight game with a close-range finish. Romania were next and he scored in a 3-2 success, then another in the quarter-final win over Peru. In the semi-finals Jairzinho scored again as Brazil beat Uruguay, and he made it a goal in every round with the third in the 4-1 win against Italy in the final, even if the ball did roll in off his chest!

Jairzinho's achievement was remarkable; one other player in World Cup history has done the same, but Uruguay's Alcide Ghiggia only had to play in four games in 1950. Jairzinho also played in the 1974 finals, scoring twice as Brazil finished fourth.

His club career was always overshadowed somewhat by his international achievements and, typically for many Brazilian players of his generation, Jairzinho rarely strayed far from his homeland. He did have a short spell with French side Marseille, but he enjoyed a highlight when he returned to more familiar surroundings with Cruzeiro, when he scored the winning goal to secure the 1976 Copa Libertadores – the South American Club Cup. He played on for Brazil's national team until the age of 38, finishing with 81 caps.

He can justifiably claim a permanent place in the World Cup Hall Of Fame.

JAIRZINHO'S RECORD-BREAKING GOALS At Mexico in 1970 Jairzinho became the only player to score in every game of every round of the finals.

1ST GROUP GAME		2ND GROUP GAME	3RD GROUP GAME	QUARTER-FINAL	SEMI-FINAL	FINAL
⚽ **v Czechoslovakia**	⚽ **v Czechoslovakia**	⚽ **v England**	⚽ **v Romania**	⚽ **v Peru**	⚽ **v Uruguay**	⚽ **v Italy**
61 mins: Puts Brazil 3-1 ahead after receiving a pass in an offside position.	**81 mins:** Beats four men to score the final goal, making it 4-1.	**59 mins:** Pelé lays off a Tostão cross for Jairzinho to fire home for a 1-0 win.	**22 mins:** The second goal in a 3-2 win, Jairzinho scores from close range.	**75 mins:** Jairzinho rounds the goalkeeper to score, completing a 4-2 win.	**76 mins:** Scores the second goal in a 3-1 win after starting move in his own half.	**71 mins:** Pelé nods on for Jairzinho to make history, scoring the third in 4-1 victory.

ALEX JAMES

Country: Scotland
Born: September 14, 1901
Position: Forward
Clubs: Raith Rovers, Preston North End, Arsenal

Lanarkshire born forward Alex James was the inspiration behind the great Arsenal side of the 1930s, winning four championship medals and two FA Cups while with The Gunners. The diminutive Scot was probably the most influential player of his generation and a huge favourite with football fans around the country. A natural showman, he was easily recognisable because of his trademark baggy shorts.

This showmanship often infuriated his managers, and it was this, coupled with a fiery temper, which probably contributed to the fact that James only gained eight Scotland caps throughout his career, though he was one of the Wembley Wizards who crushed the mighty England 5-1 in 1928. The legendary Arsenal striker of the period, Cliff Bastin, along with his contemporaries in The Gunners' attack, had much to thank him for, because it was James the creator who supplied them with the ammunition they needed.

PETAR JEKOV

Country: Bulgaria
Born: October 10, 1944
Position: Centre-forward
Clubs: Beroe, CSKA Sofia

Throughout a playing career that spanned from 1962 to 1975, Petar Jekov was an outstanding goalscorer. He was the first Bulgarian to win the Golden Boot (awarded each season to the leading scorer in the European leagues) after netting 36 goals for CSKA Sofia in the 1968-9 season, and his career total of 253 goals in 333 club appearances points to his lethal finishing ability. He won the Bulgarian championship four times with CSKA, scored 25 goals for his country and captained them to Olympic silver in 1968.

PAT JENNINGS

Country: Northern Ireland
Born: June 12, 1945
Position: Goalkeeper
Clubs: Newry Town, Watford, Tottenham Hotspur, Arsenal.

If you were designing the perfect goalkeeper on a computer, the finished article would end up very much like Pat Jennings. With all the attributes that a great keeper needs, Jennings was tall but agile, athletic but sturdy. He famously possessed huge hands, was great on crosses, superb in one-on-one confrontations with onrushing opponents, and he could improvise point-blank saves. He was also a superb shot-stopper and penalty saver.

Jennings had even more than that though, because you can add to the mix the fact that he was consistent, making very few errors in his career. Jennings was even-tempered too, and he had excellent powers of concentration. He was also incredibly durable, completing over 1,000 first class games in his long and distinguished career.

Jennings shot to fame after moving, via Watford, from his native Ireland to Tottenham Hotspur, where he kept goal for over 600 games over a 13-year spell. But the club mistakenly suspected his career was on the wane at 33 and sold him to bitter North London rivals Arsenal.

He continued his incredible career with The Gunners, winning more major honours until finally retiring in 1985 with 119 caps. He had played in four FA Cup finals, and had two Player Of The Season accolades and two World Cup campaigns under his belt.

JIMMY JOHNSTONE

Country: Scotland
Born: September 30, 1944
Position: Right-winger
Clubs: Celtic, San Jose, Sheffield United, Dundee, Shelbourne

'Jinky' Jimmy Johnstone will be remembered as one of Scotland's greatest players. The former ballboy at Celtic Park rose to become one of the stars of the great side of the late Sixties and early Seventies and was a key player in the team that won nine back-to-back league titles and seven Scottish cups. Johnstone loved the big occasion and his finest season probably came in 1967, when Celtic became the first Scottish side to lift the European Cup after beating Inter Milan in the final, crowning a season in which the club had won every competition they entered.

Johnstone, who left Celtic in 1975 to play for San Jose in the North American league, could perhaps have made even more of his career, but a typically fiery redhead, he led a less than exemplary off-the-field lifestyle. Johnstone was a superb dribbler, an accurate crosser of the ball, and an expert finisher. But like many inspirational players, consistency was his problem and he tended to have his fair share of off games. He died in 2006.

ROY KEANE

Country: Republic Of Ireland
Born: August 10, 1971
Position: Midfield
Clubs: Cobh Ramblers, Nottingham Forest, Manchester United, Celtic

A strong, fiery, ball-winning midfielder, Roy Keane was one of the Premier League's most

outstanding and consistent performers. He began his career with Cobh Ramblers in his native Cork before Brian Clough took him to Nottingham Forest as an 18-year-old. Clough gave him his debut away at Liverpool and the combative youngster instantly won many admirers with his tireless box-to-box running and his ability to score vital goals. At the end of his first full season at Forest Keane made an appearance in the 1991 FA Cup final, collecting a runners-up medal after the defeat by Tottenham. A Republic Of Ireland debut against Switzerland was to follow under the guidance of Jack Charlton.

Signed by Manchester United for £3.75 million in 1993 (at the time it was a record fee between English clubs), Keane was seen as the natural successor to Bryan Robson. His immense presence and fearless tackling in the centre of midfield, coupled with his intelligent, accurate passing, contributed greatly to United's success, and he was made club captain after Eric Cantona's retirement. However, months later a serious knee injury saw him miss much of the 1997-8 campaign, but his return coincided with his club's historic treble-winning season. After an inspired performance in the semi-final against Juventus, where he scored a goal and bossed the game majestically, Keane was unfortunate to miss the 1999 Champions League final victory over Bayern Munich due to suspension.

Highly regarded by his peers and critics alike, he was voted Player Of The Year for the 1999-2000 season by both the Football Writers Association and the PFA. A passionate and brutally honest man, Keane often courted

Above: Celtic's Jimmy Johnstone takes on Alex Miller of Rangers in the old firm derby.

notoriety throughout his time as a player. His biting 'prawn sandwich' outburst against United's executive fans was followed by a series of stinging comments about his fellow players. Those remarks were nothing compared to his fall-out with Republic Of Ireland manager Mick McCarthy. Keane had gone to the 2002 World Cup as Republic Of Ireland captain, but the personality clash with McCarthy saw him return before the tournament had kicked-off.

As Manchester United struggled to recover their dominance Keane was critical of the team in a programme for the club's television channel. The show was pulled from the schedules and by December 2005, after 13 years at the club, he was edged out of Old Trafford, finishing his career in Scotland where he helped Celtic to the Premier Division title that season.

KEVIN KEEGAN

Country: England
Born: February 14, 1951
Position: Centre-forward
Clubs: Scunthorpe United, Liverpool, Hamburg, Southampton, Newcastle United

It seems apt that Kevin Keegan was born on Saint Valentine's Day. During his career as both player and manager, the man nicknamed 'Mighty Mouse' (because of his diminutive stature and physical power) has been one of the game's great romantics, whipping up enthusiasm amongst fans and players alike.

That wasn't how Bill Shankly viewed him in 1971, however, when he bought the Scunthorpe United striker to Anfield for £33,000. But after describing him as 'playing like a rat after a weasel', Shankly was repaid for his veiled compliment as Keegan scored a goal on his debut in a 3-1 victory against Nottingham Forest.

The striker immediately became a crowd favourite (one popular Anfield chant of the day was 'Kevin Keegan walks on water') and he was arguably Shankly's best signing for the club. Certainly he had an impact, scoring 100 goals in 321 appearances and helping Liverpool to three league titles (1973, 1976, 1977), two UEFA Cups (1973, 1976) and the European Cup (1977) before moving to the German side Hamburg in 1977 for £500,000.

His England career was successful too, and after forcing his way into Alf Ramsey's side in 1972 he soon became an international regular, later forging an exciting partnership with Trevor Brooking in the early 1980s. 'He was the first person to admit he wasn't a naturally gifted player,' says Brooking now, 'but he was fabulous with man markers and would run them into the ground with his determination by twisting and turning and he was a strong little fella as well. People would knock him down and he would just get up again.'

Sadly trophies would elude England during that period and Keegan missed out on the chance of international glory when Ron Greenwood's team were knocked out of the 1982 World Cup in the second group stage, Keegan missing most of the tournament through a recurring back injury.

Despite a lack of trophies with England, he had already made his mark on the continent with Hamburg. In 1978 he claimed the European Player Of The Year award, a feat he repeated the following year when he helped Hamburg to the Bundesliga title before returning to England in 1980 to play for Southampton in a £420,000 deal.

Despite Southampton's lowly status in the old First Division, Keegan sparkled, scoring 42 goals in 80 games for the club, helping The Saints lead the title race for two months during the 1981-82 campaign before finally finishing seventh. Keegan was to pick up the PFA Player Of The Year Award that year, but, almost as quickly as he had arrived, he moved again, this time to Newcastle for £100,000.

Newcastle were languishing in the old Second Division at the time of Keegan's arrival, but after scoring on his debut against QPR he helped The Magpies to promotion in 1984. Bizarrely, as soon as this happened, Keegan announced his retirement from the game and in May of that year, directly after the end of his final match, a helicopter picked him up from the centre of the pitch at St James' Park. He was looking to a life away from the game on a golf course in Spain. Little did he know that he would be returning to football, and Newcastle United, much sooner than he thought, for an explosive period as manager. His subsequent jobs – in charge of Fulham, England and Manchester City – have been no less eventful.

MARIO KEMPES

Country: Argentina
Born: July 15, 1954
Position: Forward
Clubs: Instituto Cordoba, Rosario Central, Valencia, River Plate, Hercules, First Vienna, SV Austria Salzburg

Dubbed 'El Matador' for his incisive finishing, Kempes ranks only behind Maradona in the pantheon of Argentinian footballing heroes. Born in Cordoba, he joined local team Instituto Cordoba and then moved to Rosario, where he became top scorer in the Argentine league with 21 goals. Kempes made his international debut aged 19, against Bolivia during the qualifying rounds of the 1974 World Cup, and he was a member of the squad at the finals in West Germany.

He was to appear in three successive World Cup tournaments, making 18 of his total of 43 international appearances on the biggest stage, scoring 20 goals. At the finals in 1978 he was the only European-based player in César Luis Menotti's squad and went on to win the Golden Boot with six goals, including two in the victory over Holland in the final.

By then Kempes had made his name at Valencia where he was top scorer in the Spanish league for two successive seasons. He subsequently moved on to Austria and then to the Far East before retiring at 41. Coaching took him to obscure shores. He became a manager in Albania but was forced to flee during civil unrest and then won a league title with The Strongest in Bolivia before moving to Independiente Petrolero.

WIM KIEFT

Country: Holland
Born: November 12, 1962
Position: Centre-forward
Clubs: Ajax, Pisa, Torino, PSV Eindhoven, Bordeaux, PSV Eindhoven

Had Marco Van Basten not been around at a similar time, Wim Kieft would undoubtedly have figured in the Dutch national team on a far more regular basis than the 43 occasions he represented his country. Frequently those appearances came from the bench, but that did not stop him from scoring some important goals. As part of the squad that won the 1988 European Championship, Kieft netted the crucial winner against the Republic Of Ireland in the group stage. His goalscoring talents were equally at home in the Dutch top flight and Italy's Serie A.

Opposite: Kevin Keegan kisses the FA Cup after Liverpool's victory over Newcastle in 1974.

Below: Mario Kempes celebrates scoring against Holland in the 1978 World Cup final.

Above: The infamous Stuttgart divebomber Jurgen Klinsmann.

JURGEN KLINSMANN

Country: West Germany
Born: July 30, 1964
Position: Forward
Clubs: Stuttgart Kickers, Stuttgart, Inter Milan, Monaco, Tottenham Hotspur, Bayern Munich, Sampdoria

Klinsmann was an athletic and charismatic striker who first played for West Germany in 1987 and made an impact with his intelligent, all-round play. Club success followed when Klinsmann and fellow countrymen Lothar Matthäus and Andreas Brehme helped Inter Milan to the Serie A title. He loved testing himself in different football cultures and eventually played top-flight football in Germany, Italy, France and England.

Klinsmann is best remembered for his outstanding feats at international level, most notably in 1990 when West Germany lifted the World Cup in Italy. Klinsmann's apparent dive for the penalty that won the match added a less appealing facet to his reputation, but one that barely dimmed his popularity. Four years later, representing the newly unified Germany, he scored five more World Cup goals in the side that lost in the quarter-final.

His performances at Tottenham Hotspur made him England's Player Of The Year in 1995 and the following year he inspired Germany to the European Championship. His World Cup swansong in France in 1998 yielded another three goals. He retired with 108 caps and 47 goals, relocating to the USA, but in 2004 he was given the task of reviving the fortunes of the German national side, despite having no previous coaching experiences and took them to the 2006 World Cup semi-finals.

SANDOR KOCSIS

Country: Hungary
Born: September 23, 1929
Position: Inside-right
Clubs: Ferencváros, Honvéd, Young Fellows, Barcelona

Sandor Kocsis was top scorer at the 1954 World Cup with 11 goals and was nicknamed 'Golden Head' for his superb ability in the air. He recorded a remarkable tally of 75 goals in 68 internationals and is regarded as one of the finest Hungarian footballers of all time.

Kocsis was born in Budapest and made his international debut in 1949. During the 1950s he was three times the top scorer in the Hungarian league, won four titles, and made his name as part of the fabulous Hungary side that beat England 6-3 at Wembley in 1953.

He played for Ferencváros and Honvéd and formed a superb partnership for both club and country with Ferenc Puskás. Having won the Olympic gold medal in 1952 Kocsis went into the 1954 World Cup as a member of a Hungary side expected to claim the trophy, but despite his outstanding personal exploits, including two goals in the semi-final against Uruguay, Hungary lost to West Germany in the final.

Kocsis moved to Barcelona in 1958 and during his eight years with the Catalan giants won an impressive two Spanish league titles, two Spanish Cups and the UEFA Cup in 1960. He retired from from playing football in 1966 and died in 1979.

RONALD KOEMAN

Country: Holland
Born: March 21, 1963
Position: Central defender
Clubs: FC Groningen, Ajax, PSV Eindhoven, Barcelona, Feyenoord

Ronald Koeman's strike-rate belied his role as a defender. He netted almost 200 goals in a career spanning over 500 league games, earning himself a reputation as a set-piece specialist, both from the penalty spot and from free-kicks. His power and accuracy also meant that he was capable of delivering precision passes into the attacking third of the field for his strikers and he was comfortable on the ball in any area of the pitch.

He began his career alongside his brother Erwin at FC Groningen before joining Ajax. It was with PSV Eindhoven though, and then Barcelona, that Koeman was to enjoy his most successful spells, winning the European Cup with both clubs, becoming only the second player, after Belododici the year before, to win the competition with two different sides. He also had a key role to play in both finals, netting for PSV in the penalty shoot-out victory over Benfica in 1988 and then scoring Barcelona's winner against Sampdoria at Wembley in 1992.

Success for Koeman wasn't consigned to club football however, as he was also a member of the Dutch side that won the European Championship in 1988. After ending his playing days in Holland with Feyenoord, he moved into coaching, joining the staff of the Dutch national side before moving on to Barcelona. His first managerial role was with Vitesse Arnhem, before he took over at Ajax in 2001, Benfica in 2005 and PSV Eindhoven in 2006.

KALMAN KONRAD

Country: Hungary, Austria
Born: March 23, 1896
Position: Inside-forward
Clubs: MTK Budapest, FK Austria Vienna, Brooklyn Wanderers

Kalman Konrad was part of the dominant MTK Budapest side that ruled the Hungarian game from 1914 to 1925. By the mid 1920s after scoring 88 goals in 94 games for MTK, Konrad was lured to Vienna to play for FK Austria. In 1926 he travelled to the USA to join Brooklyn Wanderers for one successful season, before ending his career back with MTK in 1928 and becoming a respected coach. Konrad was an overtly skilful ball player, making him the grandfather of the 'Magical Magyars' – his abilities inspired a generation of Hungarian footballers, including Alfred Schaffer and Gyorgy Orth. These players in turn inspired the players that were to become legends in their own right in the 1950s.

RAYMOND KOPA

Country: France
Born: October 13, 1931
Position: Centre-forward
Clubs: Angers, Stade de Reims, Real Madrid, Stade de Reims

Raymond Kopa became France's first winner of the European Footballer Of The Year prize in 1958 and was his country's greatest player until Michel Platini came along. He made his name as a deep-lying centre-forward at Reims and helped the side reach the first European Cup final, where they lost to Real Madrid. The Spaniards snapped him up in 1956 and he played as a right-winger when Real Madrid won the European Cup in 1957, 1958 and 1959. He was outstanding at the World Cup in Sweden in 1958, helping France reach the semi-finals. In total he scored 18 goals in 45 international appearances.

HANS KRANKL

Country: Austria
Born: February 14, 1953
Position: Centre-forward
Clubs: Rapid Vienna, Vienna AC, Barcelona, First Vienna, Barcelona, Rapid Vienna, Wiener Sportclub

Hans Krankl was one of Austria's most successful footballers and a prolific goalscorer, racking up a staggering 320 goals in 427 Austrian league appearances, as well as 34 goals in a 69-game international career which ran from 1973 to 1985. Included in this total for the national side was a six-goal haul in April 1977 when Austria thrashed Malta 9-0. The following season Krankl was the winner of Europe's Golden Boot with 41 goals for Rapid Vienna. It was the second of four occasions when he was the Austrian league's top scorer, and in 1979 he became the Spanish league's top scorer while playing for Barcelona, with whom he won the European Cup Winners' Cup in 1979.

RUUD KROL

Country: Holland
Born: March 24, 1949
Position: Defender
Clubs: Ajax, Napoli, Cannes, Vancouver Whitecaps

Rudolf Josef Krol epitomised Holland's Total Football philosophy. Described as an all-round defender he could play at full-back on either flank or in the centre of defence. Indeed, he was one of the first attacking full-backs. He played 83 times for the Dutch, including successive appearances in the World Cup final in 1974 and 1978 – the second time as captain. Krol was also a European Cup and European Super Cup winner in 1972 and 1973 with the great Ajax side that featured Cruyff, Neeskens and Haan and formed the backbone of the Holland's national team.

LADISLAV KUBALA

Country: Czechoslovakia, Hungary, Spain
Born: June 10, 1927
Position: Forward
Clubs: Ferencváros, Bratislava, Vasas, Barcelona, Espanyol, FC Zurich, Toronto Falcons

Ladislav Kubala is revered at Barcelona and was voted the club's greatest player above Cruyff and Maradona in a poll carried out in the club's 1999 centenary year. Born to Slavic parents in Budapest in 1927, he began his career at Ferencváros and had just moved to Vasas when he defected in 1949, a decision that saw him banned from playing by FIFA.

A powerful, hard-running striker, good in the air and a lethal finisher, he was approached by Real Madrid in 1950 but snatched by Barcelona who made him their highest paid player. He went on to win four titles and five cups for them between 1950 and 1961, playing 329 times and scoring 256 goals. He also had the distinction of playing international football for three countries, Hungary, Czechoslovakia and Spain, with whom he won 19 caps, scoring 11 goals.

After stints with Espanyol and Toronto Falcons, he managed Malaga, then Barcelona, before coaching the Spanish national team for 68 games between 1969 and 1980, spending longer in the job than any other incumbent. There were further coaching stints with Barcelona, before he became president of the Barcelona Veterans Association in 1990. He died aged 74 on May 17, 2002 and was posthumously awarded FIFA's Order Of Merit.

ANGEL AMADEO LABRUNA

Country: Argentina
Born: September 26, 1918
Position: Inside-left
Clubs: River Plate, Platense, Green Cross, Rampla Juniors

At the age of 40, and nicknamed 'El Viejo' (the old one), Labruna represented Argentina at the 1958 World Cup finals. His two appearances in Sweden took his tally to 36 international appearances, in which he scored 17 goals and reaped two South American Championships in 1946 and 1955. Labruna also served River Plate like no other player, turning out for them in 1,150 games and scoring 457 goals over a 29-year period, finally retiring at the age of 41. He won the league championship nine times, earning a feared reputation as part of the club's famed 'Maquina' forward line.

GRZEGORZ LATO

Country: Poland
Born: April 8, 1950
Position: Winger
Clubs: Stal Mielec, KSC Lokeren, Atlanta de Mexico, Toronto

Grzegorz Lato is Poland's most capped player and also one of their leading goalscorers. His international career, spanning 13 years, saw him make 100 appearances for Poland, scoring 45 goals. He starred in three consecutive World Cups and was the tournament's top goalscorer in 1974, scoring seven of Poland's 14 goals in an attacking team that featured him alongside Gadocha, Deyna and Szarmach. In 1982 his international swansong brought him closest to success, Lato bowed out with a third place at the World Cup in Spain.

BRIAN LAUDRUP

Country: Denmark
Born: February 22, 1969
Position: Forward/Midfield
Clubs: Brondby, Bayer Uerdingen, Bayern Munich, Fiorentina, AC Milan, Rangers, Chelsea, FC Copenhagen, Ajax

A skilful dribbler and crowd entertainer, Brian Laudrup is the brother of Denmark's 1986 World Cup star Michael Laudrup. Starting his career at Brondby in 1986, the forward moved to Germany in 1989, first with Bayern Uerdingen and later Bayern Munich, before making the glamorous move to Italian side

Left: Ruud Krol of Holland in action against West Germany's Horst Hrubesch at the 1980 European Championship.

Fiorentina after winning the 1992 European Championship with Denmark. A brief stint at AC Milan followed a season later but Laudrup left after only nine games to become a crowd favourite at Glasgow Rangers in 1994.

After four seasons and 44 goals he left Scotland for Chelsea (on a free 'Bosman' deal), before controversially returning home to FC Copenhagen after a bout of homesickness. He retired in 2000 after a recurring Achilles heel problem hampered his performances.

MICHAEL LAUDRUP

Country: Denmark
Born: June 15, 1964
Position: Midfield/Forward
Clubs: Brondby, Lazio, Juventus, Barcelona, Real Madrid, Vissel Kobe, Ajax

Laudrup was the most elegant cog in the Danish side that electrified world football in the mid-1980s. Supremely gifted, Ajax wooed him at 13 and by the age of 18 he was scoring on his international debut. His list of super clubs is testament to a player of sublime skill. Laudrup won the European Cup while with Barcelona in 1992 and league titles in three countries. Highly technical and unselfish, he shone in both midfield and attack. Laudrup played in the 1986 and 1998 World Cup finals before retiring with 37 goals in 104 games. He missed Denmark's European Championship success in 1992 after falling out with the coach. In 2005 he coached Brondby to the league and cup double.

LUCIEN LAURENT

Country: France
Born: December 10, 1907
Position: Midfield/Left-wing
Clubs: Cercle Athletique de Paris, Sochaux, Rennes, RC Strasbourg

Lucien Laurent scored the first-ever World Cup goal with his 19th minute volley from a right-wing cross that put France ahead on their way to a 4-1 victory over Mexico. He was injured against Argentina in the next game and didn't appear in the World Cup again. The short but tenacious Laurent was only to play 10 times in all for France between 1930 and 1935 and cruelly injury ruled him out of the 1934 World Cup. He died at the age of 97 in April 2005.

DENIS LAW

Born: February 24, 1940
Country: Scotland
Position: Forward
Clubs: Huddersfield Town, Manchester City, Torino, Manchester United, Manchester City

Nicknamed 'The King' at Old Trafford, Denis Law was one of the most popular players to have worn a Manchester United shirt during his reign in the Sixties, with his trademark oversized shirt and his one-armed goal celebrations. Starting his career at Huddersfield Town, Law made his professional debut in 1956, aged 16. By 18 he was wearing the Scotland jersey and a move to Maine Road followed in 1960 at the age of 20. He later moved to Torino in Italy in 1961, where despite a car crash, he still scored a creditable ten goals in 27 games.

In August 1962, Manchester United paid a British record fee of £115,000 for his services and Law's impact on the club was immediate. He scored two goals on his debut, notching up a total of 160 goals during his 222 matches for the club, winning a European Player Of The Year award in 1964, as well as two league titles (1965 and 1967). He was ruled out of the club's 1968 European Cup triumph through injury.

He was later transferred to Manchester City in 1973, where he made headlines by famously back-heeling the goal at Old Trafford that helped to consign his former club to relegation in 1974. Distraught, he retired after the game.

TOMMY LAWTON

Country: England
Born: October 6, 1919
Position: Forward
Clubs: Burnley, Everton, Chelsea, Notts County, Brentford, Arsenal

A big, powerful, bustling centre-forward, recognisable as much by his centre parting as his physique, Lawton's best years were probably lost to the Second World War. Even so he can still claim an impressive record of 231 goals in 390 league games, and 22 goals in 23 internationals. For England his record was helped by the regular supply he received from the likes of Finney and Matthews.

Lawton famously scored on his league debut for Burnley aged just 16 before being picked up by Everton, keen to find a replacement for the great Dixie Dean. Lawton first donned an England shirt at just 19 and his career took him to numerous clubs.

LEÔNIDAS

Country: Brazil
Born: November 11, 1910
Position: Centre-forward
Clubs: Havanesa, Barroso, Sul Americano, Sirio Libanes, Bomsucesso, Nacional, Vasco da Gama, Botafogo, Flamengo, São Paulo

Leônidas da Silva, dubbed the 'Black Diamond', enjoyed his 90 minutes of fame at the 1938 World Cup finals when he starred in the game of the tournament, Brazil beating Poland 6-5 in the first round. Leônidas, renowned for his overhead kick, scored a hat-trick in the game, although many records incorrectly credit him with four goals in the game. He ended the World Cup as top scorer, but the competition ended in disappointment as he was rested for the semi-final against Italy and Brazil lost. After returning home, such was his fame that a chocolate bar and a brand of cigarettes were named after him: Diamante Negro.

NILS LIEDHOLM

Country: Sweden
Born: October 8, 1922
Position: Inside-forward/Wing-half/Sweeper
Clubs: Norrköping, AC Milan

Nils Liedholm was the longest serving member of the Milan's famed 'Grenoli' midfield trio. He played for the Italians in 367 league games, scoring 60 goals and helping them win the championship in 1951, 1955, 1957 and 1959. He also helped the club to their first European Cup final appearance in 1958, and followed it up by captaining Sweden to the World Cup final ten years after winning the Olympic Games title as an amateur. He won just 18 caps because of Sweden's reluctance to select professionals for the national team. In the latter part of his career Milan converted him into a formidable sweeper.

GARY LINEKER

Country: England
Born: November 30, 1960
Position: Forward
Clubs: Leicester City, Everton, Barcelona, Tottenham Hotspur, Nagoya Grampus Eight

Gary Lineker, the son of a market trader, enjoyed a glittering career as one of England's finest ever goalscorers. After seven seasons with his hometown club Leicester, Lineker became a target for England's bigger outfits and Everton clinched his prized signature in 1985 for £800,000. In his first and only season on Merseyside, Lineker's performances were phenomenal. He hit 30 league goals, but The Toffees finished runners-up in the league, beaten into second place by Liverpool. When the two teams clashed again in the 1986 FA Cup final Lineker scored early to put Everton ahead, only for The Reds to triumph 3-1.

The striker didn't have long to mope about the defeat, as in the summer he headed off to the World Cup finals in Mexico as England's number one goalscorer. It was a tournament which was to change the direction of his career. With Bobby Robson's team lurching towards a disastrous first round exit, Lineker hit a first-half hat-trick in the must-win game against Poland and his name made international headlines. Two further goals against Paraguay, then one in the quarter-final defeat against Argentina, put the England man on six goals – enough to win the Golden Boot and earn the

Above: Bayern Munich's Sepp Maier celebates after winning the 1975 European Cup final.

attentions of Spanish giants Barcelona. Lineker swapped Goodison Park for the Nou Camp.

He spent three seasons with Barça, initially under English coach Terry Venables and then the Dutchman Johan Cruyff. In Spain, Lineker was an immediate success, far more so than Mark Hughes, another Venables recruit, as he scored goals freely and pleased the critical Nou Camp faithful with his pace and sharp finishing. A hat-trick against Barça's bitter rivals Real Madrid in 1987 cemented his popularity, but when Venables was replaced by Cruyff, Lineker found his status marginalised as the new coach inexplicably deployed him as a right-winger. Despite winning the European Cup Winners' Cup in 1989, a parting of the ways was inevitable. Lineker returned to English football, teaming up with Venables again at Tottenham.

He quickly showed that he had lost none of his ability. At international level he remained a permanent threat, claiming four goals in the 1990 World Cup as England reached the semi-finals, including the equaliser in the epic encounter with West Germany. For Spurs, Lineker developed a fine understanding with Paul Gascoigne and in 1991 he won his only English domestic trophy when Tottenham toppled Nottingham Forest 2-1 to win the FA Cup. Lineker actually missed a penalty during the game, yet still ended up a winner.

The following year he accepted a lucrative offer to play for Grampus Eight in Japan, and although a toe injury limited his appearances, he proved a wonderful ambassador for a developing league until his retirement two years later opened up a second successful profession as a presenter on British television. Alongside all the goalscoring acclaim, one other major statistic stands out; throughout his career, Lineker's disciplinary record was exemplary – he wasn't booked once.

DANNY McGRAIN

Country: Scotland
Born: May 1, 1950
Position: Right-back
Club: Celtic

Despite the fact his father is said to have been a lifelong Rangers fan, Danny McGrain was an attacking full-back who spent a long and distinguished career at Celtic, for whom he made his debut in 1970. McGrain was a member of Celtic's famous 'Quality Street Gang' which included the likes of David Hay, Lou Macari and Kenny Dalglish, and he made over 600 appearances for The Bhoys, clinching a total of seven league titles during a 20-year spell with the club.

McGrain gained 62 caps in a distinguished career, but his period at the club could have been even more impressive if he hadn't been afflicted by a string of injuries and illnesses which began in 1972 with a fractured skull. He also suffered a broken ankle and was afflicted with arthritis and diabetes.

RABAH MADJER

Country: Algeria
Born: February 15, 1958
Position: Midfield/Forward
Clubs: Sempac, MA Hussein Dey, Racing Paris, Porto, Qatar

No-one will ever forget Rabah Madjer's outrageous back-heeled goal in the 1987 European Cup final. He later set-up the winner as Porto beat Bayern Munich. Later in the year he scored the winner in the World Club Cup and was a deserving winner of the 1987 African Player Of The Year Award. Not that he was an unknown, as five years earlier he had been part of Algeria's 1982 World Cup victory over West Germany, scoring the first goal in a 2-1 win. He also appeared in the 1986 finals and helped Algeria to the quarter-finals of the 1980 Olympics.

SEPP MAIER

Country: West Germany
Born: February 28, 1944
Position: Goalkeeper
Clubs: TSV Haar, Bayern Munich

Josef-Dieter 'Sepp' Maier spent 19 seasons at Bayern Munich, including a run of 422 consecutive games in goal (of a total of 473 appearances in all) for the German giants.

Maier played in each of Bayern's three consecutive European Cup successes between 1974 and 1976, keeping clean sheets in three of the four games involved. 'Die Katze' (the Cat), as he was nicknamed, had established himself as his country's first choice goalkeeper in time for the 1970 World Cup, and although West Germany only reached the semi-finals, success was just around the corner for both Maier and West Germany.

Under coach Helmut Schön and captained by Franz Beckenbauer, the West Germans were crowned champions of Europe in 1972 and world champions two years later, Maier memorably stopping a formidable Neeskens volley as his side beat Holland 2-1 in the final. The Germans had gone 1-0 behind to a first minute penalty in the 1974 game; when Maier picked the ball out of the net, he was the first German to have touched it up until that point.

Named German Player Of The Year three times in the 1970s, a car accident in 1979 ended Maier's career at the age of just 35 (still relatively young for a goalkeeper). Following his retirement, Maier returned to his first sporting love, setting up a tennis school.

JOSEF MASOPUST

Country: Czechoslovakia
Born: February 9, 1931
Position: Midfield
Clubs: SK Most, Teplice, Dukla Prague, Molenbeek

Known as the 'Czech Cavalier', Josef Masopust was named Czechoslovakian Player Of The Century. Born in Most, he began his career in 1950 playing up front but was switched to midfield where his stamina and vision covered his lack of speed. He joined Dukla Prague in 1952 and went on to win eight championships and three cups with them, making 386 appearances, including the 1967 European Cup semi-final against Celtic.

At international level Masopust won 63 caps, scoring ten goals, and he was part of the 1958 World Cup squad before reaching the semi-final of the 1960 European Championship. The high point of his career was leading his country to the runners-up spot in the 1962 World Cup, scoring the 15th minute goal that gave them the lead in the final over Brazil. His performance and his legendary sportsmanship saw him named 1962 European Footballer Of The Year. He remained the only Czech player to win the coveted award until Pavel Nedved in 2003.

Offers flooded in from Italy and West Germany, but the communist regime did not allow him to leave until 1969 when, aged 38, he moved to Molenbeek in the Belgian second division, taking them up into the top flight. He later returned to coach them, then Dukla, and became assistant manager of the national side in 1984.

DIEGO MARADONA

Country: Argentina

Born: October 30, 1960

Position: Centre-forward

Clubs: Argentinos Juniors, Boca Juniors, Barcelona, Napoli, Seville, Newell's Old Boys, Boca Juniors

As well as being one of the greatest players to ever grace the world game, Maradona is also one of the most controversial. Indeed, there are times when the Argentine's career history reads more like a rap sheet than the biography of the world's greatest sportsmen. But his various bans, drug problems and occasionally perverse behaviour (he once shot at journalists with an air rifle) shouldn't detract from Diego Maradona's formidable achievements in a game he bestrode like a colossus throughout the 1980s.

Born to working class parents in a Buenos Aires suburb, Maradona and football were inseparable from an early age. After playing for a couple of local boys clubs (one of whom he inspired to go 136 matches unbeaten), he joined first division Argentinos Juniors, making his debut as a raw but undoubtedly talented 15-year-old on October 20, 1976. Barely four months later Maradona was making another debut, this time as a fully-fledged Argentine international, coming on as a substitute in a friendly against Hungary. Although he was angry at missing out on a place in the squad for the 1978 World Cup finals, Maradona was a vital part of the Argentine side that won the World Youth Championship in 1979 in Japan.

After scoring 116 goals in 166 appearances for Argentinos Juniors, Maradona was transferred to Boca Juniors (35 goals in 71 appearances) for £1 million in 1981. He stayed only one season, before Barcelona snapped him up for £3 million. Although again prodigious in front of goal, netting 38 times in 58 appearances, his two-year stay in Spain was undermined by injury. Far more successful was his transfer to Napoli for £5 million in 1984. He led Napoli to their first league title in 1987 and again in 1990, and helped the team to a UEFA Cup win in 1989.

Maradona's first World Cup finals in 1982 ended badly for the Argentines as they failed to make it beyond the second round, while Maradona himself was sent-off against Brazil. It was a very different story in Mexico at the 1986 tournament, as Argentina became world champions for the second time and Maradona lived up to his reputation as the world's best but most controversial player. The Argentine's schizophrenic nature was perfectly illustrated by his performance in the quarter-final against England, where he scored both goals in a 2-1 win. The first he pushed past goalkeeper Shilton with his hand ('a little of the hand of God, a little of the head of Maradona' is how he impishly described it at the time) but the second saw Maradona weave the ball around an army of defenders from the halfway line before stroking it into the net.

The 1986 finals proved to be the high point of Maradona's career, although he inspired a below par Argentina to another World Cup final in 1990. The following year he was banned from the game for 15 months after testing positive for cocaine and then arrested in Argentina for possession of the drug. His World Cup swansong came in 1994 and ended in ignominy when he was sent home for failing a dope test. Short spells as a coach back home with Argentine club sides came to nothing and he soon returned as a player with Newell's Old Boys. The curtain finally fell on Maradona's incredible playing career on October 29, 1997, when he turned out for Boca Juniors against rivals River Plate.

Top: The young Diego Maradona of Boca Juniors in 1981. Above left: Argentina's captain with the World Cup in 1986. Above right: In action for Napoli against AC Milan's Franco Baresi in 1991.

1976: Makes his debut for Argentinos Juniors as a 15-year-old and a week later plays his first full match against Newell's Old Boys.

1977: Makes his debut for Argentina as a sub in a 5-1 friendly victory against Hungary.

1978: Makes the squad of 25 players for World Cup, but César Menotti elects not to take him.

1979: Member of Argentina's World Youth Cup winning side in Japan.

1982: Sent-off in World Cup against Brazil. Bought by Barcelona for £3 million, a new record transfer fee.

1983: Suffers the worst injury of his career after a tackle by Goicoechea, the 'Butcher of Bilbao'.

1984: Joins Serie A's Napoli for £5 million, another record transfer fee.

1986: Captains Argentina to World Cup win, and is the star of the show. Remembered for his two goals against England.

1987: Leads Napoli to their first ever Scudetto title.

1990: Cannot prevent Argentina from losing in the World Cup final against West Germany.

1991: Fails a drugs test and is banned for 15 months.

1992: After completion of the ban he refuses to rejoin Napoli, and makes a disappointing comeback for Seville.

1994: Fails another drugs test at the World Cup finals in the USA.

1997: Plays his last match for Boca Juniors, retires from football on his 37th birthday.

2000: He is named as FIFA's internet Player Of The Century following an online poll.

SILVIO MARZOLINI

Country: Argentina
Born: October 4, 1940
Position: Left-back
Clubs: Ferro Carril Oeste, Boca Juniors

Silvio Marzolini is a Boca Juniors legend and was part of the team that dominated the Argentine league in the mid-Sixties, winning three championships. One of the first of a new breed of full-backs to make a mark in the modern game, his dynamic, all-round style of play still gets him selected in many people's all-time XIs. He appeared in two World Cups for his country, in 1962 and 1966, and played in the infamous quarter-final against England at Wembley. After retirement he went on to manage Boca Juniors, and even took them to a league title in 1981.

LOTHAR MATTHÄUS

Country: West Germany, Germany
Born: March 21, 1961
Position: Midfielder
Clubs: Borussia Mönchengladbach, Bayern Munich, Inter Milan, Bayern Munich, New York Metro Stars

For a man who is Germany's most capped star, Lothar Matthäus's popularity appears to be inversely low. A powerful but arrogant and often outspoken midfielder, Matthäus made his debut for Mönchengladbach in 1979, before moving to Bayern Munich in 1984. He won seven championships in two spells there, broken by a move to Inter Milan in 1988 where he won the Scudetto as captain in 1989 and a UEFA Cup, scoring the first goal at the San Siro in the home leg of the 2-1 aggregate win over Roma in 1991.

Matthäus made his international debut at 19 in a 3-2 European Championship win over Holland on June 14, 1980, picking up a winners' medal in the final against Belgium, and he became a fixture in the side for 20 years, winning an incredible 150 caps. He made his first World Cup appearance in 1982, but his two games as a substitute didn't include the final, which Germany lost to Italy. He went on to play in no less than five World Cups and he holds the record for the most appearances in the tournament with 25 games.

After finishing a World Cup runner-up in 1986, Matthäus lifted the trophy as captain four years later in Italy, and he was named European Footballer Of The Year. He extended his playing career to 39 years of age by moving to sweeper and finishing with New York Metro Stars, before taking over as coach of Rapid Vienna, Partizan Belgrade and Hungary. He caused a scandal by resigning his life membership of Bayern Munich and threatening to sue the club over the gate money from his testimonial game.

STANLEY MATTHEWS

Country: England
Born: February 1, 1915
Position: Winger
Clubs: Stoke City, Blackpool, Stoke City

Regarded as 'The Wizard Of The Dribble', Stanley Matthews made his league debut for hometown club Stoke City just six weeks after his 17th birthday. The son of a featherweight boxer, his appearance was slight against his more burly opponents, but it was his lightning burst of pace, balance and timing that few defenders could live with. Within two seasons Matthews had already made his England debut and, as the most exciting young player to emerge in the First Division at the time, it was reported that his presence regularly put 10,000 extra fans on the gate wherever Stoke played.

In 1938, Matthews fell out with manager Bob McGrory and asked to be put on the transfer list, but such was the furore in the local area that business managers claimed that production was being affected by the ongoing saga. Following a massive protest meeting, Stan decided to stay. But following the war, hostilities resumed with McGrory and in 1947 he was sold to Blackpool for £11,500, aged 32.

Despite his veteran status, Matthews reached new heights as he led his club to three FA Cup finals in six years. Defeats against Manchester United and Newcastle led many to believe that a Cup hoodoo had a hold and with 20 minutes to go of the 1953 final against Bolton, that appeared to ring true for the 38-year-old. With Blackpool having fallen 3-1 behind, Matthews suddenly sprang into action and, having set up Stan Mortensen for his second goal of the game, he took a hold of the match and ran his opposing number, Ralph Banks, ragged. Then with just three minutes remaining, he skipped past his marker yet again to give Mortensen his hat-trick, and deep into stoppage time he reached the by-line one last time to set up South African winger Bill Perry to snatch a dramatic winner. Despite Mortensen's heroics and Perry's goal, the game became known as 'The Matthews Final'.

In 1961, Matthews decided to end his career back at Stoke and, having paid £3,500 for his services, the club recouped their money by regularly putting an extra 26,000 on their gate at the Victoria Ground. Matthews acted as a catalyst as The Potters marched to the 1962-3 Second Division championship and incredibly, at the age of 48, he played 35 of the club's 42 league games. Two years later, he finally bowed out of top-flight football, aged 50 years and five days.

Although he won few honours in his career, Matthews was a truly unique phenomenon, and as a result of his exemplary disciplinary record on the pitch, he was also regarded as a true gentleman. He received the Footballer

Of The Year trophy twice, in 1948 and 1963, and was knighted in the 1965 New Year's Honours list.

He played for England between 1934 and 1957 and, although scoring on his first outing for his country, he found himself in and out of the team. In all, he played only 54 of 119 full internationals during that period, a statistic that consistently outraged fans.

SANDRO MAZZOLA

Country: Italy
Born: November 8, 1942
Position: Forward
Club: Inter Milan

Sandro followed in the footsteps of his father Valentino to become an Italian football legend. Though Torino star Valentino died in the Superga plane crash when Sandro was just seven, his passion for the game had already been instilled in Mazzola junior. Inter Milan was to be his sole club, and he made more than 400 top flight appearances for the Nerazzurri, winning consecutive European and World Club Cups with them.

Although not as effective at international level, he did still make 70 appearances for his country and was in the Italian side that won the 1968 European Championship.

Above: Lothar Matthäus in action for Germany.

Opposite: The Wizard of Dribble, Stanley Matthews on the ball in the 1953 FA Cup final. The match became known as 'The Matthews Final'.

Above: Roger Milla trips past England's Paul Gascoinge in the 1990 World Cup quarter-final.

VALENTINO MAZZOLA

Country: Italy
Born: January 26, 1919
Position: Inside-left
Clubs: Venezia, Torino

Mazzola formed one half of a formidable strike partnership with Ezio Loik, with whom he combined superbly, initially at Venezia and then, from 1942 onwards, with Torino who bought both men as a pair. The move was a shrewd one because Mazzola went on to lead the dominant Torino side to five league titles between 1943 and 1949. Tragically killed in his prime in 1949 in the Superga aircrash alongside 17 of his team mates, with only 12 caps to his name, Mazzola would surely have gone on to achieve greater international recognition in the following year's World Cup finals.

PATRICK MBOMA

Country: Cameroon
Born: November 15, 1970
Position: Forward
Clubs: Stade de L'Est, Chateauroux, Paris Saint-Germain, Metz, Gamba Osaka, Cagliari, Parma, Sunderland, Al-Ittihad, Tokyo Verdy, Vissel Kobe

Patrick Mboma turned down the chance to play for Cameroon at the 1994 World Cup because, although born in Douala, he had been raised in France. Two years later he succumbed to Cameroon's call and went on to win the African Nations Cup in 2000 and 2002, the Olympic Games in 2000, and play in two World Cups. He was also voted African Player Of The Year for 2000. He was initially overlooked for France 98 but was drafted into the squad as a replacement for the injured Marc-Vivien Foe. He has graced the French League, Italy's Serie A and England's Premier League, while in Japan's J.League he became known as the 'black panther of Osaka', becoming the league's top

Right: The Welsh Wizard Billy Meredith, a legend from the early days of football.

scorer in 1997. He made three appearances at the World Cup in 2002 and retired from international football in 2004 after Cameroon's exit from the African Nations Cup. After quitting Tokyo Verdy because of differences with coach Ossie Ardíles, he ended his club career in May 2005 with J.League side Vissel Kobe.

GIUSEPPE MEAZZA

Country: Italy
Born: August 23, 1910
Position: Inside-forward
Clubs: Inter Milan, AC Milan, Juventus, Varese, Atalanta, Inter Milan

The man after whom the San Siro stadium in Milan is now formally named was considered the complete forward player; a perfect predator in front of goal, but skilled enough to create chances for others as well as himself. He made his debut for Inter in 1927 at the age of 17 and remained with the club for the next 12 seasons. In that time he was Serie A's top scorer on three occasions, hitting 33 goals in the 1929-30 season, including six in a 10-2 win against Venezia.

Having hit 241 goals for Inter in 344 games, Meazza succumbed to a leg injury and missed the whole of the 1939-40 season, before joining Inter Milan's arch-rivals AC Milan the following year. Further moves to Juventus and Atalanta followed, but Meazza returned to Inter for the 1946-7 season as player-coach to help them battle against relegation.

Meazza's time on the international stage proved to be equally impressive, scoring twice on his debut for Italy as a 19-year-old against Switzerland in 1930, and hitting a hat-trick against Hungary later that year, in a 5-0 win. Meazza was one of only two players to have played in both Italian World Cup wins in 1934 and 1938. He died in 1979 aged 68.

BILLY MEREDITH

Country: Wales
Born: July 24, 1874
Position: Outside-right/Winger
Clubs: Chirk, Wrexham, Northwich Victoria, Manchester City, Manchester United, Manchester City

Billy Meredith was the 'Welsh Wizard', a goalscoring winger who played for both Manchester United and Manchester City in his career, making his debut for the latter in 1894. He played until he was 50 for club and country and in such a long career he won both major honours in England, as well as the Welsh Cup. He also helped Wales to their first Home International Championship. A driving force behind the Players' Union, he also suffered the ignominy of suspension following a match-fixing scandal. But he returned as a match-winner and artist, whether it was beating players

on his way to the byline to deliver the perfect cross, or finding the net himself. He died in 1958 and after years lying in an unmarked grave, the PFA, the Welsh FA and both Manchester clubs agreed to pay for a new headstone and held a service to mark the new gravestone.

ROGER MILLA

Country: Cameroon
Born: May 20, 1952
Position: Forward
Clubs: Eclair de Douala, Léopard de Douala, Valenciennes, Monaco, Bastia, Saint-Etienne, Montpellier, JS Saint-Pierroise

Dancing the Makossa around a corner flag, Albert Roger Milla gave the World Cup one of its most memorable goal celebrations in 1990. A natural goalscorer, he won the African Golden Ball and played in France for 12 years. He scored on his international debut in 1978 and was part of the squad that returned unbeaten from the 1982 World Cup. At 38 he was playing on Reunion Island when the Cameroon president begged him to come back for Italia 90. Milla became a talisman with four goals from the bench as his team reached the quarter-finals. At 42 he was back at USA '94, with a goal against Russia making him the oldest World Cup goalscorer ever.

LUÍS MONTI

Country: Argentina, Italy
Born: May 15, 1901
Position: Central defender
Clubs: Huracán, Boca Juniors, San Lorenzo, Juventus

Luís Monti tasted both victory and defeat in World Cup finals, but for different nations. He was on the losing side with Argentina in 1930, going down to hosts Uruguay, but four years later he helped Italy beat Czechoslovakia. His eligibility to play for Italy came after he moved to Juventus. A tough, uncompromising and sometimes ruthless defender, at club level Monti won league titles with both Huracán and San Lorenzo in Argentina, and four consecutive Serie A titles in Turin.

BOBBY MOORE

Country: England
Born: April 12, 1941
Position: Central defender
Clubs: West Ham United, Fulham, San Antonio Thunder, Herning FC, Seattle Sounders

In the pantheon of English sporting heroes no footballer ranks above Bobby Moore, the only England captain ever to lift the World Cup. His name remains synonymous with honour, dignity and sportsmanship.

Bobby Moore was born in Barking, East London, and joined West Ham as a schoolboy, turning professional at 17. He rose rapidly to the first team, playing flawlessly in a 3-2 win over Manchester United on his debut on September 8, 1958. He did not establish himself fully until 1960, but thereafter became a fixture in the side. In 1964 he led the team to an FA Cup final win over Preston and he was voted Footballer Of The Year. The following season he was back at Wembley to guide West Ham to victory over TSV 1860 Munich in the European Cup Winners' Cup.

Bobby Moore won his first England cap against Peru en route to the 1962 World Cup finals in Chile, when deputising for the injured Bobby Robson, and he played in all four of England's games at the tournament. At 22 he became the country's youngest ever captain when he led the team against Czechoslovakia on May 20, 1963.

Just three years later his crowning moment arrived when he lifted the World Cup at Wembley following the historic 4-2 win over West Germany in the final. The famous fourth goal was the result of Moore measuring a long pass to striker Geoff Hurst rather than listening to the entreaties of his partner Jack Charlton to put the ball over the stand.

Yet Moore's finest performance was not

Wembley 66, but Mexico 70. Before that summer's World Cup tournament had even kicked-off he was falsely accused of the theft of a bracelet from a jeweller in Bogota, Columbia. Moore, held under house arrest, remained calm, destroyed the false testimony of the main witness and rejoined the squad.

Three weeks later he played the best game of his life against Brazil in the heat of Guadalajara, thwarting the tide of yellow shirts that flooded towards him. When the final whistle blew, signifying a narrow 1-0 defeat, Pelé stepped past everyone, including

Alan Mullery who had marked him through the game, to swap shirts with Moore. The moment became an iconic football image.

Moore would win 108 caps for England, 90 of them as captain, but his international career was virtually ended by England's failure to qualify for the 1974 World Cup finals. The following month, in November 1973, he made his last England appearance against Italy.

After 544 league games for West Ham he moved across London to Fulham in March 1974 and enjoyed one more Wembley appearance in the FA Cup final, ironically against his old club, but this time he collected a loser's medal. Thereafter, his career tailed off as he joined Seattle Sounders, Herning FC in Denmark, then San Antonio Thunder in Texas.

Bizarrely he won three caps for Team America, playing alongside his old adversary Pelé and finishing his international career playing against England.

Back home Moore struggled to make a mark in management. He began at non-league Oxford City in 1979, coached in Hong Kong and took over for an unsuccessful stint at Southend. By the late Eighties he had fallen out of the game and was working as a radio summariser. He was diagnosed with bowel cancer and died on February 24, 1993.

In June 2000, West Ham United purchased Bobby Moore's World Cup memorabilia for their museum, having named a stand at the Boleyn Ground after him six years earlier.

Top: England's greatest ever football hero, Bobby Moore kisses the World Cup in 1966. Left: The rising West Ham star in 1958. Above: Hurst is held aloft by his West Ham team-mates after winning the Cup Winners' Cup in 1965.

1958 Turned professional for West Ham aged 17.

1962 Won first England cap in World Cup warm-up match against Peru in Lima.

1963 Played for England against Rest Of The World team at Wembley.

1964 Captained West Ham to FA Cup final victory against Preston.

1964 Voted England's Footballer Of The Year.

1965 Wins European Cup Winners' Cup at Wembley.

1966 Lifts World Cup trophy as England captain after final victory over West Germany.

1967 Awarded OBE for services to football.

1970 Falsely accused of stealing bracelet in Bogota in run up to World Cup finals. Arrested and arrives in Mexico late.

1973 Plays 108th and final game for England in friendly against Italy at Wembley.

1974 Leaves West Ham after 16 years and 642 games. Signs for Fulham.

1975 Takes Fulham to FA Cup final but loses 2-0 to West Ham.

1976 Plays summer football with San Antonio Thunder and turns out alongside Pelé in a Team America XI against England.

1977 His final match for Fulham is the 1000th of his career.

1979 Takes over as manager of non league Oxford City.

1984 Becomes manager of Southend.

1993 Died February 24, seven days after attending his final England game, against San Marino.

JUAN MORENO

Country: Argentina
Born: August 3, 1916
Position: Inside-forward
Clubs: River Plate, Espana, Universidad Catolica, Boca Juniors, Defensor, Ferrocarril Oeste, Independiente Medellin

Juan Moreno is one of the greatest Argentine players of all time and a winner of five league titles with River Plate, where he spent most of his playing career. The first of Moreno's league winners' medals came in 1936 when he broke into the side from the youth team as a raw but talented 20-year-old. He was part of the legendary River Plate 'Máquina' attack in the 1940s which included the likes of Munoz, Pedernera, Labruna and Loustau. Morena played for two years with the Mexican club Espana before returning to River Plate for a second spell and then spending the later years of his career representing different clubs in Chile, Uruguay and Columbia. He scored 20 goals in 33 games for his country.

GERD MÜLLER

Country: West Germany
Born: November 3, 1945
Position: Forward
Clubs: TSV Nordingen, Bayern Munich, Fort Lauderdale Strikers

Gerd Müller held a special place in World Cup history. Until his record was broken by Ronaldo in 2006, he was the the all-time highest scorer in the finals. Müller's 14 goals in two World Cups were the high points of an astonishing international career which saw him average more than a goal a game. He remains his country's highest goalscorer, and he also struck the winning goal in the 1974 World Cup final.

The early 1970s were a golden period for West German football, forged on the athleticism and unquenchable spirit that Müller typified. Besides reaching the World Cup semi-final of 1970 and winning in 1974, the West Germans also won the European Championship in 1972. Müller, inevitably, scored twice in the final.

Gerd Müller's international success was repeated at club level with the Bayern Munich side that dominated European football in the mid Seventies. With them he won the European Cup in 1974, 1975 and 1976. That he enjoyed such a glittering career is even more remarkable given his background. Short and stocky, he grew up in a small village with no football ground, but he trained hard to make the most of his ability. Never giving less than 100 per cent in a game, he acquired a fearsome reputation as the ultimate predator in the penalty area, earning the nickname 'Der Bomber'.

Müller had made his international debut in 1966, shortly after West Germany had lost the World Cup final to England. When the 1970 tournament arrived he was already known as one of the great strikers in world football. But despite the pressure, Müller delivered in spectacular style, hitting ten goals in six games. He recorded hat-tricks against Bulgaria and Peru and the winner against Morocco. He also got the deciding goal in a quarter-final which saw West Germany come from 2-0 down to beat defending champions England. In the semi-final Müller scored twice more but West Germany bowed out of the competition 4-3 against Italy. He was, however, the top scorer at the tournament.

Four years later Müller was less prolific, but was to prove equally lethal when it mattered most. Determined to make amends for their recent near misses, West Germany ground their way to a final on home soil against the more fluent and outrageously talented team from Holland. Despite going a goal down, the hosts weren't going to slip up this time and after equalising it was Müller who scored the winning goal just before half-time. The moment couldn't have been sweeter: not only had he achieved the greatest dream in football but he had done so in the Olympic Stadium, where he had scored so many of his 365 goals in 427 games for Bayern.

Müller retired from the international game after the 1974 final and considered quitting altogether, but instead he decided to continue playing club football with Bayern, with whom he had won his first European honour – the European Cup Winners' Cup – in 1967. It was an inspired decision. In a fruitful autumn to his career, he achieved his three European Cup triumphs before leaving Bayern in 1979 to wind down his career in the United States with Fort Lauderdale.

Named European Footballer Of The Year in 1970, Müller was a two-time winner of the European Golden Boot, and scored a total of 628 first class goals.

MIGUEL MUNOZ

Country: Spain
Born: January 19, 1922
Position: Inside-right/Centre-half/Right-half
Clubs: Imperio, Girod, Imperio, Logrones, Santander, Celta Vigo, Real Madrid

Miguel Munoz was the scorer of Real Madrid's first goal in Europe back in 1955 against Servette. He was also the first captain to lift the coveted European Cup with Real's triumph in the inaugural competition in 1956. Madrid-born Munoz was to lead Real to a successful defence in the Bernabéu a year later. He retired as a player in 1958 and just two years later he became the first man to win the trophy as both a player and a coach, after Real's mesmerising 7-3 win over Eintracht Frankfurt.

HONG MYUNG-BO

Country: South Korea
Born: February 12, 1969
Position: Sweeper
Clubs: Posco Atoms, Pohang Steelers, Bellmare Hiratsuka, Kashiwa Reysol, Pohang Steelers, Los Angeles Galaxy

Hong Myung-bo was regarded as Asia's best sweeper. His experience and leadership was gained through playing in four successive World Cups with South Korea. His influence was apparent in South Korea's run to the semi-finals in 2002. It was Hong, the captain, who converted the decisive penalty that knocked out Spain and inspired the win over Italy. He has been equally successful in club football, being voted Most Valuable Player in the Korean League in 1992 and the Japanese League in 1999. In 2000 he became the first Korean to captain a Japanese club, Kashiwa Reysol, and in 2002 he signed for Los Angeles Galaxy. He retired in July 2004. Just before his retirement he was included by Pelé and FIFA in their list of the 125 greatest living footballers. In September 2005 he became Assistant Coach of the South Korean national team.

HIDETOSHI NAKATA

Country: Japan
Born: January 22, 1977
Position: Midfield
Clubs: Bellmare Hiratsuka, Perugia, Roma, Parma, Bologna, Fiorentina, Bolton Wanderers

Quite simply the greatest player Japan has ever produced, he was voted Asia's Player Of The Year in 1997 and 1998. Individualistic, skilful and with an iron will, through his career playmaker Nakata managed to show that players from the fledgling J.League could hold their own in Europe. Nakata carried the weight of his country on his shoulders, with massive media and public

Below: A familiar sight for West Germany and Bayern fans alike, Gerd Müller finding the back of the net. This one for Bayern, against St Etienne, was disallowed.

interest in his every move. He impressed at the 2002 World Cup, where Japan proved a surprise package, but despite helping Roma to their first league title in 18 years, his career at club level was always frustrated. An £18 million move to Parma saw Nakata win the Italian Cup in 2002 but he was loaned to Bologna and finally sold to Fiorentina in July 2004. After just one season he was loaned to English Premiership side Bolton Wanderers. He played in his third World Cup at Germany 2006 and announced his retirement from the game shortly afterwards, aged just 29.

JOSE NASAZZI

Country: Uruguay
Born: May 24, 1901
Position: Right-back
Clubs: Lito, Roland Moor, Nacional, Bella Vista

Right-back Jose Nasazzi is not only one of Uruguay's most famous players, but one of the great captains in the history of the game. His leadership qualities and organisational skills earned him the nickname 'The Marshall'. As Uruguay captain Nasazzi won Olympic gold in 1924 and 1928, as well as the Copa América in 1923, 1924 and 1926. But the best was yet to come, and Nasazzi etched himself into football history when he became the first man to lift the Jules Rimet cup after his country's 4-2 triumph over Argentina in the inaugural 1930 World Cup final. This was no mean feat, as Nasazzi was captaining a side who competed without a team manager and whose players made all the tactical decisions. When asked to coach the national team in 1945, he did so for just one South American Championship. He didn't believe in coaches.

JOHAN NEESKENS

Country: Holland
Born: September 15, 1951
Position: Midfield
Clubs: Ajax, Barcelona, New York Cosmos, Fort Lauderdale Strikers, FC Groningen, FC Baar

Although he often lived in the shadows of Johan Cruyff, Neeskens was regarded as one of the greatest midfielders of the 1970s and was an integral part of the talented Dutch side that reached the final at both the 1974 and 1978 World Cups. In the 1974 match against West Germany he scored the fastest goal in a World Cup final – converting the first ever World Cup final penalty kick in the second minute of the match – and his terrific pace, skill and control was also a key feature of the Ajax side that swept all before them, both domestically and in the European Cup.

He followed his Ajax team-mate Johan Cruyff to Barcelona after the 1974 final before moving to play in the NASL in America five years later. Having returned home to Groningen, he saw out his career as a player-coach in Switzerland.

IGOR NETTO

Country: Soviet Union
Born: January 9, 1930
Position: Left-half
Club: Spartak Moscow

Netto will be remembered by his countrymen as the man who led the Soviet Union to success at the Olympic Games in 1956 in Australia, and then four years later, to glory at the European Championship in France. All this during an international career that saw him gain 57 caps and score four goals. Sadly for Netto, injury kept him out of all but one game of the 1958 World Cup but he was an ever present member of the team in 1962, when the Soviets got as far as the quarter-finals before losing to Chile. A strong tackler, Netto moved into central defence when he had lost a little of his pace later in his career. A one-club man, he made more than 350 appearances for Spartak Moscow in his career, winning five league titles in that time.

GUNTER NETZER

Country: West Germany
Born: September 14, 1944
Position: Midfield
Clubs: Borussia Mönchengladbach, Real Madrid, Grasshoppers

A flamboyant, long-haired playmaker who was the star of West Germany's European Championship winning side of 1972. Netzer played a crucial hand in his country's advance to the final with a match-winning performance against England in the quarter-finals at Wembley, and he was equally inspirational in the 3-0 defeat of the Soviet Union in the final. Known for his long, accurate passing and ability to inspire others, Netzer usually operated just behind the strikers. He made 38 international appearances before losing his place in the national team in 1974. After hanging up his boots, he went on to become a leading commentator and businessman.

THOMAS NKONO

Country: Cameroon
Born: July 19, 1955
Position: Goalkeeper
Clubs: Douala, Canon Yaoundé, Espanyol

Thomas Nkono was twice voted African Footballer Of The Year, in 1979 and 1982. On the second occasion it was for his magnificent performance at the 1982 World Cup. Dubbed the 'Black Spider' he conceded just one goal in three unbeaten games. He had become a goalkeeper by accident. Initially a winger with Douala he went between the posts when the regular goalkeeper failed to turn up. His performances at the 1982 World Cup led to a move to Europe with, most notably, Espanyol, with whom he reached the 1988 UEFA

Above: One of the greatest midfielders of the 1970s, Johan Neeskens gets stuck in to some Total Football.

Cup final. During 2002's African Championship in Mali, while working as goalkeeping coach to Cameroon, he was arrested for witchcraft!

GUNNAR NORDAHL

Country: Sweden
Born: October 19, 1921
Position: Forward
Clubs: Degerfors, Norrköpping, AC Milan, Roma, Karlstad

Former fireman Gunnar Nordahl set a blazing goal trail wherever he went. In Sweden, he scored 77 goals in 58 games for Degerfors, followed up with a sensational 93 goals in 92 appearances for Norrköpping, before leading the charge for Sweden's gold medal success at the 1948 London Olympics. A chance to turn professional with AC Milan saw no change in his abilities as a goalscorer, netting 225 goals in 257 Serie A matches, playing alongside fellow Swedes Gren and Liedholm. For Sweden he racked up some 44 goals in 33 internationals, including the 1958 World Cup where Sweden finished as runners-up.

ERNST OCWIRK

Country: Austria
Born: March 10, 1926
Position: Centre-half/Midfield
Clubs: Floridsdorfer, FK Austria, Sampdoria

Ernst Ocwirk was the last of a dying breed of attacking centre-halves – and he was excellent at the role. While the rest of Europe went for a stopper, FK Austria Vienna and the Austrian national side exploited Ocwirk's skill and intuition. FK won the Austrian championship three times, in 1949, 1950 and 1953.

Ocwirk, nicknamed 'Clockwork' by the English for his ability to create and dictate matches, helped make Austria one of the strongest teams in Europe, playing 62 times for his country. Later in his career he had a five-year spell with Italian club Sampdoria where he was re-modelled as a midfielder.

MORTEN OLSEN

Country: Denmark
Born: August 14, 1949
Position: Defender/Forward/Midfield
Clubs: Vodingborg, B1901 Nykobing, Cercle Brugge, Racing White Bruxelles, Anderlecht, Köln

Morten Olsen's 18-year playing career saw him play in every outfield position, but he will be remembered as a gifted libero in the thrilling Denmark side of the 1980s. The role had come to him care of his Anderlecht coach, Tomislav Ivic, after Olsen had recovered from injury. To extend his playing career Ivic cast him as libero and this was embraced by Danish national coach Sepp Piontek. Olsen was instrumental in Denmark's exciting performances at the 1984 European Championship and 1986 World Cup. He later became a coach and in his first season he won the Danish championship with Brondby. He became coach of the national team in 2000.

WOLFGANG OVERATH

Country: West Germany
Born: September 29, 1943
Position: Midfield
Clubs: SV Siegburg 04, Köln

When Wolfgang Overath helped West Germany to World Cup success on home soil in 1974, not only did he bring his international career to a fitting end, but he also completed a remarkable treble. Having been a beaten finalist in the 1966 final, he scored the winner in the third placed play-off in 1970, so he can claim to be the only player to have finished first, second and third in the World Cup (Beckenbauer was in all three teams, but he didn't play in the third place play-off match in 1970). Overath won the Bundesliga in his first season with Köln and, almost 800 games later, he bowed out of football after helping them to German Cup success in 1977.

MARC OVERMARS

Country: Holland
Born: March 29, 1973
Position: Winger
Clubs: Go Ahead Eagles, Willem II, Ajax, Arsenal, Barcelona

The career of Marc Overmars really took off when he joined Ajax in 1992 and became a member of the side that won three titles and the Champions League final in 1995. The following season he was already eyeing a move abroad when he suffered a cruciate ligament injury and was sidelined for 12 months. Once recovered, he joined Arsenal and in his first season proved an influential team member as the club won the league and FA Cup double. He moved to Barcelona for £25 million a year later, at the time making him the most expensive Dutch player ever. He featured in Holland's Euro 2004 side as a regular substitute, but he retired from the game after the tournament, having had persistent problems with an injured knee.

JEAN-PIERRE PAPIN

Country: France
Born: November 5, 1963
Position: Forward
Clubs: INF Vichy, Valenciennes, Club Brugge, Marseille, AC Milan, Bayern Munich, Bordeaux, Guingamp

Jean-Pierre Papin won the European Footballer Of The Year award in 1991 and was one of the most prolific goalscorers of his era. A stocky striker with a powerful shot on either foot, he starred at the 1986 World Cup for France and finished top scorer in the French league for Marseille for five consecutive seasons. Papin found the net from every angle and became synonymous with Marseille's success across Europe. He flourished at international level too, helping France qualify for the 1992 European Championship with nine goals in eight matches.

He struggled to make an impact after moving to AC Milan and injuries marred his spell at Bayern Munich. Yet he won four French titles, two Italian titles, one UEFA Cup with Bayern and scored an impressive 30 goals in 54 appearances for France, a total that puts him among the country's top scorers.

DANIEL PASSARELLA

Country: Argentina
Born: May 25, 1953
Position: Defender
Clubs: Sarmiento, River Plate, Fiorentina, Inter Milan

Passarella, who captained Argentina to World Cup glory in 1978 aged only 25, was an instinctive sweeper who exuded calm. His leadership in the face of huge expectations earned him the nickname 'El Gran Capitan'. Passarella was an unusually skilful defender who contributed enormously in attack, scoring 22 goals in 70 internationals. He was particularly dangerous at set pieces and scored three goals in 12 World Cup games in 1978 and 1982. Passarella was selected for the 1986 finals but withdrew through injury. He achieved notoriety as a coach, banning players with long hair, or who wore earrings, for being homosexual.

BERT PATENAUDE

Country: USA
Born: November 4, 1909
Position: Centre-forward
Clubs: Philadelphia, J&P Coats, Fall River Marksmen, Newark Americans, St Louis' Central Breweries, New York Yankees, New York Giants

Bertram Patenaude may, or may not, have scored the first hat-trick in World Cup history with his goals against Paraguay at the 1930 tournament. For many years Patenaude had been credited with just two goals in the game but team manager Wilfred Cummings' official report to his football association, written at the end of the tournament, duly credits Patenaude with all three goals. This report, coupled with some contemporary news reports and the testimonies of several squad members in interviews years later, indicate that Patenaude probably should be attributed with the first World Cup hat-trick. In total he only played four times for his country but did score six goals, four of them at the World Cup.

ADOLFO PEDERNERA

Country: Argentina
Born: November 15, 1918
Position: Forward
Clubs: River Plate, Atlanta, Huracán, Millonarios

Pedernera provided the cutting edge of the devastating River Plate 'Máquina' forward line of Munoz-Moreno-Pedernera-Labruna-Loustau in the 1930s and 1940s. Nicknamed 'the Maestro', he is credited with evolving the deep-lying centre-forward role and to great success. He won the Argentine championship with River Plate five times between 1936 and 1945 and he played 21 times for his country. In 1948, during the Argentine players strike, he moved to Colombia to play for Millonarios of Bogota. He attracted huge crowds when he was presented to the fans for the first time, tripling their normal gate receipts of $18,000, and on his debut, that figure doubled again. Pedernera's move began an exodus of top South American talent to Colombia, beginning a golden age for the league called 'El Dorado'. Pedernera himself recruited the top talent to Columbia, including his replacement at River Plate, Alfredo Di Stéfano.

Below: Fans lift Argentina captain Daniel Passarella as he holds aloft the World Cup in 1978.

PELÉ

Country: Brazil
Born: October 23, 1940
Position: Forward
Clubs: Santos, New York Cosmos

Edson Arantes do Nascimento, or Pelé as he is more commonly known, began kicking a ball around the yard of his Três Corações home at the age of two and had the perfect role model in his father, Dondinho, who was a striker for leading Brazilian side Fluminese.

After playing for a few amateur teams, including Baquinho and Sete Setembro, Pelé was discovered by the former Brazilian World Cup player Waldemar de Brito, who recognized the 11-year-old's potential and invited him to join his Clube Atlético Bauru team. Within four years, de Brito had seen enough and took his protégé to top São Paulo outfit Santos for a trial, telling the club at the time: 'This boy will be the greatest soccer player in the world.'

Pelé went on to score on his debut that September and, although appearances were extremely limited in that opening campaign, he netted 32 times the following season, leading the São Paulo league goal charts in the process.

Brazil's national coach Sylvio Pirilo gave Pelé his international debut on July 7, 1957, and the 16-year-old scored in a 2-1 defeat against Argentina. His appearances in a gold shirt made Pelé a worldwide phenomenon and the early signs of his greatness were seen at the 1958 World Cup finals in Sweden.

Already guaranteed their place in the quarter-finals, Pelé made his bow in Brazil's final group game against the Soviet Union.

Above: Pelé, during his 18 year career with Santos. Below left: Queen Elizabeth presents a trophy to Pelé at the Maracanã. Below right: Taking the beautiful game to the world at Mexico 70.

He then went on to score the only goal against Wales in the quarter-finals. His pace, trickery and eye for goal ensured he remained in the side and a semi-final hat-trick in a 5-2 defeat of France, and a further two goals in the final against Sweden, made sure he was not out of the headlines.

Although Brazil successfully defended their title four years later in Chile, a pulled muscle prematurely ended Pelé's tournament, and the 1966 campaign would also end in tears and frustration. The greatest player in the world became a marked man in England and was brutally fouled against Bulgaria and Portugal as Brazil crashed out at the first stage. 'I don't want to end my life as an invalid,' moaned Pelé, as he threatened to boycott the next World Cup in Mexico.

Pelé's frustrations eased though, and his performances in 1970 proved to be the pinnacle of an illustrious career. He was again the focal point in a Brazil team that is still regarded as the greatest ever. A free-flowing brand of football swept all challengers aside and the team's 4-1 final victory against Italy emphasised their dominance. Pelé scored in that game, taking his tally to four and his overall World Cup tally to 12 in 14 matches. He would eventually end his international career with 96 goals in 111 appearances.

In 1974, Pelé left Santos, having made 1,036 appearances and scoring an alleged 1,216 goals. He helped the team to win numerous trophies before bringing down the curtain on his career in the North American Soccer League with the New York Cosmos. He scored a further 65 goals for Cosmos before playing his final game, a friendly match against Santos, on October 1, 1977.

1950: Begins playing for local team Bauru Athletic Club, where his father was a coach.

1956: Joins Santos, scores as a 15-year-old on his debut against Corinthians; finishes the season as top scorer with 32 goals.

1957: Scores on his international debut for Brazil against Argentina.

1958: At 17 he becomes the youngest ever World Cup winner and scores twice in the final in a 5-2 victory over the hosts.

1962: Misses the World Cup through injury but helps Santos to win the World Club Cup.

1966: Brutal opposition tactics see the world's best player fouled out of the World Cup.

1969: Scores his 1,000th first-class goal, a penalty against Vasco Da Gama.

1970: Star of the World Cup finals, he inspires Brazil to win the Jules Rimet trophy for the third time in Mexico.

1971: Makes his 111th and final appearance for Brazil, against Yugoslavia.

1974: Plays his final game for Santos against Ponte Preta.

1975: Comes out of retirement to appear for New York Cosmos in NASL.

1977: Retires after helping Cosmos win their second NASL championship.

1994: Appointed as Brazil's Minister for Sport.

Above: Abedi Pele of Marseille shields the ball from AC Milan's Paolo Maldini.

ABEDI PELE

Country: Ghana
Born: January 5, 1962
Position: Winger/Midfield
Clubs: Real Tamale United, Al Satar, Dragons de Louéme, FC Zurich, Niort, Marseille, Mulhouse, Lille, Torino, TSV 1860 Munich

At the age of 17 Abedi Ayew Pele won the 1982 African Nations Cup with Ghana. The precocious teenager, although not yet an automatic choice, was a sensation. A European club career beckoned, with his greatest success achieved with the French club Olympique Marseille, where he won the 1993 European Cup, beating the mighty AC Milan 1-0 just two years after losing the final on penalties to Red Star Belgrade. He was given an influential free role in a talented team that included Barthez, Desailly, Deschamps, Boksic and Völler and he excelled. In 1991 he was voted African Player Of The Year for his outstanding performances in Europe.

SILVIO PIOLA

Country: Italy
Born: September 29, 1913
Position: Forward
Clubs: Pro Vercelli, Lazio, Torino, Juventus, Novara

Silvio Piola was an early Italian football hero and one of the great pre-war strikers. He scored five goals at the 1938 World Cup in France, including two in the final as Italy triumphed with a 4-2 win over Hungary. At times he was impossible to play against, his strength and skill showing he was ahead of his peers.

At club level Piola started at Pro Vercelli,

Above: Real Madrid's Pirri shakes hands with Celtic's Danny McGrain before the European Cup quarter-final in 1980.

earning his international debut in 1935. He continued after the war but he will always be remembered for 1938, when he was a pivotal figure and, alongside Leônidas of Brazil, arguably the greatest striker of his era.

PIRRI

Country: Spain
Born: March 11, 1945
Position: Striker/Midfield/Defender
Clubs: Grenada, Real Madrid, Puebla FC

Few players have ever served one club as loyally as Pirri did Real Madrid. For three decades he was at the heart of the Spanish giants, firstly as a player, then in a variety of positions, including sports director. He made his debut for the club as a striker in 1964 but over the years moved back first into midfield and then defence, playing until 1979, after which he became the club doctor and later a scout. A long career with a great club inevitably yields honours but Pirri's with Madrid were particularly numerous, totalling eight Spanish championships, three domestic cups and the European Cup. He also played 44 times for Spain between 1966 and 1978.

FRANTISEK PLÁNICKA

Country: Czechoslovakia
Born: June 2, 1904
Position: Goalkeeper
Club: Slovan Prague, Bubenec, Slavia Prague

Frantisek Plánicka was one of Czechoslovakia's most successful players as part of Slavia Prague's unstoppable side of the 1920s and 1930s. Plánicka won nine league titles, six Czech Cups and the 1938 Mitropa Cup. He was an automatic choice for the national team between 1925 and 1938, captaining them in two World Cups in 1934 and 1938.

In the 1934 competition his magnificent, agile performances helped the Czechs to the runners-up spot, while in the 1938 quarter-final clash with Brazil, Plánicka played much of the game with a broken arm. All in all Plánicka made 73 appearances for his country in a 13-year international career.

MICHEL PLATINI

Country: France
Born: June 21, 1955
Position: Midfield
Clubs: Nancy, St Etienne, Juventus

Michel Platini is firmly established as one of the greatest players of all time. With his remarkable technique, superb passing and sublime free-kicks, he was the world's best player during the first half of the 1980s. His astonishing goalscoring record from midfield made him a match-winner at the highest level and his ability to peak on the biggest occasions set him apart from his peers.

Platini excelled for France throughout an 11-year international career and he won a string of club honours at Juventus, wowing football followers across the world. He started his career at Nancy, who took a chance on him after others famously turned him down because of his frail physique. He showed elegant natural skills and worked hard on his technique on the training field. At the relatively small club he was able to develop after making his league debut at 17 and emerged as a bright French talent, making his international debut against Czechoslovakia on March 27, 1976.

He took part impressively in the 1978 World Cup finals, hinting at things to come, and moved to St Etienne after the tournament. But the club's golden era was over and despite brilliant individual performances, Platini returned to the international spotlight only in 1982. That year he helped France to the semi-

finals of the World Cup, where they lost on penalties to West Germany following a thrilling 3-3 draw. Platini was the leader of their gifted generation, showing the vision and goalscoring ability that was his trademark.

At 27 he was coming to the peak of his powers and he moved to Juventus. It was in Serie A that he truly developed into the world's greatest player, helping the squad win the Italian title in 1984 and 1986, the Italian Cup in 1983, the European Cup Winners' Cup and the European Super Cup in 1984, and the European Cup and the World Club Cup in 1985. Platini was the master, his range of skill unrivalled in the toughest league in the world and his achievements at the highest level overshadowing those of any other player. More remarkable still was his goals record. Three times he finished as the highest goalscorer in the Italian league, thanks largely to his ability with free-kicks and penalties.

In the midst of club success Platini also tasted victory with France, inspiring them to win the European Championship in 1984 with a series of astonishing displays in the finals. He struck nine goals in five matches, including two hat-tricks and the winner in the semi-final. The opener in the 2-0 final win over Spain completed a remarkable run.

He was voted European Footballer Of The Year in 1983, 1984 and 1985, becoming only the second player to win the award three times after Johan Cruyff. He appeared at the 1986 World Cup as France again reached the semi-final, but he retired aged 31 in May 1987. He won 72 caps for France and scored 41 goals, becoming their all-time highest goalscorer. Alongside his haul of trophies, he averaged more than a goal every two games throughout his career.

DAVID PLATT

Country: England
Born: June 10, 1966
Position: Midfield
Clubs: Manchester United, Crewe Alexandra, Aston Villa, Bari, Juventus, Sampdoria, Arsenal

After a modest start to his professional career – released by Manchester United then moving to Crewe and Aston Villa – Platt made his

name during the 1990 World Cup, where one goal effectively changed his life. His fantastic volley against Belgium gave England victory in the final minute of extra-time and sent his team into the quarter-finals.

Having established his place in the starting line-up, he returned from the tournament as a player in demand. After one more season with Aston Villa he established a fine career in Italian football, first with Bari, who bought him for a British record transfer fee of £5.5 million. He then played for Juventus, where he won the UEFA Cup in 1993 despite not holding down a regular first team place, and finally he signed for Sampdoria.

At the same time his international career boomed. He was one of England's key players during the Nineties, playing in the 1992 and 1996 European Championships, eventually winning a total of 62 caps and scoring 27 goals. He was also captain on several occasions. Platt's Italian adventure ended in 1995 when he signed for Arsenal, and although he was troubled by knee problems, he won the league and FA Cup double in 1998 with The Gunners before moving into coaching.

Above: One of the world football's true greats, Michel Platini on the ball for France in 1986.

Above: Hardly the classic build for a footballer Ferenc Puskás, seen here turning out for his native Hungary, was a true legend with Honvéd and Real Madrid.

ERNEST POL

Country: Poland
Born: November 3, 1932
Position: Centre-forward
Clubs: Legia Warsaw, Gornik Zabrze

Ernest Pol was one of Poland's greatest ever strikers, having led the line in 49 internationals and scoring 39 goals. His 16-year international career spanned the 1950s and 1960s. In October 1956 he scored four times in a 5-3 friendly win over Norway and four years later at the Olympics in Rome he scored five goals in the 6-1 thrashing of Tunisia. He scored two other international hat-tricks against Finland and Denmark. He won the Polish title twice with army side Legia and five times with Gornik Zabrze. He scored 186 league goals as Gornik dominated Polish football during this period, but the political situation of the day meant that he was never able to play for any of the big European clubs.

TONI POLSTER

Country: Austria
Born: March 10, 1964
Position: Forward
Clubs: Austria Vienna, Torino, Seville, Logrones, Rayo Vallecano, Köln, Borussia Mönchengladbach, SV Salzburg

Toni Polster remains the biggest name in Austrian football. Such was his importance to the national side he was still considered one of their key players at the age of 34 during France 98. He made his final appearance for Austria against Iran, by which time he was 36, bringing down the curtain on a career spanning 95 internationals and making him Austria's most-capped player of all time.

In a side that was only able to qualify for the 1990 and 1998 World Cups during Polster's career, his haul of 44 international goals made him a feared opponent all over the world.

FERENC PUSKÁS

Country: Hungary, Spain
Born: April 2, 1927
Position: Forward
Clubs: Honvéd, Real Madrid

Football can have few more unlikely stars than Ferenc Puskás, the short, barrel-chested Hungarian goal machine who became known as the 'Galloping Major'. Puskás possessed one of the most powerful and accurate left feet in the history of the game and his goalscoring record is phenomenal: 83 goals in 84 matches for Hungary and 35 goals in 39 European matches for Real Madrid from 1961 to 1965.

As a small child Puskás was entranced by the roar of the Kispest crowd, audible from his kitchen window in Budapest. The smallest kid on the block, he became inseparable from the five-year-old next door, József Bózsik. Their fathers worked together in a slaughterhouse and when Bózsik was picked up by Kispest (renamed Honvéd after 1949 and turned into the army side, hence Puskás's nickname) his friend went with him. Together they forged one of the most dynamic strike partnerships in the history of the game.

Puskás scored on his international debut against Austria on August 20, 1945, and in the epochal 6-3 victory at Wembley in 1953 he underlined the gulf between the Magical Magyars and England with a memorable drag back and shot past the home side's goalkeeper Gil Merrick.

In the 1954 World Cup he captained the side and came back from an injury in the first match to play in the final. Though clearly unfit he opened the scoring after six minutes and had a late equaliser disallowed.

In a time of hardship he became chief smuggler among the Hungarian players, returning from away fixtures loaded with razor blades or machine parts, twice having to talk himself out of trouble with the secret police.

Puskás won four Hungarian league titles with Honvéd but his life took a dramatic turn in 1956 when the Soviet Union invaded his country to quell the nationalist uprising. Honvéd were touring Europe at the time, and Puskás, along with Kocsis and several others, refused to return and was banned by UEFA from playing football for anyone else.

Real Madrid arranged for the ban to be rescinded and he made his debut for them in 1958 aged 30, rapidly forging a devastating partnership with Argentine Alfredo Di Stéfano that yielded six league championships and a staggering 240 goals in 260 appearances, explaining his Spanish nickname 'Cañoncito Pum' (the Little Cannon).

Puskás became the first player to score a hat-trick in the European Cup final, against Eintracht Frankfurt in 1960 (Di Stéfano became the second in the same game, while

Puskás finished with a fourth from the penalty spot). He was the competition's top scorer in three campaigns, scoring another hat-trick when losing to Benfica in 1962, aged 35.

Puskás picked up four caps as a naturalised Spaniard, three of which were at the 1962 World Cup finals before eventually retiring at 40. He moved to Athens to coach Panathinaikos, taking the club to their only European Cup final in 1971, and finally resettled in Budapest. In 1993 he became caretaker manager of the national side but failed to guide Hungary to the 1994 World Cup. This did not deter the Hungarian government from marking his 75th birthday in 2002 by renaming the Népstadion (which he had helped build as a youth) as the Ferenc Puskás Stadium. A fitting tribute to a genuine football legend.

HELMUT RAHN

Country: West Germany
Born: August 16, 1929
Position: Forward
Clubs: Altenessen 12, Oelde 09, Sportfreunde Katernberg, Rot-Weiss Essen, Köln, Enschede, Duisburg

Helmut Rahn will be best remembered for the part he played in an unfancied West German side's World Cup success in 1954. Rahn scored twice in the final against the red-hot favourites Hungary, netting the equaliser and then the late winner. Yet Rahn nearly didn't get to Switzerland as he was on the verge of signing for Nacional of Uruguay while on a tour with club side Rot-Weiss Essen, before West German coach Sepp Herberger summoned him home to join the World Cup squad. Rahn was well known for having a thunderous shot and he also figured strongly in the 1958 finals when he scored six goals, to take his total World Cup tally to ten.

THOMAS RAVELLI

Country: Sweden
Born: August 13, 1959
Position: Goalkeeper
Clubs: Osters Vaxjo, IFK Gothenburg, Tampa Bay Mutiny

The adage that you have to be a bit mad to be a goalkeeper was never more appropriate than when applied to Ravelli. Known as the clown prince of Swedish football for his humourous approach to the game, he was a magnificent, agile keeper who helped his country to the semi-finals of the 1994 World Cup in America.

Ravelli made an incredible 143 appearances for his country between 1981 and 1997, a period in which Swedish football grew in stature. The commanding six-footer was the international game's most capped player until Lothar Matthäus surpassed his total.

ROBBIE RENSENBRINK

Country: Holland
Born: July 3, 1947
Position: Left-winger
Clubs: OVVO, OSV, DWS Amsterdam, Club Brugge, Anderlecht, Portland Timbers, Toulouse

The outstanding Dutch winger spent much of his career in Belgium with Anderlecht, helping them to two European Cup Winners' Cup victories, while on the international scene he was a leading figure in the exciting Dutch team of the Seventies. He played in two successive World Cup finals in 1974 and 1978, taking a runners-up medal in each, but he does hold the honour of scoring the 1,000th goal in World Cup history – that came with a penalty against Scotland in the 1978 tournament. He ended his playing career with brief spells in both America and France.

FRANK RIJKAARD

Country: Holland
Born: September 30, 1962
Position: Midfield/Central defender
Clubs: Ajax, Sporting Lisbon, Real Zaragoza, AC Milan, Ajax

Enormously versatile, Frank Rijkaard made his Ajax debut in 1979 under Johan Cruyff, but left the club for brief spells in Portugal and Spain after the two men fell out. He ended up in Italy where he was an integral part of the all-conquering AC Milan team of the late Eighties and early Nineties, along with fellow Dutchmen Ruud Gullit and Marco van Basten.

Milan won two European Cups, two league titles and two World Club Cups with Rijkaard in the side and his return to Ajax resulted in another European Cup triumph 1995. Having made his international debut at just 19 years of age, he also went on to play an important role in the exciting Holland side that won the European Championship in 1988. Following his retirement from playing Rijkaard became national team coach in 1998. He resigned, however, immediately after his promising Dutch tournament favourites were eliminated from Euro 2000 on penalties by Italy at the semi-final stage. Since then he has guided Barcelona to successive Spanish league titles in 2005 and 2006.

GIGI RIVA

Country: Italy
Born: November 7, 1944
Position: Left-wing/Centre-forward
Clubs: Legnano, Cagliari

Originally a left-winger, Riva's pace saw him develop into a prolific and popular striker, both for Italy and Cagliari. He helped the Sardinian side into Serie A and to the Scudetto, scoring 21 goals in 28 games that season. He was also Italy's top scorer in the 1970 World Cup, scoring in extra-time during the semi-final victory over West Germany. It was his 22nd international goal in 21 games. Riva then suffered the second broken leg of his career in a European Championship qualifier before turning down the opportunity of a big money move to Juventus. The 1974 tournament was not such a success for Riva and he subsequently lost his place in the Italian side.

Below: Frank Rijkaard, an integral part of AC Milan's all conquering team of the late Eighties and early Nineties.

ROBERTO RIVELINO

Country: Brazil
Born: January 1, 1946
Position: Midfield
Clubs: Corinthians, Fluminese, El Hilal

The arrival of Mario Zagalo as Brazil manager in the lead up to the 1970 World Cup finals proved to be a watershed in the career of Roberto Rivelino. Under former coach João Saldanha, the Corinthians midfielder had to be content with fleeting appearances, but as the tournament got underway in Mexico, it became evident that the first exponent of the 'banana shot' free-kick was ready to unleash his talents on a worldwide audience.

Rivelino joined in perfect harmony with Pelé, Gerson, Jairzinho and Tostão to form the most potent attacking force that Brazil has ever had. The highlight of his career came against Czechoslovakia, where a swerving long-range shot inspired his team-mates to victory.

Brazil were victorious in the final, beating Italy 4-1, and with three tournament goals to his name, Rivelino had played his part. He would play in two further World Cups, representing his country a total of 92 times, scoring 26 goals.

GIANNI RIVERA

Country: Italy
Born: August 18, 1943
Position: Inside-forward
Clubs: US Alessandria, AC Milan

Gianni Rivera was an Italian hero who made his Serie A debut for his local team aged just 15, transferring to AC Milan just a year later. Staying at the San Siro throughout his long and successful career, he starred in four consecutive World Cups and helped Milan to become Italian champions in 1962 and European Cup winners in 1963. His superb passes twice put José Altafini through the Benfica defence to score the goals that made Milan champions of Europe. Slender and graceful, he was a technically superb player with tremendous passing skills and a powerful shot, particularly from distance.

He was the dominating figure when Milan became Italian champions again in 1968 and followed this triumph by winning the European Cup and the World Club Cup the following year. He landed the European Footballer Of The Year award in 1969 and by the time he wound up his club career with a third title in 1979, he had also won the Italian Cup four times.

Internationally Rivera featured at the 1968 European Championship, which Italy won, but had to battle for his place in the national team with great rival Sandro Mazzola. Indeed, he was left on the bench for the 1970 World Cup final against Brazil, getting on for just the last eight minutes. He won 60 caps, scoring 14 goals.

BRYAN ROBSON

Country: England
Born: January 11, 1957
Position: Midfield
Clubs: West Bromwich Albion, Manchester United, Middlesbrough

Robson earned the nickname 'Captain Marvel' for his unflinching and inspiring midfield performances in what was an undistinguished era for club and country. For a decade he was consistently the most outstanding player to wear England and Manchester United's colours. Signed by United for a then British record fee of £1.5 million, Robson's battling, defensive qualities, combined with regular goals, made him a natural leader. He managed 26 strikes for England, including a 27-second effort against France in the 1982 World Cup, and a total of 97 for Manchester United.

He led Manchester United to three FA Cup triumphs, but at the time of Liverpool's great dominance he looked destined to become one of the greatest players never to win the title. However, Manchester United finally achieved back-to-back Premiership wins in 1993 and 1994, in the autumn of Robson's career. He then joined Middlesbrough as player-manager. Capped 90 times by England, 65 as captain, Robson paid the price for his fearlessness by suffering regular injuries, most significantly in the 1986 World Cup finals.

ROMARIO

Country: Brazil
Born: January 29, 1966
Position: Forward
Clubs: Olario, Vasco Da Gama, PSV Eindhoven, Barcelona, Flamengo, Valencia, Flamengo, Vasco Da Gama, Fluminese, Al Sadd, Fluminese, Vasco Da Gama, Miami

Frustrating to coaches, adored by fans and feared by defenders, Romario was one of the most exciting and colourful players in the world in his heyday. At his peak in the early 1990s, Romario was arguably the greatest striker on earth and a worthy heir to the tradition of great Brazilian attackers. In 1994, the year in which Brazil won the World Cup, he was at his deadliest. He was named FIFA World Footballer Of The Year after scoring five goals in the tournament, although he failed to get on the scoresheet in the final itself, a drab 0-0 draw with Italy. He was, however, among the successful penalty takers.

A year before the World Cup, Romario had joined Barcelona for £3 million. It was a move that brought the Spanish championship but by now he was attracting as much coverage for his playboy lifestyle as for his feats on the pitch. In 1996 he returned to Brazil to join Flamengo, only to be sacked three years later. By then injury had denied him a place alongside Ronaldo at the

Above: Italy's star of the 1982 World Cup, Paolo Rossi outpaces Junior of Brazil.

1998 World Cup and he was not selected by Luiz Felipe Scolari for the 2002 squad, despite huge public outcry. With his international career in decline, he remained in demand at club level, hopping between clubs according to whichever coach most tolerated his indulgences. Despite his intention to retire, Romario continued to play for Brazil until April 2005 and played on at club level with Vasco Da Gama and Miami, aged 40.

JULIO CESAR ROMERO

Country: Paraguay
Born: August 28, 1960
Position: Forward
Clubs: Sportivo Luquero, New York Cosmos, Fluminese, Barcelona, Puebla, Sportivo Luquero, Olimpia, La Serena, Club Cerro Corá

The 1985 South American Footballer Of The Year, Romero was the star of the Paraguay side that reached the second round of the 1986 World Cup. Alongside strike partner Cabanas, he spearheaded his team to a win over Iraq and creditable draws with hosts Mexico and Belgium, finishing second in their group before losing to England. Nicknamed 'Romerito', he lit up the Brazilian league as one of the leading lights of the Fluminese team of the mid-1980s, winning the title in 1984. He was twice a champion in the North American Soccer League with New York Cosmos, in 1980 and 1982.

PAOLO ROSSI

Country: Italy
Born: September 23, 1956
Position: Centre-forward
Clubs: Prato, Juventus, Como, Lanerossi Vicenza, Perugia, Juventus, AC Milan

Although Rossi retired young, at the age of 29, he packed a great deal of incident into a short, controversial career. A problematic knee injury saw Juventus release him in 1975 but he recovered, prospered and eventually joined

Opposite: Roberto Rivelino of Brazil is tackled by an Italian defender in the 1970 World Cup final.

Perugia for £3.5 million. Despite being banned for two years in the early 1980s, following his alleged involvement in a match-fixing scandal, Rossi received a surprise late call up for the Italian squad for the 1982 World Cup finals in Spain. It was there that his ailing reputation enjoyed an extraordinary resurrection as he ended up top scorer with six goals (including a hat-trick against Brazil) and Italy ended up as world champions. He was named European Player Of The Year in the same year. Injuries blighted his later career and he retired at 29.

KARL-HEINZ RUMMENIGGE

Country: West Germany
Born: September 25, 1955
Position: Forward
Clubs: Bayern Munich, Inter Milan, Servette

For several years, Rummenigge was the leading player in West German football. A prolific goalscorer, he was twice a European Cup winner and starred for Bayern Munich in the 1976 victory over St Etienne. He reached his peak four years later, helping Germany to win the European Championship. Twice European Footballer Of The Year (1980 and 1981), he scored 45 goals in 95 games for his country but didn't have the best of luck: he was captain when the Germans lost the 1982 World Cup to Italy, and again four years later in defeat to Argentina. He later became president of Bayern Munich,

IAN RUSH

Country: Wales
Born: October 20, 1961
Position: Striker
Clubs: Chester City, Liverpool, Juventus, Liverpool, Leeds United, Newcastle United, Sheffield United, Wrexham, Sydney Olympic

Ian Rush was one of the greatest goalscorers of his, or any other era. Signed by Bob Paisley

from Chester City for £300,000, he became a Liverpool stalwart for 16 years, barring a short spell in Italy with Juventus, where he failed to settle. As a result Ian Rush now stands as Liverpool's highest goalscorer of all time, with an impressive 346 goals to his name (he is the club's second highest scorer in the league with 229, just behind the record set by Roger Hunt).

Rush can also claim to be one of the most highly-decorated players in English football as his career peaked in conjunction with the greatest period in Liverpool's history, when league titles, FA Cups and European Cups flowed. Aside from his Italian sojourn, which was not quite as disastrous as has been made out, Rush's other great career disappointment was failing to grace the finals of any major international championship, but he was still capped 73 times by Wales, scoring 28 goals.

HUGO SANCHEZ

Country: Mexico
Born: June 11, 1958
Position: Forward
Clubs: UNAM, Atlético Madrid, Real Madrid, América, Rayo Vallecano, Dallas Burn

Human jack-in-the-box Hugo Sanchez is probably the greatest-ever player to emerge from Central America. The livewire Mexican, whose trademark was an acrobatic somersault celebration after each goal (taught to him by his Olympic gymnast sister), was the top goalscorer in Spanish league football for an incredible five consecutive seasons. He totted up 234 goals, mainly for Madrid's senior clubs, and his partnership with Emilio Butragueño at the Bernabéu remains the stuff of legend – as does his propensity for the bicycle kick. His international career lasted from 1977 to 1998, and he captained his country during several World Cup tournaments, scoring for Mexico 29 times in 58 appearances.

LEONEL SANCHEZ

Country: Chile
Born: April 25, 1936
Position: Left-winger
Club: Universidad de Chile, Colo Colo, Palestino, Ferrobadminton

Leonel Sanchez was the star player of the Chilean team that finished third as hosts in the 1962 World Cup. Raiding from the left-wing in typically direct fashion, Sanchez ended the tournament as the Golden Boot winner with four goals, a distinction he shared with five other players (Florian Albert, Valentin Ivanov, Vavá, Garrincha and Drazan Jerkovic). He is also remembered for his part in the infamous 'Battle of Santiago' between Chile and Italy at the 1962 World Cup. Initially he was the unfortunate victim of a disgraceful neck-high challenge from

Italian Mario David, but his punch that flattened Humberto Maschio was inexcusable, even if it did show impressive timing.

JOSÉ SANTAMARIA

Country: Uruguay, Spain
Born: July 31, 1929
Position: Centre-half
Clubs: Nacional, Real Madrid

The hard-as-nails Uruguayan centre-back was the defensive lynchpin of the all-conquering Nacional de Montevideo and Real Madrid teams of the 1950s and 1960s. With Nacional he won five Uruguayan championship titles in the Fifties, breaking into the national team. The move to Europe brought glory with Real Madrid. Playing behind the attacking talents of Puskás, Di Stéfano and Gento, he won a hat-trick of European Cups and six Spanish championships. Santamaria is also one of five players to have represented two countries at the finals of the World Cup. In 1954 he was one of the stars of the tournament playing in the centre of defence for Uruguay. In 1962, however, he was to be found in Spanish colours, and collected 17 caps for his adopted country. He later went on to become manager of a disappointing Spain side during the 1982 World Cup finals.

DJALMA SANTOS

Country: Brazil
Born: February 27, 1929
Position: Right-back
Clubs: Portuguesa, Palmeiras, Atletico Paranaenese

Santos was aged 37 when he played in his fourth World Cup, the 1966 tournament in England. However, it was not to be a happy competition for the outstanding full-back and he lost his place after the defeat to Hungary. Four years previously, though, he was at the height of his powers as he formed a terrific understanding with Garrincha. He set up the third goal as Brazil retained their world crown with a victory over Czechoslovakia, while in Sweden in 1958 his sole appearance was in Brazil's final victory over the hosts.

NILTON SANTOS

Country: Brazil
Born: May 16, 1925
Position: Left-back
Clubs: Botafogo

Referred to as a left-back Nilton Santos loved to push forward, more like a modern wing-back. He represented his country over a 14-year spell, which included two victorious World Cup campaigns in 1958 and 1962 and saw him make 82 international appearances before he retired

in 1963 at the age of 37. He made his debut for Brazil in 1949 and the following year embarked upon Brazil's ill-fated World Cup campaign but failed to make it on to the pitch. In 1954 Brazil fared slightly better, making the quarter-finals, but its was four years later in Sweden when he tasted glory as part of the Brazil side who became the first nation to lift the trophy outside of their own continent. Santos earned the respect of team-mates and opponents wherever he played. At club level he represented Río de Janeiro side Botafogo throughout his career.

GYORGY SÁROSI

Country: Hungary
Born: September 12, 1912
Position: Centre-forward/Centre-half
Club: Ferencváros

Gyorgy Sárosi was an educated man with a law degree and was duly nicknamed 'The Doctor' because of it. Between the wars he truly was one of the best footballers in the game, enhancing the reputation of both his club Ferencváros – eight times Hungarian league champions and Mitropa Cup winners in 1937 – and his country. Sárosi captained Hungary to the 1938 World Cup final. The previous year he scored seven goals against Czechoslovakia in an 8-3 win, the haul contributing to his overall tally of 42 goals. Later, he carved out an impressive coaching career in Italy and Switzerland.

HECTOR SCARONE

Country: Uruguay
Born: December 28, 1898
Position: Forward/Inside-right
Clubs: Nacional, Inter Milan, Palermo, Barcelona, Montevideo Wanderers, Peñarol

Hector Pedro Scarone is 'The Magician', a player who was famed for his ability to produce extraordinary skills or astounding goals from nothing. He was a star of the inaugural World Cup as Uruguay won the trophy, having already won Olympic gold in 1924 and 1928, as well as the South American Championship in 1917, 1923, 1924 and 1926. In all he scored a national record 31 goals in 51 appearances.

JUAN SCHIAFFINO

Country: Uruguay, Italy
Born: July 28, 1925
Position: Inside-forward
Clubs: Peñarol, AC Milan, Roma

Small but lethal, Schiaffino was the key striker in the Uruguay team which won the 1950 World Cup in Brazil, scoring the first goal in a 2-1 win against the hosts in the final. He played again in the 1954 finals and was his country's most dynamic performer as they fell at the semi-final stage to the might of Hungary. This prompted AC Milan to pay a then world

record fee of £72,000 for his services, and once there he crafted a reputation as one of the greatest imports ever to play in Serie A. Schiaffino could have represented Italy at the World Cup in 1958 due to his mixed ancestry, but couldn't stop them from losing out to Northern Ireland in qualification.

SALVATORE SCHILLACI

Country: Italy
Born: December 1, 1964
Position: Centre-forward
Clubs: Messina, Juventus, Inter Milan, Jubilo Iwata

Lasting less than a year and a half after his debut against Switzerland in March 1990, 'Totò' Schillaci's international career was nothing if it wasn't short. His place in history is assured, however, thanks to the six goals he netted for Italy in the 1990 World Cup finals, which made him the tournament's top scorer.

The Juventus hitman claimed crucial strikes against Austria (a game in which he came on as a substitute to score after four minutes) and the Republic Of Ireland. He also put Italy ahead in their semi-final clash with Argentina, only to see Diego Maradona's team come back to win on penalties. Despite his heroics, Schillaci played just eight more games for his country after the finals ended and scored just one more goal.

Above: Juan Schiaffino of Milan clears the ball in the 1958 European Cup final at the Heysel Stadium.

Opposite: Uwe Seeler trains with the West German squad before their 1954 match against England at Wembley.

IMRE SCHLOSSER

Country: Hungary
Born: October 11, 1889
Position: Inside-Left
Clubs: Ferencváros, MTK Budapest

Imre Schlosser was perhaps the first Hungarian player to gain a reputation beyond his homeland. Between 1906 and 1927, he played for Hungary 68 times and scored an incredible 59 goals, including a six-goal haul against Switzerland in 1911 and five goals against Tsarist Russia in Moscow a year later. The goals flowed in the Hungarian league where he was top scorer in seven successive seasons between 1909 and 1914 and won 13 league titles (five with Ferencváros, and eight with MTK). After his playing career ended he became a referee.

PETER SCHMEICHEL

Country: Denmark
Born: November 18, 1963
Position: Goalkeeper
Clubs: Gladsaxe, Hvidovre, Brondby, Manchester United, Sporting Lisbon, Aston Villa, Manchester City

For ten years, the Danish giant was regarded as the best goalkeeper in the world, collecting numerous domestic trophies and making over 100 international appearances (even scoring once). He formed an impregnable barrier behind Denmark's European Championship-winning side in 1992. But his greatest period was at Manchester United. While Eric Cantona was the enigmatic talisman up front, Schmeichel was the brick wall at the back, equally important to the winning of the club's first domestic title for more than a quarter of a century – and the many that followed.

Athletic and domineering, he was always shouting at – and organising – his defenders, never letting them lose their concentration. Schmeichel pulled off many memorable saves through his agility and speed of thought, and his long throws and accurate kicks set up many successful attacking moves from the back. Keen not to be exposed by the advancing years, he left

Below: Manchester United's Peter Schmeichel makes a spectacular save against Tottenham Hotspur in the 1992-3 season.

United after their Champions League triumph in 1999, spending two years in Portugal before returning to the English Premiership with Aston Villa. A year later he was on the move again, playing a vital role in stabilising Kevin Keegan's Manchester City on their return to the top flight. He finally announced his retirement at the end of his first season with the club, making his farewell appearance at City's last ever game at their Maine Road ground.

KARL-HEINZ SCHNELLINGER

Country: West Germany
Born: March 31, 1939
Position: Right-half/Left-back/Sweeper
Clubs: Duren, Köln, Roma, Mantua, AC Milan, Tennis Borussia Berlin

Karl-Heinz Schnellinger represented West Germany at four World Cups, as a right-half at the 1958 World Cup and subsequently in 1962, 1966 and 1970 as a left-back. He had performed impressively at the 1957 UEFA Youth Tournament in Madrid but by the time he was back from his first World Cup he had signed for Köln. In 1962 he was voted German Player Of The Year, primarily as a result of his performances at the World Cup in Chile. A £72,000 move to Roma in 1963 did not initially work out but when he joined Milan Schnellinger went on to win the Italian Cup, European Cup Winners' Cup, Serie A, European Cup and World Club Cup between 1967 and 1969.

GAETANO SCIREA

Country: Italy
Born: May 25, 1953
Position: Inside-forward/Sweeper
Clubs: Atalanta, Juventus

Gaetano Scirea was both Juventus and Italy's top sweeper of the late 1970s and early 1980s. At club level Scirea won a series of trophies with Juventus, including the European Cup in 1985, the Cup Winners' Cup in 1984, the UEFA Cup in 1977 and the European Super Cup in 1984. At home he also won seven Serie A titles and two Italian Cups, while at international level he represented Italy 78 times, ten as captain. He was a World Cup winner in 1982.

DAVID SEAMAN

Country: England
Born: September 19, 1963
Position: Goalkeeper
Clubs: Peterborough United, Birmingham City, QPR, Arsenal, Manchester City

Shown the door by Leeds United as an apprentice, David Seaman was Arsenal's first-choice goalkeeper for 13 years, winning every

domestic honour at Highbury, including the league and FA Cup double in both 1998 and 2002. He signed from QPR for £1 million and helped the team secure the 1991 league title in his debut season, conceding just 18 league goals. Within three years Seaman went on to win the FA Cup, League Cup and Cup Winners' Cup.

As an integral member of the club's fabled 'back five', Seaman's consistent performances won him international recognition, and although he missed England's 1990 World Cup campaign through injury, he was firmly established as first choice by the time of the 1996 European Championship. He was, arguably, the finest goalkeeper in the world at the time, and he kept Scotland and Spain at bay with a number of top-class saves as England progressed to the semi-finals.

At 38 years of age David Seaman remained England's first choice at the 2002 World Cup, and although his tournament was tainted by conceding Ronaldinho's long-range free-kick, his performances against Sweden and Argentina justified Sven Goran Eriksson's faith in the veteran keeper. His England career came to an end after conceding a goal straight from a corner in a Euro 2004 qualifier against Macedonia in October 2002, but his desire to continue playing club football was demonstrated by his decision to move to Manchester City in 2003, rather than remain at Arsenal in a coaching position. Time finally caught up with 'Safe Hands' Seaman when injury forced him to retire in January 2004.

UWE SEELER

Country: West Germany
Born: November 5, 1936
Position: Centre-forward
Club: Hamburg

The son of a Hamburg player, Seeler spent his entire 18-year career with the club, scoring more than 550 goals and becoming the country's top scorer in the inaugural Bundesliga season, 1963-4. But while his individual achievements are many, the sides in which he featured regularly fell at the last hurdle.

He made his international debut at 17, and his career took him to four World Cups, reaching one final, two semi-finals and one quarter-final. He scored in each tournament, an achievement matched only by Pelé, and his 21 appearances in the finals was a record that was broken by Lothar Matthäus.

Having skippered the West German side to defeat in the World Cup final at Wembley of 1966, Seeler had dropped back into a deeper role by the 1970 tournament as he turned into creator for Gerd Müller, who was to succeed him as Germany's most prolific striker. He scored 43 goals in 72 appearances for Germany and was voted German Player Of The Year on three occasions, in 1960, 1964 and 1970.

ALAN SHEARER

Born: August 13, 1970
Country: England
Position: Forward
Clubs: Southampton, Blackburn Rovers, Newcastle United

It's a shame Newcastle United didn't recognise the talents of a young schoolboy by the name of Alan Shearer when he failed his trial at the club. It certainly would have saved them the world record fee of £15 million that they paid to Blackburn Rovers for the highly sought-after England captain. Nevertheless, in his ten years leading the line at St James' Park, Shearer became a Geordie hero, in January 2006 beating Jackie Milburn's club scoring record of 200 goals that had stood for 49 years.

After failing his Newcastle trials, he was signed on schoolboy forms by Southampton, progressing through the ranks. After two substitute appearances, he made an impressive full debut in 1988, scoring a hat-trick against Arsenal to become the youngest player ever to do so in the English Football League. It was just an injury that prevented Shearer making the journey to Sweden for the 1992 European Championship, and during that summer Blackburn paid a record £3.6 million for him.

The sizeable transfer fee was repaid almost immediately. After scoring more than 30 goals in each of his first three seasons at the club, in 1995 Shearer helped manager Kenny Dalglish take Blackburn to their first league title in 81 years, pipping Manchester United to the trophy.

In 1996, Shearer had his most successful spell for England, helping Terry Venables' team win through to the European Championship semi-finals, forming a devastating partnership with Spurs striker Teddy Sheringham. Shearer notched up an impressive five goals, including a brace in the 4-1 demolition of Holland, and became the tournament's top scorer.

The disappointment of losing to Germany on penalties in the semi-final was soon washed away as Alan Shearer announced he would be returning to St James' Park on August 6 of that year. Manager Kevin Keegan was aware that the cost of Shearer's services would place a strain on the club's finances, but that was quickly forgotten as the England hitman forged a prolific partnership with Les Ferdinand in attack, complementing the guile and vision of Ginola and Beardsley in midfield.

Sadly, trophies eluded Kevin Keegan's side and the team also failed to win trophies under a succession of managers, including Kenny Dalglish, Ruud Gullit, Bobby Robson and Graeme Souness. Alan Shearer had retired from international football after Euro 2000, playing on with Newcastle, but just a few games short of his planned retirement at the end of the 2005-6 season, injury brought the curtain down on a fantastic playing career.

PETER SHILTON

Country: England
Born: September 18, 1949
Position: Goalkeeper
Clubs: Leicester City, Stoke City, Nottingham Forest, Southampton, Derby County, Plymouth Argyle, Wimbledon, Bolton Wanderers, Coventry City, West Ham United, Leyton Orient

Shilton is England's most capped player with 125 international appearances, yet his final tally could have been higher. For years he vied with Ray Clemence for the goalkeeper's jersey and it wasn't until his early 30s that Shilton clearly emerged as England's regular shot stopper.

Shilton enjoyed an extraordinarily long career: he played for England until the age of 40 and club football up to 48. He succeeded Gordon Banks, another England legend, at Leicester City when he was just 16 years of age but, although towards the end of his career he became increasingly nomadic, at club level his name is forever associated with Nottingham Forest, who enjoyed a fairytale story of success in the late 1970s. Under Brian Clough they won the league championship in 1978 at the first attempt after promotion to the top flight and went on to win back-to-back European Cups in 1979 and 1980.

When Ron Greenwood selected Shilton as his first choice goalkeeper for the 1982 World Cup it signalled the end of the Shilton-Clemence rivalry. For the next eight years and three eventful World Cups, Shilton would be a regular fixture in the England goal. He kept ten clean sheets in 17 World Cup matches, at one point holding the record for minutes played without conceding a goal, but he is most remembered for the two goals that Diego Maradona put past him in 1986: the first to a handball, the second to one of the greatest goals ever. He quit the international game after helping England to fourth place in the World Cup in Italy in 1990 but carried on playing club football down the divisions for the following seven years, ending his career at Leyton Orient.

DIEGO SIMEONE

Country: Argentina
Born: April 28, 1970
Position: Midfield
Clubs: Velez Sarsfield, Pisa, Sevilla, Atlético Madrid, Inter Milan, Lazio, Atlético Madrid, Racing Club

Diego Simeone is perhaps best remembered on the international stage for his role in the sending-off of England's David Beckham at the 1998 World Cup finals, but there is far more to the tough-tackling midfielder than that one moment of controversy. Making his international debut against Australia as far back as 1988, Simeone became the first Argentine player to win 100 caps for his country, a feat not even achieved by the great Diego Maradona. He was also part of his country's silver medal winning team at the 1996 Olympics. He made his last international appearance in Argentina's defeat to England at the 2002 World Cup.

In club football, he was a part of the Atlético Madrid side that won the Spanish league in 1996 and he scored the winner for Lazio in the 2000 Italian Cup final, helping them to a first league and cup double. After a second spell with Atlético, he returned to Buenos Aires to end his playing career with Racing Club, the team he supported as a child. On retiring in February 2006 he moved into coaching.

ALLAN SIMONSEN

Country: Denmark
Born: December 15, 1952
Position: Forward
Clubs: Vejle, Borussia Mönchengladbach, Barcelona, Charlton Athletic, Vejle

Simonsen was the man for the big occasion, scoring in the finals of all three major European club competitions. He was on target twice for Borussia Mönchengladbach in the 1975 UEFA Cup final and once in the 2-1 aggregate defeat of Red Star Belgrade in the 1979 UEFA Cup final, a season which saw him finish as the competition's top scorer with nine goals. He also netted in the 1977 European Cup final defeat against Liverpool and for Barcelona in the 1982 European Cup Winners' Cup final with Standard Liege, which the Spanish giants won 2-1. In 1977 he celebrated his third consecutive Bundesliga title along with the accolade of being named European Footballer Of The Year.

MATTHIAS SINDELAR

Country: Austria
Born: February 10, 1903
Position: Forward
Clubs: Hertha Vienna, FK Austria Vienna

A certain amount of mystery still surrounds the death of Matthias Sindelar, a slight man who was known on the football field as 'The Man of Paper'. Some sources have claimed that he was murdered for his anti-fascist beliefs at the time of the Anschluss, others that he committed suicide rather than live in Nazi-run Austria. But that he died of carbon monoxide poisoning remains the only certainty.

Sindelar was the star of Austria's talented 'Wunderteam' of the Thirties, falling to the hosts in the semi-finals of the 1934 World Cup in Italy. A knee injury almost ended his career before it began, and following surgery he was always easy to spot due to what became a trademark bandage on his right knee.

OMAR ENRIQUE SIVORI

Country: Argentina, Italy
Born: October 2, 1935
Position: Inside-left
Clubs: River Plate, Juventus, Napoli

Omar Enrique Sivori had a remarkable career, playing international football for Argentina, the country of his birth, and Italy. Sivori started at Argentinian club River Plate and established himself as an extremely gifted inside-left, playing for Argentina before Italian side Juventus paid a world record £91,000 for him in 1957. Defecting to Turin cost Sivori his international place with Argentina, but his club career took off spectacularly.

With Juventus he struck up a fabulous understanding with Welshman John Charles, and inspired the Bianconeri to a trio of league championships in 1958, 1960 and 1961. His personal contribution to these triumphs was significant. In the 1960 championship, he was the league's leading scorer with 27 goals from 31 games, and in 1961 he was named as the European Footballer Of The Year. In the following year he represented his adopted country in the 1962 World Cup, playing three times in the finals in Chile.

Sivori's glorious reign at Juve ended in 1965, but to this day he is fondly remembered as one of club's legends. He joined Napoli and played until a knee injury forced retirement in 1968.

Opposite: One of England's greatest goalscorers, Alan Shearer celebrates scoring against Luxembourg in 1999.

Below: A player for the big occasion, Barcelona's Allan Simonsen.

Above: Bulgarian legend Hristo Stoichkov of Barcelona in 1997.

JOSIP SKOBLAR

Country: Yugoslavia
Born: March 12, 1941
Position: Outside-left
Clubs: NK Zadar, OFK Belgrade, Marseille, Hanover 96, Marseille

Josip Skoblar became a legend at Marseille for his goalscoring exploits. Capable of playing on both wings or as a central forward, he struck 44 times in the 1970-1 season to win the European Golden Boot and help the club win the league. He topped the scoring charts the next year as they won the double and was league top scorer in 1972-3 for a third successive season.

He turned out for Yugoslavia at the 1962 World Cup when they reached the semi-finals, but in total he made only 35 appearances for his country because of a rule that prevented players based abroad playing for the national team. He will always be best remembered for his exploits at club level, particularly in France where he became known as Monsieur Goal.

SOCRATES

Country: Brazil
Born: February 19, 1954
Position: Midfield
Clubs: Botafogo, Corinthians, Fiorentina, Flamengo, Santos

An unlikely footballer, Socrates emanated from an educated middle-class background, and played as an amateur for Botafogo while studying for a medical degree. After qualifying as a doctor he put his stethoscope in storage and signed pro forms for São Paulo side Corinthians in 1977. A tall, lean and elegant midfielder, he captained his country with great distinction but limited success in the 1982 and 1986 World Cup finals. At the 1982 finals he scored a wondergoal against the Soviet Union, yet was unable to prevent his side being eliminated by eventual winners Italy. A similar pattern occurred four years later, where his mercurial performances were eclipsed by the pain of defeat in the quarter-finals against France. His brother Raí was a member of Brazil's 1994 World Cup-winning squad.

GUILLERMO STÁBILE

Country: Argentina, France
Born: January 17, 1906
Position: Forward
Clubs: Huracán, Genoa, Napoli, Red Star Paris

For many years Stábile had his name in the history books as the first player to score a World Cup hat-trick, until the USA staked the claim of Bert Patenaude. Stábile's hat-trick came in the inaugural tournament in 1930 when he helped Argentina to a 6-3 defeat of Mexico. He had begun the tournament as a reserve but his three goals earned him a regular place in the starting line-up. He proved he was no one-hit wonder by finishing the competition as leading scorer with eight goals. He scored and hit the woodwork in the final but ended up on the losing side. Stábile, whose game was based on blistering pace, also played for France after moving to Europe to play club football.

FRANK STAPLETON

Country: Republic Of Ireland
Born: July 10, 1956
Position: Forward
Clubs: Arsenal, Manchester United, Ajax, Derby County, Le Havre, Blackburn Rovers, Anderlecht, Huddersfield Town, Bradford City

Frank Stapleton was the Republic Of Ireland's all-time leading scorer, with 20 goals in 71 internationals until surpassed by both Niall Quinn and Robbie Keane. Stapleton also registered 149 goals at club level, leading the line admirably in a 17-year career for many outstanding sides. Strong and powerful in the air, he was a model professional who worked hard on his game after joining Arsenal as an apprentice in 1973. Signed by Manchester United for £900,000 in 1981, Stapleton became the first player to score for different teams in the FA Cup final. After leaving United in 1987 he failed to make an impact at Ajax and returned to England to finish a career that included appearances in five FA Cup finals.

HRISTO STOICHKOV

Country: Bulgaria
Born: August 2, 1966
Position: Midfield
Clubs: Plovdiv, CSKA Sofia, Barcelona, Parma, Al Nasr, CSKA Sofia, Kashiwa Reysol, Chicago Fire, DC United

Stoichkov came to prominence as an integral figure in the CSKA side that reached the semi-finals of the European Cup Winners' Cup in 1989. He also won the European Golden Boot award the following year, prompting Barcelona coach Johan Cruyff to splash out £3 million for his services. It proved to be an inspirational signing as Barça went on to win the European Cup for the first time. He also fired the club to five Spanish league titles between 1991 and 1997.

In the mid-Nineties Stoichkov was arguably the greatest footballer on the planet and at the 1994 World Cup he inspired Bulgaria to third place, winning the Golden Boot in the process. A temperamental player, his clash of personality with Johan Cruyff led to a brief spell with Parma in 1995, but he returned to inspire the Barça side under Louis Van Gaal before his playing career petered out with spells in the Middle East, Japan and USA. He took over as coach of the Bulgarian national team in 2004, but failed to take them to the 2006 World Cup.

LUIS SUAREZ

Country: Spain
Born: May 2, 1935
Position: Inside-forward
Clubs: Barcelona, Inter Milan, Sampdoria

Luis Suarez was one of the most gifted inside-forwards of his generation. Despite a fiery nature, he was voted European Footballer Of The Year in 1960, which led to Inter Milan to pay a staggering £210,000 to sign him the following year. He became Inter's midfield general and was influential in the European Cup-winning teams of 1964 and 1965. He was already a fully established international by the late 1950s but his moment of glory came when Spain won the 1964 European Championship. His Inter career came to an abrupt end when the club sold him to Sampdoria while he was on holiday in Spain. Aged 37 he was recalled to the injury-ravaged national team in 1972.

HAKAN SÜKÜR

Country: Turkey
Born: September 1, 1971
Position: Forward
Clubs: Sakaryaspoor, Bursaspor, Galatasaray, Torino, Galatasaray, Inter Milan, Parma, Blackburn Rovers, Galatasaray

Known as the 'Bull of the Bosphorus', Hakan Sükür is Turkey's greatest striker ever and a legend with Galatasaray supporters, having scored well over 200 goals during his three spells with the club, winning six championships and four Turkish cups, plus the 2000 UEFA Cup. However, Sükür struggled to make an impact abroad. He could not settle at Torino in the 1995-6 season and returned to Galatasaray, moving on to Inter Milan for £4.9 million in 2000,

and then to Parma in January 2002 after failing to hold down a regular first team place at the San Siro. He signed for Blackburn Rovers but broke his leg before he could make his debut, returning once again to Galatasaray having scored just twice in nine games for the English side.

The Turkish national team's top scorer, he was outstanding at Euro 2000, but he laboured at the 2002 World Cup, scoring only once – in the third place place play-off. Ilhan Mansiz latched on to a Korean blunder and Sükür scored, timed at 10.8 seconds, it was the fastest ever goal in World Cup history. Such is his fame in Turkey that his wedding in 2002 was televised. He made his 100th appearance for his country in a World Cup qualifier in September 2005, the third Turkish player to pass this milestone.

Left: Scorer of the fastest goal in World Cup history, Turkey's Hakan Sukur at the World Cup in 2002.

JEAN TIGANA

Country: France
Born: June 23, 1955
Position: Midfield
Clubs: Toulon, Lyon, Bordeaux, Marseille

Jean Tigana became a star in the 1980s when a glorious France side ruled Europe and shone as one of the greatest teams on earth, despite never managing to win the ultimate trophy, the World Cup. His tireless performances for Les Bleus, notably at the World Cup finals in 1982 and 1986, and at the European Championship that France won on home soil in 1984, made him hugely admired the world over.

Born in Mali, Tigana moved to France aged just three years old. Starting his professional career at Toulon, having been spotted playing part-time while working in a spaghetti factory and as a postman, he went on to make his name at Lyon before joining Bordeaux for £2 million in 1980. He played successfully there under the coaching of Aimé Jacquet, winning the French league championship in 1984, 1985 and 1987, and the French Cup in 1986 and 1987.

Tigana made his international debut in 1980 and became a fixture in the line-up alongside fellow midfielders Michel Platini, Alain Giresse and Luis Fernandez. Slight and wiry, he was a prodigious worker and a great reader of the game. His most famous moment came during the 1984 European Championship when he ran half the length of the pitch deep in extra-time and crossed for Platini to score the winning goal in the 3-2 semi-final victory over Portugal. He won 52 caps for France, scoring one goal.

Tigana finished his career at Marseille, adding league titles in 1990 and 1991, before moving into coaching at Lyon, whom to took to second in the league in his second season. He took over from Arsene Wenger at Monaco in 1995 and has subsequently enjoyed spells with Lyon, Marseille, Fulham and Besiktas.

JAN TOMASZEWSKI

Country: Poland
Born: January 9, 1948
Position: Goalkeeper
Clubs: Legia Warsaw, LKS Lodz, Beerschot, Hercules

Brian Clough dubbed him 'a clown' in 1973, but after the Polish goalkeeper's memorable performance that kept England from the World Cup finals, no-one in England was laughing. Tomaszewski made his international debut in 1971 but his fifth game was a home victory over England in a World Cup qualifier. Poland were not expected to survive the return leg at Wembley, but held out for a crucial 1-1 draw with Tomaszewski pulling off a string of improbable saves.

At the finals in West Germany, Poland demonstrated the result was no fluke as Tomaszewski conceded just five goals and saved two penalties on the way to third place. Two years later he won a silver medal at the 1976 Olympics and returned for the 1978 World Cup. His 59 appearances for Poland in total make him his country's most capped goalkeeper. The communist regime finally let him move abroad to Belgium in 1978, before subsequently moving to Spain. He retired in 1982 and entered sports journalism.

TOSTÃO

Country: Brazil
Born: January 25, 1947
Position: Forward
Clubs: Cruzeiro, Vasco Da Gama

Tostão played in two successive World Cup tournaments for Brazil – in 1966 and 1970 – but in between faced the biggest challenge of his career when he battled against a serious eye injury. The striker needed surgery to repair

a detached retina and, though the problem eventually took its toll, he recovered to win the 1970 World Cup. As a member of the Brazilian team regarded as the greatest of all time, Tostão played in all six matches, where he was joined in a fearsome forward line by Pelé, Jairzinho and Rivelino. Although he didn't score in the final, he will be remembered for the cross which led to Brazil's winner against England, and his two goals against Peru in the quarter-finals. His eye injury eventually forced him into early retirement.

Below: A member of France's magical midfield, Jean Tigana in 1986.

CARLOS VALDERRAMA

Country: Colombia
Born: September 2, 1961
Position: Midfield
Clubs: Santa Marta, Millonarios, Atlético Nacional, Montpellier, Real Valladolid, Medellin, Atletico Junior Barranquilla, Tampa Bay Mutiny, Miami Fusion, Tampa Bay Mutiny, Colorado Rapids

Carlos Valderrama's crazy hair overshadowed a special football talent. An elegant player, during the Nineties, Valderrama orchestrated Colombia's play from midfield with an unhurried air and he is rightly recognised as the country's best-ever player. Making his first international appearance in a 3-0 defeat to Paraguay in October 1985, it wasn't long before he was captaining the side. Twice South American Footballer Of The Year, he played in three World Cups between 1990 and 1998 and became the first Colombian to pass the 100-cap mark, eventually finishing with 111 international appearances and 11 goals.

Nicknamed 'El Pibe' (The Kid), Valderrama perhaps didn't deliver as often as he should have done through his career. Aside from his stint in the USA, he didn't shine outside his native country at club level, and in 1994, when great things were expected of Colombia at the World Cup (they had beaten Argentina 5-0 in Buenos Aires during qualification), the team didn't get past the first round.

MARCO VAN BASTEN

Country: Holland
Born: October 31, 1964
Position: Centre-forward
Clubs: Ajax, AC Milan

Some goals are so stunning they will never be forgotten. Marco Van Basten scored such a goal. During the 1988 European Championship final against the Soviet Union, Arnold Muhren hoisted a high ball towards the penalty area, Van Basten met the ball as it dropped, and from a tight angle sent a volley screaming into the net. It clinched the trophy for the Dutch and set the seal on a tournament of great personal success for the striker. Van Basten had earlier destroyed England with a hat-trick in the group stage and beaten Germany with a semi-final winner.

After astounding performances for Ajax – he once scored 37 goals in a season – he joined Italian giants AC Milan in 1987. Even in Serie A, the goals didn't dry up and the Dutchman helped Milan to league glory in 1988, 1992 and 1993, and European Cup wins in 1989 (when he scored twice) and 1990. But against Marseille in the 1993 final, Van Basten sustained an ankle injury that forced his retirement before the age of 30. He went into management and was coach of Holland at the 2006 World Cup.

WIM VAN HANEGEM

Country: Holland
Born: February 20, 1944
Position: Midfielder
Clubs: Velox, Xerxes/DHC, Feyenoord, AZ 67, Chicago Sting, FC Utrecht, Feyenoord.

Wim Van Hanegem was a gifted left-footed midfielder who made his name with European Cup-winning Feyenoord and the stylish Dutch side of the 1974 World Cup. Perceived as arrogant, Van Hanegem commanded midfield with his vision, precision and power that made his lack of pace seem like an asset. He played 52 times for Holland but missed out on the 1978 World Cup after a disagreement with the coach on the eve of the tournament.

PAUL VAN HIMST

Country: Belgium
Born: October 2, 1943
Position: Forward
Clubs: Anderlecht, RWD Molenbeek, Eendracht Aalst

Paul Van Himst is arguably the most decorated player in Belgian history. Four times the Belgian Player Of The Year, he made 81 appearances for the national side, scoring 30 goals. A product of the Anderlecht youth team, Van Himst made his club debut at the age of 16 and just a year later he was drafted into the national side. A technically outstanding and elegant player, he was so highly regarded that he was once dubbed 'the White Pelé'. He won the Belgian title eight times with Anderlecht and later led them as coach to UEFA Cup success in 1983.

OBDULIO VARELA

Country: Uruguay
Born: September 20, 1917
Position: Centre-half
Clubs: Wanderers, Peñarol

Obdulio Varela, a gifted attacking centre-half, was the inspiration behind Uruguay's 1950 World Cup triumph. In the decisive match against hosts Brazil, team captain Varela magnificently held his defence firm against relentless Brazilian attacks. After the break he drove his team forward and helped them turn a single goal deficit into a shock 2-1 win to lift the Jules Rimet trophy. Varela was in charge again for his swansong four years later when Uruguay finished third in Switzerland. He was injured shortly after scoring in the quarter-final victory against England and missed the semi-final defeat against Hungary.

He had won his first international honour aged 24 in Uruguay's triumphant 1942 Copa América team. He was subsequently signed by Peñarol, with whom he won six league titles.

VELIBOR VASOVIC

Country: Yugoslavia
Born: October 3, 1939
Position: Left-Half
Clubs: Partizan Belgrade, Red Star Belgrade, Partizan Belgrade, Ajax

Velibor Vasovic captained Ajax to their 1971 European Cup success, beating Panathinaikos 2-0 in the final at Wembley. It was third time lucky for Vasovic after featuring in the losing side for Partizan in 1966 and Ajax in 1969. Vasavic subsequently retired after the 1972 triumph, ending a career in which he had won five successive Yugoslav championships with two different clubs (Partizan 1961, 1962, 1963, 1965; Red Star 1964) and followed up with three Dutch league title and three Dutch Cups. He also made 34 appearances for Yugoslavia.

VAVÁ

Country: Brazil
Born: November 12, 1934
Position: Forward
Clubs: Recife, Vasco Da Gama, Atlético Madrid, Palmeiras, América, Elche, Toros Neza, San Diego Toros

Real name Edvaldo Izidio Neto, Vavá originally played as a winger but converted to centre-forward to accommodate Pelé in the 1958 Brazil starting line-up. Curiously underused, he only played 20 full internationals spread over a decade – scoring 15 goals – but he was the ultimate big stage player. He scored two of Brazil's five goals in the 1958 World Cup final victory against Sweden, and another in the 3-1 win over the Czechs in 1962. At club level his spell at Atlético Madrid was successful in terms of goals, but cut short due to homesickness.

GIANLUCA VIALLI

Country: Italy
Born: July 9, 1964
Position: Forward
Clubs: Cremonese, Sampdoria, Juventus, Chelsea

Vialli started his career with hometown club Cremonese, before joining Sampdoria in 1984. His eight seasons with the Genoa-based side coincided with the most successful period in their history. Sampdoria won three Italian Cups, the European Cup Winners' Cup in 1990 and enjoyed a first league title in 1991, Vialli scoring 19 goals in 26 games. He signed for Juventus for £12 million in 1992 and his success story continued, captaining the side to European Cup glory against Ajax in 1996. He joined Chelsea the same year, winning both the League Cup and European Cup Winners' Cup in 1998 as player-coach and the FA Cup in 2000 as coach.

Opposite: Vavá celebrates scoring Brazil's third goal in the 1962 World Cup final.

IVO VIKTOR

Country: Czechoslovakia
Born: May 21, 1942
Position: Goalkeeper
Club: Dukla Prague

Ivo Viktor will always be remembered for his magnificent performances for Czechoslovakia on their way to winning the 1976 European Championship, an achievement that helped him to third in the European Player Of The Year Award, behind Beckenbauer and Rensenbrink. The keeper, who was never booked in his career, was outstanding in the two-legged quarter-final clash with the Soviet Union, equally superb in both the semi-final against Holland and in the final against West Germany, where he made the decisive save in a 5-4 penalty shoot-out win. In that year he was voted the Czech Player Of The Year for the fifth time. Hffle played 63 times for his country, making his debut at the Maracanã Stadium against Brazil.

RUDI VÖLLER

Country: West Germany, Germany
Born: March 13, 1960
Position: Forward
Clubs: Stuttgart Kickers, Munich 1860, Werder Bremen, Roma, Marseille, Bayer Leverkusen

A classic poacher, Rudi Völler is remembered as much for his bubble perm and the spittle Frank Rijkaard deposited in it in 1990. He began his career in 1978 with Stuttgart Kickers but established his reputation as a top predator with Werder Bremen, being named German Footballer Of The Year in 1982. He joined Roma in 1987 where he scored 69 goals in 197 appearances and reached a UEFA Cup final. He left for Marseille in 1992, winning the European Cup before finishing at Bayer Leverkusen.

England captain Billy Wright with Wolverhampton Wanderers in the 1949-50 season.

Playing 90 times for his country, and with 47 goals, Völler ranks only behind Gerd Müller as his nation's top scorer. Having made his international debut in 1982, he came on to score the equaliser that took the 1986 World Cup final with Argentina to extra-time. Four years later he was a winner when West Germany had their revenge in a scrappy final.

Despite his lack of managerial experience he was appointed national manager in 2000 and surprised doubters by taking the team to the final of the 2002 World Cup.

FRITZ WALTER

Country: West Germany
Born: October 31, 1920
Position: Midfield/Forward
Club: Kaiserslautern

Only Franz Beckenbauer outranks Fritz Walter in the list of German football legends. Making his debut for home town club Kaiserslautern in 1937, Walter remained there for his entire career, playing 379 games and scoring an impressive 306 goals. He won two league titles in 1951 and 1953 with the club, top-scoring in the latter campaign with 38 goals. In 1985 Kaiserslautern recognised his achievements by renaming their stadium after him.

Walter made his international debut in 1940, scoring a hat-trick against Romania, but World War II interrupted his career. In 1948 he returned to football, now alongside his brother Ottmar. At the age of 33, national team coach Sepp Herberger made him captain of the West German team for the 1954 World Cup in Switzerland. Walter scored three goals in the tournament, and his brother two, as the West Germans came back from a disastrous start against Hungary to win the final in the 'Miracle of Berne', making them the first siblings to win a World Cup.

Walter led his team again at the 1958 World Cup in Sweden, this time losing at the semi-final stage to the hosts. He retired the following year after 61 matches and 33 goals, but could have gone to Chile in 1962 had he listened to Herberger's entreaties. As Germany closed in on another World Cup final in June 2002, Walter died aged 81.

GEORGE WEAH

Country: Liberia
Born: October 1, 1966
Position: Centre-forward
Clubs: Young Survivors, Bongrang, Mighty Barolle, Tonnerre de Yaoundé, Monaco, Paris Saint-Germain, AC Milan, Chelsea, Manchester City, Marseille

Although born in Liberia, Weah holds French citizenship and played for many different clubs in five different countries. He helped Monaco win the French league title in 1991 and repeated the trick with Paris Saint-Germain in 1995. The striker's most successful period came in Italy with AC Milan, who he joined for £3.5 million in 1995, his goals firing the club to the Serie A title in both 1996 and 1999. The former African, European and World Footballer Of The Year, Weah was also part of the Chelsea team which won the FA Cup in 2000, the last one ever to be staged at the old Wembley Stadium.

Weah was also very well known for his charity work. He acted as a goodwill ambassador for UNICEF and also provided substantial financial support to the Liberian national team. He stood for the Presidency of Liberia in 2005 but his bid failed at the polls.

ERNEST WILIMOWSKI

Country: Poland, Germany
Born: June 23, 1916
Position: Inside-Left
Clubs: Katowice, Ruch Wielkie Hajduki, PSV Chemnitz, 1860 Munich, Chemnitz West, Hameln, Detmond, Augsburg, Offenburg, Singen, Kaiserslautern, Kehl

Ernest Wilimowski's name has gone down in football history as the player who scored four goals in a World Cup match but still end up on the losing side! Wilimowski was in the Poland team beaten 6-5 by Brazil at 1938 World Cup. A prolific goalscorer, he netted 21 goals in 22 appearances for Poland. Invasion by Germany saw Wilimoski become a German citizen and during the war he scored 13 goals in eight games for Germany. In the Polish league he scored 112 goals in 86 games, including a ten-goal haul in Ruch's 12-1 thrashing of Union-Touring Lodz.

BILLY WRIGHT

Country: England
Born: February 6, 1924
Position: Centre-half
Club: Wolverhampton Wanderers

One of the most celebrated footballers of his day, Billy Wright joined the Wolverhampton Wanderers ground staff as a boy in 1938 and stayed at Molineux in a one-club career that spanned 13 seasons and 490 appearances. During his tenure at the club he led them to FA Cup success in 1949, and three league titles in the 1950s. He was hardly the tallest centre-half in the world, but he still managed to command the game both in the air and on the ground. Wright's popularity wasn't confined to the Black Country either, and as an automatic pick for the national team, he was captain of his country for 90 of the 105 games in which he played, leading England in three World Cup campaigns: 1950, 1954 and 1958. He died of cancer in North London on September 3, 1994.

Above: Bobby Smith sees his effort stopped by Yashin in an England v Rest Of The World XI match. Below: Soviet hero Yashin playing England again, this time for his country in 1958.

LEV YASHIN

Country: Soviet Union
Born: October 22, 1929
Position: Goalkeeper
Club: Dynamo Moscow

Goalkeeping legends don't come much larger or imposing than Lev Yashin. Dressed in black, possessed of huge hands and, according to Gordon Banks, 'fingers the size of bananas', his nickname, the 'Black Spider' (also the 'Black Panther'), was not hard to fathom.

Lev Ivanovich Yashin went to work in the same Moscow tool factory as his father at the age of 13 and played in goal for their football team. He was spotted by Dynamo Moscow but was on the verge of taking up a career as keeper for the club's ice hockey team when an injury to first choice football goalkeeper Aleksei 'Tiger' Khomich opened the door for him. He made his league debut in 1949 and went on to play 326 matches for the club, staying for a total of 22 years and winning five league championships and three cups.

Yashin is seen as the greatest goalkeeper in the history of the game and the first of the modern era. Extremely vocal, he kept his defence constantly on its toes and was one of the first goalkeepers to venture out of his area to kick the ball away. His huge throws helped launch rapid counter-attacks and he was also a penalty specialist, saving 150 in his career.

In 1963 he was named European Footballer Of The Year after letting in a miserly 14 goals in 38 league games, the only time the award has ever gone to a goalkeeper.

Yashin made his debut for the Soviet Union on September 8, 1954, in a 6-0 win over Sweden. In 1956 he won a gold medal with the Soviet team at the Melbourne Olympics, marking the beginning of a golden era for Soviet football. Yashin proved instrumental in securing the Soviet Union its only major trophy of the modern era, making a string of crucial saves in the inaugural European Nations Cup in 1960 to deny Yugoslavia. Four years later he was still between the posts when the Soviets were runners-up.

Yashin was also instrumental in taking the Soviet Union to the quarter-finals of the World Cups of 1958 and 1962, where they were eliminated by the hosts on both occasions. However, he was blamed for both goals against Chile in 1962 and he subsequently went into premature retirement.

Four years later he was back at the World Cup in England as the side recorded its best performance in the tournament, reaching the semi-finals and losing narrowly to West Germany with ten men. Named in the squad for the 1970 World Cup in Mexico, he would have set new records had he appeared in a match. In total he won 78 caps.

By the time of his retirement Yashin was regarded as a Soviet national hero to rank

alongside cosmonaut Yuri Gagarin. He received the Order Of Lenin and Honoured Master Of Soviet Sport, and in 1971 some 120,000 spectators turned up for his final testimonial game between Dynamo Moscow and a Rest Of The World XI.

Sadly he suffered pain from a knee injury in his later years and had a leg amputated in 1986. He died on March 20, 1990, following complications from surgery. To celebrate his achievements in 1994 FIFA introduced the Lev Yashin Award for the best goalkeeper at the World Cup. Its recipients so far have included Michel Preud'Homme of Belgium, France's Fabian Barthez, Germany's Oliver Khan and Italy's Gianluigi Buffon.

1946: Joins Dynamo Moscow ice hockey team as a goaltender.

1953: Opting for football, establishes himself as Dynamo Moscow's first-choice goalkeeper.

1954: Wins first of 78 caps for the Soviets in a 3-2 victory against Sweden.

1956: Forms part of the Soviet Union's Olympic gold medal winning team in Melbourne.

1959: Wins Soviet championship with Dynamo Moscow.

1960: Wins his first European Championship with the Soviet Union, with a 2-1 victory against Yugoslavia in the final.

1963: The 'Black Panther' is named European Footballer Of The Year.

1964: Soviet Union are beaten by Spain in the European Championship final.

1966: Stars in World Cup, as Soviet Union reach semi-finals.

1968: Receives the Order Of Lenin awarded by the Soviet government.

1970: Retires from the game with a testimonial match watched by 120,000 at the Lenin Stadium in Moscow.

1986: Has leg amputated after complications with a knee injury.

1990: Lev Yashin passes away on March 20 at the age of 60.

MARIO ZAGALO

Country: Brazil
Born: August 9, 1931
Position: Left-winger
Club: Botafogo

Mario Zagalo's name is synonymous with the World Cup, and he is the most successful individual in the history of the tournament, having won it on four occasions with Brazil in various roles. In 1958 he played in his country's World Cup team as a left-winger. An intelligent player, Zagalo had a great match against Sweden in the final, scoring the fourth goal and creating Pelé's second of the match as Brazil ran out 5-2 winners. He struck gold again in 1962, having dropped back to midfield and assuming a harder working role (he was known as 'the Little Ant' for his industry on the pitch). Ultimately it was his versatility that converted Brazil from the 4-2-4 formation to their trademark 4-3-3 playing style. In 1970, Zagalo coached one of the greatest attacking teams in World Cup history to success, and in 1994 he repeated the trick as technical adviser to coach Carlos Alberto.

Below: Brazil's Zico in action against Argentina at the 1982 World Cup.

IVAN ZAMARANO

Country: Chile
Born: January 18, 1967
Position: Forward
Clubs: Cobresal, St Gallen, Seville, Real Madrid, Inter Milan, América, Colo Colo

Ivan Luis Zamarano Zamora was one of the greatest footballers to have played for Chile, scoring 34 goals in his 69 international appearances for the country, which included reaching the second round of the 1998 World Cup finals. At the 2000 Olympics he was also in Chile's bronze medal-winning team, brought in at the last minute to replace the injured Marcelo Salas as one of the three overaged players permissible in the largely youth competition. He scored both goals in the team's 2-0 win over the US to claim the bronze medal. He had a successful 13-year club career in Europe, including Real Madrid's 1995 Spanish championship-winning season, in which Zamarano finished top scorer with 27 goals.

RICARDO ZAMORA

Country: Spain
Born: January 21, 1901
Position: Goalkeeper
Clubs: Espanyol, Barcelona, Espanyol, Real Madrid, OGC Nizza

Zamora was the first hero of Spanish football, making 46 appearances for Spain, a record that lasted for 38 years. He also became the first goalkeeper to save a World Cup penalty, against Brazil in 1934. His first club was Espanyol, the city of Barcelona's 'other team', and after a short stint with Barça he returned to Espanyol and then completed a record-breaking transfer to Real Madrid. He won two titles and two Spanish cups at Real, having already won the cup twice with Barça and once with Espanyol. He retired in 1936 after moving to France at the start of the Spanish Civil War. He moved into coaching with Atlético Madrid, and later took over at Espanyol. He also had a period in charge of the Spain. Fittingly it was in his home city of Barcelona that Zamora died at the age of 77.

ZICO

Country: Brazil
Born: March 3, 1953
Position: Forward/Midfield
Clubs: Flamengo, Udinese, Flamengo, Kashima Antlers

The great Zico represented Brazil in three consecutive World Cups from 1978, and was seen at his best in Spain in 1982 where he was the outstanding player of the tournament. One of the game's greatest ever dead-ball strikers, he scored with one of his speciality free-kicks on his debut against Uruguay in 1977. He went on to add a further 51 goals to this total in his 72 internationals, to leave himself second only behind Pelé in Brazil's all-time goalscoring list. A wiry, dynamic yet tricky forward, he was just as adept at setting up his centre-forward as he was finding the goal for himself.

At club level he inspired Flamengo to victory in the Copa Libertadores in 1981, and was almost single-handedly responsible for the subsequent undoing of Liverpool in the World Club Cup in the same year. After the 1982 World Cup finals he moved to Italy's Udinese, and was voted World Footballer Of The Year in 1983. He added this title to the three South American Player Of The Year awards he already possessed.

After a spell as Brazil's Minister of Sport, he joined Kashima Antlers at the start of the J-League in 1993. He took over as the coach of the Japan after the 2002 World Cup and took them to the 2006 World Cup finals, before resigning to become coach of Fenerbahçe.

ZINÉDINE ZIDANE

Country: France
Born: June 23, 1972
Position: Midfield
Clubs: Cannes, Bordeux, Juventus, Real Madrid

It is impossible to overstate the talent that Zinédine Zidane possessed. At the height of his powers the Marseille-born midfielder was quite rightly mentioned in the same breath as Puskás, Pelé, Cruyff and Maradona, and in the modern game he was just untouchable. His awareness on the ball, his sublime skill, peerless touch, and his unmatched big-game mentality marked him out as a genuine footballing superstar.

The world first took note of Zidane in 1996 when, as the master of Bordeaux's midfield, his incisive passing and instinctive skill inspired the French side to the UEFA Cup final. Bayern Munich scuppered their hopes of glory but for Zidane, it marked the entrance to football's hall of fame. The same summer he was bought by Italian giants Juventus and helped the club to the Serie A title. Appearances in consecutive Champions League finals underlined what every football fan knew about his exceptional talent, but at France 98 he bettered that, inspiring his country to World Cup triumph. Despite blotting his copy book early on in the tournament with an ugly stamping incident, 'Zizou' ran rings around the world's best players and scored the two goals that killed off Brazil in the final.

It was no surprise, after his superlative performance on the world's biggest stage, that the game's top honours soon came his way – in 1998 FIFA announce Zidane as their World Player Of The Year. The honour was repeated in 2000, but, as is fitting for such a talent, an even greater compliment was soon to be bestowed upon him. In the summer of 2001, Zidane became the world's most expensive player. It was Real Madrid who lured him away from Juventus, and they did it with the kind of deal that the game will probably never see again. The exact figure paid is still unclear, and the arrangements for payment were typically complicated, but the most accurate estimates put it at around £45 million.

The unassuming playmaker continued to demonstrate his utter genius on the world stage, and although injury prevented him from rescuing France's 2002 World Cup campaign from disaster, the volley that he scored to win the Champions League earlier the same year was a perpetual reminder of the sheer class of the man. He retired from international football after the 2004 European Championship, but in August 2005 he was encouraged to make a comeback after France struggled in their World Cup qualification campaign.

After an injury plagued season at Real Madrid, he announced that he would retire after the 2006 World Cup, but it was to be a sad ending to an illustrious career. In the World Cup final against Italy he converted a seventh minute penalty and by half-time in the game the world's press had voted him the tournament's best player. However, after the game went into extra-time he was sent-off for violent conduct, goaded into butting Italian defender Marco Materazzi in the chest. Minutes after the world saw the last of Zidane, France lost the World Cup on penalties.

DINO ZOFF

Country: Italy
Born: February 28, 1942
Position: Goalkeeper
Clubs: Udinese, Mantova, Napoli, Juventus

One of the finest goalkeepers of all-time, Zoff's career is packed with honours. He captained Italy to World Cup glory in Spain in 1982, held the Italian record for international appearances (112, with 59 as captain) and between 1973 and 1974 went 1,142 minutes without conceding a goal (an international record).

Initially rejected as a 14-year-old by Inter Milan and Juventus for being too small, he first signed professional forms with Udinese in 1961. But on his debut he was beaten five times by Fiorentina and the club were soon relegated. A more successful spell at Mantova followed, but it was at Napoli that Zoff's career truly took off, leading to an international call-up.

He made his debut for Italy in a European Championship quarter-final match against Bulgaria in April 1968, and he retained his place as the Italians went on to win the tournament. At the 1970 World Cup he missed the chance of playing in another final as Albertosi was selected at first choice keeper. Zoff then joined Juventus in 1972, and went on to win six titles, two Italian cups and a UEFA Cup in 11 years at the club. His only major career disappointment was that he never won the European Cup,

despite reaching the final twice.

He retired from playing as a 40-year-old in 1982, going on to coach Italy's Olympic team, Juventus and Lazio, before taking the Italian senior team all the way to the final of the European Championship in 2000, where after leading until the last minute of the game, they were beaten by France in extra-time, provoking his immediate resignation.

GIANFRANCO ZOLA

Country: Italy
Born: July 5, 1966
Position: Inside-forward
Clubs: Nuorese, Torres, Napoli, Parma, Chelsea, Cagliari

Learning his trade as Diego Maradona's understudy at Napoli in the early Nineties, Sardinian-born Gianfranco Zola soon became known as a creative but hard-working attacker with a speciality in long-range free-kicks. He joined Parma in 1993, and helped them lift the Super Cup in 1994 and beat Juventus over two legs to win the UEFA Cup in 1995. Following his countrymen Gianluca Vialli and Roberto Di Matteo to Chelsea in December 1996 for £4.5 million proved to be a great move for Zola. He came off the bench to score the London side's winner in the final of the Cup Winners' Cup against Stuttgart in 1998, and in 2003 fans voted him the club's best ever player.

His international career has been one of few highlights. He is probably best remembered for missing a penalty at Euro 96 that effectively eliminated Italy from the tournament. He was also sent-off in a World Cup game against Nigeria in 1994, minutes after coming on as a substitute. But neither incident should

overshadow his superb winner in a World Cup qualifier against England at Wembley in 1997.

In July 2003 he decided to return home to Sardinia to fulfil a promise to end his career with his local team, Serie B side Cagliari. In his first year he helped them to promotion to Serie A, and the following season ensured that the club reached the semi-final of the Italian cup and a secured mid-table finish in the league before retiring just days shy of his 39th birthday in June 2005. The previous year he had been awarded an OBE for services to British football.

ANDONI ZUBIZARRETA

Country: Spain
Born: October 23, 1961
Position: Goalkeeper
Clubs: Athletic Bilbao, Barcelona, Valencia

In January 1985 Andoni Zubizarreta made his international debut for Spain against Finland. Some 13 years later he played his 126th game for his country, capping an incredible career which included appearances in four separate World Cup tournaments – in 1986, 1990, 1994 and 1998. He started out with Athletic Bilbao, winning two Spanish titles, before switching to Barcelona and enjoying the most successful spell of his club career. As well as further domestic honours, Zubizarreta triumphed in Europe, with Barça winning the European Cup Winners' Cup in 1989 and the European Cup in 1992, both times against Sampdoria.

Zubizarreta left the Nou Camp in 1994 to join Valencia but continued to defy the years with top-level performances. He bowed out of international football after captaining Spain in the 1998 World Cup at the age of 37.

Above: Zinédine Zidane of France celebrates scoring his second goal in the 1998 World Cup final.

GREAT PLAYERS OF TODAY

Above: Adriano fends off a Roma challenge while playing for Inter.

ADRIANO

Country: Brazil
Born: February 17, 1982
Position: Centre-forward
Clubs: Flamengo, Inter Milan, Fiorentina, Parma, Inter Milan

Leite Ribeiro Adriano first caught the eye at the 1999 FIFA Under-17 World Championship, where his strength, agility and balance caught the eye of many watching scouts. Having later top-scored for Brazil with six goals at the 2001 World Youth Championships, he was transferred to Inter Milan for £18 million, scoring a ferocious free-kick on his debut in a friendly game against Real Madrid. Following loan spells at Fiorentina and Parma, he returned to Inter Milan in 2005, scoring 15 goals in 16 appearances. Adriano won the 2004 Copa América with Brazil, where he was named Player Of The Tournament. He also won the 2005 Confederations Cup. He was the top scorer at both events. At the 2006 World Cup he scored Brazil's 200th World Cup goal.

PABLO AIMAR

Country: Argentina
Born: November 3, 1979
Position: Midfield
Clubs: River Plate, Valencia

Pablo Cesar Aimar, son of Newell's Old Boys' Ricardo Aimar, made his name at River Plate as an excellent playmaker. At 18 he inherited the great Uruguayan Enzo Francescoli's number 10 shirt. Aimar, dubbed 'The Little Clown', was part of Argentina's triumphant 1997 World Youth Cup team. In 2000, Valencia coach Hector Cuper signed the 21-year-old for £13.6 million. He went on to win the Spanish league twice, played in the European Champions League final in his first season and then lifted the UEFA Cup in 2004. In June

Right: Micahel Ballack in action for Germany.

2000 he made his international debut against Bolivia and was also voted Argentina's Player Of The Year. Aimar played in Argentina's ill-fated 2002 World Cup attempt, while four years later an attack of acute meningitis threatened his participation at the 2006 World Cup but he recovered in time to make the squad.

SAMI AL-JABER

Country: Saudi Arabia
Born: December 11, 1972
Position: Forward
Clubs: Al Hilal, Wolverhampton Wanderers, Al Hilal

Discovered as a 15-year-old by Al Hilal, Sami Al-Jaber has been Saudi Arabia's golden boy. He has won the Saudi championship on four occasions, in 1996, 1998, 2002 and 2005 (a league and cup double), and the Asian Cup Winners' Cup in 1997 and 2002. For Saudi Arabia he played in four successive World Cups until 2006 and also lifted the Asian Cup in 1996. At his height he was an attacking player who ran at defenders and was one of the most feared strikers in Asia.

MICHAEL BALLACK

Country: Germany
Born: September 29, 1976
Position: Midfield
Clubs: BSG Motor Karl-Marx-Stadt, Chemnitzer FC, Kaiserslautern, Bayer Leverkusen, Bayern Munich, Chelsea

Chelsea got the deal of the century when they signed Michael Ballack on a free transfer from Bayern Munich in May 2006. In his native Germany he is revered as a skilful goalscoring midfielder for both club and country. Ballack has played at the highest level of German football from a young age, having won the 1998 Bundesliga title with Kaiserslautern, steered Bayer Leverkusen to a European Cup final in 2002, and spearheaded Bayern Munich to three league and cup doubles: the first in 2003, then as captain in 2005, and once again in 2006. He has been voted Germany's Player Of The Year on three occasions.

He missed the 2002 World Cup final through suspension but still managed to score the winning goal in the semi-final clash with South Korea. For the 2006 World Cup he was captain, the Germans reaching the semi-finals.

FABIEN BARTHEZ

Country: France
Born: June 28, 1971
Position: Goalkeeper
Clubs: Toulouse, Marseille, Monaco, Manchester United, Marseille

Ever the extrovert, Barthez has won all the major honours in the game, with domestic titles in both France and England and success in the European Cup with Marseille. He played a leading role in helping France to the magnificent double of the World Cup on home soil in 1998 and the European Championship in 2000. Superbly athletic and excellent at distributing the ball from the hand or with his feet, he is one of the most entertaining goalkeepers in the game. The son of a top class rugby player, in 2005 Barthez was banned for six months for spitting at a referee. He fought off the challenge of Gregory Coupet to once again become France's first-choice goalkeeper, reaching the 2006 World Cup final, but he failed to stop any of Italy's spot-kicks in the deciding shoot-out.

DAVID BECKHAM

Country: England
Born: May 2, 1975
Position: Right midfield
Clubs: Manchester United, Real Madrid

On the opening day of the 1996-7 season David Beckham chipped the opposition keeper from the halfway line, and in scoring the type of goal that had eluded even Pelé, he began his inexorable rise to football superstardom. The London-born Manchester United trainee's subsequent marriage to Spice Girl, Victoria Adams, did little to take the media spotlight off him. His assured performances and long-range goals helped United to the Premier League title that season, and earned him a place in Glenn Hoddle's England team.

Despite rattling in a trademark free-kick against Colombia in the World Cup group stages, France 98 was a personal disaster for Beckham, who was sent-off against Argentina for a petulant kick at Diego Simeone in his country's narrow quarter-final defeat. As a result, the Manchester United number 7 was made into a national pariah, and booed by

opposing fans whenever he played for his club the following season.

A testament to his strength of character, the barracking failed to have a detrimental effect on his football. Beckham played a vital role in United's 1999 treble-winning team (Premier League, FA Cup and Champions League), his efforts also earning him second place behind Rivaldo in the voting for both the World and European Player Of The Year awards. His main attributes are his fantastic range of passing and crossing, coupled with a world-class ability at free-kicks. However, his game is also based on tireless running, a steely determination, and a ferocious will to win.

Caretaker England manager Peter Taylor rewarded his accomplishments with the England captaincy for a friendly against Italy in November 2000, and 'Becks' was to retain the armband with the appointment of Sven-Göran Eriksson. The winning goal in the 2002 World Cup qualifier against Finland at Anfield signalled the start of David Beckham's rehabilitation from scapegoat to national hero, the culmination of which was a remarkable individual performance against Greece at Old Trafford, where he scored the last-ditch free-

kick equaliser that took England to the World Cup in Japan. It also landed him the BBC's coveted Sports Personality Of The Year Award.

A broken metatarsal received in a game against Deportivo La Coruña threatened Beckham's participation in the tournament, and his lack of fitness hampered much of his play. However, he was still able to gain a degree of revenge when he slotted home the winning penalty against Argentina. Much speculation about a move to Spanish giants Real Madrid surrounded Beckham at the end of the 2003 season, but he still managed to pick up a sixth league winner's medal with United before moving to the Spanish giants. Although popular in Spain, his time at the Bernabéu has coincided with an unexpected lack of success by Madrid, who have been eclipsed by a revival of arch enemies Barcelona.

Beckham captained a disappointing England at the 2006 World Cup where he became the first Englishman to score at three World Cups. He led the side to the quarter-finals but, after he had left the pitch through injury, England lost on penalties to Portugal. He resigned the captaincy immediately afterwards, having worn the armband on 58 occasions.

Above: Real Madrid's David Beckham celebrates with Robinho and Gutierrez after scoring against Rosenborg Trondheim in 2005.

CUAUHTEMOC BLANCO

Country: Mexico
Born: January 17, 1973
Position: Forward
Clubs: América, Necaxa, América, Real Valladolid, América, Veracruz, América

Cuauhtemoc Blanco is the fans' favourite in Mexico and his controversial exclusion from the 2006 World Cup squad because he did not fit into coach Ricardo Lavolpe's plans drew protests but to no avail. He had not helped his cause by quitting the 2005 Confederations Cup squad on the eve of the tournament. Blanco is a gifted player who is unpredictable and exciting to watch, as well as being a prolific goalscorer. His two-footed trickery at the 1998 World Cup against the South Koreans will always be remembered.

TIM BOROWSKI

Country: Germany
Born: May 2, 1980
Position: Midfield
Clubs: FCT Neubrandenburg, Werder Bremen

Tim Borowski is one of Germany's most talented and adaptable players who can perform in the middle of defence or anywhere in midfield. He made his international debut back in August 2002, but he didn't really establish himself until the World Cup qualifiers. He has improved enormously for Werder Bremen, boosted by his club's league and cup double in 2004. He has developed superb timing, with attacking runs from deep, and he is an excellent passer of the ball and a lethal finisher.

GIANLUIGI BUFFON

Country: Italy
Born: January 28, 1978
Position: Goalkeeper
Clubs: Juventus

Gianluigi Buffon deservedly won the Lev Yashin Award for the best goalkeeper at the 2006 World Cup. Buffon, who played in all seven matches as Italy went on to win the competition for the fourth time, was only beaten twice in the tournament – by an own goal and a penalty. It was Buffon's third World Cup after being a non-playing member in 1998 and a part of the team that suffered the shock exit at the hands of South Korea in 2002. He had made his Italy debut in October 1997 in a World Cup play-off against Russia, coming on as a substitute for Gianluca Pagliuca and impressed with several fine saves. Some 15 months earlier he helped Italy win the 1996 European Under-21 Championship. In July 2001 Juventus signed him for a staggering £32.6 million from Parma, with whom he had won the UEFA Cup in 1999. He went on to win Serie A four times between 2002 and 2006.

CAFU

Country: Brazil
Born: June 19, 1970
Position: Right-back
Clubs: São Paulo, Real Zaragoza, Palmeiras, Roma, AC Milan

Better known as Cafu, Marcos Evangelista de Moraes was the first person to play in the final of three World Cups and ended up a winner twice, in 1994 and 2002. The latter was extra

special as he was captain of the side that defeated Germany 2-0 to lift the trophy. Cafu is regarded as Brazil's greatest right-back. He succeeded Jorginho in the role and made his international debut in September 1990 against Spain. He gained success with São Paulo in the Copa Libertadores in 1992 and 1993, and went on to win the UEFA Cup with Real Zaragoza in 1995. He won the Serie A title with Roma in 2001 and AC Milan in 2004, and he played in the 2005 European Champions League final for Milan, losing out to Liverpool on penalties.

SOL CAMPBELL

Country: England
Born: September 18, 1974
Position: Defender
Clubs: Tottenham Hotspur, Arsenal

Sol Campbell stunned British football when he quit Tottenham for arch-rivals Arsenal in the summer of 2001. As a free agent, it was expected Campbell would join either Barcelona or Bayern Munich, but when he was paraded at a press conference in an Arsenal shirt, his actions outraged Spurs fans who felt a real sense of betrayal. Fine displays at the 1998 World Cup saw Campbell's status elevated, and as a fiercely ambitious individual, a lack of silverware at White Hart Lane ultimately prompted him to take such decisive action. The move was controversial, but justified as he won the league and cup double in his first season and the league again in 2004. After an ill-fated 2005-6 season, Campbell regained his place in the Arsenal team just in time to play in the 2006 Champions League final, scoring Arsenal's only goal in the 2-1 defeat to Barcelona. He decided to leave Arsenal for a 'fresh start' after the 2006 World Cup.

FABIO CANNAVARO

Country: Italy
Born: September 13, 1973
Position: Defender
Clubs: Napoli, Parma, Inter Milan, Juventus, Real Madrid

Fabio Cannavaro captained Italy to World Cup glory in 2006, winning his 100th cap against France in the final. He is a cultured centre-back who makes up for what he lacks in height with an uncanny ability to read a game and intercept attacks. Born in Naples, he turned professional with his home town side, making his senior debut aged 20, but quit for Parma four years later. His seven seasons at the club established him as one of the world's best defenders and a regular for the Italian team at the World Cups in 1998, 2002 and 2006 and at the European Championships in 2000 and 2004. A big money move to Inter Milan came in 2002 but it wasn't until he joined Juventus (and was

Below: Fabio Cannavaro's outstanding performances at the 2006 World Cup helped Italy to lift the trophy.

reunited with former Parma team-mates Lilian Thuram and Gianluigi Buffon) that he finally got his hands on the Italian title. After Juventus were relegated in 2006 for their part in a match-fixing scandal, he signed for Real Madrid.

ROBERTO CARLOS

Country: Brazil
Born: April 10, 1973
Position: Left-back
Clubs: União São João, Palmeiras, Inter Milan, Real Madrid

As a regular starter for both Brazil and Real Madrid, Roberto Carlos is one of the most admired players in world football, and his dynamic, rampaging style of play from left-back has won him many of the game's major honours, including the World Cup in 2002. After failing to settle at Inter Milan following his move from Brazil in 1995, he found himself part of a very talented Real Madrid side. Legendary for his ability with a dead ball, Carlos scored one of the most memorable free-kicks the game has ever seen in the pre-World Cup Tournoi in France in 1997. In a silverware-laden career Robert Carlos has won the World Cup, two Copa Américas, three Champions Leagues and four Spanish titles. Following Brazil's surprise quarter-final exit at the 2006 World Cup, he announced his international retirement.

DANIEL CARVALHO

Country: Brazil
Born: March 1, 1983
Position: Midfield
Clubs: Internacional, CSKA Moscow

In a national team overflowing with attacking talents, one man who has made a big name for himself in unlikely surroundings was Brazilian Under-23 star Daniel Da Silva Carvalho. New money flooding in to Russian football lured a number of foreigners to CSKA, traditionally the army club of Russia, but perhaps the most exciting is the deft creator and goalscorer Carvalho. He has strength, pace and a terrific left foot, and has proven himself on the European club stage by inspiring CSKA to UEFA Cup glory. Carvalho is a star player of the near future, with full international honours and a more attractive club inevitable.

IKER CASILLAS

Country: Spain
Born: May 20, 1981
Position: Goalkeeper
Club: Real Madrid

Iker Casillas was born in Madrid and his potential came to fruition when he helped

Spain to both World Youth Championship and Meridian Cup success in 1999. His progress continued when he replaced the injured Bodo Illgner to perform heroics as Real Madrid defeated Valencia in the 2000 Champions League final, but at the tender age of 19 he failed to live up to his newly-found fame and was replaced in the Real goal by Cesar Sanchez. A little older and wiser, he reclaimed the jersey for the 2002 final against Bayer Leverkusen and, having helped preserve a slender 2-1 lead with a number of fine saves, he has remained in goal for club and country ever since.

PETR CECH

Country: Czech Republic
Born: 20 May, 1982
Position: Goalkeeper
Clubs: Chmel Blsany, Sparta Prague, Rennes, Chelsea

Widely regarded as one of the best goalkeepers in the world, Cech made his name as a member of the Czech Republic side that won the Under-21 European Championship in 2002. He has since established himself as first choice goalkeeper for his country's senior team, helping them to the semi-finals of the European Championship in 2004 and a place at the World Cup in 2006.

At club level, he joined Sparta Prague in 2001 and there set a national record of 855 minutes without conceding a goal. A move to French side Rennes followed in 2002 but it was after his £9 million move to Chelsea in summer 2004 that his career really took off.

A supreme shot-stopper and commanding in the penalty area, Cech's consistently excellent displays were vital as Chelsea won their first league title in 50 years in 2005. The 6ft 5ins goalkeeper also set a new Premiership record of 1,025 minutes without conceding a goal in his first season with the club.

JOE COLE

Country: England
Born: November 8, 1981
Position: Midfield
Clubs: West Ham, Chelsea

A product of West Ham's youth academy, as a 16-year-old Cole was the hottest property in English football with Manchester United rumoured to be ready to break the bank to secure the services of 'the new Paul Gascoigne'. However, the player remained at Upton Park, made his senior debut at 17 and became club captain in his early twenties.

Cole's failure to live up to the early hype surrounding him didn't deter Chelsea from paying £6.6 million for him in 2003. After a long period where he found it difficult to hold

down a regular place in the starting line-up, Cole finally came good in the 2005-6 season, operating very effectively as a left-sided winger for Chelsea. He became an England regular under Sven-Göran Eriksson and featured in the 2006 World Cup, scoring one of the best goals of the tournament against Sweden.

Above: Petr Cech played a major role in Chelsea's back-to-back title wins in 2005 and 2006.

HERNAN CRESPO

Country: Argentina
Born: July 5, 1975
Position: Forward
Clubs: River Plate, Parma, Lazio, Inter Milan, Chelsea, AC Milan, Chelsea, Inter Milan

In 2000 Hernan Crespo moved from Parma to Lazio in a staggering £36 million deal, that saw Lazio part with Maitias Almeyda (£14 million), Sergio Conceicao (£10 million) and £12 million in cash. Crespo had been instrumental in Parma's success in winning the UEFA Cup, the Italian Cup and the Italian Super Cup in 1999. Parma themselves had parted with £10 million for Argentina's 1994 Young Player Of The Year.

Crespo made his Argentina debut in February 1995 against Bulgaria. River Plate coach Daniel Passarella groomed Crespo to become a prolific goalscorer for club and country and in 1996 he scored twice for River in their Copa Libertadores victory. A move to Chelsea included a loan spell at AC Milan, where he played in the 2005 Champions League final, but he returned to Stamford Bridge to play a part in the 2006 title-winning team before signing for Inter.

DECO

Country: Portugal
Born: August 27, 1977
Position: Midfield
Clubs: Corinthians Alagoano, Benfica, Alverca, Salgueiros, Porto, Barcelona

A gifted playmaker, Brazilian-born Deco – or Anderson Luiz de Sousa – attracts as much controversy as praise for his combative midfield style, that often brings as many yellow cards as goals. Once deemed not good enough by Benfica boss Graeme Souness, he really came to prominence under José Mourinho at Porto. The key figure in their 2003 UEFA Cup win, he capped that the following season with a league title and Champions League victory, scoring in the 3-0 win over Monaco.

Never picked to play for the land of his birth, he qualified to represent Portugal and scored on his debut – against Brazil. A key player for both Barcelona and Portugal, winning the European Champions League in 2006 and playing in his first World Cup in Germany.

ALESSANDRO DEL PIERO

Country: Italy
Born: November 9, 1974
Position: Centre-forward/Midfield
Clubs: Padova, Juventus

Signed from Serie B side Padova in 1993 as a 19-year-old, it wasn't long before the mercurial Alessandro Del Piero had forced himself into the Juventus first team, where he has since become an inspirational figure. Although mostly known for his passing and creative play,

it isn't unusual for Del Piero to get among the goals: he scored an impressive 21 times in 32 league appearances during the 1997-8 season as Juventus went on to win the title, the first of his seven championship wins with the club.

Del Piero has never really hit the same heights for the Italian national team, his slow recovery from a knee ligament injury that had kept him sidelined for nine months limited his effectiveness at the 1998 World Cup finals. He started Euro 2000 in fine form, netting an exquisite goal against Sweden, but having come on as a second-half substitute in the final, missed two gilt-edged opportunities to score.

Coach Giovanni Trapattoni used Del Piero only sparingly in the 2002 World Cup, but he still came off the bench against Mexico to score the equaliser five minutes from time that helped Italy qualify for the second round. Marcello Lippi again used Del Piero at the 2006 World Cup, the 86th minute substitute converting Italy's fourth spot-kick in their 5-3 penalty shoot-out win over France in the final.

EL HADJI DIOUF

Country: Senegal
Born: January 15, 1981
Position: Forward
Clubs: Linguere, Sochaux, Rennes, Lens, Liverpool, Bolton Wanderers

El Hadji Diouf is one of the brightest talents to emerge from Africa. This gifted footballer, like many of his fellow Senegalese players, was quickly snapped up by the French league as a teenager. Initially he earned a reputation as a wild player but he has matured into one of the most dangerous strikers in European football.

In April 2000 Diouf made his international debut against Benin. His nine-goal haul in eight appearances, including successive hat-tricks against Algeria and Namibia, helped Senegal

to their first World Cup in 2002 and led to a £10 million move to the English Premiership with Liverpool. His period at Anfield was less than successful and he subsequently transferred to Bolton Wanderers.

LANDON DONOVAN

Country: United States
Born: March 4, 1982
Position: Forward
Clubs: Clubs: Bayer Leverkusen, San Jose Earthquakes, Bayer Leverkusen, Los Angeles Galaxy

Donovan is the golden boy of American football. He has represented his country at every level, becoming Player Of The Tournament at the 1999 Under-17 World Championship. After appearing at the Olympics in 2000 and making his full international debut against Mexico a month later, Donovan went on to help the USA to the World Cup quarter-finals in 2002. In club football he has won the MLS championship three times and, in 2006, became the all-time top scorer in the MLS play-offs. He has twice been voted USA's Athlete Of The Year, in 2003 and 2004. Despite two brief, unhappy spells in Germany with Bayer Leverkusen, he has always delivered for the USA.

DIDIER DROGBA

Country: Ivory Coast
Born: March 11, 1978
Position: Forward
Clubs: Le Mans, Guingamp, Marseille, Chelsea

A powerful and athletic striker, Didier Yves Drogba Tébily enjoyed successful spells at Le Mans and Guingamp before joining Marseille in 2003. He was only with the club for a season but scored 18 goals, was named French Player

Of The Year and collected a UEFA Cup runners-up medal after his side lost to Valencia in the final. In July 2004, Drogba joined Roman Abramovich's high-spending Chelsea for £24 million but in two seasons at Stamford Bridge the striker has only intermittently lived up to his enormous transfer fee, despite Chelsea's impressive haul of trophies in the same period. On the international stage, the 28-year-old captained the Ivory Coast to the final of the African Nations Cup in 2006 (they lost to Egypt on penalties, Drogba among those missing a spot-kick) and he also helped the West African nation to its first World Cup finals appearance in the same year.

EDMILSON

Country: Brazil
Born: July 10, 1976
Position: Centre-back
Clubs: São Paulo, Lyon, Barcelona

Edmilson Jose Gomes de Moraes, the son of an orange picker and amateur footballer, was Brazil's attack-minded centre-back in a three-man defence in the 2002 World Cup winning team. He magnificently dealt with Germany's aerial attack in the final, while his desire to cross the halfway line at every opportunity led to a spectacular first international goal with an overhead kick against Costa Rica. He made his name with São Paulo as a midfielder and was captain of the Paulista state championship-winning team in 2000 before joining Lyon, with whom he won a hat-trick of French titles. A move to Barcelona coincided with a revival in the club's fortunes and he notched up successive Spanish league wins in 2005 and 2006 and picked up a Champions League winner's medal in 2006. Injury ruled him out of the 2006 World Cup.

EMERSON

Country: Brazil
Born: April 4, 1976
Position: Midfield
Clubs: Gremio, Botafogo, Gremio, Bayer Leverkusen, Roma, Juventus, Real Madrid

Emerson Ferreira da Rosa is that rare breed: a tenacious Brazilian who has the reputation as a hard man. His propensity to commit fouls is offset by his versatility – he can play just about anywhere in any formation. He made his international debut against Ecuador in 1997, won the 1999 Copa América and was named captain of Brazil's 1999 Confederations Cup squad. He missed out on the 2002 World Cup, dislocating his shoulder before the tournament after going in goal in training for the benefit of photographers. He proved equally adept in the German and Italian leagues before signing for Real Madrid in 2006 after Juventus were punished with relegation to Serie B.

MICHAEL ESSIEN

Country: Ghana
Born: December 3, 1982
Position: Midfield
Clubs: Liberty Professionals, Bastia, Lyon, Chelsea

A powerful, combative midfielder, Essien began his club career with Ghanian side Liberty Professionals. Impressive performances for his home country in the Under-17 World Cup in 1999 brought him to the attention of French side Bastia, who signed him in 2001. After a couple of false starts, Essien settled very nicely into a central midfield role for his club and was soon doing likewise for his country, making his debut for Ghana in 2002's African Nations Cup.

He joined Lyon in 2003 and helped them to back-to-back titles in his two seasons, picking up a player of the year award from France's National Union Of Professional Footballers along the way. After a protracted summer transfer saga, Chelsea signed Essien in August 2005 for a club record £24.4 million. His battling displays helped the club mount a fine defence of their league title but an over-the-top tackle on Liverpool's Dietmar Hamann also earned him a two-match European ban and widespread criticism. He helped Ghana to the 2006 World Cup, reaching the second round before losing to Brazil, a game Essien missed through suspension.

SAMUEL ETO'O

Country: Cameroon
Born: March 10, 1981
Position: Centre-forward
Clubs: Real Madrid, Barcelona

Three-time African Player Of The Year, Samuel Eto'o joined Real Madrid's youth academy at the age of 15 but he was unable to break into a squad littered with world-class signings and he spent four-and-a-half years on loan at Real Mallorca. While at the Son Moix he won the 2003 Spanish Cup and established himself as a prolific striker.

Eto'o won gold with Cameron at the 2000 Olympics in Sydney, and was also a winner at both the 2000 and 2004 African Nations Cup, before joining Barcelona in 2004, where his £16 million transfer fee was split between Mallorca and Real Madrid. Real's president Florentino Perez sanctioned the transfer as he didn't feel that Eto'o would be able to break into his side ahead of Raúl and Ronaldo, but it has since left the club extremely red faced. Eto'o top-scored with 24 goals in his debut season at the Nou Camp as Barcelona cantered to the league title. They won the championship again the following season, while Eto'o picked up another yet winner's medal after victory over Arsenal in the 2006 Champions League final in Paris.

Below: Cameroon's Samuel Eto'o fends off Togo's Assemoassa at the 2006 African Nations Cup.

RIO FERDINAND

Country: England
Born: November 8, 1978
Position: Defender
Clubs: West Ham, Leeds United, Manchester United

Rio Ferdinand is the trainee from Peckham who became the world's most expensive defender. Signed to West Ham United in 1995 he soon earned comparisons to local legend Bobby Moore for his composure on the ball. He made his league debut in May 1996 and his England debut against Cameroon in November 1998, demonstrating the class that would later make him such a success at the 2002 World Cup. He joined Leeds United in November 2000 for a record fee of £18 million and helped them to the semi-final of the Champions League before Manchester United signed him for another British record fee of £30 million and he won a championship medal in his first season with the club. He was banned for eight months after forgetting to attend a drugs test in 2003, missing the 2004 European Championship, but on returning to action he reclaimed his place for both club and country.

LUIS FIGO

Country: Portugal
Born: November 4, 1972
Position: Midfield
Clubs: Sporting Lisbon, Barcelona, Real Madrid, Inter Milan

A strong, tricky winger, Luis Felipe Madeira Figo has enthralled fans across Europe, particularly in Spain where he has worn the shirts of both Barcelona and Real Madrid. His career began in the alleyways of Lisbon where he played for the street team Os Pastilhas, and it was here that he attracted the attentions of Sporting Lisbon, signing schoolboy forms at 11.

As a teenager Figo received international acclaim, helping Portugal to third place in the FIFA Under-16s tournament in 1989, before winning the FIFA World Junior Championship two years later with the Under-20s team. After making his full debut for Sporting Lisbon at the age of 17, and helping them to second place in the league and a Portuguese Cup win in 1995, he attracted the attention of Europe's big guns and signed for Barcelona for £1.5 million.

Under coaches Johan Cruyff, Bobby Robson and Louis Van Gaal, Figo developed into a world-class player, mesmerising fans and defenders with his quick feet and acute football brain. He drove the team to success in the Cup Winners' Cup and the European Super Cup in 1997, two Spanish league titles in 1998 and 1999, and two Spanish Cups in 1997 and 1998.

After a three-year love affair with the Nou Camp and a hugely successful Euro 2000 (Figo

helped Portugal to the semi-finals and was viewed by many as the player of the tournament), he made a controversial big-money move to arch rivals Real Madrid. His impact was immediate, both on an off the pitch. Alongside team-mates Roberto Carlos and Raúl, and later Zinédine Zidane and Ronaldo, Figo steered the best club side in the world to the title in 2001 and 2003, plus the Champions League in 2002.

Away from the field he had caused an outrage that would never be forgiven in Barcelona, but the anger that greeted his departure (a pig's head was thrown at him during a clash between the two teams) was as much to do with his talent as it was to do with traditional rivalry, as testified by Real's technical director, Jorge Valdano: 'We are so used to Figo playing brilliantly, that we think he's playing badly when he just plays normally.'

After losing his place in the Real team to David Beckham Figo moved to the San Siro on a free transfer, signing a two-year deal with Inter. With Portugal he reached the semi-finals of the 2006 World Cup.

DIEGO FORLAN

Country: Uruguay
Born: May 19, 1979
Position: Centre-forward
Clubs: Danubio FC, Peñarol, Independiente, Manchester United, Villarreal

Much derided for his spell at Manchester United, it took Diego Forlan eight months and 27 games to record his first goal for the club, a Champions League strike against Maccabi Haifa in August 2002. Signed for £6.9 million from Independiente that January, Forlan managed just 17 goals in 95 appearances and Wayne Rooney's arrival signalled the end of a difficult two-and-a-half years. But a move to Villarreal in the Spanish Liga has suited the Uruguayan and he showed his worth by ending 2004-5 as the league's top scorer with 25 goals, jointly winning the European Golden Boot with Thierry Henry in the process.

STEVEN GERRARD

Country: England
Born: June 16, 1976
Position: Midfield
Club: Liverpool

A product of the Liverpool youth academy, Steven Gerrard is one of the brightest talents in English football. Making his debut for Liverpool in a European tie against Celta Vigo at Anfield during the 1998-9 season, his robust, all-action style from the centre of midfield has seen him establish a regular place in the first team at club level, and he was an integral part of the Liverpool side that won a trio of cup competitions in 2001 (UEFA Cup, League Cup and FA Cup). He is also a valuable member of the national team,

and scored England's second goal from long range in the historic 5-1 demolition of Germany in the 2002 World Cup qualifier. Gerrard missed the subsequent finals through injury but recoverd to become a permanent fixture in the England side at Euro 2004 and the 2006 World Cup. There was further success with Liverpool, Gerrard inspiring his team's dramatic comebacks to win both the 2005 European Champions League final and the 2006 FA Cup.

RYAN GIGGS

Country: Wales
Born: November 29, 1973
Position: Winger
Club: Manchester United

As one of the original members of Sir Alex Ferguson's 'Fledglings', Ryan Giggs has become the most decorated player in Manchester United's history. He made his debut as a 17-year-old substitute against Everton in March 1991 and immediately caught the eye with his unmatchable pace and dribbling skills. The comparisons with United legend George Best were plentiful and although he became a regular the following season, making his debut for Wales and winning the PFA Young Player Of The Year in the process, the campaign would end in disappointment as Leeds United pipped their rivals to the championship.

The title finally arrived at Old Trafford in 1993 for the first time in 26 years, signalling the start of the most illustrious period in the club's history. Giggs has played a prominent role every season and, despite constant links with a move to Serie A, he has remained loyal to the club, winning eight Premiership titles, four FA Cups, two League Cups, one World Club Cup, and most famously, the Champions League in 1999.

THIERRY HENRY

Country: France
Born: August 17, 1977
Position: Forward
Clubs: Monaco, Juventus, Arsenal

In a prolific career with Arsenal, Thierry Henry has been one of the most influential players in England's Premiership. A wonderfully fast and powerful striker, Henry is among the finest goalscorers in the world. He has been top scorer of the Premiership on four occasions (2002, 2004, 2005 and 2006) and won the European Golden Boot in both 2004 and 2005. The club's all-time top goalscorer, he surpassed Ian Wright's 185-goal record in October 2005.

In 2003 and 2004 Henry was voted the Premiership's Player Of The Year by both the Professional Footballers' Association and the Football Writers' Association, winning the FWA award for a third time in 2006. He has also been French player of the year a record four times. He

Opposite: One of the best strikers in the world game, Thierry Henry broke all of Arsenal's goalscoring club records.

326

Above: Oliver Kahn in action for Germany in 2006.

won the Premiership title in 2002 and 2004 and lifted the FA Cup in 2002, 2003 and 2005. Although disappointed to lose the Champions League final in 2006, he signed an extension to his Arsenal contract after the defeat.

Arsene Wenger signed Henry in August 1999 in a £10.5 million deal, rescuing him from a disappointing season with Juventus, who had paid Monaco £14 million just a year earlier. Henry had originally been given his debut in the French league as a 17-year-old by Wenger in the 1994-5 season, winning the French title with Monaco in 1997. The following season he made his France debut against South Africa.

Although an important part of France's 1998 World Cup-winning squad, scoring three goals, he failed to get on the pitch in the final – he was warming up to come on as a second-half substitute but the sending-off of Marcel Desailly resulted in a tactical change. Two years later and Henry was the main France striker in the team's European Championship triumph, but although reaching the World Cup final in 2006, Henry was sustituted in extra-time and had to look on as France were beaten 5-3 on penalties.

ZLATAN IBRAHIMOVIC

Country: Sweden
Born: October 3, 1981
Position: Centre-forward
Clubs: Malmö, Ajax, Juventus

Born of Bosnian immigrants, Ibrahimovic started his career at Malmö. With 16 goals in 40 games, Ajax boss Leo Beenhaker signed the leggy striker in a £5 million deal in March 2001. Handed the number nine shirt previously worn by Patrick Kluivert, he ended his injury-hit first full season by scoring 13 goals in 16 games as Ajax won the double. A regular for Sweden alongside Henrik Larsson, Ibrahimovic's international credentials were heightened by a stunning strike that sent Italy crashing out of the 2004 European Championship. His form that summer won him a £13 million move to Juventus, where he netted 16 goals as the Turin club won the Serie A title.

FILIPPO INZAGHI

Country: Italy
Born: August 9, 1973
Position: Centre-forward
Clubs: Piacenza, Leffe, Piacenza, Parma, Atalanta, Juventus, AC Milan

A lethal opportunist in the penalty area, Filippo Inzaghi's best season to date as a striker came with Atalanta in 1996-7, when he netted 24 times in 33 league games. He was immediately snapped up by Juventus and stayed in Turin for four seasons, winning a league title in 1998 and losing 1-0 to Real Madrid in the final of the 1998 Champions League.

Inzaghi played three matches for Italy at the 1998 World Cup finals, and scored twice for his country at the European Championship two years later. He also scored seven times in six games for Italy during their qualification campaign for the 2002 World Cup finals. He was included in Italy's victorious 2006 World Cup squad, but he did not play in the final.

With AC Milan, Inzaghi was a winner of the European Champions League in 2003, beating his former club Juventus 3-2 in a penalty shoot-out after a goalless draw. He also won the Serie A title the following year.

OLIVER KAHN

Country: Germany
Born: June 15, 1969
Position: Goalkeeper
Clubs: Karlsrühe, Bayern Munich

Highly motivated and imposing, Oliver Khan is one of the contemporary game's great keepers. He started his career at Karlsrühe but was snapped up by Bayern Munich in 1994 for £1.6 million, a record fee for a goalkeeper in the Bundesliga. At Bayern he has won seven league titles, a UEFA Cup and the 2001 Champions League, crucially saving three times in the penalty shoot-out. It was a performance that saw him voted German Player Of The Year for the second successive season.

Khan made his international debut in 1995 and was a non-playing squad member in two World Cups until he captained the side at Japan and Korea in 2002. He was instrumental in guiding the team to the final and was named Player Of The Tournament, the first time a goalkeeper has received the award. By the 2006 World Cup, however, he had been demoted to deputy behind Jens Lehmann, but played in the third place play-off against Portugal.

KAKÁ

Country: Brazil
Born: April 22, 1982
Position: Attacking midfield
Clubs: São Paulo, Milan

Often overlooked in Brazil's line-up, Ricardo Izecson dos Santos Leite is better known as Kaká, allegedly so-called because his young brother couldn't say Ricardo. After demonstrating an impressive goalscoring record at club level in Brazil while still a teenager, he gained a big-money move to Milan in 2003 and helped his new side to the Serie A title and the European Super Cup in his first season. In 2005, playing in the 'hole' behind striker Andriy Shevchenko, he provided the vital ammunition for the Ukrainian star, and chipped in with vital goals of his own en-route to second place in Serie A and a Champions League final against Liverpool.

NWANKWO KANU

Country: Nigeria
Born: August 1, 1976
Position: Forward
Clubs: Federation Works, Iwuanyanwu Nationale, Ajax, Inter Milan, Arsenal, West Bromwich Albion

Nwankwo Kanu signed for Ajax aged 16 and was a teenage member of the side that won the 1995 Champions League against AC Milan. The following season he captained Nigeria to gold at the Olympic Games in Atlanta, where his unpredictability and breathtaking skill earned him the first of his African Footballer Of The Year awards and a glamour move to Inter Milan.

A life-threatening heart problem, which required surgery, brought an end to his Serie A career before it really begun, but he was given a lifeline by Arsenal boss Arsene Wenger, who signed him for £4 million in January 1999. By the year's end he was African Footballer Of The Year a second time.

Kanu failed to establish a regular place in the starting line-up. Nevertheless he won the Premiership and FA Cup double in 2002, picked up another FA Cup winner's medal in 2003, albeit as an unused substitute, and earned another Premiership title the following season. In 2004 Kanu was given a free transfer to West Bromwich Albion. He played for Nigeria at the World Cups of 1998 and 2002.

ROBBIE KEANE

Country: Republic Of Ireland
Born: July 8, 1980
Position: Forward
Clubs: Wolves, Coventry, Inter Milan, Leeds United, Tottenham Hotspur

Robbie Keane made the breakthrough with both Wolves and the Republic Of Ireland at the age of 17, his creative skills not only forging goalscoring opportunities for himself, but for his strike partners too. While few expected the midlands club to be able to hold on to such a hot talent for long, not many would have predicted that within six years he would have moved club four times and commanded combined transfer fees of almost £40 million. His spell in Italy with Inter Milan was short and unsuccessful but he has shown with both Leeds United and Tottenham that he is one of the most expressive players in the Premiership. On the international stage he remains one of the Republic Of Ireland's greatest talents, with plenty still to come.

HARRY KEWELL

Country: Australia
Born: September 22, 1978
Position: Midfield
Clubs: Leeds United, Liverpool

The young Australian was brought to the UK at the age of 16, having been recruited from the New South Wales Soccer Academy. Leeds United manager Howard Wilkinson threw the young Australian international into the first team at the age of 17, but under George Graham he was forced to bide his time on the sidelines. Kewell really blossomed when David O'Leary gave him, and several other Leeds youngsters, a chance in the first team and the 1999-2000 campaign saw him pick up the PFA Young Footballer Of The Year Award.

Since then, Kewell has risen to become a genuine world star, signing for Liverpool in July 2003 for £5 million. His performance in Australia's 3-1 win over England in February 2003 was hailed by many as the greatest individual performance by an Australian football international for his country.

In 2005 Kewell was part of Liverpool's Champions League-winning team, although he had to hobble off injured early in the first-half,. He was also a member of the side that won the 2006 FA Cup, but he again failed to finish the game. His greatest achievement has been in helping Australia to reach the 2006 World Cup, where they reached the second round. He has been voted Oceania Player Of The Year on three occasions, in 1999, 2001 and 2003.

KLEBERSON

Country: Brazil
Born: June 19, 1979
Position: Midfield
Clubs: Atletico Paranaense, Manchester United, Besiktas

Just five months after making his international debut, Kleberson became a World Cup winner at the age of 23. Although he had made an immediate impact, scoring on his Brazilian debut against Bolivia, he began the World Cup on the bench. But when coach Luis Felipe Scolari opted to strengthen the heart of his midfield, he turned to the man from Atletico Paranaense. Not surprisingly his performances at the 2002 World Cup in Japan and Korea earned Kleberson many new admirers among the major clubs in Europe. He signed for Manchester United for £6.5 million in August

2003 but his two years at the club saw limited opportunities that were not helped by injuries. He made a £2.5 million move to Turkish side Besiktas in August 2005. He also lost his place in the Brazil squad.

MIROSLAV KLOSE

Country: Germany
Born: June 9, 1978
Position: Forward
Clubs: SG Blaubach-Diedelkopf, FC Homburg, Kaiserslautern, Werder Bremen

Miroslav Klose's meteoric rise from regional football to the 2002 World Cup final took less two years. Signed by Kaiserslautern in 2000, within seven months he had made a dramatic match-winning international debut as a substitute for Germany against Albania. He did likewise in his next appearance against Greece. The striker's blistering pace and sharp reactions in the box were a godsend for a national team crying out for a lethal striker. A World Cup hat-trick against Saudi Arabia followed on the way to the final and he finished the tournament as second-highest scorer behind Ronaldo.

Polish-born Klose moved to Germany with his family as a child in 1987 and declined an opportunity to play for the Polish national team. He is a natural athlete with a sporting family history: his father was a professional footballer, playing for Odra Opole and Auxerre, while his mother was a Poland handball international. Werder Bremen signed Klose in 2004 and he finished top scorer in the Bundesliga in the 2005-6 season, with 26 goals in 26 appearances. At the 2006 World Cup Klose finised the tournament as top scorer with five goals.

Below: Miroslav Klose celebrates his second goal against Ecuador at the 2006 World Cup finals. He finished the tournament as winner of the Golden Boot.

PATRICK KLUIVERT

Country: Holland
Born: July 1, 1976
Position: Forward
Clubs: Ajax, AC Milan, Barcelona, Newcastle United, Valencia

Following in the footsteps of his father Kenneth, who was a professional footballer in Surinam, Patrick Kluivert was given his Ajax debut by Louis Van Gaal in 1994. The following season he scored the only goal against AC Milan in the team's Champions League final triumph, which became a defining moment in the 18-year-old's life. As the most talked about young striker in Europe, his 39 league goals in 70 games for Ajax prompted a move to Milan the following year, although it proved to be an unhappy spell at the San Siro. In a star-studded side, which included international team-mates Edgar Davids and Michael Reiziger, Kluivert failed to command a regular place in a team that struggled to make an impression in the title race.

He was made a scapegoat by the fans but managed to rediscover his form when Holland reached the semi-finals of the 1998 World Cup. When Van Gaal invited him to join Barcelona that September, he needed little persuading. In his first season he helped Barcelona to the league title and continued his form at the 2000 European Championship, where he was joint leading scorer with five goals.

In 2004 Kluivert was given a free transfer and spent one poor season at Newcastle in England's Premiership before returning to Spain with Valencia. For Holland, although out of favour under Marco Van Basten, he remains the nation's all-time top goalscorer with 40 goals.

FRANK LAMPARD

Country: England
Born: 20 June, 1978
Position: Midfielder
Clubs: West Ham United, Chelsea

Named the world's second best player (behind Brazilian Ronaldinho) in December 2005, Frank Lampard is the complete midfielder with prodigious attacking and defensive qualities. In 1995 he turned professional at West Ham (where his father Frank Lampard Snr was a former player and the assistant manager) but was briefly loaned out to Swansea City. He captained the West Ham youth team to the final of the FA Youth Cup in 1996 and made his debut in the senior side the same year. The 1998-9 season saw Lampard make his senior England debut and he was also an ever-present in the West Ham side that finished fifth in the Premiership. After six years at Upton Park (39 goals in 187 appearances in all competitions), Lampard signed for Chelsea for £11 million in May 2001. Since then, his form has just got better and better, culminating in him being named the Football Writers' Association's Player Of The Year in 2005.

In the same year he helped Chelsea to the Carling Cup and league title, and he also set a Premiership record of playing 159 consecutive league matches between October 13, 2001 and November 26, 2005. The following year he won a second Premiership title, along with the PFA Player Of The Year award.

Lampard became an integral part of the England team, featuring in the side that made it to the Euro 2004 quarter-finals – where he scored three goals in four appearances. In 2006 he took part in his first World Cup, where despite not performing at the top of his game he still had more shots at goal than any other player – although he failed to find the net.

HENRIK LARSSON

Country: Sweden
Born: September 20, 1971
Position: Forward
Clubs: Hogaborg, Helsingborgs, Feyenoord, Celtic, Barcelona, Helsingborgs

Celtic had an amazing return for the £650,000 they paid for Henrik Larsson in 1997. Despite serious injuries the Swedish striker topped the Scottish league goal charts in five of the seven seasons he was there. He was twice voted Scotland's Player Of The Year in 1998 and 2001 by both the football writers and by the players' association. He was also Europe's top league goalscorer and, inevitably with Celtic, won a host of domestic honours, including four Scottish Premier Division titles, the Scottish Cup twice and the Scottish League Cup four times.

With an incredible strike rate – 242 goals in 315 games – he was the darling of the Celtic fans and was not only the most feared striker in Scottish football but one with a reputation that spread worldwide. Success followed him to Barcelona where he won the Spanish league title twice in his two seasons at the Nou Camp, and he also won the European Champions League in 2006 after victory over Arsenal. The Champions League final was his last appearance for Barcelona as he fulfilled a longstanding desire to return to Sweden to play for his home town club of Helsingborgs.

With the Sweden national side he has played in three World Cups: in 1994 (where Sweden reached the semi-finals), 2002 and 2006. The Swedish football association regard him as 'the greatest Swedish player of the last 50 years'.

Tricky, fast and good in the air, Larsson has the full repetoire of skills required of a world-class striker. It is not just at club level that he has been prolific. He is Sweden's third highest goalscorer at international level, averaging better than a goal every three games.

In 2006, Larsson was awarded an MBE for his services to Scottish football.

Above: Henrik Larsson in action for Barcelona in April 2006, his last season with the club.

PAOLO MALDINI

Country: Italy
Born: June 26, 1968
Position: Left-back/Sweeper
Club: AC Milan

Paolo Maldini is one of the finest defenders ever to grace the world stage. An unflappable, cultured and resilient presence at left-back for Milan, he is equally proficient when deployed at sweeper or centre-half. He is world famous for his ability to bring the ball out of defence, but he is more than capable of helping out in attack when needed.

He began his long and exclusive association with his local club AC Milan when only a boy. Making his debut for the first team as a 16-year-old substitute against Udinese in January 1985, Maldini was following in the footsteps of his father, Cesare, who had won the European Cup with Milan in 1963 and played for Italy in the Sixties, later coaching the national team. To say Paolo's time at Milan has been successful is a great understatement; in 21 years in the first team he has helped them accrue a vast collection of silverware, including seven Italian league titles, two World Club Cups, three European Super Cups, and four European Champions Cups.

The 1994 Champions League final saw Milan thrash Barcelona 4-0 and Maldini deputise at sweeper for the suspended Franco Baresi. Maldini was also part of the Milan sides that lost Champions League finals in 1993 and 1995, to Marseille and Ajax respectively.

Maldini made his international debut as a 19-year-old, against Yugoslavia on March 31, 1988, and has subsequently become Italy's most capped player. But he has failed translate his successful club career to the international arena: Italy came third in the World Cup in 1990 and reached the final in 1994, before losing to Brazil on penalties. The Italian captain was unlucky

Left: Frank Lampard was voted second to Ronaldinho in FIFA's World Player Of The Year Award in 2005.

331

Above: Pavel Nedved celebrates after scoring for Juventus against Sampdoria in 2006.

again at the 2000 European Championship. Despite missing a penalty in the semi-final shoot-out against Holland, Maldini found himself in the final and seconds away from lifting the Henri Delaunay trophy. But Italy's slender 1-0 lead over France was obliterated in the game's final minute and the French went on to win in extra-time.

Maldini announced his retirement from international football after Italy's exit from the 2002 World Cup finals with a record-breaking 126 caps for his country. He is expected to bring down the curtain on his club career with Milan at the end of the 2006-7 season as he nears his 36th birthday.

GAIZKA MENDIETA

Country: Spain
Born: March 27, 1974
Position: Midfield
Clubs: Castellón, Valencia, Lazio, Barcelona, Middlesbrough

Basque-born Gaizka Mendieta became one of the hottest properties in football for his contribution to Valencia's run to two successive Champions League finals. Signed from second division Castellón at 19 years of age, he blossomed rapidly under Claudio Ranieri, drifting out wide and helping launch rapid counter-attacks. He made his international debut against Austria in 1999 and figured at both the European Championship of 2000 and the World Cup of 2002. However, a subsequent £30 million move to Lazio turned sour as he struggled to make an impact in Serie A. Barcelona brought him back on loan, where he attempted to piece his game back together. Middlesbrough signed Mendieta, initially on loan but then permanently. He helped the club

to win their first significant honour – the League Cup in 2004 and was in the team that reached the 2006 UEFA Cup final. He played 40 times for Spain between 1999 and 2002, including the 2000 European Championship and the 2002 World Cup.

LIONEL MESSI

Country: Argentina
Born: June 24, 1987
Position: Centre-forward
Clubs: Barcelona

Lionel Messi started his career with hometown club Newell's Old Boys but because he was suffering from a hormone deficiency that his parents were unable to afford to treat in Argentina, they decided to move to Barcelona. Messi had a trial with Barcelona at 13 and soon found himself in the club's B team, averaging more than a goal a game.

At 16 years of age Messi became the third youngest player ever to feature in the Barcelona first team, making his bow against local rivals Espanyol in October 2004, and the following June he picked up the Golden Boot as Argentina won the World Youth Championships. Dubbed 'the New Maradona', Messi made his full international debut against Hungary in August 2005 and impressed at the 2006 World Cup, despite making most of his appearances from the bench. He scored in the 6-0 rout of Serbia and Montenegro. For Barcelona he has gone on to claim a regular place in the starting line-up of Frank Rijkaard's team, although he failed to recover from a thigh injury in time to play in the European Champions League final of 2006.

FERNANDO MORIENTES

Country: Spain
Born: April 5, 1976
Position: Forward
Clubs: Albacete, Real Zaragoza, Real Madrid, Monaco, Real Madrid, Liverpool, Valencia

Fernando Morientes is a talented forward who has not been able to fulfil his maximum potential. Despite being named in Spain's preliminary 2006 World Cup squad, he was overlooked by coach Luis Aragones, even though he had played at the two previous tournaments. In 1998 Spain crashed out of the World Cup in the opening phase despite beating Bulgaria 6-1 in their final game, with Morientes scoring twice. In 2002 Spain were surprisingly beaten by hosts South Korea on penalties.

Not that silverware and success have eluded him. Morientes has won two Spanish titles and three Champions League medals, while in his early international career he raced to 20 goals in just 26 appearances. Even with Liverpool he won the FA Cup in 2006 before signing for Valencia.

PAVEL NEDVED

Country: Czech Republic
Born: August 30, 1972
Position: Midfield
Clubs: Dukla Prague, Sparta Prague, Lazio, Juventus

Dubbed the 'Czech Cannon' for his powerful but cultured left-foot, Pavel Nedved is the most talented and charismatic Czech footballer since Josef Masopust, a tireless runner capable of leading the line or acting as playmaker. He played for two of Prague's major sides, winning three league championships with Sparta, and became an automatic choice for the national side, starring in the final of the 1996 European Championship.

He joined Lazio, becoming the club's top scorer in 1998 and clinching the winning goal in the last ever Cup Winners' Cup final. He won the Scudetto in 2000 and was nominated the Best Foreign Player In Serie A before Juventus secured him for £26 million as a replacement for Zinédine Zidane.

In 2003 he was voted European Football Of The Year and he has been instrumental in the revival of Juventus, winning four Serie A titles in 2002, 2003, 2005 and 2006. In September 2004 Nedved announced his international retirement – three months earlier he had captained the Czech Republic to the European Championship semi-finals – but he was lured back in November 2005 for the World Cup play-offs with Norway and successfully helped the Czechs to qualify for the 2006 World Cup.

ALESSANDRO NESTA

Country: Italy
Born: March 19, 1976
Position: Central defender
Clubs: Lazio, AC Milan

A product of the Lazio youth system, Nesta made his senior debut for the Rome side when he was 17. After a marathon 18-year association with the club, which included winning the European Cup Winners' Cup in 1999, the Italian league title in 2000, and a long spell as captain, he transferred to Italian rivals AC Milan in August 2002 for £19 million. With Milan he won the European Champions League, European Super Cup and Italian Cup in 2003 and won another Serie A title in 2004.

On the international stage he was a member of Italy's Under-21 European Championship-winning team in 1996 and became a non-playing member of the Euro 96 squad, although he was not to make his full international debut until October that year. A defensive rock with sublime ball control, Nesta has gone on to become a regular fixture in the national side under a succession of coaches, and effectively marked Patrick Kluivert out of the game in

Italy's win over Holland in the semi-final at the 2000 European Championship. He appeared in the World Cups of 1998, 2002 and 2006, as well as the European Championship in 2004, but injury meant that he wasn't in the team that won the final, his replacement Marco Materazzi scoring Italy's goal in the game.

MICHAEL OWEN

Country: England
Born: December 14, 1979
Position: Forward
Club: Liverpool, Real Madrid, Newcastle United

A prolific goalscorer, Michael Owen made his Liverpool debut against Wimbledon in May 1997, and as a regular in the side the following season, he showed his predatory instincts by netting 18 league goals. He was rewarded with an England debut against Chile in February 1998, making him the youngest player of the last century to represent his country. He went on to make a real impact at the World Cup that year, scoring one of the tournament's most outstanding goals against Argentina.

In each of his six full seasons at Anfield, Owen was Liverpool's leading scorer, and even a serious hamstring injury, sustained against Leeds United at the tail end of the 1998-9 season, did not dent a goalscoring ratio of more than one goal in every two league games. Although he had already enjoyed many career highs, in 2001 he helped Liverpool to success in three cup competitions – the UEFA Cup, the League Cup and the FA Cup – and he was voted European Footballer Of The Year. Owen also scored more goals for England than any other Liverpool player.

In August 2004, after 158 goals in 257 games with Liverpool, Owen joined Spanish giants Real Madrid but lasted just one season. He was not guaranteed a first team place but still managed to score 16 goals for the club. Owen returned to the Premiership with Graeme Souness's Newcastle United after a £17 million transfer. Unfortunately, on New Year's Eve 2005, Owen suffered a broken foot that ruled him out of action for much of the remainder of the 2005-6 season. He recovered just in time to lead England's bid for the 2006 World Cup. However, yet another injury ended his

tournament in the first minute of England's final group game with Sweden.

JI-SUNG PARK

Country: South Korea
Born: February 25, 1981
Position: Midfield
Clubs: Kyoto Purple Sanga, PSV Eindhoven, Manchester United

Park began his J-League career in 2000 and was the first Korean to make it into Japan's top division without having to start out in the K-League. He broke into the South Korea national team at 18 and rose to fame with his performances at the 2002 World Cup. The following year Park teamed up with his former international coach Guus Hiddink at PSV Eindhoven and after Arjen Robben's departure to Chelsea in 2004, he began to flourish. His Champions League performances, as PSV reached the 2005 semi-finals, prompted Sir Alex Ferguson to splash out £4 million on his services and the versatile midfielder has excelled in a host of positions.

Above: Michael Owen heads home against Argentina in 2005, but the goal was disallowed.

PAULETA

Country: Portugal
Born: April 28, 1973
Position: Striker
Clubs: Uniao Micaelense, Estoril-Praia, UD Salamanca, Deportivo La Coruna, Bordeaux, Paris Saint-Germain

Possessing a good touch, excellent in the air and powerful, Pauleta could well end up being remembered for two quirky facts. He is the first player from the Azores to play for Portugal, and he is also the first Portuguese international never to have played in that nation's top division, making his name in the Spanish and French leagues. On the fringes of the national side at Euro 2000, by the World Cup of 2002 he was leading the line and scored three times, while at Euro 2004 he failed to register as Portugal lost out in the final. But he is a proven goalscorer, and in October 2005 overtook legend Eusébio as Portugal's all-time top scorer.

ROBERT PIRÈS

Country: France
Born: January 29, 1973
Position: Midfield
Clubs: Metz, Marseille, Arsenal, Villareal

Robert Pirès came to life at Arsenal following a £6 million move from Marseille in 2000 and was voted England's Footballer Of The Year in 2002 after helping the club win the league and FA Cup double. He went on to win the FA Cup twice and the Premiership once more before joining Spanish club Villareal in 2006, just after playing in Arsenal's Champions League final defeat. A gifted attacker, he can play in a variety of positions and is capable of both creating and scoring goals. Earlier in his career, he won the French Young Player Of The Year award while at Metz in 1996 and was a squad member at both the World Cup in 1998 and the European Championship in 2000. He had to endure two disappointing seasons as he struggled at Marseille before returning to prominence in England with Arsenal. Pirès missed out on selection for the World Cup in 2006 after criticising coach Raymond Domenech in October 2004. Despite apologising he did not add to his 79 caps and failed to make the squad.

ANDREA PIRLO

Country: Italy
Born: May 19, 1979
Position: Midfield
Clubs: Brescia, Inter Milan, Reggina, Inter Milan, Brescia, AC Milan

Andrea Pirlo was an outstanding member of Italy's 2006 World Cup-winning team and he came close to being voted player of the tournament, finishing in third place behind Zinédine Zidane and Fabio Cannavaro for FIFA's Golden Ball Award. Pirlo had also been voted Man Of The Match in Italy's semi-final win over hosts Germany, a match regarded as the best in the tournament.

Pirlo has been an impressive deep-lying midfielder for Milan and Italy, imposing his will on matches as ball-winner and playmaker. He is also a free-kick specialist and was a member of Milan's Champions league-winning team in 2003, before clinching the Serie A title, his first domestic honour, the following year.

Success has not come easily as Pirlo made his Serie A debut for Brescia back in May 1995. A move to Inter Milan followed but he was largely overlooked by coach Marcello Lippi (who went on to select him for Italy's 2006 World Cup win). Loan spells with Reggina and Brescia followed before a move to Milan where, at Pirlo's own suggestion, coach Carlo Ancelotti found him a regular place in the starting line-up as a deep-lying midfielder. At the end of that season Pirlo made his international debut against Azerbaijan and he hasn't looked back since.

LUKAS PODOLSKI

Country: Germany
Born: June 4, 1985
Position: Centre-forward
Club: Köln, Bayern Munich

Lukas Podolski made his international bow at the 2004 European Championships, aged just 19, but showed his undoubted potential at the 2005 Confederations Cup, where he scored three times. A powerful forward, he grabbed ten goals in 19 games in his first full Bundesliga season with Köln in 2003-4 and then netted 24 goals in 30 games in Bundesliga Two as the club made an immediate return to the top division. His outstanding performances at the 2006 World Cup saw him voted FIFA Young Player Of The Tournament and he has a big future ahead of him.

DADO PRSO

Country: Croatia
Born: November 5, 1974
Position: Forward
Clubs: NK Zardar, Hajduk Split, NK Pazinka, Rouen, San Raphael, Monaco, AC Ajaccio, Monaco, Rangers

After Rangers clinched the 2006 Scottish championship, helped in no small way by 12 goals from Dado Prso, departing boss Alex McLeish described Prso as 'the best signing ever'. He had risen to prominence at Monaco, under Jean Tigana, winning the French league title in 2000 and playing in the 2004 European Champions League final. Prso was a late-comer to the international scene, not making his debut until he was 28. His goals helped to propel Croatia to the 2004 European Championship and, although the team made an early exit, Prso scored with a spectacular volley past Fabien Barthez in a 2-2 draw with France. His goals also helped Croatia to the 2006 World Cup. He announced he was to make his international retirement after the tournament. Prso has twice been voted Croatia's Player Of The Year.

CARLES PUYOL

Country: Spain
Born: April 13, 1978
Position: Defender
Clubs: Barcelona

A one-club man, and a Catalan at that, Carles Puyol is the type of player the fans of Barcelona adore. With the club once again in the ascendancy, the big money imports may grab the headlines, but it is club captain Puyol who helps the team bond. He made his first team debut in 1999 against arch-rivals Real Madrid and developed into a superb full-back, gaining Spain Under-21 and full international honours, including the 2002 and 2006 World Cups. Now a centre-back, his never-say-die attitude is popular and has attracted interest from many top clubs, but it is unlikely he can be lured away, particularly after lifting the Champions League trophy for the club in 2006.

RAÚL

Country: Spain
Born: June 27, 1977
Position: Forward
Club: Real Madrid

Raúl became the first player to score 50 goals in the European Cup in September 2005 when he netted against Olympiakos in the Champions League. In so doing he beat the 49-goal record held by former Real Madrid great Alfredo Di Stéfano which had been established some 41 years and 145 days before. Raúl has been a

Below: Raúl of Real Madrid became the first player to score 50 goals in the European Cup.

sensation at Real ever since becoming the youngest player ever to make his debut for the club, at 17 years and four months old in 1994. He has won the European Champions league on three occasions, in 1998 beating Juventus 1-0, in 2000 scoring the third goal in a 3-0 win over Valencia, and, in 2002, scoring the opener in a 2-1 win over Bayer Leverkusen. In domestic football Raúl has notched up four Spanish league titles and three Spanish Cups.

He made his debut for Spain at the age of 19 and has been a permanent fixture ever since. Raúl is the nation's all-time top goalscorer, the most-capped outfield player and, since 2002, he has been captain. He has played in three World Cups and two European Championships. He had the distinction of scoring both Spain's 800th and 900th international goal against Austria in 1999 and Greece in 2002.

ALVARO RECOBA

Country: Uruguay
Born: March 17, 1976
Position: Forward
Clubs: Danubio, Nacional, Venezia, Inter Milan

Alvaro Recoba is reputedly among the highest-paid players in Serie A, but Inter Milan must be happy with what they are getting for their money as, bar a six-month loan spell at Venezia, he has been at the club since 1997. He made an immediate impact, scoring twice on his debut in a 2-1 victory over Brescia, with one strike from more than 30 yards. A technically-gifted player with a fantastic left foot, he is dangerous with his pace, is a set-piece specialist and is equally adept at playing as a central striker or in a free role behind the front men. In his time at the club, they have won the Italian Cup twice, although after Juventus were stripped of their Serie A title in 2006, Inter were retrospectively awarded the championship. He has had injury problems too. However, with Uruguay he has been as popular as ever, despite missing a golden opportunity in a World Cup play-off with Australia, which cost his nation a place at the 2006 finals.

JUAN ROMAN RIQUELME

Country: Argentina
Born: June 26, 1978
Position: Midfield
Clubs: Argentinos Juniors, Boca Juniors, Barcelona, Villarreal

In 1996 Riquelme took the same journey as Maradona, moving from Argentinos Juniors to Boca Juniors, where his flair, vision and eye for goal soon made him a star. Within a year he had made his international debut against Colombia, but it was his match-winning performances in the 2000 Copa Libertadores against Palmeiras and the World Club Championship against Real Madrid that earned him a host of European

admirers. Another Copa Libertadores win the following season, beating Mexico's Cruz Azul in the final led to both the Argentinian and South American Player Of The Year awards. He signed for Barcelona in a £17 million deal in 2002 but after one indifferent season was loaned to Villarreal. His numerous assists for Diego Forlan and Antonio Guayre helped the club to third place in La Liga in 2005 and he celebrated by signing a permanent contract with the club.

For the national side he wears the coveted number 10 shirt and, under Jose Pekerman, became the team's playmaker in an attacking midfield role, a position he played at his first World Cup in 2006.

RIVALDO

Country: Brazil
Born: April 19, 1972
Position: Forward/Midfield
Clubs: Santa Cruz, Mogi Mirim, Corinthians, Palmeiras, Deportivo La Coruna, Barcelona, AC Milan, Cruzeiro, Olympiakos

Reinaldo Vitor Borba Ferreira, or Rivaldo as he is more commonly known, began his road to fame and fortune with local club Paulista at the age of 17. Following spells at Santa Cruz and Corinthians, he joined Palmeiras in 1994, helping the club to two championships. His goalscoring potential was spotted by Spanish side Deportivo La Coruna in 1996, and in one season at the Riazor, he scored an incredible 30 goals in 30 games.

A regular for Brazil, he moved to Barcelona for £18 million as a replacement for Ronaldo and his impact was immediate, as he inspired Barcelona to league and cup success in his first season. Rivaldo's outstanding form at the Nou Camp was rewarded with the FIFA World Player Of The Year and European Player Of The Year awards in 1999 and his worth to the side was never more evident than on the final day of the 2000-1 season when his hat-trick secured Barcelona a place in the following season's Champions League tournament. It is widely regarded as one of the best hat-tricks ever scored, but with the club's continued lack of success both in Europe and domestically, Rivaldo was offloaded to AC Milan in the summer of 2002, despite an exceptional showing at the World Cup in Japan.

Rivaldo performances at the World Cup helped Brazil to their fifth world title and he was their most consistent performer, playing in all seven games. He scored in each of the three group games against Turkey, China and Costa Rica and in the knockout stages against Belgium and England. He finished as the tournament's joint second highest scorer. In the final against Germany it was his dummy that led Ronaldo to score Brazil's second goal. His other honours for Brazil include winning the Copa América in 1997 and 1999, where he was top scorer.

Rivaldo helped Milan to reach the Champions League final in 2003 but missed the game itself. He did win the Italian Cup. He was to return to Brazil at the end of the season but then signed for Olympiakos, with whom he won the Greek league and cup double in 2004-5 and 2005-6.

ROBINHO

Country: Brazil
Born: January 25, 1984
Position: Centre-forward
Clubs: Santos, Real Madrid

Robson de Souza, nicknamed Robinho, or Little Robson, caught the eye with Santos in 2002, scoring seven goals as he helped the club to the Brazilian title. Comparisons were quickly drawn with the legendary Garrincha and although the following season was a relatively quiet one, he netted 21 goals in 36 matches in 2004, alerting a host of European clubs to his undoubted talents. Having seen his mother kidnapped for two months late in the year, Robinho decided to quit Brazil and eventually moved to Real Madrid in 2005 for a fee of £17 million.

RONALDINHO

Country: Brazil
Born: March 21, 1980
Position: Forward
Clubs: Gremio, Paris Saint-Germain, Barcelona

One of the best players at the 2002 World Cup finals, Ronaldinho helped Brazil to victory by forming a spectacular attacking trio with Ronaldo and Rivaldo. He was shortlisted for FIFA Player Of The Tournament and made headlines with his free-kick goal that beat

Above: Twice voted FIFA World Player Of The Year, Ronaldinho of Barcelona and Brazil.

Above: Manchester United's Wayne Rooney celebrates scoring against Birmingham City in 2005.

England keeper David Seaman from great distance in the quarter-final. He first came to prominence at the Copa América in 1999, which Brazil won beating Uruguay 3-0 in the final. He was to win the Copa América again in 2005, along with the Confederations Cup.

A sublimely gifted player, he took time to settle in France after a protracted move to Paris SG but he only established his credentials as one of the world's most exciting players when he moved to Barcelona in 2003. He was named FIFA World Player Of The Year in both 2004 and 2005, and was selected as European Player Of The Year after winning his first Spanish league title in 2005. That year he was also the inaugural winner of the FIFPro Player Of The Year award voted for by players. Further glory followed in 2006 with another Spanish league title, plus victory over Arsenal in the European Champions League final in Paris.

RONALDO

Country: Brazil
Born: September 22, 1976
Position: Forward
Clubs: Cruzeiro, PSV Eindhoven, Barcelona, Inter Milan, Real Madrid

Right: The Phenomenon, Ronaldo on the ball for Real Madrid.

Once dubbed 'The Phenomenon', Ronaldo is the closest thing to a modern day Pelé that Brazil has managed to produce. At the peak of his

football powers he demonstrated searing pace, unbelievable skill and a razor sharp finishing ability, whether breaking from his own half to score alone or tapping in from a few feet.

Ronaldo Luiz Nazario de Lima was born in Bento Ribeiro, in the suburbs of Río De Janeiro. He made his debut for Cruzeiro aged 16 and earned a place in the squad for the World Cup in 1994, having made his debut that year against Argentina. He left Brazil to join Bobby Robson's PSV Eindhoven, following in the footsteps of another great Brazilian predator, Romario. In two seasons in Holland he scored 42 goals, despite playing only 13 matches in the 1995-6 season. When Robson took over at Barcelona in 1996 he promptly spent £20 million on Ronaldo, who scored 47 goals in his one season with the Catalan club, winning the European Cup Winners' Cup in the process.

At the 1998 World Cup in France, Ronaldo's world began to unravel. The team leant heavily on him but he managed only four goals on the way to the final. On the eve of the big match Ronaldo suffered a fit, which led to his name being struck-off the team sheet in the hour leading up to the kick-off. However, when the Brazilians took to the pitch he was there, though patently unfit. Brazil lost the game amid much acrimony, but worse was to come.

He joined Inter Milan for £19 million and scored 25 goals in his first season, but wear and tear after years of playing top-level football from

a young age resulted in a serious knee injury in November 1999. Five months later he made his return in the final of the Italian Cup, but collapsed in agony after just seven minutes without being touched.

Many wrote off his chances of returning to football but he fought back after extensive rehabilitation to prove his fitness in time for the 2002 World Cup finals. The tournament proved his redemption as he scored eight goals, including two in the final against Germany, on the way to lifting the trophy and winning the Golden Boot. He was also named FIFA World Player Of The Year for the third time. There was bitterness at Inter Milan, however. After spending long periods of his contract injured, as soon as he was fit he jumped ship to join Real Madrid for £23 million in September 2002.

Carrying extra weight he struggled to convince Real Madrid fans that he merited a place above favourite Morientes, but eventually proved his worth in the Champions League. At the 2006 World Cup his performances were criticised but he nevertheless netted three goals to become the competition's all-time top scorer with 15 goals.

WAYNE ROONEY

Country: England
Born: October 24, 1985
Position: Forward
Club: Everton, Manchester United

Becoming England's youngest international when he made his debut as a substitute against Australia aged just 17 years and 111 days, Rooney has the natural talent to become a major international star. England boss Sven-Göran Eriksson certainly thought so. He selected Rooney for the crucial away European Championship qualifier against Turkey and the youngster impressed with a confident display.

He signalled his arrival in the Premiership with a fabulous late goal to help Everton to victory over Arsenal, and his power and touch belie his youth. Wayne Rooney had a sensational European Championship in 2004, netting four goals in the tournament, scoring two each against Switzerland and Croatia respectively. However, in the quarter-final clash with hosts Portugal, with England leading 1-0, Rooney suffered a serious foot injury and was substituted after just 27 minutes. England went on to squander the lead twice and ultimately lost out on penalties.

A lucrative £27 million move to Manchester United followed and he began his career at Old Trafford with a stunning hat-trick in the Champions League clash against Fenerbahçe. Since joining United the Premiership title has eluded him, as has the FA Cup – he was in the team that lost the 2005 final on penalties. He did finally win his first piece of silverware with the 2006 League Cup.

Towards the end of the 2005-6 season he suffered a broken metatarsal in his foot seriously affected his plans to take part in the 2006 World Cup finals. In the run up to the tournament his medical reports fascinated the nation and dominated news bulletins. Rooney was included in the England squad and his impressive powers of recovery saw him return by the second group game against Trinidad And Tobago. Although England reached the last eight, Rooney – largely due to Eriksson's tactics – did not perform at his best and against Portugal he was sent-off for violent conduct and had to look on as England once again went out on penalties.

TOMAS ROSICKY

Country: Czech Republic
Born: October 4, 1980
Position: Midfield
Clubs: Sparta Prague, Borussia Dortmund, Arsenal

In 2001 Borussia Dortmund paid a Bundesliga record £18 million to Sparta Prague for Czech Republic international Tomas Rosicky. It was the most money any German club had paid for a foreign player. Dortmund had been impressed with his superb performances for Sparta in the European Champions League and were looking for a player to replace the recently transferred Andreas Moller. Rosicky helped Dortmund to the UEFA Cup final in his first season, but they were a club on the slide and facing bankruptcy.

With Dortmund facing increasing financial pressures, and with Rosicky's own loss of form and injury problems, a sale was inevitable. In his five seasons at the Westfalen Stadium he had played 154 matches and scored 20 goals. Arsenal were interested and paid £6.8 million for the Czech midfielder just prior to the 2006 World Cup. On the international stage he has remained indispensable, his seven goals in qualifying helped propel the Czech Republic team to the 2006 World Cup finals.

RUI COSTA

Country: Portugal
Born: March 29, 1972
Position: Midfield
Clubs: Fafe, Benfica, Fiorentina, AC Milan, Benfica

On his day a brilliant playmaker, the man around whom his national and club sides tick, Rui Costa was a member of Portugal's 'Golden Generation' which won the World Under 17 title in 1989 and the World Youth Cup in 1991. His passing and creativity have seen him lured to some of Europe's top clubs, AC Milan paying £28 million for him in 2001. In his homeland many believed him more vital to the side than Luis Figo. Able to score spectacular goals, injury has hampered

his career. Inconsistency has proved his only weakness – he had an outstanding Euro 2000, but was disappointing at the 2002 World Cup when not fully fit. He retired from international football after defeat in the Euro 2004 final and decided to play out his career at Benfica, rejoining the Lisbon club for the 2006-7 season.

MARCELO SALAS

Country: Chile
Born: December 24, 1974
Position: Forward
Clubs: Universidad de Chile, River Plate, Lazio, Juventus, River Plate, Universidad de Chile

Marcelo Salas is Chile's all-time top goalscorer having netted 35 goals in a 64-match nine-year international career. In 1997 he was South America's Player Of The Year. Dubbed 'The Matador' for his finishing, Marcelo Salas is a quicksilver forward with a dynamic left foot. Born of Indian blood in Temuco, he joined Universidad de Chile in 1990 but moved to River Plate in 1996, winning three Argentine league titles. He made his name at the World Cup in 1998, beating the record of Chilean legend Zamorano with four goals, a tally that helped him secure a move to Lazio, scoring 12 goals in their 2000 double-winning season.

He left for Juventus in 2001 but was sidelined by a knee ligament injury. He did manage to win one Serie A title with Juve before returning to River Plate in a £6.5 million deal in 2004. In July 2005 he rejoined his first club but his appearances were limited due to injury and the national team missed him as they failed to qualify for the 2006 World Cup.

WALTER SAMUEL

Country: Argentina
Born: March 23, 1978
Position: Centre-Back
Clubs: Newell's Old Boys, Boca Juniors, Roma, Real Madrid, Inter Milan

Walter Samuel's towering presence came to prominence with Argentina's 1997 World Youth Championship-winning team. Three years later he was part of the Boca Juniors side that lifted the Copa Libertadores. He was lured to play in Italy by Roma and in four seasons with the club he earned the nickname 'The Wall' for his prized defensive abilities. In his first season Roma won the 2001 Italian title. After a brief, unhappy season in Spain with Real Madrid in 2004-5, his fortunes were revived with a move to Inter Milan, who won the Italian Cup in his first season. The club were also retrospectively awarded the league title after the Italian match-fixing enquiry stripped Juventus of the honour. On the international stage he has formed a formidable central defensive partnership with Roberto Ayala, helping Argentina cruise to two World Cups.

Above: Argentinian Javier Saviola in action for Seville.

JAVIER SAVIOLA

Country: Argentina
Born: December 11, 1981
Position: Forward
Clubs: River Plate, Barcelona, Monaco, Seville

At £18 million Javier Saviola was the world's most expensive teenager when he signed for Barcelona in 2001. By then he had already cemented his reputation as a gifted footballer and prolific goalscorer. He was only 16 when he made his debut with River Plate and at the tender age of 18 he was South America's Footballer Of The Year. In 2001 he was player of the tournament at the World Youth Championships and he finished top scorer as his goals helped Argentina to the trophy.

A year later he was playing at his first World Cup. However, Saviola fell out of favour with successive Barcelona bosses Louis Van Gaal and then Frank Rijkaard. Unable to feature in the first team his place in the Argentina national squad was threatened. He was loaned out to Monaco and then Seville. The season with Seville rehabilitated his reputation as he won the UEFA Cup with the club and secured his place in Argentina's World Cup squad.

PAUL SCHOLES

Country: England
Born: November 16, 1974
Position: Midfield
Club: Manchester United

Paul Scholes may not get the same media attention as some of his team-mates, but there are few players who are as effective on the pitch. His fantastic runs into the box, and his shooting and heading ability, have meant that his goalscoring record from midfield for club and country is impressive. But there is a discipline to his game that is rarely found in attacking midfielders. Never one to neglect his defensive duties, Scholes is a terrifically hard-working and tough-tackling player.

After winning the FA Youth Cup in 1992 he had to wait two more seasons before making his breakthrough into first team. Inevitably the honours flowed, including the 1998-9 treble winning season of FA Cup, Premiership and Champions League, although he missed the European final through suspension. In all Scholes has won the Premiership on six occasions and the FA Cup three times.

His international career began in 1997 against South Africa at Old Trafford and he went on to play at two World Cups, in 1998 and 2002, and the European Championships of 2000 and 2004. After 65 appearances in which he scored 14 goals, Scholes announced his international retirement following Euro 2004.

ANDRIY SHEVCHENKO

Country: Ukraine
Born: August 29, 1976
Position: Forward
Clubs: Dynamo Kiev, AC Milan, Chelsea

Just before the 2006 World Cup Andriy Shevchenko signed for English Premiership champions Chelsea from AC Milan for a British record £31 million. Ukrainian international Shevchenko ended a seven-year association with the Italian giants despite being offered an extension to his contract. During his years at the San Siro, Shevchenko, who cost the club £16 million in 1999, was a prolific goalscorer.

In his first season he scored 24 goals, making him Serie A highest scorer, while in 2003 he scored the decisive penalty in the shoot out with Juventus in the all-Italian Champions League final. By December that year he had scored his 100th Serie A goal and went on to be the season's top scorer again with 24 goals as Milan won the league title. At the year's end he was crowned European Footballer Of The Year.

In 2005 Milan once again reached the

Below: Andriy Shevchenko of Ukraine looks to pull away from a Greece defender in 2005.

Champions League final, but they squandered a 3-0 lead against Liverpool. In the penalty shoot-out this time Shevchenko missed his kick and the trophy went to England. The following season he became only the second player to score over 50 goals in the European Cup.

In his native Ukraine, Shevchenko is a major star and in 2004 he was given the Hero Of Ukraine award by the country's president. He was brought up through the ranks at Dynamo Kiev and his first trophy was presented to him at age 13 by Ian Rush at a tournament in Wales. He formed a lethal partnership with Sergei Rebrov in Dynamo Kiev's 1997 Champions League campaign, scoring a hat-trick at Barcelona. He was later to improve on that with a four-goal haul for Milan against Fenerbahçe in November 2005. With Kiev he won five Ukrainian league title, including two doubles.

For the national side, since making his debut in April 1995 against Croatia, Shevchenko has been the team's driving force, scoring an array of goals that make him by far the nation's all-time top goalscorer. He is also the captain of the side and helped guide them to their first major tournament, the 2006 World Cup.

RIGOBERT SONG

Country: Cameroon
Born: July 1, 1976
Position: Defender
Clubs: Metz, Salernitana, Liverpool, West Ham United, Köln, Lens, Galatasaray

Rigobert Song came to prominence during the 1994 World Cup in the United States, and he was a key man for his nation in both the 1998 and 2002 finals. He has gone on to set a Cameroon record for international appearances, representing them on more than a hundred occasions. He signed for Liverpool from Italian Serie A club Salernitana, operating at both full-back and centre-back for the Reds. A move to West Ham didn't really work out for him, and further moves across Europe followed. But it is on the international stage that he really excels. The personification of his nation's nickname, he led the Indomitable Lions to the African Nations Cup, although in the final against Senegal in 2002 he had a penalty saved.

JUAN PABLO SORIN

Country: Argentina
Born: May 5, 1976
Position: Midfield
Clubs: Argentinos Juniors, Juventus, River Plate, Cruzeiro, Lazio, Barcelona, Paris Saint-Germain, Villarreal

After just one season in his homeland, former Argentina Under-19 captain Juan Pablo Sorin set off to Europe in 1995 to find fame and fortune with Juventus. Unfortunately, the

classy midfielder found it hard to adapt to life in Serie A and returned home after just two games. With River Plate he was far happier, helping the club to four league championships and a Copa Libertadores title before switching to Brazilian side Cruzeiro, where he won two domestic cups. His return to Europe took in loan spells with Lazio, Barcelona and Paris Saint-Germain, before he signed a four-year deal with Villarreal in 2004, adding guile to the club's Champions League campaign in the 2005-6 season.

JAAP STAM

Country: Holland
Born: July 17, 1972
Position: Centre-back
Clubs: Zwolle, Cambuur, Willem II, PSV Eindhoven, Manchester United, Lazio, AC Milan, Ajax

Jaap Stam became the world's most expensive defender when he joined Manchester United in 1998, and he enjoyed a dream first season, winning the Premiership, the FA Cup and the European Champions League. But after falling out with manager Alex Ferguson the imposing defender forced out of the club only three years in to his five-year contract.

Signing for Lazio, his career in Italy didn't get off to the best of starts and he had to serve a five-month ban for testing positive for nandralone. Following his time in Rome, which climaxed with an Italian Cup win, Jaap Stam joined AC Milan for two seasons and featured in the team that surrendered a three-goal lead in the Champions League final before being defeated on penalties by Liverpool. He returned home to Holland with Ajax in 2006.

Stam played 67 times for his country and scored three goals before his international retirement after the Euro 2004. Stam has been losing semi-finalist on three occasions at major tournaments. At France 98 in his only World Cup Holland were beaten 4-2 on penalties after a 1-1 draw with Brazil. He was twice a European Championship semi-finalist: in 2000 his penalty miss, one of three failed Dutch kicks in the shoot-out, saw Holland lose to Italy, while four years later they lost 2-1 to hosts Portugal.

JOHN TERRY

Country: England
Born: December 7, 1980
Position: Defender
Clubs: Chelsea

A strong, no nonsense centre-back with inspirational leadership qualities, John Terry is captain of Chelsea and an England regular. The Barking-born defender was spotted by the Blues playing Sunday League football and worked his way up through the club's youth and reserve teams before eventually making his senior debut in October 1998. A first team regular under Chelsea boss Claudio Ranieri, Terry was quickly installed as club captain when José Mourinho took the reins at Stamford Bridge in the summer of 2004. The following season saw him named PFA Player Of The Year as he led Chelsea to their first league title in 50 years, conceding only 15 goals as they did so.

He made his England debut against Serbia and Montenegro in 2003 and was an integral part of the side that made it to the quarter-final stages of Euro 2004 and the 2006 World Cup. He is England's first-choice centre-back.

CARLOS TEVEZ

Country: Argentina
Born: February 5, 1984
Position: Forward/Midfield
Clubs: Boca Juniors, Corinthians

It is little wonder that Carlos Tevez has been dubbed the 'new Maradona' after winning a hat-trick of South American Player Of The Year awards in 2003, 2004 and 2005. He has all the makings of a world star. Signed by Argentine giants Boca Juniors from youth side All Boys (whom he joined aged eight), he was part of Boca's all-conquering team that claimed the national championship, the Copa Libertadores and the World Club Cup in 2003, and the Copa Sudamericana in 2004. But it was at the 2004 Olympics he shot to world attention, becoming the football tournament's top scorer. In 2004 he shocked many by signing for Corinthians of Brazil in a big money deal, instead of moving to Europe. A real livewire, perhaps his best quality is that he can perform the unexpected with apparent ease.

LILIAN THURAM

Country: France
Born: January 1, 1972
Position: Defender
Clubs: Monaco, Parma, Juventus, Barcelona

Lilian Thuram came to prominence at the 1998 World Cup as one of the best players of the tournament and produced an unforgettable performance by scoring both goals in the 2-1 semi-final win over Croatia. He started his career at Monaco and joined Parma in 1996, quickly becoming one of the outstanding defenders in Serie A. Capable at centre-back or right-back, his strengths are power and man-marking. He added another honour when France won the European Championship in 2000 and became the world's most expensive defender when he joined Juventus for £22 million in 2001, helping them win the Italian title the following year.

Further titles followed in 2003, 2005 and 2006, along with Italian Cup triumphs in 2002 and 2003. After Euro 2004 Thuram retired from international football, having made 111 appearances, but he returned to Les Bleus a year later and took part in his third successive World Cup in 2006, picking up a runners-up medal. After the World Cup he signed for Barcelona.

FRANCESCO TOLDO

Country: Italy
Born: February 12, 1971
Position: Goalkeeper
Clubs: AC Milan, Verona, Trento, Ravenna, Fiorentina, Inter Milan

Part of Italy's Under-21 side which won the European Championship in 1994, Francesco Toldo had begun his club career with AC Milan's youth team. As a 19-year-old he joined Trento of Italy's Serie C2, but two years later was playing in Serie A with Fiorentina, where he stayed for eight seasons. When Italy's first choice goalkeeper, Gianluigi Buffon, broke his hand a week before the start of the 2000 European Championship, Toldo stepped in to deputise. His penalty saves in the semi-final against Holland – first from Frank De Boer in normal time, and then from De Boer (again) and Paul Bosvelt in the shoot-out that followed – took Italy to the final and had many proclaiming him as the tournament's best goalkeeper. Although part of the Italian squad for the 2002 World Cup finals, he was left on the bench for all four of his country's matches, as was the case for four of the five successive tournaments he attended with Italy between 1996 and 2004.

LUCA TONI

Country: Italy
Born: May 26, 1977
Position: Striker
Clubs: Modena, Treviso, Vicenza Calcio, Brescia Calcio, Palermo, Fiorentina

Derided by many after playing for a string of 'unfashionable' clubs, for evidence of Toni's quality, look no further than his goals tally in season 2005-6, a campaign in which he shattered the 26-goal Fiorentina club record held jointly by Gabriel Batistuta and Swedish legend Kurt Hamrin. Toni is more than just a goalscorer, but he has managed to bang them in throughout his career, especially at Palermo, where his 30-goal tally in one season helped them gain promotion. His 20 goals the following year attracted the attention of Fiorentina, who paid £7 million for his services.

Toni had looked to have just missed out on international honours, but crucial goals in qualifying for the World Cup in 2006, including a hat-trick against Belarus, meant that he travelled to the finals as his country's leading striker. In the 2006 World Cup final he hit the crossbar and had a goal disallowed as Italy became world champions for the fourth time.

FRANCESCO TOTTI

Country: Italy
Born: September 27, 1976
Position: Midfield/Forward
Club: Roma

Above: Roma's Francesco Totti in full flight as he powers through the Siena defence at the Olympic Stadium in Rome.

Francesco Totti made his debut for AS Roma in March 1993, aged just 16, but didn't become a first-team regular until two years later. In 2001 he captained the club to their first Italian title for 18 years and scored 13 goals in 30 league appearances. Preferring to play as an attacking midfielder or deep-lying forward, Totti made his first appearance for the Italian national side against Switzerland in October 1998. He went on to impress at the Euro 2000, scoring a superb goal against Romania and converting a crucial penalty in the semi-final shoot-out with Holland. He was Italy's best player in the final defeat to France, however, his red card against South Korea in Italy's disastrous 2002 World Cup campaign, and the ban he received at Euro 2004 after spitting at Denmark's Christian Poulsen, put Totti under the microscope for the wrong reasons. He bounced back, however, and picked up a World Cup winners medal in 2006.

KOLO TOURE

Country: Ivory Coast
Born: March 19, 1981
Position: Centre-Back
Clubs: ASEC Mimosas, Beveren, Arsenal

Kolo Toure was discovered by Ivory Coast's most successful club ASEC Mimosas. In 2002 he was given a trial and subsequently signed by English Premiership club Arsenal. He made his first team debut later that year and was converted from being a midfielder to a central defender by Arsene Wenger. In his four seasons with the club Toure has won the Premiership title in 2004 and won the FA Cup in 2005. He has been an influential figure in Ivory Coast's young side that reached the 2006 African Nations Cup final and took them to their first World Cup later that year.

Above: After signing for Real Madrid, Ruud Van Nistelrooy poses between club legend Alfredo Di Stéfano and club president Ramon Calderon.

DAVID TREZEGUET

Country: France
Born: October 15, 1977
Position: Centre-forward
Clubs: Platense, Monaco, Juventus

Son of Argentine footballer Jorge Trezeguet, David was born in France but started his career with Argentinian side Platense in 1994. His pace and directness caught the eye of Monaco, who brought him home a year later, and in his final season he bagged 22 goals in 20 matches as the club won the French title. Since joining Juventus in 2000 he has won three Serie A titles, scoring an impressive 24 goals along the way to their 2002 league championship win. Trezeguet has often been forced to play wide for France. Although he didn't play in the 1998 World Cup final, he can still boast a winners' medal as a squad member, while his golden goal against Italy in 2000 won the European Championship. In the 2006 World Cup final, however, it was his penalty that hit the bar in the shoot-out, handing the World Cup trophy to Italy.

EDWIN VAN DER SAR

Country: Holland
Born: October 29, 1970
Position: Goalkeeper
Clubs: Ajax, Juventus, Fulham, Manchester United

Goalkeeper Edwin Van Der Sar won a host of domestic trophies with his first club Ajax. There were four Dutch league titles and three Dutch Cups, including a league and cup double in 1998, but the highlight was the European Champions League triumph of 1995, when he kept a clean sheet against AC Milan in the final to help the club to a 1-0 win in Vienna. After 226 appearances with Ajax, he joined Italian giants Juventus in 1999 for two seasons.

It was a shock to many that after his time at the biggest club in Italy, Van Der Sar chose to sign for unfashionable Fulham for the start of their English Premiership adventure in 2001, but it was an excellent signing for Jean Tigana. The Dutch keeper proved an instant crowd favourite in West London, helping Fulham to an FA Cup semi-final and to top-flight survival with some inspirational performances.

He struggled with injuries in 2003 but still remained enough of dominant force between the posts to attract the attention of Manchester United, who were desperate for a reliable and settled keeper. In June 2005 Van Der Sar signed for United for an undisclosed fee (thought to be around £2 million) and established himself as first choice goalkeeper, helping the club win the League Cup in 2006.

He has played at five major tournaments with Holland, seeing the team knocked out of the first three – the European Championships of 1996 and 2000, and the World Cup in 1998 – by the lottery of the penalty shoot-out. Holland failed to qualify for the 2002 World Cup, while at Euro 2004 Van Der Sar and Holland were losing semi-finalists for a third time in four tournaments. During 2006 Van Der Sar became the most-capped Dutchman after overtaking Frank de Boer's record of 112 appearances.

RUUD VAN NISTELROOY

Position: Forward
Born: July 1, 1976
Country: Holland
Clubs: Den Bosch, Heerenveen, PSV Eindhoven, Manchester United, Real Madrid

Strong, fast and with a killer instinct for goal, Dutch striker Ruud Van Nistelrooy plied his trade for a while in the Dutch league, eventually making his name with PSV Eindhoven. It was at PSV that he first attracted the attentions of Manchester United manager, Sir Alex Ferguson, but a proposed deal in 2000 fell through after a medical revealed a weak right knee. The knee was to rupture two days later, but after a lengthy spell on the sidelines, Van Nistelrooy signed for United for £19 million in April 2001.

He had scored over 150 goals for the club by the end of the 2005-6 season, a year that had seen him recover from injury and develop a good partnership with Wayne Rooney. But after an alleged training ground altercation with team-mate Cristiano Ronaldo, the Dutchman was overlooked for the League Cup final, and he remained out-of-favour with Ferguson for the remainder of the season. During his time at Old Trafford he helped United win the Premiership in 2003 and the FA Cup – scoring twice in the final – in 2004, while he scored regularly in Europe for the club.

At the age of 29, Van Nistelrooy, as Holland's recognised first-choice striker under Marco Van Basten, played in his first World Cup in 2006. On his return he signed for Real Madrid.

JUAN SEBASTIÁN VERÓN

Country: Argentina
Born: March 9, 1975
Position: Midfield
Clubs: Estudiantes de la Plata, Boca Juniors, Sampdoria, Parma, Lazio, Manchester United, Chelsea, Inter Milan, Estudiantes de la Plata

The son of striker Juan Ramon Verón, 'Seba' was born in Buenos Aires and joined his father's team, Estudiantes de la Plata, before moving to Boca Juniors in 1996. He made his international debut against Poland that year and has starred in two World Cups. He moved to Sven-Göran Eriksson's Sampdoria in August 1996 before a £15 million move to Parma. He rejoined Eriksson at Lazio for £18 million in 1999 and was instrumental in the team's championship run. He then moved on to Manchester United for £28 million in July 2001.

Despite question marks over his impact, in his second season at Old Trafford he became the first Argentinian to win the league title in England, before moving to Chelsea for a fee of £15 million. First team appearances restricted by a back injury, Veron was on the fringes during his first season at Chelsea. With arrival of José Mourinho as coach, Veron was part of the clear out and was loaned to Inter Milan until the expiry of his contract. Veron celebrated by winning the Italian Cup in 2006, before returning home to Argentina to sign for his first club, Estudiantes.

MARK VIDUKA

Country: Australia
Born: October 9, 1975
Position: Centre-forward
Clubs: Melbourne Croatia, Croatia Zagreb, Celtic, Leeds United, Middlesbrough.

With Croatian parentage, Mark Viduka joined Croatia Zagreb at the request of President Franjo Tudjman, and while the country's leader was a fan, Zagreb's fans were not and after three years he was on his way to Celtic in a £3.5 million deal. Having netted 27 goals in his one full season, the burly striker with a lightweight touch joined Leeds United for £6 million in 2000 and helped the club reach the 2001 Champions League semi-final. United's financial troubles ensured his departure in 2004, having netted an impressive 59 league goals in 126 games. Middlesbrough were the benefactors, and while his performances since have been erratic, he helped the club to the UEFA Cup final in 2006. On the international stage Viduka is a mainstay of the Australia team and in 2006 he captained the country to their second World Cup.

PATRICK VIEIRA

Country: France
Born: June 23, 1976
Position: Midfield
Clubs: Cannes, AC Milan, Arsenal, Juventus, Inter Milan

Patrick Vieira's nine years at Arsenal between 1996 and 2005 coincided with a period when the club seriously challenged the supremacy of Alex Ferguson's Manchester United and reaped deserved silverware, winning the Premiership title on three occasions – the first as a league and cup double in 1997-8. The success was largely thanks to his midfield partnership with Emmanuel Petit. After three seasons as runners-up, Arsenal repeated the league and cup double with Vieira as captain. An FA Cup victory in 2003 was followed by a remarkable third title the following season, Vieira leading Arsenal through the league campaign unbeaten. The sliverware that he brought the club more than justified the £3.5 million that the London club had paid AC Milan for his services.

It was Juventus who finally lured Vieira away from Highbury in July 2005 in a £13.5 million deal. His last match for the Gunners was the 2005 FA Cup final in which Arsenal beat bitter rivals Manchester United 5-4 on penalties, with Vieira striking home the decisive spot kick.

Vieira, although born in Senegal, has also driven France to unprecedented success. He was part of the side that won the World Cup in 1998, beating Brazil 3-0 in the final. Vieira had started on the substitutes' bench but came on with 15 minutes remaining and was involved in creating the third goal. Two years later he was on the field from start to finish as France beat Italy 2-1 with an extra-time golden goal to win the European Championship. In the 2006 World Cup he held his place despite suggestions that he should be dropped, and he twice scored vital goals that helped France on the way to the final. Injury forced his substitution in the final before the cup was lost on penalties to Italy.

CHRISTIAN VIERI

Country: Italy
Born: July 12, 1973
Position: Centre-forward
Clubs: Prato, Torino, Pisa, Ravenna, Venezia, Atalanta, Juventus, Atlético Madrid, Lazio, Inter Milan, AC Milan, Monaco, Sampdoria

As famous for the number of clubs he has joined as for his goalscoring exploits, Christian Vieri rose to prominence while at Juventus. Originally acquired from Atalanta as a squad player, Vieri stepped into the first team after injuries to Alessandro Del Piero and Alen Boksic. He joined Spanish side Atlético Madrid in July 1997 and scored 24 goals in 24 games before a move to Lazio, with whom he won the European Cup

Winners' Cup. In July 1999 he was transferred to Inter for a world record fee of £31 million.

Vieri shone at the 1998 World Cup finals, scoring five goals in five games, including a superb chip over the goalkeeper in a 3-0 win against Cameroon. The tournament proved less fruitful in 2002, however. Vieri had put Italy ahead in the second round game against South Korea but they ultimately crashed out 2-1 in one of the tournament's biggest shocks.

Born in Bologna but raised in Sydney, his family had returned to Italy when he was a teenager, where as with his brother, he started off at Prato. But while both forged careers in Italy, his brother Max went on to play his international football for Australia.

SYLVAIN WILTORD

Country: France
Born: May 10, 1974
Position: Forward
Clubs: Rennes, Bordeaux, Deportivo La Coruna, Arsenal, Lyon

Sylvain Wiltord became Arsenal's record signing when he joined the club from Bordeaux

for £13 million in the summer of 2000, but the transfer was drawn out as Deportivo, the club he was on loan to, demanded a share of the fee. Once he took his place, Wiltord was shunted on to the wing as Thierry Henry and Dennis Bergkamp limited his chances in attack. He still netted 15 goals in his first season, and followed up with a further 17 as the club won the league and FA Cup double. A second Premiership and FA Cup double followed in 2004 before Wiltord, after netting 49 goals in four seasons, was sold to Lyon. Success continued as Lyon won successive French titles in 2005 and 2006, adding to the one he had secured with Bordeaux in 1999.

Wiltord was a part of France's European Championship-winning team in 2000. In the final against Italy, it was Wiltord, coming on as a 58th minute substitute, who struck the injury time equaliser that set up extra-time and David Trezeguet's golden goal. Since then he has had Confederations Cup success in 2001 and 2003 as France beat Japan and Cameroon respectively. He missed out on the biggest prize, however, making a substitute appearance in the 2006 World Cup final defeat to Italy, scoring France's first spot-kick in the penalty shoot-out.

Below: Christian Vieri in action during Italy's World Cup qualifier against Scotland in 2005.

GREAT MANAGERS

343

ENZO BEARZOT

Born: September 26, 1927
Management Career: Prato, Italy
Major honours: World Cup 1982

Enzo Bearzot masterminded Italy's first World Cup triumph since 1938. After qualifying as a coach he joined the national set-up in 1969, becoming sole manager in 1977. Little was expected of his team in the 1978 World Cup, but Bearzot's commitment to teamwork, loyalty and a more adventurous approach, meant they finished fourth. The 1982 World Cup campaign began badly, but again his loyalty was rewarded when he stuck by out-of-form striker Paolo Rossi. 'Pablito' went on to bag the goals that won the trophy. Bearzot's ageing side failed at the World Cup in 1986, but that should not devalue his reputation as a canny tactician and superb man-manager.

RAFAEL BENÍTEZ

Born: April 16, 1960
Management career: Real Valladolid, Osasuna, Extremadura, Tenerife, Valencia, Liverpool
Major honours: European Cup 2005; UEFA Cup 2004

Despite starting at Real Madrid, Benítez never made the first team and a knee injury cut short his playing career in the lower leagues at 25. His early coaching days were far from distinguished. He was sacked following two wins from 23 games as Valladolid manager in 1995-6 and shown the door the following season at Osasuna. Things improved at Extremadura, whom he led to promotion, and he achieved the same feat for Tenerife in 2000 before guiding them to a third-placed finish in the top-flight.

Courted by Valencia in 2001, he led the club to two league victories and a UEFA Cup success against Marseille in 2004, before joining Liverpool in June of that year. He finished the season by writing his name in the Reds' history books, leading the club to Champions League glory with an epic final victory against AC Milan in Istanbul, his team coming back from 3-0 down. He also guided the club to the 2006 FA Cup final, where they again won on penalties after clawing their way back from 2-0 down.

FULVIO BERNARDINI

Born: December 28, 1905
Management Career: Lazio, Fiorentina, Bologna, Italy

Fulvio Bernardini was an educated and elegant centre-half who earned the nickname 'Il Dottore' (the Doctor). However, he really made his name as one of the best coaches in the Italian game, taking modest clubs and making them successful. In 1956 he guided Fiorentina to their first ever Italian championship success and followed it up by taking them to the 1957 European Cup final. In 1964 he took Bologna to their first title in 23 years. In the mid-Seventies he took charge of the national team, helping Italy through the World Cup qualifiers before handing the reins to Enzo Bearzot.

VICENTE DEL BOSQUE

Born: December 23, 1950
Management career: Real Madrid, Besiktas
Major honours: European Cup 2000, 2002; World Club Cup 2002; European Super Cup 2002

Opinion is divided on Vicente del Bosque. Some class him as the luckiest coach ever, a man for whom Luis Figo, Zinédine Zidane and Ronaldo were bought in successive seasons to add to a Real Madrid squad already packed with talent. With such a team, they argue, how could he fail?

Others think the Spaniard was terribly unlucky to be sacked in June 2003 after delivering two Champions League triumphs and two Spanish league titles in four years. When he desperately needed to bolster a failing defence, he was instead given more of the world's finest attacking stars and he did magnificently to smooth over the super-egos of the dressing room and fashion a style of play that fitted his attack-heavy side.

Whatever the truth and whatever else he may do in his coaching career, Del Bosque will forever be associated with Madrid. As a player, he turned out for Cordoba and Castellon, but it was at the Bernabéu that he enjoyed his greatest success, collecting five league titles, four cups and 18 caps. So enamoured was Del Bosque with the club that when his playing days came to an end, he stayed there, filling a variety of roles, initially as manager of Madrid's B-team, Castilla.

Having stepped in as Real Madrid's first-team boss for an 11-game spell in the 1993-4 season, and for one game during the 1995-6 campaign, he did so for a third time during 1999-2000, a season that culminated in a glorious Champions League final victory over Valencia at the Stade de France in Paris.

Asked to stay on in the role, he delivered another Champions League victory, two league titles, the European Super Cup and the World Club Cup, but when Madrid lost to Juventus in the Champions League semi-finals in 2003, the writing was on the wall. Offered a role as technical director, Del Bosque instead decided to finally sever his ties with the club.

After being linked with the Spanish national job after Euro 2004, Del Bosque instead settled for a move to Besiktas in Turkey, but he was to last just eight months in the job, sacked after a run of poor results.

MATT BUSBY

Born: May 26, 1909
Management career: Manchester United
Major honours: European Cup 1968

Revered at Manchester United's Old Trafford stadium, Sir Matt Busby remains one of the greatest post-war British managers, a man who built a succession of great teams and forged a dynasty. Like Jock Stein and Bill Shankly, Busby hailed from Scottish mining stock. Born in Orbiston, Lanarkshire, he escaped a life at the coal-face through football. He played at half-back, winning one international cap for Scotland in 1933 and an FA Cup winner's medal for Manchester City the following year before finishing his career with Liverpool.

Manchester United was his first managerial appointment and, although just 36 years old, he quickly asserted his authority, demonstrating a tough disciplinary approach and a ruthless streak, belied by his amiable exterior. When he took over in 1945 the club was in disarray. Old Trafford was being rebuilt following severe

Left: Manchester United manager
Matt Busby enjoys his team's
1968 European Cup victory.

FABIO CAPELLO

Born: June 18, 1946
Management career: AC Milan, Real Madrid,
AC Milan, Roma, Juventus, Real Madrid
Major honours: European Cup 1994

One of the most decorated coaches in Italy, Fabio Capello commands a massive salary, and usually delivers the silverware in return, winning league titles with AC Milan, Roma, Real Madrid and Juventus. A no-nonsense and fiery character, he has often had run-ins with opposition players and coaches, as well as top officials at his own clubs. He controversially quit Milan in 1996 after winning the Serie A title four times in five seasons. But his record speaks for itself and his hard-working teams often play in his own image.

He rarely hides his emotions, but he is always linked with every big job that comes up. Back-to-back titles with Juventus in 2005 and 2006 kept him in Italy until a match-fixing scandal saw the team punished with relegation. Capello quit and rejoined Real Madrid. An excellent player in his own right, Capello won 32 Italian caps between 1972 and 1976 while playing for Juventus and AC Milan.

HERBERT CHAPMAN

Born: January 19, 1878
Management career: Northampton Town,
Leeds City, Huddersfield Town, Arsenal

One of English football's great managers, Herbert Chapman was a visionary who, in his career, advocated numbered shirts, European football, white balls, floodlit matches and attempted to keep pace with the best of foreign tactical developments. Chapman enjoyed an undistinguished playing career, spending time with, among others, Northampton Town and Tottenham reserves.

He returned to Northampton as player-manager in 1907 and began to demonstrate his ability, leading them to the Southern League title in his second season. He moved on to Leeds City, finishing fourth in Division Two in 1914. However, he was suspended over illegal payments to guest players and quit the game, only returning in 1920 when his appeal was upheld. He took over at Huddersfield Town and began a golden era for the club, winning consecutive league titles in 1924 and 1925 with limited resources.

He moved to Arsenal and sparked a revival in the club's fortunes, toying with their formation in the wake of changes to the offside rule. The reversal of north-south power was demonstrated when Arsenal won the 1930 FA Cup, beating Huddersfield 2-0. With some bold transfer coups, including Alex James and David Jack, Arsenal embarked on an era of dominance that included five league titles. Sadly Chapman did not live to see them all: he died in January 1934 after contracting pneumonia watching his third team.

---

bomb damage, money was short and the team was struggling in the league.

Busby began his own rebuilding process, setting up a coherent youth policy at the club and reorganising the scouting system. The first sign of progress was the 1948 FA Cup win which was followed, after a couple of close calls, by the 1952 league title, United's first since 1911. His team scored prolifically that season but Busby was not content and began rebuilding immediately, bringing in talented youth squad players. The era of the Busby Babes was born, with Bobby Charlton, Duncan Edwards, Dennis Viollet, Tommy Taylor and Jackie Blanchflower.

Two successive championships followed in 1956 and 1957 before Busby defied the Football League to enter Manchester United in to the European Cup, making them the first English club to take part in the competition. His decision rebounded with tragic consequences when the team plane crashed on a Munich airfield in 1958 en route home from an encounter with Red Star Belgrade. Eight of the team were killed and Busby himself was severely injured.

He recovered and began rebuilding the team with iron determination, unearthing major international talents like Denis Law and George Best. Two more league championships followed before Manchester United finally triumphed in Europe, beating Benfica 4-1 in 1968 to become the first English team to win the coveted trophy.

Busby's retirement in 1969 did not sever his influence on the team and a succession of managers, including Wilf McGuinness, Frank O'Farrell and Tommy Docherty, struggled to fill the vacuum he left and deal with the influence he continued to wield in the boardroom. It took another Scotsman to restore the club to its former glory. Busby lived long enough to see the club dominate the league again before dying, aged 84, on January 20, 1994.

Nottingham Forest manager
Brian Clough poses with the
European Cup, a trophy that
he won twice.

JAVIER CLEMENTE

Born: March 12, 1950
Management Career: Athletic Bilbao, Espanyol,
Athletic Bilbao, Spain, Real Betis, Real
Sociedad, Marseille, Tenerife, Athletic Bilbao

Injury ended Javier Clemente's playing career
at the age of 23, and he went straight on to the
coaching staff of the club he had played for:
Athletic Bilbao. He quickly rose through the
ranks, eventually leading them to the Spanish
title in 1983 and the league and cup double in
1984. His next job saw him move to Espanyol,
and although he failed to win them trophies he
reached the 1988 UEFA Cup final, before
returning to Bilbao for a short but unsuccessful
spell in 1991. Taking charge of the Spanish
national team in 1992, he coached the side to
three successive tournaments before his sacking
in 1998, following an embarrassing defeat to
Cyprus. He took on successful relegation battles
at Real Betis, Real Sociedad and Marseille, but
was unable to do the same for Tenerife in a three-
month spell with the club in 2002. He returned
for his third stint at Athletic Bilbao in 2005.

BRIAN CLOUGH

Born: March 21, 1935
Management career: Hartlepool United, Derby
County, Brighton & Hove Albion, Leeds United,
Nottingham Forest
Major honours: European Cup 1979, 1980

Brian Clough was a free-scoring centre-forward
before injury ended his playing days. Aged 30,
he embarked on one of the greatest managerial
careers in history. At Fourth Division Hartlepool
he forged an enduring partnership with Peter
Taylor. The pair moved to Derby, and in five
seasons rebuilt the club, taking them from 18th

in Division Two to their first league title. The
duo left after interference from the board and
brief and eccentric sojourns at Brighton and
Leeds United followed (Clough lasted 44 days
at Elland Road before player-power had him
removed), but Nottingham Forest were similar
to Derby – a club he could mould.

This time it took four seasons to go from
Division Two to the league championship. He
cemented his reputation as England's foremost
club boss by winning the European Cup in
consecutive seasons, against Malmö and
Hamburg. League Cup victories followed in the
Eighties, but in 1993 his final season was
marred by relegation from the newly-established
Premiership. Always outspoken, he knew how
to motivate ordinary players, but wasn't afraid
to buy big either, signing the first million-pound
player, Trevor Francis. He believed football was
a simple game, but his teams always played it
skilfully and wholeheartedly.

JOHAN CRUYFF

Born: April 25, 1947
Management career: Ajax, Barcelona
Major honours: European Cup 1992; European
Cup Winners' Cup 1987, 1989; European
Super Cup 1992

One of the game's greatest playing talents, the
three-time European Footballer Of The Year
proved to be almost as gifted in the manager's
office at Ajax and Barcelona, the clubs that had
seen his best as a player. Without any coaching
qualifications, Cruyff guided Ajax to the title,
two Dutch Cups and the 1987 European Cup
Winners' Cup before returning to Barcelona.

Two years later Barcelona defeated Sampdoria
to lift the Cup Winners' Cup at the start of what
was to be a golden era for the Catalan giants.
Playing sumptuous attacking football, his team

won two Spanish Cups, four consecutive league
titles and, finally, in 1992, the European Cup.
Again Sampdoria were the victims as Ronald
Koeman's stunning extra-time free-kick gave
Barça the one trophy they most desired.

Two years later Barcelona again reached the
European Cup final, only to find themselves on
the receiving end of a 4-0 thumping from Milan.
With his side's success waning, Cruyff was
forced out in 1996 and, though he remains
enormously popular with Barcelona fans,
serious heart problems make a permanent
return to football management unlikely.

SVEN-GÖRAN ERIKSSON

Born: February 5, 1948
Management Career: Degerfors, IFK
Gothenburg, Benfica, Roma, Fiorentina,
Benfica, Sampdoria, Lazio, England
Major honours: UEFA Cup 1982; European Cup
Winners' Cup 1999; European Super Cup 1999

After an unremarkable playing career, Sven-
Göran Eriksson has proved to be one of the
game's most successful coaches, his ice cool,
intellectual approach rubbing off on his players,
his teams often performing with confidence and
intelligence. Eriksson made his name in Sweden,
winning a league, cup and UEFA Cup 'treble'
with Gothenburg in 1982, before taking Benfica
to the league title and the UEFA Cup final in his
first season in Portugal.

After retaining the title the following season,
Eriksson quit Benfica for Roma, where he won
the Coppa Italia. After a spell with Fiorentina,
he returned to Benfica, losing the European Cup
final to AC Milan in 1990 and winning another
league title in 1991. After victory in the Coppa
Italia with Sampdoria in 1994, he won it twice
more with Lazio (1998 and 2000), along with
the European Cup Winners' Cup in 1999 and
the Italian league title in 2000.

Taking charge of England's national team in
2001 after the resignation of Kevin Keegan the
previous year, Eriksson controversially became
the country's first foreign manager and best paid
international coach. With David Beckham as his
captain, he led England to three tournaments,
but despite initially constructing a team capable
of winning, he failed to inspire his players at the
moments that really counted. He watched his
team throw away a 1-0 lead over Brazil in the
2002 World Cup quarter-finals, and oversaw a
penalty shoot-out defeat to hosts Portugal at the
same stage of Euro 2004.

After being linked with several high profile
clubs, Eriksson found himself at the centre of a
series of tabloid newspaper exposés which proved
too much for the Football Association. He led
England to the 2006 World Cup knowing that
he would leave his post after the tournament.
His team again lost to Portugal on penalties in
the quarter-finals and his tactics were openly
criticised, even by FIFA president Sepp Blatter.

ALEX FERGUSON

Born: December 31, 1941

Management career: East Stirlingshire, St Mirren, Aberdeen, Scotland, Manchester United

Major honours: European Cup 1999; European Cup Winners' Cup 1983, 1991; World Club Cup 1999; European Super Cup 1991

A handy but limited player with a string of Scottish clubs, most notably Rangers, Alex Ferguson got his chance in management with Scottish minnows East Stirling. There he began to develop the motivational skills that would make him one of the world's most successful coaches, before moving to St Mirren and winning the First Division title.

Offered the manager's job at Aberdeen, Ferguson seized his opportunity to shake up Scottish football and break the 'Old Firm' duopoly. Between them Rangers and Celtic had won 14 successive league titles, but driven on by their workaholic manager's extraordinary hunger for success, Aberdeen snatched the 1980 championship. Two further league titles followed, along with four Scottish Cups and a memorable victory over Real Madrid in the 1983 European Cup Winners' Cup final.

In 1986, Ferguson led Scotland at the World Cup finals after the sudden death of Jock Stein, and three months later Manchester United asked him to become their manager. After decades of underachievement, England's biggest club were desperate for success. But for four years Ferguson struggled as he sought to revolutionise United, cutting out the dead wood and shaping the club in his image.

Above left: Ferguson at Aberdeen in 1983. Above: Lifting the 1999 Premier League trophy with Manchester United.

As results dipped, and the pressure on Ferguson's job intensified, the Glaswegian finally delivered his first trophy, the 1990 FA Cup, to kickstart a golden era for United. The European Cup Winners' Cup and League Cup were added before, in 1993, after 26 years of trying, the league championship finally returned to Old Trafford.

The following year, United won their first league and FA Cup double, adding a second two years later as the team racked up eight league titles and four FA Cups in an 11-year spell. But it was 1999's historic and seemingly impossible treble that really established Ferguson in the pantheon of great managers.

Faced with mounting challenges in the league, FA Cup and Champions League, Ferguson brilliantly juggled his resources, tweaking and tinkering, resting players where he could, and all the while exhorting his team to play thrilling, attacking football. It made for memorable games, none more so than the Champions League final against Bayern Munich, where two injury-time goals saw United crowned European champions for the first time since 1968.

Knighted for his achievements, Ferguson announced his intention to retire at the end of the 2001-2 season. But as United faltered, he could not resist one last challenge, extending his contract and leading his team to another league title in 2003. Free-spending Chelsea have made league success harder to achieve in recent years, but Ferguson led United to victory in the FA Cup in 2004 and the League Cup in 2006, while challenging hard in the league.

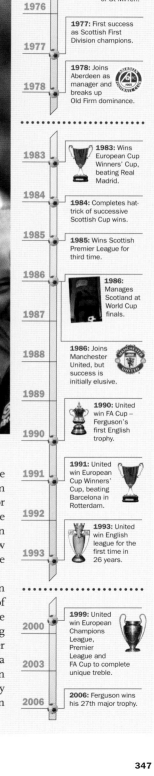

1964
1964: Signs on as a professional at Dunfermline.

1966

1967
1967: Moves to boyhood heroes Rangers for £65,000.

1968

1969: Joins Falkirk and tries coaching.

1975
1975: Appointed manager of St Mirren.

1976

1977
1977: First success as Scottish First Division champions.

1978
1978: Joins Aberdeen as manager and breaks up Old Firm dominance.

1983
1983: Wins European Cup Winners' Cup, beating Real Madrid.

1984
1984: Completes hat-trick of successive Scottish Cup wins.

1985
1985: Wins Scottish Premier League for third time.

1986
1986: Manages Scotland at World Cup finals.

1987

1988
1986: Joins Manchester United, but success is initially elusive.

1989

1990
1990: United win FA Cup – Ferguson's first English trophy.

1991
1991: United win European Cup Winners' Cup, beating Barcelona in Rotterdam.

1992

1993
1993: United win English league for the first time in 26 years.

2000
1999: United win European Champions League, Premier League and FA Cup to complete unique treble.

2003

2006
2006: Ferguson wins his 27th major trophy.

BELA GUTTMAN

Born: March 13, 1900
Managerial career: AC Milan, Peñarol, Benfica
Major honours: European Cup 1961, 1962

A hugely respected coach, Hungarian Bela Guttman retired as a player in 1935 and embarked on a 40-year management career. He coached several teams in Eastern Europe, took the reins of AC Milan in Italy, and was one of the first from Europe to work in South America when he led Peñarol. The highlights of his career came at Benfica, whom he led to European Champions Cup triumph in 1961. He was feted for taking the trophy away from Real Madrid for the first time and retained it the following year. Guttman won a total of seven national titles during his trek around the globe. He died in 1981.

ERNST HAPPEL

Born: June 25, 1929
Management Career: Wacker Innsbruck, Feyenoord, Den Haag, Club Brugge, Holland, Hamburg, FC Swarovski Tirol, Austria
Major honours: European Cup 1970, 1983; World Club Cup 1970

Ernst Happel was one of the world's most successful and disciplined coaches, winning a staggering 17 trophies, including the national league titles of Austria, Belgium, Holland and West Germany. He was the first manager to have won the European Cup with two different clubs: Feyenoord in 1970 and Hamburg in 1983. He was also in charge of losing finalists Club Brugge at the 1978 final. In that same year he almost won the World Cup with Holland, but Rob Rensenbrink's shot late in the game hit the post and the Dutch went on to lose 3-1 in extra-time to Argentina.

JOSEF 'SEPP' HERBERGER

Born: March 28, 1897
Management Career: Germany, West Germany
Major honours: World Cup 1954

Josef 'Sepp' Herberger was coach of Germany from 1938 to 1963 without ever managing a club side. He proved to be tactically shrewd, a great motivator, pragmatic yet adaptable. He built the foundation that was to make West Germany one of the strongest teams in the world. In 1954 Herberger's strategies earned West Germany the World Cup. The late call-up of Rot Weiss Essen winger Helmut Rahn was a stroke of genius, as was the bold gamble of fielding a second-string side against the mighty Hungary early on in the competition – the result earned them the easier route to the final, where a full strength Germany beat Hungary 3-2 with two goals from Rahn.

HELENIO HERRERA

Born: April 17, 1917
Management career: Puteaux, Red Star 93, Stade Francais, Atlético Madrid, Malaga, Valladolid, Seville, Barcelona, Italy, Spain, Inter Milan, Roma
Major honours: European Cup 1964, 1965; World Club Cup 1964, 1965

In terms of trophies, Helenio Herrera's record is impressive enough, but the impact of the man they called 'Il Mago' (the Magician) cannot be measured in silverware alone. Herrera was a revolutionary manager, a well-paid control freak who dominated his club and whose use of man-management techniques was way ahead of its time. His tactical innovations can still be felt in the game today, most notably his role in the development of the highly-defensive system of 'catenaccio' with which Inter Milan enjoyed such success in the mid-1960s.

Herrera used tough man-for-man markers supported by a sweeper, asking his team to focus primarily on defence, pressing their opponents hard and then hitting them on the counter-attack at pace. So successful was this approach that Inter won three league titles and successive European and World Club Cups in 1964 and 1965. However, it would be wrong to remember Herrera merely as the godfather of defensive Italian football.

Born in Argentina, but raised in Morocco, Herrera played his club football in France and it was there that he began his managerial career with little Puteaux. On moving to Spain, he guided Atlético Madrid to back-to-back league titles before embarking on a tour of the country that ended with Barcelona and another league title. Far from being defensive, at Barcelona Herrera earned a reputation for coaching a wildly attacking team, often playing forwards in defensive positions and encouraging them to go forward in search of goals.

He coached the Italian national team during qualification for the 1962 World Cup finals, but by the time the tournament came round, he was at the helm of the Spanish team, though he could do nothing to stop them finishing bottom of their group. After the glorious successes of 'Il Grande Inter', Herrera was snapped up by Roma, but could only add an Italian Cup.

MICHEL HIDALGO

Born: March 22, 1933
Management career: RC Menton, France, Olympique Marseille, Congo
Major honours: European Championship 1984

Hidalgo had a distinguished playing career, scoring a consolation goal in the European Cup final of 1956 for Reims against Real Madrid. He also played for Monaco, where he won two league medals before taking over at RC Menton

Above: PSV Eindhoven coach Guus Hiddink holds the Dutch league trophy in 2006.

as player-manager. He later became president of the UNFP, the French players' union, before his appointment as coach of the French national team in 1976.

Having succeeded Stefan Kovacs, he helped groom a young Michel Platini as the team reached the semi-finals of the 1982 World Cup, dramatically losing the decisive tie with West Germany despite having led the game. Two years later, on home soil, he guided France to victory at the European Championship, winning the final against Spain. After the victory he became France's technical director, before returning to full-time management with Marseille in 1986, where he won two league titles. In 2004 Hidalgo came out of retirement to manage Congo and today he is an advisor to the French FA.

GUUS HIDDINK

Born: November 8, 1946
Management Career: De Graafschap, PSV Eindhoven, Fenerbahçe, Valencia, Holland, Real Madrid, Real Betis, South Korea, PSV Eindhoven, Australia, Russia
Major honours: European Cup 1988

Guus Hiddink rose to prominence during his time at PSV Eindhoven, where he won the league and cup three times each, and topped his reign by claiming the European Cup in 1988. His attractive, free-flowing football won many admirers, and after spells at Fenerbahçe and Valencia he took charge of the Dutch national team, where only a penalty shoot-out prevented an appearance in the final of the 1998 World Cup. A move back to Spain followed, to take charge of Real Madrid and then Real Betis.

Left: Helenio Herrera, whose defensive tactics brought him success with Inter Milan.

He may well be best remembered for taking co-hosts and underdogs South Korea to the semi-finals of the 2002 World Cup. After the tournament the stadium in Gwangju was renamed the Guus Hiddink Stadium.

Returning to PSV, he won the league and cup double in 2005 and the Dutch title in 2006, while in his spare time guiding Australia to the 2006 World Cup finals. Despite being linked with the England manager's job, he announced that after the World Cup he would leave PSV to take charge of Russia's national team.

OTTMAR HITZFELD

Born: January 12, 1949.
Management career: Zug, Aarau, Grasshoppers Zurich, Borussia Dortmund, Bayern Munich
Major honours: European Cup 1997, 2001

Composed, determined, steely – all could apply to the man who became the first coach to win the new format of the Champions League with two different clubs following its inception in the early 1990s. There wasn't much of a stir when he took over at Borussia Dortmund in 1991, but within four years they were dominating the Bundesliga and then Europe, with a Champions League win in 1997.

Poached by Bayern Munich in 1998, his authoritarian style was just what was needed. He transformed the club in his own image, winning four league titles in five years, as well as the Champions League in 2001, beating

Valencia on penalties. After six successful years with Bayern, Hitzfeld was sacked in May 2004 and has subsequently turned down the opportunity to coach the German national side on health grounds.

ROY HODGSON

Born: August 9, 1947
Management Career: Halmstad, Bristol City, Orebro SK, Malmö, Xamax Neuchatel, Switzerland, Inter Milan, Blackburn Rovers, Inter Milan, Grasshoppers, FC Copenhagen, Udinese, UAE, Viking FK, Finland

Roy Hodgson has been one of the most successful English coaches abroad. He made his name in Sweden with the championship-winning sides of Halmstad and Malmö. With the latter he reached the 1979 European Cup final before losing out to Nottingham Forest. He went on to manage clubs in Switzerland, Italy, Denmark and England, reaching the UEFA Cup final with Inter Milan in 1997. He succeeded Uli Stielike as Switzerland's national team coach, taking them to the 1996 European Championship, their first major tournament since 1966. In 2002 he became national coach of the United Arab Emirates and in 2006 he took over as coach of Finland.

JIMMY HOGAN

Born: October 16, 1882
Management Career: Holland, Austria, MTK Hungaria, Fulham, Aston Villa

Moderately successful as an inside-forward for Burnley and Fulham, Jimmy Hogan was enticed to coach in Vienna in 1912 by Hugo Meisl. He failed to get his message across to the educated university students, but the unwavering support of Meisl encouraged Hogan to persist with the principles of ball control and intelligent passing that was to be the hallmark of football in Austria, Germany and Hungary. The Vienna School's emphasis on skill led to the 'Wunderteam' of Austria, the rise of West Germany as a football force after the war and the 'Magical Magyars' of Hungary. By way of an acknowledgement of his influence on Hungarian football, Hogan was the team's guest of honour when Hungary memorably defeated England 6-3 at Wembley. He died in January 1974.

AIMÉ JACQUET

Born: November 27, 1941
Management career: Lyon, Bordeaux, Montpellier, Nancy, France
Major honours: World Cup 1998

Aimé Jacquet led France to their greatest-ever sporting triumph, victory on home soil at the 1998 World Cup. A decent player in his time,

he picked up five league titles and three French Cups at St Etienne in the 1960s and 1970s. He had a brief international spell, playing twice for France, before turning to management at Lyon, where his talent was quickly spotted.

He took over at Bordeaux in 1980 and led the club through the most successful period in their history. Under Jacquet, Bordeaux won three titles, two French Cups and starred impressively in Europe, reaching the semi-finals of the European Cup and the European Cup Winners' Cup, confirming his reputation as France's foremost club manager. A meticulous planner, he prided himself on knowing his players well and paid rigorous attention to detail – qualities that would serve him well during international tournaments.

After leaving Bordeaux in 1989 he took a Montpellier side including Eric Cantona to an unexpected French Cup triumph. However, a downturn in fortunes followed when he left for Nancy. He was sacked and moved into the French Football Federation set-up, working as assistant to Gerard Houllier before taking over the national team in 1993 and leading a side built around a solid defence to the semi-finals of the European Championship in 1996.

Despite press criticism he held on to his job to deliver the ultimate prize in 1998. He quit immediately after the final, becoming the FFF's technical director and elder statesman.

ROGER LEMERRE

Born: June 18, 1941
Management Career: Red Star, Lens, Paris FC, Strasbourg, Espérance, Red Star, France Military, Lens, France, Tunisia
Major honours: European Championship 2000; Confederations Cup 2001; African Nations Cup 2004

Roger Lemerre is unique in being the only coach to have won both the European Championship and the African Nations Cup. In 1995 he guided the French Military team to the Military World Championship; he was Aimé Jacquet's assistant when France won the World Cup in 1998; and on taking over as coach in his own right, he lifted the 2000 European Championship after his team beat Italy 2-1 in final, thanks to an injury time equaliser from Sylvain Wiltord and a David Trezeguet golden goal. He went on to win the 2001 Confederations Cup, but after a disastrous first round exit from the World Cup in 2002 he was sacked. Taking over as Tunisia's coach, he guided the North Africans to a 2-1 win over Morocco in the 2004 African Nations Cup final, with goals from Francileudo dos Santos and Ziad Jaziri, and he led them to the 2006 World Cup.

MARCELLO LIPPI

Born: April 12, 1948
Management Career: Sampdoria, Pontedera, Siena, Pistoiese, Carrarese, Cesena, Lucchese, Atalanta, Napoli, Juventus, Inter Milan, Juventus
Major honours: World Cup: 2006; European Cup 1996; World Club Cup 1996; European Super Cup 1996

Just one glance at Marcello Lippi's Serie A titles confirms his managerial greatness, but he has worked hard to get where he is. After being in charge of an endless succession of minor Italian clubs, it wasn't until he finished seventh and sixth with Atalanta and Napoli respectively – on shoestring budgets – that his reputation was sealed. His achievements earned him a chance to take over at the helm of Juventus, where he delivered the Champions League, beating Ajax on penalties, the Italian Cup, and a series of three Serie A titles in four seasons between 1995 and 1998. He spent a brief period at Inter Milan, before returning to Juventus to pick up the title in both 2002 and 2003, and led the team to defeat in the 2003 Champions League final.

He took charge of the Italian national side in July 2004 and led them to the 2006 World Cup in Germany after a two-year unbeaten run. Despite the distraction of the ongoing match-fixing scandal dominating domestic Italian football, Lippi was much praised for his tactical acumen as he guided the country to a fourth World Cup win, beating France 5-3 on penalties after a 1-1 draw.

VALERY LOBANOVSKY

Born: January 6, 1939
Management career: Dnepr Dnepropetrovsk, Dynamo Kiev, Soviet Union, United Arab Emirates, Kuwait, Dynamo Kiev, Ukraine
Major honours: European Cup Winners' Cup 1975, 1986

Notorious for his solemn expression and ruling teams with an iron fist, Valery Lobanovsky was the man responsible for making Dynamo Kiev a force in European football. As coach he took the club to victory in the European Cup Winners' Cup in 1975 and 1986, and to the

semi-finals of the Champions League in 1999. He also had three stints as coach of the Soviet Union, reaching the final of the 1988 European Championship before defeat to Holland. A left-winger, as a player he won the league and cup with Dynamo before moving to Chernomorets Odessa. But he made his name as a coach, starting in the late 1960s. Teamwork was the cornerstone of his teams, but he also brought through outstanding individuals such as Oleg Blokhin, and latterly Sergei Rebrov and Andriy Shevchenko. He died on May 13, 2002.

CESARE MALDINI

Born: February 5, 1932
Management Career: Foggia, Ternana, Parma, Italy, Paraguay

Cesare Maldini believed in the traditional Italian values of a solid defence, with teams that win games by the odd goal. It worked for him though. He was second in command to Enzo Bearzot when Italy won the 1982 World Cup, and his highly successful spell in charge of the Italy Under-21s was enough to earn him the stewardship of the national team, but a quarter-final exit from the 1998 World Cup cost him his job. He went on to manage Paraguay, although the appointment proved controversial with Paraguayan coaches who were unhappy at what they saw as the selection of an old-fashioned foreigner. He retired after the 2002 World Cup campaign.

HUGO MEISL

Born: November 16, 1881
Management Career: Amateure, Austria

Hugo Meisl developed the famed Vienna School alongside Englishman Jimmy Hogan.

Meisl was a highly educated man and a believer in 'pure' football. He was an admirer of the British game and his recruiting and encouragement of Hogan not only had a profound effect on football in Austria – notably with 'Wunderteams' of the 1930s and 1950s – but also on football in Hungary and Germany. Austria finished fourth at the 1934 World Cup but the country had been annexed by the Nazis' Greater Germany by the time of the 1938 tournament. He founded Amateure (later FK Austria) and was an advocate of FIFA and the international game.

CÉSAR LUIS MENOTTI

Born: November 5, 1938.
Management career: Independiente, Argentina, Barcelona, Peñarol, Boca Juniors, River Plate, Mexico, Atlético Madrid, Sampdoria, Valencia, Rosario Central, Independiente
Major honours: World Cup 1978

A decent player, it was not until chain-smoking César Luis Menotti went into management that he became a football legend, reviving the fortunes of Argentina. 'El Flaco' (The Thin One) was a highly-strung coach who had already enjoyed a spell as manager of Independiente when he took over the national team before the 1978 World Cup. He broke the mould by going for all-out attack, with stars such as Mario Kempes and Osvaldo Ardíles at the heart of his teams. After beating Holland to lift the World Cup in 1978 he stayed loyal to many of his ageing stars four years later, but despite having Diego Maradona in the line-up, his team hadn't the stomach for the campaign. He has variously enjoyed and endured short spells at many clubs. In 2005 he returned to Independiente for a third stint at the club, but he only lasted nine matches.

Above: One of the great coaches of modern times, Marcello Lippi lifts the World Cup in 2006

1940
1940s/50s: Enjoys a career as a centre-forward with Ajax during which time he wins five caps with Holland.

1950

1965
1965: Becomes head coach of Ajax, where he develops the Total Football concept.

1967
1967: Success arrives with a Dutch league and cup double.

1968
1968: Ajax win third successive Dutch championship.

1971
1971: Ajax win European Cup for the first time, beating Panathinaikos at Wembley.

1972
1971: Moves to Spain to take over as manager at Barcelona.

1973
1973: Signs Cruyff, who epitomised Total Football.

1974
1974: Wins Spanish league title.

1975
1974: Takes Holland to World Cup final, but loses to West Germany.

1975: Returns to Ajax as coach.

1980
1980: Tackles the German Bundesliga by joining Köln.

1984
1984: Returns to international coaching with Holland.

1986
1988: Holland win European Championship with a team which includes the talents of Gullit, Rijkaard and Marco Van Basten.

1988
1988: Takes over at Bayer Levekusen.

1990
1990: Becomes Dutch coach for third time, only to retire in 1992.

2002
2002: Recognised with UEFA Lifetime Achievement Award.

2005
2005: Died aged 77, in a hospital in Belgium, March 3, 2005

MARINUS 'RINUS' MICHELS

Born: February 9, 1928
Management career: Ajax, Barcelona, Holland, Barcelona, Los Angeles Aztecs, Köln, Holland, Bayer Leverkusen, Holland
Major honours: European Cup 1971; European Championship 1988

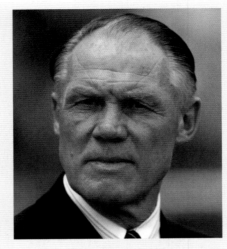

An Ajax centre-forward who won five caps for Holland, it is as the coach who invented Total Football that Michels will always be remembered. With Johan Cruyff as its heartbeat, Total Football – a philosophy dependent on versatility, adaptability and all-round ball skills – was first developed with Ajax in the late 1960s, and then with the brilliant Dutch team of the Seventies.

But 'Iron Rinus' was no soft touch. For him, playing beautiful football was a serious business and he demanded a high level of professionalism from his players. That combination of silk and steel took Ajax to their first European Cup final in 1969, and although they lost to Milan, the foundations for future success had been firmly laid. Ajax went on to win three successive European Cups and, while Michels left for Barcelona after the first victory, he could still claim much of the credit for the legacy he left behind.

At Barcelona he at first found progress hard but, having taken Cruyff to the Nou Camp, he celebrated league success in 1974 and lifted the Spanish Cup in 1978 during a second spell in charge. He also found time to lead an outstanding Holland team to the 1974 World Cup final, captivating fans across the world. Unfortunately his talented team threw away a 1-0 lead against West Germany and finished the competition as runners-up.

In 1978 Michels joined the Los Angeles Aztecs in the NASL before going back to Germany for a successful spell with Köln. He returned as coach of Holland in time to mould individuals like Ruud Gullit and Marco Van Basten into a disciplined Dutch unit good enough to win their first international trophy, the 1988 European Championship.

After a spell with Bayer Leverkusen, Michels led Holland to the 1992 European Championship, but when they slipped up on penalties to surprise winners Denmark, he called time on a glorious career. In 1999 FIFA named him Coach Of The century. He died in March 2005, aged 77.

Above: Rinus Michels capped his return to managing the Dutch national side by taking them to the 1988 European Championship, but retired after defeat to Denmark in the same competition four years later.

BORA MILUTINOVIC

Born: September 7, 1944
Management Career: Pumas UNAM, Mexico, San Lorenzo, Almagro, Costa Rica, Udinese, USA, Mexico, Nigeria, MetroStars, China, Honduras, Al Saad
Major honours: CONCACAF Championship 1989; Gold Cup 1991, 1996

Bora Milutinovic is a coaching legend, having taken charge of five different countries at five successive World Cups: Mexico (1986), Costa Rica (1990), USA (1994), Nigeria (1998) and China (2002). He started the 2006 World Cup qualification campaign with Honduras but he resigned in June 2004 after just ten games in charge. The Yugoslav-born coach has the ability to get teams to exceed expectations and his sides have been responsible for a number of World Cup shocks over the years, including Costa Rica's defeat of Scotland in 1986 and Nigeria's win over Spain in 1998. His best World Cup finals performance was taking hosts Mexico to the quarter-finals of the competition in 1986. His coaching career began in Mexico with Pumas UNAM in 1977 and, between international appointments, he has managed clubs in Argentina, Italy, USA and Qatar.

MIGUEL MUÑOZ

Born: September 15, 1924
Management Career: Plus Ultra, Real Madrid, Hercules, Sevilla, Las Palmas, Spain
Major honours: European Cup 1960, 1966

Miguel Muñoz was, arguably, the greatest manager that Real Madrid ever had. During his 14-year reign in charge Real won the Spanish championship nine times and the Spanish Cup twice. Of greater significance were the European Cup wins of 1960 and 1966. The 1960 victory was the classic 7-3 triumph over Eintracht Frankfurt at Hampden Park in Glasgow, regarded as one of the best matches of all time. It was Real Madrid's fifth successive European Cup triumph. As a player, Muñoz had won the trophy twice with Real in 1956 and 1957. Inevitably, Muñoz became coach of the Spanish national team, taking them to the 1984 European Championship final and the 1986 World Cup quarter-finals.

JOSÉ MOURINHO

Born: 26 January 1963
Management Career: Benfica, Uniao de Leiria, Porto, Chelsea
Major honours: European Cup 2004; UEFA Cup 2003

Mourinho is an outspoken and controversial figure but even his fiercest detractors would be hard pressed to criticise his exemplary record in club management. The Chelsea manager cut his teeth in the game first as Bobby Robson's translator at Sporting Lisbon and Porto, and then as Robson's assistant coach at Barcelona. His first job as head coach came at Benfica in 2000, but it ended with Mourinho walking out after only nine games, frustrated at problems in the boardroom. Next Mourinho guided the Portuguese minnows Uniao de Leiria into the top five of their domestic league before he jumped ship in January 2002 to coach Porto. It was there that his career went into overdrive, guiding them to an extraordinary trophy triple in 2003 and trumping it the following season with both league and Champions League glory. Mourinho took over at Chelsea in 2004 and has already guided the super-rich West Londoners to back-to-back league title wins.

BILL NICHOLSON

Born: January 26, 1919
Management Career: Tottenham Hotspur
Major honours: UEFA Cup 1972; European Cup Winners' Cup 1963

Bill Nicholson guided Tottenham Hotspur to a host of domestic and European trophies between 1958 and 1974. However, his most famous and enduring achievement was winning the 1961 league championship and FA Cup double. In their 42 league games that season Tottenham scored 115 goals, playing outstanding and attractive football. Nicholson achieved the double after spending more money than any other British manager in history. His Tottenham side, featuring Danny Blanchflower and the skilful John White, began the season with 11 straight wins and ended up winning 31 games (including 16 away). The double was successfully completed by defeating Leicester City 2-0 in the FA Cup final at Wembley Stadium.

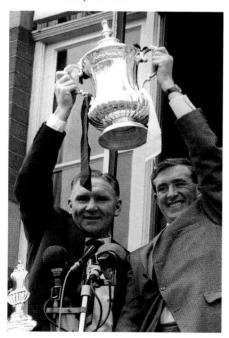

Under Nicholson Tottenham became the first British club to lift a major European trophy, beating Atlético Madrid 5-1 in Rotterdam to win the Cup Winners' Cup, and nine years later he took the club to glory in the UEFA Cup after beating Wolverhampton Wanderers over two legs. He resigned shortly after defeat in the final of the 1974 UEFA Cup but later returned to the club as a consultant, working with them until 1991. He died in October 2004.

BOB PAISLEY

Born: January 23, 1919
Management career: Liverpool
Major honours: European Cup 1977, 1978, 1981; UEFA Cup 1976;

Bob Paisley began his playing career with the famous amateur side Bishop Auckland in his native North-East, but from just before the war in 1939 until his retirement from the board in 1992, he was Liverpool through and through. Few football professionals can have been a player, a coach, a physiotherapist, a manager and a director of the same club.

Paisley fulfilled all these roles at Anfield. He forged his 'odd couple' partnership with Bill Shankly in 1959, and for 15 years was happy to play second fiddle to the extrovert Scotsman. Shankly relied heavily on Bob Paisley's shrewd judgment of a player's strengths and weaknesses, and when Shankly suddenly resigned in 1974, the unassuming Paisley was reluctant to take on the mantle. With the support of his senior players, he agreed to take on the challenge, continuing to develop at Liverpool the footballing philosophy that he had helped formulate.

His teams, like Shankly's before him, played a simple, fast, passing game, the players working tirelessly for each other. Soon Paisley's Liverpool were surpassing the achievements of the Shankly era. After a worryingly trophyless first season, his side went on to win the league the following year, and a 4-3 aggregate victory over Club Brugge gave them the UEFA Cup too.

In 1977 Liverpool won the title by a point from Manchester City and, four days after an FA Cup final defeat to Manchester United, they outplayed Borussia Mönchengladbach to win the European Cup in Rome. As a member of the British Army in World War II, Paisley was able to joke that the last time he had visited the city he had helped liberate it! That was Kevin Keegan's last game for the club, but in keeping with his reputation as a good judge of a player, Paisley replaced Keegan with Kenny Dalglish. The Scotsman went on to score the winner against Club Brugge the following year as Liverpool retained the European Cup. Other useful investments included Alan Hansen, Graeme Souness and Mark Lawrenson, as he strove to renew his incredibly successful side.

The Reds continued to dominate in the league, winning four of the five titles between 1979 and

1983. In that year off, 1981, they added a third European Cup, beating Real Madrid 1-0. Paisley also managed three League Cup triumphs in his final three years, before he called it a day in 1983, staying on as an advisor to Joe Fagan and then Kenny Dalglish. He died on February 14, 1996.

Above: Liverpool manager Bob Paisley celebrates winning the league title.

CARLOS ALBERTO PARREIRA

Born: February 27, 1943
Management career: São Cristovao, Ghana, Kotoko, Fluminense, Kuwait, Brazil, UAE, Saudi Arabia, UAE, Bragantino, Brazil, Valencia, Fenerbahçe, São Paulo, MetroStars, Saudi Arabia, Atletico Mineiro, Santos, Internacional, Corinthians, Brazil, South Africa
Major honours: World Cup 1994

In charge of Brazil on three occasions, to many people the man known as 'The Professor' is modern Brazilian football. He is famous for combining modern coaching techniques with the exciting tradition of his national team. Parreira was not a distinguished player himself, arriving instead from a background of physical preparation, having been on the coaching staff when Brazil won the 1970 World Cup in Mexico. He then married the attacking and exciting play forever demanded by the public following that success to a more pragmatic, match-winning approach. But for his 1994 World Cup-winning side he was also blessed with stars such as Bebeto

Left: Danny Blanchflower and Tottenham Hotspur manager Bill Nicholson lift the FA Cup at the Town Hall in 1962.

and Romario, enabling the team to claim Brazil's first World Cup win for 24 years. He is one of only two men to lead four different nations to World Cup finals (Kuwait, United Arab Emirates, Saudi Arabia and Brazil), Bora Multinovic being the other. His most recent spell as Brazil coach saw him lead the team to the 2006 World Cup.

VITTORIO POZZO

Born: March 2, 1886
Management Career: Torino, Italy
Major honours: World Cup 1934, 1938; Olympics 1936

Many believe Vittorio Pozzo only won the World Cup because the all-powerful Mussolini 'arranged' it – others see him as a managerial genius. He is certainly the only manager to win the World Cup twice, and he was the first man to lead Italy in a competitive game. The war broke up his career, and 'Il Vecchio Maestro' (the Old Master) never really rediscovered his touch, despite remaining manager of the national team. Part of the problem was that Italy had been largely ignored by the footballing world after its involvement in the war, but Pozzo had already done enough to earn his reputation.

ALF RAMSEY

Born: January 21, 1920
Management Career: Ipswich Town, England, Birmingham City
Major honours: World Cup 1966

Though he never coached a major club, Alf Ramsey was one of the game's top managers for his success at both ends of the spectrum: in piloting a relatively minor club to the First Division championship and in guiding the national team to World Cup triumph.

A high grade full-back who played for Southampton and Tottenham, Ramsey was a natural leader and an instinctive reader of the game. He won 32 caps, captaining both club and country. Retiring at the age of 35 in 1955, he took up management with Ipswich, then in the Third Division South. Playing with a deep-lying striker and his wide players tucked, the club embarked on an extraordinary seven-year run of success, moving swiftly through the divisions until they secured the First Division title in 1962.

An enigmatic character, he was unflappable, pragmatic and iron-willed. His clipped vowels concealed a working-class upbringing in Dagenham, but while he was never close to his players, he commanded their utmost respect. It was these characteristics that led to his appointment as England manager in 1962, following the retirement of Walter Winterbottom. On taking the job he promptly announced that England would win the World Cup, but in his first match in charge they exited the European Nations Cup with a 2-5 defeat to France.

Ramsey set about building a team with the ability to take on the world, shoring up the defence with the addition of goalkeeper Gordon Banks and refining his 'wingless wonders' system. Captain Bobby Moore became the heartbeat of his side. England's World Cup victory was a triumph for Ramsey's preparation and planning. He drafted Geoff Hurst in to the squad late, but when injury ruled Jimmy Greaves out of the confrontation with Argentina, Ramsey put Hurst in and then played him in the final, with match-winning consequences.

A knighthood did not go to Ramsey's head and his preparation for the World Cup in 1970 was even more meticulous. Bad luck played its part in undermining an even better squad, but the quarter-final defeat to West Germany raised questions about his cautious tactics.

Two disastrous results against Poland home and away in 1973 led to failure to qualify for the 1974 tournament and to Ramsey's eventual dismissal. He had a brief spell at Birmingham as caretaker-manager in 1977, and was later technical director with Panathinaikos in 1979, before retiring from the game completely. He died on April 28, 1999, but will always be remembered for his role in England's greatest sporting achievement.

GEORGE RAYNOR

Born: January 13, 1907
Management Career: Sweden, AIK Stockholm, Atvidaberg, Juventus, Lazio, Skegness Town, Djurgardens, Skegness Town, Doncaster
Major honours: Olympics 1948

Englishman George Raynor took Sweden to Olympic Games gold in 1948 and to the 1958 World Cup final as hosts. Chairman of the FA, Stanley Rous, noticed Raynor when he was coaching in Iraq during the Second World War. After the war Raynor moved from reserve trainer at Aldershot to national team coach of Sweden. In his first game in charge he made his mark by devising a strategy to outwit Switzerland's revolutionary 'Swiss bolt' system. A series of training camps were then set up aimed at improving young players. The scheme was a roaring success and by 1948 he had helped Sweden to gold at the Olympics with a team that included Gren, Nordahl and Liedholm.

OTTO REHHAGEL

Born: August 9, 1938
Management career: Kickers Offenbach, Borussia Dortmund, Werder Bremen, Bayern Munich, Kaiserslautern, Greece
Major honours: European Championship 2004

Rehhagel's playing career at Hertha Berlin and Kaiserslautern was less than distinguished and, having cut his managerial teeth at Kickers Offenbach in 1972, a run of 12 games without a

Above: Vittorio Pozzo leads the celebrations after Italy's 1938 World Cup win in France.

win in the hot-seat at Dortmund suggested another unassuming career in the making. Yet 15 years at Bremen spawned such players as Rudi Völler, Karlheinz Reidle and Andreas Herzog, as the club won two league titles and the European Cup Winners' Cup. One disastrous season at Bayern Munich followed in 1996 but he restored his reputation taking Kaiserslautern to the title in 1998. His greatest triumph, however, came at the European Championship in 2004, when he pulled off one of the greatest shocks in the history of international football, guiding outsiders Greece to the title. His team beat host nation Portugal in the final, even if they gained few admirers for their defence-first policy.

DON REVIE

Born: July 10, 1927
Management Career: Leeds United, England, United Arab Emirates, Al Nasr, Al-Al FC
Major honours: Fairs Cup 1968, 1971

Between the mid-Sixties and mid-Seventies, Revie turned Leeds into the fiercest contenders in British football, winning six trophies and finishing as runners-up to a further 11. Revie had been a decent centre-forward for Leicester, Hull, Manchester City and Sunderland before joining a broke and demoralised Leeds in the Second Division as player-manager in 1958.

By 1964 he had taken the club from the relegation zone of the Second Division to the brink of the Division One title and to the FA Cup final, where they lost to Liverpool. The following ten seasons saw Revie construct a team renowned for a win-at-all-costs attitude. And win they did: the league in 1969 and 1974; the FA Cup in 1972; the Fairs Cup in 1968 and 1971; and the League Cup in 1968.

In 1974 Revie left Leeds to replace Sir Alf

Opposite: England's World Cup-winning manager Sir Alf Ramsey on the training pitch with players Tommy Smith, Chris Lawler and Gordon Banks.

Above: Bobby Robson displays the UEFA Cup after Ipswich Town's victory in 1981.

Ramsey as manager of the England team. But he couldn't recreate the same magic on the international stage and, midway through the qualification campaign for the 1978 World Cup finals, he caused consternation when he resigned to take up a £340,000 four-year contract to manage the United Arab Emirates.

Revie subsequently coached Saudi side Al Nasr and had a short spell in Cairo with Al-Al FC, before returning home in 1984. After his resignation from the England job, the FA had banned him from the English game for ten years. The ban was overturned but, despite brief negotiations with QPR, Revie never returned to club management. He died in May 1989.

FRANK RIJKAARD

Born: September 30, 1962
Management career: Holland, Sparta Rotterdam, Barcelona.
Major honours: European Cup 2006

On becoming Dutch coach in 1998, Frank Rijkaard had no previous experience but took his team to the semi-finals of the 2000 European Championship, playing some of the most thrilling football of the tournament. In a shock decision, he resigned the post just minutes after his teams had been knocked out of the competition on penalties by Italy. He spent one unsuccessful year at Sparta Rotterdam, overseeing the first relegation in the club's history, before rebuilding his coaching career with Barcelona.

At the Nou Camp he has turned around the fortunes of the club, winning back-to-back league titles in 2005 and 2006. He also managed to win the Champions League in 2006, making Barcelona champions of Europe for only the second time in their history. Perhaps more significantly to fans at the Nou Camp, he became the only Barça coach ever to win twice at the Bernabéu, home of rivals Real Madrid.

BOBBY ROBSON

Born: February 18, 1933
Management career: Vancouver Royals, Fulham, Ipswich Town, England, PSV Eindhoven, Sporting Lisbon, Porto, Barcelona, PSV Eindhoven, Newcastle United
Major honours: UEFA Cup 1981; European Cup Winners' Cup 1997

Bobby Robson started his coaching career in 1967 with a brief spell in Canada, returning to coach Fulham, where he had spent much of his distinguished playing career. He was sacked after less than a year in the job, and in 1969 he began his long and successful stint at Ipswich. He turned the small-town club into one of the country's best and most attractive sides, winning the FA Cup in 1978 and the UEFA Cup against AZ 67 Alkmaar in 1981.

Robson was rewarded for his achievements in 1982 when he was offered the England job. His side lost to Argentina, and to Maradona's dextrous subterfuge, in the quarter-finals of the 1986 World Cup; performed badly in the 1988 European Championship; and nearly made it to the World Cup final of 1990. Robson then began his decade-long journey around the continent, winning numerous domestic trophies in Holland, Portugal and Spain, plus the European Cup Winners' Cup in 1997 with Barcelona. Returning to England in 1999 he helped breathe fresh life in to Newcastle, the team he supported as a child.

His stay at St James' Park cost him the opportunity to take charge of England once more after the resignation of Kevin Keegan in 2000. He was controversially sacked by Newcastle in 2004 and became a consultant to the Republic Of Ireland team in 2006.

ARRIGO SACCHI

Born: April 1, 1946
Management career: Rimini, Parma, AC Milan, Italy, AC Milan, Atlético Madrid, Parma
Major honours: European Cup 1989, 1990; World Club Cup 1989, 1990

Having never played the game professionally, Arrigo Sacchi's big break came after his up-and-coming Parma team knocked AC Milan out of the 1986-7 Italian Cup. The following summer Milan president Silvio Berlusconi moved to bring Sacchi to the San Siro and within a year he had created a brilliant attacking team. The Serie A league title in his first season in charge was followed by two successive European Cup triumphs in 1989 and 1990, before he was tempted away to coach the Italian national side.

He guided the Azzurri to the 1994 World Cup final in the USA, where they were beaten on penalties by Brazil, but resigned after the 1996 European Championship and returned to Milan for a brief, unsuccessful spell. He then had a short stint at Atlético Madrid, and an even shorter one (just 28 days) back at Parma, who he left for health reasons before resurfacing at the club as general manager in December 2001. He subsequently became director of football at Real Madrid, before resigning in 2005.

HELMUT SCHÖN

Born: September 15, 1915
Management Career: Saarland, West Germany
Major honours: World Cup 1974; European Championship 1972

Helmut Schön scored 17 goals in 16 international games before the war forced him to flee his native Dresden. His first 'national' coaching job was with the postwar limbo state, Saarland. Then from 1955 he was West Germany's assistant manager, taking over the reins from Sepp Herberger in 1964. Schön's fine, undervalued team nearly upset England in the 1966 World Cup final, eventually losing in extra-time. In the 1970 quarter-final the Germans exacted revenge, beating England, and eventually finishing third.

Schön's natural inclination, as an inside-forward, was to produce ball-playing teams. His truly great 1972 European Championship-winning side, boasting Franz Beckenbauer, Gerd Müller and Gunter Netzer, epitomised that Dutch ideal of Total Football. Despite arguments over money – which depressed the benign, erudite Schön deeply – his flexible, powerful 1974 World Cup team pulled through to beat Holland and win the ultimate prize.

West Germany lost in the final of the 1976 European Championship, before failing again at the 1978 World Cup. That final performance, however, cannot devalue Helmut Schön's many achievements in a long career. He died in 1996.

LUIZ FELIPE SCOLARI

Born: November 9, 1948.
Management career: Gremio, Criciuma, Palmeiras, Cruzeiro, Brazil, Portugal
Major honours: World Cup 2002; Copa Libertadores 1995, 1999

'Big Phil' led Brazil from the doldrums to a record fifth World Cup, but his style is different to many in that country. With a reputation for making tough decisions and sticking by them – especially over selection – Scolari preferred home-based stars to some playing in Europe. He placed an emphasis on a workmanlike midfield and strong defence, and he put the team before all individuals. His playing career was hardly sparkling, being a defender for modest Brazilian teams, but when called upon by his nation as a manager, he transformed their fortunes from Copa América strugglers to world champions in just over a year. He coached hosts Portugal to the final of Euro 2004, but lost to outsiders Greece. He subsequently led the team to the 2006 World Cup semi-final.

BILL SHANKLY

Born: September 2, 1919
Management Career: Carlisle United, Grimsby Town, Workington, Huddersfield Town, Liverpool
Major honours: UEFA Cup 1973

Bill Shankly was the founding father of the great Liverpool dynasty of the Sixties, Seventies and Eighties. After a good playing career, which included several caps for Scotland, he spent a decade as manager at various lowly clubs who lacked his drive and vision. In 1959, he finally alighted at Liverpool, languishing in Division Two. He dispensed with the services of 24 players, but was canny enough to retain two members of the coaching staff, Joe Fagan and Bob Paisley. Together they would go on to form the legendary Anfield 'Boot Room'.

With their help, and through his own willpower, charisma and native intelligence, he transformed the club, taking them to promotion to Division One in 1962, and to the league championship in 1964. He emphasised a neat passing game, with constant movement and indefatigable teamwork, hallmarks which stayed with Liverpool teams through the decades.

The FA Cup was collected in 1965 after beating Leeds United 2-1, and the league title was won again in 1966, though they failed at the final hurdle in the European Cup Winners' Cup against Borussia Dortmund the same year. As the team built around Ron Yeats, Ian St John and Roger Hunt began to fade, Shankly set about rebuilding. His enthusiasm was embodied on the pitch in the shape of new signing, Kevin Keegan. The pocket-sized powerhouse helped The Reds to another Division One title in 1973.

That year they also achieved one of Shankly's much-coveted ambitions: a European honour, in the shape of a UEFA Cup victory over Borussia Mönchengladbach. After the 3-0 FA Cup final trouncing of Newcastle in 1974, Shankly unexpectedly announced his retirement.

He left behind a powerful legacy at Anfield, and will be eternally venerated by the club's fans for his passion for the game, his commitment to good football, and his witticisms ('This city has two great teams: Liverpool and Liverpool reserves,' he once famously quipped). He died on September 29, 1981.

JOCK STEIN

Born: October 1, 1922
Management Career: Dunfermline Athletic, Hibernian, Celtic, Leeds United, Scotland
Major honours: European Cup 1967

Jock Stein, 'The Big Man', announced his arrival as a manager by guiding unfancied Dunfermline Athletic to the Scottish Cup of 1961, beating Celtic – the team Stein had captained to the double of 1954. Stein moved to Hibs for a spell, but by 1965 he was in charge at Celtic Park. With a determination born of his background as a miner, he quickly built one of the best British club sides ever. In 1966 he won the first of an unprecedented nine titles in succession. Their exuberant, skilful victory over dour Inter Milan in the European Cup final of 1967 was also a victory for football. They nearly repeated the feat in 1970, losing narrowly to Feyenoord.

Celtic tried to move Stein into a more senior role after his final title in 1977, but he decided instead on a new challenge at Leeds. This lasted mere weeks before he returned north to manage the Scottish national team. He steered them to the 1982 World Cup finals, but they failed to progress beyond the first round. Tragically he died of a heart-attack immediately after the game which ensured Scotland a place at the 1986 finals in Mexico. His balance of honesty, intelligence, steel and likeability marked him as one of the very greatest managers.

GUY THYS

Born: December 6, 1922
Management Career: Racing Lokeren, Wezel Sport, Herentals, SK Beveren, Union St Gilloise, Antwerp, Belgium

When Guy Thys, a club manager with no real success, was appointed national team coach of Belgium in 1976 he inherited an old team from his predecessor Raymond Goethals. Thys embarked on a policy of developing young players and went on to build one of the best national sides in the history of Belgian football. Thys's team proved to be the surprise package of the 1980 European Championship, only losing the final with West Germany to a goal

two minutes from time. Belgium played exciting open football and also reached the World Cup semi-finals under Thys in 1986. He left the job in 1989 but returned less than a year later to take the side to the second round of the 1990 World Cup. He died in 2003.

GIOVANNI TRAPATTONI

Born: March 17, 1939
Management Career: AC Milan, Juventus, Inter Milan, Bayern Munich, Cagliari, Bayern Munich, Fiorentina, Italy, Benfica, Stuttgart
Major honours: European Cup 1985; UEFA Cup 1977, 1991, 1993; European Cup Winners' Cup 1984; World Club Cup 1985; European Super Cup 1984

Italy's most successful coach actually won two European Cups as a player with AC Milan, but it was as coach of Juventus that he really made his name, winning all three major European trophies, the European Super Cup, the World Club Cup, six Italian league titles and two Italian Cups. He added another league title and UEFA Cup with Inter Milan before succeeding Franz Beckenbauer at Bayern Munich. He struggled with the language in Germany, but after a spell at Cagliari he returned to the club to become the first foreign manager to win the German league. He became coach of the Italian national side in July 2000, taking the team to the finals of the 2002 World Cup and to the 2004 European Championship, but he couldn't replicate his club success on the international stage.

Left: Bill Shankly with the UEFA Cup trophy after Liverpool's aggregate victory over Borussia Mönchengladbach in 1973.

PHILIPPE TROUSSIER

Born: March 21, 1955

Management career: INF Vichy, Alencon, Red Star, ASEC Abidjan, Ivory Coast, Kaizer Chiefs, CA Rabat, FUS Rabat, Nigeria, Burkino Faso, South Africa, Japan, Qatar, Marseille, Morocco

Major honours: Asian Nations Cup 2000

Paris-born Philippe Troussier started coaching in France but only found success after moving to Africa, where he led ASEC Abidjan to three consecutive league titles. He gained a huge reputation with spells in charge of Ivory Coast, Nigeria and Burkina Faso, who he led to fourth place in the African Nations Cup on home soil in 1998. Nicknamed 'The White Sorcerer', Troussier took South Africa to the 1998 World Cup finals, but switched to Japan afterwards, revolutionising the team and winning the Asian Nations Cup and reaching the last 16 of the 2002 World Cup. He spent just two months in charge of the Morocco team in 2005 before he was sacked. He and his wife converted to Islam in 2006 and he changed his name to Omar.

LOUIS VAN GAAL

Born: August 8, 1951

Management career: Ajax, Barcelona, Holland, Barcelona, AZ Alkmaar

Major honours: European Cup 1995; UEFA Cup 1992; World Club Cup 1995; European Super Cup 1995

A fine creative midfielder in the 1970s, Louis Van Gaal became head coach of his former club Ajax in 1991. Putting his faith in youth, he created a fast, accomplished, ball-playing side who peaked with their 1995 Champions League triumph over AC Milan. Having lost the 1996 final, and seen his best players leave, Van Gaal headed for Barcelona in 1997, winning back-to-back Spanish league titles but proving unpopular with the fans who resented his preference for Dutch players. He resigned in 2000, becoming Holland coach, but failure to qualify for the 2002 World Cup forced him out and he returned to Barcelona for a short, unsuccessful spell. After a brief period as technical director of Ajax he took charge of AZ Alkmaar in 2005, taking them to second in the Dutch league in his first season, finishing above Feyenoord and Ajax.

TERRY VENABLES

Born: January 6, 1943

Management career: Crystal Palace, Queens Park Rangers, Barcelona, Tottenham Hotspur, England, Australia, Crystal Palace, Middlesbrough, Leeds United

Terry Venables represented England at every level as a player, but after a bright start with Chelsea and Spurs his career was fading by the time Malcolm Allison offered him a coaching post at Crystal Palace. As manager from 1976, Venables guided The Eagles to two promotions with a young side dubbed 'The Team of the Eighties', but then left in 1980 for QPR, who he led to the FA Cup final.

In 1984 he took over at Barcelona, earning the nickname 'El Tel' as he brought the club their first league title in 11 years and took them to the 1986 European Cup final. Back in England Venables collected his only major English trophy in 1991, winning the FA Cup with Tottenham, before falling out with chairman Alan Sugar. In 1994 he took charge of England, leading them to the semi-finals of the 1996 European Championship on home turf, but left the job amid controversy. He then dabbled in ownership at Portsmouth, coached Australia, narrowly missing out on a place at the 1998 World Cup finals after a play-off defeat to Iran, and returned to Palace.

In December 2000 he joined Bryan Robson at Middlesbrough and saved the club from relegation, but decided not to stay. It was a surprise when he accepted the manager's job at Leeds United in 2002, but after the club's severe financial troubles saw their best players sold, Venables was sacked in March 2003. In 2006 he joined England as assistant to Steve McClaren.

ARSENE WENGER

Born: September 22, 1949

Management career: Nancy, Monaco, Nagoya Grampus Eight, Arsenal

An average player with Strasbourg, Arsene Wenger joined the club's coaching staff in 1981, going on to become head coach at Nancy and then Monaco in 1987, where he won the league, the French Cup and reached the European Cup Winners' Cup final before departing for Japan. Having transformed Grampus Eight from also-rans into title hopefuls, Wenger took over at Arsenal, arriving in September 1996 to newspaper headlines of 'Arsene Who?' In 1998, however, he became the first foreign coach to win the English championship, throwing in the FA Cup for good measure. After a series of near misses, a second double followed in 2002. He brought the league title back to Highbury again in 2004 and the FA Cup in 2005 and although he finally took the club to their first Champions League final in 2006, they lost 2-1 to Barcelona.

WALTER WINTERBOTTOM

Born: January 31, 1913

Management Career: England

Between 1946 and 1962 Winterbottom was England manager and director of FA coaching. He was in charge for 139 games, winning 78 times, lifting the British Championship outright on seven occasions and taking charge of England at four World Cups. Winterbottom considered coaching as the most important aspect of his job. For much of his tenure he did not have control over team selection: that was done by committee. It is a testament to his abilities that England still had the reputation of being one of the world's best teams during this period.

MARIO ZAGALO

Born: August 9, 1931

Management career: Botafogo, Brazil, Fluminense, Flamengo, Brazil, Kuwait, Saudi Arabia, UAE, Brazil, Portuguesa de Desportes, Flamengo

Major honours: World Cup 1970; Copa América 1997

Famously spelling his surname 'Zagalo' as a player and 'Zagallo' as a coach, he won the 1958 and 1962 World Cups as a player (scoring as Brazil defeated Sweden 5-2 in the 1958 final). He began his coaching career as youth team boss at Botafogo before becoming manager in 1967. He won two Río State Championships, before his big opportunity came just three months before the 1970 World Cup finals, when he was asked to take charge of the national side. He allowed his team to play with such freedom and panache that many regard their performances as the greatest ever seen. Continuing as Brazil coach, he also led Fluminense and Flamengo to State Championships before a fourth-place finish with Brazil at the 1974 World Cup.

After a seven-year stint in the Middle East with Kuwait, Saudi Arabia and the UAE (who he led to the 1990 World Cup finals), Zagalo became Brazil's technical co-ordinator in 1991, teaming up with coach Carlos Alberto Parreira to win the 1994 World Cup in the USA, and becoming the first man ever to be involved in four World Cup victories. He again took over as Brazil coach later in 1994 and came close to making it five victories, had his team not stalled in the 1998 World Cup final. After winning another State Championship with Flamengo, in autumn 2002 he returned for one last crack with the national team, again working as technical director alongside coach Parreira at the 2006 World Cup.

Opposite clockwise from top left: Japanese coach Philippe Troussier lifts the Asian Cup in 2000; Arsene Wenger parades the Premiership trophy in 2004; 'El Tel' at Barcelona; Louis Van Gaal enjoys Ajax's 1995 European Cup win.

Below: Mario Zagalo hoists aloft his fourth World Cup as Brazil's technical co-ordinator in 1994.

WOMEN'S FOOTBALL

THE HISTORY OF WOMEN'S FOOTBALL

Above from left to right: Sun Wen of China scores at the Olympics in 2000; a women's football match in Treharris, Wales, in 1951; Briana Scurry, Mia Hamm and Brandi Chastain celebrate gold at the 2004 Olympics.

Opposite top: Dick, Kerr's Ladies in their England kit in the 1920s. Lily Parr holds the ball.

Opposite bottom: Sweden's Malin Andersson is congratulated after scoring against Brazil in the 2003 World Cup quarter-final.

Below: The women's football team of Welshpool munitions factory, pictured in 1915.

Women's football may not have come to the public's attention until the last decade of the 20th Century, but its history began in Europe 100 years earlier. The first recorded women's football match in the world was staged in England at Crouch End Athletic Ground on March 23, 1895.?The game saw a North London team convincingly beat a side from the south of the city 7-1.

The match was organised by educated middle class feminist, Miss Nettie Honeyball, and her British Ladies Football Club. They had advertised in the Daily Graphic for women to play 'a manly game and show that it could be womanly as well'. The game proved a qualified success, although reports indicate that the ladies forgot the rules and failed to change ends at half-time. 'When the novelty has worn off, I do not think that women's football will attract the crowds,' wrote a 'Lady Correspondent' in the Manchester Guardian. This idea of football for the middle classes indeed failed to take off. It took the Great

War to really kick start women's football, this time as a sport for the working class.

The development of women's football in the early 20th Century happened in the work teams of the munitions factories during?World?War I. After the war, the popularity of women's football continued to grow in England and crowds of up to 53,000 watched teams such as Dick, Kerr's Ladies from Preston play matches to raise money for charity. However, the FA banned women from playing on league grounds in 1921 and this destroyed the game in England for more than 40 years. The Dutch and German federations followed suit in the 1950s, although they were to adopt the women's game 20 years later.

The sport continued to develop in other European countries, most notably in Italy and Scandinavia. By the early 1970s the Italian women's league, run by the amateur women's football association, was attracting players from across Europe, offering to pay living expenses while some of the better home-grown players were earning weekly wages.

A key step forward in the development of the game came from UEFA in 1971. Dismayed that its member nations had participated in two 'unofficial' World Cups in Italy and Mexico between 1970 and 1971, UEFA held a vote of its states where an overwhelming majority voted in favour of national associations taking over the governance of women's football in their countries. Most European nations did this, although Italy (1986) and England (1993) left it until much later. Germany, Sweden and Norway, whose associations did take control of the

women's game in the 1970s, are three of the top teams in the world today, while Italy and England have struggled to qualify for recent World Cup competitions.

This change allowed for official international competition to begin, albeit limited to just friendlies at first. A UEFA women's committee established in 1971 (and composed entirely of men) folded seven years later, having failed to successfully create an official championship tournament for nations.

Across the Atlantic, another political decision was being taken that would help to shape the future development of women's football. The US government introduced an equity funding programme, Title IX, which ensured that the same investment would be put into women's collegiate sport as men's. The entire North American sports structure relies on competitive college sport, from which the country's top leagues draft their talent. While the men's scholarships were centred around basketball, baseball and American football, the minority sport of 'soccer' soon began to emerge as the preferred women's scholarship sport.

Today more than 300 colleges in America provide football scholarships, drawing on the best young players from across the world to supplement their own talented players. This programme has helped drive the participation rates to more than eight million by giving the players an exit route. It also enables the national team to cherry-pick their world-beating squad. It wasn't until 1985 that the USA first took part in an international fixture, but by playing many

Above left: Dick, Kerr's Ladies represented England against France in Paris in 1920.

Above right: Pohler and Carlson of Germany celebrate winning Euro 2005.

competitive games each year, with funding most national women's teams across the world could only dream of, the side became the world's first official champions just six years later.

With the growing number of national teams and competitions, FIFA followed up UEFA's call to member associations in 1983 with an announcement three years later that a Women's World Cup would be established, the first one to be staged in China in 1991. An official world tournament would not only give more credibility to the women's game, but it would have an impact on the development of the sport through elite competition. It was to be an occasion where the USA, and star striker Michelle Akers, would stamp their mark on the game. The potential of women's football as a serious spectator sport became apparent for all to see, with 65,000 attending the final to see USA beat Norway.

At the 1995 World Cup FIFA president Sepp Blatter outlined that, 'the future of football is feminine'. The sentiment turned out to be more than just lip service because following the 1995 World Cup in Sweden, the next two major women's tournaments ensured that the game could live up to those expectations. Women's football was launched at the 1996 Atlanta Olympics, with the host nation sweeping all before them to take the gold medal from China in front of 76,000 cheering fans. But while a section of the American audience was being won over, it was the 1999 World Cup that launched women's football across the world as a sport in

its own right – a sport that could complement the men's game, rather than be forever regarded as its poor relation. Over half a million fans packed into stadia to watch the games, while a global audience of 40 million tuned in to watch the tournament on television.

It is a valid question whether the cup would have left such a legacy had the United States not triumphed on home soil. But triumph they did, giving rise to a wave of enthusiasm across the country that enabled the successful formation of the world's first fully professional women's league, the Women's United Soccer Association (WUSA), launched 18 months later to modest, yet encouraging audiences.

However, despite average crowds of 6,000 for the eight WUSA teams, in Autumn 2003, on the eve of the FIFA Women's World Cup, the league announced it was to close. The darlings of the 1999 tournament – Mia Hamm, Kristine Lilly and Julie Foudy – may still have been fronting TV advertising campaigns, but sponsorship income was not hitting targets and the world's only professional league collapsed. Players were forced to join semi-pro sides in the USA, China or northern Europe.

The 2003 World Cup did not have the same impact in the USA as it did four years earlier, largely due to the late switch from China, caused by a SARS outbreak in the country. It also suffered because its September scheduling clashed with American Football and basketball seasons. Still, the USA team regularly sold-out

smaller venues but only finished third after a play-off with Canada, paving the way for an all-European final for the first time. That shift in power highlighted the advance of the North European nations, although the United States still beat World Champions Germany to the 2004 Olympics crown.

In some continents the sport is in its infancy. Africa and South America still remain areas for major improvement in women's football, while many countries don't operate a national league or a national team and the opportunity for girls to play organised football is limited. FIFA's plans to introduce both Under-17 and Under-19 World Championships has helped to encourage associations to appreciate the value of developing the women's game, while the AFC president Mohamed bin Hammam has set the target of having as many as 20 nations (from 44 member states) competing at the 15th Asian Women's Football Championships in 2005.

Despite a survey in 2001 showing that there are now 22 million girls and women playing affiliated football across the world, most of these are concentrated in the North Americas, Europe, Oceania and China. Of the 207 FIFA member states, there are 120 countries now actively competing on the international stage in women's football, all of which were grouped into the first world rankings launched on July 16, 2003. The battle for top spot over the past three years has been an interesting one between the USA and Germany.

DICK, KERR'S LADIES

Dick, Kerr's Ladies were pioneers of women's football.?At a time when women had barely secured the right vote in Great Britain, this team of Lancashire factory workers were attracting crowds as large as 53,000 and were deemed to be a genuine threat to the men's game.

The firm of Dick, Kerr and Co Ltd was the leading British manufacturer of light railway equipment, but in 1917 the needs of a country at war necessitated that the production lines of the Dick, Kerr factory were converted to the manufacture of munitions and a new workforce of uniformed women was recruited. It was felt that these young women needed some kind of sporting release to run off their excess energy, and lunchtime workyard football games proved popular. The women were even playing against men, a practice that had been officially banned by the FA in 1902. Factory teams sprang up around the country, often with the aim of raising money for charity.

At the Dick, Kerr factory, the women had already played one match against the men of the plant in a game organised by factory worker Grace Sibbert, whose husband was a prisoner of war. Office administrator Alfred Frankland joined with Sibbert in a plan to stage a charity match on Christmas Day 1917, the intention being to raise money for the local hospital for wounded soldiers at Moor Park. Frankland brought his organisational skills to bare on the challenge and, for the princely sum of £20 (£4,000 in today's money) he hired Deepdale, home of the legendary Preston North End.

By staging the game at Deepdale, Frankland was putting women's football on a level playing field with the men's game. It was a gamble that paid off as 10,000 spectators passed through the turnstiles to watch Dick, Kerr's beat Arundel Coulthard Foundry 4-0. 'Dick, Kerr's were not long in showing that they suffered less than their opponents from stage fright, and they had a better all round understanding of the game,' reported The Daily Post. 'Their forward work, indeed, was often surprisingly good, one or two of the ladies showing quite admirable ball control.' With the match raising a much needed £200 for the hospital (about £40,000 today), Frankland immediately booked the stadium for a further three matches and prepared to build the team into a force to be reckoned with.

Charitable causes were benefiting greatly from these games and women's football was flourishing, but although Dick,?Kerr's started as a part-time project for factory workers, after the armistice it was obvious that there was still a need for charitable donations and Frankland continued to bring a level of professionalism to the team. Pushing back the boundaries of football again, in December 1920 he staged one of the first floodlit matches in England, getting special permission from Secretary Of State For War, Winston Churchill, to borrow two anti-aircraft spotlights to illuminate the proceedings. He also had the brown leather footballs whitewashed to enable them to be better seen.

After dominating women's football in England in the immediate post-war era, the only way that Alfred Frankland could offer his team a fresh challenge was to go international. In the years after the war France was a country in need of rebuilding and Dick, Kerr's Ladies extended a hand of friendship to the Federation Française Sportive Feminine, inviting them for a series of exhibition games. Frankland would eventually bill the team as Dick, Kerr's International Ladies, dressing them when required in the white shirts and blue shorts of England, but for the first international clashes with France, his team would keep their traditional black and white striped shirts and caps.

The four-game series kicked off at Deepdale, with captain Alice Kell leading Dick, Kerr's to a convincing 2-0 victory in front of a crowd of 25,000. The following day they repeated the feat with a 5-2 result in Stockport, before the French finally hit their stride, securing a 1-1 draw at Manchester's Hyde Road. One of their players even indulged in the most outlandish of goal celebrations for the time: she performed a full somersault, landing gracefully on her feet.

The final game of the tour was at Stamford Bridge in London, but Dick, Kerr's suffered an early blow when Jennie Harris was knocked unconscious by a shoulder charge. With the team reduced to ten women, Florrie Redford's sole strike for the English was not enough to prevent a 2-1 defeat.

In the wake of the French games, the popularity of Dick, Kerr's Ladies soared. Players like Lily Parr became minor celebrities, featuring regularly in the newsreels of the day. They played to some of their biggest crowds: a record 53,000 saw them beat St Helens 4-0 at Goodison Park, with a reported 14,000 turned away; 35,000 spectators watched them take on Bath at Old Trafford; 25,000 people turned out to witness them destroy a Rest Of Britain team 9-1 at Anfield; and 22,000 watched the return fixture with the French in Paris before a pitch invasion ended the game at 1-1 five minutes from time.

Those within football who felt threatened by the women's game campaigned for it to be banned, perpetuating a myth expounded in newspapers by 'medical experts' that football was a dangerous game for women to play. The FA finally succumbed, citing unsubstantiated rumours about the legitimacy of the charitable fundraising as the main excuse. In an FA decree of December 5, 1921, they concluded that all women's games should be banned from the grounds of its member clubs.

Dick, Kerr's rescheduled their games at Rugby League grounds, but the FA ban was more damaging to their weaker rivals who

Above: The first picture of Dick, Kerr's Ladies in October 1917.

found they were unable to compete in the new environment. Dick, Kerr's best days would soon be behind them, but in September 1922 the team embarked on their most ambitious challenge, a North American tour.

Problems beset the trip. On arrival the team found that the Canadian leg of the tour had been cancelled after pressure from the FA. Worse still, their US fixtures were to be played against men, including immigrants from England and Scotland who had turned out for teams such as Chelsea, Blackpool, Kilmarnock and Morton, plus at least one local who would go on to represent the USA at the 1930 World Cup finals. Dick, Kerr's acquitted themselves well, losing just three out of nine games, and even in defeat they proved tough opponents. 'I played against them in 1922,' recalled Paterson keeper Pete Renzulli. 'We were national champions and we had a hell of a job beating them.'

In the years after the US tour the climate changed. Dick, Kerr and Co Ltd had become English Electric and were less tolerant of sponsoring the activities of a football team that no longer carried the company's brand name. In 1926 they parted company with Alfred Frankland and severed all ties with the team. Frankland persevered, rechristening the side as Preston Ladies, but they would continue to be known as Dick, Kerr's for many years.

The team outlived the 1957 death of Alfred Frankland, but eventually ran out of steam – and fixtures – in 1965. Lily Parr, possibly the greatest woman footballer of all time, continued playing until 1951, scoring over 900 goals. Not a bad return for a winger. She died in 1978.

With the huge growth of the game in recent times, it seems that history has finally caught up with the pivotal role played by the team in the history of women's football. 'It is fast becoming a world sport,' concluded Tom Finney in the early Nineties. 'Perhaps this is due in some way to the determination of Dick, Kerr's Ladies, who played on after the FA ban and helped lay the foundations for today's game.'

LEGENDS OF WOMEN'S FOOTBALL

BRANDI CHASTAIN

Country: USA
Born: July 21, 1968
Position: Defender
Club: San Jose CyberRays

Chastain has the glory of being the most recognisable player in women's football. However, most would only recognise the endearing image of her celebrating victory at the 1999 World Cup rather than know her name or where she plays. After scoring the winning penalty against China at the Pasadena Rose Bowl in front of a TV audience of 40 million, Chastain sunk to her knees and whipped off her shirt to reveal her sports bra – 'momentary insanity' she claimed in the subsequent press conference.

She started off her early career as a striker, before a two-year injury-enforced break, after which she returned in defence, from where she earned the majority of her 192 caps. She retired on December 8, 2004 in the same game as Mia Hamm and Julie Foudy, the USA beating Mexico 5-0 in front of a crowd of excited, young female players to whom she had become a heroine five years earlier.

DORIS FITSCHEN

Country: Germany
Born: October 25, 1968
Position: Central defender
Clubs: FC Hesedorf, Eintracht Wolfsburg, TSV Siegen, SG Praunheim, Philadelphia Charge

Fitschen was the first great star of women's football in Germany, helping to lead the team from defence and turning the traditional also-rans in to a leading nation of European football. Playing an important role as sweeper for the international team, she managed to achieve an outstanding four European Championship triumphs (two unofficial) and a bronze medal at Sydney Olympic Games in 2000.

At club level in Germany, she picked up three league titles, three German Cups and a Super Cup, before switching her career to the United States early in 2001. She had the honour of scoring the first ever goal in professional women's football, a penalty for Philadelphia Charge on the opening day of WUSA in 2001. After just one season as a professional, and after winning thousands of fans in America, Fitschen was forced to retire from the game due to injury.

JULIE FOUDY

Country: USA
Born: January 23, 1971
Position: Central midfielder
Club: San Diego Spirit

For many years the captain of the all-conquering USA national team, Foudy made her debut in 1988 at 17 years old and went on to play until December 2004. In her 16-year international career Foudy played in 271 games scoring 45 goals, and somehow found time to give birth to her three children during this phenomenal career.

Foudy played as an attacking midfielder, showing the typical all-American desire to win every ball and every game. Aged 20 she played every minute of the USA's victorious inaugural World Cup campaign in 1991 and helped her team to win the gold medal in the first women's football event at the 1996 Olympics in Atlanta. She was also part of the 1999 World Cup team that captured the attention of the American nation, lifting the trophy in front of over 90,000 fans at the Pasadena Rose Bowl.

Although she couldn't lead her United States side to victory in the 2003 World Cup, when they finished in third place, she finished her career on a high after winning a second Olympic gold medal at Athens in 2004. Among a team of high profile, successful players, including Mia Hamm and Kristine Lilly, Julie Foudy's achievements have sometimes been overlooked but her record speaks for itself.

MIA HAMM

Country: USA
Born: March 17, 1972
Position: Centre-forward
Club: Washington Freedom

Hamm is the most famous player in women's football history. After helping to shoot the USA to World Cup victory in 1999 in front of 90,185 home fans, she became the most-requested world footballer – male or female – on internet search engines. Her profile is such that she has fronted a campaign to promote milk, signed a multi-million pound sponsorship deal

Opposite: Mia Hamm, the most famous footballer in the women's game, takes a shot at Denmark's goal in 2004.

Below left: Germany's Doris Fitschen at Euro 2001.

Below right: Julie Foudy holds the Women's Gold Cup trophy after America beat Brazil 1-0 in 2000.

Above: Charmaine Hooper of Canada raises her arms in celebration after scoring against Costa Rica in 2004.

with Nike, written a best-selling autobiography and even had a high profile marriage to LA Dodgers baseball star Nomar Garciaparra.

She was the player to launch the world's first professional league, WUSA, attracting the biggest league attendances wherever she played with her team Washington Freedom. Being an out-and-out striker and having scored more international goals than any footballer in the world certainly helped endear Hamm to the glory-thirsty American public.

Born in Alabama, Hamm didn't have much time to call it a home, being dragged halfway around the USA and back with her soldier father. She began playing football, as many young girls did at that time, and at 15 she became the youngest player to debut for America, in what would be the first of many important matches in her career against China. Four years later she was the youngest member of the squad that travelled to China and lifted the inaugural World Cup, playing in five of the six matches. She was a part of the unsuccessful World Cup squad in 1995, where she stepped in as keeper after a sending-off. She also played with a sprained ankle but helped the US win the 1996 Olympic gold medal, and she netted the opening goal of the 1999 World Cup.

In 2003 it was always going to be hard for

USA to repeat their 1999 World Cup success on home soil once more. After recovering from a series of injuries to be fit for the tournament, Hamm's team went out in the semi-finals to eventual winners Germany, America settling for a third place play-off victory over Canada.

It was to be left to the 2004 Olympic Games in Athens to provide a suitable epilogue to an unbelievable career and the United States beat all before them to once again triumph in the competition they had first won in 1994. Hamm retired in December 2004 with 275 caps and 158 goals.

CHARMAINE HOOPER

Country: Canada
Born: January 15, 1968
Position: Centre-forward
Clubs: Rockford Dactyls, Chicago Cobras, Atlanta Beat, New Jersey Wildcats

Hooper was never a particularly fast or skilful striker, her main attribute being that she hit the net in virtually every game she played. She holds the record for the number of caps and goals scored by a Canadian international, and she was voted Player Of The Year for Atlanta Beat in the first two seasons of America's pro

league WUSA. Hooper travelled far to play in the best leagues in the world, having semi-professional contracts in Italy, Norway and Japan, and she regularly topped goalscoring charts along the way. She played in her third World Cup in 2003, making a breakthrough for Canada as the team reached the semi-finals of the competition. Hooper's side lost out on a place in the final to Sweden and then lost a pulsating third place play-off match with hosts USA in Los Angeles, but there was some small consolation when she found herself named in the World Cup's All-Star Team.

MAREN MEINERT

Country: Germany
Born: August 5, 1973
Position: Centre-forward
Club: Boston Breakers

The biggest compliment that was ever paid to Meinert is that teams would regularly change their defensive tactics when playing against her, often employing a man-marker in the hope of stopping the German striker from finding the back of the net.

Meinert was the sixth overseas player selected to play for WUSA in 2000, a month after Germany had won the bronze medal at the Sydney Olympics. A season later she shot her country to the European Championship title in 2001, but then surprised the women's game by retiring from international football. She was tempted out of retirement to help Germany win the 2003 World?Cup and continued playing club football for Boston Breakers until the end of WUSA in August 2003. At the end of her career she showed in the 2003 WUSA All Star game that she was still one of the hardest players to defend against in the world.

CAROLINA MORACE

Country: Italy
Born: December 5, 1964
Position: Striker
Clubs: Spinea, Belluno, Verona, Trani 80, Lazio, Reggiana Zambelli, Milan Salvarani, Torres, Agliana, Verona, Modena

Morace was a prolific goalscorer in the semi-professional Italian women's league and was the top scorer in the league for 11 consecutive seasons from 1988 to 1999, helping eight different clubs to a combined 12 league titles, scoring more than 500 goals. She made her international debut at just 14 years of age in 1978 against Yugoslavia and went on to hit a spectacular 105 goals in 153 appearances. She played in two European Championships.

After finishing her playing days, she pursued a coaching career and attracted mass media attention when she became the first woman to manage a professional men's team,

Serie C1 side Viterbese, but she resigned after two games due to the press attention. She then became the manager of the Italian national women's side, but resigned after the 2005 European Championship.

LILLY PARR

Country: England
Born: April 26, 1905
Position: Left-wing
Clubs: St Helens, Dick, Kerr's Ladies, Preston Ladies

Lily Parr was the undisputed star of Dick, Kerr's Ladies, a team of factory workers who formed in 1917 to play charity matches, raising money for wounded soldiers. The team was already well established when they poached 14-year-old Lily Parr from St Helens, and in her first season with the club (1919-20), she scored 43 goals. A six-foot tall left-winger who had quick feet, a fierce shot and a sharp eye for goal, Lily Parr fast forged a reputation for scoring, or setting up, many of the team's goals. In the early 1920s Dick, Kerr's Ladies started playing international matches and before a tour of France The Daily News described Lily Parr as 'a 15-year-old girl back who is said to kick like a First Division man'.

Parr went on to score over 1,000 goals in a career that lasted until 1951, long after the Football Association had tried to extinguish the growing popularity of women's football by banning it from Football League grounds. By the time Parr retired, Dick, Kerr's Ladies had long since become formally known as Preston Ladies and she was playing at left-back.

She died of cancer on May 24, 1978, but she was recognised for her contribution to women's football when she was inducted into the National Football Museum's Hall of Fame in 2002.

HEGE RIISE

Country: Norway
Born: July 18, 1969
Position: Midfield
Clubs: Nikko Securities, Asker, Carolina Courage, Team Strommen

While the Americans have dominated recent women's football through their strength, fitness and desire to win, their players still don't have the same understanding that their European peers nurture in countries where football is the national sport. Riise, however, had the two biggest attributes required to make the ultimate player: strength and superb technical ability. The Norwegians are technically gifted at football and their record at world level is testimony to that: they were runners-up at the 1991 World Cup and lifted the European Championship in 1993. Riise helped Norway to finally secure victory at the 1995 World Cup, where she

scored first in the final to help beat Germany 2-0 and lift the cup. At the inaugural women's football event at the 1996 Olympics in Los Angeles she won a bronze medal, and in 2000 in Sydney she added the gold medal to her collection when Norway beat the USA.

After a spell as a professional with Nikko Securities in Japan between 1995 and 1997, with whom she won the league and cup titles, she was voted the Player Of The Year in Norway for her performances for Asker in 2000. She was then signed by Carolina Courage in October 2001 and continued to impress, winning the Player Of The Year award for the first two seasons and leading them to victory in the 2002 Founders' Cup.

Riise made her last appearance for Norway at a major tournament at the 2003 World Cup finals in?America, recovering from a serious knee ligament injury to make the squad. Riise then retired from international football in 2004 and now helps to coach the country's Under-19 side, while still playing club football for Team Strommen.

PIA SUNDHAGE

Country: Sweden
Born: February 13, 1960
Position: Midfield
Clubs: Hammarby IF, ROI Lazio, Osters IF, Jitex BK, Falkopings KIK, Ulricehamn IFK

Sundhage is the record holder for the greatest number of caps won and goals scored by any Swedish women's international, with 71 goals in 146 games. For many years she also held the record for the most international appearances in the history of women's football. She kicked off her glittering international career at the age of 15 in 1975 and ended it at the 1996 Atlanta Olympic Games, the first time women's football had been contested.

She scored her team's last penalty to beat England on spot-kicks in the unofficial 1984 European Championship final, after two legs had failed to separate the sides. She also was a part of the side that finished as runners-up in the unofficial 1987 World Cup, and she played in the 1991 and 1995 World Cup finals.

During her club career in Sweden's top flight, she won four league championship titles, four cup competitions and even enjoyed a year as a semi-professional playing in Italy with Lazio. Sundhage continued her career in women's football after her playing days had ended, coaching at club level in Sweden, at international youth level and as assistant national coach to the Sweden team.?She also worked in Women's United Soccer Association with Philadelphia Charge and she now manages KIF Orebro in the Swedish league.

Left: Lily Parr, a pioneer of women's football and star of Dick, Kerr's Ladies.

Below left: Carolina Morace becomes the first woman coach of a men's football team in Italy.

Below: Carolina Courage's Hege Riise, wearing the number 10 shirt, battles with Steffi Jones of Washington Freedom in the Founders Cup in 2002.

GREAT PLAYERS OF WOMEN'S FOOTBALL

SHANNON BOXX

Country: USA
Born: June 29, 1977
Position: Midfield
Club: Boston Renegades, Saarbrucken, San Diego Spirit, New York Power

Boxx was suddenly catapulted into the big time in Autumn 2003 when she received a call-up for the United States squad for the 2003 World Cup despite never having played an international. After impressing national coach April Heinrichs playing for San Diego Spirit in WUSA, she played in two warm-up games and went on to score in the opening World Cup match against Sweden and in the third place play-off victory against Canada. A year later, she was an ever present in the team and helped her side win the gold medal at the Athens Olympics.

Now with over 50 caps to her name, the defensive midfielder who likes to get forward

has become one of the world's finest players. Alongside Marta, she was voted a runner-up in the 2005 FIFA Player Of The Year Award to Birgit Prinz and captained the World All-Star XI that beat world champions Germany in 2004 as part of FIFA's Centenary celebrations.

MARIBEL DOMINQUEZ

Country: Mexico
Born: November 18, 1978
Position: Centre-forward
Clubs: Kansas City Mystics, Atlanta Beat, Barcelona, FC Indiana

The captain of the Mexican national team, Maribel Dominquez had been a closely-guarded secret in the American amateur W-League for Kansas City Mystics. But her consistent good form in 2002, when she was named as the league's Player Of The Year, caught the eye of several WUSA teams and she was signed by Atlanta Beat for 2003. A small and fast forward who regularly hits the back of the net, Dominquez made an immediate impact on the professional league in America and became popular with fans.

After the collapse of WUSA in 2003, Dominquez returned home to Mexico. She has a fantastic goalscoring rate of nearly a goal in every game at international level, and was the team's top scorer at the 2004 Olympics where they lost to Brazil in the quarter-finals. She captured the headlines in 2004 when she was set to sign for a Mexican men's Second Division side, Celaya, before FIFA stepped in to reiterate their policy of keeping men's and women's senior football competition separate. She is now player/assistant coach for FC Indiana.

JULIE FLEETING

Country: Scotland
Born: December 18, 1980
Position: Centre-forward
Clubs: Ayr United, San Diego Spirit, Ross County, Arsenal

Born into a footballing family, Julie Fleeting's father Jim played for Norwich City. Like many British girls, Fleeting's early footballing years

were served playing alongside boys until she followed in her father's footsteps by playing for Ayr United, where she won several honours. She caught the eye of US scouts in 2002 and, after the end of the Scottish season, Fleeting made the switch to San Diego Spirit. A tall striker who is both comfortable running at defenders and good in the air, her typical British-style of play helped her flourish in WUSA.

When the American professional league closed in 2003, Julie returned home to Scotland and Ayr United but she was soon tempted to try her luck in the English Women's Premier League, with Arsenal flying her down to London every Sunday. She made an immediate impact, helping Arsenal to a league and cup double in 2004, scoring a hat-trick in the FA Women's Cup final just a day after playing an international match for Scotland.

Undoubtedly the star of the Scotland team since her debut at the age of 16, Fleeting ended the 2005-6 season with 92 goals from 85 international appearances. But sadly, with the Scotland team struggling to compete in qualification campaigns, it seems unlikely that Fleeting will ever grace a major international tournament.

SOLVEIG GULBRANDSEN

Country: Norway
Born: January 12, 1981
Position: Striker
Club: Kolbotn IL

The striker has never played for a club outside her native Norway, but her performances on the international scene have won her much acclaim. She won a gold medal at the Sydney Olympics in 2000 at the age of just 19. Norway struggled to maintain their form over the next few years, losing to Germany in the semi-finals of Euro 2001 and going out to hosts USA in the 2003 World Cup quarter-finals.

It was Gulbrandsen who helped secure Norway's rise back to the top of women's football, first scoring a hat-trick in a 9-3 aggregate annihilation of Iceland in the play-off to reach the 2005 UEFA European Championship in England. Despite carrying an injury going into the finals, Gulbrandsen was undoubtedly the

Below: Arsenal's Julie Fleeting lifts the Premier League trophy at Highbury in 2004.

star of the tournament, helping Norway to perform beyond expectation and reach the final. By this time Gulbrandsen had become the darling of the English crowds and was cheered on by much of the 21,000-strong crowd at Blackburn's Ewood Park, where they lost a tough game to Germany.

STEFFI JONES

Country: Germany
Born: December 22, 1972
Position: Defender/Midfield
Clubs: FSV Frankfurt, SG Praunheim, Niederkirchen, SG Praunheim, FSV Frankfurt, SC 07 Bad Neuenahr, FFC Frankfurt, Washington Freedom, FFC Frankfurt

Born to an American soldier father and German mother, Jones has been a regular in the German defence since she made her debut in 1993. She has won numerous honours as Germany have battled their way to the top of the FIFA World Rankings, including two Olympic bronze medals in 2000 and 2004, and three European Championships (a new trophy had to be cast for the 2005 tournament as Germany had retained the original after their third win). However, the defender missed out on the ultimate achievement of playing in a World Cup final after sustaining a career-threatening injury in a group game against Argentina at USA 2003. She was flown home immediately to have surgery and, alongside eight million other Germans, watched her team-mates lift the World Cup live on television. For FFC Frankfurt she has won many domestic honours, including the German league and cup double, and the UEFA Women's Cup in 2002 and 2006. She also won the WUSA championship in 2003 with Washington Freedom.

KARA LANG

Country: Canada
Born: October 22, 1986
Position: Centre-forward
Club: Vancouver Whitecaps

Kara Lang made her breakthrough on the world stage at the age of just 15, scoring three goals in six games at the inaugural FIFA Under-19 World Championship, staged in August 2002 in her homeland Canada. Her height, combined with her deadly pace when running on to long balls and the ability to shoot from seemingly anywhere in the opposition's half, was enough to see Canada through to the final, losing only on penalties to the Americans in front of a crowd of 48,000.

She made the transition to the senior national team with ease, notching a brace against Wales in her second international while still a 15-year-old student, setting an international record for the youngest goalscorer. She had scored 14 goals by her 24th game. The signing of a semi-professional contract in February 2003 with W-League side Vancouver Whitecaps has added further to her potential. She is currently on a football scholarship at the University of California studying communications and will grace the international women's football stage for many years to come.

KRISTINE LILLY

Country: USA
Born: July 22, 1971
Position: Winger
Clubs: Boston Breakers, KIF Orebro

Kristine Lilly's finest moment in a 16-year international career was undoubtedly the 1999 World Cup final: a speedy winger and an occasional forward, she jumped to clear a goal-bound header from China's Fan Yunjie in the last minute of extra-time to force penalties. Lilly then netted the USA's third spot-kick to put them ahead after China had missed, leading them to a 5-4 win. Like fellow legends Julie Foudy and Mia Hamm, it was her second World Cup win after the victory in China in 1991.

A year after that famous second World Cup victory, Lilly was making history again: this time becoming the first player in footballing history, male or female, to reach the 200-cap mark.

A more illuminating fact is that she has played in more than 85 per cent of all internationals played by the USA, a testimony to the influence this midfielder has had on the success of the American team.

In January 2006 Lilly broke world records yet again when, in a match against Norway, she became the first ever player to reach the 300-cap mark. She also equalled Michelle Akers' record for highest number of international goals scored; at 105 goals that averages at one goal every three games, which is outstanding for a midfielder at international level.

At club level, Lilly captained the Boston Breakers in the WUSA for three years and now plays for KIF Orebro in the Swedish league. One of the fittest players in the game, she can dictate the pace of play and is a prolific creator of attacking moves. Nicknamed the 'Ironwoman', Lilly now runs her own soccer school, while her former school named a football pitch after her and her home town had a parade in her honour when she was part of the USA team that won Olympic gold in 1996.

RENATE LINGOR

Country: Germany
Born: October 11, 1975
Position: Midfielder
Clubs: SC Klinge Seckach, FFC Frankfurt

It took a while for Renate Lingor to make the breakthrough, but she has become the player at the heart of the Germany team and has contributed hugely to their international success in the last six years. At Under-20 level she won the Nordic Cup with Germany, ending the competition as top goalscorer, but Lingor had to wait longer to make the grade at senior level. She made her international debut in 1995, but was only a fringe player and even though she made the 1999 World Cup squad she was limited to just substitute appearances.

The Sydney Olympics in 2000 presented her with the opportunity to establish herself as a regular first team player and win some recognition for her country. She scored the opening goal in the third-place play-off victory against Brazil to win the bronze medal and hasn't looked back since. She was a regular in the side that won the European Championship final of 2001 on home soil in front of 18,000 fans, the 2003 World Cup in the USA, and also the 2005 European Championship staged in England.

In club football, Lingor began playing for SC Klinge Seckach in the German Bundesliga at just 14. The club reached the German Cup final in 1996 and Lingor scored an equaliser, although they eventually lost 2-1 to FSV Frankfurt in front of a massive 40,000 crowd at the Olympic Stadium in Berlin. Lingor then joined the new incarnation of FFC Frankfurt,

and helped them to win the inaugural UEFA Women's Cup in 2002. In her first season at the club she secured a league runners-up medal, but has gone on to win three league titles and four German cups.

HANNA LJUNGBERG

Country: Sweden
Born: January 8, 1979
Position: Centre-forward
Club: Umea IK

Hanna Ljungberg made a name for herself as one of the best emerging players in world football when she burst on to the scene at the 2001 European Championship. A fast and tricky striker, she starred up front as Sweden reached the final, losing to hosts Germany. She saw heartbreak again in October 2003 when Sweden were once more on the losing end of a final to Germany, this time in Los Angeles at the World Cup. Back home in Sweden 3.8 million people (nearly half the population watching TV that day) watched the final and the team were treated to a triumphant welcome home, with two jets accompanying their landing.

Ljungberg has played a major role in putting her club on the map. In 2002 she scored a record 39 league goals in one season and she virtually put on a one-player show as Umea IK won the 2003 UEFA Women's Cup, netting two goals and setting up two more in the first leg over Fortuna Hjorring. She added another goal to her tally in the return leg.

After the World Cup she underwent knee surgery and had to battle hard to secure a place in the final squad for the 2004 Athens Olympics, eventually helping Sweden to finish in fourth place. She has the enviable record of more than a goal every game at international level and still has time to fulfil her ambition of finally bringing success home to Sweden.

MARTA

Country: Brazil
Born: February 2, 1986
Position: Striker
Club: Umea IK

Marta Vieira Da Silva may only be 20 years of age but she has already made her mark on world football and she has the target of ensuring more of her countrywomen can follow in her footsteps. A skilful and prolific striker, Marta first brought her skills to the attention of the world at FIFA's 2002 Under-19 World Championship before helping the senior Brazil team to the quarter-finals of the 2003 World Cup. A year later Brazil proved the surprise attraction at the 2004 Olympic football tournament, reaching the final, only to lose in extra-time to the USA.

Before winning the silver medal at the Athens Olympics, Marta had made her name on the club circuit after joining Umea of Sweden in March 2004. She came in as a replacement for the injured Hanna Ljungberg and made an immediate impact, helping the team to the domestic league title and the UEFA Women's Cup.

After beginning her career playing in boys' teams as a youngster, as well as excelling at Futsal and handball, her ambition remains to set up a domestic league in Brazil to help develop young female football talent. Currently the top five Brazilian players are plying their trade in Europe due to the lack of a domestic league or cup competition for women in their home country.

DAGNY MELLGREN

Country: Norway
Born: June 19, 1978
Position: Centre-forward
Clubs: Klepp, Bjornar, Boston Breakers, Klepp, Bjornar

Mellgren is a short, but tricky forward who has an aptitude for playing the offside trap and getting into the space behind defenders. The best moment of her career was scoring the 'golden goal' that helped Norway to a 3-2 victory over world champions USA to win a surprise gold medal the 2000 Olympics in Sydney. She was in good form a year later at the 2001 European Championship, but she couldn't help Norway to overcome hosts and eventual winners Germany in the semi-finals. She was one of the first overseas players to be selected for WUSA, where she was a key player for Boston Breakers.

After the collapse of America's professional league, Dagny returned home to finish her studies as a radiographer and rejoined Klepp, where she works part-time. From a footballing family, Mellgren's father played top-flight football in Norway and both her brother and sister play the game.

MARINETTE PICHON

Country: France
Born: November 26, 1975
Position: Centre-forward
Clubs: Saint-Memmie, Philadelphia Charge, New Jersey Wildcats, Juvisy FCF

Pichon is a tall, strong forward who has a great presence in the penalty area. She played two seasons of professional football in the WUSA for Philadelphia Charge, initially stepping in to the boots of the injured fans' favourite Kelly Smith to shoot Charge to the semi-finals of the 2002 Founders Cup. She was the second highest scorer in the league that year, was voted the Player Of The Year and also Striker Of The Year. She then played alongside England's

Smith for the New Jersey Wildcats after the closure of the WUSA, before returning home to her native France.

At international level, Pichon's biggest achievement was helping France to qualify for the World Cup for the first time in 2003, netting a goal in the first leg of the UEFA play-off against England. But Pichon's talents couldn't help the team to get past the group stage in that World Cup, or at the 2005 European Championship. Despite a fall-out with manager Elisabeth Loisel, Pichon's aim is to shoot France to qualification for China 2007 and she plans to retire at the end of that campaign.

BIRGIT PRINZ

Country: Germany
Born: October 25, 1977
Position: Centre-forward
Clubs: FFC Frankfurt, Carolina Courage, FFC Frankfurt

Birgit Prinz is undoubtedly the princess of women's football today. Voted FIFA World Player Of The Year for three consecutive years, she led Germany to international success at the 2003 World Cup, collecting the Golden Boot en route. She also led the team to victory at the 2001 and 2005 European Championships.

A tall, strong, athletic figure, Birgit Prinz could be regarded as the nearest thing the women's game has to a male player: she dominates matches from her centre-forward role, often tracking back in order to win the ball in midfield, before creating as many opportunities for her team-mates as herself.

A European champion for her club as well as her country, she lifted the inaugural UEFA Women's Cup with Frankfurt in 2002. That victory brought her to the attention of WUSA, America's professional league, in the summer of 2002 when she signed for Carolina Courage, immediately making her mark by scoring the winning goal in the Founders Cup final to secure the 2002 WUSA title.

Prinz has won numerous domestic honours in Germany, where she is now back playing with FFC Frankfurt. The one title which has eluded her career is the Olympic gold medal and she will have her sights set on Beijing 2008 to put that right, but more immediately Germany will defend their title at the World Cup in September 2007 and all eyes will be on Prinz.

SILKE ROTTENBERG

Country: Germany
Born: January 25, 1972
Position: Goalkeeper
Club: Grun-Weiss Brauweiler, SF Siegen, FFC Brauweiler, FCR 2001 Duisburg, FFC Frankfurt

Renowned as the greatest women's goalkeeper ever, Germany's shot stopper has won well over 100 caps for the women's national side since her international debut against the USA

in 1993. With over 13 years between the sticks for Germany, Rottenberg was in unstoppable form during the 2005 Women's European Championship in England, conceding just two goals on the way to lifting the trophy for a third time – she had already tasted victory in the competition in Scandinavia in 1997 and on home turf in 2001.

It hasn't just been on the European stage that Rottenberg has received universal acclaim. She was voted goalkeeper of the 2003 Women's World Cup in the USA, after helping Germany to defeat the hosts in the semi-finals and Sweden after extra-time in the final. During her long career Rottenberg has also won two Olympic bronze medals in 2000 and 2004, two German league titles and two German Cup finals.

In a sport where female goalkeepers are often derided for their lack of height and presence, Rottenberg commands the penalty box and has been the backbone of Germany's international success in recent years.

SISSI

Country: Brazil
Born: June 2, 1967
Position: Midfield
Clubs: San Jose CyberRays, Sacramento Storm

A veteran of three World Cup finals and two Olympic campaigns for her native Brazil, Sisleide do Amor Lima is regarded as one of the most entertaining players in the world. When she was a young girl, she would tear the heads off her dolls to kick around and her obvious hero was Pelé. Formerly a teacher, she was one of a handful of foreign stars integrated into the WUSA professional league at its launch in 2001 and for three seasons she was a virtual ever present for her club side.

Although she is more likely to set up goals, free-kicks have become her trademark and she jointly won the Golden Boot at the 1999 World Cup. Although she has played in three World Cups and two Olympic football tournaments, the Brazil team has not played an international fixture since the Athens Olympics in 2004, so Sissi may never grace the international stage again. She now works as a FIFA ambassador and is still playing semi-professional football in the American W-League with Sacramento Storm, with whom she is also involved in a coaching capacity.

KELLY SMITH

Country: England
Born: October 29, 1978
Position: Centre-forward/central midfield
Clubs: Philadelphia Charge, New Jersey Wildcats, Arsenal

Scouted for a soccer scholarship in America while playing football in Watford, Smith went

Below left: Sissi flies the flag for Brazil.

Below right: England's number 10, Kelly Smith.

on to break college and league goalscoring records and was so highly regarded at Seton College that they decided to retire her shirt number. She stayed on in the United States for a year, coaching young girls, in anticipation of the launch of WUSA, the world's first professional women's football league, in 2001. She was an immediate success and became a firm fans' favourite, running successful soccer camps under her own name and having her own website.

USA national coach April Heinrichs voted Kelly Smith as her World Player Of The Year after the England striker debuted in WUSA's inaugural year, but her four seasons in professional football were blighted by injury.

Smith joined the New Jersey Wildcats after the collapse of WUSA, but further injury curtailed her time with the club and she returned home to sign for Arsenal and to begin the long preparation for the 2005 European Championship in her home country.

While not 100 per cent fit for the European Championship, she was by far England's best player and captured the imagination of the new found home audience for women's football. A welcome injury-free season followed, along with the league title, FA Cup and being crowned both Players' Player and England International Player Of The Year.

Smith is at her best with the ball at her feet, taking players on and carving out opportunities from the tightest of angles. She plays as an out-and-out striker for England, but for Philadelphia Charge she played as a central midfielder, enjoying being able to track back deep into her own team's half to fetch the ball before trying to dribble it past a full defence and shooting for goal.

VICTORIA SVENSSON

Country: Sweden
Born: May 18, 1977
Position: Winger
Club: Djurgarden/Alvsjo

Victoria Svensson was undoubtedly the star of the Sweden team that reached the 2003 Women's World Cup final, only to see her team lose out to an extra-time free-kick against Germany in Los Angeles. In fact it was Svensson who was harshly adjudged to have fouled a German player, with Nia Kunzer scoring from the resulting free-kick.

Shortly after returning from the World Cup finals, Svensson made headlines when Italian men's club Perugia approached her to play for them, but in response FIFA set stringent guidelines disallowing women from playing for men's football clubs.

Svensson's club side Djurgarden/Alvsjo beat arch rivals Umea to the Swedish league title in 2004 and finished as runners-up in the 2005 UEFA Women's Cup.

Above: One of the true greats of the women's game, China's Sun Wen attempts to score against Germany in 2003.

ABBY WAMBACH

Country: USA
Born: June 2, 1980
Position: Striker
Club: Washington Freedom

One of the greatest strikers to ever pull on the USA shirt, Wambach sits alongside Mia Hamm as one of the national side's legends, and has a list of honours to match. Winner of a gold medal at the 2004 Athens Olympics after scoring four goals, including the extra-time winning header against Brazil in the final, Wambach's speed, skill and dominance in the air was used to devastating effect.

Earlier that year she scored all five goals in the second half against Ireland – levelling a USA record – and added to her accolades by winning the Footballer Of The Year award for the second year in a row. The previous year Wambach secured a place in the 2003 World Cup team, scoring three, including a vital goal in the memorable 1-0 win over Norway in the quarter-finals.

Wambach's WUSA career was just as incredible, joining Washington Freedom after becoming the University of Florida's all-time leading goalscorer. In 2003 the number 28's stunning strikes helped the Freedom win the Founders Cup where she became the game's Most Valuable Player. She also earned the WUSA Goal Of The Year award for a sensational diving header. She still plays for Washington Freedom in America's amateur W-League. Not bad for a girl who was once a high school basketball star!

SUN WEN

Country: China
Born: April 6, 1973
Position: Midfielder
Clubs: Atlanta Beat

Many fans of women's football regard Sun Wen as the best player in the world. She perhaps hasn't had the opportunity to play as many matches or score as many goals as Mia Hamm or Birgit Prinz, but she has all the qualities you would expect from a world class star: pace, vision, accuracy of passing and the ability to score not only on a regular basis, but often spectacularly so.

She is undoubtedly the star of the Chinese team. As well as achieving domestic success in China, she won the Golden Boot at the 1999 World Cup, a small consolation for losing the final in front of 90,000 people to home team USA on penalties. She has suffered a career-threatening injury recently, but is working hard to get back to fitness in anticipation of two exciting milestones in her career: the 2007 FIFA World Cup and the 2008 Olympics, both of which will be held in China. A well known face in her homeland and star of chat shows, she was named as the FIFA World Player Of The Century alongside Michelle Akers in 2000.

THE HISTORY OF THE WOMEN'S WORLD CUP

Above from left to right: Mia Hamm kisses the World Cup in 1999; USA's Brandi Chastain celebrates her World Cup goal in 1999; Germany's 2003 World Cup victory.

Below from left to right: The USA do a lap of honour in 1999; action from the 2003 World Cup final at the Home Depot Stadium.

The inaugural women's World Cup in 1991 came 20 years after women had first contested an official international match. In the early 1970s the women's game had taken its first steps on the road to recognition, with numerous national federations taking the running of the female game under their own governance, or at least forming links with amateur women's associations to allow national sides to be established. This move was widely encouraged by FIFA, the world governing body, which had issued directives to its member states to run the women's game alongside the men's.

As an increasing number of national sides emerged, international games became more competitive, with the Scandinavians' technique and fitness proving to be a generation ahead of their peers. Indeed, Denmark had the honour of being champions at the first unofficial world cup held in Mexico in 1971. USA exploded on to the world football stage in the early Eighties and competed twice in the 'Little World Cup' held in Italy in 1985 and 1988, both of the small tournaments won by England.

With an increasing number of unofficial world championships, and with UEFA having already staged a European Championship, FIFA felt under pressure to launch an official Women's World Cup. FIFA President João Havelange announced at the 1986 Congress in Mexico City, prior to the men's World Cup of that year, that a women's tournament would be launched, to take place every four years in the year directly following the men's competition.

In November 1991, 12 nations arrived in China for the first official Women's World Cup. The host media swarmed to see the home side thrash Norway 4-0 in the opening match. Norway returned to form to reach the final, where they met new kids on the block, the United States. The Americans had benefitted from a significant investment in female 'soccer' scholarships, making US colleges a hotbed of football development. Their forward line of Michelle Akers, April Heinrichs and Carin Jennings – labelled the 'Triple-Edged Sword' by local journalists – hit 18 of the team's 23 goals in just five games to reach the final.

Even without the home nation competing, an unexpected crowd of 65,000 witnessed the the first World Cup final, China having lost to Sweden in the quarter-finals. Akers hit two goals to take the trophy to America for the first time, snatching a 2-1 victory late in the game. The move to have an official women's competition on the world stage had been fully justified.

The first Women's World Cup had been a unanimous success and the second tournament had a lot to live up to. Staged in Sweden, where participation rates were high and where there was a culture of acceptance of women playing football, it gave the European sides a chance to show a superior tactical awareness.

More than 14,000 packed into the national stadium for the opening match, only to see Brazil steal a surprise 1-0 victory against the home side. After that defeat Sweden had to battle hard to progress to the final eight, where they were cruelly knocked out by China on penalties. In the semi-finals Norway avenged their 1991 final defeat by securing a tight 1-0 victory against the United States, before Hege Riise and Marianne Pettersen netted a goal each to beat Germany 2-0 in the final in front of a 17,000 crowd.

While the 1995 World Cup had been a step forward in terms of performance, it was the 1999 tournament that would change women's football forever. The American media was highly sceptical that the tournament could be a success; after all, football was a minority sport and the women's team had previously attracted minimal crowds. But the Americans had a potential audience of seven million female players to draw upon and tickets began selling out as early as Mia Hamm and her team-mates began their preparations.

As the tournament gained momentum, the interest spiralled. With 90,185 supporters in the stadium, and another 40 million homes around America switching on to watch, the final was a success, with USA's Brandi Chastain creating headlines when she whipped off her shirt in celebration of her winning penalty against China. Spectator figures for the tournament reached 660,000, around six times that of the 1995 tournament in Sweden, while images of the winning team adorned *Sports Illustrated* and even the illustrious *Time* magazine – as well as every American schoolgirl's bedroom wall.

The World Cup has played a vital role in the development of the game: as competitiveness has increased, each tournament has raised the profile of the game and has driven interest in women's football as a spectator sport. The stars of the 1999 World Cup became household names and the first professional women's league was launched in the USA.

The 2003 World Cup was awarded to China, but FIFA made the decision in early 2003 to move the tournament due to the outbreak of SARS. The United States pitched for the finals and so the tournament was to return to North America four years after the huge success of 1999. With a short lead time to organise and promote the finals, smaller venues were used, but despite USA not progressing to the final, a sell-out 26,000 crowd at the Home Depot Arena, Los Angeles, saw Germany beat Sweden 2-1. The Swedes had taken the lead in the 41st minute, Hanna Ljungberg scoring on the break, but Germany equalised through Maren Meinert just one minute after the break. Both teams squandered chances to finish off the tie, and early in extra-time the Germans secured their first world title, Nia Kuenzer heading in a 98th-minute free-kick from Renate Lingor. The result made Tina Theune-Meyer the first female coach to win the Women's World Cup.

While television audiences in the USA were focussed on the gridiron season, in Germany eight million watched the Women's World Cup final. The viewing figures in Sweden were even higher than those achieved by the men's team's appearance in the quarter-finals of the previous year's World Cup. It seems that Women's football has made a significant breakthrough in Europe, both on and off the pitch.

Above: Germany lift the Women's World Cup trophy for the first time in 2003.

THE WOMEN'S WORLD CUP
WINNERS
1991: USA
1995: Norway
1999: USA
2003: Germany

INDEX

CHRIS HUNT: EDITOR

Writer and broadcaster Chris Hunt has travelled the world covering football. A freelance editor and journalist, his travels around Japan for the World Cup in 2002 were documented in the BBC TV programme *Beckham For Breakfast*. His definitive history of football's biggest prize – *World Cup Stories: The Hsitory Of The FIFA World Cup* – was published in 2006 to accompany the BBC television series of the same name.

For eight years he was Managing Editor of Britain's biggest-selling football magazine, *Match*. Now a regular contributor to *Four Four Two*, he was also Editor of many of the acclaimed special editions of leading music magazines *Mojo, Q, Uncut* and *NME*, covering subjects as diverse as The Beatles, U2, Kurt Cobain, Oasis, punk rock and mod. In the past he has worked as a broadcast journalist for BBC Radio 5 and was a regular columnist for *Ice, Sport First* and *Football First*. He has also written for *The Sportsman* and *The Times*. When major football tournaments allow, he spends his summers as Editor of *The Official Wayne Rooney Annual* and *The Match Of The Day Annual*. He can be contacted through his website: www.ChrisHunt.biz

DAVID HOUGHTON: ART DIRECTOR

An experienced designer, David Houghton often specialises in football or music projects. Working with Editor Chris Hunt, as the design half of the 'Mile Away Club' magazine and book production team, David has been the Art Director of *Match's Euro 2000 Guide, The Match Diary, The Official Wayne Rooney Annual* and *The Match Of The Day Annual*. He has also worked as Art Director of monthly music magazine *Hip-Hop Connection*. Not only were his travels around Japan in 2002 with author Chris Hunt featured in the BBC TV programme *Beckham For Breakfast*, but he managed to come back from Tokyo with a wife, Ayumi. His photography of football fans has been published in *Four Four Two, Sport First, Football First* and *Match*. He has also had two collections of his arthouse photographs published in book form, *Penumbra* and *Telefon*. He has watched England play all over the world, and tries to live as near to the Cambridge United ground as possible.

CONTRIBUTORS

NICK GIBBS is an international football journalist who has written for a host of publications, including *Match*, World Soccer, *European Football Yearbook* and preview specials of every World Cup and European Championship since 1988. He is also the author of the FA endorsed book *England – The Football Facts*.

LUKE NICOLI has worked in senior roles at both *Match and Shoot*, and has contributed to *Four Four Two, The Guardian, Observer* and *Daily Star On Sunday*. He was co-author of *Second Time Around*, the autobiography of Kevin Phillips and author of *William, The People's Prince*.

ANDREW WINTER has worked on a variety of sports magazines, including *Match* and *Sported!* He was also Editor of *Shoot!* between 1997 and 2000.

JAMES EASTHAM was editor of weekly national newspapers *Sport First* and *Soccerbet*. Twice nominated for Young Journalist Of The Year, he currently works for *The Sportsman*.

HUGH SLEIGHT was deputy editor of *Match* and is currently editor of *Four Four Two* magazine.

GARY TIPP was formerly the Editor of *Total Football* magazine. A Pompey fan, he is a regular contributor to a number of the club's websites.

KEVIN HUGHES was Associate Editor of *Match*. He has spent the last ten years interviewing the biggest names that football has to offer.

PAUL ROBSON has worked on both *Match* and *Total Football*, but allows himself to be distracted from his current job writing about guitars by the varying fortunes of Swindon Town.

MIKE PATTENDEN has written regular features about football for *The Times, The Daily Mail, Esquire, Goal* and *Four Four Two*. He was also the author of *Last Orders At The Liars' Bar*, the official biography of The Beautiful South.

JOE CUSHLEY has contributed to many football fanzines, and has written about stadia for the *Architects' Journal*.

STEVE CRESSWELL was a staff writer with *Match*, before spending two seasons in the press department at Leicester City. He joined the BBC Sport website as a journalist in 2000.

TIM HARTLEY was formerly Deputy Editor of *Match* and for five years was Editor of the *Boston Standard*. He works for the Press Association and has edited magazine's for Sport England and the Professional Rugby Players' Association.

MATT ALLEN was Assistant Editor of *Four Four Two*. He is author of *Jimmy Greaves: The Biography*.

RICHARD ADAMS spent three years as a writer for *Match*, and has written on football for numerous titles. He is the founding Editor of thefootyroom.co.uk.

ALISTAIR PHILLIPS was editor of *Sports Trader* for three years before joining *Match* in 1998. He now works as a freelance journalist, writing about sport and fitness.

BEV WARD was a journalist on *Match* for four years. She now works for the Football Association and is involved in promoting the women's game.

JOHN PLUMMER is a London-based freelance journalist who specialises in sport and fitness. He has written widely about football for many newspapers and magazines.

Many thanks for additional contributions and assistance: Sara Hunt, Alan Beeson, John Glover, Jonathan Wilson and Mark Rosselli at Cambridge Publishers Ltd.

The publisher would like to thank: David Jacobs, Gavin Clay and Paul Langan at Action Images.

INTRODUCTION

The carpus is a complex unit of bony articulations that transfers the force and motion of the hand to the supporting forearm and upper extremity. It allows a wide range of motion in two major planes and, with its adjacent radioulnar joints, permits a substantial rotatory arc around the longitudinal axis of the forearm. Unlike a simple hinge joint such as the elbow, the wrist involves a delicate interaction between eight carpal bones that are divided into two carpal rows.[39,100,110] While the main motions are flexion–extension and radioulnar deviation, the primary axis of motion of the carpal bones resides within the head of the capitate, which is not a singular point, but rather an oblique screw axis for combined motions of wrist extension/flexion and radial/ulnar deviation.[38,99,124] To produce this natural movement, individual carpal bones not only turn up and down and back and forth, but also spin and roll about their own axes.

GENERAL, TOPOGRAPHIC, SURGICAL, AND APPLIED ANATOMY

Bones and Joints

The carpus is composed of eight bones in two rows (Fig. 29-1). The articular surfaces of the joints that make up the wrist have important roles in subsequent integrated movements of the wrist. The eight carpal bones are influenced by the shape of the distal radius, the distal ulna, and the triangular fibrocartilage complex (TFCC).

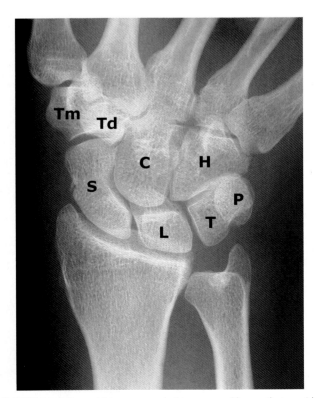

FIGURE 29-1 The wrist is composed of two rows of bones that provide motion and transfer forces. C, capitate; H, hamate; L, lunate; S, scaphoid; T, triquetrum; P, pisiform; Td, trapezoid; Tm, trapezium.

The proximal row consists of the scaphoid, the lunate, and the triquetrum. The proximal carpal row is regarded by many authors as an "intercalated segment" between the radius and the distal row, the keystone in the coordination of motions of the wrist as well as in the control of forces that are transmitted from the hand to the forearm and vice versa. To cope with such an important role, the three proximal row bones continuously need to adapt their position and orientation to guarantee the necessary joint congruency between the radius and distal row. Articular joint congruency depends on joint geometry and the integrity of the ligaments that connect the three bones to each other and to the surrounding bones, as the proximal carpal row has no direct tendon attachments.[56,100,110,113]

The pisiform is a sesamoid bone enclosed in the sheath of the flexor carpi ulnaris tendon; accordingly, it does not belong directly to the proximal carpal row. It may stabilize the proximal carpal row indirectly by acting on the triquetrum via the pisotriquetral joint.

The distal row, which is more stable and moves as a unit, consists of the trapezium, the trapezoid, the capitate, and the hamate. The distal row forms a rigid, supportive transverse arch upon which the five metacarpals of the hand are supported. The trapezium articulates with the first metacarpal, the trapezoid with the second, and the capitate with the third one. The capitate and trapezoid are tightly connected to the metacarpals, whereas there is 30 to 40 degrees of flexion–extension and rotation at the metacarpotrapezial joint. The hamate articulates with the fourth and fifth metacarpal.

Ligaments of the Wrist

The carpal bones are supported by both extrinsic and intrinsic ligaments.[113,121,174]

Extrinsic Ligaments

Extrinsic ligaments link the carpal bones to the radius, ulna, and metacarpals and are attached to roughened areas on the dorsal and palmar surfaces. The transverse carpal ligament is an extrinsic ligament that connects the scaphoid tuberosity and trapezial ridge with the hamate and pisiform to provide structural integrity to the proximal carpal arch. It also constrains the flexor tendons.

The deeper extrinsic ligaments are intracapsular ligaments best observed from within the radiocarpal and midcarpal joints. From an external view, the ligaments appear as condensations of the fibrous capsule (Fig. 29-2) and are difficult to distinguish through the superficial adventitia. They are, however, quite prominent from the intra-articular aspect of the joint.[39]

Palmar Wrist Ligaments. The palmar wrist ligaments originate laterally from a radial-palmar facet of the radial styloid and are directed in a distal ulnar direction, where they meet ligaments originating medially from the TFCC and the distal ulna.

The stronger and more oblique radial ligaments prevent the carpus from translating ulnarly on the medially angulated slope of the distal radius. The palmar extrinsic ligaments consist of two V-shaped ligamentous bands: one is proximal and connects the forearm to the proximal carpal row and one is distal and connects the forearm to the distal carpal row. The distal limb of the palmar extrinsic ligaments consists of the radioscaphocapitate ligament laterally and the ulnocapitate ligament medially